# Exploring
# Macroeconomics

## Fifth Canadian Edition

Robert L. Sexton
Pepperdine University

Peter N. Fortura
Algonquin College

Colin C. Kovacs
Algonquin College

Darren Chapman, Contributor
Fanshawe College

**NELSON**

# NELSON

**Exploring Macroeconomics, Fifth Canadian Edition**

by Robert L. Sexton, Peter N. Fortura, and Colin C. Kovacs

**VP, Product Solutions, K–20:**
Claudine O'Donnell

**Publisher, Digital and Print Content:**
Katherine Baker-Ross

**Marketing Manager:**
Marcia Siekowski

**Technical Reviewer:**
Racquel Lindsay

**Content Manager:**
My Editor Inc.

**Photo and Permissions Researcher:**
Jessie Coffey

**Senior Production Project Manager:**
Imoinda Romain

**Production Service:**
SPi Global

**Copy Editor:**
June Trusty

**Proofreader:**
SPi Global

**Indexer:**
SPi Global

**Design Director:**
Ken Phipps

**Higher Education Design PM:**
Pamela Johnston

**Cover Design:**
Courtney Hellam

**Cover Image:**
Ed Norton/Getty

**Compositor:**
SPi Global

**Library and Archives Canada Cataloguing in Publication**

Sexton, Robert L., author

Exploring macroeconomics / Robert L. Sexton, Pepperdine University, Peter N. Fortura Algonquin College, Colin C. Kovacs, Algonquin College, Darren Chapman, contributor, Fanshawe College. — Fifth Canadian edition.

Previously published as part of: Exploring economics. 1st Canadian ed.

Includes bibliographical references and index.

Issued in print and electronic formats.

ISBN 978-0-17-687704-0 (softcover).
ISBN 978-0-17-687718-7 (PDF)

1. Macroeconomics—Textbooks.
2. Textbooks.

I. Fortura, Peter, 1961-, author
II. Kovacs, Colin C., 1969-, author
III. Chapman, Darren, author
IV. Sexton, Robert L. Exploring economics.
V. Title.

HB172.5.S49 2019
339   C2018-906420-X
      C2018-906421-8

ISBN-13: 978-0-17-687704-0
ISBN-10: 0-17-687704-5

To Cynthia, Laura, and Nicholas

P.N.F.

To Lindsay, Rowan, Seth, and Myles

C.C.K.

To Elizabeth, Katherine, and Tommy

R.L.S.

# Brief Contents

# Detailed Contents

# About the Authors

**Robert L. Sexton** is Distinguished Professor of Economics at Pepperdine University. Professor Sexton has also been a Visiting Professor at the University of California at Los Angeles in the Anderson Graduate School of Management and the Department of Economics.

Professor Sexton's research ranges across many fields of economics: economics education, labour economics, environmental economics, law and economics, and economic history. He has written several books and been published in many top economic journals such as the *American Economic Review,* the *Southern Economic Journal, Economics Letters,* the *Journal of Urban Economics,* and the *Journal of Economic Education.* Professor Sexton has also written more than 100 other articles that have appeared in books, magazines, and newspapers.

Professor Sexton received the Pepperdine Professor of the Year Award in 1991, the Harriet and Charles Luckman Teaching Fellow in 1994, the Tyles Professor of the Year in 1997, and the Howard A. White Award for Teaching Excellence in 2011.

Pepperdine University

**Peter N. Fortura** earned his undergraduate degree from Brock University, where he was awarded the Vice-Chancellor's Medal for academic achievement, and his Master of Arts from the University of Western Ontario in London, Ontario. He has taught economics at Algonquin College in Ottawa for over 20 years. Prior to that, he was an economist in the International Department of the Bank of Canada in Ottawa.

Professor Fortura has published articles on Canadian housing prices, Canada's automotive industry, and Canada's international competitiveness. As well, he is an author of the *Study Guide* to accompany *Principles of Macroeconomics* by Mankiw, Kneebone, and McKenzie (Nelson Education, 7th edition), and co-author of the statistics textbook *Contemporary Business Statistics with Canadian Applications* (Pearson, 3rd edition).

He lives in Ottawa with his wife, Cynthia, and their children, Laura and Nicholas.

Peter Fortura

**Colin C. Kovacs** received his Master of Arts degree from Queen's University after completing his Bachelor of Arts degree at the University of Western Ontario. He has taught economics, statistics, and finance for nearly 25 years at both the DeVry College of Technology in Toronto and Algonquin College in Ottawa. His research papers have included *Determinants of Labour Force Participation Among Older Males in Canada* and *Minimum Wage—The Past and Future for Ontario.*

He lives in Ottawa with his wife, Lindsay, and their children, Rowan, Seth, and Myles.

Algonquin College

# Preface

*Exploring Macroeconomics,* Fifth Canadian Edition, offers students a lively, back-to-the-basics approach designed to take the intimidation out of economics. With its short, self-contained active learning units and its carefully chosen pedagogy, graphs, and photos, this text helps students master and retain the principles of economics. In addition, the current-events focus and modular format of presenting information makes *Exploring Macroeconomics* a very student-accessible and user-friendly text. Driven by more than 70 years of combined experience teaching the economic principles course, the dedication and enthusiasm of Bob Sexton, Peter Fortura, and Colin Kovacs shine through in *Exploring Macroeconomics.*

## NEW TO THE FIFTH CANADIAN EDITION

### Overall Highlights

As with previous editions of *Exploring Macroeconomics,* attention has been paid to the structure and layout of each chapter to ensure that the material is presented in as clear and consistent a manner as possible. In addition, special attention has been given to the numerous examples and illustrations presented in each chapter to ensure they are meaningful and relevant to today's student.

The end-of-chapter *For Your Review* questions and problems have been continued in this edition. *Blueprint Problems,* the review feature introduced in the previous edition, have been retained and have undergone revision to ensure they continue to provide relevant and meaningful insight into the methodologies surrounding key economic concepts. As in the previous edition, all *Blueprint Problems* are accompanied by full and annotated solutions.

Also returning in this fifth edition are the *Debate* and *Business Connection* features. Both have undergone revision and updating. While their content has been revised, the purpose of each feature remains the same—*Debate* features are designed to promote in-class discussion and self-exploration, and *Business Connection* features are designed to highlight the link between economic theory and business principles.

Finally, where relevant, Canadian content has been added and all statistical information has been updated. For example, the data accompanying the discussion of unemployment, inflation, and economic growth in Chapter 5 has been updated to include the most recent figures available and expanded to cover a variety of other economies. The addition of international data gives the reader the opportunity to evaluate the performance of the Canadian economy from a global perspective, thereby deepening understanding of these central macroeconomic goals.

## CHAPTER HIGHLIGHTS

### Chapter 4: Bringing Supply and Demand Together

In this chapter, readers will find an expanded discussion of the existence of price controls in the Canadian economy. An investigation of Canadian dairy production and the pricing of dairy products in Canada are provided, giving the reader a more in-depth understanding of this key topic and how it impacts the efficiency of market forces in Canada.

## Chapter 5: Introduction to the Macroeconomy

International unemployment, the inflation rate, and economic growth data have been integrated into the domestic discussion of these three central economic topics. Their inclusion provides a valuable global context in which the performance of the Canadian economy can be better evaluated. A second feature added to Chapter 5 relates to the accuracy of the Consumer Price Index (CPI) as a measure of prices and of price level changes. This added discussion provides necessary insight into the complexities involved in measuring changes to an economies price level using the CPI methodology.

## Chapter 6: Measuring Economic Performance

The discussion detailing the income approach to calculating gross domestic product has been re-worked in the latest edition of this chapter. This revised discussion provides greater clarity and detail to this key measure of economic performance.

## Chapter 7: Economic Growth in the Global Economy

An expanded discussion explaining the impact of physical capital on labour productivity is now part of the Determinants of Economic Growth section of Chapter 7. In addition, a detailed numerical example accompanies the discussion to provide valuable illustration and clarification.

## Chapter 11: Money and the Banking System

Greater detail has been added to the section outlining the evolution of the monetary aggregates M2 and M2+ in Canada. This added detail provides valuable insight into the evolving nature of savings among Canadian households.

## Chapter 13: Monetary Policy

The nonconventional forms of monetary policy that emerged as a result of the global financial crisis are acknowledged and detailed in the newly expanded discussion of monetary policy.

## FEATURES OF THE BOOK
## The Section-by-Section Approach

*Exploring Macroeconomics* uses a section-by-section approach in which economic ideas and concepts are presented in short, self-contained units rather than in large blocks of text. Each chapter is composed of approximately four to six bite-sized sections, with each section typically presented in two to eight pages that include all of the relevant graphs, tables, applications, features, photos, and definitions for the topic at hand. Our enthusiasm for and dedication to this approach stems from studying research on *learning theory,* which indicates that students retain information much better when it is broken down into short, intense, and exciting bursts of "digestible" information. Students prefer information divided into smaller, self-contained sections that are less overwhelming, more manageable, and easier to review before going on to new material. In short, students will be more successful in mastering and retaining economic principles using this approach, which is distinctly more compatible with modern communication styles.

But students aren't the only ones to benefit from this approach. The self-contained sections allow instructors greater flexibility in planning their courses. They can simply select or delete sections of the text as it fits their syllabus.

# Highlighted Learning Tools

**Key Questions** Each section begins with key questions designed to preview ideas and to pique students' interest in the material to come. These questions are then used to structure the section material that follows, each question being prominently displayed as a section heading, with additional subheadings provided as needed. In addition to ensuring a clear instructional layout of each section and chapter, these key questions can also be used by students as a review resource. After reading the section material, if students are able to answer the key questions, they can go forward with confidence.

**Section Checks** A *Section Check* appears at the end of each section and is designed to summarize the answers to the key questions posed at the beginning of the section. The summaries provided by the *Section Check* give students an opportunity to evaluate their understanding of major ideas before proceeding.

**Debate Features** *Debate* features are designed to provide students with an opportunity to develop and express their opinions about a variety of economic issues. The "For" and "Against" arguments that accompany each debate topic make it easy to use these features to initiate in-class discussions. By engaging in informal debate regarding current economic policy, students will be able to link course content to current events as well as to their own personal lives. Questions have been added to encourage critical thinking.

**Business Connection Features** *Business Connection* features are designed to help students see the link between economic theory and business fundamentals. They help students better understand the reasoning behind the empirical validity of economic theory and also aid in the grounding of abstract economic theory in modern business principles. Accompanying each *Business Connection* feature are questions that can be used to either evaluate student understanding or initiate in-class discussion.

**Photos** *Exploring Macroeconomics* contains a large number of colourful photos, which are an integral part of the book for both learning and motivation. The photos are carefully placed where they reinforce important concepts, and they are accompanied by captions designed to extend students' understanding of particular ideas.

**For Your Review** Provided at the end of each chapter, these problems allow students to test their understanding of chapter concepts. The *For Your Review* problems are organized into sections to match the corresponding sections in the text so that students and instructors can easily identify particular topics. To assist in the learning process, solutions to all odd-numbered problems are provided at the back of the text. With a variety of both problems and application-style questions to choose from, this section can also be used by instructors to assign homework directly from the text.

**Blueprint Problems** Integrated into the end-of-chapter *For Your Review* sections, these fully annotated problems and their solutions are intended to provide additional insight into key economic topics and issues. Intentionally designed to mirror the accompanying *For Your Review* problems, each *Blueprint Problem* allows students to "walk through" a complete solution, seeing the essential steps necessary to successfully complete a key economic question.

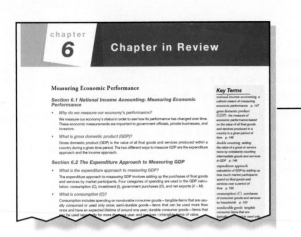

**Chapter in Review Cards**   Located at the back of the textbook, these detachable *Chapter in Review* cards are designed to give students a summary overview of key chapter concepts at a glance. Each *Chapter in Review* card contains the following information:

- **Chapter Summary** A point-form summary response to the section's key questions, highlighting the most important concepts of each section, is provided.
- **Key Terms** A list of key terms allows students to test their mastery of new concepts. Both the definition and the page number are included so that students can easily find a key term in a chapter.
- **Key Exhibits/Graphs** Given the importance and explanatory ability of exhibits and graphical representations in economics, a list of key figures is provided for each chapter.
- **Key Equations** A list of key equations enables students to quickly refer to important formulas.

## INSTRUCTORS

The **Nelson Education Teaching Advantage (NETA)** program delivers research-based instructor's resources that promote student engagement and higher-order thinking to enable the success of Canadian students and educators. Be sure to visit Nelson Education's **Inspired Instruction** website at www.nelson.com/inspired to find out more about NETA. Don't miss the testimonials of instructors who have used NETA supplements and watched student engagement increase!

The following instructor's resources have been created for *Exploring Macroeconomics*, Fifth Canadian Edition. Access these ultimate tools for customizing lectures and presentations at www.nelson.com/instructor.

**Instructor's Solutions Manual:** Answers to all *For Your Review* questions in the textbook are provided in this manual, now separated from the Instructor's Manual for easier reference. Students can access only the odd-numbered solutions in the Answer Key at the back of the book. The solutions were prepared by the text co-author, Colin Kovacs, and independently checked for accuracy by Racquel Lindsay, University of Toronto.

**NETA Test Bank:** This resource was prepared by Russell Turner, Fleming College. It includes over 1775 multiple-choice questions written according to NETA guidelines for effective construction and development of higher-order questions. Also included are more than 290 true/false and more than 130 essay-type questions.

The NETA Test Bank is available in a new, cloud-based platform. **Nelson Testing Powered by Cognero®** is a secure online testing system that allows you to author, edit, and manage test bank content from any place you have Internet access. No special installations or downloads are needed, and the desktop-inspired interface, with its drop-down menus and familiar, intuitive tools, allows you to create and manage tests with ease. You can create multiple test versions in an instant, and import or export content into other systems. Tests can be delivered from your learning management system, your classroom, or wherever you want. Nelson Testing Powered by Cognero for

*Exploring Macroeconomics* can also be accessed through http://www.nelson.com/login and http://login.cengage.com. Printable versions of the Test Bank in Word and PDF versions are available with the instructor's resources for the textbook.

**NETA PowerPoint:** Microsoft® PowerPoint® lecture slides for every chapter have been adapted by Ifeanyichukwu Uzoka of Sheridan College. We offer two separate collections. The Basic PowerPoint collection contains an average of 40 slides per chapter. This collection is a basic outline of the chapter and contains key figures, tables, and photographs from the fifth Canadian edition of *Exploring Macroeconomics*. The Expanded PowerPoint collection includes an average of 60 slides per chapter and provides a more complete overview of the chapter. NETA principles of clear design and engaging content have been incorporated throughout, making it simple for instructors to customize the deck for their courses.

**Image Library:** This resource consists of digital copies of figures, short tables, and photographs used in the book. Instructors may use these images to customize the NETA PowerPoint or create their own PowerPoint presentations.

**Instructor's Manual:** The *Instructor's Manual* to accompany *Exploring Macroeconomics*, Fifth Canadian Edition, has been prepared by Phil Ghayad and Michel Mayer of Dawson College. This manual is organized according to the textbook chapters and includes teaching tips and active learning exercises. (Answers to all *For Your Review* exercises in the text are now provided in the separate Instructor's Solutions Manual supplement described earlier.)

**DayOne:** Day One—Prof InClass is a PowerPoint presentation that instructors can customize to orient students to the class and their textbook at the beginning of the course.

## Aplia + MindTap

**MindTap** is the digital platform that propels students from memorization to mastery, helping to challenge them, build their confidence, and empower them to be unstoppable. **Aplia**™ is an application in the MindTap platform that has proven to significantly improve outcomes and elevate thinking by increasing student effort and engagement. Aplia makes it easy to assign frequent online homework assignments and assessments, ensuring students master important concepts. Developed by teachers, Aplia assignments connect concepts to the real world and focus on the unique course challenges faced by students. The MindTap content for *Exploring Macroeconomics*, Fifth Canadian Edition, was updated and revised by Jason Dean of Sheridan College. The Aplia problems for *Exploring Macroeconomics*, Fifth Canadian Edition, were updated and revised by Hanika Bhojwani-Chen of Centennial College.

The challenging and interactive activities within Aplia guide students through assignments, moving them from basic knowledge and understanding to application and practice. Look for the Aplia logo in the MindTap app dock to explore all that Aplia has to offer. With Aplia, instructors can do the following:

- easily set their course with pre-built, flexible homework assignments;
- author questions (single choice, multiple choice, true/false, essay and numeric entry);
- create custom assignments and populate them with self-authored—and Aplia-authored—questions; and
- inspire students to learn from their mistakes and reward them for effort with the Grade It Now feature that enables three attempts at different versions of a question.

## STUDENT ANCILLARIES

## Aplia + MindTap

Stay organized and efficient with MindTap—a single destination with all your course materials and study tools you need to succeed. Leverage the latest learning technology to stay on track with your learning. For this generation of digital natives, guidance is key to student confidence and engagement. MindTap makes learning a more constant part of your life, motivating you to take a more active role in learning and course preparedness.

- Personalized content in an easy-to-use interface helps you achieve better grades.
- The new MindTap Mobile App allows for learning anytime, anywhere with flashcards, quizzes and notifications.
- The MindTap Reader lets you highlight and take notes online, right within the pages, and easily reference them later.
- ReadSpeaker will read the text to you.

Aplia guides you through assignments, moving from basic knowledge and understanding to application and practice. These challenging and interactive activities are designed to reinforce important concepts. With Aplia, you can do the following:

- learn from mistakes and reinforce your learning with Grade It Now, which provides three attempts at a question;
- get immediate step-by-step feedback; and
- gain understanding through real-world application of concepts.

# Acknowledgments

Producing the fifth Canadian edition of *Exploring Macroeconomics* has truly been a team effort. We would like to thank the editorial, production, and marketing teams at Nelson Education for their hard work and effort. First, our appreciation goes to Claudine O'Donnell, Vice President, Product Solutions, who has provided the vision and leadership for the Canadian editions of the text.

We would like to thank Katherine Baker-Ross, publisher at Nelson, for her continuing support. Thank you to Katherine Goodes, Content Manager, for her helpful advice and constant encouragement. Thanks also to Imoinda Romain, Senior Production Project Manager; June Trusty, Copy Editor; Marcia Siekowski, Marketing Manager; and all the marketing and sales representatives at Nelson. Special thanks are extended to Darren Chapman at Fanshawe College for providing the engaging and insightful *Business Connection* and *Debate* features.

We are grateful to our families for their patience and encouragement.

Finally, we would like to acknowledge the reviewers of the Canadian editions, past and present, for their comments and feedback:

Sarah Arliss, *Seneca College*
Vick Barylak, *Sheridan College*
Aurelia Best, *Centennial College*
Ramesh Bhardwaj, *George Brown College*
Michael Bozzo, *Mohawk College*
Jim Butko, *Niagara College*
Lewis Callahan, *Lethbridge College*
Darren Chapman, *Fanshawe College*
Robert Dale, *Algonquin College*
Carol Derksen, *Red River College*
Jeffrey Dzikowicz, *Red River College*
Bruno Fullone, *George Brown College*
Alexander Gainer, *University of Alberta*
Phillipe Ghayad, *Dawson College*
James Hnatchuk, *Champlain College Saint-Lambert*
Michael Leonard, *Kwantlen Polytechnic University*
Margaret Rose Olfert, *University of Saskatchewan*
Geoffrey Prince, *Centennial College*
Norm Smith, *Georgian College*
Martha Spence, *Confederation College*
Sarah J. Stevens, *Georgian College*
Carl Weston, *Mohawk College*

Their thoughtful suggestions were very important to us in providing input and useful examples for the fifth Canadian edition of this book.

P.N.F.
C.C.K.

# The Role and Method of Economics

**section**

**1.1**

# Economics: A Brief Introduction

- What is economics?
- Why study economics?
- What distinguishes macroeconomics from microeconomics?

## WHAT IS ECONOMICS?

Some individuals think economics involves the study of the stock market and corporate finance, and it does—in part. Others think that economics is concerned with the wise use of money and other matters of personal finance, and it is—in part. Still others think that economics involves forecasting or predicting what business conditions will be like in the future, and again, it does—in part.

### Growing Wants and Scarce Resources

Precisely defined, **economics** is the study of the allocation of our limited resources to satisfy our unlimited wants. **Resources** are inputs—such as land, human effort and skills, and machines and factories—used to produce goods and services. The problem is that our wants exceed our limited resources, a fact that we call *scarcity*. Scarcity forces us to make choices on how to best use our limited resources. This is **the economic problem**: Scarcity forces us to choose, and choices are costly because we must give up other opportunities that we value. This economizing problem is evident in every aspect of our lives. Choosing between a trip to the gym or the coffee shop, or between finishing an assignment or chatting online, can be understood more easily when one has a good handle on the "economic way of thinking."

**economics**
*the study of the allocation of our limited resources to satisfy our unlimited wants*

**resources**
*inputs used to produce goods and services*

**the economic problem**
*Scarcity forces us to choose, and choices are costly because we must give up other opportunities that we value.*

Anatoliy Babiy/iStock/Thinkstock

**Articles related to economics—either directly or indirectly—are common in the news media. News headlines might trumpet: Gasoline Prices Soar; Stocks Rise; Stocks Fall; Prime Minister Vows to Increase National Defence Spending; Health-Care Costs Continue to Rise.**

## Economics Is All Around Us

Although many things that we desire in life are considered to be "noneconomic," economics concerns anything that is considered worthwhile to some human being. For instance, love, sexual activity, and religion have value for most people. Even these have an economic dimension. Consider love and sex, for example. One product of love—the institution of the family—is an important economic decision-making unit. Also, sexual activity results in the birth of children, one of the most important "goods" that many humans want. Economic forces have played a central role in the evolution of the family unit, from the traditional "nuclear family" (Dad, Mom, and two kids) to dual-income families, to dual-income no-kids (DINKs) families. Concerns for spiritual matters have likewise received economists' scrutiny, as they have led to the development of institutions such as churches, mosques, and temples that provide religious and spiritual services. These services are goods that many people want.

Even time has an economic dimension. In fact, perhaps the most precious single resource is time. We all have the same limited amount of time per day, and how we divide our time between work and leisure (including perhaps study, sleep, exercise, etc.) is a distinctly economic matter. If we choose more work, we must sacrifice leisure. If we choose to study, we must sacrifice time with friends, or time spent sleeping or watching TV. Virtually everything we decide to do, then, has an economic dimension.

Living in a world of scarcity involves trade-offs. As you are reading this text, you are giving up other things you value, such as shopping, spending time on Facebook, text messaging with friends, going to the movies, sleeping, or working out. When we know what the trade-offs are, we can make better choices from the options all around us, every day.

## WHY STUDY ECONOMICS?

Among the many good reasons to study economics, perhaps the best reason is that so many of the things of concern in the world around us are at least partly economic in character. A quick look at media headlines reveals the vast range of problems that are related to economics—global warming, health care, education, and social assistance. The study of economics improves your understanding of these concerns. A student of economics becomes aware that, at a basic level, much of economic life involves choosing among alternative possible courses of action—making choices between our conflicting wants and desires in a world of scarcity. Economics provides some clues as to how to intelligently evaluate these options and determine the most appropriate choices in given situations. But economists learn quickly that there are seldom easy, clear-cut solutions to the problems we face: The easy problems were solved long ago!

Many students take introductory postsecondary economics courses because these are part of the core curriculum requirements. But why do the committees that establish these requirements include economics? In part, economics helps develop a disciplined method of thinking about problems as opposed to simply memorizing solutions. The problem-solving tools you will develop by studying economics will prove valuable to you in both your personal and professional life, regardless of your career choice. In short, the study of economics provides a systematic, disciplined way of thinking.

## Using This Stuff

The basic tools of economics are valuable to people in all walks of life and in all career paths. Journalists benefit from economics because the problem-solving perspective it teaches trains them to ask intelligent questions whose answers will better inform their readers. Engineers, architects, and contractors usually have alternative ways to build. Architects learn to combine technical expertise and artistry with the limitations imposed by finite resources. That is, they learn how to evaluate their options from an economic perspective. Business owners face similar problems, because costs are a constraint in both creating and marketing a new product. Will the added cost of developing a new and improved product be outweighed by the added sales revenues that are expected to result? Economists can, however, pose these questions and provide criteria that business owners can use in evaluating the appropriateness of one design as compared to another. The point is that the economic way of thinking causes those in many types of fields to ask the right kind of questions.

## WHAT DISTINGUISHES MACROECONOMICS FROM MICROECONOMICS?

Like psychology, sociology, anthropology, and political science, economics is considered a social science. Economics, like the other social sciences, is concerned with reaching generalizations about human behaviour. Economics is the study of people. It is the social science that studies the choices people make in a world of limited resources.

Economics and the other social sciences often complement one another. For example, a political scientist might examine the process that led to the adoption of a certain tax policy, whereas an economist might analyze the impact of that tax policy. Or, whereas a psychologist may try to figure out what makes the criminal mind work, an economist might study the factors causing a change in the crime rate. Social scientists, then, may be studying the same issue but from different perspectives.

Conventionally, we distinguish two main branches of economics: macroeconomics and microeconomics. **Macroeconomics** is the study of the **aggregate** or total economy; it looks at economic problems as they influence the whole of society. Topics covered in macroeconomics include discussions of inflation, unemployment, business cycles, and economic growth. **Microeconomics** is the study of the smaller units within the economy. Topics include the decision-making behaviour of firms and households and their interaction in markets for particular goods or services. Microeconomic topics also include discussions of health care, agricultural subsidies, the price of everyday items such as running shoes, the distribution of income, and the impact of labour unions on wages. To put it simply, microeconomics looks at the trees whereas macroeconomics looks at the forest.

**macroeconomics**
*the study of the aggregate economy, including the topics of inflation, unemployment, and economic growth*

**aggregate**
*the total amount—such as the aggregate level of output*

**microeconomics**
*the study of the smaller units within the economy, including the topics of household and firm behaviour and how they interact in the marketplace*

## SECTION CHECK

- Economics is the study of the allocation of our limited resources to satisfy our unlimited wants.
- Economics is a problem-solving social science that teaches you how to ask intelligent questions.
- Macroeconomics deals with the aggregate, or total, economy, while microeconomics focuses on smaller units within the economy.

# section
# 1.2

# Economic Theory

- What are economic theories?
- Why do we need to abstract?
- What is a hypothesis?
- What is the *ceteris paribus* assumption?
- Why are observations and predictions harder in the social sciences?
- What distinguishes between correlation and causation?
- What are positive analysis and normative analysis?

## WHAT ARE ECONOMIC THEORIES?

**theory**
*an established explanation that accounts for known facts or phenomena*

A **theory** is an established explanation that accounts for known facts or phenomena. Specifically, economic theories are statements or propositions about patterns of human behaviour that are expected to take place under certain circumstances. These theories help us to sort out and understand the complexities of economic behaviour. We expect a good theory to explain and predict well. A good economic theory, then, should help us to better understand and, ideally, predict human economic behaviour.

## WHY DO WE NEED TO ABSTRACT?

How is economic theory like a GPS? Because of the complexity of human behaviour, economists must abstract to focus on the most important components of a particular problem. This is similar to how a GPS highlights the important information (and does not register many minor details) to help people get from here to there.

Economic theories cannot realistically include every event that has ever occurred. This is true for the same reason that a newspaper or history book does not include every world event that has ever happened. We must abstract. Without abstraction or simplification, the world is too complex to analyze.

Economic theories and models make some unrealistic assumptions. For example, we may assume there are only two countries in the world, producing two goods. Obviously, this is an abstraction from the real world. But if we can understand trade in a simplified world, it will help us understand trade in a more complex world. Similarly, sometimes economists make very strong assumptions, such as the assumption that all people seek self-betterment or all firms attempt to maximize profits. That is, economists use simplifying assumptions in their models to make the world more comprehendible. But only when we test our models using these assumptions can we find out if they are too simplified or too limiting.

How are economic theories and models like a road map? A road map of Canada may not include every creek, ridge, and valley between Vancouver and Halifax—indeed, such an all-inclusive map would be too complicated and confusing to be of much value. However, a GPS programmed to guide the traveller while referencing key details encountered along the way, such as highways and major attractions, will provide enough

Rafal Olechowski/iStock/Thinkstock

information to travel by car from Vancouver to Halifax. Likewise, an economic theory provides a broad view, not a detailed examination, of human economic behaviour.

## WHAT IS A HYPOTHESIS?

The beginning of any theory is a **hypothesis**, a testable proposition that makes some type of prediction about behaviour in response to certain changes in conditions. In economic theory, a hypothesis is a testable prediction about how people will behave or react to a change in economic circumstances. For example, if the price of iPads increased, we might hypothesize that fewer iPads would be sold, or if the price of iPads fell, we might hypothesize that more iPads would be sold. Once a hypothesis is stated, it is tested by comparing what it predicts will happen to what actually happens.

**hypothesis**
*a testable proposition*

## Using Empirical Analysis

To see whether a hypothesis is valid, we must engage in an **empirical analysis**. That is, we must examine the data to see whether the hypothesis fits well with the facts. If the hypothesis is consistent with real-world observations, it is accepted; if it does not fit well with the facts, it is "back to the drawing board."

Determining whether a hypothesis is acceptable is more difficult in economics than it is in the natural or physical sciences. Chemists, for example, can observe chemical reactions under laboratory conditions. They can alter the environment to meet the assumptions of the hypothesis and can readily manipulate the variables (chemicals, temperatures, and so on) crucial to the proposed relationship. Such controlled experimentation is seldom possible in economics. The laboratory of economists is usually the real world. Unlike a chemistry lab, economists cannot easily control all the other variables that might influence human behaviour.

**empirical analysis**
*the examination of data to see whether the hypothesis fits well with the facts*

## From Hypothesis to Theory

After gathering their data, economic researchers must then evaluate the results to determine whether the hypothesis is supported or refuted. If supported, the hypothesis can then be tentatively accepted as an economic theory.

Economic theories are always on probation. A hypothesis is constantly being tested against empirical findings. Do the observed findings support the prediction? When a hypothesis survives a number of tests, it is accepted until it no longer predicts well.

## WHAT IS THE *CETERIS PARIBUS* ASSUMPTION?

Virtually all economic theories share a condition usually expressed by use of the Latin expression ***ceteris paribus***. This roughly means "let everything else be equal" or "holding everything else constant." In trying to assess the effect of one variable on another, we must isolate their relationship from other events that might also influence the situation that the theory tries to explain or predict. To make this clearer, we will illustrate this concept with a couple of examples.

***ceteris paribus***
*holding everything else constant*

Suppose you develop your own theory describing the relationship between studying and exam performance: If I study harder, I will perform better on the test. That sounds logical, right? Holding other things constant (*ceteris paribus*), this is likely to be true. However, what if you studied harder but inadvertently overslept the day of the exam? What if you were so sleepy during the test that you could not think clearly? Or what if you studied the wrong material? Although it may look as if additional studying did not improve your performance, the real problem may lie in the impact of other variables, such as sleep deficiency or how you studied.

## WHY ARE OBSERVATIONS AND PREDICTIONS HARDER IN THE SOCIAL SCIENCES?

Working from observations, scientists try to make generalizations that will enable them to predict certain events. However, observation and prediction are more difficult in the social sciences than in physical sciences such as chemistry, physics, and astronomy. Why? The major reason for the difference is that the social scientists, including economists, are concerned with *human* behaviour. And human behaviour is more variable and often less readily predictable than the behaviour of experiments observed in a laboratory. However, by looking at the actions of a large group of people, economists can still make many reliable predictions about human behaviour.

### Economists Predict on a Group Level

Economists' predictions usually refer to the collective behaviour of large groups rather than to that of specific individuals. Why is this? Looking at the behaviours of a large group allows economists to discern general patterns of actions. For example, consider what would happen if the price of air travel from Canada to Europe was drastically reduced, say from $1500 to $500, because of the invention of a more fuel-efficient jet. What type of predictions could we make about the effect of this price reduction on the buying habits of typical consumers?

### Individual Behaviour

Let's look first at the responses of individuals. As a result of the price drop, some people will greatly increase their intercontinental travel, enjoying theatre weekends in London or week-long trips to France to indulge in French food. Some people, however, are terribly afraid to fly, and a price reduction will not influence their behaviour in the slightest. Others might detest Europe and, despite the lowered airfares, prefer to spend a few days in Vancouver instead. A few people might respond to the airfare reduction very negatively: At the lower fare, they might make fewer trips to Europe, because they might believe (rightly or wrongly) that the price drop would be accompanied by a reduction in the quality of service, greater crowding, or reduced safety. In short, we cannot predict with any level of certainty how a given individual will respond to this airfare reduction.

### Group Behaviour

Group behaviour is often more predictable than individual behaviour. When the weather gets colder, more firewood is sold. Some individuals may not buy firewood (e.g., if they don't have a fireplace in their home), but we can predict with great accuracy that a group of individuals will establish a pattern of buying more firewood. Similarly, while we cannot say what each individual will do, within a group of persons, we can predict with great accuracy that more flights to Europe from Toronto will be sold at lower prices, holding other things such as income and preferences constant. We cannot predict exactly how many more airline tickets will be sold at $500 than at $1500, but we can predict the direction of the impact and approximate the extent of the impact. By observing the relationship between the price of goods and services and the quantities people purchase in different places and during different time periods, it is possible to make some reliable generalizations about how much people will react to changes in the prices of goods and services. Economists use this larger picture of the group for most of their theoretical analysis.

## WHAT DISTINGUISHES BETWEEN CORRELATION AND CAUSATION?

Without a theory of causation, no scientist could sort out and understand the enormous complexity of the real world. But one must always be careful not to confuse correlation with causation. In other words, the fact that two events usually occur together (**correlation**) does not necessarily mean that one caused the other to occur (**causation**). For example, say a groundhog awakes after a long winter of hibernation, climbs out of his hole, sees his shadow, and then six weeks of bad weather ensue. Did the groundhog cause the bad weather? It is highly unlikely.

Perhaps the causality may run in the opposite direction. Although a rooster may always crow before the sun rises, it does not cause the sunrise; rather, the early light from the sunrise causes the rooster to crow.

### The Positive Correlation between Ice Cream Sales and Crime

Did you know that when ice cream sales rise, so do crime rates? What do you think causes the two events to occur together? Some might think that a sugar "high" caused by the ice cream causes the higher crime rate. Excess sugar in a snack was actually used in court testimony in a murder case—the so-called "Twinkie defence." However, it is more likely that crime peaks in the summer because of weather, more people on vacation (leaving their homes vacant), teenagers out of school, and so on. It just happens that ice cream sales also peak in those months because of weather. The lesson: One must always be careful not to confuse correlation with causation and to be clear on the direction of the causation.

### The Fallacy of Composition

One must also be careful with problems associated with aggregation (summing up all the parts), particularly the **fallacy of composition**. This fallacy states that even if something is true for an individual, it is not necessarily true for many individuals as a group. For example, say you are at a concert and you decide to stand up to get a better view of the stage. This works as long as no one else stands up. But what would happen if everyone stood up at the same time? Then, standing up would not let you see better. Hence, what may be true for an individual does not always hold true in the aggregate. The same can be said of arriving to class early to get a better parking place—what if everyone arrived early? Or studying harder to get a better grade in a class that is graded on a curve—what if everyone studied harder? All of these are examples of the fallacy of composition.

## WHAT ARE POSITIVE ANALYSIS AND NORMATIVE ANALYSIS?

### Positive Analysis

Most economists view themselves as scientists seeking the truth about the way people behave. They make speculations about economic behaviour, and then (ideally) they try to assess the validity of those predictions based on human experience. Their work emphasizes how people *do* behave, rather than how people *should* behave. In the role of scientist, an economist tries to observe, objectively, patterns of behaviour without

People tend to drive slower when the roads are covered with ice. In addition, more traffic accidents occur when the roads are icy. So, does driving slower cause the number of accidents to rise? No, it is the icy roads that lead to both lower speeds and more accidents.

**correlation**
*two events that usually occur together*

**causation**
*when one event causes another event to occur*

**fallacy of composition**
*Even if something is true for an individual, it is not necessarily true for a group.*

**positive analysis**
*an objective, value-free approach, utilizing the scientific method*

reference to the appropriateness or inappropriateness of that behaviour. This objective, value-free approach, utilizing the scientific method, is called **positive analysis**. In positive analysis, we want to know the impact of variable A on variable B. We want to be able to test a hypothesis. For example, the following is a positive statement: If rent controls are imposed, vacancy rates will fall. This statement is testable. A positive statement does not have to be a true statement, but it does have to be a testable statement.

However, keep in mind that it is doubtful that even the most objective scientist can be totally value-free in his or her analysis. An economist may well emphasize data or evidence that supports his hypothesis, putting less weight on other evidence that might be contradictory. This, alas, is human nature. But a good economist/scientist strives to be as fair and objective as possible in evaluating evidence and in stating conclusions based on the evidence.

## Normative Analysis

**normative analysis**
*a subjective, biased approach*

Like everyone, economists have opinions and make value judgments. When economists, or anyone else for that matter, express opinions about some economic policy or statement, they are indicating in part how they believe things should be, not just facts as to the way things are. **Normative analysis** is a subjective, biased approach, where one expresses opinions about the desirability of various actions. Normative statements involve judgments about what should be or what ought to happen. For example, one could judge that incomes should be more equally distributed. If there is a change in tax policy that makes incomes more equal, there will be positive economic questions that can be investigated, such as how work behaviour will change. But we cannot say, as scientists, that such a policy is good or bad; rather, we can point to what will likely happen if the policy is adopted.

## Positive vs. Normative Statements

The distinction between positive and normative analysis is important. It is one thing to say that everyone should have universal health care, a normative statement, and quite another to say that universal health care would lead to greater worker productivity, a testable positive statement. It is important to distinguish between positive and normative analysis because many controversies in economics revolve around policy considerations that contain both. When economists start talking about how the economy should work rather than how it does work, they have entered the normative world of the policymaker. Anytime you see the word *should*, be aware that you are in the realm of normative economics. Positive statements are about *what is*, normative statements are about what *ought to* or *should be*. In short, positive statements are attempts to *describe* what happens and why it happens, while normative statements are attempts to *prescribe* what should be done. But sometimes the two are intertwined.

## Why Economists Disagree

Although economists differ frequently on economic policy questions, there is probably less disagreement than the media would have you believe. Disagreement is common in most disciplines: Tech-savy consumers cannot agree which operating system is superior—Windows or Mac; historians can be at odds over the interpretation of historical events; psychologists disagree on proper ways to rear children; and nutritionists debate the merits of large doses of vitamin C.

The majority of disagreements in economics stem from normative issues, as differences in values or policy beliefs result in conflict. For example, a policy might increase efficiency at the expense of fairness or equity, or it might help a current generation at the expense of a future generation. Because policy decisions involve trade-offs, they will always involve the potential for conflict.

## Freedom vs. Fairness

Some economists are concerned about individual freedom and liberty, thinking that any encroachment on individual decision making is, other things equal, bad. People with this philosophic bent are inclined to be skeptical of any increased government involvement in the economy.

On the other hand, some economists are concerned with what they consider an unequal, "unfair," or unfortunate distribution of income, wealth, or power, and view governmental intervention as desirable in righting injustices that they believe exist in a market economy. To these persons, the threat to individual liberty alone is not sufficiently great to reject governmental intervention in the face of perceived economic injustice.

## The Validity of an Economic Theory

Aside from philosophic differences, there is a second reason why economists may differ on any given policy question. Specifically, they may disagree as to the validity of a given economic theory for the policy in question. Suppose two economists have identical philosophical views that have led them to the same conclusion: To end injustice and hardship, unemployment should be reduced. To reach the objective, the first economist believes the government should lower taxes and increase spending, whereas the second economist believes increasing the amount of money in public hands by various banking policies will achieve the same results with fewer undesirable consequences. The two economists differ because the empirical evidence for economic theories about the cause of unemployment appears to conflict. Some evidence suggests government taxation and spending policies are effective in reducing unemployment, whereas other evidence suggests that the prime cause of unnecessary unemployment lies with faulty monetary policy. Still other evidence is consistent with the view that, over long periods, neither approach mentioned here is of much value in reducing unemployment, and that unemployment will be part of our existence no matter what macroeconomic policies we follow.

Although you may not believe it after reading the previous discussion, economists don't always disagree. In fact, according to a survey among members of the American Economic Association, most economists agree on a wide range of issues, including rent control, import tariffs, export restrictions, the use of wage and price controls to curb inflation, and the minimum wage.

## SECTION CHECK

- Economic theories are statements used to explain and predict patterns of human behaviour.
- Economic theories, through abstraction, provide a broad view of human economic behaviour.
- A hypothesis makes a prediction about human behaviour and is then tested.
- In order to isolate the effects of one variable on another, we use the *ceteris paribus* assumption.
- With its focus on human behaviour, which is more variable and less predictable, observation and prediction are more difficult in the social sciences.
- The fact that two events are related does not mean that one caused the other to occur.
- Positive analysis is objective and value-free, while normative analysis involves value judgments and opinions about the desirability of various actions.

**section**

**1.3**

# Scarcity

- What is scarcity?
- What are goods and services?

Most of economics is knowing certain principles really well and knowing when and how to apply them. In the following sections, some important tools are presented that will help you understand the economic way of thinking. These few basic ideas will repeatedly occur throughout the text. If you develop a good understanding of these principles and master the problem-solving skills inherent in them, they will serve you well for the rest of your life.

## WHAT IS SCARCITY?

**scarcity**
*the situation that exists when human wants exceed available resources*

As we have already mentioned, economics is concerned primarily with **scarcity**—the situation that exists when human wants exceed available resources. We may want more "essential" items like food, clothing, schooling, and health care. We may want many other items like vacations, cars, computers, and concert tickets. We may want more friendship, love, knowledge, and so on. We also may have many goals—perhaps an A in this class, a university education, and a great job. Unfortunately, people are not able to fulfill all of their wants—material desires and nonmaterial desires. And as long as human wants exceed available resources, scarcity will exist.

## Scarcity and Resources

The scarce resources used in the production of goods and services can be grouped into four categories: labour, land, capital, and entrepreneurship.

**labour**
*the physical and mental effort used by people in the production of goods and services*

**Labour** is the total of both physical and mental effort used by people in the production of goods and services.

**land**
*the natural resources used in the production of goods and services*

**Land** includes the "gifts of nature" or the natural resources used in the production of goods and services. Trees, animals, water, minerals, and so on are all considered to be "land" for our purposes, along with the physical space normally thought of as land.

**capital**
*the equipment and structures used to produce goods and services*

**Capital** is the equipment and structures used to produce goods and services. Office buildings, tools, machines, and factories are all considered capital goods. When we invest in factories, machines, research and development, or education, we increase the potential to create more goods and services in the future. Capital also includes **human capital**, the productive knowledge and skills people receive from education and on-the-job training.

**human capital**
*the productive knowledge and skill people receive from education and on-the-job training*

**entrepreneurship**
*the process of combining labour, land, and capital together to produce goods and services*

**Entrepreneurship** is the process of combining labour, land, and capital together to produce goods and services. Entrepreneurs make the tough and risky decisions about what and how to produce goods and services. Entrepreneurs are always looking for new ways to improve production techniques or to create new products. They are lured by the chance to make a profit. It is this opportunity to make a profit that leads entrepreneurs to take risks.

However, entrepreneurs are not necessarily a John Molson (Molson Brewery), a Wallace McCain (frozen food empire), or a William or Alfred Billes (Canadian Tire). In some sense, we are all entrepreneurs when we try new products or when we find better ways to manage our households or our study time. Rather than money, then, our profits might take the form of greater enjoyment, additional time for recreation, or better grades.

## WHAT ARE GOODS AND SERVICES?

**Goods** are those items that we value or desire. Goods tend to be tangible—objects that can be seen, held, heard, tasted, or smelled. **Services** are intangible acts for which people are willing to pay, such as legal services, medical services, and dental care. Services are intangible because they are less overtly visible, but they are certainly no less valuable than goods. All goods and services, whether tangible or intangible, are produced from scarce resources and can be subjected to economic analysis. If there are not enough goods and services for all of us, we will have to compete for those scarce goods and services. That is, scarcity ultimately leads to competition for the available goods and services, a subject we will return to often in the text.

**goods**
*items we value or desire*

**services**
*intangible acts that people want*

### Bads

In contrast to goods, **bads** are those items that we do not desire or want. For most people, garbage, pollution, weeds, and crime are bads. People tend to eliminate or minimize bads, so they will often pay to have bads, like garbage, removed. The elimination of the bad—garbage removal, for example—is a good.

**bads**
*items that we do not desire or want*

## Business CONNECTION

### ECONOMICS IN BOTH BUSINESS AND LIFE

Why are business students required to study economics, and why so early in their chosen programs? The simple answer is that economics is really the game of life and that studying it can help students in business and other disciplines learn and appreciate how to better manage both their professional careers and their private households. Economics is, at its foundation, learning how decisions are made—whether the decisions are for consumers and firms or for households and governments. In making these decisions, we analyze (1) choices, benefits, and costs; (2) the way our decisions affect individual wants and needs; and (3) the way individual decisions affect people in general (consumers and society).

In today's economy, there is less emphasis on content (as it changes so quickly and is readily available online) and more emphasis on learning how to learn. In this respect, studying economics helps students to learn critical thinking skills. Students must also disengage from their phones and learn communication skills—these are the major skills that employers will be looking for. So, learning economics is not only for and about business, it is also a medium we can use to hone our thinking and communication skills—skills we'll use for the rest of our lives. It can be an important, high-impact course for everybody.

From a purely business point of view, profit is the ultimate goal, yet maximizing profits is just one of a number of strategies that a firm may follow. Others include focusing on growth, revenue generation, cash flow, cost reduction, product/service differentiation, product/service elimination, and vertical or horizontal integration. Each of these strat-

egies will have a different effect on the decisions of price and quantity over short, medium, or longer terms. All of these strategies seek to answer the three basic economic questions: (1) What to produce? (2) How to produce it? and (3) For whom? Finding the answers requires a knowledge of the basics of economics decision making.

Students should also recognize that there is only one constant, that time and circumstances change. What worked months or years ago may not work today or in the future, and what's good for individuals is not necessarily good for everyone and vice versa. Individuals and firms need to appreciate these changes, and economics and economic thinking teach us how to recognize and respect our changing environment so that we can make the changes that will be best for our particular goal(s).

Historically, business was all about maximizing profit for the benefit of shareholders. But this world is changing because of three significant realities that our parents never dealt with: (1) globalization, (2) environmental limitations to growth, and (3) automation and artificial intelligence (AI). Profits will still be required to keep firms in business, but all stakeholders—including firms, consumers, and governments—may no longer expect profits to be the main goal. In fact, AI and automation may force firms and governments to actually pay people *not* to work—and that will require a complete redefinition of many of the macroeconomic foundations we've relied on for centuries. Many firms now see themselves as socially responsible and emphasize other factors, such as the sustainability of the business and using the firm as a vehicle for employment and for achieving

*(continued)*

a higher standard of living for all. How those goals are achieved require economic decisions.

No matter what choice you make in terms of what you do in your career, where you work, what you produce, where you live, what you do in your leisure time, or even where you spend your time, economics will play a role in your decisions. So now you can appreciate why economics is not restricted to business, but rather why we see it as a major player in the game of life.

1.  What do you think is the single most important thing you'll learn from studying economics that will assist you in your business/working career?
2.  From an economic perspective, what do you think differentiates entrepreneurs from others working in business?
3.  Do you think entrepreneurs are born, or do you think anyone can learn to be an entrepreneur? What are your reasons for your opinion?

### Everyone Faces Scarcity

We all face scarcity because we cannot have all of the goods and services that we desire. However, because we all have different wants and desires, scarcity affects everyone differently. For example, a child in a developing country may face a scarcity of food and clean drinking water, whereas a rich person may face a scarcity of garage space for his growing antique car collection. Likewise, a harried middle-class working mother may find time for exercise particularly scarce, whereas a pharmaceutical company may be concerned with the scarcity of the natural resources it uses in its production process. Although its effects vary, no one can escape scarcity.

### SECTION CHECK

- Scarcity exists when our wants exceed the available resources of land, labour, capital, and entrepreneurship.
- Goods and services are things that we value.

## section 1.4

# Opportunity Cost

- Why do we have to make choices?
- What do we give up when we have to choose?
- Why are "free" lunches not free?

### WHY DO WE HAVE TO MAKE CHOICES?

We may want nice homes, two luxury cars in every garage, wholesome and good-tasting food, personal trainers, and therapists, all enjoyed in a pristine environment with zero pollution. If we had unlimited resources, and thus an ability to produce all of the goods and services anyone wanted, we would not have to choose among those desires. If we did not have to make meaningful economic choices, the study of economics would not be necessary. The essence of economics is to understand fully the implications that scarcity has for wise decision making. This suggests another way to define economics: *Economics is the study of the choices we make among our many wants and desires.*

## WHAT DO WE GIVE UP WHEN WE HAVE TO CHOOSE?

We are all faced with scarcity and, as a consequence, we must make choices. Because none of us can afford to buy everything we want, each time we do decide to buy one good or service, we reduce our ability to buy other things we would also like to have. If you buy a new car this year, you may not be able to afford your next best choice—the vacation you've been planning. You must choose. The cost of the car to you is the value of the vacation that must be forgone. The highest or best forgone opportunity resulting from a decision is called the **opportunity cost**. For example, time spent running costs time that could have been spent doing something else that is valuable—perhaps spending time with friends or studying for an upcoming exam. Another way to put this is that "to choose is to lose" or "an opportunity cost is an opportunity lost." To get more of anything that is desirable, you must accept less of something else that you also value.

**opportunity cost**
*the highest or best forgone opportunity resulting from a decision*

One of the reasons why vehicle drivers talk so much on their cellphones is that they have little else to do with their time while driving—a low opportunity cost. However, drivers should not use cellphones while driving because this is a distraction; by not giving full attention to their driving, they are giving up safety. Trade-offs are everywhere. This particular trade-off is why many jurisdictions have made the use of a cellphone while driving illegal.

Bill Gates, Tiger Woods, and Mark Zuckerberg all quit university or college to pursue their dreams. Tiger Woods dropped out of Stanford to join the PGA golf tour. Bill Gates dropped out of Harvard to start a software company. Mark Zuckerberg also dropped out of Harvard to continue working on his social networking site Facebook. Staying in school would have cost each of them millions of dollars. We cannot say it would have been the wrong decision to stay in school, but it would have been costly. For each of them, the opportunity cost of staying in school was high.

**Drivers who talk on their cellphones or put on make-up while driving are attempting to make better use of their time while in the vehicle. However, the distractions these activities cause can result in a tragic trade-off.**

## Money Prices and Costs

If you go to the store to buy groceries, you have to pay for the items you buy. This amount is called the *money price*. It is an opportunity cost, because you could have used the money to purchase other goods and services. However, additional opportunity costs include the nonprice costs incurred to acquire the groceries—time spent getting to the grocery store, finding a parking space, actually shopping, and waiting in the checkout line. The nonprice costs are measured by assessing the sacrifice involved—the value you place on what you would have done with the time if you had not gone shopping. So the cost of grocery shopping is the price paid for the goods plus the nonprice costs incurred.

Minerva Studio/iStock/Thinkstock

Remember that many costs do not involve money but are still costs. Should I major in accounting or human resources? Should I go to college or university? Should I get an MBA now or work and wait a few years to go back to school?

Policymakers are unavoidably faced with opportunity costs too. Consider airline safety. Both money costs and time costs affect airline safety. New airline safety devices cost money (luggage inspection devices, fuel tank safeguards, new radar equipment, and so on), and time costs are quite relevant with the new safety checks. Time waiting in line costs time that could be spent doing something that is valuable. New airline safety requirements could also actually cost lives. If the new safety equipment costs are passed on in the form of higher airline ticket prices, people may choose to travel by car, which is far more dangerous per kilometre than air travel is. Opportunity costs are everywhere! And the real cost of anything is what you have to give up to get it.

### The Opportunity Cost of Going to School or Having a Child

The average person often does not correctly consider opportunity costs when thinking about costs. For example, the opportunity cost of going to school is not just the direct expense of tuition and books; of course, those expenses do involve an opportunity cost, because the money used for books and tuition could be used for other things that you value. But what about the nonmoney costs? That is, going to school also includes the opportunity cost of your time. Specifically, the time spent going to school is time that could have been spent on a job earning, say, $30 000 a year. And how often do people consider the opportunity cost of raising a child to the age of 18? There are the direct costs: food, visits to the dentist, clothes, piano lessons, and so on. But there are also additional costs incurred in rearing a child. Consider the cost if one parent chooses to give up his or her job to stay at home: Then, the time spent in child-rearing is time that could have been used making money and pursuing a career.

### WHY ARE "FREE" LUNCHES NOT FREE?

The expression *there's no such thing as a free lunch* clarifies the relationship between scarcity and opportunity cost. Suppose the school cafeteria is offering "free" lunches today. Although the lunch is free to you, is it really free from society's perspective? The answer is no, because some of society's scarce resources will have been used in the preparation of the lunch. The issue is whether the resources that went into creating that lunch could have been used to produce something else of value. Clearly, the scarce resources that went into the production of the lunch, such as the labour and materials (food-service workers, lettuce, meat, plows, tractors, fertilizer, and so forth) could have been used in other ways. They had an opportunity cost, and thus were not free. Whenever you hear the word "free"—free libraries, free admission, and so on—an alarm should go off in your head. Very few things are free in the sense that they use none of society's scarce resources. So what does a free lunch really mean? It is, technically speaking, a "subsidized" lunch—a lunch using society's scarce resources, but one for which you personally do not have to pay.

## SECTION CHECK

- Scarcity means we all have to make choices.
- When we are forced to choose, we give up the next highest-valued alternative.
- Because the production of any good uses up some of society's resources, there is no such thing as a free lunch.

# Marginal Thinking

- What do we mean by *marginal thinking*?
- What is the rule of rational choice?

## WHAT DO WE MEAN BY *MARGINAL THINKING*?

Most choices involve how *much* of something to do, rather than whether or not to do something. It is not *whether* you eat, but *how much* you eat. Hopefully, the question is not *whether* to study this semester but instead *how much* to study this semester. For example, "If I studied a little more, I might be able to improve my grade," or "If I had a little better concentration when I was studying, I could improve my grade." This is what economists call **marginal thinking** because the focus is on the additional, or incremental, choices. Marginal choices involve the effects of adding to or subtracting from the current situation. In short, it is the small (or large) incremental changes to a plan of action.

Always watch out for the difference between average and marginal costs. Suppose the cost to an airline of flying 250 passengers from Edmonton to Montreal was $100 000. The average cost per seat would be $400 (the total cost divided by the number of seats— $100 000/250). If ten people are on standby and willing to pay $300 for a seat on the flight, should the airline sell them a ticket? Yes! The unoccupied seats earn nothing for the airline. The airline pays the $400 average cost per seat regardless of whether or not someone is sitting in the seat. What the airline needs to focus on are the additional (marginal) costs of a few extra passengers. The marginal costs are minimal—slight wear and tear on the airplane, handling some extra baggage, and ten extra in-flight meals. In this case, thinking at the margin can increase total profits, even if it means selling at less than-average cost of production.

Auctions are another good example of marginal thinking. Prices are bid up marginally as the auctioneer calls out one price after another. When a bidder views the new price (the marginal cost) to be greater than the value she places on the good (the marginal benefit), she withdraws from further bidding.

**marginal thinking**
*focusing on the additional, or incremental, choices*

## WHAT IS THE RULE OF RATIONAL CHOICE?

In trying to make themselves better off, individuals will pursue an activity if the expected marginal benefits are greater than the expected marginal costs—this is the **rule of rational choice**. The term *expected* is used with marginal benefits and costs because the world is uncertain in many important respects, so the actual result of changing behaviour may not always make people better off—but on average it will. However, as a matter of rationality, people are assumed to engage only in behaviour that they think ahead of time will make them better off. That is, individuals will pursue an activity only if the expected marginal benefits are greater than the expected marginal costs, or *E(MB) > E(MC)*. This fairly unrestrictive and realistic view of individuals seeking self-betterment can be used to analyze a variety of social phenomena.

Suppose that you have to get up for an 8 A.M. class but have been up very late. When the alarm goes off at 7 A.M., you are weighing the marginal benefits and marginal costs of an extra 15 minutes of sleep. If you perceive the marginal benefits of

**rule of rational choice**
*Individuals will pursue an activity if the expected marginal benefits are greater than the expected marginal costs.*

15 minutes of sleep to be greater than the marginal costs of those extra minutes, you may choose to hit the snooze button. Or perhaps you may decide to blow off class completely. But it's unlikely you will choose that action if it is the day of the final exam, because it is now likely that the **net benefits**—the difference between the expected marginal benefits and expected marginal costs—of skipping class have changed. When people have opportunities to better themselves, they usually take them. And they will continue to seek those opportunities as long as they expect a net benefit from doing so.

**net benefits**
*the difference between the expected marginal benefits and expected marginal costs*

The rule of rational choice is simply the rule of being sensible, and most economists believe that individuals act *as if* they are sensible and apply the rule of rational choice to their daily lives. It is a rule that can help us understand our decision to study, walk, shop, exercise, clean house, cook, and perform just about every other action. It is also a rule that we will continue to use throughout the text because whether we are consumers, producers, or policymakers, we all must compare the expected marginal benefits and the expected marginal costs to determine the best level to consume, produce, or develop policies.

To help illustrate the concepts of marginal thinking and rational choice, consider the number of cakes a small neighbourhood bakery in suburban Vancouver can produce daily. The bakery employs three people. After performing a business analysis, we are able to determine the following daily production schedule: one employee, 25 cakes; two employees, 45 cakes; three employees, 60 cakes. What each employee can individually (or incrementally) produce represents that person's marginal benefit (*MB*)—these values are determined in the following table.

**What would you be willing to give up to eliminate the rush-hour congestion you face? Think of the number of hours drivers waste each year sitting in traffic in Canada's largest cities. It costs the Canadian economy hundreds of millions of dollars a year in lost wages and wasted fuel.**

Vladikpod/Dreamstime.com

| Employees | Total Production | Marginal Benefit (*MB*) |
|---|---|---|
| 0 | 0 | |
| | | 25 |
| 1 | 25 | |
| | | 20 |
| 2 | 45 | |
| | | 15 |
| 3 | 60 | |

How the bakery pays its employees provides us with another illustration of marginal thinking. If each employee is paid $55 a day, this is the individual (or incremental) cost of each employee—interpreted as the marginal cost (*MC*) of each worker.

We can now use these two illustrations of marginal thinking to help determine whether the bakery has the right number of employees. If a cake sells for $3, the daily *MB* of each employee would be as follows: first employee $75 (25 cakes × $3); second employee $60 (20 cakes × $3); third employee $45 (15 cakes × $3). Based on this information, the first employee represents $20 of positive net benefit [$75(*MB*) − $55(*MC*) = $20 net benefit]; the second employee represents $5 of positive net benefit [$60(*MB*) − $55(*MC*) = $5 net benefit]; while the third employee represents $10 of negative net benefit [$45(*MB*) − $55(*MC*) = −$10 net benefit]. The rule of rational choice would indicate that the bakery should hire the first two employees, but not the third employee.

## Zero Pollution Would Be Too Costly

Let's use the concept of marginal thinking to evaluate pollution levels. We all know the benefits of a cleaner environment, but what would we have to give up—that is, what marginal costs would we have to incur—in order to achieve zero pollution? A lot! You could not drive a car, fly in a plane, or even ride a bike, especially if everybody else was riding bikes too (because congestion is a form of pollution). How would you get to school or work, or go to the movies or the grocery store? Everyone would have to grow their own food because transporting, storing, and producing food uses

## DEBATE

### SHOULD EVERY NEW POLITICIAN HAVE TO BE EDUCATED IN ECONOMIC THEORY BEFORE BEING ALLOWED TO SIT AS A LAWMAKER OR POLICYMAKER?

Economics is about making decisions; for microeconomics, it's primarily about how individuals and firms make decisions, and for macroeconomics, it's about how decisions are made based on how the possible outcome looks from a wider perspective and how it might affect society as a whole.

For many years, almost any individual could stand for office in our democracies—the person just needed to put his or her name forward. However, as our society has become more complex and regulated (by both government and corporate policies), it is no longer sufficient that a layperson can understand the outcomes, effects, and costs well enough to make a good "gut" decision. Perhaps it's time that any elected politician should possess at least a basic understanding of micro- and macroeconomic theory. People who had taken such courses in postsecondary study would be free to sit immediately after election. Those who hadn't taken such courses would be required to do so before they could construct and vote on the bills that affect their constituents.

### For:

As many of society's problems and conflict originate as an economic problem (scarcity of something, an allocation issue, a choice between alternatives with both benefits and costs to each), it makes sense that those who make decisions for a society have an open and objective mind that can understand and appreciate the gravity of such decisions, both in the short and long term, and especially the impact on those that it affects. They need to understand that not all costs can be quantified, especially those that put values over monetary benchmarks. Economically well-schooled politicians would understand that there are not only explicit costs in making decisions, but implicit as well—and that the choice of not doing something has itself a cost associated with it.

A politician who appreciates the lens of an economist would appreciate the complexities of decisions where

what's good for the individual is not necessarily good for the masses, and what's good for the masses may not be good for individuals, where decisions are based not solely on one's intellect, but on knowledge as well. Surely, we should expect that those who make decisions for society should bring a higher level of thinking to the process, not just a "gut" instinct.

### Against:

Politics is a process in which many individuals from diverse backgrounds can come together and develop and debate different policies, regardless of their formal education. Requiring some form of formal education (even just some economics courses) should not be the case for someone who wants to represent a society. Countless individuals have served their country well without ever having finished high school, let alone having acquired a postsecondary education.

What if an otherwise well-qualified individual failed to get even a passing grade in an economics course? Should that mark the end of that person's political aspirations, or should the voters pass judgment on his or her qualifications?

1. How could a requirement for basic economic understanding be constructed so that it doesn't serve as a barrier to those who might be challenged in passing such a course but could still serve our society?

2. If you don't believe in your elected representatives having a basic understanding of economics, do you think there should be some form of competence that they need before making laws? What might that look like?

3. Having a requirement of completing a theoretical course stinks of elitism, and sets a standard that only those who can understand some complex theory can serve as community leaders. Does this not then marginalize those on the lower socioeconomic scale?

machinery and equipment that pollutes. And even growing your own food would be a problem because many plants emit natural pollutants. We could go on and on. The point is *not* that we shouldn't be concerned about the environment; rather, we have to weigh the expected marginal benefits of a cleaner environment against the expected marginal costs of a cleaner environment. This is not to say the environment should not be cleaner, only that zero pollution levels would be far too costly in terms of what we would have to give up.

## Optimal (Best) Levels of Safety

Just as we can have optimal (or best) levels of pollution that are greater than zero, it is also true for crime and safety. Take crime. What would it cost society to have zero crime? It would be prohibitively costly to divert a tremendous amount of our valuable resources toward the total elimination of crime. In fact, it would be impossible to eliminate crime totally. But it would also be costly to reduce crime significantly. Since lower crime rates are costly, society must decide how much it is willing to give up: The additional resources for crime prevention can come only from limited resources, which could be used to produce something else possibly valued even more.

The same is true for safer products. Nobody wants defective tires on their cars, or cars that are unsafe and roll over at low speeds. However, there are optimal amounts of safety that are greater than zero too. The issue is not safe versus unsafe products but rather *how much* safety consumers want. It is not risk versus no risk but rather *how much* risk are we willing to take? Additional safety can come only at higher costs. To make all products perfectly safe would be impossible, so we must weigh the benefits and costs of safer products. In fact, according to one U.S. study by Sam Peltzman, a University of Chicago economist, additional safety features in cars (mandatory safety belts, padded dashboards) in the late 1960s may have had little impact on highway fatalities. Peltzman found that making cars safer led to more reckless driving and more accidents. Although the safety regulations did result in fewer deaths per automobile accident, the total number of deaths remained unchanged because there were more accidents.

Reckless driving has benefits—getting somewhere more quickly—but it also has costs—possibly causing an accident or even a fatality. Rational people will compare the marginal benefits and marginal costs of safer driving and make the choices that they believe will get them to their destination safely. We would expect that even thrill-seekers would slow down if there were higher fines and/or increased law enforcement. It would change the benefit–cost equation for reckless driving (as would bad brakes, bald tires, and poor visibility). On the other hand, compulsory seat belts and air bags might cause motorists to drive more recklessly.

## SECTION CHECK

- Economists are usually interested in the effects of additional, or marginal, changes in a given situation.
- The rule of rational choice states that individuals will pursue an activity if they expect the marginal benefits to be greater than the marginal costs, or $E(MB) > E(MC)$.

# Incentives Matter

- Can we predict how people will respond to changes in incentives?
- What are positive and negative incentives?

## CAN WE PREDICT HOW PEOPLE WILL RESPOND TO CHANGES IN INCENTIVES?

In acting rationally, people are responding to incentives. That is, they are reacting to the changes in expected marginal benefits and expected marginal costs. In fact, much of human behaviour can be explained and predicted as a response to incentives. Consider the economic view of crime. Why do criminals engage in their "occupation"? Presumably because the "job," even with its risks, is preferred to alternative forms of employment. For criminals, the benefits of their actions are higher and/or the opportunity costs of them are lower than is the case for noncriminals. In some cases, criminals cannot get a legitimate job at a wage they would find acceptable, so the cost of crime in terms of other income forgone may be quite low. At other times, the likelihood of being caught is small, so the expected cost is negligible. Also, for some, the moral cost of a crime is low, whereas for others it is high. The benefits, in terms of wealth gained, are clear. If the expected gains or benefits from committing a crime outweigh the expected costs, the activity is pursued.

For most policy purposes, the primary concern is not what causes the level of crime to be what it is but, rather, what causes the level of crime to change. Changes in the crime rate can be largely explained in terms of such a benefit–cost framework. If the benefits of crime rise, say, in the form of larger real "hauls," and/or if the costs fall due to a reduced likelihood of being caught or of being imprisoned if caught, then economists would expect the amount of crime to rise. Likewise, economists would expect the crime rate to fall in response to increased police enforcement, stiffer punishments, or an increase in the employment rate. Whether this analysis tells the complete story is debatable, but use of the economic framework in thinking about the problem provides valuable insight.

## WHAT ARE POSITIVE AND NEGATIVE INCENTIVES?

Almost all of economics can be reduced to incentive [$E(MB)$ versus $E(MC)$] stories, where consumers and producers are driven by incentives that affect expected costs or benefits. Prices, wages, profits, taxes, and subsidies are all examples of economic incentives. Incentives can be classified into two types: positive and negative. **Positive incentives** are those that either increase benefits or reduce costs and thus result in an increased level of the related activity or behaviour. **Negative incentives**, on the other hand, either reduce benefits or increase costs, resulting in a decreased level of the related activity or behaviour. For example, a tax on cars that emit lots of pollution (an increase in costs) would be a negative incentive that would lead to a reduction in emitted pollution. On the other hand, a subsidy (the opposite of a tax) for hybrid cars—part electric, part internal combustion—would be a positive incentive

**positive incentives**
*incentives that either reduce costs or increase benefits, resulting in an increase in the activity or behaviour*

**negative incentives**
*incentives that either increase costs or reduce benefits, resulting in a decrease in the activity or behaviour*

A subsidy for hybrid electric vehicles (HEVs) would be a positive incentive that would encourage greater production and consumption of these vehicles. A wide variety of incentives are offered by governments to encourage the expanded use of alternative-fuel vehicles.

WENN Ltd/Alamy Stock Photo

that would encourage greater production and consumption of hybrid cars. Human behaviour is influenced in predictable ways by such changes in economic incentives, and economists use this information to predict what will happen when the benefits and costs of any choice are changed. In short, economists study the incentives and consequences of particular actions.

Because most people seek opportunities that make them better off, we can predict what will happen when incentives are changed. If salaries increase for engineers and decrease for MBAs, we would predict fewer people would go to a business graduate school and more would go into engineering. A permanent change to a much higher price of gasoline would lead us to expect fewer gas guzzlers on the highway. People who work on commission tend to work harder. If the price of downtown parking increased, we would predict that commuters would look for alternative methods to get to work that would save money.

If households were taxed to conserve water, economists would expect people to use less water—and substantially less water than if they were simply asked to conserve water. Some people are charitable and some people are stingy, but if you change the tax code to give even greater deductions for charitable contributions, we can predict that more people will be charitable, even some of those who are stingy. Incentives matter.

## SECTION CHECK

- People respond to incentives in predictable ways.
- A positive incentive decreases costs or increases benefits, thus encouraging consumption or production, while a negative incentive increases costs or reduces benefits, thus discouraging consumption or production.

# Specialization and Trade

- Why do people specialize?
- How do specialization and trade lead to greater wealth and prosperity?

## WHY DO PEOPLE SPECIALIZE?

As you look around, you can see that people specialize in what they produce. They tend to dedicate their resources to one primary activity, whether it be child-rearing, driving a bus, or making bagels. Why is this? The answer, short and simple, is opportunity costs. By concentrating on the production of one, or a few, goods or services, individuals are **specializing**. This allows them to make the best use of (and thus gain the most benefit from) their limited resources. A person, a region, or a country can gain by specializing in the production of the good or service in which they have a comparative advantage. That is, if they can produce a good or service at a lower opportunity cost than others, we say that they have a **comparative advantage** in the production of that good or service.

For example, should a lawyer who types 100 words per minute hire an administrative assistant to type her legal documents if the assistant can type only 50 words per minute? The answer to this question depends on the particular comparative advantages of the lawyer and the administrative assistant. Consider a job that would take the lawyer five hours and the administrative assistant ten hours to complete. If the lawyer makes $100 an hour, and the administrative assistant earns $15 an hour, who has the comparative advantage?

If the lawyer types her own documents, it will cost $500 ($100 per hour × 5 hours). If she has the administrative assistant type her documents, it will cost $150 ($15 per hour × 10 hours). Clearly, then, the lawyer should hire the administrative assistant to type her documents because the administrative assistant has the comparative advantage (lower opportunity cost) in this case, despite being half as good in absolute terms.

**specializing**
*concentrating on the production of one, or a few, goods or services*

**comparative advantage**
*occurs when a person or a country can produce a good or service at a lower opportunity cost than others can*

## We All Specialize

We all specialize to some extent and rely on others to produce most of the goods and services we want. The work that we choose to do reflects our specialization. For example, we may specialize in selling or fixing automobiles. The wages from that work can then be used to buy goods from a farmer who has chosen to specialize in the production of food. Likewise, the farmer can use the money earned from selling his produce to get his tractor fixed by someone who specializes in that activity.

Specialization is evident not only among individuals but among regions and countries as well. In fact, the story of the economic development of Canada involves specialization. Within Canada, the prairies with their wheat, the Maritime provinces of eastern Canada with their fishing fleets, and Alberta with its oil and gas are all examples of regional specialization.

## The Advantages of Specialization

In a small business, employees may perform a wide variety of tasks—from hiring to word processing to marketing. As the size of the company increases, each employee can perform a more specialized job, with a consequent increase in output per worker.

The primary advantages of specialization are that employees acquire greater skill from repetition, they avoid wasted time in shifting from one task to another, and they do the types of work for which they are best suited. Specialization also promotes the use of specialized equipment for specialized tasks.

The advantages of specialization are seen throughout the workplace. For example, in larger firms, specialists conduct personnel relations and accounting is in the hands of full-time accountants; such jobs are too critical in large firms to be done by someone with half a dozen other tasks to perform. The owner of a small retail store selects the location for the store primarily through guesswork, placing it where she believes sales will be high or where an empty, low-rent building is available. In contrast, larger chains have store sites selected by experts who have experience in analyzing the factors that make different locations relatively more desirable, like traffic patterns, income levels, demographics, and so on.

## HOW DO SPECIALIZATION AND TRADE LEAD TO GREATER WEALTH AND PROSPERITY?

Trade, or voluntary exchange, directly increases wealth by making both parties better off (or they wouldn't trade). It is the prospect of wealth-increasing exchange that leads to productive specialization. That is, trade increases wealth by allowing a person, a region, or a nation to specialize in those products that it produces at a lower opportunity cost and to trade for those products that others produce at a lower opportunity cost. That is, we trade with others because it frees up time and resources to do other things that we do better. For example, say Canada is better at producing wheat than Brazil, and Brazil is better at producing coffee than Canada. Canada and Brazil would each benefit if Canada produces wheat and trades some of it to Brazil for coffee. Coffee growers in Canada could grow coffee in expensive greenhouses, but it would result in higher coffee costs and prices, while leaving fewer resources available for employment in more productive jobs, such as wheat production. This is true for individuals, too. Imagine Tom had 10 kilograms of tea and Katherine had 10 kilograms of coffee. However, Tom preferred coffee to tea and Katherine preferred tea to coffee. So if Tom traded his tea to Katherine for her coffee, both parties would be better off. Trade simply reallocates existing goods, and voluntary exchange increases wealth by making both parties better off, or they would not agree to trade.

In short, if we divide the tasks and produce what we do *relatively* best and trade for the rest, we will be better off than if we were self-sufficient—that is, without trade. Imagine life without trade, where you were completely self-sufficient—growing your own food, making your own clothes, working on your own car, building your own house. Do you think you would be better off?

### SECTION CHECK

- Specialization is important for individuals, businesses, regions, and nations. It allows them to make the best use of their limited resources.
- Specialization and trade increase wealth by allowing a person, a business, a region, or a nation to specialize in those products that it produces at a lower opportunity cost and to trade for those products that others produce at a lower opportunity cost.

# The Three Economic Questions Every Society Faces

- What is to be produced?
- How are the goods and services to be produced?
- Who will get the goods and services?

Collectively, our wants far outstrip what can be produced from nature's scarce resources. So how should we allocate those scarce resources? Some methods of resource allocation might seem bad and counterproductive, like the "survival of the fittest" competition that exists in the jungle. Physical violence has been used since the beginning of time, as people, regions, and countries attack one another to gain control over resources. One might argue that governments should allocate scarce resources on the basis of equal shares or according to need. However, this approach poses problems because of diverse individual preferences, the problem of ascertaining needs, and the negative work and investment incentives involved. In reality, society is made up of many approaches to resource allocation. For now, we will focus on one form of allocating goods and services found in most countries—the market system.

Because of scarcity, certain economic questions must be answered, regardless of the level of affluence of the society or its political structure. We will consider three fundamental questions that inevitably must be faced: (1) What is to be produced? (2) How are the goods and services to be produced? (3) Who will get the goods and services? These questions are unavoidable in a world of scarcity.

## WHAT IS TO BE PRODUCED?

How do individuals control production decisions in market-oriented economies? Questions arise such as "Should we produce lots of cars and just a few school buildings, or relatively few cars and more school buildings?" The answer to this and other such questions is called **consumer sovereignty**—how consumers vote on economic affairs with their dollars (or pounds or yen) in a market economy. Consumer sovereignty explains how individual consumers in market economies determine what is to be produced. High-definition televisions, digital cameras, cellphones, digital video recorders (DVRs), iPods, and tablets, for example, became part of our lives because consumers "voted" hundreds of dollars apiece on these goods. As they bought more plasma TVs, consumers "voted" fewer dollars for tube TVs. Similarly, CDs gave way to downloadable music as consumers voted for these items with their dollars. As consumers vote for more fuel-efficient cars and healthier foods, firms that want to remain profitable must listen and respond.

**consumer sovereignty**
*Consumers vote on economic affairs with their dollars in a market economy.*

### How Different Types of Economic Systems Answer the Question "What Is to Be Produced?"

Economies are organized in different ways to answer the question of what is to be produced. The dispute over the best way to answer this question has inflamed passions for centuries. Should central planning boards make the decisions, as in China and North Korea? In **command economies**, the government uses central planning

**command economy**
*The government uses central planning to coordinate most economic activities.*

to coordinate most economic activities. Under this type of regime, decisions about how many tractors or automobiles to produce are largely determined by a government official or a committee associated with the central planning organization. That same group decides on the number and size of school buildings, refrigerators, shoes, and so on. Other countries—including Canada, the United States, much of Europe, and, increasingly, Asia and elsewhere—have largely adopted a decentralized decision-making process in which literally millions of individual producers and consumers of goods and services determine what and how many will be produced. An economy that allocates goods and services through the private decisions of consumers, input suppliers, and firms is often referred to as a **market economy**. Actually, no nation has a pure market economy. Most countries, including Canada, are said to have a **mixed economy**. In such economies, the government and the private sector together determine the allocation of resources.

**market economy**
*Goods and services are allocated based on the private decisions of consumers, input suppliers, and firms.*

**mixed economy**
*Government and the private sector together determine the allocation of resources.*

## HOW ARE THE GOODS AND SERVICES TO BE PRODUCED?

Because of scarcity, all economies, regardless of their political structure, must decide how to produce the goods and services that they want. Goods and services can generally be produced in several ways. For example, a ditch can be dug by many workers using their hands, by a few workers with shovels, or by one person with a backhoe. Someone must decide which method is most appropriate. The larger the quantity of the good and the more elaborate the form of capital, the more labour that is saved and is thus made available for other uses. (Remember, goods like shovels and large earth-moving machines used to produce goods and services are called *capital*.) From this example, you might be tempted to conclude that it is desirable to use the biggest, most elaborate form of capital. But would you really want to plant your spring flowers with huge earth-moving machinery? That is, the most capital-intensive method of production might not always be the best. The best method is the least-cost method.

### The Best Form of Production

The best or optimal form of production will usually vary from one economy to the next. For example, earth-moving machinery is used to dig large ditches in Canada, the United States, and Europe, whereas in developing countries, such as India, China, or Pakistan, shovels are often used. Similarly, a person in Canada might use a power lawn mower to cut the grass, whereas in a developing country, a hand mower might be used or grass might not be cut at all. Why do these "optimal" forms of production vary so drastically? Compared to capital, labour is relatively cheap and plentiful in developing countries but relatively scarce and expensive in Canada. In contrast, capital (machines and tools, mainly) is comparatively plentiful and cheap in Canada but scarcer and more costly in developing countries. That is, in developing countries, production tends to be more **labour-intensive**, using a large amount of labour. In Canada, production tends to be more **capital-intensive**, using a large amount of capital. Each nation tends to use the production processes that conserve its relatively scarce (and thus relatively more expensive) resources and use more of its relatively abundant resources.

**labour-intensive**
*production that uses a large amount of labour*

**capital-intensive**
*production that uses a large amount of capital*

## WHO WILL GET THE GOODS AND SERVICES?

In every society, some mechanism must exist to determine how goods and services are to be distributed among the population. Who gets what? Why are some people able to consume or use far more goods and services than others? This question of distribution is so important that wars and revolutions have been fought over it. Both the French and Russian revolutions were concerned fundamentally with the distribution of goods and services. Even in societies where political questions are usually settled peacefully, the question of the distribution of income is an issue that always arouses strong emotional responses. As we will see, in a market economy with private ownership and control of the means of production, the amount of goods and services one is able to obtain depends on one's income, which in turn depends on the quantity and quality of the scarce resources that the individual controls. For example, Connor McDavid makes a lot of money because he has unique and marketable skills as a hockey player.

To say that this may or may not be "fair" is an opinion at the centre of the *efficiency* versus *equity* dilemma in economics. As an economy, do you focus on getting the most you can from your scarce resources (efficiency) or should the emphasis be on equally distributing the benefits of those resources to all (equity)? Some economists believe that individual freedom and choice are central to economic well-being. When limitations are placed on these individual freedoms, these economists believe that economic efficiency will suffer. On the other hand, some economists are concerned with the economic inequalities and unfairness created by production and distribution. For example, to these economists, government intervention is a valuable tool in making society more equitable. Regardless of which side of the debate is chosen, one truth is certain: Decisions regarding the three economic questions raised in this section play a central role in shaping the efficiency and equity of an economy.

Photo by Jeff Vinnick/NHLI via Getty Images

**Connor McDavid gets paid a lot of money because he controls a scarce resource: his talent and name recognition. As we will see in later chapters, people's talents and other goods and services in limited supply relative to demand will command high prices.**

## SECTION CHECK

- Every economy has to decide what to produce. In a market economy, millions of buyers and sellers determine what and how much to produce, while in a command economy, the government coordinates economic activity. In a mixed economy, the government and the private sector determine the allocation of resources.
- The best form of production is the one that conserves the relatively scarce (more costly) resources and uses more of the abundant (less costly) resources. When capital is relatively scarce and labour is plentiful, production tends to be labour-intensive. When capital is relatively abundant and labour is relatively scarce, production tends to be capital-intensive.
- In a market economy, the amount of goods and services one is able to obtain depends on one's income. The amount of one's income depends on the quantity and the quality of the scarce resources that the individual controls.

# For Your Review

## Section 1.1

1. Write your own definition of *economics*. What are the main elements of the definition?

2. Would the following topics be covered in microeconomics or macroeconomics?

   a. the effects of an increase in the supply of lumber on the home-building industry

   b. changes in the national unemployment rate

   c. the effect of interest rates on the machine-tool industry

   d. the effect of interest rates on the demand for investment goods

   e. the way a firm maximizes profits

## Section 1.2

3. Are the following statements normative or positive, or do they contain both normative and positive statements?

   a. A higher income tax rate would generate increased tax revenues. Those extra revenues should be used to give more government aid to the poor.

   b. The study of physics is more valuable than the study of sociology, but both should be studied by all postsecondary students.

   c. An increase in the price of wheat will decrease the amount of wheat purchased. However, it will increase the amount of wheat supplied to the market.

   d. A decrease in the price of butter will increase the amount of butter purchased, but that would be bad because it would increase Canadians' cholesterol levels.

   e. The birth rate is reduced as economies urbanize, but that also leads to an increased average age of developing countries' populations.

4. Which of the following economic statements are positive and which are normative?

   a. A tax increase will increase unemployment.

   b. The government should reduce funding for social assistance programs.

   c. Tariffs on imported wine will lead to higher prices for domestic wine.

   d. A decrease in the capital gains tax rate will increase investment.

   e. Goods purchased on the Internet should be subject to provincial sales taxes.

   f. A reduction in interest rates will cause inflation.

5. Do any of the following statements involve fallacies? If so, which ones do they involve?

   a. Because sitting in the back of classrooms is correlated with getting lower grades in the class, students should always sit closer to the front of the classroom.

   b. Historically, the stock market rises in years the NFC team wins the Super Bowl and falls when the AFC wins the Super Bowl. I am rooting for the NFC team to win for the sake of my investment portfolio.

c. When a hockey team spends more to get better players, it is more successful, which proves that all the teams should spend more to get better players.

d. Gasoline prices were higher last year than in 1970, yet people purchased more gas, which contradicts the law of demand.

e. An increase in the amount of money I have will make me better off, but an increase in the supply of money in the economy will not make Canadians as a group better off.

6. Why are observation and prediction more difficult in economics than in chemistry?

7. Why do economists look at group behaviour rather than individual behaviour?

## Section 1.3

8. Explain the difference between poverty and scarcity.

9. The automotive revolution after World War II reduced the time involved for travel and shipping goods. This innovation allowed the Canadian economy to produce more goods and services since it freed resources involved in transportation for other uses. The transportation revolution also increased wants. Identify two ways in which vehicle manufacturers evoked new wants.

10. Which of the following goods are scarce?

a. garbage

b. salt water in the ocean

c. clothes

d. clean air in a big city

e. dirty air in a big city

f. public libraries

## Section 1.4

11. The price of a one-way bus trip from Toronto to Ottawa is $150. Sarah, a school-teacher, pays the same price in February (during the school year) as in July (during her vacation), so the cost is the same in February as in July. Do you agree?

12. You work as a tutor at your school, making $15 per hour. Yesterday, you decided to cancel your two-hour tutoring appointment in order to meet friends for a coffee. The coffee cost you $3.50. What was the opportunity cost of this decision in dollars?

13. List the opportunity costs of the following:

a. going to college or university

b. missing a lecture

c. withdrawing and spending $100 from your savings account, which earns 5 percent interest annually

d. going snowboarding on the weekend before final examinations

14. Why does inaction have consequences?

15. In most countries, the birth rate has fallen as incomes and the economic opportunities for women have increased. Use economics to explain this pattern.

## Blueprint Problem

Assume that the total cost to Steve of producing additional sets of headphones at his factory is represented by the following schedule: 1 pair, $9; 2 pairs, $21; 3 pairs, $35; 4 pairs, $53; 5 pairs, $75 (for simplicity, assume all costs are variable, there are no fixed costs).

    a.  Calculate the marginal cost (*MC*) of each pair of headphones.

    b.  Suppose Steve sells each pair of headphones for $16. How many pairs of headphones will he make if his decision is based on rational choice?

## Blueprint Solution

| Number of Headphones Produced | Total Production Cost |
|:---:|:---:|
| 0 | $0 |
| 1 | 9 |
| 2 | 21 |
| 3 | 35 |
| 4 | 53 |
| 5 | 75 |

This problem is better understood if it is presented in a table.

Notice that if Steve decides not to make any headphones, his total cost is zero. This is due to the assumption that all of Steve's costs are variable and none are fixed.

a.

| Number of Headphones Produced | Total Production Cost | Marginal Production Cost of Each Pair of Headphones |
|:---:|:---:|:---:|
| 0 | $0 | |
| 1 | 9 | $9 |
| 2 | 21 | 12 |
| 3 | 35 | 14 |
| 4 | 53 | 18 |
| 5 | 75 | 22 |

To determine the marginal production cost of each pair of headphones, calculate the incremental cost resulting from the production of each additional pair of headphones. The third column displays the marginal cost (*MC*) of each pair of headphones.

b.

| Number of Headphones Produced | MC | MB | Net Benefit | Production Decision |
|---|---|---|---|---|
| 1 | $9 | $16 | $7 | Produce |
| 2 | 12 | 16 | 4 | Produce |
| 3 | 14 | 16 | 2 | Produce |
| 4 | 18 | 16 | −2 | Do not produce |
| 5 | 22 | 16 | −6 | Do not produce |

This question involves using the rule of rational choice. The determination of the marginal benefit (*MB*) is based on the assumption that Steve sells all of his pairs of headphones at the same price of $16.

Steve will make only those pairs of headphones that generate positive net benefit for his business, that is *E*(*MB*) > *E*(*MC*). The determination of net benefit provides the rationale for the production decision.

## Section 1.5

16. Assume the total benefits to Mark from trips to a local amusement park during the year are given by the following schedule: 1 trip, $60; 2 trips, $115; 3 trips, $165; 4 trips, $200; 5 trips, $225; 6 or more trips, $240.

   a. What is Mark's marginal benefit of the third trip? The fifth trip?

   b. If the admission price to the amusement park was $45 per day, how many times would Mark be willing and able to go in a year? What if the price was $20 per day? Explain.

   c. If the amusement park offered a year-long pass for $200 rather than a per-day admission price, would Mark be willing to buy one? If so, how many times would he go? Explain.

17. Assume the total cost of producing widgets was $4200 for 42 units; $4257 for 43 units; $4332 for 44 units; and $4420 for 45 units.

   a. What is the marginal cost of producing the 43rd unit? The 45th unit?

   b. If the widget producer could sell at $60 per unit—however many he could produce—how many would he choose to produce? If he could sell at $80 per unit—however many he could produce—how many would he choose to produce? Explain.

18. Imagine that you are trying to decide whether to cross a street without using the designated crosswalk at the traffic signal. What are the expected marginal benefits of crossing? What are the expected marginal costs? How would the following conditions change your benefit–cost equation?

    a. The street was busy.

    b. The street was empty and it was 3:00 A.M.

    c. You were in a huge hurry.

    d. There was a police officer 10 metres away.

    e. The closest crosswalk was 1 kilometre away.

    f. The closest crosswalk was 5 metres away.

19. Which of the following activities require marginal thinking, and why?

    a. studying

    b. eating

    c. driving

    d. shopping

    e. getting ready for a night out

20. Explain why following the rule of rational choice makes a person better off.

## Section 1.6

21. Which of the following are positive incentives? Negative incentives? Why?

    a. a fine for not cleaning up after your dog defecates in the park

    b. a trip to Hawaii paid for by your parents or significant other for earning an A in your economics course

    c. a higher tax on cigarettes and alcohol

    d. a subsidy for installing solar panels on your house

22. The penalty for drug trafficking in Singapore is death. Do you think there would be more drug traffickers in Singapore if the mandatory sentence was five years, with parole for good behaviour?

23. Under China's former family planning law (commonly referred to as its one-child policy), those who followed the policy were offered rewards, loans, and other forms of social assistance, depending on socioeconomic status. People who did not comply with the policy were subject to penalties such as fines and confiscation of personal property. Excess children could also be subject to educational and health sanctions. What behaviour was the Chinese government attempting to promote with these types of incentives? Identify which aspects of the law were negative incentives and which were positive incentives.

## Section 1.7

24. Throughout history, many countries have chosen the path of autarky, choosing to not trade with other countries. Explain why this path would make a country poorer.

25. Farmer Fran can grow soybeans and corn. She can grow 1500 kilograms of soybeans or 3000 kilograms of corn on a hectare of her land for the same cost. The price of soybeans is $1.50 per kilogram and the price of corn is $0.60 per kilogram. Show the benefits to Fran of specialization. What should she specialize in?

26. Which region has a comparative advantage in the following goods?
    a. wheat: Colombia or Canada
    b. coffee: Colombia or Canada
    c. lumber: Alberta or British Columbia
    d. oil: Alberta or British Columbia

27. a. Why is it important that the country or region with the lower opportunity cost produce the good?
    b. How would you use the concept of comparative advantage to argue for reducing restrictions on trade between countries?

## Section 1.8

28. What are the three basic economic questions? How are decisions made differently in a market economy than in command economies?

29. Adam was a university graduate with a double major in economics and art. A few years ago, Adam decided that he wanted to pursue a vocation that utilized both of his talents. In response, he shut himself up in his studio and created a watercolour collection, "Graphs of Famous Recessions." With high hopes, Adam put his collection on display for buyers. After several years of displaying his econ art, however, the only one interested in the collection was his eight-year-old sister, who wanted the picture frames for her room. Recognizing that Adam was having trouble pursuing his chosen occupation, Adam's friend Karl told him that the market had failed. What do you think? Is Karl right?

# Appendix

## GRAPHS ARE AN IMPORTANT ECONOMIC TOOL

Sometimes the use of visual aids, such as graphs, greatly enhances our understanding of a theory. It is much the same as finding your way to a friend's house with the aid of a map rather than with detailed verbal or written instructions. Graphs are important tools for economists. They allow us to understand better the workings of the economy. To economists, a graph can be worth a thousand words. This text will use graphs throughout to enhance the understanding of important economic relationships. This appendix provides a guide on how to read and create your own graphs.

The most useful graph for our purposes is one that merely connects a vertical line (the **Y-axis**) with a horizontal line (the **X-axis**), as seen in Exhibit 1. The intersection of the two lines occurs at the origin, which is where the value of both variables is equal to zero. In Exhibit 1, the graph has four quadrants or "boxes." In this textbook we will be primarily concerned with the shaded box in the upper right-hand corner. This portion of the graph deals exclusively with positive numbers. Always keep in mind that moving to the right on the horizontal axis and up along the vertical axis each lead to higher values.

**Y-axis**
*the vertical axis on a graph*

**X-axis**
*the horizontal axis on a graph*

**pie chart**
*a circle divided into proportionate slices that represent various quantities that add up to 100 percent*

**bar graph**
*represents data using vertical bars rising from the horizontal axis*

**time-series graph**
*shows changes in the value of a variable over time*

## USING GRAPHS AND CHARTS

Exhibit 2 presents three common types of graphs. A **pie chart** is a circle divided into proportionate slices that represent various quantities that add up to 100 percent. The pie chart in Exhibit 2(a) shows what college students earn. That is, each slice in the pie chart represents the percentage of college students in a particular earnings category.

A **bar graph** represents data using vertical bars rising from the horizontal axis. Exhibit 2(b) is a bar graph that shows the sales of wireless phone service by province for a new company that has just entered the Canadian market. The height of the line represents sales in millions of dollars. Bar graphs are used to show a comparison of the sizes of quantities of similar items.

Exhibit 2(c) is a **time-series graph**. This type of graph shows changes in the value of a variable over time. This is a visual tool that allows us to observe important trends over a certain time period. In Exhibit 2(c) we see a graph that shows trends in the stock price of the company Fly-by-Chance for the period January to December. The horizontal axis shows us the passage of time, and the vertical axis shows us the stock price in dollars per share.

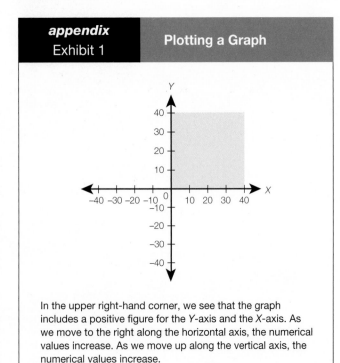

| appendix Exhibit 1 | Plotting a Graph |
| --- | --- |

In the upper right-hand corner, we see that the graph includes a positive figure for the *Y*-axis and the *X*-axis. As we move to the right along the horizontal axis, the numerical values increase. As we move up along the vertical axis, the numerical values increase.

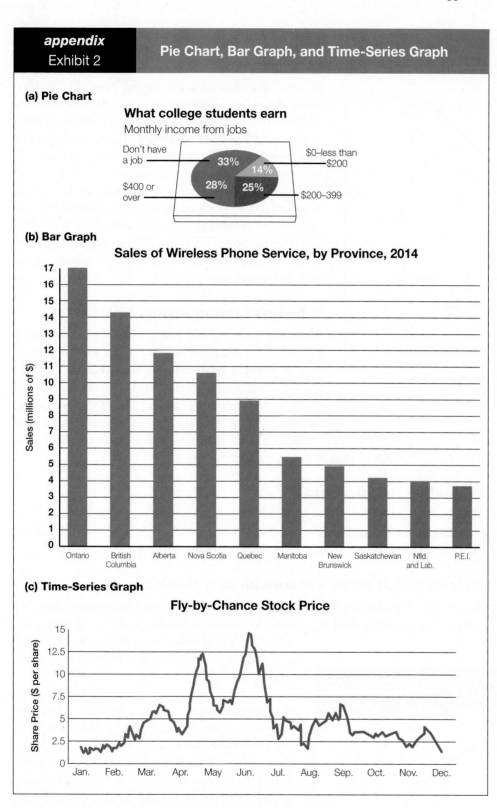

**appendix**
Exhibit 2     **Pie Chart, Bar Graph, and Time-Series Graph**

**(a) Pie Chart**

**What college students earn**

Monthly income from jobs

Don't have a job — 33%

$0–less than $200 — 14%

$400 or over — 28%

25% — $200–399

**(b) Bar Graph**

**Sales of Wireless Phone Service, by Province, 2014**

Sales (millions of $)

Ontario, British Columbia, Alberta, Nova Scotia, Quebec, Manitoba, New Brunswick, Saskatchewan, Nfld. and Lab., P.E.I.

**(c) Time-Series Graph**

**Fly-by-Chance Stock Price**

Share Price ($ per share)

Jan. Feb. Mar. Apr. May Jun. Jul. Aug. Sep. Oct. Nov. Dec.

## USING GRAPHS TO SHOW THE RELATIONSHIP BETWEEN TWO VARIABLES

Although the graphs and chart in Exhibit 2 are important, they do not allow us to show the relationship between two variables (a **variable** is something that is measured by a number, such as your height). To more closely examine the structure and functions of graphs, let us consider the story of Katherine, an avid snowboarder who has aspirations of

**variable**

*something that is measured by a number, such as your height*

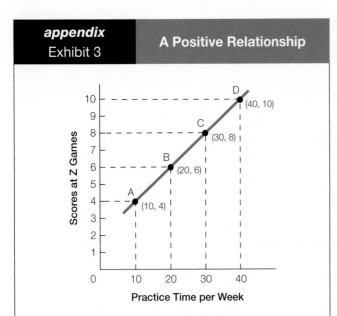

winning the Z Games next year. To get there, however, she will have to put in many hours of practice. But how many hours? In search of information about the practice habits of other snowboarders, she logged onto the Internet, where she pulled up the results of a study conducted by ESPM 3 that indicated the score of each Z Games competitor and the amount of practice time per week spent by each snowboarder. The results of this study (see Exhibit 3) indicated that snowboarders had to practise 10 hours per week to receive a score of 4.0, 20 hours per week to receive a score of 6.0, 30 hours per week to get a score of 8.0, and 40 hours per week to get a perfect score of 10. What does this information tell Katherine? By using a graph, she can more clearly understand the relationship between practice time and overall score.

## A Positive Relationship

The study on scores and practice times revealed what is called a direct relationship, also called a *positive relationship*. A **positive relationship** means that the variables change in the same direction. That is, an increase in one variable (practice time) is accompanied by an increase in the other variable (overall score), or a decrease in one variable (practice time) is accompanied by a decrease in the other variable (overall score). In short, the variables change in the same direction.

**positive relationship**
*when two variables change in the same direction*

## A Negative Relationship

When two variables change in opposite directions, we say they are inversely related, or have a **negative relationship**. That is, when one variable rises, the other variable falls, or when one variable decreases, the other variable increases.

**negative relationship**
*when two variables change in opposite directions*

## Variables That Have a Maximum or a Minimum

Many relationships described in economic models have maximum or minimum values. For example, firms are always looking to make the maximum possible profits; one way they can achieve this is by minimizing their costs. Exhibits 4 and 5 show relationships that have maximum and minimum values.

Exhibit 4 shows the first case—a relationship that begins positive, reaches a maximum, and then ends with a negative relationship. This example of the relationship between tax rates and tax revenue shows what economists refer to as the *Laffer curve*. When the tax rate is zero, the government receives no tax revenue. As the tax rate rises, tax revenue increases because the government receives a larger percentage of people's incomes. In the exhibit, a tax rate of 50 percent generates the maximum tax revenue of $15 million. As the tax rate continues to rise, it may be the case that the incentive to earn more income begins to decline, causing tax revenue to fall. If the tax rate was increased to 100 percent,

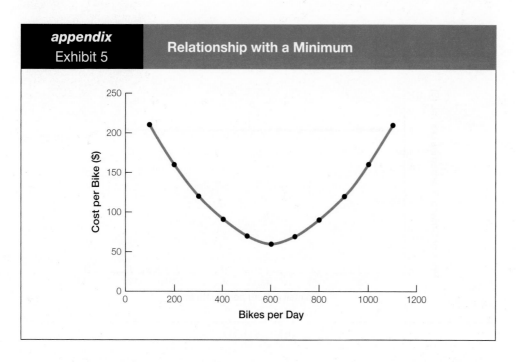

**appendix**
Exhibit 5

**Relationship with a Minimum**

there would be no incentive to earn income because it would all be taxed away; as a result, no tax revenue would be generated.

Exhibit 5 illustrates the opposite case—a relationship that begins negative, reaches a minimum, and then returns positive. Most economic costs are seen as following this relationship. As a bicycle manufacturer increases its output, per bike costs of production begin to fall, perhaps as workers develop special skills and the benefits of teamwork emerge. At a level of 600 bikes per day, the cost per bike is minimized at $60 per bike. However, as production is increased beyond 600 bikes per day, the cost per bike begins to rise, perhaps as the bike factory is forced to operate beyond its efficient capacity.

## Variables That Are Not Related

There are still other situations in economics in which the change in one variable has no impact on the value of another variable. Exhibit 6 provides a graphical depiction of a curious relationship—a student's grade in economics and the lunar cycle. Since a

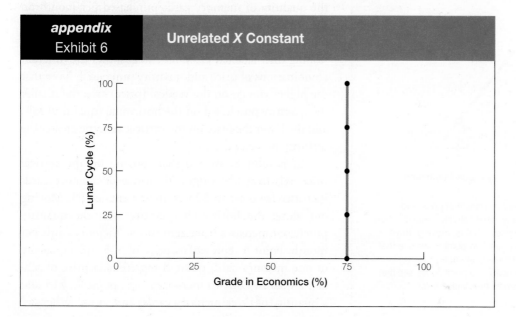

**appendix**
Exhibit 6

**Unrelated *X* Constant**

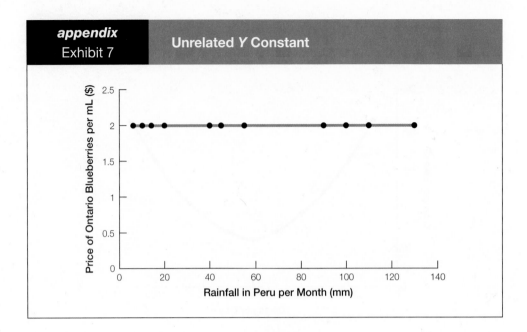

**appendix**
Exhibit 7

**Unrelated Y Constant**

student's grade in economics is not affected by the lunar cycle, no relationship exists. If a student grade of 75 percent is plotted on the horizontal axis, with the lunar cycle plotted on the vertical axis, the curve is vertical.

Exhibit 7 illustrates another curious relationship—the price of blueberries grown in Ontario and the average rainfall in Peru. Since the price of blueberries grown in Ontario, plotted on the vertical axis, does not vary with the monthly rainfall in Peru, plotted on the horizontal axis, the curve is horizontal.

**appendix**
Exhibit 8

**A Negative Relationship**

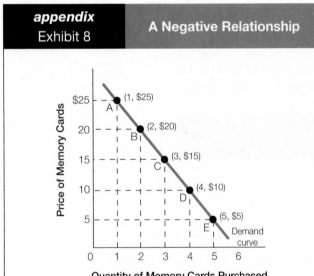

The downward slope of the curve means that price and quantity purchased are inversely, or negatively, related: when one increases, the other decreases. That is, moving down along the demand curve from point A to point E, we see that as price falls, the quantity purchased increases. Moving up along the demand curve from point E to point A, we see that as the price increases, the quantity purchased falls.

## THE GRAPH OF A DEMAND CURVE

One of the most important graphs in all of economics is the demand curve. In Exhibit 8, we see Emily's individual demand curve for digital camera memory cards. It shows the price of memory cards on the vertical axis and the quantity of memory cards purchased per month on the horizontal axis. Every point in the space shown represents a price and quantity combination. The downward-sloping line, labelled *Demand curve*, shows the different combinations of price and quantity purchased. Note that the higher you go on the vertical (price) axis, the smaller the quantity purchased on the horizontal (quantity) axis, and the lower the price on the vertical axis, the greater the quantity purchased.

In Exhibit 8, we see that moving up the vertical price axis from the origin, the price of memory cards increases from $5 to $25 in increments of $5. Moving out along the horizontal quantity axis, the quantity purchased increases from zero to five memory cards per month. Point A represents a price of $25 and a quantity of one memory card, point B represents a price of $20 and a quantity of two memory cards, point C, $15 and a quantity of three memory cards, and so on. When we

**appendix**
Exhibit 9

**Shifting a Curve**

**(a) Demand Curve with Higher Income**

Price of Memory Cards

0

Quantity of Memory Cards Purchased

D

D (with higher income)

**(b) Demand Curve with Lower Income**

Price of Memory Cards

0

Quantity of Memory Cards Purchased

D (with lower income)

D

connect all the points, we have what economists call a *curve*. As you can see, curves are sometimes drawn as straight lines for ease of illustration. Moving down along the curve, we see that as the price falls, a greater quantity is demanded; moving up the curve to higher prices, a smaller quantity is demanded. That is, when memory cards become less expensive, Emily buys more memory cards. When memory cards become more expensive, Emily buys fewer memory cards, perhaps choosing to go to the movies or download some music instead.

## USING GRAPHS TO SHOW THE RELATIONSHIP AMONG THREE VARIABLES

Although only two variables are shown on the axes, graphs can be used to show the relationship among three variables. For example, say we add a third variable—income—to our earlier example. Our three variables are now income, price, and quantity purchased. If Emily's income rises, say she gets a raise at work, she is now able and willing to buy more memory cards than before at each possible price. As a result, the whole demand curve shifts outward (rightward) compared to the old curve. That is, she uses some of her additional income to buy more memory cards. This is seen in the graph in Exhibit 9(a). On the other hand, if her income falls, say she quits her job to go back to school, she now has less income to buy memory cards. This causes the whole demand curve to shift inward (leftward) compared to the old curve. This is seen in the graph in Exhibit 9(b).

### The Difference between a Movement along and a Shift in the Curve

It is important to remember the difference between a movement between one point and another along a curve and a shift in the whole curve. A change in one of the variables on the graph, like price or quantity purchased, will cause a movement along the curve, say from point A to point B, as shown in Exhibit 10. A change in one of the variables not shown (held constant in order to show only the relationship between price and quantity), like income in our example, will cause the whole curve to shift. The change from $D_0$ to $D_1$ in Exhibit 10 shows such a shift.

**appendix**
Exhibit 10 — **Shifts vs. Movements**

Price of Memory Cards

A

B

$D_0$   $D_1$

0

Quantity of Memory Cards Purchased

## SLOPE

In economics, we sometimes refer to the steepness of the lines or curves on graphs as the **slope**—the ratio of the rise over the run. A slope can be either positive (upward sloping) or negative (downward sloping). A curve that is downward sloping represents an inverse, or negative, relationship between the two variables and slants downward from left to right, as seen in Exhibit 11(a). A curve that is upward sloping represents a direct, or positive, relationship between the two variables and slants upward from left to right, as seen in Exhibit 11(b). The numeric value of the slope shows the number of units of change of the $Y$-axis variable for each unit of change in the $X$-axis variable. Slope provides the direction (positive or negative) as well as the magnitude of the relationship between the two variables.

**slope**

*the ratio of rise (change in the Y variable) over the run (change in the X variable)*

## Measuring the Slope of a Linear Curve

A straight-line curve is called a *linear curve*. The slope of a linear curve between two points measures the relative rates of change of two variables. Specifically, the slope of a linear curve can be defined as the ratio of the change in the $Y$ value to the change in the $X$ value. The slope can also be expressed as the ratio of the rise to the run, where the rise is the change in the $Y$ variable (along the vertical axis) and the run is the change in the $X$ variable (along the horizontal axis).

In Exhibit 12, we show two linear curves, one with a positive slope and one with a negative slope. In Exhibit 12(a), the slope of the positively sloped linear curve from point A to point B is 1/2, because the rise is 1 (from 2 to 3) and the run is 2 (from 1 to 3). In Exhibit 12(b), the negatively sloped linear curve has a slope of $-4$, a rise of $-8$ (a fall

**appendix**
Exhibit 11 — **Downward- and Upward-Sloping Linear Curves**

**(a) Downward-Sloping Linear Curve**

25
20
15
10
5
0   5   10   15   20   25

Downward sloping

**(b) Upward-Sloping Linear Curve**

25
20
15
10
5
0   5   10   15   20   25

Upward sloping

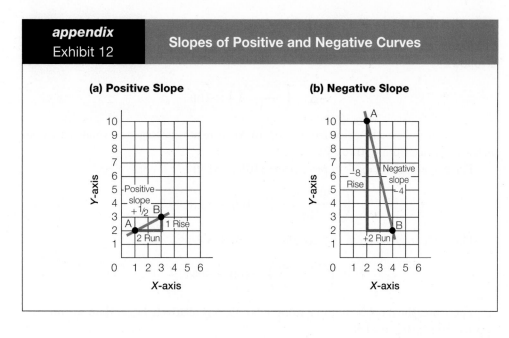

**appendix**
Exhibit 12

**Slopes of Positive and Negative Curves**

**(a) Positive Slope**

**(b) Negative Slope**

of 8 from 10 to 2), and a run of 2 (from 2 to 4), which gives us a slope of −4 (−8/2).
Note the appropriate signs on the slopes: The negatively sloped line carries a minus sign
and the positively sloped line, a plus sign.

## Finding the Slope of a Nonlinear Curve

In Exhibit 13, we show the slope of a nonlinear curve. A nonlinear curve is a line that
actually curves. Here the slope varies from point to point along the curve. However,
we can find the slope of this curve at any given point by drawing a straight-line tangent to that point on the curve. A tangency is when a straight line just touches the
curve without actually crossing it. At point A, we see that the positively sloped line
that is tangent to the curve has a slope of 1—the line rises one unit and runs one unit.
At point B, the line is horizontal, so it has zero slope. At point C, we see a slope of −2
because the negatively sloped line has a rise of −2 units (a fall of two units) for every
one unit run.

Remember, many students have problems with economics simply because they fail to understand graphs, so
make sure that you understand this material before going
on to Chapter 2.

## Percentage Change

In economics, the determination of the percentage change
in a quantity is a common calculation. The advantage of
calculating percentage change (as opposed to simple absolute change) is that percentage change provides a more
accurate measure of the magnitude of the change. For
example, is an increase in price from $105 to $130 relatively larger or smaller than an increase in price from $50
to $75? In both cases, the difference (absolute increase) is
the same at $25, but what about the relative (percentage)
change?

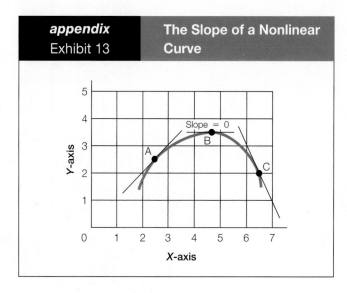

**appendix**
Exhibit 13

**The Slope of a Nonlinear Curve**

### The Formula for Percentage Change

The percentage change in a value that is originally $x_0$ and changes to $x_1$ can be expressed as follows:

$$\%\Delta = \left(\frac{X_1 - X_0}{X_0}\right) \times 100$$

So, is an increase in price from \$105 to \$130 relatively larger or smaller than an increase in price from \$50 to \$75?

The percentage increase in price from \$105 to \$130 is

$$\left(\frac{130 - 105}{105}\right) \times 100 = 23.81\%$$

The percentage increase in price from \$50 to \$75 is

$$\left(\frac{75 - 50}{50}\right) \times 100 = 50\%$$

Therefore, the increase in price from \$50 to \$75 is relatively larger than the increase in price from \$105 to \$130.

# For Your Review    (Chapter 1 Appendix)

1. What are the coordinates of the points of the following graph?

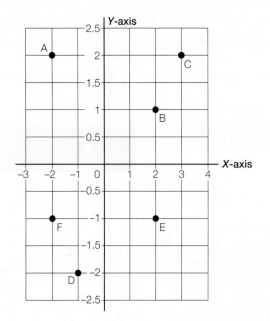

2. Refer to the following pie chart, which shows the percentage of sales by vehicle type in 2018.

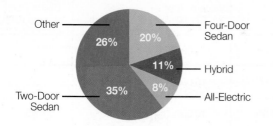

a. What percentage of the cars sold in 2018 were all-electric vehicles?

b. What percentage of the cars sold in 2018 were four-door sedans?

c. What was the most popular vehicle type for 2018 based on sales?

d. What was the least popular vehicle type for 2018 based on sales?

3. Refer to the following bar graph, which shows the number of boys and girls participating in campus recreational leagues in each of four semesters.

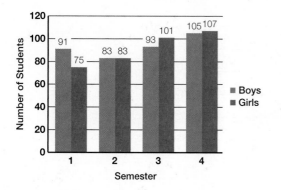

a. In which semesters were more boys than girls registered in campus recreational leagues?

b. In which semesters were more girls than boys registered in campus recreational leagues?

c. In which semesters did the same number of girls and boys register in campus recreational leagues?

d. Looking at all four semesters, what was the total number of boys registered in campus recreational leagues?

4. Plot the relationships described in the following tables on separate graphs (plot the variables in the left-hand columns on the horizontal axis and the variables in the right-hand columns on the vertical axis).

| Graph 1 | | Graph 2 | | Graph 3 | |
|---|---|---|---|---|---|
| Temperature (°C) | Ice Cream Sales (cones) | Year | Value of Tom's Car ($) | Shoe size | Grade Point Average (GPA) |
| 20 | 30 | 2018 | 14 000 | 8 | 3.5 |
| 22 | 50 | 2017 | 15 000 | 9 | 3.5 |
| 24 | 70 | 2016 | 16 000 | 10 | 3.5 |
| 26 | 90 | 2015 | 17 000 | 11 | 3.5 |
| 28 | 110 | 2014 | 18 000 | 12 | 3.5 |

How would you describe the resulting graphs: upward sloping, downward sloping, or unrelated?

5. Refer to the following graph.

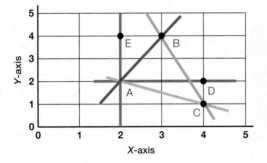

Calculate the slope between the following sets of points.

a. A to B

b. B to C

c. A to C

d. E to A

e. A to D

6. Calculate the percentage change in each of the following scenarios.

a. The temperature increases from 12°C to 18°C.

b. The price of a laptop computer falls from $800 to $760.

c. The Consumer Price Index (CPI) increases from 105.3 to 106.1.

d. The number of emergency calls to campus security decreased from 912 last semester to 862 this semester.

# Scarcity, Trade-Offs, and Production Possibilities

# The Production Possibilities Curve

section

2.1

- What is a production possibilities curve?
- What is efficiency?
- How is opportunity cost measured?
- What is the law of increasing opportunity costs?

## WHAT IS A PRODUCTION POSSIBILITIES CURVE?

The economic concepts of scarcity, choice, and trade-offs can be shown with a simple graph called a *production possibilities curve*. The **production possibilities curve** represents the potential total output combinations of any two goods for an economy, given the inputs and technology available to the economy. That is, it illustrates an economy's potential for allocating its limited resources in producing various combinations of goods in a given time period.

**production possibilities curve**

*the potential total output combinations of any two goods for an economy, given the inputs and technology available*

**Because you have only so many hours a week to study, studying more for economics and less for accounting might hurt your grade in accounting, *ceteris paribus*. Life is full of trade-offs.**

### A Straight-Line Production Possibilities Curve—Grades in Economics and Accounting

What would the production possibilities curve look like if you were "producing" grades in two of your classes—say, economics and accounting? In Exhibit 1, we draw a hypothetical production possibilities curve for your expected grade in economics on the vertical axis and your expected grade in accounting on the horizontal axis. Assume, because of a part-time restaurant job, you choose to study ten hours a week and that you like both courses and are equally adept at studying for both courses.

We see in Exhibit 1 that the production possibilities curve is a straight line. For example, if all ten hours are spent studying economics, the expected grade in economics is 85 percent (an A) and the expected grade in accounting is 45 percent (an F). Moving down the

## Production Possibilities Curve: "Producing" Grades in Economics and Accounting

The production possibilities curve highlights the concept of trade-offs. Assuming you choose to study a total of ten hours a week, moving down the production possibilities curve shows that if you use your time to study accounting instead of economics you can raise your expected grade in accounting but only at the expense of lowering your expected grade in economics. With a straight-line production possibilities curve, the opportunity costs are constant.

production possibilities curve, we see that as you spend more of your time studying accounting and less on economics, you can raise your expected grade in accounting but only at the expense of lowering your expected grade in economics. Specifically, moving down along the straight-line production possibilities curve, the trade-off is one letter-grade lower in economics for one higher letter-grade in accounting. That is, with a straight-line production possibilities curve, the opportunity costs are constant.

The trade-offs between expected grades in economics and accounting are the result of holding study time constant (ten hours per week) and all other factors that could increase your ability to learn, such as software study packages.

Of course, if you increased your study time it would be possible to expect higher grades in both courses. But that would be on a new production possibilities curve; along this production possibilities curve we are assuming that technology and the number of study hours are given. In the next section, the coverage is expanded to cover the more realistic case of a bowed production possibilities curve.

### Production Alternatives on the Bowed Production Possibilities Curve

To more clearly illustrate the production possibilities curve, imagine an economy that produces just two goods: food and shelter. The fact that we have many goods in the real world makes actual decision making more complicated, but it does not alter the basic principles being illustrated. Each point on the production possibilities curve shown in Exhibit 2 represents the potential amounts of food and shelter that can be produced in a given time period, given the quantity and quality of resources available in the economy for production.

Note in Exhibit 2 that if we devoted all of our resources to making units of shelter, we could produce 10 units of shelter, but no food (point A). If, on the other hand, we chose to devote all of our resources to food, we could produce 80 units of food, but no shelter (point E).

In reality, nations would rarely opt for production possibility A or E, preferring instead to produce a mixture of goods. For example, the economy in question might produce 9 units of shelter and 20 units of food (point B), or perhaps 7 units of shelter and 40 units of food (point C). Still other combinations along the curve, such as point D, are possible.

### Production Alternatives Off the Production Possibilities Curve

The economy cannot operate at point N (not attainable) during the given time period because there are presently not enough resources to produce that level of output. However, it is possible the economy can operate inside the production possibilities curve, at point I (inefficient). If the economy is operating at point I, or at any other point inside the production possibilities curve, it is not at full capacity and is operating inefficiently. In short, the economy is not using all of its scarce resources efficiently; as a result, actual output is less than potential output.

| section 2.1 Exhibit 2 | Production Possibilities Curve: The Trade-Off between Shelter and Food |
|---|---|

| Combi- nations | Shelter (units) | Food (units) |
|---|---|---|
| A | 10 | 0 |
| B | 9 | 20 |
| C | 7 | 40 |
| D | 4 | 60 |
| E | 0 | 80 |

Each point on the production possibilities curve represents the potential amounts of food and shelter that can be produced in a given time period, given the quantity and quality of resources available in the economy to use for production. All the points on the production possibility curve are efficient. Any points in the shaded area, like point I, are inefficient. Any point outside the production possibilities curve, like point N, is not attainable at the present time.

## WHAT IS EFFICIENCY?

Most modern economies have resources that are idle, at least for some period of time—like during periods of high unemployment. If those resources were not idle, people would have more scarce goods and services available for their use. Unemployed resources create a serious problem. For example, consider an unemployed construction worker who is unable to find work at a "reasonable" wage, or those unemployed in depressed times when factories are already operating below capacity. Clearly, the resources of these individuals are not being used efficiently.

The fact that factories can operate below capacity suggests that it is not just labour resources that should be most effectively used. Rather, all resources entering into production must be used effectively. However, for several reasons, social concern focuses on labour. First, labour costs are the largest share of production costs. Also, unemployed or underemployed labourers (whose resources are not being used to their full potential) may have mouths to feed at home, whereas an unemployed machine does not (although the owner of the unemployed machine may).

### Inefficiency and Efficiency

Suppose for some reason there is widespread unemployment or resources are not being put to their best use. The economy would then be operating at a point, such as I, inside the production possibilities curve where the economy is operating inefficiently. At point I, 4 units of shelter and 40 units of food are being produced. By putting unemployed resources to work or by putting already employed resources to better use, we could expand the output of shelter by 3 units (moving to point C) without giving up any units of food. Alternatively, we could boost food output by 20 units (moving to point D) without reducing shelter output. We could even get more of both food and shelter moving to a point on the curve between C and D. Increasing or improving the utilization of resources, then, can lead to greater output of all goods. An efficient use of our resources means that more of everything we want can be available for our use. Thus, efficiency requires society to use its resources to the fullest extent—getting the most from our scarce resources; that is, there are no wasted resources. If resources are being used efficiently, that is, at some point along a production possibilities curve, then more of one good or service requires the sacrifice of another good or service. Efficiency does not tell us which point along the production possibilities curve is *best*, but it does tell us that points inside the curve cannot be best because some resources are wasted.

## HOW IS OPPORTUNITY COST MEASURED?

When an economy is operating efficiently, the decision to increase the production of one good or service will carry with it a related opportunity cost. Within the framework of the production possibility model, the determination of opportunity cost is greatly simplified since the next best alternative is the only alternative—therefore, in our example, the opportunity cost of increasing the production of shelter would be measured in corresponding forgone units of food, and the opportunity cost of expanding food production would be measured in units of forgone shelter.

Note in Exhibit 2 that if the economy is currently operating at point D (producing 4 units of shelter and 60 units of food), the decision to increase the amount of shelter it produces to 7 units will have an opportunity cost of 20 units of food—as this is the amount of food that the economy must give up to gain the additional units of shelter. In the diagram, this gain of shelter and related opportunity cost would involve the movement along the production possibilities curve from point D to point C.

## WHAT IS THE LAW OF INCREASING OPPORTUNITY COSTS?

Note that in Exhibits 2 and 3, the production possibilities curve is not a straight line like that in Exhibit 1. It is concave from below (i.e., bowed outward from the origin). Looking at the figures, you can see that at very low food output, an increase in the amount of food produced will lead to only a small reduction in the units of shelter produced. For example, increasing food output from 0 to 20 (moving from point A to point B on the curve) requires the use of resources capable of producing 1 unit of shelter. This means that for the first 20 units of food, 1 unit of shelter must be given up. When food output is higher, however, more units of shelter must be given up when switching additional resources from the production of shelter to food. Moving from point D to point E, for example, an increase in food output of 20 (from 60 to 80) reduces the production of shelter from 4 to 0. At this point, then, the cost of those 20 additional units of food is 4 units of shelter, considerably more than the 1 unit of shelter required in the earlier scenario. This difference shows us that opportunity costs have not remained constant, but have risen, as more units of food and fewer units of shelter are produced.

**law of increasing opportunity cost**

*As more of one item is produced by an economy, the opportunity cost of additional units of that product rises.*

The **law of increasing opportunity cost** refers to the concept that, as more of one item is produced by an economy, the opportunity cost of additional units of that product rises. It is this increasing opportunity cost, then, that is represented by the bowed production possibilities curve.

### The Reason for the Law of Increasing Opportunity Cost

The basic reason for the law of increasing opportunity cost is that some resources and skills cannot be easily adapted from their current uses to alternative uses. For example, at low levels of food output, additional increases in food output can be obtained easily

## section 2.1
### Exhibit 3
### Increasing Opportunity Cost and the Production Possibilities Curve

The production possibilities curve also illustrates the opportunity cost of producing more of a given product. For example, if we were to increase food output from 40 units to 60 units (moving from point C to point D), we must produce 3 fewer units of shelter. The opportunity cost of those 20 additional units of food is the 3 units of shelter we must forgo. We can see that moving down the curve from A to E, each additional 20 units of food costs society more and more shelter—the law of increasing opportunity cost.

by switching relatively low-skilled carpenters from making shelter to producing food. However, to get even more food output, workers who are less well suited or appropriate for producing food (i.e., they are better adapted to making shelter) must be released from shelter making in order to increase food output. For example, a skilled carpenter may be an expert at making shelter but a very bad farmer, because he lacks the training and skills necessary in that occupation. So, using the skilled carpenter to farm results in a relatively greater opportunity cost than using the poor carpenter to farm. Hence, the production of additional units of food becomes increasingly costly as progressively even lower-skilled farmers (but good carpenters) convert to farming.

In short, resources tend to be specialized. As a result, we lose some of their productivity when we transfer those resources from producing what they are relatively good at to producing something they are relatively bad at.

# Business *CONNECTION*

## WHAT CAN THE PPC OFFER MANAGERS?

The production possibilities curve (PPC) can be extremely helpful to entrepreneurs, especially those in small and medium-sized businesses. The curve represents the potential total output combinations of any two goods for an economy, given the inputs and technology available to the economy. It's not so much that managers will construct their own PPCs, but rather that using the model can help their thinking. The PPC demonstrates a number of economic concepts: growth, choice, opportunity cost, law of diminishing returns, marginal benefits, and inflationary pressures. It can be used in a broad context (e.g., when thinking about investing in consumer goods versus capital

goods) or in a narrow perspective (e.g., when deciding on whether a plant should produce Smooth Joy bars versus Chewy Delight bars).

In general terms, the marketing side of the business is responsible for revenue (as opposed to the operations side, which is responsible for expenses). If managers of the firm feel that demand is growing, they may decide to increase the production of their plant. In terms of the PPC, the firm could presently be operating at three different levels: (1) significantly below capacity, or the PPC curve's boundary, (2) slightly below capacity, or (3) at capacity. If the firm is operating significantly below capacity, it can comfortably

*(continued)*

increase production without any concern about rising costs of production—it may actually lower average unit prices as it increases production. As the plant approaches full production, it will experience increased costs—for example, managers might have to pay overtime to employees. At capacity, there is no way to increase production without investing in expanding capacity, which can mean investing in capital (equipment) and/or plant size (land).

The PPC also helps the managers to visualize what the level of production should be. Producing at capacity does not allow the plant to look for new accounts, because the increased production increases the company's costs, but producing at levels slightly below capacity allows for a company to increase production both in the short and long term without major cost increases. If the occasional increase turns out to be more permanent, then managers look to expand the business.

It is vital that the marketing and operations side of the business be in sync—the last thing the firm needs is new business if it is at capacity, because that means higher costs and the pressures of meeting delivery times. This situation illustrates one reason why some young businesses fail by growing too fast they think all growth is good. In fact, however, only managed growth is good, because taking on more than the firm can deal with can lead it into failure.

The PPC can be helpful to both the marketing and operations sides when they are making decisions on the firm's product mix. For example, the firm can produce product A or product B. On the PPC, this is demonstrated by moving along the curve toward one axis or another. If demand dictates that more of product A should be made, the plant has to decide whether to make less of product B in order to make more of product A (opportunity cost). But what do managers do when demand for product B remains high and demand for product A increases significantly?

Here, the firm has to decide if it wants to expand. If it can't expand, then the decision could be to meet the increase in demand for product A and decrease production of product B, or the firm could actually increase the price of product A and leave existing production levels where they are. You'll see why this is when you learn about supply and demand in the next few chapters.

Finally, managers should be aware that as they near the plant's capacity, they have to spend considerably more for just a little bit of return. It's the same concept for you as a student—you have to spend a lot more time to move your grade up from 95 percent to 98 percent than you do to raise your grade from 50 to 60 percent. For managers, this means higher costs, and even though they could reach near capacity, would they really want to from a profitability perspective? This demonstrates the mindset of why operation managers might decide to operate at levels slightly below capacity.

Keeping the concepts of the PPC model in mind while making both marketing and operations decisions will be of great benefit to managers. This is more strategic thinking than tactical thinking—areas that successful managers have to be good at all of the time.

1. There are a number of reasons why a firm shouldn't be producing at its capacity. Can you think of some other reasons not discussed here? In each case, in your opinion, why should the firm be operating at less than capacity?

2. It is true that one of the main reasons new firms fail is that they grow too fast. Thinking of the PPC, what are other risks or reasons that could lead to business failure?

3. Why do you think costs increase for a firm the closer it gets to operating at capacity?

## SECTION CHECK

- The production possibilities curve represents the potential total output combinations of two goods available to a society, given its resources and existing technology.
- Efficiency requires society to use its resources to the fullest extent—no wasted resources. If the economy is operating within the production possibilities curve, the economy is operating inefficiently.
- The cost of altering production within the production possibilities curve framework, at efficiency, is measured in forgone units of the sole alternative.
- A bowed production possibilities curve means that the opportunity costs of producing additional units of a good rise as society produces more of that good (the law of increasing opportunity costs).

# Economic Growth and the Production Possibilities Curve

- How do we show economic growth on the production possibilities curve?
- How can we summarize the production possibilities curve?

## HOW DO WE SHOW ECONOMIC GROWTH ON THE PRODUCTION POSSIBILITIES CURVE?

How have some nations been able to rapidly expand their output of goods and services over time, whereas others have been unable to increase their standards of living at all?

The economy can grow only with qualitative or quantitative changes in the factors of production—land, labour, capital, and entrepreneurship. Advancement in technology, improvements in labour productivity, or new sources of natural resources (such as previously undiscovered oil) could all lead to outward shifts of the production possibilities curve.

This idea can be clearly illustrated by using the production possibilities curve (Exhibit 1). In terms of the production possibilities curve, economic growth means an outward shift in the possible combinations of goods and services produced. With growth comes the possibility to have more of both goods than were previously available. Suppose we were producing at point C (7 units of shelter, 40 units of food) on our original production possibilities curve. Additional resources and/or new methods of using them (technological progress) can lead to new production possibilities, creating the potential for more of all goods (or more of some with no less of others). These increases would shift the production possibilities curve outward. For example, if the government introduces programs that make it easier for workers to get an education and relevant workplace expertise (called *human capital*), such as training workers to make shelter, this increases the productivity of these workers. As a result, they will produce more units of shelter. This means, ultimately, that fewer resources will be used to make shelter, freeing them to be used for farming—resulting in more units of food. Notice that at point F (future) on the new curve, it is possible to produce 9 units of shelter and 70 units of food, more of both goods than was previously produced, at point C. Alternatively, as evidenced by land degradation and depletion of natural resources, resources can be lost over time. This has a negative impact on production, shifting the production possibilities curve inward.

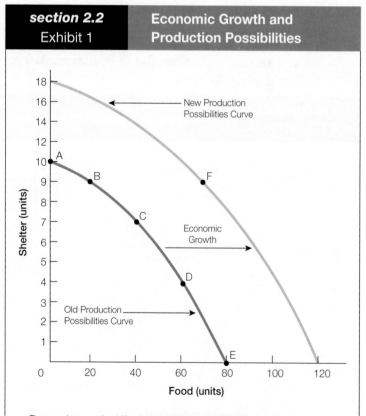

| section 2.2 Exhibit 1 | Economic Growth and Production Possibilities |

Economic growth shifts the production possibilities curve outward, allowing increased output of both food and shelter (compare point F with point C).

## Growth Doesn't Eliminate Scarcity

With all of this discussion of growth, it is important to remember that growth, or increases in a society's output, does not make scarcity disappear. Even when output has grown more rapidly than the population so that people are made better off, they still face trade-offs: At any point along the production possibilities curve, in order to get more of one thing, you must give up something else. There are no free lunches on the production possibilities curve.

## Capital Goods vs. Consumption Goods

Economies that choose to invest more of their resources for the future will grow faster than those that don't. To generate economic growth, a society must produce fewer consumer goods—like pizza, digital cameras, cellphones, cars, and so on—in the present and produce more capital goods. The society that devotes a larger share of its productive capacity to capital goods (machines, factories, tools, and education), rather than consumption goods (computer games, cups of coffee, and vacations), will experience greater economic growth. It must sacrifice some present consumption of consumer goods and services in order to experience growth in the future. Why? Investing in capital goods, like computers and other new technological equipment, as well as upgrading skills and knowledge, expands the ability to produce in the future. It shifts the economy's production possibilities outward, increasing the future production capacity of the economy. That is, the economy that invests more now (consumes less now) will be able to produce, and therefore consume, more in the future. In Exhibit 2, we see that Economy A invests more in capital goods than Economy B. Consequently, Economy A's production possibilities curve shifts out farther than Economy B's over time.

To better understand the significance of these two production alternatives, it may help to apply the distinction to the Canadian economy. Which type of economy is Canada, Economy A or Economy B? In Canada, consumption expenditure is nearly three times that of investment. As a result, the Canadian economy is best represented by the

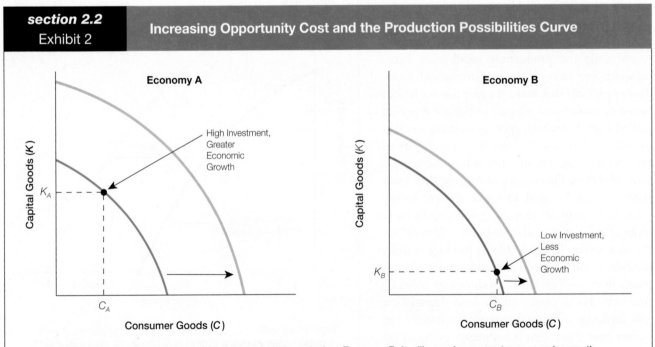

| section 2.2 | Increasing Opportunity Cost and the Production Possibilities Curve |

Because Economy A invests relatively more in capital goods than Economy B, it will experience greater economic growth.

Economy B illustration. By comparison, China's gross savings amount is more than double that of Canada's. Clearly then, China is best represented by the Economy A illustration.

## The Effects of a Technological Change on the Production Possibilities Curve

In Exhibit 3, we see that a technological advance does not have to impact all sectors of the economy equally: There is a technological advance in food production but not in housing production. The technological advance in agriculture causes the production possibilities curve to extend out farther on the horizontal axis, which measures food production. We can move to any point on the new production possibilities curve. For example, the move from point A on the original curve to point B on the new curve would result in 150 more units of food (500 − 350) and the same amount of housing—200 units. Or, we could move from point A to point C, which would allow us to produce more units of both food and housing. How do we produce more housing, when the technological advance occurred in agriculture? The answer is that the technological advance in agriculture allows us to produce more from a given quantity of resources. That is, it allows us to shift some resources out of agriculture into housing. This is actually an ongoing story in Canadian economic history. In colonial days, almost all of the Canadian population made a living in agriculture. Today, it is less than 3 percent.

## HOW CAN WE SUMMARIZE THE PRODUCTION POSSIBILITIES CURVE?

The production possibilities curve shown in Exhibit 4 illustrates the choices faced by an economy that makes military goods and consumer goods. How are the economic concepts of scarcity, choice, opportunity costs, efficiency, and economic growth illustrated in this production possibilities curve framework? In Exhibit 4, we can show scarcity because resource combinations outside the initial production possibilities curve, like point D, are unattainable without economic growth. If the economy is operating efficiently, we are somewhere on that production possibilities curve, like point B or point C. However, if the economy is operating

POM POM/Shutterstock.com

**From the analogue type to touch-screen devices, technological progress has had a dramatic impact on the cellphone industry. At first, cellphones had only one purpose—to allow a person to call someone else while on the move. Today, smartphones can send and receive emails, text message, store music and images, take and send pictures, and even provide television and the Internet.**

| **section 2.2** Exhibit 3 | The Effects of Change on the Production Possibilities Curve |
|---|---|

A move from point A to point C will lead to more housing and food. A move from point A to point B will lead to more food and the same level of housing.

| **section 2.2** Exhibit 4 | **Production Possibilities Curve** |

Point A, inside the initial production possibilities curve, represents inefficiency. Points B and C, on the curve, are efficient points and represent two possible output combinations. Point D can be attained only with economic growth, illustrated by the outward shift in the production possibilities curve.

inefficiently, we are operating inside that production possibilities curve, like point A. We can also see in this graph that to get more military goods you must give up consumer goods—that is, there is an opportunity cost. Finally, we see that over time, with economic growth, the whole production possibilities curve can shift outward, making point D now attainable.

# DEBATE

## COSTS AND BENEFITS: SHOULD HIGHER EDUCATION BE FULLY SUBSIDIZED FOR THE CONSUMER/STUDENT?

One of the most pressing issues facing students lately is their ability to pay higher tuition fees for college or university courses. There are many reasons why higher education is good for individuals and for society at large, so many students and politicians (because students vote!) are attempting to make education more accessible without raising tuition fees. In fact, many are advocating for the elimination of tuition fees completely.

While there are some compelling reasons to eliminate tuition costs, there are also some very solid reasons not to eliminate them. Which side of the debate are you on? Sometimes you should be careful what you wish for—it might come true!

### For:

As the cost of education has increased significantly over the last decades, students are having to shoulder a higher percentage of the costs of their education, thus making a higher education less accessible for many. And many of those attending college or university face acquiring a significant amount of debt to pay for their tuition fees. The elimination of these fees altogether would provide access to individuals who want a higher education without the acquisition of a heavy debt load. This is especially true for those who come from families that have

lower income levels. Paying for tuition is generally the largest barrier to attaining a higher education.

Some countries already pick up the full cost of higher education because they recognize that the benefits of educating individuals are more than offset by the benefits that society gains from their education. In all societies, higher levels of education lead to more productivity for the nation and higher rates of income for successful graduates. Also, people with more education usually draw less from social services and social safety nets provided by the state, so not only are the costs of providing those services lower, but so too are the administrative costs to the system as a whole.

### Against:

As you have already realized from reading this textbook, there is no "free lunch." For everything there is a cost—perhaps not to you directly, but somewhere there is a cost that must be paid. In the case of higher education, it is recognized that the major benefit of education accrues to the individual gaining it; therefore, the individual should be paying the lion's share of the cost of that education. However, we've seen that there are social benefits to achieving an education. As a result, society has agreed to pay the greater share, leaving the individual student to pay a lesser, but still significant, share.

Some students argue that they will pay for their education through the taxes they will pay throughout life. This is true, but if one's taxes were to reflect the amount of cost for the education one gets, should those that don't have an education get a tax rebate for the portion of their taxes that go to general education for the population? And what about those who have many kids—should their taxes be increased to pay for their kids' education?

What about students who receive an education in Canada, and then move to another country far away? Canada has paid for their education but receive very little or no future benefit from that investment. The same argument can be made for immigrants who have recently arrived and therefore have not paid into the system but gain immediate benefits, such as free tuition. Should that be the case, or should individuals have to reside in Canada for a set time period before becoming eligible for a free college or university education?

A common belief is that when there is no personal payment for a good or service, individuals value that good or service less than if they had paid for it. With free tuition, for example, there would be less incentive for students to do well in courses or even to finish their education.

As a professor, I would have no qualms about subsidizing students who are serious about gaining an education, but if a student failed my course *for lack of effort or not showing up,* I think that student should pay the international student rate (which is 100 percent of the cost of the course) to take it again. If the student legitimately failed the course because they had difficulty in understanding the content but attended the majority of classes and did all the assignments/tests, then I would have no problem subsidizing them to take the course again.

1. There are multiple compelling arguments for governments to fully subsidize education. Can you provide other reasons not mentioned here that might convince a politician to support tuition-free education?

2. Since an education is a major benefit for the individual gaining it, shouldn't the individual pay at least a majority of the cost of that education?

3. How would you structure a tuition-free program for students that is fair and equitable to both students and the taxpayer? Do you agree with the professor's suggestion of a middle ground? What improvements would you make?

## SECTION CHECK

- Economic growth is represented by an outward shift of the production possibilities curve, indicating an increase in the possibility of producing more of all goods. Despite this, scarcity inevitably remains a fact of life.
- The production possibilities model is an effective way of illustrating the economic concepts of scarcity, choice, opportunity costs, efficiency, and economic growth.

**section**

# 2.3

# Market Prices Coordinate Economic Activity

- What is a market?
- What are the roles of buyers and sellers in a market?
- How does a market system allocate scarce resources?
- What is a market failure?

## WHAT IS A MARKET?

Although we usually think of a market as a place where some sort of exchange occurs, a market is not really a place at all. A **market** is the process of buyers and sellers exchanging goods and services. This means that supermarkets, the Toronto Stock Exchange, drugstores, roadside stands, garage sales, Internet stores, and restaurants are all markets.

**market**
*the process of buyers and sellers exchanging goods and services*

Every market is different. That is, the conditions under which the exchange between buyers and sellers takes place can vary. These differences make it difficult to precisely define a market. After all, an incredible variety of exchange arrangements exists in the real world—organized securities markets, wholesale auction markets, foreign exchange markets, real estate markets, labour markets, and so forth.

Goods being priced and traded in various ways at various locations by various kinds of buyers and sellers further compound the problem of defining a market. For some goods, such as housing, markets are numerous but limited to a geographic area. Homes in Niagara Falls, Ontario, for example (about 130 kilometres from downtown Toronto), do not compete directly with homes in Toronto. Why? Because people who work in Toronto will generally look for homes within commuting distance. Even within cities, there are separate markets for homes, differentiated by amenities such as bigger houses, newer houses, larger lots, and better schools.

In a similar manner, markets are numerous but geographically limited for a good such as cement. Because transportation costs are so high relative to the selling price, the good is not shipped any substantial distance and buyers are usually in contact only with local producers. Price and output are thus determined in a number of small markets. In other markets, like those for gold or automobiles, markets are global. The important point is not what a market looks like, but what it does—it facilitates trade.

## WHAT ARE THE ROLES OF BUYERS AND SELLERS IN A MARKET?

The roles of buyers and sellers in markets are important. The buyers, as a group, determine the demand-side of the market. Buyers include the consumers who purchase the goods and services and the firms that buy inputs—labour, capital, and raw materials. Sellers, as a group, determine the supply side of the market. Sellers include the firms that produce and sell goods and services, and the resource owners who sell their inputs to firms—workers who "sell" their labour and resource owners who sell raw materials and capital. It is the interaction of buyers and sellers that determines market prices and output—through the forces of supply and demand.

In Chapter 3, we focus on how supply and demand work in a competitive market—one in which there are a number of buyers and sellers. Because most markets contain a large degree of competitiveness, the lessons of supply and demand can be applied to many different types of problems.

The supply and demand model is particularly useful in markets like agriculture, finance, labour, construction, services, wholesale, and retail. In short, a model is only as good as it explains and predicts. The model of supply and demand is very good at predicting changes in prices and quantities in many markets, large and small.

## HOW DOES A MARKET SYSTEM ALLOCATE SCARCE RESOURCES?

In a world of scarcity, competition is inescapable, and one method of allocating resources among competing uses is the market system. The market system provides a way for millions of producers and consumers to allocate scarce resources. For the most part, markets are efficient. To an economist, **efficiency** is achieved when the economy gets the most out of its scarce resources. In short, efficiency makes the economic pie as large as possible.

**efficiency**
*getting the most from society's scarce resources*

Buyers and sellers indicate their wants through their action and inaction in the marketplace, and it is this collective "voice" that determines how resources are allocated. But how is this information communicated? Market prices serve as the language of the market system. By understanding what these market prices mean, you can get a better understanding of the vital function that the market system performs.

Markets may not always conform to your desired tastes and preferences. You may think that markets produce too many fast foods, face-lifts, and Justin Bieber albums. Some markets are illegal—the market for cocaine, the market for stolen body parts, and the market for child pornography. Markets do not come with a moral compass; they simply provide what buyers are willing and able to pay for and what sellers are willing and able to produce.

## Market Prices Provide Important Information

Market prices communicate important information to both buyers and sellers. These prices communicate information about the relative availability of products to buyers, and they provide sellers with critical information about the relative value that consumers place on those products. In effect, market prices provide a way for both buyers and sellers to communicate about the relative value of resources. This communication results in a shifting of resources from those uses that are less valued to those that are more valued. We will see how this works beginning in Chapter 3.

The basis of a market economy is the voluntary exchange and the price system that guide people's choices and produce solutions to the questions of what goods to produce and how to produce and distribute them. Take something as simple as the production of a pencil. Where did the wood come from? Perhaps British Columbia or Quebec. The graphite may have come from the mines in northern Ontario, and the rubber may be from Malaysia. The paint, the glue, the metal piece that holds the eraser—who knows? The point is that market forces coordinated this activity among literally thousands of people, some of whom live in different countries and speak different languages. The market system brought these people together to make a pencil that sells for $1.50 for 20 of them. It all happened because the market system provided the incentive for people to pursue activities that benefit others. This same process produces millions of goods and services around the world, from automobiles and computers to pencils and paper clips. The same is true of the iPod and iPhone.

In countries that do not rely on the market system, there is no clear communication between buyers and sellers. In the former Soviet Union, where quality was virtually nonexistent, there were shortages of quality goods and surpluses of low-quality goods. For example, there were thousands of tractors without spare parts and millions of pairs of shoes that were left on shelves because the sizes did not match those of the population.

## Property Rights and the Legal System

In a market economy, private individuals and firms own most of the resources. For example, when consumers buy houses, cars, or pizzas, they have purchased the right to use these goods in ways they, not someone else, see fit. These rights are called *property rights*. Property rights are the rules of our economic game. If well defined, property rights give individuals the incentive to maintain, improve, and conserve their property to preserve or increase its value.

The market system can work only if the government enforces the rules. That is, one of the key functions of the government is to provide a legal framework that protects and enforces property rights and contracts. Markets, like baseball games, need umpires. It is the government that plays this role when it defines and protects the rights of people and their property through the legal system and police protection. That is, by providing rules and regulations, government can make markets work more efficiently. Private enforce-

**Apple employees have learned how to combine almost 500 generic parts to make something of much greater value. The whole is greater than the sum of the parts. There is not one person at Apple or in the world who could put together an iPhone all alone. It takes many people, making many parts, living all over the world.**

Tanjala Gica/Shutterstock.com

ment is possible, but as economic life becomes more complex, political institutions have become the major instrument for defining and enforcing property rights.

The government defines and protects property rights through the legal system and public policy. The legal system ensures the rights of private ownership, the enforcement of contracts, and the legal status for businesses. The legal system serves as the referee, imposing penalties on violators of our legal rules. Property rights also include intellectual property—the property rights that an owner receives through patents, copyrights, and trademarks. These rights give the owner long-term protection that encourages individuals to write books, music, and software programs and to invent new products. In short, well-defined property rights encourage investment, innovation, exchange, conservation, and economic growth.

## WHAT IS A MARKET FAILURE?

**market failure**

*when the economy fails to allocate resources efficiently on its own*

The market mechanism is a simple but effective and efficient general means of allocating resources among alternative uses. When the economy fails to allocate resources efficiently on its own, however, it is known as **market failure**. For example, a steel mill might put soot and other forms of "crud" into the air as a by-product of making steel. When it does this, it imposes costs on others not connected with using or producing steel from the steel mill. The soot may require homeowners to paint their homes more often, entailing a cost. And studies show that respiratory diseases are greater in areas with more severe air pollution, imposing costs and often shortening life itself. In addition, the steel mill might discharge chemicals into a stream, thus killing wildlife and spoiling recreational activities for the local population. In this case, the steel factory emits too much pollution but does not bear the cost of its polluting actions. In other words, by transferring the pollution costs onto society, the firm has lowered its costs of production and is now producing more than the ideal output. This is inefficient because it is an overallocation of resources.

Markets can also produce too little of a good—research, for example. The government might decide to subsidize promising scientific research that may benefit many people, such as cancer research.

Whether the market economy has produced too little (underallocation) or too much (overallocation), the government can improve society's well-being by intervening.

In addition, we cannot depend on the market economy to always communicate accurately. Some firms may have market power to distort prices in their favour. For example, the only regional cement company in the area has the ability to charge a higher price and provide a lower-quality product than if the company was in a highly competitive market. In this case, the lack of competition can lead to higher prices and reduced product quality. And without adequate information, unscrupulous producers may be able to misrepresent their products to the disadvantage of unwary consumers.

### The Market Distribution of Income

Sometimes a painful trade-off exists between how much an economy can produce efficiently and how that output is distributed—the degree of equality. There is no guarantee that the market economy will provide everyone with adequate amounts of food, shelter, and transportation. That is, not only does the market determine what goods are going to be produced and in what quantities, but it also determines the distribution of output among members of society.

As with other aspects of government intervention, the degree-of-equity argument can generate some sharp disagreements. What is "fair" for one person may seem highly "unfair" to someone else. Although one person may find it terribly unfair for some individuals to earn many times the amount earned by other individuals who work equally hard, another person may find it highly unfair to ask one group, the relatively rich, to pay a much higher proportion of their income in taxes than another group.

Government policymakers make decisions recognizing that there is a trade-off between efficiency (creating a bigger pie) and equality (dividing that pie). Some policies, like a progressive income tax system, Employment Insurance, and welfare programs, are aimed at redistributing the pie. While these programs aim to achieve a more equal distribution of income, they also may distort incentives for others to work hard and produce more goods and services. But that does not mean the poor should be ignored because helping them distorts incentives. We just need to recognize that there are trade-offs.

## Government Does Not Always Have the Solution

Just because the government could improve the distribution of income situation does not mean it will. After all, the political process has its own set of problems, such as special interests, short-sightedness, and imperfect information. For example, government may reduce competition through tariffs and quotas, or it may impose inefficient regulations that restrict entry. Consequently, government, like markets, has shortcomings and imperfections; the cost of government policies can exceed the benefits. Citizens failing to understand the difference between actual and ideal government performance will find it difficult to decide the appropriate role for government.

## SECTION CHECK

- Markets consist of buyers and sellers exchanging goods and services with one another.
- Buyers determine the demand-side of the market and sellers determine the supply-side of the market.
- Through voluntary exchange and the price system, the market system provides a way for producers and consumers to allocate scarce resources.
- A market failure occurs when an economy fails to allocate resources efficiently on its own.

**section**

**2.4**

# The Circular Flow Model

- What are product markets?
- What are factor markets?
- What is the goods and services flow?
- What is the income flow?
- What is the circular flow model?

How do we explain how millions of people in an economy interact when it comes to buying, selling, producing, working, hiring, and so on? A continuous flow of goods and services is bought and sold between the producers of goods and services (which we call *firms*) and the buyers of goods and services (which we call *households*). A continuous flow of income also moves from firms to households, as firms buy inputs to produce the goods and services they sell. In our simple economy, these exchanges take place in product markets and factor markets.

## WHAT ARE PRODUCT MARKETS?

**product markets**
*the markets for consumer goods and services*

**Product markets** are the markets for consumer goods and services. In the product market, households are buyers and firms are sellers. Households buy the goods and services that firms produce and sell.

## WHAT ARE FACTOR MARKETS?

**factor (input) markets**
*the market in which households sell the use of their inputs (capital, land, labour, and entrepreneurship) to firms*

**Factor**, or **input**, **markets** are the markets where households sell the use of their inputs (capital, land, labour, and entrepreneurship) to firms. In the factor markets, households are the sellers and the firms are the buyers.

## WHAT IS THE GOODS AND SERVICES FLOW?

**goods and services flow**
*the continuous flow of inputs and outputs in an economy*

The **goods and services flow** represents the continuous flow of inputs and outputs in an economy. Households make inputs available to producers through the factor markets. These inputs are then turned into outputs which are then bought by households.

## WHAT IS THE INCOME FLOW?

**income flow**
*the continuous flow of income and expenditure in an economy*

The **income flow** represents the continuous flow of income and expenditure in an economy. Households receive money payments from firms as compensation for the labour, land, capital, and entrepreneurship needed to produce goods and services. These payments take the form of wages (salaries), rent, interest payments, and profits, respectively. The payments from households to firms are for the purchase of goods and services.

## WHAT IS THE CIRCULAR FLOW MODEL?

**circular flow model of income and output**
*an illustration of the continuous flow of goods, services, inputs, and payments between firms and households*

The simple **circular flow model of income and output** is an illustration of the continuous flow of goods, services, inputs, and payments between firms and households. A simple depiction of the model is presented in Exhibit 1. In the top half of the exhibit, product markets, households purchase goods and services that firms have produced. In the lower half of the exhibit, factor (or input) markets, households sell the inputs that firms use to produce goods and services. The income flow (going clockwise in Exhibit 1) describes how households receive income—money income—and use that income to buy goods and services—consumption spending. The goods and services flow (going counterclockwise in Exhibit 1) details how households supply inputs—capital, land, labour, and entrepreneurship—to firms that use them in the production of outputs—goods and services.

Let's take a simple example to see how the circular flow model works. Suppose a teacher's supply of labour generates personal income in the form of wages (the factor market), which she can use to buy automobiles, vacations, food, and other goods (the product market). Suppose she buys an automobile (product market); the automobile dealer now has revenue to pay for his inputs (factor market)—wages to workers, purchase of new cars to replenish his inventory, rent for his building, and so on. So we see that in the simple circular flow model, income flows from firms to households (factor markets) and spending flows from households to firms (product markets). The simple circular flow model shows how households and firms interact in product markets and in factor markets and how product markets and factor markets are interrelated.

**section 2.4**
Exhibit 1

**The Circular Flow Model**

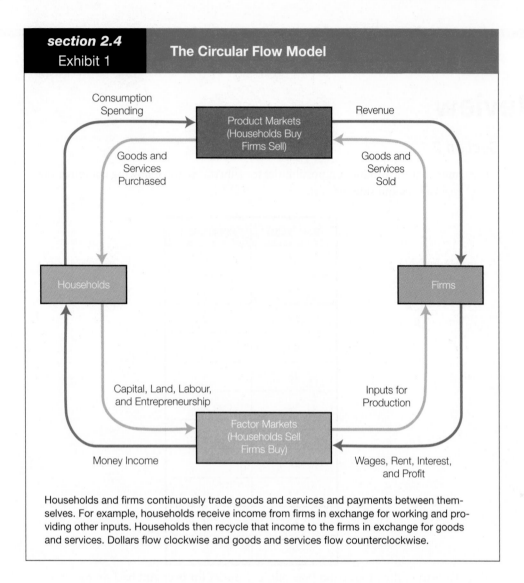

Households and firms continuously trade goods and services and payments between themselves. For example, households receive income from firms in exchange for working and providing other inputs. Households then recycle that income to the firms in exchange for goods and services. Dollars flow clockwise and goods and services flow counterclockwise.

The circular flow model can become much more complex but here it is presented merely to introduce the major markets and players in the economy. For example, the model can be extended to show the role of government, the financial sector, and foreign markets. Our simple model also does not show how firms and households send some of their income to the government for taxes or how households save some of their income for savings. Households are not the only buyers in the economy—firms, government, and foreigners buy some of the goods and services.

## SECTION CHECK

- In the product market, households are buyers and firms are sellers.
- In the factor markets, households are the sellers and firms are the buyers.
- The goods and services flow represents the continuous flow of inputs and outputs in an economy.
- The income flow represents the continuous flow of income and expenditure in an economy.
- The circular flow model illustrates the flow of goods, services, and payments among firms and households.

# For Your Review

## Section 2.1

1. Assume that the production possibilities for Alberta are the following combinations of kegs of beer and sides of beef.

| Beer (kegs) | Beef (sides) |
|---|---|
| 55 | 0 |
| 54 | 1 |
| 52 | 2 |
| 49 | 3 |
| 45 | 4 |
| 40 | 5 |
| 34 | 6 |
| 27 | 7 |
| 19 | 8 |
| 10 | 9 |
| 0 | 10 |

a. Construct the production possibilities frontier for beer and beef on the grid below.

b. Given the information above, what is the opportunity cost of the 55th keg of beer in Alberta? Of the 6th side of beef? Of the 9th side of beef?

c. Suppose Alberta is currently producing 4 sides of beef and 45 kegs of beer. What is the opportunity cost of 5 more sides of beef in Alberta?

d. Would the combination of 40 kegs of beer and 4 sides of beef be efficient? Why or why not?

e. Is the combination of 9 kegs of beer and 10 sides of beef possible for Alberta? Why or why not?

## Blueprint Problem

Assume that an economy is characterized by the following production possibilities.

| Bread (loaves) | Computers (units) |
|:---:|:---:|
| 75 | 0 |
| 70 | 1 |
| 60 | 2 |
| 45 | 3 |
| 25 | 4 |
| 0 | 5 |

a. Construct the production possibilities curve (PPC) for this economy.

b. Does this economy's production possibilities curve exhibit the law of increasing opportunity cost? Provide sufficient proof.

c. Suppose that a new technique for baking loaves of bread is invented and the production of bread doubles, while computer production remains unchanged. Illustrate this outcome using the PPC model.

## Blueprint Solution

a.

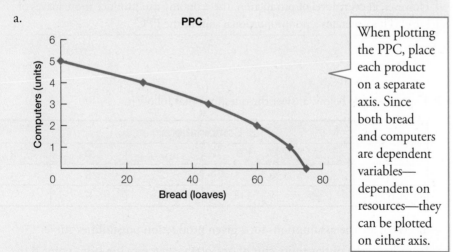

When plotting the PPC, place each product on a separate axis. Since both bread and computers are dependent variables—dependent on resources—they can be plotted on either axis.

b.

| Bread (loaves) | | Computers (units) | |
|---|---|---|---|
| Total Production | Marginal Production | Total Production | Marginal Production |
| 75 | | 0 | |
| 70 | 5 loaves of bread | 1 | 1st computer |
| 60 | 10 loaves of bread | 2 | 2nd computer |
| 45 | 15 loaves of bread | 3 | 3rd computer |
| 25 | 20 loaves of bread | 4 | 4th computer |
| 0 | 25 loaves of bread | 5 | 5th computer |

By calculating the marginal changes in both production schedules, we are able to answer this question. Notice that the opportunity cost of computer production—the amount of bread production that is forgone as computer production is increased—is increasing. Therefore, the law of increasing opportunity cost is proven.

c.

Notice that the number of computers this economy can produce remains unchanged. However, at every level of production, the economy can produce more loaves of bread. This generates a nonproportional shift of the PPC.

2. Using the table below, answer the questions that follow it.

| Combinations | | | | | |
|---|---|---|---|---|---|
| | A | B | C | D | E |
| Pizza | 0 | 1 | 2 | 3 | 4 |
| Robots | 20 | 18 | 14 | 8 | 0 |

a. What are the assumptions for a given production possibilities curve?

b. What is the opportunity cost of one pizza when moving from point B to point C? When moving from point D to point E?

c. Do these combinations demonstrate constant or increasing opportunity costs?

3. Imagine that you are the sole inhabitant of a small island that produces only two goods: cattle and wheat. About a quarter of the land is not fertile enough for growing wheat, so cattle graze on it. What would happen if you tried to produce more and more wheat, extending your planting even to the less fertile soil?

## Sections 2.1 and 2.2

4. How would the following events be shown using a production possibilities curve for shelter and food?

   a. The economy is experiencing double-digit unemployment.

   b. Economic growth is increasing at over 5 percent per year.

   c. Society decides it wants less shelter and more food.

   d. Society decides it wants more shelter and less food.

5. Suppose the following production possibility table represents the province of Quebec.

| | A | B | C | D | E | F |
|---|---|---|---|---|---|---|
| Cheese | 45 | 42 | 36 | 27 | 15 | 0 |
| Tractors | 0 | 10 | 20 | 30 | 40 | 50 |

   a. Construct the production possibilities frontier (PPF) for cheese and tractors.

   b. Does this production possibilities frontier illustrate the law of increasing opportunity cost? Explain.

   c. Suppose a technological advance increases the efficiency of cheese production, leaving tractor production unaffected. What impact would this have on the PPF for the province of Quebec?

   d. Suppose tractors represent *capital goods* and cheese represents *consumption goods*. If the province of Quebec altered its production from combination B to combination E, what impact could this have on the future economic growth of the province?

6. Given the following production possibilities curve, answer the questions that follow it.

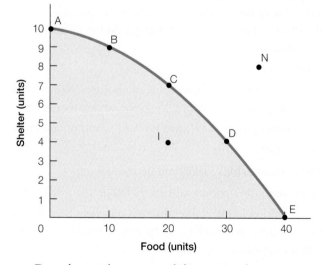

   a. Does this production possibilities curve show increasing opportunity costs? Explain.

   b. What is the opportunity cost of moving from point I to point D? Explain.

   c. What is the opportunity cost of moving from point C to point B?

   d. Which of points A–E is the most efficient? Explain.

e. Which of the identified production alternatives is currently impossible for this economy to achieve? What must happen in order for this production alternative to become attainable?

f. Which of the identified production alternatives is currently attainable but inefficient? What must happen in order for this production alternative to become efficient?

## Section 2.2

7. Economy A produces more capital goods and fewer consumer goods than Economy B. Which economy will grow more rapidly? Draw two production possibilities curves, one for Economy A and one for Economy B. Demonstrate graphically how one economy can grow more rapidly than the other.

8. A politician running for prime minister of Canada promises to build new schools and new prisons if elected, without sacrificing any other goods and services. Using the production possibilities curve between schools and prisons, explain under what conditions the politician would be able to keep her promise.

9. Why one nation experiences economic growth and another does not is a question that has intrigued economists since Adam Smith wrote *An Inquiry into the Nature and Causes of the Wealth of Nations* in 1776. Explain why each of the following would limit economic growth.

   a. The politically connected elite secure a large share of a country's output and put the proceeds into foreign banks.

   b. The national philosophy is "Live for the moment and forget about tomorrow."

   c. The government closes all of the schools so more people will be available for work.

   d. The country fears military invasion and spends half of its income on military goods.

10. How does education add to a nation's capital stock?

## Section 2.3

11. Evaluate the validity of the following statement: "Canadians spend millions of dollars every year shopping online, buying everything from investment products to children's toys. However, due to the virtual nature of these transactions (buyers and sellers do not actually meet in person), these exchanges do not occur in what economists would consider markets."

12. What role do buyers and sellers have in a market?

13. Prices communicate information about the relative value of resources. Which of the following would cause the relative value and, hence, the price, of potatoes to rise?

   a. A fungus infestation wipes out half of the Prince Edward Island potato crop.

   b. The price of potato chips rises.

   c. Scientists find that eating potato chips makes you better-looking.

   d. The prices of wheat, rice, and other potato substitutes fall dramatically.

14. People communicate with each other in the market through the effect their decisions to buy or sell have on prices. Indicate how each of the following would affect prices by putting a check mark in the appropriate space.

   a. People who see an energetic and lovable Jack Russell terrier in a popular TV series want Jack Russell terriers as pets. The price of Jack Russell terriers ___ rises ___ falls.

b. Retirees flock to Tampa, Florida, to live. The price of housing in Tampa ___ rises ___ falls.

c. Weather-related crop failures in Colombia and Costa Rica reduce coffee supplies. The price of coffee ___ rises ___ falls.

d. Wheat fields in Alberta are replaced with oil rigs. The price of wheat ___ rises ___ falls.

e. More and more students graduate from Canadian medical schools. The income of Canadian doctors ___ rises ___ falls.

15. Is the market for laptop computers local, national, or global?

## Section 2.4

16. Identify where the appropriate entries go in the circular flow diagram below.

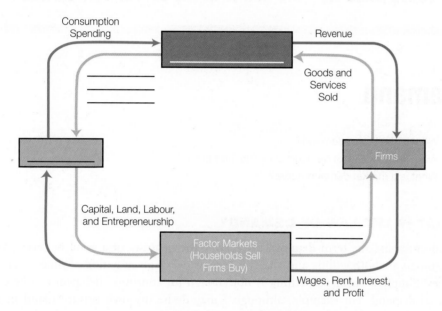

17. Identify whether each of the following transactions takes place in the factor market or the product market.

a. Billy buys a sofa from Home Time Furniture for his new home.

b. Home Time Furniture pays its manager her weekly salary.

c. The manager buys dinner at Billy's Café.

d. After he pays all of his employees their wages and pays his other bills, the owner of Billy's Café takes his profit.

18. Consider the following scenario.

Claire works as a rental agent for Hanson Car Rentals, earning $800 a week. She has set up an automatic $40 withdrawal each week to pay for her gym membership at Fit for Life. Fit for Life pays Markus $70 to teach a weekly kickbox-cardio class. Next week, Markus plans to spend $200 on a rental car from Hanson to visit his aunt in Winnipeg.

a. Which of the events in this scenario occur in the factor market?

b. Which of the events in this scenario occur in the product market?

# chapter 3

# Supply and Demand

## section 3.1

# Demand

- What is the law of demand?
- What is an individual demand schedule and curve?
- What is a market demand curve?

### WHAT IS THE LAW OF DEMAND?

**demand**
*the quantity of a good or service that consumers are both willing and able to purchase over a period of time at various prices*

Economists use the term **demand** to describe the quantity of a good or service that consumers are both willing and able to purchase over a given period of time at various prices. Simply desiring something is not enough for consumer behaviour to be considered demand. For example, although I may desire my own private island in the Bahamas, since I do not possess the financial ability to buy one, my quantity demanded is zero. Similarly, although I may have the income to buy a new expensive Armani suit, since I have no desire to do so, again my quantity demanded is zero.

Sometimes, observed behaviour is so pervasive it is considered to be a law—like the law of demand. According to the **law of demand**, the quantity of a good or service demanded varies inversely (negatively) with its price, *ceteris paribus*. More directly, the law of demand says that, other things being equal, when the price ($P$) of a good or service falls, the quantity demanded ($Q_D$) increases, and conversely, if the price of a good or service rises, the quantity demanded decreases.

**law of demand**
*the quantity of a good or service demanded varies inversely (negatively) with its price, ceteris paribus*

$$P \uparrow \Rightarrow Q_D \downarrow \text{ or } P \downarrow \Rightarrow Q_D \uparrow$$

### The Negative Relationship between Price and Quantity Demanded

The law of demand describes a negative (inverse) relationship between price and quantity demanded. When price goes up, the quantity demanded goes down, and vice versa. But why is this so? One reason for the negative relationship is what economists call *diminishing marginal utility*—the concept that in a given time period, an individual will receive less satisfaction from each successive unit of a good consumed. For example, a second ice cream cone will yield less satisfaction than the first, a third will yield less satisfaction than the second, and so on. It follows from diminishing marginal utility that if people derive decreasing amounts of satisfaction from successive units, consumers will buy additional units only if the price is reduced.

Other reasons for this inverse relationship are the substitution and income effects. According to the **substitution effect**, at higher prices, buyers increasingly substitute other goods for the good that now has a higher relative price. For example, if the price of orange juice increases, some consumers may substitute other juices for orange juice, such as apple or tomato juice, or perhaps water, milk, or coffee. According to the **income effect**, higher prices make the buyer feel poorer, causing a lowering of quantity demanded (since they cannot buy the same quantity of goods as they did when prices were lower). For example, when the price of pizza rises, this results in a decrease in the purchasing power of the consumer's income, which will usually lead to the consumer buying less pizza.

**substitution effect**
*At higher prices, buyers increasingly substitute other goods for the good that now has a higher relative price.*

**income effect**
*At higher prices, buyers feel poorer, causing a lowering of quantity demanded.*

## WHAT IS AN INDIVIDUAL DEMAND SCHEDULE AND CURVE?

The **individual demand schedule** is a table that shows the relationship between the price of the good and the quantity demanded. For example, suppose Elizabeth enjoys eating apples. How many kilograms of apples would Elizabeth be willing and able to buy at various prices during the year? At a price of $3 a kilogram, Elizabeth buys 15 kilograms of apples over the course of a year. If the price is higher, at $4 per kilogram, she might buy only 10 kilograms; if it is lower, say $1 per kilogram, she might buy 25 kilograms of apples during the year. Elizabeth's demand for apples for the year is summarized in the demand schedule in Exhibit 1. Elizabeth might not be consciously aware of the amounts that she would purchase at prices other than the prevailing one, but that does not alter the fact that she has a schedule in the sense that she would have bought various other amounts had other prices prevailed. It must be emphasized that the schedule is a list of alternative possibilities. At any one time, only one of the prices will prevail, so a certain quantity will be purchased.

**individual demand schedule**
*a table that shows the relationship between price and quantity demanded*

### An Individual Demand Curve

An **individual demand curve** is a graphical representation that shows the inverse relationship between price and quantity demanded. By plotting the different prices and corresponding quantities demanded in Elizabeth's demand schedule in Exhibit 1 and then connecting them, we can create an individual demand curve for Elizabeth (Exhibit 2). From the curve, we can see that when the price is higher, the quantity demanded is lower, and when the price is lower, the quantity demanded is higher. The demand curve shows how the quantity demanded of the good changes as its price varies.

**individual demand curve**
*a graphical representation that shows the inverse relationship between price and quantity demanded*

| *section 3.1* Exhibit 1 | Elizabeth's Demand Schedule for Apples |
|---|---|
| **Price (per kilogram)** | **Quantity Demanded (kilograms per year)** |
| $5 | 5 |
| 4 | 10 |
| 3 | 15 |
| 2 | 20 |
| 1 | 25 |

## WHAT IS A MARKET DEMAND CURVE?

Although we introduced this concept in terms of the individual, economists usually speak of the demand curve in terms of large groups of people—a whole nation, a community, or a trading area. As you know,

| section 3.1 Exhibit 2 | Elizabeth's Demand Curve for Apples |
| --- | --- |

The dots represent various quantities of apples that Elizabeth would be willing and able to buy at different prices in a given time period. The demand curve shows how the quantity demanded varies inversely with the price of the good when we hold everything else constant—*ceteris paribus*. Because of this inverse relationship between price and quantity demanded, the demand curve is downward sloping.

**market demand curve**
*the horizontal summation of individual demand curves*

every single individual has his or her demand curve for every product. The horizontal summation of individual demand curves is called the **market demand curve**.

Suppose the consumer group comprises Homer, Marge, and the rest of their small community, Springfield, and that the product is still apples. The effect of price on the quantity of apples demanded by Marge, Homer, and the rest of Springfield is given in the demand schedule and demand curves shown in Exhibit 3. At $4 per kilogram, Homer would be willing and able to buy 20 kilograms of apples per year, Marge would be willing and able to buy 10 kilograms, and the rest of Springfield would be willing and able to buy 2970 kilograms. At $3 per kilogram, Homer would be willing and able to buy 25 kilograms of apples per year, Marge would be willing and able to buy 15 kilograms, and the rest of Springfield would be willing and able to buy 4960 kilograms. The market demand curve is simply the (horizontal) sum of the quantities Homer, Marge, and the rest of Springfield demand at each price. That is, at $4, the quantity demanded in the market would be 3000 kilograms of apples (20 + 10 + 2970 = 3000), and at $3, the quantity demanded in the market would be 5000 kilograms of apples (25 + 15 + 4960 = 5000).

In Exhibit 4, we offer a more complete set of prices and quantities from the market demand for apples during the year. Remember, the market demand curve shows the amounts that all the buyers in the market would be willing and able to buy at various prices. For example, if the price of apples is $2 per kilogram, consumers in the market would collectively be willing and able to buy 8000 kilograms per year. At $1 per kilogram, the amount demanded would be 12 000 kilograms per year.

The market demand curve is the negative (inverse) relationship between price and the total quantity demanded, while holding constant all other factors that affect how much consumers are able and willing to pay, *ceteris paribus*. For the most part, we are interested in how the market works, so we will primarily use the market demand curves.

**Every Boxing Day, eager consumers line up at the break of dawn in front of retailers that are advertising deep discounts and two-for-one deals. Although they didn't want to buy the televisions, game consoles, clothing, and computers at the regular asking prices, many clearly want these goods at a lower price—the law of demand.**

Toronto Star via Getty Images

## section 3.1
### Exhibit 3
**Creating a Market Demand Curve**

### a. Creating a Market Demand Schedule for Apples

| Price (per kilogram) | Quantity Demanded (kilograms per year) | | | | | | | |
|---|---|---|---|---|---|---|---|---|
| | Homer | + | Marge | + | Rest of Springfield | = | Market Demand |
| $4 | 20 | + | 10 | + | 2970 | = | 3000 |
| $3 | 25 | + | 15 | + | 4960 | = | 5000 |

### b. Creating a Market Demand Curve for Apples

## section 3.1
### Exhibit 4
**A Market Demand Curve**

### a. Market Demand Schedule for Apples

| Price (per kilogram) | Total Quantity Demanded (kilograms per year) |
|---|---|
| $5 | 1000 |
| 4 | 3000 |
| 3 | 5000 |
| 2 | 8000 |
| 1 | 12 000 |

### b. Market Demand Curve for Apples

The market demand curve shows the amounts that all buyers in the market would be willing to buy at various prices. If the price of apples is $2 per kilogram, consumers in the market would collectively be willing to buy 8000 kilograms per year. At $1 per kilogram, the amount demanded would be 12 000 kilograms per year.

## section 3.2

# Shifts in the Demand Curve

- What is the difference between a change in demand and a change in quantity demanded?
- What are the determinants of demand?
- Can we review the distinction between changes in demand and changes in quantity demanded?

### WHAT IS THE DIFFERENCE BETWEEN A CHANGE IN DEMAND AND A CHANGE IN QUANTITY DEMANDED?

**change in quantity demanded**
*a change in a good's price leads to a change in quantity demanded, a move along a given demand curve*

**change in demand**
*a change in a determinant of demand leads to a change in demand, a shift of the entire demand curve*

Understanding the relationship between price and quantity demanded is so important that economists make a clear distinction between it and the various other factors that can influence consumer behaviour. A change in a good's price is said to lead to a **change in quantity demanded**. That is, it "moves you along" a given demand curve. The demand curve is drawn under the assumption that all other things are held constant, except the price of the good. However, economists know that price is not the only thing that affects the quantity of a good that people buy. The other factors that influence the demand curve are called *determinants of demand* and a change in these other factors *shifts the entire demand curve*. These determinants of demand are called *demand shifters* and they lead to a **change in demand**.

### WHAT ARE THE DETERMINANTS OF DEMAND?

An increase in demand shifts the demand curve to the right; a decrease in demand shifts the demand curve to the left, as seen in Exhibit 1. Changes in demand such as these are the result of demand shifters. Some of the possible demand shifters are the prices of related goods, income, number of buyers, tastes, and expectations. We will now look more closely at each of these variables.

### The Prices of Related Goods

In deciding how much of a good or service to buy, consumers are influenced by the price of that good or

**section 3.2**
Exhibit 1

**Demand Shifts**

An increase in demand shifts the demand curve to the right.
A decrease in demand shifts the demand curve to the left.

service, a relationship summarized in the law of demand. However, consumers are also influenced by the prices of *related* goods and services—substitutes and complements.

**Substitutes**    Substitutes are generally goods for which one could be used in place of the other. To many, substitutes would include butter and margarine, domestic and foreign cars, movie tickets and on-demand TV programs, jackets and sweaters, Petro Canada and Shell gasoline, and Nikes and Adidas.

Suppose you go into a store to buy a couple of six packs of Coca-Cola and you see that Pepsi is on sale for half its usual price. Is it possible that you might decide to buy Pepsi instead of Coca-Cola? Economists argue that this is the case, and empirical tests have confirmed that people are responsive to both the price of the good in question and the prices of related goods. In this example, Pepsi and Coca-Cola are said to be substitutes. Two goods are **substitutes** if an increase (a decrease) in the price of one good causes an increase (a decrease) in the demand for another good, a direct (or positive) relationship. In Exhibit 2(a), we see that as the price of Coca-Cola increased—a movement up along your demand curve for it—you increased your demand for Pepsi, resulting in a shift in the demand for Pepsi (Exhibit 2[b]).

**substitute**
*An increase (a decrease) in the price of one good causes an increase (a decrease) in the demand for another good.*

**Complements**    Complements are goods that "go together," often consumed and used simultaneously, such as skis and bindings, peanut butter and jam, hot dogs and buns, digital music players and downloadable music, and printers and ink cartridges. If an increase (a decrease) in the price of one good causes a decrease (an increase) in the demand of another good (an inverse or negative relationship), the two goods are called **complements**. For example, in Exhibit 3(a), we see that as the price of computers increases, the quantity demanded of computers falls (a movement in demand). And with fewer computers being purchased, we would expect people to decrease their demand (a leftward shift) for printers (Exhibit 3[b]).

**complement**
*An increase (a decrease) in the price of one good causes a decrease (an increase) in the demand of another good.*

### Income

Economists have observed that generally the consumption of goods and services is positively related to the income available to consumers. Empirical studies support the notion that as individuals receive more income, they tend to increase their purchases

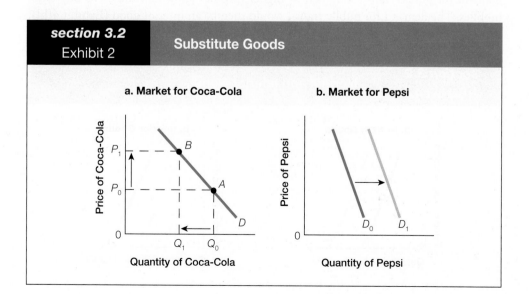

**section 3.2**
Exhibit 2          **Substitute Goods**

a. Market for Coca-Cola

b. Market for Pepsi

**section 3.2**
Exhibit 3

**Complementary Goods**

**a. Market for Computers**

**b. Market for Printers**

of most goods and services. Other things held equal, rising income usually leads to an increase in the demand for goods (a rightward shift of the demand curve), and decreasing income usually leads to a decrease in the demand for goods (a leftward shift of the demand curve).

### Normal and Inferior Goods

**normal good**
*If income increases, the demand for a good increases; if income decreases, the demand for a good decreases.*

**inferior good**
*If income increases, the demand for a good decreases; if income decreases, the demand for a good increases.*

If when income increases, the demand for a good increases and decreases when income decreases, the good is called a **normal good**. Most goods are normal goods. Consumers will typically buy more cellphones, clothes, pizzas, and trips to the movies as their incomes rise. However, if when income increases, the demand for a good decreases and increases when income decreases, the good is called an **inferior good**. For example, for most people inferior goods might include inexpensive cuts of meat, used cars, gently used clothing, and macaroni and cheese. The term *inferior* in this sense does not refer to the quality of the good in question but shows that when income changes, demand changes in the opposite direction (inversely).

Consider how an increase in income can affect the market for automobiles and the market for public transit. Automobiles are generally considered a normal good, so a rise in income will increase the demand for automobiles (Exhibit 4[a]). However, the demand for public transit may fall, as higher incomes allow consumers to buy automobiles. The demand for public transit would then be an inferior good (Exhibit 4[b]).

**section 3.2**
Exhibit 4

**Normal and Inferior Goods**

**a. Normal Goods**

**b. Inferior Goods**

For example, if people's incomes rise and they increase their demand for movie tickets, we say that movie tickets are a normal good. But if people's incomes fall and they increase their demand for bus rides, we say bus rides are an inferior good. Whether goods are normal or inferior, the point here is that income influences demand—usually positively, but sometimes negatively.

## Number of Buyers

The demand for a good or service will vary with the size of the potential consumer population. The demand for wheat, for example, rises as population increases because the added population wants to consume wheat products, like bread or cereal. Marketing experts, who closely follow the patterns of consumer behaviour with regard to a particular good or service, are usually vitally concerned with the "demographics" of the product—the vital statistics of the potential consumer population, including size, income, and age characteristics. For example, market researchers for baby-food companies keep a close watch on the birth rate.

**Body piercing and tattoos have risen in popularity in recent years. As the preference for these types of personal expression increases, the demand for these services is shifted to the right. According to the Pew Research Center, 32 percent of 18- to 29-year-olds acknowledged having at least one tattoo.**

## Tastes

The demand for a good or service may increase or decrease suddenly with changes in fashions or fads. Taste changes may be triggered by advertising or promotion, by a news story, by the behaviour of some popular public figure, and so on. Taste changes are particularly noticeable in apparel. Skirt lengths, coat lapels, shoe styles, and tie widths change frequently.

Changes in preferences naturally lead to shifts in demand. Much of the predictive power of economic theory, however, stems from the assumption that tastes are relatively stable, at least over a substantial period of time. Tastes *do* change, though. A person may grow tired of one type of recreation or food and try another type. Changes in occupation, number of dependants, state of health, and age also tend to alter preferences. The birth of a baby may cause a family to spend less on recreation and more on food and clothing. Illness increases the demand for medicine and lessens purchases of other goods. A cold winter increases the demand for natural gas. Changes in customs and traditions also affect preferences, and the development of new products draws consumer preferences away from other goods. Digital music files have replaced compact discs, just as flat-screen TVs have replaced traditional tube TVs. A change in information can also impact consumers' demand. For example, an outbreak of *Escherichia coli* or new information about a defective and/or dangerous product, such as a baby crib, can reduce demand.

## Expectations

Sometimes the demand for a good or service in a given period will increase or decrease because consumers expect the good to change in price or availability at some future date. If people expect the future price to be higher, they will purchase more of the good now before the price increase—an increase in the demand today. If people expect the future price to be lower, they will purchase less of the good now and wait for the price decrease—a decrease in the demand today. For example, if you expect the price of computers to fall soon, you may be less willing to buy one today. Or you might buy next year's Halloween decorations on November 1 during a post-Halloween sale. That is, expectations of higher prices in the future could increase your demand now.

A change in consumers' expectations about their future incomes can also shift the demand curve. For example, if you expect to earn additional income next month, you may be more willing to dip into your current savings to buy something this month. If you expect your income to fall in the future, you may choose to save more today and reduce your demand for some goods.

## CAN WE REVIEW THE DISTINCTION BETWEEN CHANGES IN DEMAND AND CHANGES IN QUANTITY DEMANDED?

Economists put particular emphasis on the impact on consumer behaviour of a change in the price of a good. We are interested in distinguishing between consumer behaviour related to the price of a good itself (movement *along* a demand curve) from behaviour related to other factors changing (shifts of the demand curve).

As indicated earlier, if the price of a good changes, we say that this leads to a *"change in quantity demanded."* In Exhibit 5, the movement from A to B is called an *increase in quantity demanded,* and the movement from B to A is called a *decrease in quantity demanded.* Economists use the phrase "increase in quantity demanded" or "decrease in quantity demanded" to describe movements along a given demand curve. If one of the other factors (determinants) influencing consumer behaviour changes, we say there is a *change in demand.* In Exhibit 5, the change from A to C is called an *increase in demand,* and the change from C to A is called a *decrease in demand.* The phrase "increase in demand" or "decrease in demand" is reserved for a shift in the whole curve. So if an individual buys more CDs because the price fell, we say there was an increase in quantity demanded. However, if she buys more CDs even at the current price, say $10, we say there is an increase in demand. The effects of some of the other determinants that cause a change in demand (shifters) are reviewed in Exhibit 6.

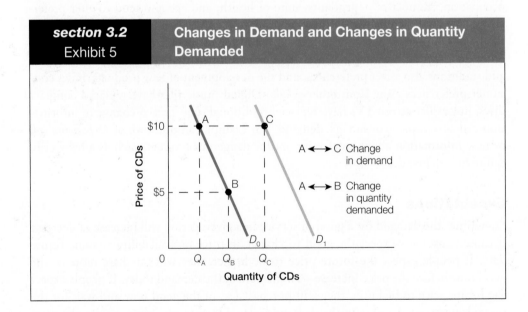

| **section 3.2** Exhibit 5 | **Changes in Demand and Changes in Quantity Demanded** |
| --- | --- |

| **section 3.2**<br>Exhibit 6 | **Possible Demand Shifters** |

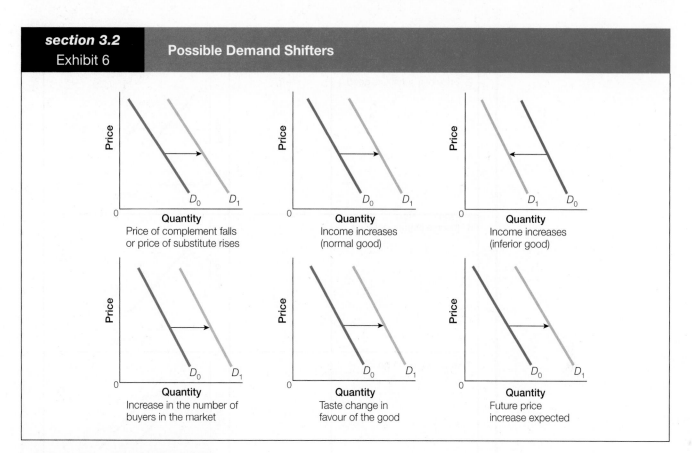

## SECTION CHECK

■ A change in the quantity demanded describes a movement along a given demand curve in response to a change in the price of the good. A change in demand shifts the entire demand curve in response to a change in some determinant of demand.

■ Some possible determinants of demand (demand shifters) are the prices of related goods, income, number of buyers, tastes, and expectations.

Change in Variable and Change in Demand

| | Variable | Change in Variable | Change in Demand |
|---|---|---|---|
| 1. | Price of a complement good | ↑ | |

(*continued*)

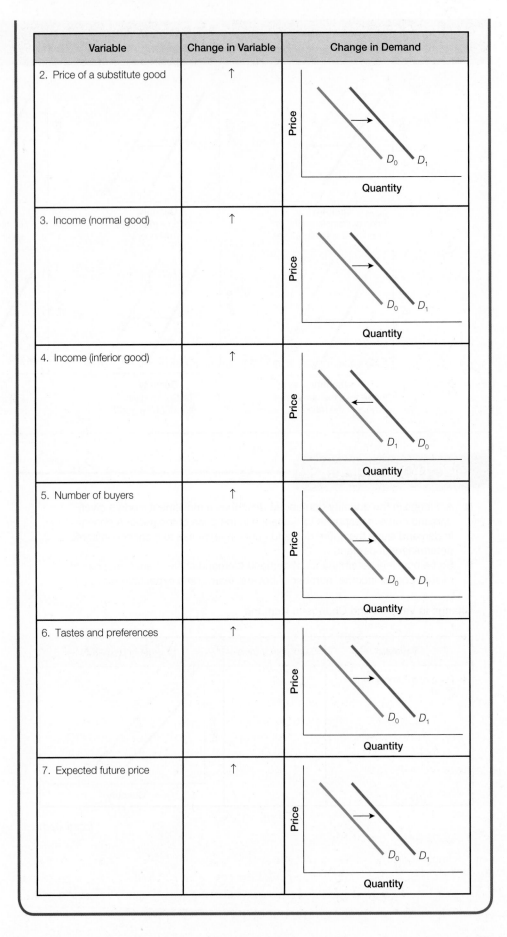

| Variable | Change in Variable | Change in Demand |
|---|---|---|
| 2. Price of a substitute good | ↑ | |
| 3. Income (normal good) | ↑ | |
| 4. Income (inferior good) | ↑ | |
| 5. Number of buyers | ↑ | |
| 6. Tastes and preferences | ↑ | |
| 7. Expected future price | ↑ | |

**section**
# 3.3

# Supply

- What is the law of supply?
- What is an individual supply curve?
- What is a market supply curve?

## WHAT IS THE LAW OF SUPPLY?

In a market, the answer to the fundamental question "What do we produce, and in what quantities?" depends on the interaction of both buyers and sellers. Demand is only half the story. The term **supply** refers to the quantity of a good or service that producers are both willing and able to make available for sale. It is an equally important factor that must be weighed by decision makers in all societies. As with demand, the price of the good is an important factor. And just as with demand, factors other than the price of the good are also important to suppliers, such as the cost of inputs or advances in technology. Although behaviour will vary among individual suppliers, economists expect, other things being equal, that the quantity supplied will vary directly with the price of the good, a relationship called the **law of supply**. According to the law of supply, the higher the price of the good ($P$), the greater the quantity supplied ($Q_s$), and the lower the price of the good, the smaller the quantity supplied, *ceteris paribus*.

$$P \uparrow \Rightarrow Q_s \uparrow \text{ or } P \downarrow \Rightarrow Q_s \downarrow$$

    The relationship described by the law of supply is a direct, or positive, relationship, because the variables move in the same direction.

### A Positive Relationship between Price and Quantity Supplied

Firms supplying goods and services want to increase their profits, and the higher the price per unit, the greater the profitability generated by supplying more of that good. For example, if you were an apple grower, wouldn't you much rather be paid $5 a kilogram than $1 a kilogram, *ceteris paribus*?

    There is another reason that supply curves are upward sloping. In Chapter 2, the law of increasing opportunity costs demonstrated that when we hold technology and input prices constant, producing additional units of a good will require increased opportunity costs. That is, when we produce something, we use the most efficient resources first (those with the lowest opportunity cost) and then draw on less efficient resources (those with a higher opportunity cost) as more of the good is produced. Because costs per unit rise as more are produced, sellers must receive a higher price to increase the quantity supplied, *ceteris paribus*.

## WHAT IS AN INDIVIDUAL SUPPLY CURVE?

To illustrate the concept of an individual supply curve, consider the amount of apples that an individual supplier, John Macintosh, is willing and able to supply in one year. The law of supply can be illustrated, like the law of demand, by a table or a graph. John's supply schedule for apples is shown in Exhibit 1(a). The price–quantity supplied combinations were then plotted and joined to create the individual supply curve

**In order to get more oil, drillers must sometimes drill deeper or go into unexplored areas, and they still may come up with a dry hole. If it costs more to increase oil production, then oil prices would have to rise in order for producers to increase their output.**

**supply**
*the quantity of a good or service that producers are both willing and able to make available for sale*

**law of supply**
*The higher (lower) the price of the good, the greater (smaller) the quantity supplied, ceteris paribus.*

### section 3.3
Exhibit 1 — An Individual Supply Curve

**a. John's Supply Schedule for Apples**

| Price (per kilogram) | Quantity Supplied (kilograms per year) |
|---|---|
| $5 | 80 |
| 4 | 70 |
| 3 | 50 |
| 2 | 30 |
| 1 | 10 |

**b. John's Supply Curve for Apples**

**individual supply curve**

*a graphical representation that shows the positive relationship between price and quantity supplied*

shown in Exhibit 1(b). The resulting **individual supply curve** is a graphical representation that shows the positive relationship between the price and the quantity supplied. Note that the individual supply curve is upward sloping as you move from left to right. At higher prices, it will be more attractive to increase production. Existing firms, or growers, will produce more at higher prices than at lower prices.

## WHAT IS A MARKET SUPPLY CURVE?

**market supply curve**

*the horizontal summation of individual supply curves*

The **market supply curve** can be thought of as the horizontal summation of individual supply curves. The market supply schedule, which reflects the total quantity supplied at each price by all of the apple producers, is shown in Exhibit 2(a). Exhibit 2(b) illustrates the resulting market supply curve for this group of apple producers.

### section 3.3
Exhibit 2 — A Market Supply Curve

**a. Market Supply Schedule for Apples**

| | | | Quantity Supplied (kilograms per year) | | |
|---|---|---|---|---|---|
| Price | John | + | Other Producers | = | Market Supply |
| $5 | 80 | + | 7920 | = | 8000 |
| 4 | 70 | + | 6930 | = | 7000 |
| 3 | 50 | + | 4950 | = | 5000 |
| 2 | 30 | + | 2970 | = | 3000 |
| 1 | 10 | + | 990 | = | 1000 |

**b. Market Supply Curve for Apples**

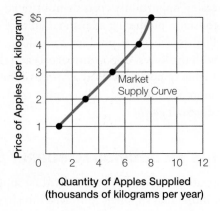

The dots on this graph indicate different quantities of apples that producers would be willing and able to supply at various prices. The line connecting those combinations is the market supply curve.

# Shifts in the Supply Curve

**section
3.4**

● What is the difference between a change in supply and a change in quantity supplied?
● What are the determinants of supply?
● Can we review the distinction between a change in supply and a change in quantity supplied?

## WHAT IS THE DIFFERENCE BETWEEN A CHANGE IN SUPPLY AND A CHANGE IN QUANTITY SUPPLIED?

Changes in the price of a good lead to changes in quantity supplied by suppliers, just as changes in the price of a good lead to changes in quantity demanded by buyers. Similarly, a change in supply, whether an increase or a decrease, will occur for reasons other than changes in the price of the product itself, just as changes in demand are due to factors (determinants) other than the price of the good. In other words, a change in the price of the good in question is shown as a movement along a given supply curve, leading to a change in quantity supplied. A change in any other factor that can affect supplier behaviour (input prices, the prices of related products, expectations, number of suppliers, technology, regulation, taxes and subsidies, and weather) results in *a shift in the entire supply curve, leading to a change in supply.*

## WHAT ARE THE DETERMINANTS OF SUPPLY?

An increase in supply shifts the supply curve to the right; a decrease in supply shifts the supply curve to the left, as seen in Exhibit 1. We will now look at some of the possible determinants of supply—factors that determine the position of the supply curve—in greater depth.

### Input Prices

Suppliers are strongly influenced by the costs of inputs used in the production process, such as steel used for

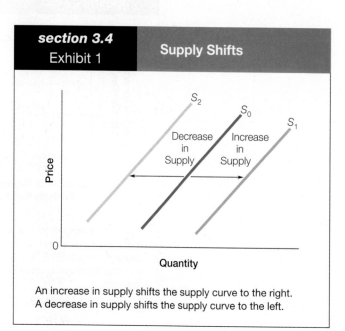

**section 3.4**
Exhibit 1

**Supply Shifts**

An increase in supply shifts the supply curve to the right.
A decrease in supply shifts the supply curve to the left.

automobiles and microchips used in computers. For example, higher labour, materials, energy, or other input costs increase the costs of production, causing the supply curve to shift to the left at each and every price. If input prices fall, this will lower the costs of production, causing the supply curve to shift to the right—more will be supplied at each and every price.

## The Prices of Related Products

Consider a car manufacturer that produces both electric and natural gas models of its vehicles. If the price of the natural gas vehicles falls, producers will reduce their quantity supplied, as seen in Exhibit 2(a). What effect would this lower price of the natural gas vehicles have on the manufacturer's decision to produce electric models of their cars? Easy question—it would increase the supply of the electric models because electric and natural gas models of car are *substitutes in production* because both goods can be produced using the same resources. You would want to produce relatively fewer of the model that had fallen in price (natural gas) and relatively more of the now more attractive other model (electric).

This example demonstrates why the price of related products is important as a supply shifter as well as a demand shifter. Producers tend to substitute the production of more profitable products for that of less profitable products. This is desirable from society's perspective as well because more profitable products tend to be those considered more valuable by society, whereas less profitable products are usually considered less valuable. Hence, the lower price in the natural gas vehicle market has caused an increase in supply (a rightward shift) in the electric vehicle market, as seen in Exhibit 2(b).

Alternatively, if the price of natural gas vehicles, a substitute in production, increases, then that model becomes more profitable. This leads to an increase in the quantity supplied of natural gas vehicles. Consequently, manufacturers will shift their resources out of the relatively lower priced models (electric); the result is a decrease in supply of electric vehicles.

**section 3.4**
Exhibit 2

**Substitutions in Production**

**a. Market for Natural Gas Vehicles**

**b. Market for Electric Vehicles**

If plant and equipment can be used to produce either natural gas or electric vehicles, a decrease in the price of natural gas vehicles (a movement along the supply curve) may cause some automobile manufacturers to shift out of the production of natural gas vehicles and into the production of electric vehicles—shifting the electric vehicle supply curve to the right.

Other examples of substitutes in production include farmers who have to decide between producing wheat or corn, or construction companies that have to choose between building single-family houses or commercial buildings.

Some goods are *complements in production.* Producing one good does not prevent the production of the other, but actually enables production of the other. For example, asphalt (which is used in road construction and roof shingles) is a marketable by-product obtained from the process of refining crude oil. Refined crude oil itself has a wide variety of applications, such as gasoline, jet fuel, diesel fuel, and home heating oil. Suppose the price of refined crude oil, say gasoline, rises and as a result, refineries increase the quantity supplied of gasoline, moving up the supply curve for gasoline, as seen in Exhibit 3(a). When refineries produce more gasoline, they automatically produce more asphalt. Thus, when the price of gasoline increases, the supply of the related good, asphalt, shifts to the right, as seen in Exhibit 3(b). Suppose the price of gasoline falls, and as a result, the quantity supplied of gasoline falls; this leads to a decrease (a leftward shift) in the supply of asphalt.

**section 3.4**
Exhibit 3

**Complements in Production**

**a. Market for Gasoline**

**b. Market for Asphalt**

If the price of the complement in production increases (gasoline), it becomes more profitable and as a result, refineries increase the quantity of gasoline supplied, moving up the supply curve for gasoline, as seen in Exhibit 3(a). When refineries produce more gasoline, they also produce more asphalt. Thus, when the price of gasoline increases, the supply of the related good, asphalt, shifts to the right, as seen in Exhibit 3(b).

Other examples of complements in production where goods are produced simultaneously from the same resource include a lumber mill that produces lumber and sawdust and a dairy that produces skim milk and cream.

## Expectations

Another factor shifting supply is suppliers' expectations. If producers expect a higher price in the future, they will supply less now than they otherwise would have, preferring to wait and sell when their goods will be more valuable. Similarly, if producers expect now that the price will be lower later, they will supply more now. For example, oil refiners will often store some of their spring supply of gasoline to sell it in the summer because gasoline prices typically peak in summer. In addition, some of the heating oil for the fall is stored for sale in the winter when heating oil prices peak.

## Number of Suppliers

We are normally interested in market demands and supplies (because together they determine prices and quantities) rather than in the behaviour of individual consumers and firms. As we discussed earlier, the supply curves of individual suppliers can be summed horizontally to create a market supply curve. An increase in the number of suppliers leads to an increase in supply, denoted by a rightward shift in the supply curve. For example, think of the number of smartphones that have entered the market over the last ten years, shifting the supply curve of smartphones to the right. An exodus of suppliers has the opposite impact, a decrease in supply, which is indicated by a leftward shift in the supply curve.

# Business *CONNECTION*

## USING DEMAND AND SUPPLY

Just as economics is the game of life, so demand and supply are the game of business. Students sometimes ask whether firms construct their own demand and supply curves, and if so, how. In reality, few firms actually do such analysis and those that do are usually larger firms that have the resources. Most of our economy is built on small and medium-sized enterprises (SMEs) and they simply don't have the time, money, or know-how to build such elaborate models. That triggers another question: Why do we have to learn this anyway if it's not used? The fact is that entrepreneurs and managers use their knowledge of demand and supply every day to make business decisions, even though you won't see evidence of the graphs on their desks.

These decision makers have learned the basics of demand and supply and they know instinctively how certain stimuli will affect their firm. They spend hours trying to understand where their firm's strengths, weaknesses, opportunities, or threats (SWOT) lie, as well as considering how they will respond. Threats generally shift the demand curves leftward, whereas positive responses are opportunities that may shift the curves rightward. A firm building on its strengths will shift demand (and supply) rightward, and ignoring the weaknesses will likely bring leftward shifts of the curves. The process relies less on having to literally illustrate the movements of the curves than it does on understanding that they will move. Managing both internal and external change is what business is all about. Let's investigate a bit more.

Managers constantly face the realities of external changes, and if you've taken basic business courses you will likely be thinking now about political, economic, social, and technological (PEST) factors analysis. A PEST analysis looks at the external issues that entrepreneurs cannot change. All of the PEST factors affect demand for a company's products and how it responds in supplying the product. Managers ignore these factors at their peril.

Once confronted with the external environment, managers do respond. They may want to increase revenues, increasing quantity (Q) or perhaps they leave Q as is and increase prices (P). Remember that an increase in price will result in a decrease in quantity demanded. Perhaps the managers need to seek new markets, or compete against substitutions—here they are shifting the demand curve. How do they do that? Remember that managers can't change the PEST factors, they can only use that information. What they can change are the 4Ps (price, product, place, and promotion). Managers can, and do, change Ps to try to meet or change the market demand, shifting the demand curve rightward if they want to grow the market, or shifting it leftward if they are contracting (which they sometimes do).

Once the demand curve has shifted, it's the operations side of the business that responds to meeting the new realities by shifting the supply curve. If the firm doesn't respond and leaves the supply curve static, and the demand has shifted rightward, then it will have produced its own shortage and consumers may turn to competitors to buy the goods they want—which means lost sales, or opportunity costs, to the firm. If on the other hand, the firm ramps up production beyond what consumers want, the firm will have produced its own surplus, which will require lowering prices later or having to accept sunk costs if the firm has to scrap the product. Either way, those are losses to the firm.

Clearly a dance between the theory and the practical application of economics goes on in every firm every day. You don't necessarily have to see evidence of theory to know that it's working—you just have to look at what's happening within the firm daily to see the practical application of demand and supply at work.

1. Which do you think occurs first in the economy: businesses responding to changes in demand or consumers responding to changes in the supply of goods and services? What do you think would happen if the opposite occurred?

2. In your opinion, has the rise of e-commerce and online purchasing increased growth in the economy? In what other ways has e-commerce affected the economy?

3. There is a plethora of "dollar stores" that purchase the oversupply of many manufacturers and sell it at a discount. Do you think this is efficient for the economy? Thinking broadly, do you think consumers and businesses benefit or not? Explain.

## Technology

Technological change can lower the firm's costs of production through productivity advances. These changes allow the firm to spend less on inputs and produce the same level of output. Human creativity works to find new ways to produce goods and services using fewer or less costly inputs of labour, natural resources, or capital. In recent years, despite generally rising prices, the prices of electronic equipment such as computers, cellphones, and flat-screen TVs have fallen dramatically. At any given price this year, suppliers are willing to provide many more (of a given quality of) computers than in previous years simply because technology has dramatically reduced the cost of providing them. Graphically, the increase in supply is indicated by a shift to the right in the supply curve.

## Regulation

Supply may also change because of changes in the legal and regulatory environment in which firms operate. Government regulations can influence the costs of production to the firm, leading to cost-induced supply changes similar to those just discussed. For example, if new safety or anti-pollution requirements increase labour and capital costs, the increased cost will result, other things equal, in a decrease in supply, shifting the supply curve to the left, or up. An increase in a government-imposed minimum wage may have a similar effect by raising labour costs and decreasing supply in markets that employ many low-wage workers. However, deregulation—the process by which governments reduce or outright eliminate restrictions on individuals or businesses—can shift the supply curve to the right.

## Taxes and Subsidies

Certain types of taxes can also increase the costs of production borne by the supplier, causing the supply curve to shift to the left at each price. The opposite of a tax (a subsidy) can lower the firm's costs and shift the supply curve to the right. For example, the government sometimes provides farmers with subsidies to encourage the production of certain agricultural products.

## Weather

In addition, weather can certainly affect the supply of certain commodities, particularly agricultural products and transportation services. A drought or freezing temperatures will almost certainly cause the supply curves for many crops to shift to the

## DEBATE

### IS IT ETHICAL TO GROW CORN FOR FUEL?

**For:**
Over the past decade, the market has adjusted to rising gas prices by blending ethanol into gasoline. The widespread use of corn-based ethanol has been a boon for farmers, who are free to choose which markets to participate in. Most farmers will choose to grow the crop that provides the greatest return on their investment and at present, corn is an extremely lucrative crop.

Note, though, that as there is a rise in the number of hectares devoted to corn, there is a drop in the number of hectares devoted to wheat and soy crops, which increases the price of wheat and soy crops and benefits the farmers who grow those crops.

This is the market in action and there is nothing unethical about it. Surely you can defend the farmers' decisions.

**Against:**
In the long term, growing crops for fuel rather than for food will mean higher prices for food around the world and that will hurt the poorest people the most. This is unethical because the market, rather than an act of nature, is causing famine—the poor simply can't afford food.

Clearly, the benefits flow to those who can afford fuel, so the poor get relatively little marginal benefit and those who cannot afford the higher costs of basic food staples now pay a much higher marginal cost than they otherwise would.

Those who believe the market should consider ethical issues along with prices would likely support a less efficient market. Just because farmers can supply a crop for an alternative use, should they?

**Questions:**
1. Why has the price of gas at the pumps risen—because of increased consumption (more people driving) or because of an increasing scarcity in the supply of crude oil?
2. Should we promote growing corn for our transportation needs?
3. Is there a conflict between the wider society's needs and the individual farmer's needs?

**section 3.4**
Exhibit 4

**Change in Supply vs. Change in Quantity Supplied**

A ⟷ B   Change in quantity supplied

B ⟷ C   Change in supply

left, whereas exceptionally good weather can shift a supply curve to the right. For example, during the summer of 2015, record-breaking temperatures and extremely low rainfalls across western Canada caused chaos for farmers as they grappled with the worst drought in more than a decade. Several counties in Alberta were forced to declare states of agricultural emergency, while the Saskatchewan government loosened crop insurance rules to aid impacted farmers.

## CAN WE REVIEW THE DISTINCTION BETWEEN A CHANGE IN SUPPLY AND A CHANGE IN QUANTITY SUPPLIED?

If the price of a good changes, we say this leads to a *change in the quantity supplied.* For example, in Exhibit 4, if the price of wheat rises from $P_0$ to $P_1$, the market for wheat experiences a movement from A to B. If one of the other factors influences sellers' behaviour, we say this leads to a *change in supply.* For example, if production costs fall because of a wage decrease or lower fuel costs, other things remaining constant, we would expect an increase in supply—that is, a rightward shift in the supply curve as illustrated by the change from B to C in Exhibit 4. Alternatively, if some variable, like lower input prices, causes the costs of production to fall, the supply curve will shift to the right. Exhibit 5 illustrates the effect of some of the determinants that cause shifts in the supply curve.

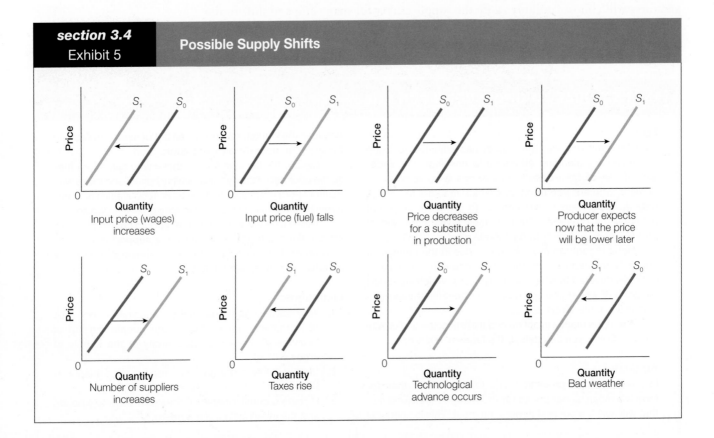

**section 3.4**
Exhibit 5

**Possible Supply Shifts**

Input price (wages) increases

Input price (fuel) falls

Price decreases for a substitute in production

Producer expects now that the price will be lower later

Number of suppliers increases

Taxes rise

Technological advance occurs

Bad weather

## SECTION CHECK

- A movement along a given supply curve is caused by a change in the price of the good in question. As we move along the supply curve, we say there is a change in the quantity supplied. A shift of the entire supply curve is called a *change in supply*.
- Input prices, the prices of related products, expectations, the number of suppliers, technology, regulation, taxes and subsidies, and weather can all lead to changes in supply (shifts in supply).

**Change in Variable and Change in Supply**

| Variable | Change in Variable | Change in Supply |
|---|---|---|
| 1. Input prices | ↑ | |
| 2. Price of substitute in production | ↑ | |
| 3. Price of complement in production | ↑ | |
| 4. Expected future price | ↑ | |

*(continued)*

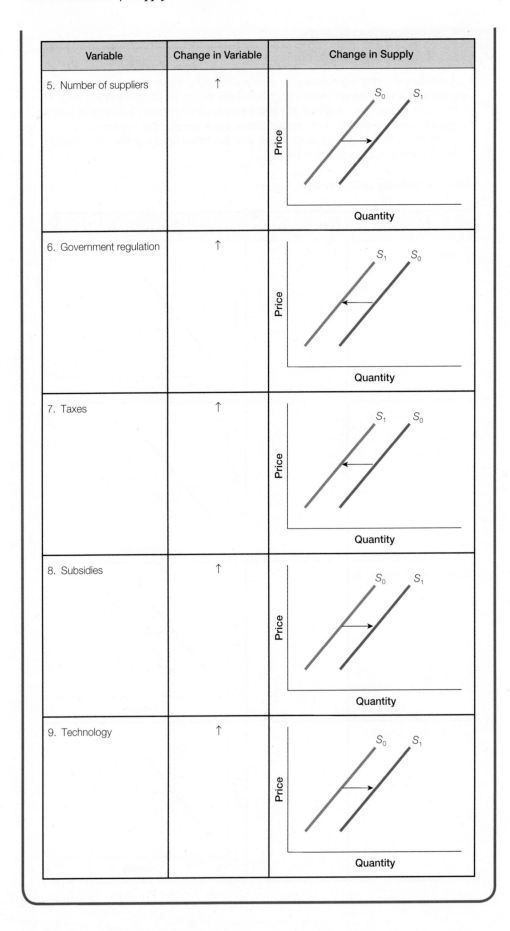

| Variable | Change in Variable | Change in Supply |
|---|---|---|
| 5. Number of suppliers | ↑ | |
| 6. Government regulation | ↑ | |
| 7. Taxes | ↑ | |
| 8. Subsidies | ↑ | |
| 9. Technology | ↑ | |

# For Your Review

## Section 3.1

1. Assume the following demand schedule information:

| Ben | | Boris | | Bilal | |
|---|---|---|---|---|---|
| $P$ | $Q_D$ | $P$ | $Q_D$ | $P$ | $Q_D$ |
| $5 | 1 | $5 | 2 | $5 | 3 |
| 4 | 2 | 4 | 4 | 4 | 6 |
| 3 | 3 | 3 | 6 | 3 | 9 |
| 2 | 4 | 2 | 8 | 2 | 12 |
| 1 | 5 | 1 | 10 | 1 | 15 |

a. Complete the market demand schedule if Ben and Bilal are the only demanders, and graph the market demand curve.

| $P$ | $Q_D$ |
|---|---|
| $5 | |
| 4 | |
| 3 | |
| 2 | |
| 1 | |

b. Complete the market demand schedule if Boris joins Ben and Bilal in the market, and graph the market demand curve.

| $P$ | $Q_D$ |
|---|---|
| $5 | |
| 4 | |
| 3 | |
| 2 | |
| 1 | |

c.  Complete the market demand schedule if Ben now leaves the market and only Boris and Bilal remain, and graph the market demand curve.

| P | $Q_D$ |
|---|---|
| $5 | |
| 4 | |
| 3 | |
| 2 | |
| 1 | |

2.  What is the difference between an individual demand curve and a market demand curve?

3.  The following table shows Hillary's demand schedule for Cherry Blossom lotion. Graph Hillary's demand curve.

| Price (dollars per mL) | Quantity Demanded (mL per week) |
|---|---|
| 15 | 5 |
| 12 | 10 |
| 9 | 15 |
| 6 | 20 |
| 3 | 25 |

4.  The following table shows Cherry Blossom lotion demand schedules for Hillary's friends, Marita and Jacquie. If Hillary, Marita, and Jacquie constitute the whole market for Cherry Blossom lotion, complete the market demand schedule and graph the market demand curve.

| Quantity Demanded (mL per week) | | | | |
|---|---|---|---|---|
| Price (dollars per mL) | Hillary | Marita | Jacquie | Market |
| 15 | 5 | 0 | 15 | _____ |
| 12 | 10 | 5 | 20 | _____ |
| 9 | 15 | 10 | 25 | _____ |
| 6 | 20 | 15 | 30 | _____ |
| 3 | 25 | 20 | 35 | _____ |

## Section 3.2

5. What would be the effects of each of the following on the demand for hamburger in Swift Current, Saskatchewan. In each case, identify the responsible determinant of demand.

   a. The price of chicken falls.

   b. The price of hamburger buns doubles.

   c. Scientists find that eating hamburger prolongs life.

   d. The population of Swift Current doubles.

6. What would be the effect of each of the following on the demand for Chevrolets in Canada? In each case, identify the responsible determinant of demand.

   a. The price of Fords plummets.

   b. Consumers believe that the price of Chevrolets will rise next year.

   c. The incomes of Canadians rise.

   d. The price of gasoline falls dramatically.

7. The following graph shows three market demand curves for cantaloupe. Starting at point A, which point represents

   a. an increase in quantity demanded?

   b. an increase in demand?

   c. a decrease in demand?

   d. a decrease in quantity demanded?

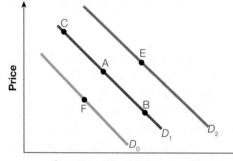

8. Using the demand curve, show the effect of the following events on the market for beef.

   a. Consumer income increases.

   b. The price of beef increases.

   c. An outbreak of mad cow disease occurs.

   d. The price of chicken (a substitute) increases.

   e. The price of barbecue grills (a complement) increases.

9. Draw the demand curves for the following goods. If the price of the first good listed rises, what will happen to the demand for the second good, and why?

   a. hamburgers and ketchup

   b. Coca-Cola and Pepsi

   c. iPhones and iPhone cases

   d. golf clubs and golf balls

   e. skateboards and razor scooters

10. If plane travel is a normal good and bus travel is an inferior good to plane travel, how will each respond to an increase in people's incomes?

11. Using the graph below, answer the following questions:
    a.  What is the shift from $D_0$ to $D_1$ called?
    b.  What is the movement from B to A called?
    c.  What is the movement from A to B called?
    d.  What is the shift from $D_1$ to $D_0$ called?

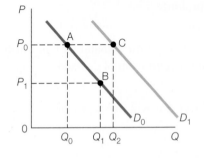

12. Show and describe what would happen to the market demand curve for a good in each of the following cases:
    a.  an increase in the price of a substitute and a decrease in the price of a complement
    b.  a decrease in the price of a substitute and an increase in the price of a complement
    c.  an increase in the number of buyers and an increase in income, for a normal good
    d.  a decrease in the number of buyers and an increase in income, for an inferior good
    e.  a decrease in expected future prices and a shift in tastes away from the good

## Section 3.3

13. Felix is a wheat farmer who has two fields he can use to grow wheat. The first field is right next to his house and the topsoil is rich and thick. The second field is 16 kilometres away in the mountains and the soil is rocky. At current wheat prices, Felix produces only from the field next to his house because the market price for wheat is just high enough to cover his costs of production, including a reasonable profit. What would have to happen to the market price of wheat for Felix to have the incentive to produce from the second field?

14. The following table shows the supply schedule for Rolling Rock Oil Co. Plot Rolling Rock's supply curve on a graph.

| Price<br>(dollars per barrel) | Quantity Demanded<br>(barrels per month) |
|---|---|
| 5 | 10 000 |
| 10 | 15 000 |
| 15 | 20 000 |
| 20 | 25 000 |
| 25 | 30 000 |

15. The following table shows the supply schedules for Rolling Rock and two other petroleum companies, Armadillo Oil and Pecos Petroleum. Assuming these three companies make up the entire supply side of the oil market, complete the market supply schedule and draw the market supply curve on a graph.

| Quantity Supplied (barrels per month) | | | | |
|---|---|---|---|---|
| Price (dollars per barrel) | Rolling Rock | Armadillo | Pecos | Market |
| 5 | 10 000 | 8000 | 2000 | _____ |
| 10 | 15 000 | 10 000 | 5000 | _____ |
| 15 | 20 000 | 12 000 | 8000 | _____ |
| 20 | 25 000 | 14 000 | 11 000 | _____ |
| 25 | 30 000 | 16 000 | 14 000 | _____ |

16. Assume the following supply schedule information.

| Sacha | | Steve | | Sean | |
|---|---|---|---|---|---|
| P | $Q_s$ | P | $Q_s$ | P | $Q_s$ |
| $5 | 10 | $5 | 15 | $5 | 5 |
| 4 | 8 | 4 | 12 | 4 | 4 |
| 3 | 6 | 3 | 9 | 3 | 3 |
| 2 | 4 | 2 | 6 | 2 | 2 |
| 1 | 2 | 1 | 3 | 1 | 1 |

a. Complete the market supply schedule if Sacha and Steve are the only suppliers, and graph the market supply curve.

| P | $Q_s$ |
|---|---|
| $5 | |
| 4 | |
| 3 | |
| 2 | |
| 1 | |

b. Complete the market supply schedule if Sean joins Sacha and Steve in the market, and graph the market supply curve.

| P | $Q_s$ |
|---|---|
| $5 | |
| 4 | |
| 3 | |
| 2 | |
| 1 | |

c.  Complete the market supply schedule if Sacha now leaves the market and only Steve and Sean remain, and graph the market supply curve.

| P | $Q_s$ |
|---|---|
| $5 | |
| 4 | |
| 3 | |
| 2 | |
| 1 | |

## Section 3.4

17.  Using the graph below, answer the following questions:

a.  What is the shift from $S_0$ to $S_1$ called?

b.  What is the movement from A to B called?

c.  What is the movement from B to A called?

d.  What is the shift from $S_1$ to $S_0$ called?

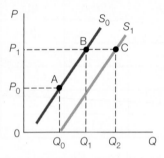

18.  Show and describe what would happen to the market supply curve for a good in each of the following cases.

a.  an increase in the number of suppliers and an increase in subsidies

b.  a decrease in the number of suppliers and an increase in taxes

c.  an increase in input prices and increasing costs of regulation

d.  producers expect now that the price will be lower later

19.  Many farmers in western Canada have the choice between growing fields of wheat or growing fields of corn, due to the nearly identical resources required to cultivate each crop. If the price of corn increased, what would be the effect on

a.  the supply of corn?

b.  the supply of wheat?

20.  What would be the effect of each of the following on the supply of ketchup in Canada? In each case, identify the responsible determinant of supply.

a.  Tomato prices skyrocket (ketchup is made from tomatoes).

b.  Parliament places a 26 percent tax on ketchup production.

c.  Entrepreneurs invent a new, faster tomato crusher to make ketchup.

21.  What would be the effects of each of the following on the supply of coffee worldwide? In each case, identify the responsible determinant of supply.

a.  Freezing temperatures wipe out half of Brazil's coffee crop.

b.  The wages of coffee workers in Latin America rise as unionization efforts succeed.

c. Indonesia offers big subsidies to its coffee producers.

d. Genetic engineering produces a super coffee bean that grows faster and needs less care.

e. Coffee suppliers expect prices to be higher in the future.

22. What would be the effect of each of the following on the supply of automobiles in Canada? In each case, identify the responsible determinant of supply.

a. North American automobile makers are successful in negotiating wage reductions with their unionized workforce.

b. Automobile manufacturers in India and China begin to sell their vehicles in Canada.

c. The Canadian government decides to implement a specific tax on automobiles (the tax is to be paid by the automobile producers).

d. Technological innovation in computer design and robotic assembly dramatically increase the efficiency of manufacturing automobiles in Canada.

23. The following graph shows three market supply curves for cantaloupe. Compared to point A, which point represents

a. an increase in quantity supplied?

b. an increase in supply?

c. a decrease in quantity supplied?

d. a decrease in supply?

24. Molasses is a marketable by-product of sugar refining. That is, the more product that sugar refineries produce, the more molasses they generate. Molasses itself is used as an additive in livestock feed as well as the principal ingredient in the distillation of rum. If the price of sugar increased, what would be the effect on

a. the supply of sugar?

b. the supply of molasses?

25. If a guitar manufacturer increased its wages in order to keep its workers, what would happen to the supply of guitars as a result?

## Sections 3.2 and 3.4

26. Show the impact of each of the following events on the oil market.

[***Note:*** The 15 countries that comprise the Organization of the Petroleum Exporting Countries (OPEC) exert considerable control of the world market for oil.]

a. OPEC becomes more effective in limiting the supply of oil.

b. OPEC becomes less effective in limiting the supply of oil.

c. The price for natural gas (a substitute for heating oil) rises.

d. New oil discoveries occur in Alberta.

e. Electric and hybrid cars become subsidized and their prices fall.

# chapter 4

# Bringing Supply and Demand Together

## section 4.1

# Market Equilibrium Price and Quantity

- What are the equilibrium price and the equilibrium quantity?
- What is a shortage and what is a surplus?

In the last chapter, we learned about demand and supply separately. We now bring the market supply and market demand together.

### WHAT ARE THE EQUILIBRIUM PRICE AND THE EQUILIBRIUM QUANTITY?

**market equilibrium**
*the point at which the market supply and the market demand curves intersect*

**equilibrium price**
*the price at the intersection of the market supply and demand curves; at this price, the quantity demanded equals the quantity supplied*

**equilibrium quantity**
*the quantity at the intersection of the market supply and demand curves; at this quantity, the quantity demanded equals the quantity supplied*

The **market equilibrium** is found at the point at which the market supply and the market demand curves intersect. It is at market equilibrium that two important values are determined: equilibrium price and equilibrium quantity. The **equilibrium price** is the price at the intersection of the market supply and demand curves. At this price, the quantity demanded equals the quantity supplied; that is, the amount that buyers are willing and able to buy is exactly equal to the amount that sellers are willing and able to produce. The **equilibrium quantity** is the quantity at the intersection of the market supply and demand curves. At this quantity, the quantity demanded equals the quantity supplied.

The equilibrium market solution is best understood with the help of a simple graph. Let's return to the apple example we used in our earlier discussions of supply and demand in Chapter 3. Exhibit 1 combines the market demand curve for apples with the market supply curve. At $3 per kilogram, buyers are willing to buy 5000 kilograms of apples and sellers are willing to supply 5000 kilograms of apples. Neither may be "happy" about the price, because the buyers would like a lower price and the sellers would like a higher price. But both buyers and sellers are able to carry out their purchase and sales plans at that $3 price. However, at any other price, either suppliers or demanders would be unable to trade as much as they would like.

## section 4.1
### Exhibit 1
## A Hypothetical Market Supply and Demand Schedule for Apples

| Price | Quantity Supplied | Quantity Demanded | Difference | State of Market |
|---|---|---|---|---|
| $5 | 8000 kg | 1000 kg | 7000 kg | Surplus |
| 4 | 7000 | 3000 | 4000 | Surplus |
| 3 | 5000 | 5000 | 0 | Equilibrium |
| 2 | 3000 | 8000 | −5000 | Shortage |
| 1 | 1000 | 12 000 | −11 000 | Shortage |

The equilibrium is $3 per kilogram and 5000 kilograms of apples, where quantity demanded and quantity supplied are equal. At higher prices, quantity supplied exceeds quantity demanded, resulting in a surplus. Below $3, quantity demanded exceeds quantity supplied, leading to a shortage.

## WHAT IS A SHORTAGE AND WHAT IS A SURPLUS?

What happens when the market price is not equal to the equilibrium price? As you can see in Exhibit 1, at $4 per kilogram, the quantity of apples demanded would be 3000 kilograms, but the quantity supplied would be 7000 kilograms. At that price, a **surplus** would exist, where quantity supplied exceeded quantity demanded. That is, at this price, growers would be willing to sell more apples than demanders would be willing to buy. To cut growing inventories, frustrated suppliers would cut their price and cut back on production. And as price falls, consumers buy more, ultimately eliminating the unsold surplus and returning the market to the equilibrium.

**surplus**
*where quantity supplied exceeds quantity demanded*

What would happen if the price of apples was cut to $1 per kilogram? The yearly quantity demanded of 12 000 kilograms would be greater than the 1000 kilograms that producers would be willing to supply at that low price. So, at $1 per kilogram, a **shortage** would exist, where quantity demanded exceeded quantity supplied. Because of the apple shortage, frustrated buyers would be forced to compete for the existing supply, bidding up the price. The rising price would have two effects: (1) Producers would be willing to increase the quantity supplied; and (2) the higher price would decrease the quantity demanded. Together, these two effects would ultimately eliminate the shortage, returning the market to the equilibrium.

**shortage**
*where quantity demanded exceeds quantity supplied*

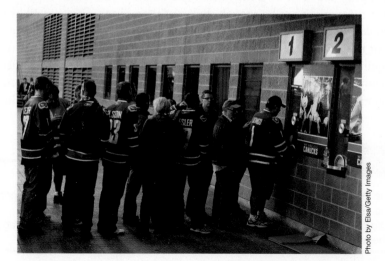

**An NHL playoff game is a high-demand, limited-supply sporting event. With a number of tickets going to corporate sponsors and individuals affiliated with the two teams playing in the game, in addition to the heightened interest because the home team has made the playoffs, the quantity demanded far exceeds the quantity supplied at the face value of the tickets. Consequently, some fans are willing to pay much more for these tickets from scalpers who buy the tickets at face value and try to resell them at a higher price.**

# DEBATE

## WHERE THERE'S A MARKET, SHOULD PEOPLE BE ALLOWED TO TRADE FREELY, WITHOUT STATE LIMITATIONS OR INTERVENTION?

### For:

Just as all humans are said to have a price, so every *thing* has its price. That applies equally to ice cream, school uniforms, bagels, drugs, weapons, sexual favours, and human organs. Trading a product at a price acceptable to at least one buyer satisfies both the consumer and the producer, and so ensures that the market trades at the most efficient level—regardless of legal or moral issues.

Both the demand side and the supply side should be free to establish their own trade criteria. After all, trade means satisfying the needs and wants of both the demanders and the suppliers, and if both parties agree, who is the state or society to interfere in the transactions?

Anyone who advocates for the superiority of a free market system should have no difficulty with moral or ethical issues, because what matters is the superiority of the market, not its particulars. Drug users and sellers should make their own decisions about their actions, for example. The same should be true for weapons and those who sell their bodies.

There are also a number of individuals in dire economic situations, especially those in underdeveloped countries, who could benefit from selling one of their kidneys. Don't all markets trade at the most efficient levels, so that people should be allowed to trade freely?

### Against:

Not everything has its price. In exploring demand and supply, we find that goods or services trade at levels where both the consumer and the supplier are mutually satisfied at an agreed-on price. But not all markets trade at the most efficient levels, and in fact, some markets are unethical or illegal. Some products and services should simply not be offered or sold in a civilized society.

While individual choice and need generally take precedence in an open market, we still need to have limitations for the public good. Some people can't make informed decisions—those who are underage, for example, or those who lack the necessary intellectual ability. Even if individuals have the capacity to make informed decisions, do they always have enough information to do so? For example, do individuals in developing countries appreciate the long-term risks associated with donating a kidney, or is the lure of available money unduly influencing their decisions?

There are also cases where the public good overrides the individual's benefit, such as in the selling of automatic assault weapons. At some point, individual freedom gives way to society's best interests and safety.

Surely society has seen the harm that can come from lack of intervention when these trades take place in the open market, making state limitations and intervention necessary. In fact, aren't there situations where the state should intervene proactively?

### Questions:

1. Since individuals are allowed to donate organs (such as kidneys), why can't they sell their organs to someone who is willing to pay?
2. What practical, moral, or ethical issues might there be in relation to selling an organ?
3. Who should decide what is practical, moral, or ethical in such a case?

---

Producers independently decide how much they are going to produce and at what price, and consumers will show up at websites, garage sales, restaurants, and stores to buy those goods and services. Sometimes there might be too much supplied, while at other times there might not be enough. But over time, these mistakes will be corrected by the process of adjustment in supply and demand. So whether the price starts off too high or too low, the activities of the many buyers and sellers will move the market toward equilibrium. Once equilibrium is reached, buyers and sellers are satisfied in their ability to buy and sell at that price, and there is no longer any pressure on prices. How quickly do markets adjust to equilibrium? It depends on the type of market. But in most competitive markets, shortages and surpluses tend to be temporary.

## SECTION CHECK

- The intersection of the supply and demand curves shows the equilibrium price and equilibrium quantity in a market.
- A surplus is where quantity supplied exceeds quantity demanded. A shortage is where quantity demanded exceeds quantity supplied.

# Changes in Equilibrium Price and Quantity

- What happens to equilibrium price and equilibrium quantity when the demand curve shifts?
- What happens to equilibrium price and equilibrium quantity when the supply curve shifts?
- What happens when both supply and demand shift in the same time period?

When one of the many determinants of demand or supply (input prices, prices of related products, number of suppliers, expectations, technology, and so on) changes, the demand and supply curves will shift, leading to changes in the equilibrium price and equilibrium quantity. To accomplish an objective and ultimately accurate analysis of a change in demand and supply, it is important that the theoretical concepts first developed in Chapter 3 are correctly applied. One way you can ensure that your demand–supply analysis of a given event is complete is by asking yourself the following three questions:

1. Which side of the market is being affected by the event in question, demand or supply?
2. Is the event in question a "shift" or a "movement"?
3. Is the event in question having an expansionary or contractionary impact on the market?

We first consider a change in demand.

## WHAT HAPPENS TO EQUILIBRIUM PRICE AND EQUILIBRIUM QUANTITY WHEN THE DEMAND CURVE SHIFTS?

A shift in the demand curve—caused by a change in the price of a related good (a substitute or a complement), income, the number of buyers, tastes, or expectations—results in a change in both equilibrium price and equilibrium quantity. But how and why does this happen? This result can be best explained through the presentation of a brief case.

The energy drink market in Canada has experienced dramatic growth. In both 2011 and 2012, sales growth for this sector of the beverage market exceeded 20 percent. The industry leader, Red Bull, with a 42 percent share of the energy drink market, sold an impressive $2.9 billion worth of product in 2012—a 28 percent improvement over the previous year's sales.

With names like Rockstar and Monster, these beverages appeal to and are aggressively marketed to the urban fast-paced consumer. How can the record growth in this market segment best be explained? The following are the answers to those three important questions:

1. The case describes how consumer behaviour (fuelled by advertising and lifestyle demands) is impacting market growth; therefore, the event is demand-side.

Getty Images

| section 4.2 | Growth in the Energy |
| Exhibit 1 | Drink Market |

The demand for energy drinks has increased significantly. These increases in demand, coupled with a fixed supply, mean a higher price and a greater quantity.

2. The case makes no reference to the price of energy drinks changing; therefore, the event will be illustrated as a shift.

3. The case details how the aggressive and targeted advertising of energy drink manufacturers has resonated with busy, time-constrained consumers; therefore, the event is expansionary.

In conclusion, due to the fast-rising demand for energy drinks, this market segment has experienced rapid growth. As shown in Exhibit 1, the rightward shift of the demand curve results in an increase in both equilibrium price and equilibrium quantity.

Let's look at a second case of how changing demand can impact equilibrium price and equilibrium quantity. In 2008 to 2009, measured economic activity in the Canadian economy declined by nearly $20 billion (producing what economists refer to as a *recession*). In response to this recession, while median after-tax family income remained virtually unchanged (for example a family of two or more people consistently received around $65 500), many Canadian families experienced a decline in income due to job loss or reduction in hours worked.

Over this same time period, according to data compiled by the Conference Board of Canada, limited-service restaurants (such as McDonald's and Subway) surpassed full-service restaurants (such as The Keg and Earls) in terms of their overall percentage of sales. From these observations, what conclusions can be drawn about these two segments of the restaurant market? Again, let's answer this using our three questions:

1. The case describes how consumers, in response to a decline in their income, make adjustments to the types of restaurants they visit; therefore, the event is demand-side.

2. The case focuses on the impact of consumer income on demand; therefore, the event will be illustrated as a shift.

3. The case reveals that as consumers' incomes declined due to recession pressures, the demand for full-service restaurants declined, while the demand for limited-service restaurants increased; therefore, depending on the particular market segment, the event is either expansionary or contractionary.

| section 4.2 | Decline in Consumer |
| Exhibit 2 | Income |

A change in consumers' incomes can have a variety of effects on demand, depending on the type of good or service. In the case of full-service restaurants, 2008 to 2009 declines in family incomes resulted in lower demand, whereas for limited-service restaurants, that same decline in income produced an increase in demand.

In conclusion, the case seems to indicate that full-service restaurants fit the definition of a normal good, and limited-service restaurants fit the definition of an inferior good. As shown in Exhibit 2, the restaurant market exhibited two distinct responses. In the full-service segment (a), demand declined, shifting the demand curve leftward, causing equilibrium price and quantity to decline. However, in the limited-service segment (b), demand increased, shifting the demand curve rightward, causing equilibrium price and quantity to increase.

## WHAT HAPPENS TO EQUILIBRIUM PRICE AND EQUILIBRIUM QUANTITY WHEN THE SUPPLY CURVE SHIFTS?

Like a shift in demand, a shift in the supply curve also influences both equilibrium price and equilibrium quantity, assuming that demand for the product has not changed. Let's look at another case. Between 2000 and 2013, the price of flat-screen TVs declined dramatically. Industry data reveal that in 2000, a 20-inch flat-screen TV would have cost around $1200, whereas by 2013, that same 20-inch TV cost less than $100. Furthermore, an investigation into the technology of manufacturing flat-screen displays reveals that, since 2000, the machines necessary for producing the displays have increased in capacity by 800 percent. Translation: Bigger machines, cheaper TVs. How can this technological development explain the dramatic reduction in the price of flat-screen TVs?

1. The case describes how a technological innovation in production is impacting the ability of electronic manufacturers to produce their product; therefore, the event is supply-side.
2. The case highlights the impact of technology on production; therefore, the event will be illustrated as a shift.
3. The case indicates that as production technology has improved, the ability of manufacturers to make more product available has also increased; therefore, the event is expansionary.

In conclusion, as shown in Exhibit 3, the lower cost of producing flat-screen TVs—and the subsequent increase in profitability—shifts the supply curve to the right. This increase in supply lowers equilibrium price and increases equilibrium quantity.

Let's look at a second case of how equilibrium price and quantity can be impacted by a change in supply. Tequila, originally associated with Mexican ranchers and cowboys and increasingly the choice of mainstream North American consumers, is an alcoholic beverage produced from the agave plant. With its production carefully regulated and limited to five Mexican states, the 2007 failure of the agave crop had a devastating impact on the industry. The price of a bottle of tequila increased 50 to 60 percent in Canada, translating into about a $10 jump in price at the liquor store. How can demand supply analysis explain the significantly higher price of tequila?

1. The case details how the availability of inputs in a market is a factor in determining market price; therefore the event is supply-side.
2. The case's focus on production inputs as the independent variable means the event will be illustrated as a shift.
3. The case draws a relationship between the failure of the agave crop and the higher price of tequila worldwide (results for Canada provided specifically). As a result, the event is contractionary.

**section 4.2**
Exhibit 3

**Advances in Production Technology**

Advances in the technology of producing flat-screen displays enable manufacturers to produce flat-screen TVs more efficiently and therefore more profitably. This increase in profit encourages more supply, shifting the supply curve rightward. Equilibrium price decreases and equilibrium quantity increase as a result.

**section 4.2**
Exhibit 4

**Loss of a Critical Input**

Price of Tequila

Quantity of Tequila

Tequila is produced by extracting the juice from the agave plant. Therefore, failure of the agave crop shifts the supply curve for tequila leftward, leading to a higher equilibrium price and lower equilibrium quantity, *ceteris paribus*.

Therefore, the supply of tequila shifts leftward due to the failure of the agave crop, without which tequila cannot be produced. As shown in Exhibit 4, this decline in supply results in the predicted increase in equilibrium price and decrease in equilibrium quantity.

## WHAT HAPPENS WHEN BOTH SUPPLY AND DEMAND SHIFT IN THE SAME TIME PERIOD?

We have discussed that as part of the continual adjustment process that occurs in the marketplace, supply and demand can each shift in response to many different factors, with the market then adjusting toward the new equilibrium. We have, so far, considered what happens when just one such change occurs at a time. In these cases, we learned that the results of these adjustments in supply and demand on the equilibrium price and quantity are predictable. However, both supply and demand very often will shift in the same time period. Can we predict what will happen to equilibrium prices and equilibrium quantities in these situations?

As you will see, when supply and demand move at the same time, we can predict the change in one variable (price or quantity), but we are unable to predict the direction of the effect on the other variable with any certainty. This change in the second variable, then, is said to be indeterminate because it cannot be determined without additional information about the size of the relative shifts in supply and demand. This concept will become clearer to you as we work through the following example.

### An Increase in Supply and a Decrease in Demand

When considering this scenario, it might help you to break it down into its individual parts. As you learned in the last section, an increase in supply (a rightward shift in the supply curve) results in a decrease in the equilibrium price and an increase in the equilibrium quantity. A decrease in demand (a leftward movement of the demand curve), on the other hand, results in a decrease in both the equilibrium price and the equilibrium quantity. These shifts are shown in Exhibit 5(a). Taken together, then, these changes will clearly result in a decrease in the equilibrium price because both the increase in supply and the decrease in demand work to push this price down. This drop in equilibrium price (from $P_0$ to $P_1$) is shown in the movement from $E_0$ to $E_1$.

The effect of these changes on equilibrium price is clear, but how does the equilibrium quantity change? The impact on equilibrium quantity is indeterminate because the increase in supply increases the equilibrium quantity and the decrease in demand decreases it. In this scenario, the change in the equilibrium quantity will vary depending on the relative changes in supply and demand. If, as shown in Exhibit 5(a), the decrease in demand is greater than the increase in supply, the equilibrium quantity will decrease. If, however, as shown in Exhibit 5(b), the increase in supply is greater than the decrease in demand, the equilibrium quantity will increase.

**section 4.2**
Exhibit 5

**Shifts in Supply and Demand**

**a. A Little Increase in Supply and a Big Decrease in Demand**

**b. A Big Increase in Supply and a Little Decrease in Demand**

If the decrease in demand (leftward shift) is greater than the increase in supply (rightward shift), the equilibrium price and equilibrium quantity will fall.

If the increase in supply (rightward shift) is greater than the decrease in demand (leftward shift), the equilibrium price will fall and the equilibrium quantity will rise.

# Business *CONNECTION*

## EQUILIBRIUM DETERMINES PRICE

Beyond knowing and understanding the equilibrium price and quantity of products in their industry, businesspeople often try to understand what will happen to prices if there is a change in the market. When asked to explain why prices are at a certain level, they quickly reply that present price levels are simply a reflection of market demand and supply. Strictly speaking, they are correct. In the absence of a detailed analysis, which most small and medium-sized enterprises cannot afford, most of these managers or owners might not realize why this is the case. A basic four-step economic analysis would show them what impact a market change might have on their revenues.

In the four-step analysis, the entrepreneur simply responds to a change in the environment by asking these four questions:

1. Which curve is affected? (Is it a demand or supply issue?)

2. Is price the issue, or is it something else? (If it's price, it's a movement *along* the curve; if it's something else, it's a *shift* of the curve. Numerous factors can shift demand and supply—work at finding which factor is affecting the change.)

3. Is the change an increase or a decrease?

4. How much change is involved? (Is the change small or large?)

Managers—and students—can use this scenario with any business problem. The following example illustrates how the analysis plays out. (You're encouraged to walk yourself through any problem to see how useful the analysis steps can be. Read a business article on the Internet for problem ideas. If you can complete the analysis, you're thinking like a manager!)

*Scenario:* An Apple ad campaign for its new iPhone was successful. At the same time, Apple announced that it's moving some of its iPhone manufacturing back to North America because it can use cheaper automated processes.

Let's deal with each situation separately, using the four-step analysis: (1) Is the ad campaign a demand or supply issue? Clearly, it's a demand issue, so it will affect the demand curve. (2) Is the issue price or something else? It's something else, so it will *shift* the demand curve—what causes the shift is a change in tastes or preferences, which is one of the factors that shift demand. (3) A positive or negative change?

*(continued)*

The ad campaign is successful, so it will shift the demand curve rightward. (4) How much? Here, you will need to draw a simple demand and supply model, shift the demand curve rightward a little, and then draw a second curve, shifting it rightward a lot.

Now analyze the second issue: (1) Is it a demand or supply issue? It's a supply issue. (2) Is it price, or something else? Something else—in this case, it's a decrease in input (capital) prices. (3) Which direction? Lower input costs will shift the supply curve rightward—Apple can make more units for the same price as before! (4) Finally, by how much? Again, you have to go to your model drawing and shift the supply curve rightward, first a little and then a lot. From the final diagram, you will see that equilibrium quantity will always be more than it was before the changes, but price is indeterminate. To see what happens to price, you look at the intersections of small (or large) changes in demand and large (or small) changes in supply. Depending on your confidence in which curve will shift more or less to the other side, your answer to a price change will come from there.

To answer these questions, companies often create powerful econometric models to simulate different economic scenarios, often referred to as "what-if" scenarios. This simple yet elegant practical application of economic theory is extremely useful to business managers in forecasting new equilibrium quantities and prices, and even a company's future revenues and profits over time.

1. What tools do you think businesses can use to establish their own demand and supply issues?

2. What role do time and time lags have on a business that is attempting to establish its own market equilibrium? What items would you think would be affected by time lags?

3. In what ways do large businesses have advantages over smaller businesses in establishing their own level of equilibrium? Give some specific examples of how these advantages would affect equilibrium.

## The Combinations of Supply and Demand Shifts

The eight possible changes in demand and/or supply are presented in Exhibit 6, along with the resulting changes in equilibrium quantity and equilibrium price. Although you could memorize the impact of the various possible changes in demand and supply, it would be more worthwhile to draw a graph, as shown in Exhibit 7, whenever a situation of changing demand and/or supply arises. Remember that an increase in either demand or supply means a rightward shift in the curve, whereas a decrease in either demand or supply means a leftward shift. Also, when both demand and supply change, one of the two equilibrium values—price or quantity—will change in an indeterminate manner (can increase, decrease, or stay the same) depending on the size of the change in demand relative to the change in supply.

| **section 4.2** Exhibit 6 | **The Effect of Changing Demand and/or Supply** | | |
|---|---|---|---|
| **If Demand** | **and Supply** | **Then Equilibrium Quantity** | **and Equilibrium Price** |
| 1. Increases | Stays unchanged | Increases | Increases |
| 2. Decreases | Stays unchanged | Decreases | Decreases |
| 3. Stays unchanged | Increases | Increases | Decreases |
| 4. Stays unchanged | Decreases | Decreases | Increases |
| 5. Increases | Increases | Increases | Indeterminate* |
| 6. Decreases | Decreases | Decreases | Indeterminate* |
| 7. Increases | Decreases | Indeterminate* | Increases |
| 8. Decreases | Increases | Indeterminate* | Decreases |

*May increase, decrease, or remain the same, depending on the size of the change in demand relative to the change in supply.

**section 4.2**
Exhibit 7

**The Combinations of Supply and Demand Shifts**

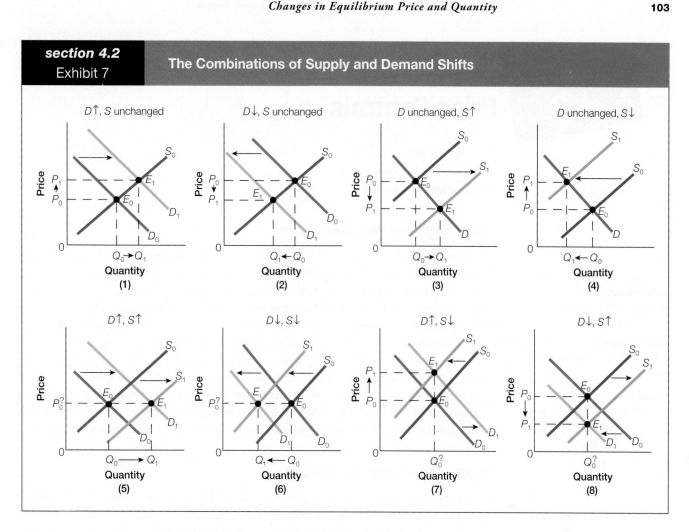

# SECTION CHECK

- Changes in demand will cause a change in the equilibrium price and quantity, *ceteris paribus.*
- Changes in supply will cause a change in the equilibrium price and quantity, *ceteris paribus.*
- When there are simultaneous shifts in both supply and demand curves, either the equilibrium price or the equilibrium quantity will be indeterminate without more information.

# Price Controls

- What are price controls?
- What are price ceilings?
- What are price floors?

## WHAT ARE PRICE CONTROLS?

**price controls**
*government-mandated minimum and maximum prices*

**price ceiling**
*a legally established maximum price*

**price floor**
*a legally established minimum price*

Although nonequilibrium prices can occur naturally, reflecting uncertainty, they seldom last for long. Governments, however, may impose nonequilibrium prices for significant time periods. **Price controls** are government-mandated minimum and maximum prices that sometimes force prices above or below what they would be in equilibrium. The motivations for price controls vary with the market under consideration. For example, a **price ceiling**—a legally established maximum price—is often set for goods deemed important to low-income households, like housing. Or a **price floor**—a legally established minimum price—may be set on wages because wages are the primary source of income for most people.

Price controls are not always implemented by the federal government. Provincial governments can and do impose local price controls. One fairly well-known example of regional price controls is rent controls, which limit how much landlords can charge for rental housing.

## WHAT ARE PRICE CEILINGS?

Rent controls have been imposed in Prince Edward Island, Quebec, Ontario, Manitoba, and British Columbia. Although the rules may vary, generally the price (or rent) of an apartment remains fixed over the tenure of an occupant, except for allowable annual increases tied to the cost of living or some other price index. When an occupant moves out, the owners can usually, but not always, raise the rent to a near-market level for the next occupant. The controlled rents for existing occupants, however, are generally well below market rental rates.

### Results of Rent Controls

Rent controls distort market signals and lead to shortages. In addition, they often do not even help the intended recipients—low-income households. Most people living in rent-controlled apartments have a good deal, one that they would lose by moving as their family circumstances or income change. Tenants thus are reluctant to give up their governmentally granted right to a below-market-rent apartment. In addition, because the rents received by landlords are constrained and below market levels, the rate of return (roughly, the profit) on housing investments falls compared to that on other forms of real estate not subject to rent controls, like office rents or mortgage payments on condominiums. Hence, the incentive to construct new housing is reduced. Where rent controls are truly effective, there is generally little new construction going on, resulting in a shortage of apartments that persists and grows over time.

Also, when landlords are limited in what rent they can charge, there is little incentive to improve or upgrade apartments, such as by putting in new kitchen appliances or new carpeting. In fact, there is some incentive to avoid routine maintenance, thereby lowering the cost of apartment ownership to a figure approximating the controlled rental price, although the quality of the housing stock will deteriorate over time.

In extreme cases, the repercussions of rent controls can be life-threatening. For example, when four floors of his building caved in, killing three of his neighbours, Uttamchand K. Soiatwala, owner of a successful textile business, refused to leave his two-bedroom, rent-controlled apartment in Mumbai, India. The city then cut off his electricity and water and threatened to arrest his wife, but he still wouldn't leave. In all, 58 tenants refused to leave a rent-controlled apartment building that was considered too dangerous by city officials. Why did these residents take this risk? Cheap rent— $8.50 a month. There is tremendous tension in the market for Mumbai rent-controlled properties between landlords who can't afford to keep up their properties and tenants who will go to extraordinary lengths and even risk their lives to keep their units.

Another impact of rent control is that it promotes housing discrimination. Where rent controls do not exist, a prejudiced landlord might willingly rent to someone he believes is undesirable simply because the undesirable family is the only one willing to pay the requested rent (and the landlord is not willing to lower the rent substantially to get a desirable family, since this could translate into the loss of thousands of dollars in income). With rent controls, many families are likely to want to rent the controlled apartment, some desirable and some undesirable as seen by the landlord, simply because the rent is at a below-equilibrium price. The landlord can indulge in his "taste" for discrimination without any additional financial loss beyond that required by the controls.

Consequently, he will be more likely to choose to rent to a desirable family, perhaps a family without children or pets, rather than an undesirable one, perhaps one with a lower income and so a greater risk of nonpayment.

Exhibit 1 shows the impact of rent control. If the price ceiling is set below the market price, the quantity demanded will increase to $Q_D$ from $Q^*$ and the quantity supplied will fall to $Q_S$ from $Q^*$. The rent control policy will therefore create a shortage, the difference between $Q_D$ and $Q_S$.

**section 4.3**
Exhibit 1

**Rent Controls**

The impact of a price ceiling (a rent control law) set below the equilibrium price is a shortage.

## WHAT ARE PRICE FLOORS?

The argument for minimum-wage legislation is simple: Existing wages for workers in some types of labour markets do not allow for a very high standard of living, and a set minimum wage allows those workers to live better than before. Provincial and territorial government legislation makes it illegal to pay most workers an amount below the current legislated minimum wage.

Let us examine graphically the impact of a minimum-wage law on low-skilled workers. In Exhibit 2, suppose the government sets the minimum wage, $W_{MIN}$, above the market equilibrium wage, $W_E$. In Exhibit 2, we see that the price floor is binding; that is, there is a surplus of low-skilled workers at $W_{MIN}$ because the quantity of labour supplied is greater than the quantity of labour demanded. The reason for the surplus of low-skilled workers (unemployment) at $W_{MIN}$ is that more people are willing to work than employers are willing and able to hire.

Notice that not everyone loses as a result of a minimum-wage law. Those workers who continue to hold jobs now have higher incomes (those workers between 0 and $Q_D$ in Exhibit 2). However, many low-skilled workers suffer as a result of minimum-wage legislation—they either lose their jobs or are unable to get them in the first place (those between $Q_D$ and $Q_S$ in Exhibit 2). Although studies disagree somewhat on the precise magnitudes, they largely agree that minimum-wage laws do create some unemployment, and that the unemployment is concentrated among teenagers—the least-experienced and least-skilled members of the labour force.

Exhibit 3 shows the provincial minimum-wage rates (including the date on which they became effective) and the 2017 provincial unemployment rates (for both the youth segment of the population and the overall population) from across Canada.

**If the minimum wage was raised to $30 an hour, one group that could experience a rise in unemployment would be teenagers.**

**section 4.3**
Exhibit 2

**The Unemployment Effects of a Minimum Wage on Low-Skilled Workers**

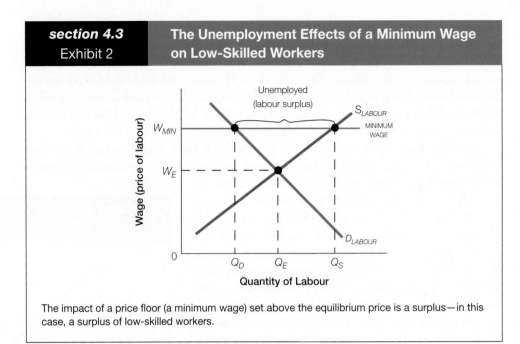

The impact of a price floor (a minimum wage) set above the equilibrium price is a surplus—in this case, a surplus of low-skilled workers.

The data in Exhibit 3 reveal two interesting facts regarding minimum-wage rates and youth unemployment: (1) Youth unemployment varies considerably, even between provinces that have similar minimum-wage levels, and (2) in all jurisdictions that impose a minimum wage on their labour market, youth unemployment exceeds the rate of unemployment in the overall population.

It is this second conclusion that economists point to when they suggest that effective minimum-wage levels produce unemployment—especially in marginal segments of the labour market, such as the youth segment. Can the entire difference between the overall rate of unemployment and youth unemployment be attributed to the existence of minimum-wage legislation? Clearly not, but we must acknowledge it is a contributing factor.

**section 4.3**
Exhibit 3

**Provincial Minimum Wages and Unemployment Rates**

| | | | Unemployment Rate (%) (2017) | |
| --- | --- | --- | --- | --- |
| **Province** | **Minimum Wage ($/hr.)** | **Effective Date** | **15–24 Years** | **15 Years and Over** |
| British Columbia | 11.35 | Sep. 15, 2017 | 8.6 | 5.1 |
| Alberta | 13.60 | Oct. 1, 2017 | 13.2 | 7.8 |
| Saskatchewan | 10.96 | Oct. 1, 2017 | 11.8 | 6.3 |
| Manitoba | 11.15 | Oct. 1, 2017 | 11.7 | 5.4 |
| Ontario | 14.00 | Jan. 1, 2018 | 12.3 | 6.0 |
| Quebec | 11.25 | May 1, 2017 | 10.3 | 6.1 |
| New Brunswick | 11.25 | Apr. 1, 2018 | 13.5 | 8.1 |
| Nova Scotia | 11.00 | Apr. 1, 2018 | 16.8 | 8.4 |
| PEI | 11.55 | Apr. 1, 2018 | 13.2 | 9.8 |
| Newfoundland and Labrador | 11.00 | Oct. 1, 2017 | 17.6 | 14.8 |
| Canada | | | 11.6 | 6.3 |

SOURCES: Minimum-wage rates, Canada: http://srv116.services.gc.ca/dimt-wid/sm-mw/rpt1.aspx; unemployment rates: Statistics Canada, Table 282-0086, *Labour Force Survey* estimates (LFS), supplementary unemployment rates by sex and age group, annual (percentage) (2).

Most Canadian workers are not affected by the minimum-wage law because in the market for their skills, they earn wages that exceed the minimum wage. For example, minimum-wage legislation will not affect the unemployment rate for accountants. In Exhibit 4, we see the labour market for skilled and experienced workers. In this market the minimum wage (the price floor) is not binding because these workers are earning wages that far exceed the minimum wage—$W_E$ is much higher than $W_{MIN}$.

The above analysis does not "prove" minimum-wage laws are "bad" and should be abolished. To begin with, there is the empirical question of how much unemployment is caused by minimum-wage legislation. Secondly, some might believe that the cost of unemployment resulting from a minimum-wage law is a reasonable price to pay for assuring that those with jobs get a "decent" wage. The analysis does point out, however, that there is a cost to having minimum-wage legislation, and the burden of this falls not only on low-skilled workers and employers but also on consumers of products made more costly by the minimum-wage law.

## Canadian Dairy Production: Another Example of a Price Floor

Another example of price floors can be found by looking at the price controls that have been imposed on dairy products produced in Canada since the 1970s. While initially implemented to ensure a fair return for farmers and greater price stability for processors and consumers, these price controls have ultimately resulted in milk prices being nearly 50 percent higher in Canada than in the United States and cheese prices being almost 25 percent higher. To understand how this discrepancy in price has happened, we need to understand the role that price controls play in the dairy industry.

The price farmers receive for raw milk is set by the Canadian Dairy Commission, a Crown corporation composed mainly of dairy farmers. This "farm gate" price is not based on what the market is willing to pay, but on the costs of production, market conditions, and what is determined to be a fair profit for producers.

Processors take the raw milk and turn it into fluid milk, yogurt, and other dairy products. The price these processors sell the finished product to retailers for is subject to a second price control. Referred to as a "floor price," processors cannot sell their dairy products for less than a minimum wholesale price. And the controls don't end there. At the final stage, retailers have a minimum price they must charge for milk. The floor price plus the retailer's expenses and margins is what consumers end up paying for a litre of milk in Canada.

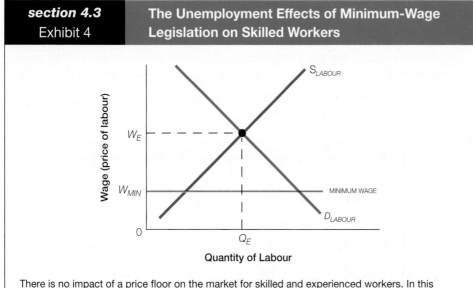

| **section 4.3** Exhibit 4 | **The Unemployment Effects of Minimum-Wage Legislation on Skilled Workers** |
| --- | --- |

There is no impact of a price floor on the market for skilled and experienced workers. In this market, the price floor (the minimum wage) is not binding.

**unintended consequences**

*the secondary effects of an action that may occur after the initial effects*

## Unintended Consequences

When markets are altered for policy reasons, it is wise to remember that actions do not always have the results that were initially intended—**unintended consequences** or secondary effects may occur after the initial effects of actions. As economists, we must always look for the secondary effects of an action that may occur, along with the initial effects. For example, the government is often well intentioned when it adopts price controls to help low-skilled workers or tenants in search of affordable housing; however, such policies can also cause unintended consequences, which may completely undermine the intended effects. For example, rent controls may have an immediate effect of lowering rents, but secondary effects may well include very low vacancy rates, discrimination against low-income and large families, and deterioration of the quality of rental units. Similarly, a sizable increase in the minimum-wage rate may help many low-skilled workers or apprentices, but will result in higher unemployment and/or a reduction in fringe benefits, such as vacations and discounts to employees. Society has to make tough decisions, and if the government subsidizes some program or group of people in one area, then something must always be given up somewhere else. The "law of scarcity" cannot be repealed!

### SECTION CHECK

- Price controls involve government mandates to keep prices above or below the market-determined equilibrium price.
- Price ceilings are government-imposed maximum prices. When price ceilings are set below the equilibrium price, shortages will result.
- Price floors are government-imposed minimum prices. When price floors are set above the equilibrium price, surpluses will result.

# For Your Review

## Section 4.1

1. If a price is above the equilibrium price, explain the forces that bring the market back to the equilibrium price and quantity. If a price is below the equilibrium price, explain the forces that bring the market back to the equilibrium price and quantity.

2. The following table shows the hypothetical monthly demand and supply schedules for bottles of maple syrup in Winnipeg.

| Price | Quantity Demanded (bottles) | Quantity Supplied (bottles) |
|-------|-----------------------------|-----------------------------|
| $6    | 700                         | 100                         |
| 7     | 600                         | 200                         |
| 8     | 500                         | 300                         |
| 9     | 400                         | 400                         |
| 10    | 300                         | 500                         |

a. What is the equilibrium price of a bottle of maple syrup in Winnipeg?

b. At a price of $7 per bottle, is there equilibrium, a surplus, or a shortage? If it is a surplus or shortage, how large is it?

c. At a price of $10, is there equilibrium, a surplus, or a shortage? If it is a surplus or shortage, how large is it?

3. The market for tablet computers is represented by the following demand and supply schedules.

| Price ($) | Quantity Demanded (millions of units) | Quantity Supplied (millions of units) |
|---|---|---|
| 100 | 8.2 | 4.7 |
| 200 | 7.6 | 5.0 |
| 300 | 7.1 | 5.2 |
| 400 | 6.3 | 6.3 |
| 500 | 5.9 | 6.9 |
| 600 | 5.1 | 7.3 |
| 700 | 4.1 | 8.1 |

a. What is the equilibrium price and quantity of tablet computers?

b. Over what range of price would the tablet computer market exhibit a shortage of computers? How would the market self-regulate a solution to this disequilibrium situation?

c. Over what range of price would the tablet computer market exhibit a surplus of computers? How would the market self-regulate a solution to this disequilibrium situation?

## Sections 4.1 and 4.2

4. Assume the following information for the demand and supply schedules for coffee.

| Price ($) | Quantity Demanded (thousands of kg ) | Quantity Supplied (thousands of kg) |
|---|---|---|
| 6 | 3 | 9 |
| 5 | 4 | 7 |
| 4 | 5 | 5 |
| 3 | 6 | 3 |
| 2 | 7 | 1 |

a. Graph the corresponding demand and supply curves and identify the equilibrium price and quantity of coffee?

b. At the price of $6, would there be a shortage or a surplus and how large would it be?

c. At the price of $3, would there be a shortage or a surplus and how large would it be?

    d. If the demand for coffee decreased by 3000 kg at every price, would there be a shortage or a surplus and how much would it be at the price of $4?

    e. Using the original amounts of supply and demand, if the supply for coffee increased by 6000 kg at every price, would there be a shortage or a surplus and how much would it be at the price of $2?

5. Assume the following information for the demand and supply schedules for Good Z.

| Price per Unit | Quantity Demanded | Quantity Supplied |
|---|---|---|
| $10 | 10 | 55 |
| 9 | 20 | 50 |
| 8 | 30 | 45 |
| 7 | 40 | 40 |
| 6 | 50 | 35 |
| 5 | 60 | 30 |
| 4 | 70 | 25 |
| 3 | 80 | 20 |
| 2 | 90 | 15 |
| 1 | 100 | 10 |

    a. Draw the corresponding supply and demand curves.

    b. What is the equilibrium price per unit and quantity traded?

    c. If the price was $9, would there be a shortage or a surplus? How large?

    d. If the price was $3, would there be a shortage or a surplus? How large?

    e. If the demand for Z increased by 15 units at every price, what would be the new equilibrium price and quantity traded?

    f. Given the original demand for Z, if the supply of Z was increased by 15 units at every price, what would be the new equilibrium price and quantity traded?

6. The market for baseball tickets at your school's stadium, which seats 2000, is the following:

| Price per Unit | Quantity Demanded | Quantity Supplied |
|---|---|---|
| $2 | 4000 | 2000 |
| 4 | 2000 | 2000 |
| 6 | 1000 | 2000 |
| 8 | 500 | 2000 |

    a. What is the equilibrium price?

    b. What is unusual about the supply curve?

    c. At what prices would a shortage occur?

d. At what prices would a surplus occur?

e. Suppose that the addition of new students (all big baseball fans) next year will add 1000 to the quantity demanded at each price. What will this increase do to next year's demand curve? What will be the new equilibrium price?

## Section 4.2

### Blueprint Problem

Using supply and demand curves, show the effect of the following events on the market for gasoline in North America:

    a. world economic growth resulting in rising consumer incomes

    b. hostilities in the Middle East and domestic refinery problems

### Blueprint Solution

    a.

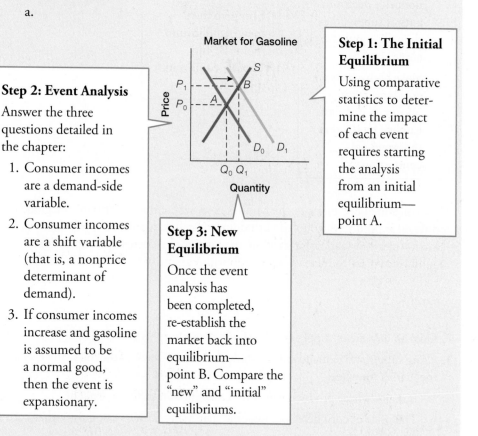

**Step 1: The Initial Equilibrium**

Using comparative statistics to determine the impact of each event requires starting the analysis from an initial equilibrium—point A.

**Step 2: Event Analysis**

Answer the three questions detailed in the chapter:

1. Consumer incomes are a demand-side variable.

2. Consumer incomes are a shift variable (that is, a nonprice determinant of demand).

3. If consumer incomes increase and gasoline is assumed to be a normal good, then the event is expansionary.

**Step 3: New Equilibrium**

Once the event analysis has been completed, re-establish the market back into equilibrium— point B. Compare the "new" and "initial" equilibriums.

As a result of world economic growth and rising consumer incomes, the gasoline market will experience an increase in demand, causing both the equilibrium price and the quantity of gasoline to rise.

b.

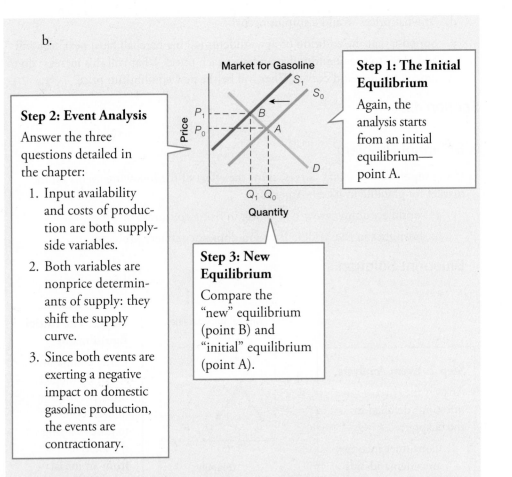

**Step 2: Event Analysis**

Answer the three questions detailed in the chapter:

1. Input availability and costs of production are both supply-side variables.

2. Both variables are nonprice determinants of supply: they shift the supply curve.

3. Since both events are exerting a negative impact on domestic gasoline production, the events are contractionary.

**Market for Gasoline**

**Step 1: The Initial Equilibrium**

Again, the analysis starts from an initial equilibrium—point A.

**Step 3: New Equilibrium**

Compare the "new" equilibrium (point B) and "initial" equilibrium (point A).

The continued hostilities in the Middle East, where the majority of the globe's crude oil is produced, coupled with domestic refinery problems, will cause the North American market for gasoline to experience a decrease in supply, causing equilibrium price to increase and equilibrium quantity to decline.

7. Does an increase in supply create a shortage or a surplus at the original price?

8. Using supply and demand curves, show the effect of each of the following events on the market for wheat.

   a. A major wheat-producing area in Saskatchewan suffers a drought.

   b. The price of corn decreases (assume that many farmers can grow either corn or wheat).

   c. The Prairie provinces have great weather.

   d. The price of fertilizer declines.

   e. More individuals start growing wheat.

9. Beginning from an initial equilibrium, draw the effects of the following changes in terms of the relevant supply and demand curves.

   a. an increase in the price of hot dogs on the hamburger market

   b. a decrease in the number of taxi companies in Halifax on cab trips

   c. the effect of El Niño rainstorms destroying the strawberry crops in Ontario

10. Use supply and demand curves to show the following:

    a. simultaneous increases in supply and demand, with a large increase in supply and a small increase in demand

    b. simultaneous increases in supply and demand, with a small increase in supply and a large increase in demand

    c. simultaneous decreases in supply and demand, with a large decrease in supply and a small decrease in demand

    d. simultaneous decreases in supply and demand, with a small decrease in supply and a large decrease in demand

11. Why do 10 A.M. classes fill up before 8 A.M. classes during class registration? Use supply and demand curves to help explain your answers.

12. What would happen to the equilibrium price and equilibrium quantity in the following cases?

    a. an increase in income for a normal good and a decrease in the price of an input

    b. a technological advance and a decrease in the number of buyers

    c. an increase in the price of a substitute and an increase in the number of suppliers

    d. producers' expectations that prices will soon fall and a reduction in consumer tastes for the good

13. In Canada, why is fresh fruit (apples, strawberries, peaches) less expensive in the summer than in the winter? Use supply and demand curves to help explain your answer.

14. If both buyers and sellers of grapes expect grape prices to rise in the near future, what will happen to grape prices and sales today?

## Section 4.3

15. Refer to the following supply and demand curve diagram.

    a. Starting from an initial equilibrium at E, what shift or shifts in supply and/or demand could move the equilibrium price and quantity to each of points A through I?

    b. Starting from an initial equilibrium at E, what would happen if both a decrease in the price of a substitute in production and an increase in income occurred, if it is a normal good?

    c. Starting from an initial equilibrium at E, what would happen if both an increase in the price of an input and an advance in technology occurred?

    d. If a price floor is imposed above the equilibrium price, which of A through I would tend to be the quantity supplied, and which would tend to be the quantity demanded? Which would be the new quantity exchanged?

    e. If a price ceiling is imposed below the equilibrium price, which of A through I would tend to be the quantity supplied, and which would tend to be the quantity demanded? Which would be the new quantity exchanged?

16. Draw a supply and demand curve diagram with a price floor above the equilibrium price, and indicate the quantity supplied and quantity demanded at that price and the resulting surplus.

    a. What happens to the quantity supplied, the quantity demanded, and the surplus if the price floor is raised? If it is lowered?

    b. What happens to the quantity supplied, the quantity demanded, and the surplus if, for a given price floor, the demand curve shifts to the right?

    c. What happens to the quantity supplied, the quantity demanded, and the surplus if, for a given price floor, the supply curve shifts to the right?

17. Draw a supply and demand curve diagram with a price ceiling below the equilibrium price, and indicate the quantity supplied and quantity demanded at that price, and the resulting shortage.

    a. What happens to the quantity supplied, the quantity demanded, and the shortage if the price ceiling is raised? If it is lowered?

    b. What happens to the quantity supplied, the quantity demanded, and the shortage if, for a given price ceiling, the demand curve shifts to the right?

    c. What happens to the quantity supplied, the quantity demanded, and the shortage if, for a given price ceiling, the supply curve shifts to the right?

18. Why do price floors and price ceilings both reduce the quantity of goods traded in those markets?

19. What would be the impact of a price floor set above the equilibrium price for dairy products? Below the equilibrium price?

20. Giving in to pressure from voters who claim that local theatre owners are gouging their customers with ticket prices as high as $10 per movie, the city council of a local municipality imposes a price ceiling of $2 on all movies. What effect is this likely to have on the market for movies in this particular city? What will happen to the quantity of tickets demanded? What will happen to the quantity supplied? Who gains? Who loses?

# chapter 5

# Introduction to the Macroeconomy

# Macroeconomic Goals

- What are the three major macroeconomic goals in Canada?
- Are these macroeconomic goals universal?

## WHAT ARE THE THREE MAJOR MACROECONOMIC GOALS IN CANADA?

Recall from Chapter 1 that macroeconomics is the study of the whole economy—the study of the forest, not the trees. A macroeconomist may study the changes in the inflation rate or the unemployment rate, the impact of changing monetary policy or fiscal policy on output and inflation, or alternative policies that may contribute to long-term economic growth.

Nearly every society has been interested in three major macroeconomic goals:

1. **Employment:** By maintaining employment of human resources at relatively high levels, jobs are relatively plentiful and financial suffering from lack of work and income is relatively uncommon. Policies targeting the *unemployment rate* are designed to address this goal.
2. **Price-level stability:** By keeping prices relatively stable, consumers and producers can make better decisions. Policies targeting the Consumer Price Index (CPI) and the *inflation rate* are designed to address this goal.
3. **Economic growth:** By achieving a high rate of growth in real output over time, standards of living improve. Policies targeting the growth rate of *real gross domestic product (real GDP)* are designed to address this goal.

While each goal is valid in its own right, of greater importance for effective macroeconomic management is how to strike a balance among all three. An economy with perfectly stable prices but no jobs and no growth is vastly inferior to an economy that is able to promote appropriate levels of economic growth and job creation while maintaining acceptable levels of price-level stability. A society will experience true economic benefit with the achievement of all three goals—a problem with no easy solution.

**real gross domestic product (RGDP)**

*the total value of all final goods and services produced in a given time period, such as a year or a quarter, adjusted for inflation*

The statistic **real gross domestic product (RGDP)** measures the total value of all final goods and services produced in a given time period, such as a year or a quarter, adjusted for inflation. The word *real* is used to indicate that the output is adjusted for general increases in prices over time. We use real gross domestic product to measure the level of output or production in the entire economy.

Exhibit 1 provides data on Canada's macroeconomic performance since 1998. The predominantly downward trend in Canada's annual growth rate in real GDP, commonly referred to as Canada's economic growth rate, was a major contributor to the nation's higher-than-normal rate of unemployment. In particular, the 2008–12 period was marked by a severe contraction of the Canadian economy (in 2009), resulting in a measured rise in the unemployment rate over this same time period. This lower rate of economic growth was also a major reason why the rate of inflation remained below 3 percent per year throughout the 1998–2017 period.

## ARE THESE MACROECONOMIC GOALS UNIVERSAL?

In addition to these primary goals, concern has been expressed at various times and places about other economic issues, some of which are essentially microeconomic in character. For example, concern about the "quality of life" has prompted some societies to try to reduce "bads" such as pollution and crime, and increase goods and services such as education and health services. Another goal has been "fairness" in the distribution of income or wealth. Still another goal pursued in many nations at one time or another has been self-sufficiency in the production of certain goods or services, such as food and energy.

## The Impact of Value Judgments on Economic Goals

In stating that nations have economic goals, we must acknowledge that nations are made up of individuals. Individuals within a society may differ considerably in their evaluation of the relative importance of certain issues, or even whether certain "problems" are really problems after all. For example, economic growth, viewed positively by most

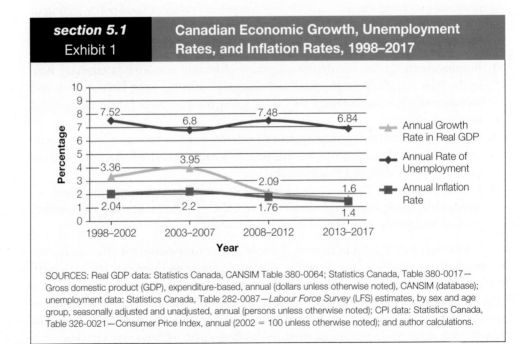

**section 5.1**
**Exhibit 1**

**Canadian Economic Growth, Unemployment Rates, and Inflation Rates, 1998–2017**

SOURCES: Real GDP data: Statistics Canada, CANSIM Table 380-0064; Statistics Canada, Table 380-0017—Gross domestic product (GDP), expenditure-based, annual (dollars unless otherwise noted), CANSIM (database); unemployment data: Statistics Canada, Table 282-0087—*Labour Force Survey* (LFS) estimates, by sex and age group, seasonally adjusted and unadjusted, annual (persons unless otherwise noted); CPI data: Statistics Canada, Table 326-0021—Consumer Price Index, annual (2002 = 100 unless otherwise noted); and author calculations.

people, is not considered as favourably by others. Although some citizens may think that income distribution is just about right, others might think it provides insufficient incomes to the poorer members of society; still others think it involves taking too much income from the relatively well-to-do and thereby reduces incentives to carry out productive, income-producing activities.

## SECTION CHECK

- The three major macroeconomic goals for Canada are full employment, price stability, and economic growth.
- People have their own reasons for valuing certain goals more than others. As a result, there is debate as to what is most important for an economy.

# Employment and Unemployment

- What is the unemployment rate?
- Are unemployment statistics accurate reflections of the labour market?
- How long is someone typically unemployed?
- What is the labour force participation rate?

News of lower unemployment usually sends stock prices higher, and the news of higher unemployment usually sends stock prices lower. Politicians are also concerned about unemployment figures because elections often hinge precariously on whether unemployment has been rising or falling.

Nearly everyone agrees that it is unfortunate when a person who wants a job cannot find one, and the loss of a job can mean financial insecurity and a great deal of anxiety. High rates of unemployment in a society can increase tensions and despair. A family without income undergoes great suffering; as its savings fade, it wonders where it is going to obtain the means to survive. Society loses some potential output of goods when some of its productive resources—human or nonhuman—remain idle, and potential consumption is also reduced. Clearly, then, there is a loss in efficiency when people willing to work and productive equipment remain idle. That is, other things equal, relatively high rates of unemployment are viewed almost universally as undesirable.

## WHAT IS THE UNEMPLOYMENT RATE?

When discussing unemployment, economists and politicians refer to the *unemployment rate*. In order to calculate the unemployment rate, you must first understand another important concept—the labour force. The **labour force** is the number of persons 15 years of age and over who are employed or are unemployed and seeking work. Exhibit 1 shows the population categories used by Statistics Canada in its analysis of the labour market. First, it calculates the population 15 years of age and over, which was 29 901.7 thousand people in 2017. This population is broken down into two categories: those in the labour force and those not in the labour force. Those not in the labour force, 10 238.7 thousand people, were people who were not working and were

**labour force**

*persons 15 years of age and over who are employed or are unemployed and seeking work*

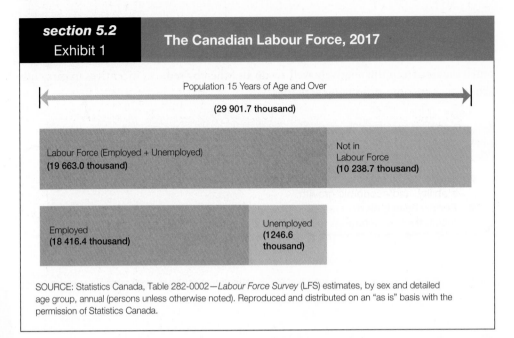

section 5.2
Exhibit 1

**The Canadian Labour Force, 2017**

Population 15 Years of Age and Over
(29 901.7 thousand)

Labour Force (Employed + Unemployed)
(19 663.0 thousand)

Not in
Labour Force
(10 238.7 thousand)

Employed
(18 416.4 thousand)

Unemployed
(1246.6 thousand)

SOURCE: Statistics Canada, Table 282-0002—*Labour Force Survey* (LFS) estimates, by sex and detailed age group, annual (persons unless otherwise noted). Reproduced and distributed on an "as is" basis with the permission of Statistics Canada.

**unemployment rate**

*the percentage of the people in the labour force who are unemployed*

not seeking work. For example, they might have been retired people, full-time home-makers, or full-time students. Those in the labour force, 19 663.0 thousand people, were people who were employed or were unemployed and seeking work.

The **unemployment rate** is defined as the percentage of the people in the labour force who are unemployed. To calculate the unemployment rate, we divide the number of unemployed people by the number of people in the labour force:

Unemployment rate = (Number of unemployed/Labour force) × 100

In 2017, 1246.6 thousand people were unemployed from a labour force of 19 663.0 thousand people:

Unemployment rate = (1246.6 thousand/19 663.0 thousand) × 100

= 0.063 × 100

= 6.3 percent

### The Worst Case of Canadian Unemployment

By far the worst employment downturn in Canadian history was the Great Depression, which began in late 1929 and continued until 1939. Unemployment rose from only 2.9 percent of the labour force in 1929 to more than 19 percent in the early 1930s, and double-digit unemployment persisted through 1939. Some economists would argue that modern macroeconomics, with its emphasis on the determinants of unemployment and its elimination, truly began in the 1930s.

### Variations in the Unemployment Rate

Exhibit 2 shows the unemployment rate since 1976. Unemployment has ranged from a high of 11.9 percent in 1983 to a low of 6.0 percent in 2007. Unemployment varies not only over time, it also varies between different segments of the population and by regions of the country. Unemployment tends to be much greater among teenagers, and female unemployment tends to be slightly lower than male unemployment. As Exhibit 3(a) indicates, the unemployment rate for teenagers (15.9 percent)

**Unemployment Rate**

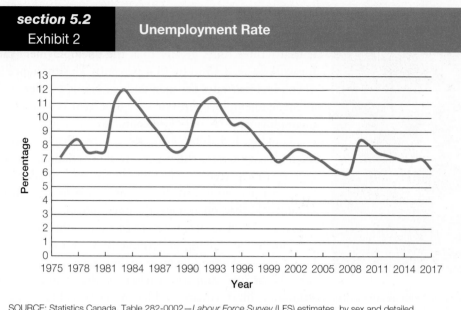

SOURCE: Statistics Canada, Table 282-0002—*Labour Force Survey* (LFS) estimates, by sex and detailed age group, annual (persons unless otherwise noted). Reproduced and distributed on an "as is" basis with the permission of Statistics Canada.

**Unemployment in Canada by Age, Sex, and Region, and Globally, 2017**

**a. Canadian Unemployment by Sex and Age**

**b. Unemployment by Province**

**c. Unemployment in Other Countries**

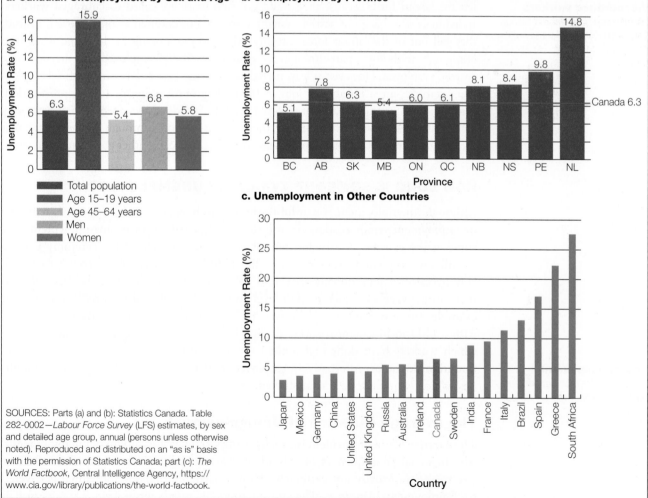

SOURCES: Parts (a) and (b): Statistics Canada. Table 282-0002—*Labour Force Survey* (LFS) estimates, by sex and detailed age group, annual (persons unless otherwise noted). Reproduced and distributed on an "as is" basis with the permission of Statistics Canada; part (c): *The World Factbook*, Central Intelligence Agency, https://www.cia.gov/library/publications/the-world-factbook.

**In Canada, teenagers have the highest rates of unemployment. A shortage of marketable skills and a lack of workplace experience are seen as two major reasons for this unequal burden.**

**discouraged workers**

*people who have left the labour force because they could not find work*

**underemployment**

*a situation in which workers have skills higher than necessary for a job*

is nearly three times greater than the unemployment rate for workers aged 45 to 64 (5.4 percent). The difference in unemployment rates for men and women is smaller, with a female unemployment rate of 5.8 percent versus a male unemployment rate of 6.8 percent.

Looking at Exhibit 3(b), we can see that provincial unemployment rates show considerable variation: from a high of 14.8 percent in Newfoundland and Labrador to a low of 5.1 percent in British Columbia. It is also clear from Exhibit 3(b) that, on average, the unemployment rate tends to rise as one moves from west to east across the country.

Finally, by looking at Exhibit 3(c) we can compare Canada's rate of unemployment to those rates in other countries. What this comparison reveals is that, while Canada has not been as successful as economies like Germany and Japan in terms of lowering its rate of unemployment, countries like Spain and South Africa have experienced rates of unemployment that are far greater than those experienced in Canada.

## ARE UNEMPLOYMENT STATISTICS ACCURATE REFLECTIONS OF THE LABOUR MARKET?

In periods of prolonged economic recession and high unemployment, some individuals think that the chances of landing a job are so bleak that they quit looking. People who have left the labour force because they could not find work are called **discouraged workers**. Individuals who have not actively sought work are not counted as unemployed; instead, they fall out of the labour force category. Also, people looking for full-time work who grudgingly settle for a part-time job are counted as "fully" employed, yet they are only "partly" employed. However, at least partially balancing these two biases in official employment statistics are a number of jobs in the underground economy (drugs, prostitution, gambling, and so on) that are not reported at all. In addition, many people may claim they are actually seeking work when, in fact, they may just be going through the motions so that they can continue to collect Employment Insurance or receive other government benefits.

## HOW LONG IS SOMEONE TYPICALLY UNEMPLOYED?

Although unemployment is painful to those who have no source of income, reducing unemployment is not costless. In the short run, a reduction in unemployment may come at the expense of a higher rate of inflation, especially if the economy is close to full capacity, where resources are almost fully employed. Also, trying to match employees with jobs quickly may lead to significant inefficiencies because of mismatches between the worker's skill level and the level of skill required for a job. For example, the economy would be wasting resources subsidizing education if people with a PhD in biochemistry were driving taxis or tending bar. That is, situations in which workers have skills higher than necessary for a job are what economists call **underemployment**. Alternatively, employees may be placed in jobs beyond their abilities, which would also lead to inefficiencies.

### The Average Duration of Unemployment

The *duration* of unemployment is equally as important as the amount of unemployment. The financial consequences of a head of household being unemployed for four or five weeks are usually not extremely serious, particularly if the individual is covered by Employment Insurance. The impact becomes much more serious if a person is unemployed for many months. Therefore, it is useful to look at the average duration of unemployment to discover what percentage of the labour force is unemployed for more than a certain time period, say, 13 weeks. Canadian data indicate that long-term unemployment (greater than 13 weeks) accounts for approximately 40 to 50 percent of total unemployment.

Exhibit 4 shows the unemployment duration for Canada from 1976 to 2017. According to the exhibit, the average duration of unemployment has ranged from 25.7 weeks in 1994 to a low of 13.7 weeks in 2008. However, the economic downturn that followed the global financial crisis, with its slow recovery, has seen the duration of unemployment return to nearly 18 weeks on average. The duration of unemployment tends to be greater when the amount of unemployment is high and smaller when the amount of unemployment is low. Unemployment of any duration, of course, means a potential loss of output. This loss of current output is permanent; it is not made up when unemployment starts falling again.

## WHAT IS THE LABOUR FORCE PARTICIPATION RATE?

The percentage of the population aged 15 years and over that is in the labour force is what economists call the **labour force participation rate**. Since 1976, the labour force participation rate has increased from 61.5 to nearly 68 percent. The increase in the labour force participation rate can be attributed in large part to the entry of the baby boomers into the labour force and a 17 percentage point increase in the women's labour force participation rate.

**labour force participation rate**
*the percentage of the population (aged 15 years and over) in the labour force*

Since 1976, the number of women working has shifted dramatically, reflecting the changing role of women in the workforce. In Exhibit 5, we see that in 1976 only 46 percent of women were working or looking for work. That figure is more than 61 percent now. In 1976, over 77 percent of men were working or looking for work. The labour force participation rate for men has fallen to roughly 70 percent now, as many men stay in school longer or opt to retire earlier.

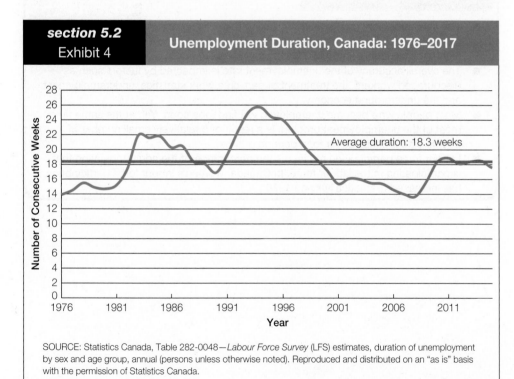

**section 5.2**
Exhibit 4

**Unemployment Duration, Canada: 1976–2017**

Average duration: 18.3 weeks

*y-axis:* Number of Consecutive Weeks (0 to 28)
*x-axis:* Year (1976, 1981, 1986, 1991, 1996, 2001, 2006, 2011)

SOURCE: Statistics Canada, Table 282-0048—*Labour Force Survey* (LFS) estimates, duration of unemployment by sex and age group, annual (persons unless otherwise noted). Reproduced and distributed on an "as is" basis with the permission of Statistics Canada.

| **section 5.2** Exhibit 5 | **Labour Force Participation Rates for Men and Women, 1976–2017** |
|---|---|

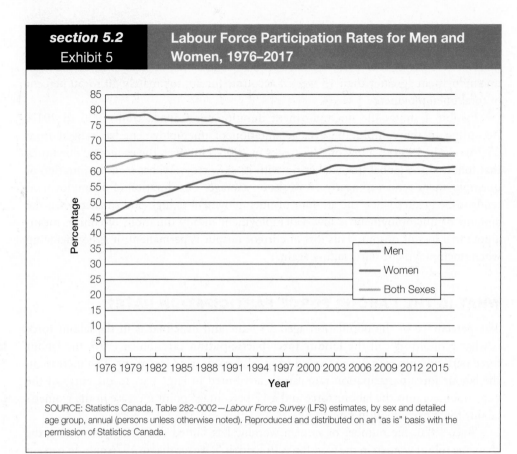

SOURCE: Statistics Canada, Table 282-0002—*Labour Force Survey* (LFS) estimates, by sex and detailed age group, annual (persons unless otherwise noted). Reproduced and distributed on an "as is" basis with the permission of Statistics Canada.

## SECTION CHECK

- The unemployment rate is found by taking the number of people officially unemployed and dividing by the number in the labour force. Unemployment rates are higher for teenagers and those living in eastern Canada.
- The overall accuracy of the unemployment rate is impacted by factors such as discouraged workers, the treatment of part-time work statistics, underemployment and the underground economy.
- Most people who become unemployed will find jobs soon. Yet, at the same time, most of the unemployment problem is a result of a relatively small number of people who are jobless for long periods of time.
- Labour force participation measures the percentage of the adult population that is participating in the labour force. In Canada, women's labour force participation has increased dramatically since 1976.

# Different Types of Unemployment

● What is frictional unemployment?
● What is structural unemployment?
● What is cyclical unemployment?
● What is the natural rate of unemployment?

In examining the status of and changes in the unemployment rate, it is important to recognize that there are numerous types of unemployment. In this section, we will examine frictional, structural, and cyclical unemployment and evaluate the relative impact of each on the overall unemployment rate. You may be surprised to find zero unemployment is not the same as full employment. In fact, some amount of unemployment is inevitable and even desirable. In this section, we will see why the two are not the same.

## WHAT IS FRICTIONAL UNEMPLOYMENT?

In a dynamic economy where people are constantly losing or leaving their jobs, some unemployment is always present. Specifically, **frictional unemployment** is temporary unemployment that results from workers searching for suitable jobs and firms looking for suitable workers. People seeking work do not usually take the first job offered to them. Likewise, firms do not usually take the first person they interview. People and firms engage in a search to match up skills and interests. While the unemployed are looking, they are frictionally unemployed.

In short, frictional unemployment is caused by (1) the normal search time that is necessary for people to find a new job and (2) the lack of information to match a job applicant with a job vacancy. It is short-run unemployment that is unavoidable and it can be caused by changes in people's lives, such as moving from one place to another, or temporary changes in the economy, such as a firm downsizing. In sum, it is a short-run job skill-matching problem, generally lasting only several weeks.

For example, consider an advertising executive who was laid off and is now actively looking for similar work. Of course, not all unemployed workers were laid off from their jobs; some may have voluntarily quit their jobs, while still others are without a job because they have just entered the labour market (such as recent college and university graduates). In any case, frictional unemployment is short term and results from normal turnover in the labour market, as when people change from one job to another.

Some unemployment occurs because certain types of jobs are seasonal in nature; this type of unemployment is called *seasonal unemployment*. For example, a ski instructor in British Columbia might become seasonally unemployed when the skiing season is over. Or a roofer in Nova Scotia may become seasonally unemployed during the winter months. In agricultural areas, employment increases during the harvest season and falls after harvesting is finished. Even a forest firefighter in a provincial park might be employed only during the months when forest fires are more likely to occur. Because the seasonal unemployment rate is of course higher in the off-season, Statistics Canada also publishes a seasonally adjusted unemployment rate.

### Frictional Unemployment—A Sign of Economic Health

A certain amount of frictional unemployment might be good for the economy because workers who are temporarily unemployed might find jobs that are better suited to their skill level, increasing output in society as well as the wage income of the mover. Hence,

**frictional unemployment**
*temporary unemployment that results from workers searching for suitable jobs and firms looking for suitable workers*

frictional unemployment, although not good in itself, can be viewed as a by-product of a healthy phenomenon, and because it is often short-lived, it is generally not viewed as a serious problem. Actually, frictional unemployment tends to be somewhat greater in periods of low unemployment, when job opportunities are plentiful. This high level of job opportunity stimulates mobility, which, in turn, creates some frictional unemployment.

## WHAT IS STRUCTURAL UNEMPLOYMENT?

**structural unemployment**
*unemployment that occurs due to a lack of skills necessary for available jobs*

A second type of unemployment is structural unemployment. Like frictional unemployment, structural unemployment is related to occupational movement or mobility, or in this case, to a lack of mobility. Specifically, **structural unemployment** refers to unemployment that occurs due to a lack of skills necessary for available jobs. For example, if a machine operator in a manufacturing plant loses his job, he could remain unemployed despite the fact that there are openings for computer programmers in his community. The quantity of unemployed workers conceivably could equal the number of job vacancies, but the unemployment persists because the unemployed lack the appropriate skills for some of the job vacancies. Given the existence of structural unemployment, it is wise to look at both unemployment and job vacancy statistics in assessing labour market conditions. Structural unemployment, like frictional unemployment, reflects the dynamic dimension of a changing economy. Over time, new jobs open up that require new skills, whereas old jobs that required different skills disappear. It is not surprising, then, that many people advocate government-subsidized retraining programs as a means of reducing structural unemployment.

Another reason for structural unemployment is that low-skilled workers are frequently unable to find desirable long-term employment. Some low-skilled jobs do not last long and involve little job training, so workers may soon be looking for a new job. Because these workers acquired no new skill from the old job, they may be stuck without long-term secure work. That is, structural workers cannot be said to be "between jobs," like those who are frictionally unemployed. Structural unemployment is more long term and serious than frictional unemployment because these workers do not have marketable skills.

The dimensions of structural unemployment are debatable, in part because of the difficulty in precisely defining the term in an operational sense. Structural unemployment varies considerably—sometimes it is low and at other times, like in the 1970s and 1980s, it is high. To some extent, in this latter period, jobs in the traditional sectors like manufacturing and mining gave way to jobs in the computer and financial services sectors. Consequently, structural unemployment was higher.

**What type of unemployment would occur if these miners lost their jobs as a result of a reduction in demand for their output and needed retraining to find other employment? Usually structural unemployment occurs because of a lack of required skills or long-term changes in demand. Consequently, it generally lasts for a longer period of time than frictional unemployment. In this situation, both might come into play.**

Jules Frazier/Photodisc/Getty Images

## Some Unemployment Is Unavoidable

Some unemployment is actually normal and important to the economy. Frictional and structural unemployment are simply unavoidable in a vibrant economy. To a considerable extent, one can view both frictional and structural unemployment as phenomena resulting from imperfections in the labour market. For example, if individuals seeking jobs and employers seeking workers had better information about each other, the level of frictional unemployment would be considerably lower. It takes time for suppliers of labour to find the demanders of labour services, and it takes time and money for labour resources to acquire the necessary skills. But because information is not costless, and because job search also is costly, the bringing of demanders and suppliers of labour services together does not occur instantaneously.

## WHAT IS CYCLICAL UNEMPLOYMENT?

Often, unemployment is composed of more than just frictional and structural unemployment. In years of relatively low economic activity some unemployment may be due to short-term cyclical fluctuations in the economy. We call this **cyclical unemployment**. That is, during a recession many firms find their sales falling and cut back on production. As production falls, firms start laying off workers. For example, Ford Motor Company, and many others, laid off many workers during the recession of 2008–09. But when the economy improved, Ford rehired many of them. During the transition between being laid off and rehired, those workers experienced cyclical unemployment. Whenever the unemployment rate is greater than the natural rate, or during a recession, there is cyclical unemployment.

**cyclical unemployment**
*unemployment due to short-term cyclical fluctuations in the economy*

## The Costs of Cyclical Unemployment

When the unemployment rate is high, numerous economic and social hardships result. The economic costs are the forgone output when the economy is not producing at its potential level. According to Okun's law (really, a rule of thumb), a 1 percent increase in cyclical unemployment reduces output by 2 percentage points, so we can actually estimate the economic costs of not producing at our potential output. The costs are particularly high for those groups with the least skills—the poorly educated and teenagers with little work experience.

## WHAT IS THE NATURAL RATE OF UNEMPLOYMENT?

It is interesting to observe that over the period in which annual unemployment data are available, the unemployment rate has never been zero; that is, some level of unemployment has always existed within a dynamic economy. Some economists call this unavoidable amount of unemployment the **natural rate of unemployment** and equate it to the sum of frictional and structural unemployment when they are at a maximum. The rate of unemployment in Canada in March 2018 was 5.8 percent, which was below what is currently believed to be Canada's natural rate of unemployment of 6 percent. The natural rate does not necessarily mean that it is the desirable rate; it merely refers to the rate that the economy normally experiences. There will always be some people without jobs, even when the economy is performing well. Some will be transitioning between jobs, others will have lost jobs, and still others may have quit to look for better jobs.

**natural rate of unemployment**
*the amount of unemployment that is unavoidable, equal to the sum of frictional and structural unemployment when they are at a maximum*

When unemployment rises well above the natural rate, we have abnormally high unemployment; when it falls well below the natural rate, we have abnormally low unemployment. Since the natural rate of unemployment roughly equals the sum of frictional and structural unemployment when they are at a maximum, we can view unemployment rates below the natural rate as reflecting the existence of below-average levels of frictional and structural unemployment. When unemployment rises above the natural rate, however, it reflects the existence of cyclical unemployment. In short, the natural rate of unemployment is the unemployment rate when the economy is experiencing neither a recession nor a boom. The natural rate of unemployment is also called the *full-employment rate of unemployment*.

The natural rate of unemployment can change over time as technological, demographic, institutional, and other conditions vary. For example, as baby boomers age, the natural rate falls because middle-aged workers generally experience lower unemployment rates than do younger workers. In addition, the Internet and job placement agencies have improved access to employment information and allowed workers to find jobs more quickly. Also, the restructuring of Canada's Employment Insurance program is believed to have increased the number of people with jobs. Thus, the natural rate is not fixed, because it can change with demographic changes over time.

In fact, it is estimated that the natural rate was as low as about 5 percent in the 1960s, and then rose to over 8 percent in the 1980s and early 1990s. Most economists estimate the natural rate of unemployment to lie in a range between 6 and 7 percent.

## Full Employment and Potential Output

**potential output**
*the amount of real output the economy would produce if its labour and other resources were fully employed—that is, at the natural rate of unemployment*

The amount of real output that an economy produces when its resources—labour, land, capital, and entrepreneurship—are fully employed is considered to be that economy's **potential output**; that is, the amount of output at the natural rate of unemployment. Literal full employment of labour means that the economy is providing employment for all who are willing and able to work, with no cyclical unemployment. It also means that capital and land are fully employed. That is, at the natural rate of unemployment, all resources are fully employed and the economy is producing its potential output and there is no cyclical unemployment. This does not mean the economy will always be producing at its potential output of resources. For example, when the economy is experiencing cyclical unemployment, the unemployment rate is greater than the natural rate. It is also possible that the economy's output can temporarily exceed the potential output as workers take on overtime or moonlight by taking on extra employment.

**Will new technology in one industry displace workers in the whole economy? No. There may be some loss of specific jobs within certain industries, but the overall effect of technological improvements is the release of scarce resources for the expansion of output and employment in other areas and ultimately more economic growth and a higher standard of living.**

## Employment Insurance and the Natural Rate of Unemployment

Losing a job can lead to considerable hardship, and Employment Insurance (EI) is designed to partially offset the severity of the unemployment problem. That is, EI allows unemployed workers to maintain some income and spending, reducing the financial hardship associated with job loss. The program does not cover those who quit their jobs. To qualify, recipients must have worked a certain length of time. Although the program is intended to ease the pain of unemployment, it also leads to more frictional unemployment, as job seekers stay unemployed for longer periods of time while searching for new jobs.

For example, some unemployed people may show little drive in seeking new employment, because EI lowers the opportunity cost of being unemployed. For example, a worker making $600 a week when employed receives $330 in compensation when unemployed; as a result, the cost of losing his job is not $600 a week in forgone income, but only $270.

Without EI, job seekers would more likely take the first job offered even if it did not match their preferences or skill levels. A longer job search might mean a better match but at the expense of lost production and greater amounts of tax dollars.

Of course, that does not mean that EI is necessarily a bad program. It still serves its desired goal of reducing income uncertainty. Workers who turn down unattractive jobs have an opportunity to find jobs that may be better suited to their tastes and skills. In summary, most economists believe that eliminating EI could reduce unemployment but they disagree on whether economic well-being is reduced or enhanced by such a change in policy.

The unemployment rates for Canada are lower than those for Spain, Greece, Italy, and France. In fact, European unemployment rates have historically been higher than Canada's rates over the last few decades. Why? Many economists believe the answer lies in differences in unemployment benefits and labour market regulations. In Europe, unemployment benefits are higher and last longer. Consequently, incentives for the unemployed to look for or accept work are reduced. Also, labour regulations in Europe make it difficult to fire employees, which makes employers more reluctant to hire new workers. Japan has lower unemployment rates because many companies give workers job security for life. Due to such differences, different places have different natural rates of unemployment.

## Technological Change and the Natural Rate of Unemployment

Although many believe that technological advances inevitably result in the displacement of workers, this is not necessarily the case. New inventions are generally cost-saving, and these cost savings will generally generate higher incomes for producers and lower prices and better products for consumers, benefits that will ultimately result in the growth of other industries. If the new equipment is a substitute for labour, then it might displace workers. For example, many fast-food restaurants have substituted self-service beverage bars for workers. However, new capital equipment requires new workers to manufacture and repair the new equipment. The most famous example of this is the computer, which was supposed to displace thousands of workers. Although it did displace workers, the total job growth it generated exceeded the number of lost jobs. The problem is that it is easy to see just the initial effect of technological advances (displaced workers), without recognizing the implications of that invention for the whole economy over time.

### SECTION CHECK

- Frictional unemployment results when a person moves from one job to another as a result of normal turnover in the economy.
- Structural unemployment results when people who are looking for jobs lack the required skills for the jobs that are available or a long-term change in demand occurs.
- Cyclical unemployment is due to short-term cyclical fluctuations in the economy, such as recessions.
- When cyclical unemployment is eliminated, our economy is said to be operating at full employment, or at a natural rate of unemployment.

**section**

**5.4**

# Inflation

- Why is the overall price level important?
- How is inflation measured using the Consumer Price Index (CPI)?
- Is the CPI accurate?
- Who are the winners and losers during inflation?
- What are the costs of inflation?
- What is the relationship between inflation and interest rates?

## WHY IS THE OVERALL PRICE LEVEL IMPORTANT?

**price level**
*the average level of prices in the economy*

**inflation**
*a continuous rise in the overall price level*

**deflation**
*a decrease in the overall price level*

Just as full employment brings about economic security of one kind, stable prices increase another form of security. Most prices in the Canadian economy tend to rise over time and economists use a statistic known as a *price level* to measure this change. A **price level** measures the average level of prices in the economy. A continuous rise in the *overall* price level is called **inflation**. Even when the level of prices is stable, some prices will be rising while others are falling. However, when inflation is present, the goods and services with rising prices will outweigh the goods and services with falling prices. Without stability in the price level, consumers and producers will experience more difficulty in coordinating their plans and decisions. When the *overall* price level is falling, there is **deflation**.

In general, the only thing that can cause a *sustained* increase in the price level is a high rate of growth in money, a topic we will discuss thoroughly in the coming chapters.

## HOW IS INFLATION MEASURED USING THE CONSUMER PRICE INDEX (CPI)?

**relative price**
*the price of a specific good compared to the prices of other goods*

We often use the term *purchasing power* when we discuss how much a dollar can buy of goods and services. In times of inflation, a dollar cannot buy as many goods and services. Thus, the higher the inflation rate, the greater the rate of decline in purchasing power.

In periods of high and variable inflation, households and firms have a difficult time distinguishing between changes in the **relative price** of individual goods and services (the price of a specific good compared to the prices of other goods) and changes in the general price level of all goods and services. Suppose the price of milk rises by 5 percent between 2017 and 2018, but the overall price level (inflation rate) increases by only 2 percent during that period. Then we could say that between 2017 and 2018, the relative price of milk rose only 3 percent (5 – 2 percent). The next year, the price of milk might increase 5 percent again, but the general inflation rate might be 6 percent. That is, between 2018 and 2019, the relative price of milk might actually fall by 1 percent (5 – 6 percent).

Remember, the relative price is the price of a good relative to all other goods and services. Because of this difficulty in establishing relative prices, inflation distorts the information that flows from price signals. Does the good have a higher price because it has become relatively more scarce and therefore more valuable relative to other goods, or did the price rise along with all other prices because of inflation?

**price index**
*a measure of the trend in prices for a certain bundle of goods and services over a given time period*

This muddying of price information undermines good decision making, so we need a method to measure inflation. We adjust for the changing purchasing power of the dollar by constructing a price index. Essentially, a **price index** is a measure of the trend in prices for a certain bundle of goods and services over a given time period.

There are many different types of price indices. The best-known price index, the **Consumer Price Index (CPI)** is a measure of the prices of a basket of consumable goods and services that serves to gauge inflation. Constructing the Consumer Price Index is complicated. Since literally thousands of consumer goods and services are involved, attempting to include all of them in the index would be cumbersome and make the index expensive to compute; in addition, it would take a long time to gather the necessary price data. Therefore, Statistics Canada bases the CPI on a basket of over 600 consumer goods and services, in 175 basic goods and services classes, that are purchased by a typical Canadian household. Each month, the prices of these goods and services are recorded all across Canada. The eight major components of the CPI appear in Exhibit 1. The weight for each component is represented as a proportion of the total expenditures for the CPI basket.

**Consumer Price Index (CPI)**

*a measure of the prices of a basket of consumable goods and services that serves to gauge inflation*

## Calculating the CPI—A Simplified Example

Suppose a consumer typically buys 24 loaves of bread and 12 kilograms of oranges in a year. The following table indicates the prices of bread and oranges and the cost of the consumer's typical market basket in the years 2017 through 2019.

| Year | Price of Bread | Price of Oranges | Cost of Market Basket |
|------|----------------|------------------|------------------------|
| 2017 | $1.00 | $2.00 | (24 × $1.00) + (12 × $2.00) = $48.00 |
| 2018 | 1.15 | 2.10 | (24 × 1.15) + (12 × 2.10) = 52.80 |
| 2019 | 1.40 | 2.20 | (24 × 1.40) + (12 × 2.20) = 60.00 |

| **section 5.4**<br>Exhibit 1 | **2017 CPI Basket Weights, Effective with the January 2015 CPI** |
|---|---|

**Consumer Price Index and Major Components, Canada**

| | Relative importance |
|---|---|
| | % |
| All-items CPI | 100.00 |
| Food | 16.23 |
| Shelter | 27.15 |
| Household operations, furnishings, and equipment | 12.97 |
| Clothing and footwear | 5.44 |
| Transportation | 19.70 |
| Health and personal care | 5.00 |
| Recreation, education, and reading | 10.89 |
| Alcoholic beverages and tobacco products | 2.63 |

Recreation, education, and reading 10.89%

Alcoholic beverages and tobacco products 2.63%

Food 16.23%

Health and personal care 5.00%

Transportation 19.70%

Shelter 27.15%

Clothing and footwear 5.44%

Household operations, furnishings, and equipment 12.97%

Statistics Canada divides the typical Canadian household's spending among various categories of goods and services.

SOURCE: Statistics Canada, Table 326-0031—Basket Weights of the Consumer Price Index (CPI) occasional (percent). Reproduced and distributed on an "as is" basis with the permission of Statistics Canada.

We calculate the CPI by comparing the cost of the market basket in the current year to the cost of the market basket in the base year. The base year is arbitrarily chosen; in our example, we will designate 2017 as the base year. The CPI for each year is calculated using the following formula:

$$\text{CPI} = \frac{\text{Cost of market basket in current year}}{\text{Cost of market basket in base year}} \times 100$$

The following table shows the CPI from 2017 through 2019. In 2017, the base year, the CPI equals 100. In 2018 and 2019, the CPI is 110 and 125, respectively, meaning that the average price level has risen in each of these two years.

| Year | Consumer Price Index |
|------|----------------------|
| 2017 | $48/$48 × 100 = 100.0 |
| 2018 | $52.80/$48 × 100 = 110.0 |
| 2019 | $60/$48 × 100 = 125.0 |

A comparison of the CPI shows that between 2017 and 2018, prices increased an average of 10 percent. Between 2017 and 2019, 25 percent inflation occurred. And between 2018 and 2019, the inflation rate was 13.6 percent, $(125 - 110)/110 \times 100$.

## IS THE CPI ACCURATE?

It is very difficult to measure changes in the price level. Statistics Canada has been eliminating or reducing biases that cause the index to overstate inflation. It is important that the CPI measure inflation accurately or that the degree of bias be known. If the CPI does not measure inflation correctly, cost-of-living adjustments for wages, Canada Pension Plan (CPP) benefits, and even alimony and child support payments will be distorted. The following four biases cause the CPI to overstate the true inflation rate.

## The Substitution Bias

The substitution bias occurs because the CPI measures the price changes of a fixed basket of goods and services. That is, it assumes that consumers purchase the same amount of each product in the basket over time. As a result, it does not capture the savings that households enjoy when they change their spending in response to relative price changes. When prices change from year to year, they do not change proportionately. Some prices rise more than others. Consumers respond to incentives—they buy less of those goods that have increased a large amount and buy more of those goods that have risen just a little or fallen. If the basket was fixed, it would miss people substituting away from the high-priced goods and the CPI would overstate the increased cost of living.

## The Quality Bias

This bias arises because some of any increase in the price of an item may be due to an improvement in quality, rather than being a price increase for the same quality. For example, take the personal computer, where greater speeds and more features have become available without substantial increases in price. If the CPI looked at only the price of a computer, it would miss the quality-change effect of these features. Quality improvements in many areas—such as education—are difficult to measure, so the quality bias is more likely to occur in such areas. And features of a product that becomes mandatory—such as seat belts, which buyers are forced to purchase—are particularly difficult to measure.

## The New Outlet Bias

This type of bias is similar to substitution bias, but refers to where households shop rather than to what they purchase. Over the past 15 years, for example, the growth of discount stores like Costco has helped consumers lower their expenditures. A similar problem arises with online shopping, which now accounts for a significant fraction of sales. So when Statistics Canada collects data on the same or similar products only from full-price retail stores, the CPI overstates the prices some buyers actually paid.

If people prefer buying in bulk at discount stores, will the CPI accurately measure inflation? The success of discount stores has grown over the last few years, indicating that for some customers, the reduction in customer service often associated with these megastores does not offset the lower prices. This change results in an upward bias in the price index.

## The New Product Bias

This bias occurs because new products, such as iPhones or iPads, are not introduced into the CPI until they are commonplace items. This means that the substantial price decreases and quality increases that occur during the early years following introduction are not captured by the index.

## The Price Level over the Years

Unanticipated and sharp changes in the price level are almost universally considered to be "bad" and to require a policy remedy. What is the historical record of changes in the overall Canadian price level? Exhibit 2(a) shows changes in the Consumer Price Index, the standard measure of inflation, from 1915 to 2017. As you can see from the chart, the Canadian economy experienced deflation in the early 1920s and the early 1930s. High rates of inflation, on the other hand, were experienced in the mid-1970s and early 1980s. Notice that since 1992, the annual inflation rate has remained below 3 percent, implying a substantial period of relatively low and stable inflation. Remember, however, that even when the inflation rate is only 3 percent per year, prices on average are rising, and the price level will double in 24 years. Exhibit 2(b) shows inflation rates from selected countries for 2017. Fortunately, Canadian inflation rates are among some of the lowest in the world, while other countries have had to endure significantly higher rates of inflation.

## Anticipated vs. Unanticipated Inflation

Before we can determine the effects of inflation, we must distinguish between anticipated and unanticipated inflation. If the annual inflation rate has been 3 percent for several years and people anticipate that the inflation rate will remain at 3 percent, then there is anticipated inflation. Anticipated inflation causes few problems. For the most part, people see it coming and prepare for it.

Unanticipated inflation occurs when people don't see it coming and have failed to prepare for it. Suppose people anticipate a 3 percent inflation rate, but the inflation rate unexpectedly jumps to 10 percent. When inflation is unanticipated, people are less able to protect themselves from its costs. But that does not mean that everybody is worse off. Unanticipated inflation leads to arbitrary gains and losses as wealth and

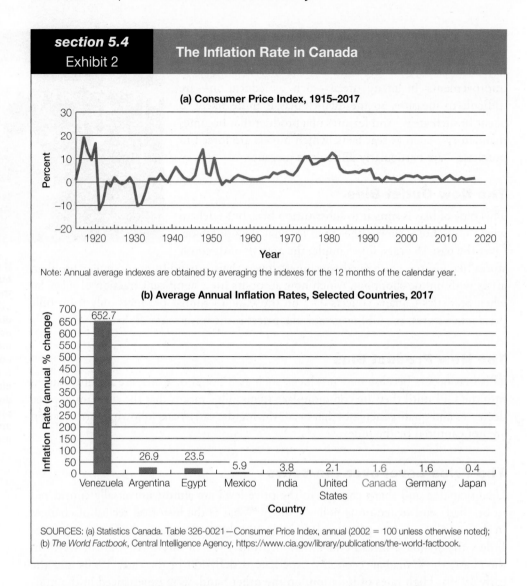

**section 5.4**
Exhibit 2

**The Inflation Rate in Canada**

**(a) Consumer Price Index, 1915–2017**

Note: Annual average indexes are obtained by averaging the indexes for the 12 months of the calendar year.

**(b) Average Annual Inflation Rates, Selected Countries, 2017**

| Country | Inflation Rate (annual % change) |
|---|---|
| Venezuela | 652.7 |
| Argentina | 26.9 |
| Egypt | 23.5 |
| Mexico | 5.9 |
| India | 3.8 |
| United States | 2.1 |
| Canada | 1.6 |
| Germany | 1.6 |
| Japan | 0.4 |

SOURCES: (a) Statistics Canada. Table 326-0021—Consumer Price Index, annual (2002 = 100 unless otherwise noted); (b) *The World Factbook*, Central Intelligence Agency, https://www.cia.gov/library/publications/the-world-factbook.

income are redistributed from one group to another. In addition, it makes it more difficult to make long-term plans, and forces people to focus more on money and prices and less on efficient choices about production and consumption in order to protect themselves from eroding purchasing power.

## WHO ARE THE WINNERS AND LOSERS DURING INFLATION?

Inflation brings about changes in people's purchasing power, and these changes may be either desirable or undesirable. Suppose you retire on a fixed pension of $3000 per month. Over time, the $3000 will buy less and less if prices generally rise. Your real income—your income adjusted to reflect changes in purchasing power—falls. Inflation lowers income in real terms for people on fixed-dollar incomes. Likewise, inflation can hurt creditors.

For example, suppose that in the early 1960s (a period of low inflation), a bank loaned someone money for a house at a 4 percent fixed rate for 20 years. However, the 1970s was a period of high inflation rates (roughly 10 percent per year). In this scenario, because the lender did not correctly anticipate the higher rate of inflation, the lender is the victim of unanticipated inflation and the borrower is the winner. That is, the borrower is paying back with dollars that have much less purchasing power than those dollars that were borrowed in the early 1960s.

Another group that sometimes loses from inflation, at least temporarily, are people whose incomes are tied to long-term contracts. For example, if inflation begins shortly after a labour union signs a three-year wage agreement, it may completely eat up the wage gains provided by the contract. The same applies to businesses that agree to sell a quantity of something, say, phone service, for a fixed price for a given number of years.

If some people lose because of unanticipated inflation, others must gain. The debtor pays back dollars worth less in purchasing power than those she borrowed. Corporations that can quickly raise the prices on their goods may have revenue gains greater than their increases in costs, providing additional profits. Wage earners sometimes lose as a result of inflation because wages may rise at a slower rate than the price level. The redistributional impact of inflation is not the result of conscious public policy—it just happens.

## WHAT ARE THE COSTS OF INFLATION?

The uncertainty that unanticipated inflation creates can also discourage investment and economic growth. When inflation rates are high, they also tend to vary considerably, which creates a lot of uncertainty. This uncertainty complicates planning for businesses and households, which is vital to capital formation, as well as adding an inflation risk premium to long-term interest rates.

Moreover, inflation can raise one nation's price level relative to that in other countries. In turn, this can make that nation's goods and services less competitive in international markets or can decrease the value of the national currency relative to that of other countries.

### Costs of High Inflation

Predictable low rates of inflation, while still a problem, are considerably better than high and variable inflation rates. A slow predictable rate of inflation makes predicting future price increases relatively easy, so setting interest rates will be an easier task and the redistribution effects of inflation will be minimized. High and variable inflation rates make it almost impossible to set long-term contracts, however, because prices and interest rates may be changing by the day or even by the hour in the case of **hyperinflation**— extremely high rates of inflation for a sustained period of time.

**hyperinflation**
*extremely high rates of inflation for a sustained period of time*

In its extreme form, inflation can lead to a complete erosion of faith in the value of the pieces of paper we commonly call money. In Germany after both world wars, prices rose so fast that people in some cases finally refused to take paper money, insisting instead on payment in goods or metals, whose prices tend to move predictably with inflation. Unchecked inflation can feed on itself and ultimately can lead to hyperinflation of 300 percent or more per year. We saw these rapid rates of inflation in Argentina and Brazil in the 1990s, when the inflation rate topped 2000 percent per year. Most economists believe we can live quite well in an environment of low, steady inflation, but no economist believes we can prosper with high, variable inflation.

### Unanticipated Inflation Distorts Price Signals

In periods of high and variable inflation, households and firms have a difficult time distinguishing between changes in the relative prices of individual goods and services and changes in the general price level of all goods and services. Inflation distorts the information that flows from price signals. Does the good have a higher price because it has become relatively more scarce, and therefore more valuable relative to other goods, or did the price rise along with all other prices because of inflation? This muddying of price information undermines good decision making.

## Menu and Shoe-Leather Costs

Whether inflation is anticipated or not, firms incur costs as a result of the need to change prices more frequently. For example, a restaurant may have to print new menus, or a department or mail-order store may have to print new catalogues to reflect changing prices. These costs are called **menu costs**—the costs incurred by a firm as a result of changing its listed prices. In some South American economies in the 1980s, inflation increased at over 300 percent per year, with prices changing on a daily, or even hourly, basis in some cases. Imagine how large the menu costs could be in an economy such as that!

There is also the **shoe-leather cost** of inflation: the time and inconvenience cost incurred when individuals reduce their money holdings because of inflation. Specifically, high rates of inflation erode the value of a currency, which means that people will want to hold less currency—perhaps going to the ATM once a week rather than twice a month, thus wearing out the leather of their shoes going to and from the ATM. That is, higher inflation rates lead to higher nominal interest rates, which may induce more individuals to put money in the bank rather than allowing it to depreciate in their pockets. The effects of shoe-leather costs of inflation, like those of menu costs, are modest in countries with low inflation rates but can be quite large in countries where inflation is anticipated and substantial.

## Unanticipated Deflation

The effects of unanticipated deflation are generally opposite to those for unanticipated inflation. As the overall price level declines with deflation, it has the effect of raising people's purchasing power, so people on fixed-dollar incomes will benefit. Savers will also discover that the purchasing power of their savings has increased, possibly stimulating additional savings at the expense of additional spending. Deflationary pressures will benefit creditors, as opposed to debtors, as the money that is repaid to lenders is worth more (in terms of purchasing power) than the money that was initially loaned out, possibly leading to a drop in bank lending.

A final note relates to the impact of deflation on wages. As the economy's price level falls, companies will find it increasingly difficult to maintain profits. As profits are reduced, an argument can be made that this can lead to rising unemployment and falling wages.

## WHAT IS THE RELATIONSHIP BETWEEN INFLATION AND INTEREST RATES?

The interest rate that is usually reported is not adjusted for inflation. This is the **nominal interest rate**. We determine the actual **real interest rate** by taking the nominal rate of interest minus the inflation rate:

$$\text{Real interest rate} = \text{Nominal interest rate} - \text{Inflation rate}$$

For example, if the nominal interest rate was 5 percent and the inflation rate was 3 percent, then the real interest rate would be 2 percent.

If people can correctly anticipate inflation, they will behave in a manner that will largely protect them against loss. Consider the creditor who believes that the overall price level will rise 6 percent a year, based on immediate past experience. Would that creditor lend money to someone at a 5 percent rate of interest? No. A 5 percent rate of interest means that a person borrowing $1000 now will pay back $1050 ($1000 plus 5 percent of $1000) one year from now. But if prices go up 6 percent, it will take $1060 to buy what $1000 does today. (That is, $1060 is 6 percent more than $1000.) Thus,

**menu costs**
*the costs incurred by a firm as a result of changing its listed prices*

**shoe-leather cost**
*the time and inconvenience cost incurred when individuals reduce their money holdings because of inflation*

**nominal interest rate**
*the reported interest rate that is not adjusted for inflation*

**real interest rate**
*the nominal interest rate minus the inflation rate*

the person who lends at 5 percent will be repaid an amount ($1050) that is less than the purchasing power of the original loan ($1060). The real interest rate, then, would actually be negative. So, to protect themselves, lenders will demand a rate of interest large enough to compensate for the deteriorating value of money.

## Creditors Don't Always Lose from Inflation

Usually lenders are able to anticipate inflation with reasonable accuracy. For example, in the early 1980s when the inflation rate was over 10 percent a year, nominal interest rates on a three-month Treasury bill were relatively high. Since 2000, with low inflation rates, the nominal interest rate has been relatively low. If the inflation rate is anticipated accurately, new creditors will not lose nor will debtors gain from a change in the inflation rate. However, nominal interest rates and real interest rates do not always run together. For example, in periods of high *unexpected* inflation, the nominal interest rates can be very high whereas the real interest rates may be very low or even negative.

## DEBATE

### SHOULD THE GOVERNMENT STAY FOCUSED ON INFLATION RATHER THAN UNEMPLOYMENT RATES?

**For:**

Although governments have three major macroeconomic goals that they try to keep in balance, they tend to zero in on one at a time. The goals are (1) to keep employment rates at relatively high levels, (2) to keep prices at relatively stable levels, and (3) to achieve high rates of growth. These are competing forces that act against each other—for example, if growth increases at too high a rate, prices (inflation) will likely rise, and if growth isn't meeting expected levels, unemployment rises.

Stable prices of goods and services, in both the consumer and the factor markets, are of top importance to a strong economy. Stable prices ensure that investment and interest rates are at manageable levels, which will ensure that growth continues and people are employed.

By managing inflation rates, the government benefits in meeting the other goals without having to directly intervene. In an open, capitalist economy, the less government intervention, the better. It can be argued that changing the dominant policy may be premature—it's too early to conclude one way or the other that the current dominant policy target is not the right policy. Surely the government should not change its dominant policy from inflation to unemployment rates under these circumstances.

**Against:**

The government's choice to control inflation came at a time when rising prices were a concern. During the late 1970s and early 1980s, the government concentrated on growth and the policies that were put in place certainly achieved growth—but inflation rates rose to around 20 percent. At

that point, the key goal changed from targeting growth to targeting inflation, so both growth and inflation rates dropped to more manageable and productive levels.

The country had undergone a period when high inflation was causing high interest rates and therefore impeded growth. At the time, targeting inflation was the proper policy. However, since the start of the Great Recession and its recovery, we have seen growth and inflation rates slightly below target levels, but corresponding increases in longer-term unemployment rates to the point where there is debate that the natural rate of unemployment has moved 2 to 3 percentage points higher than the target 6 to 7 percent rate. This means that the economy is performing relatively well in terms of productivity but there are fewer workers employed.

So, under the current economic conditions, there are more important concerns than inflation, in fact, such as putting people back to work. Further, if the unemployment rate is too high, growth is impeded and the government will be paying higher costs for social programs. Surely the government should concentrate on employment rates over rising prices in this situation.

**Questions:**

1. What are the consequences if the government changes the dominant policy too soon? What about if it changes it too late?
2. Can you think of other reasons why the government would chose inflation over the other goals?
3. Can you think of other reasons why the government should reconsider its primary target?

### Protecting Ourselves from Inflation

Some groups try to protect themselves from inflation by using cost-of-living clauses in contracts. In labour union contracts with these clauses, workers automatically get wage increases that reflect rising prices. The same is true of some private pension plans that are adjusted for inflation, as well as the government-run Canada Pension Plan. Personal income taxes also are now indexed (adjusted) for inflation. However, some of the tax laws are still not indexed for inflation. This can affect the incentives to work, save, and invest.

Some economists have argued that we should go one step further and index everything, meaning that all contractual arrangements would be adjusted frequently to take changing prices into account. Such an arrangement might reduce the impact of inflation, but it would also entail additional contracting costs. An alternative approach has been to try to stop inflation through various policies relating to the amount of government spending, tax rates, or the amount of money created.

## SECTION CHECK

- A continuous rise in the price level defines the case of inflation, whereas a fall in the overall price level defines the case for deflation.
- A price index allows us to compare prices paid for goods and services over time. The Consumer Price Index (CPI) is the best-known price index. However, substitution bias, quality bias, new outlet bias, and new product bias all cause the CPI to overstate the true inflation rate.
- Inflation generally hurts creditors and those on fixed incomes and pensions; debtors generally benefit from inflation.
- Unanticipated inflation causes unpredictable transfers of wealth and reduces the efficiency of the market system by distorting price signals.
- The nominal interest rate is the actual amount of interest you pay. The real interest rate is the nominal rate minus the inflation rate. Inflationary expectations tend to increase nominal interest rates.

## section 5.5

# Economic Fluctuations

- What are short-term economic fluctuations?
- What are the four phases of a business cycle?
- How long does a business cycle last?

### WHAT ARE SHORT-TERM ECONOMIC FLUCTUATIONS?

The aggregate amount of economic activity in Canada and most other nations has increased markedly over time, even on a per capita basis, indicating long-term economic growth. Short-term fluctuations in the economy relative to the long-term trend in output are referred to as **business cycles**. Exhibit 1 illustrates the distinction between long-term economic growth and short-term economic fluctuations. Over a long period of time, the line representing economic activity slopes upward, indicating increasing

**business cycles**

*short-term fluctuations in the economy relative to the long-term trend in output*

| section 5.5 Exhibit 1 | Business Cycles and Economic Growth |
|---|---|

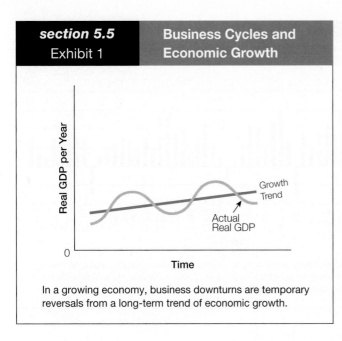

In a growing economy, business downturns are temporary reversals from a long-term trend of economic growth.

| section 5.5 Exhibit 2 | Four Phases of a Business Cycle |
|---|---|

Business cycles have four phases: expansion, peak, contraction, and trough. The expansion phase usually is longer than the contraction, and in a growing economy, output (real GDP) will rise from one business cycle peak to the next.

real output. Over short time periods, however, there are downward, as well as upward, output changes. Business cycles are the short-term ups and downs in economic activity, not the long-term trend in output, which in modern times has been upward.

## WHAT ARE THE FOUR PHASES OF A BUSINESS CYCLE?

A business cycle has four phases—expansion, peak, contraction, and trough—as illustrated in Exhibit 2. The period of **expansion** occurs when output (real GDP) is rising significantly. Usually during the expansion phase, unemployment is falling and both consumer and business confidence is high. Thus, investment spending by firms is rising, as well as expenditures for expensive durable consumer goods, such as automobiles and household appliances. The **peak** is the point in time when the expansion comes to an end, when output is at the highest point in the cycle. The **contraction** is a period of falling real output, and is usually accompanied by rising unemployment and declining business and consumer confidence. The contraction phase is measured from the peak to the trough. Investment spending by firms and expenditures on consumer durable goods fall sharply in a typical contraction. This contraction phase is also called **recession**, a period of significant decline in output and employment (lasting at least six months). The **trough** is the point in time when output stops declining; it is the moment when business activity is at its lowest point in the cycle. Unemployment is relatively high at the trough, although the actual maximum amount of unemployment may not occur exactly at the trough. Often, unemployment remains fairly high well into the expansion phase. The expansion phase is measured from the trough to the peak.

Exhibit 3 shows the growth in Canadian real GDP over the 1962–2017 period. On an annual basis, you can see that there were three major recessions during this period: 1982, 1991, and 2009. In the 1982 recession, the economy declined by 3.2 percent, whereas in 1991, the economy contracted by 2.1 percent. As for the 2009 recession, the Canadian economy experienced a 2.9 percent decline in real GDP. Of the three recessions, the sharp drop in output in 1982 was the deepest recession the economy had

**expansion**
*when output (real GDP) is rising significantly—the period between the trough of a recession and the next peak*

**peak**
*the point in time when the expansion comes to an end, when output is at the highest point in the cycle*

**contraction**
*when the economy's output is falling—measured from the peak to the trough*

**recession**
*a period of significant decline in output and employment*

**trough**
*the point in time when output stops declining; it is the moment when business activity is at its lowest point in the cycle*

SOURCE: Statistics Canada, Table 380-0064—Gross domestic product, expenditure-based (percentage change) (year-to-year), annual (dollars unless otherwise noted) (accessed: April 17, 2018). Reproduced and distributed on an "as is" basis with the permission of Statistics Canada.

experienced since the Great Depression of the 1930s. Both the 1982 and 1991 recessions were accompanied by sharp rises in unemployment, which rose from 7.6 percent (1981) to 12.0 percent (1983), and from 8.1 percent (1990) to 11.4 percent (1993). The 2009 recession, however, was different in that the unemployment rate remained relatively low at around 8.3 percent (2009), the rate being 6.1 percent in 2008.

Another distinguishing feature of these recessionary periods in Canadian economic history is their duration. The 1982 and 1991 recessions were roughly equal in duration— the 1982 recession lasted five quarters, while the 1991 recession lasted six quarters. By comparison, the 2009 recession lasted only four quarters. In the 1982 recession, the economy was experiencing negative real GDP growth by the first quarter of 1982; this lasted until the first quarter of 1983. Recovery from this recession, however, was very rapid, and by the fourth quarter of 1983, the Canadian economy was growing at a rate of 6.2 percent.

In the 1991 recession, the economy actually began to experience negative real GDP growth by the third quarter of 1990, which lasted until the end of 1991. Despite experiencing positive real GDP growth by the first quarter of 1992, the recovery this time was much less secure. Throughout 1992 and 1993, the Canadian economy continued to experience low rates of growth in real GDP and consistent positive growth was not achieved until mid-1993. While the 2009 recession was the shortest in duration, it was the most severe in contraction, with real GDP growth declining from 1.4 percent in the third quarter of 2008 to negative 3.7 percent by the second quarter of 2009. Despite an initial bounce-back in economic growth (3.4 percent in the second quarter of 2010), the recovery quickly stalled, with real GDP growth rates of 1.7 and 2.5 percent in 2012 and 2013, respectively.

You will also notice that the expansion phase of the business cycle is characterized by varying rates of economic growth. In 1962 and 1973, for example, the economy grew at a very rapid pace of 7 percent per year. In other years, economic growth can be much more sluggish, as in 1975 and 2003 when the economy grew by less than 2 percent each year.

By way of comparison, Exhibit 4 shows us Canada's 2017 growth rate relative to other selected countries. The exhibit reveals that not only have other countries recovered from the global financial crisis with varying degrees of success, but also regional economic factors can have a measured impact on an economy's rate of economic growth.

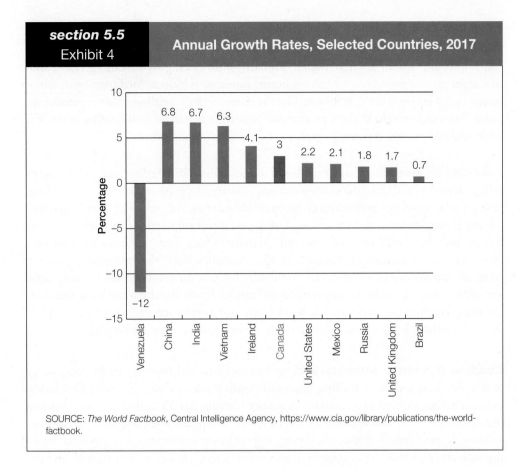

**section 5.5**
Exhibit 4

**Annual Growth Rates, Selected Countries, 2017**

SOURCE: *The World Factbook*, Central Intelligence Agency, https://www.cia.gov/library/publications/the-world-factbook.

## HOW LONG DOES A BUSINESS CYCLE LAST?

As you can see from Exhibit 3, there is no uniformity to a business cycle's length. Because it does not have the regularity that the term *cycle* implies, economists often use the term *economic fluctuation* rather than *business cycle*. In addition, economic fluctuations are almost impossible to predict. Severe recessions are called **depressions**. Likewise, a prolonged expansion in economic activity is sometimes called a **boom**. For example, during the Great Depression, real GDP contracted for four consecutive years, from 1930 to 1933. An economic boom occurred during the 1960s when real GDP grew by about 6 percent a year on average over that decade.

**depression**
*a severe recession*

**boom**
*prolonged expansion in economic activity*

### Seasonal Fluctuations Affect Economic Activity

The determinants of cyclical fluctuations in the economy are the major thrust of the next several chapters, and some fluctuations in economic activity reflect seasonal patterns. Business activity, whether measured by production or by the sale of goods, tends to be high in the two months before the winter holidays and somewhat lower in the summer, when families often are on vacation. Within individual industries, of course, seasonal fluctuations in output are often extremely pronounced, agriculture being the best example.

Often, key economic statistics, such as unemployment rates, are seasonally adjusted, meaning that the numbers are modified to account for normal seasonal fluctuations. Thus, seasonally adjusted unemployment rates in summer months are below actual unemployment rates, because employment is normally high in the summer due to the inflow of school-aged workers into the labour force.

## Forecasting Cyclical Changes

The farmer and the aviator rely heavily on weather forecasters for information on climatic conditions in planning their activities. Similarly, businesses, government agencies, and, to a lesser extent, consumers rely on economic forecasts to learn of forthcoming developments in the business cycle. If it looks like the economy will continue in an expansionary phase, businesses might expand production to meet a perceived forthcoming need; if it looks like contraction is coming, perhaps they will be more cautious.

**Forecasting Models**   Using theoretical models, which will be discussed in later chapters, economists gather statistics on economic activity in the immediate past, including, for example, consumer expenditures, business inventories, the supply of money, governmental expenditures, and tax revenues. Using past historical relationships between these factors and the overall level of economic activity (which form the basis of economic theories), they formulate *econometric models.* Statistics from the immediate past are plugged into the model and forecasts are made. Because human behaviour changes and we cannot correctly make assumptions about certain future developments, our numbers are imperfect and our econometric models are not always accurate. Like the weather forecasts, although the econometric models are not perfect, they are helpful.

**leading economic indicators**

*factors that typically change before changes in economic activity*

**Leading Economic Indicators**   One less sophisticated but very useful forecasting tool is watching trends in **leading economic indicators**—factors that typically change before changes in economic activity. Statistics Canada has identified ten such leading indicators: furniture and appliance sales, other durable goods sales, length of the average workweek, new orders in manufacturing, shipments-to-inventory ratio, housing starts, business and personal services employment, index of stock prices, money supply, and the U.S. leading indicator. Statistics Canada combines all of these into a composite index of leading indicators. If the index rises sharply for two or three months, it is likely (but not certain) that increases in the overall level of activity will follow.

Although the leading economic indicators do provide a warning of a likely downturn, they do not provide accurate information on the depth or the duration of the downturn.

## Business *CONNECTION*

### REVISITING THE PRODUCTION POSSIBILITIES CURVE FROM A MACROECONOMIC PERSPECTIVE

Business owners and managers need simple tools to be able to read the economy and make decisions. Fortunately, one of the simplest and easily adapted tools available is the production possibilities curve (PPC) model. In an earlier chapter we discussed how the PPC helps us understand how individuals or firms think when confronted with scarce resources. Interestingly, it can also be applied from a macroeconomic perspective. We'll see the same concepts of scarcity, choice, opportunity cost, growth, and capacity—but we'll also be able to visualize macroeconomic growth, unemployment, and inflation in the same model. And imagine that the goods we're making with this macroeconomic PPC are consumer goods (goods and services provided in the consumer market) on one axis of the model or capital goods (goods and services provided in the factors market) illustrated on the

other axis. The percentage of consumer and capital goods produced are both represented by points on the model.

First, let's consider the business cycle, which represents the different phases of the economy through time, and let's assume we're starting at the top of the cycle, where the economy is producing at its capacity. We have learned that we call this the "full employment" level of output.

Basically, an economy grows until it runs out of steam. The moment the growth cycle slows, firms start to see increases in their inventory levels and they respond by slowing production, perhaps reducing shifts or laying people off, and by reducing their inventory levels by reducing their prices. This period of contraction would be seen in the PPC by movement from the frontier, or limit, inward toward the origin. We sometimes experience this movement as a recession.

Once we are inside the curve, we are underemployed, meaning that labour, capital, and land are not being utilized at their capacity. Workers who are laid off and who want jobs will be willing to work for lower wages or to work for fewer hours at the same wages. Either way, the average wage decreases. At the same time, goods and services are discounted to clear inventory levels, and we begin to see evidence of a slowdown in the rate of inflation (disinflation), or even deflation. In the consumer and factors markets, average prices are either not increasing as much as they were, or are decreasing. So the PPC shows us contraction in negative growth levels, falling average prices, and higher rates of unemployment in labour, land, and capital.

As the economy bottoms out and we've experienced the sometimes painful outcomes of a recession, firms and individuals need to replace what they've done without, resulting in fully depleted inventory levels. Perhaps governments have injected funds into the economy in order to stimulate growth and get people and firms back to work. Either way, the economy starts to pick up steam, and at this point it reverses its inward slide and starts to expand. With expansion comes growth, as firms hire more workers and those workers start to purchase the very goods they've made. Growth in the economy creates even more good growth as the incomes and wealth are shared between firms and households. People are finding it easier to get jobs, so the unemployment rate drops.

As the economy edges toward full employment, times are good and individuals and firms experience increases in wages and prices. Those who have work (which is most people) will not move to other jobs unless the pay is higher than they're presently getting. (Why would you risk working for a new company without an increase in pay?) As wages increase, firms raise the price of their goods and services to maintain the desired level of profits. This increase in prices is inflation.

Now imagine that we're at the edge of the PPC or at macroeconomic full employment in the short term. Why in the short term? Because this is all that we can produce given our current state of resources (land, labour, and capital). But because individuals and firms still desire more, we invest in additional land, labour, and capital to keep this engine moving, and both capital and labour increase their outputs as work is done beyond one or two shifts. The curve is therefore pushed out to greater levels of output, but this all takes time as new land is acquired, new machines purchased, and new labour is hired and trained. Then we are growing in the long term.

As people are pushed to their limits, they start to value leisure more than the bigger paycheques they're getting, and they aren't working as hard. At the same time, consumers overextend themselves, and the buying frenzy is at its maximum. At this point, governments or monetary institutions decide to slow the growth, as it is too much. They might do this by increasing taxes, lowering government spending, increasing interest rates, or reducing the money supply. This intervention begins to slow the economy a bit, or sometimes the party's over, and the markets recognize that we've had it too good for too long and both firms and individuals purchase less. The outcome is weaker growth than in the previous period. This is when inventory levels start to increase, production slows, and we start the cycle all over again.

All of the phases of the business cycle are demonstrated with the macroeconomic PPC — we see growth (as we recover from a recession) as well as growth as we push beyond the current level of capacity. With that growth, we're seeing virtually no, or very low, inflation at the innermost point of the curve, but inflation starts with that growth and becomes its highest as we approach capacity. We also see unemployment levels increase at the start of a recession, and then reverse as we start to grow again, hitting full employment (and higher rates of inflation) at the edge of the curve. We can also see how governments intervene when we're either slowing too quickly or growing too fast.

Who would have thought that the PPC could show us all of that in one model!

1. Demonstrate on the PPC model how a government program that targets a certain industry or a certain region can increase the PPC? Illustrate on the model how both the consumer and the factors markets benefit, regardless of what sector gets the most investment.

2. People often state that governments should not intervene in an economy. Can you demonstrate, using the model, why such intervention might not be best for an economy as a whole?

3. What do you think would happen if large amounts of automation and artificial intelligence were to have a significant impact on our economy. Demonstrate your thoughts using the PPC model.

## SECTION CHECK

- Business cycles (or economic fluctuations) are short-term fluctuations in the amount of economic activity relative to the long-term growth trend in output.
- The four phases of a business cycle are expansion, peak, contraction, and trough.
- Recessions occur during the contraction phase of a business cycle. Severe, long-term recessions are called *depressions,* while prolonged expansions are referred to as *booms.* The economy often goes through short-term contractions even during a long-term growth trend. Overall, the duration of any one business cycle is uncertain.

# For Your Review

### Section 5.1

1. Visit the Statistics Canada website at www.statcan.gc.ca. After choosing your language, scroll down to the section entitled "Key indicators." Based on the most recent information, how is the Canadian economy doing in terms of the macroeconomic goals of maintaining prices, maintaining employment, and achieving a high rate of economic growth?

2. Numerous African nations have targeted food self-sufficiency as their primary economic goal. How can this fact coexist with the three primary economic goals discussed in the chapter?

### Section 5.2

3. What would be the labour force participation rate if

   a. The population = 200 million, the labour force = 160 million, and employment = 140 million?

   b. The population = 200 million, the labour force = 140 million, and employment = 120 million?

   c. Starting from the situation in (a), what would happen to the labour force participation rate if 30 million people lost their jobs and all of them exited the labour force?

   d. Starting from the situation in (a), what would happen to the labour force participation rate if employment rose from 140 to 150 million?

4. Answer the following questions about unemployment.

   a. If a country had an adult population (those 15 years of age and over) of 200 million and a labour force of 160 million, and 140 million people were employed, what would be its labour force participation rate and its unemployment rate?

   b. If 10 million new jobs were created in the country and it attracted into the labour force 20 million of the people who were previously not in the labour force, what would be its new labour force participation rate and its unemployment rate?

   c. Beginning from the situation in (a), if 10 million unemployed people became discouraged and stopped looking for work, what would be the country's new labour force participation rate and its unemployment rate?

   d. Beginning from the situation in (a), if 10 million current workers retired but their jobs were filled by others still in the labour force, what would be the country's new labour force participation rate and its unemployment rate?

5. Which of the following individuals would economists consider unemployed?

   a. Sam looked for work for several weeks, but has now given up his search and is going back to university.

   b. A 12-year-old wants to mow lawns for extra cash but is unable to find neighbours willing to hire her.

   c. A factory worker is temporarily laid off but expects to be called back to work soon.

   d. A receptionist who works only 20 hours per week would like to work 40 hours per week.

   e. A high-school graduate spends his days backpacking across the country rather than seeking work.

6. How could the official unemployment rate understate the "true" degree of unemployment? How could the official unemployment rate overstate the "true" degree of unemployment?

7. What would happen to the unemployment rate if a substantial number of unemployed people started going to school full time? What would happen to the size of the labour force?

## Section 5.3

8. Identify whether each of the following reflects structural, frictional, or cyclical unemployment.

   a. A real estate agent is laid off due to slow business after housing sales fall.

   b. An automotive worker is replaced by robotic equipment on the assembly line.

   c. A salesperson quits a job in Ontario and seeks a new career after moving to Alberta.

   d. An employee is fired for poor job performance and searches the want ads each day for work.

9. Which type of unemployment would be affected by the following changes? Would it go up or down?

   a. increased employment benefits

   b. a heavy snowfall in Saskatchewan

   c. more effective online job search

   d. a large, permanent decrease in the demand for coal

   e. more retraining of people to develop new skills

   f. a sharp fall in demand for goods and services in the economy

10. a. What is the relationship between the natural rate of unemployment and frictional, structural, and cyclical unemployment?

   b. What would happen to both unemployment and the natural rate of unemployment if

     i. cyclical unemployment increases.

     ii. frictional unemployment increases.

     iii. structural unemployment falls and cyclical unemployment rises by the same amount.

     iv. structural unemployment increases and cyclical unemployment decreases by a larger amount.

     v. frictional unemployment decreases and structural unemployment increases by the same amount.

11. Most economists consider Canada's current natural rate of unemployment to be around 6 percent.

   a. Suppose the actual rate of unemployment was 8 percent. What could be concluded about what types of unemployment are occurring?

   b. Suppose the actual rate of unemployment was 4 percent. What could be concluded about what types of unemployment are occurring?

12. Employment insurance benefits in many European countries tend to be both more generous and available for longer periods of time than those in Canada. What effect do you think these enhanced benefits might be having on the unemployment rate in those European countries? Why?

13. Why might frictional unemployment be higher in a period of plentiful jobs that is a period of overall low unemployment?

14. Why isn't it true that technological advances inevitably displace workers?

## Section 5.4

15. Answer the following questions about inflation.

    a. What would be the effect of unexpected inflation on each of the following?
       – retirees on fixed incomes
       – workers
       – debtors
       – creditors
       – shoe-leather costs
       – menu costs

    b. How would your answers change if the inflation was expected?

16. Answer the following questions about the nominal and real interest rates.

    a. What would be the real interest rate if the nominal interest rate was 14 percent and the inflation rate was 10 percent? If the nominal interest rate was 8 percent and the inflation rate was 1 percent?

    b. What would happen to the real interest rate if the nominal interest rate went from 9 to 15 percent when the inflation rate went from 4 to 10 percent? If the nominal interest rate went from 11 to 7 percent when the inflation rate went from 8 to 4 percent?

17. Calculate a price index for 2016, 2017, and 2018 using the following information about prices. Let the market basket consist of one pizza, two sodas, and three video rentals. Let the year 2016 be the base year (with an index value of 100).

| Year | Price of a Pizza | Price of a Soda | Price of a Video Rental |
|------|------------------|-----------------|-------------------------|
| 2016 | $ 9.00 | $0.50 | $2.00 |
| 2017 | 9.50 | 0.53 | 2.24 |
| 2018 | 10.00 | 0.65 | 2.90 |

How much inflation occurred between 2016 and 2017? Between 2016 and 2018? Between 2017 and 2018?

18. You borrow money at a fixed rate of interest to finance your university education. If the rate of inflation unexpectedly slows down between the time you take out the loan and the time you begin paying it back, is there a redistribution of income? What if you already expected the inflation rate to slow at the time you took out the loan? Explain.

19. Does anticipated inflation or unanticipated inflation discourage economic growth? Why?

## Blueprint Problem

The following table contains prices for items consumed by a typical college student over time.

| Year | Pizza/Slice | Energy Drink/Can | Internet |
|------|-------------|------------------|----------|
| 2016 | $4.25 | $2.75 | $45.00 |
| 2017 | 5.50 | 3.50 | 42.00 |
| 2018 | 5.00 | 4.25 | 38.00 |

Let the market basket consist of three slices of pizza, five energy drinks, and one Internet connection.

a. Based on the information presented above, calculate the price index for 2016, 2017, and 2018 if 2016 is designated as the base year.

b. How much inflation occurred during 2016 and 2017, and during 2017 and 2018?

## Blueprint Solution

The first step in determining a CPI-style index is to determine the cost of each market basket. Notice that the basket remains the same from year to year, only the prices change.

The next step is to determine the price index for each year. Recall the formula

$$CPI = \frac{\text{Cost of market basket in current year}}{\text{Cost of market basket in base year}} \times 100$$

Note that since the base year remains constant over the period of observation, the denominator in the formula does not change. Also, don't forget to multiply each index calculation by 100.

| Year | Market Basket Costs | Price Index | Inflation Rate |
|------|---------------------|-------------|----------------|
| 2016 | (3 × $4.25) + (5 × $2.75) + (1 × $45) = $71.50 | = ($71.50/$71.50) × 100 = 100 | |
| 2017 | = (3 × $5.50) + (5 × $3.50) + (1 × $42) = $76.00 | = ($76.00/$71.50) × 100 = 106.3 | = (106.3 − 100)/100 = 6.3% |
| 2018 | = (3 × $5.00) + (5 × $4.25) + (1 × $38) = $74.25 | = ($74.25/$71.50) × 100 = 103.8 | = (103.8 − 106.3)/106.3 = −2.3% |

Once price index values have been calculated for each year, inflation rates can be determined. Recall the formula

$$\text{Inflation rate} = \frac{CPI_1 - CPI_0}{CPI_0}$$

Unlike the price index calculations that use a static base year for comparison, inflation rates are typically calculated year on year.

**Special note:** When the price index—the measure of the general level of prices—declines as it did in 2017, this produces a negative inflation rate. This is referred to as *deflation*.

20. Say that the bundle of goods purchased by a typical consumer in the base year consisted of 20 litres of milk at a price of $1 per litre and 15 loaves of bread at a price of $2 per loaf. What would be the price index in a year in which

a. milk cost $2 per litre and bread cost $1 per loaf?

b. milk cost $3 per litre and bread cost $2 per loaf?

c. milk cost $2 per litre and bread cost $4 per loaf?

## Section 5.5

21. Suppose the hypothetical economy of Ecoland is characterized by the following economic data. Where along the business cycle would the economy of Ecoland be located?

| Variable | Value (%) | Trend |
|---|---|---|
| Unemployment rate | 8 | Decreasing |
| Natural rate of unemployment | 5 | — |
| Inflation rate | 1 | Increasing |
| Real gross domestic product (growth rate) | 2 | Increasing |

22. Evaluate the following statement regarding business cycles: "Typically, unemployment and inflation move in opposite directions as the economy travels through its business cycle."

23. Suppose a country experiences the following annual percentage changes in real GDP over a ten-year period.

| Year | 1 | 2 | 3 | 4 | 5 | 6 | 7 | 8 | 9 | 10 |
|---|---|---|---|---|---|---|---|---|---|---|
| % Δ real GDP | 2 | 3 | 5 | 3 | 1 | −2 | −3 | 1 | 2 | 3 |

a. Which year(s) best illustrate(s) the peak phase of the business cycle?

b. Which year(s) best illustrate(s) the recessionary (contractionary) phase of the business cycle?

c. Which year(s) best illustrate(s) the trough phase of the business cycle?

d. Which year(s) best illustrate(s) the expansionary phase of the business cycle?

# chapter 6

# Measuring Economic Performance

**section**

**6.1**

# National Income Accounting: Measuring Economic Performance

- Why do we measure our economy's performance?
- What is gross domestic product (GDP)?

## WHY DO WE MEASURE OUR ECONOMY'S PERFORMANCE?

There is a great desire to measure the success, or performance, of our economy. Are we getting "bigger" (and hopefully better) or "smaller" (and worse) over time? Aside from intellectual curiosity, the need to evaluate the magnitude of our economic performance is important to macroeconomic policymakers who want to know how well the economy is performing so that they can set goals and develop policy recommendations.

Measurement of the economy's performance is also important to private businesses because inaccurate measurement can lead to bad decision making. Traders in stocks and bonds are continually checking economic statistics—buying and selling in response to the latest economic data.

### National Income Accounting

To fulfill the desire for a reliable method of measuring economic performance, **national income accounting**—a uniform means of measuring economic performance—was born early in the twentieth century. The establishment of these accounting rules for economic performance was such an important accomplishment that one of the first Nobel Prizes in economics was given to the late Simon Kuznets, a pioneer of national income accounting in the United States.

**national income accounting**

*a uniform means of measuring economic performance*

Several measures of aggregate national income and output have been developed, the most important of which is gross domestic product (GDP). We will examine GDP and other indicators of national economic performance in detail later in this chapter.

## WHAT IS GROSS DOMESTIC PRODUCT (GDP)?

The measure of aggregate economic performance that receives the most attention in the popular media is **gross domestic product (GDP)**, which is defined as the value of all final goods and services produced in a country during a given period of time. By convention, that period of time is almost always one year. But let's examine the rest of this definition. What is meant by "value" and "final goods and services"?

### Measuring the Value of Goods and Services

Value is determined by the market prices at which goods and services sell. Underlying the calculations, then, are the various equilibrium prices and quantities for the multitude of goods and services produced. Recall that in microeconomics, we measured production in kilograms of wheat or quantity of cars purchased. However, when we measure GDP, we can't add kilograms of wheat with litres of gasoline. That would be very messy. Instead, we measure the value of the production of the goods and services in dollars.

### Final Goods and Services

The word "final" means that the good is ready for its designated ultimate use. Many goods and services are intermediate goods or services; that is, they are used in the production of other goods. For example, suppose Magna International produces auto parts that it sells to General Motors for use in making an automobile. If we counted the value of the parts used in making the car as well as the full value of the finished automobile in the GDP, we would be adding the value of auto parts twice, first in their raw intermediate form and second in their final form, the automobile. This type of error in accounting is referred to as **double counting**—adding the value of a good or service twice by mistakenly counting intermediate goods and services in GDP.

### Measuring GDP

Economic output can be calculated primarily in two ways: the expenditure approach and the income approach. Although these methods differ, their result, GDP, is the same, apart from minor "statistical discrepancies." In the following two sections, we will examine each of these approaches in turn.

### Only Current Production Is Counted in GDP

Only current, or new, production is counted in GDP. For example, if you bought a used 1995 Dodge Neon, it would *not* be counted in current GDP because it was already counted in the year that it was produced. It would be double counting to count it in the year it was produced and in the current period. Similarly, a house that was purchased this year, but built 20 years ago, would not be included in current GDP. In short, GDP does *not* include the value of used goods.

### Production, Income, and the Circular Flow Model

When we calculate GDP in the economy, we are measuring the value of total production—our total expenditures. However, we are also measuring the value of total income because every dollar of spending by some buyer

---

**gross domestic product (GDP)**

*the measure of economic performance based on the value of all final goods and services produced in a country during a given period of time*

**double counting**

*adding the value of a good or service twice by mistakenly counting intermediate goods and services in GDP*

**The paper used in this book is an intermediate good; it is the book, the final good, that is included in the GDP.**

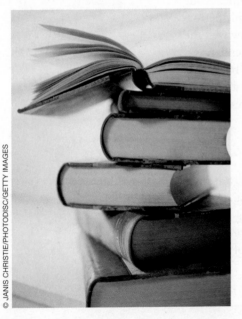

ends up being a dollar of income for some seller. In short, expenditures (spending) must equal income. And this is true whether it is a household, a firm, or a government that buys the good or service. The main point is that when we spend (the value of total expenditure) it ends up as someone's income (the value of total income). Buyers have sellers.

In Exhibit 1, we reintroduce the circular flow model to show the flow of money in the economy. For example, households use some of their income to buy domestic goods and services and some to buy foreign goods and services (imports). Households also use some of their income to pay taxes and invest in financial markets (company shares, bonds, saving accounts, and other financial assets). When income flows into the financial system as saving, it makes it possible for consumers, firms, and governments to borrow. This market for saving and borrowing is vital to a well-functioning economy.

Firms sell their goods and services to domestic and foreign consumers and foreign firms and governments. Firms use their factors of production (labour, land, capital, and entrepreneurship) to produce goods and services. Firms pay wages to workers, interest for the use of capital, and rent for land. Profits are the return to entrepreneurs for taking the risk of producing the goods and services. Wages, rent, interest, and profit comprise aggregate income in the economy. Governments provide transfer payments such as Employment Insurance payments. Whether we add up the aggregate expenditure on

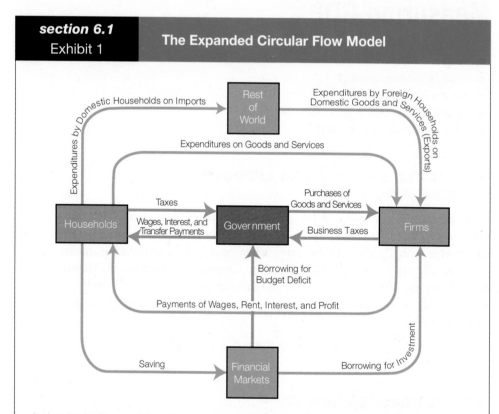

**section 6.1**
Exhibit 1

**The Expanded Circular Flow Model**

In the circular flow model of income and expenditures, we can measure GDP either by calculating the total value of expenditures or the total value of aggregate income because for the economy as a whole, expenditures must equal income. GDP equals the total amount spent by households in the market—to buy goods and services, to pay taxes, and to save. To produce goods and services, the firm uses the factors of production (labour, land, capital, and entrepreneurship), and it pays these factors wages, rent, interest, and profit. These payments are total income, which is also equal to GDP. Governments and firms borrow the funds that flow into the financial system from households.

final goods and services, or the value of aggregate income (wages, rent, interest, and profit) we get the same GDP. For an economy as a whole, expenditures and income are the same. Actually, while the two should be exactly the same, there may be a slight variation because of data issues.

## SECTION CHECK

- We measure our economy's status in order to see how its performance has changed over time. These economic measurements are important to government officials, private businesses, and investors.
- Gross domestic product (GDP) is the value of all final goods and services produced in a country during a given time period. The two different ways to measure GDP are the expenditure approach and the income approach.

## section 6.2

# The Expenditure Approach to Measuring GDP

- What is the expenditure approach to measuring GDP?
- What is consumption (*C*)?
- What is investment (*I*)?
- What are government purchases (*G*)?
- What are net exports (*X − M*)?

## WHAT IS THE EXPENDITURE APPROACH TO MEASURING GDP?

**expenditure approach**
*calculation of GDP by adding up how much market participants spend on final goods and services over a period of time*

One approach to measuring GDP is the **expenditure approach**. With this method, GDP is calculated by adding up how much market participants spend on final goods and services over a period of time. For convenience and for analytical purposes, economists usually categorize spending into four categories: consumption, identified symbolically by the letter *C;* investment, *I;* government purchases, *G;* and net exports, which equals exports (*X*) minus imports (*M*), or (*X − M*). Following the expenditure method, then

$$GDP = C + I + G + (X - M)$$

## WHAT IS CONSUMPTION (C)?

**consumption (C)**
*purchases of consumer goods and services by households*

**Consumption** refers to the purchase of consumer goods and services by households. For most of us, a large percentage of our income in a given year goes for consumer goods and services. The consumption category does not include purchases by business or government. As Exhibit 1 indicates, in 2017 consumption expenditures totalled $1242 billion. This figure was 57.9 percent of GDP.

Consumption spending, in turn, is usually broken down into four subcategories: nondurable goods, semi-durable goods, durable goods, and services.

| section 6.2 Exhibit 1 | 2017 Canadian GDP by Type of Spending | |
|---|---|---|
| **Category** | **Amount (billions of current dollars)** | **Percentage of GDP** |
| Gross domestic product | $2145 | |
| Consumption (*C*) | 1242 | 57.9% |
| Investment (*I*) | 422 | 19.7 |
| Government purchases (*G*) | 530 | 24.7 |
| Net exports of goods and services (*X – M*) | −49 | −2.3 |

Note: This exhibit is the result of source data and author calculations.

SOURCE: Statistics Canada, Table 380-0064—Gross domestic product, expenditure-based, annual (dollars unless otherwise noted). With author calculations.

## Goods

**Nondurable goods** include tangible consumer items that are typically consumed or used only once (or retain little value once used). Food and gasoline are examples, as are drugs, magazines, soap, and toys. Nearly everything purchased in a supermarket or drugstore is a nondurable good. In 2017, nondurable goods accounted for 23.5 percent of household final consumption expenditure.

**Semi-durable goods** include consumer items that can be used more than once and have an expected lifetime of around one year. Clothing and footwear are both common examples of semi-durable goods. In 2017, semi-durable goods accounted for nearly 7.0 percent of household final consumption expenditure.

**Durable goods** include those consumer goods that can be used repeatedly for more than one year. The most important single category of durable goods is automobiles and other consumer vehicles. Appliances, consumer electronics like cellphones, and furniture are also included in the durable goods category. On occasion, it is difficult to decide whether a good is durable, semi-durable, or nondurable, and the definitions are, therefore, somewhat arbitrary. In 2017, durable goods accounted for 13.4 percent of household final consumption expenditure.

The distinction between durables and nondurables is important because consumer buying behaviour is somewhat different for each of these categories of goods. In boom periods, when GDP is rising rapidly, expenditures on durables often increase dramatically, whereas in years of stagnant or falling GDP, sales of durable goods often plummet. By contrast, sales of nondurables like food tend to be more stable over time because purchases of such goods are more difficult to shift from one time period to another. You can "make do" with your car for another year, but not your lettuce.

## Services

Services are intangible items of value provided to consumers, as opposed to physical goods. Legal services, dental services, recreational services, automobile repair, haircuts, airplane transportation—all of these are services. In recent years, service expenditures have been growing faster than spending on goods; the share of household final consumption expenditure going for services reached 56.1 percent in 2017. As incomes have risen, service industries such as health, education, financial, and recreation have grown dramatically.

**nondurable goods**
*tangible consumer items that are typically consumed or used only once, such as food*

**semi-durable goods**
*consumer items that can be used more than once and have an expected lifetime of around one year, such as clothing*

**durable goods**
*consumer goods that can be used repeatedly for more than one year, such as automobiles*

## WHAT IS INVESTMENT (*I*)?

**investment (*I*)**
*the creation of capital goods to augment future production*

**Investment** (*I*), as used by economists, refers to the creation of capital goods to augment future production, that is, inputs like machines and tools whose purpose is to produce other goods. This definition of investment deviates from the popular use of that term. It is common for people to say that they invested in stocks, meaning that they have traded money for a piece of paper, called a stock certificate, that says they own a share in some company. Such transactions are not investment as defined by economists (i.e., an increase in capital goods), even though they might provide the enterprises selling the shares with the resources for new capital goods, which *would* be counted as investment by economists.

There are two categories of investment purchases measured in the expenditures approach: fixed investment and inventory investment.

### Fixed Investments

**fixed investments**
*all new spending on capital goods by producers*

**producer goods**
*capital goods that increase future production capabilities*

**Fixed investments** include all new spending on capital goods by producers—sometimes called **producer goods**—such as machinery, tools, and factory buildings. All of these goods increase future production capabilities. Residential construction is also included as an investment expenditure in GDP calculations. The construction of a house allows for a valuable consumer service—shelter—to be provided, so it is considered an investment. Residential construction is the only part of investment that is tied directly to household expenditure decisions.

### Inventory Investment

**inventory investment**
*all purchases by businesses that add to the stocks of goods kept by the firm to meet consumer demand*

**Inventory investment** includes all purchases by businesses that add to the stocks of goods kept by firms to meet customer demands. Every business needs inventory and, other things equal, the greater the inventory, the greater the amount of goods and services that can be sold to a consumer in the future. Thus, inventories are considered a form of investment. Consider a grocery store. If the store expands and increases the quantity and variety of goods on its shelves, future sales can rise. An increase in inventory, then, is presumed to increase the firm's future sales, and this is why we say it is an investment.

### Gross vs. Net Investment

The concept of investment that we have discussed so far—fixed investment plus inventory investment—is more accurately described as *gross investment*. The term *gross* refers to the fact that this measure of investment includes all forms of investment goods. That is, gross investment includes both investment goods that are new additions to the stock of capital as well as investment goods that are a replacement for plant and equipment worn out over the current period.

In contrast to gross investment, economists define *net investment* as the amount of investment that is new, the amount of investment that adds to the stock of capital in an economy. Specifically, net investment is defined as

$$\text{Net investment} = \text{Gross investment} - \text{Depreciation}$$

where depreciation (or capital consumption allowance) refers to the amount of capital that is used up over the year through the production of goods and services.

Usually the amount of gross investment is greater than the amount of depreciation. In this case, net investment is positive and the economy's capital stock is increasing. However, in cases where gross investment is less than depreciation, net investment becomes negative and an economy's capital stock declines.

## The Stability of Investment Expenditures

In recent years, investment expenditures have generally been around 20 percent of GDP. Investment spending is the most volatile category of GDP, however, and tends to fluctuate considerably with changing business conditions. When the economy is booming, investment purchases tend to increase dramatically. In downturns, the reverse happens. In addition, investment expenditure often increases in advance of an economic recovery, as firms look to position themselves for the return of economic demand. Again, the opposite happens in economic downturns. Because investment in capital goods is directly tied to a nation's future production capabilities, in those countries where expenditures on capital goods represent a smaller proportion of GDP, such as the United States, there is concern about GDP growth.

## WHAT ARE GOVERNMENT PURCHASES (G)?

Government purchases include the spending by federal, provincial/territorial, regional, and municipal governments on goods and services. For example, a government must pay the salaries of its employees, and it must also make payments to the private firms with which it contracts to provide various goods and services, such as highway construction companies and computer companies. All of these payments would be included in GDP. However, transfer payments (such as Employment Insurance benefits and Canada Pension Plan payments) are not included in government purchases because that spending does not go to purchase newly produced goods or services. Transfer payments are merely a transfer of income among that country's citizens (which is why such expenditures are called *transfer payments*). The government purchase proportion of GDP, at 24.7 percent, has grown over the last 50 years, in part because of rising spending on publicly funded health care.

## WHAT ARE NET EXPORTS (X – M)?

**Exports ($X$)** are the value of foreign expenditure on domestically produced goods and services. Consider a jar of maple syrup made in Quebec that is sold to a household in Norway. Since this item is not purchased in Canada, it would not be accounted for as part of Canada's *C, I,* or *G*. However, the fact that the maple syrup was made in Canada means that it should be included in the measure of Canadian production. The solution here is to account for its value as part of exports.

**Imports ($M$)** are the value of domestic expenditure on foreign-produced goods and services. For example, when you buy an Apple iPhone from your local telecommunications provider that is made in Shenzen, China, the value of your expenditure (being a Canadian citizen) is considered consumption (*C*). However, only a small fraction of the value of the iPhone represents expenditure on Canadian production (mostly related to the transportation and retailing of the phone in Canada). To accurately determine the total expenditure on Canadian products, the imported components of domestic expenditure need to be excluded. This is why imports are subtracted from Canada's measure of GDP.

The most common way of representing the impact of these foreign interactions on the domestic economy is by calculating **net exports ($X - M$)**, the value of total exports minus total imports.

In 2017, Canada's net exports were −$49 billion, or −2.2 percent of GDP. However, exports of goods and services themselves were $662 billion, or 30.9 percent of GDP. Likewise, imports of goods and services were $711 billion, or 33.1 percent of GDP. These numbers mean that about 31 percent of all Canadian production of goods and services is sold to foreigners, whereas about 33 percent of all Canadian expenditure is on

**exports (X)**
*the value of foreign expenditure on domestically produced goods and services*

**imports (M)**
*the value of domestic expenditure on foreign-produced goods and services*

**net exports (X – M)**
*the value of total exports minus total imports*

foreign-produced goods and services. These high proportions reflect the fact that Canada is very much an "open" economy; that is, the Canadian economy is highly dependent on foreign markets in terms of both buying and selling goods and services. In some years, the value of Canada's exports is greater than the value of its imports, net exports are a positive number, and Canada runs a trade surplus. However, in 2017, the value of imports exceeded the value of exports, net exports were a negative number, and Canada ran a trade deficit.

## Business *CONNECTION*

### HAS GDP RUN ITS TIME?

The measuring of GDP is much discussed in macro-economics. However, Herman Daly, a former senior economist at the World Bank commented, "Imagine if a corporation used GDP accounting to do its books: it would be adding all its income and expenses together to get a final number. Nobody would think that's a very good indication of how well the business is doing. The current national accounting system treats the earth as a business in liquidation" (Kubiszewski).*

Currently, GDP measures, using the expenditure approach, indicate four components: (1) the consumer spending of individuals and households; (2) the capital spending by businesses, mainly to expand their productive capacity and build up inventory levels; (3) the spending by various levels of government; and (4) the spending by those who bought goods and services produced by Canadians less the amounts Canadians spent to buy goods and services from abroad.

GDP measures do not take into account other components of our society that are equally important, such as household and volunteer work on the plus side, and social, environmental, and criminal costs on the debit side. We would all agree that including these intangible costs and benefits provides us with a more complete picture of what it is like to live in a particular society as opposed to just capturing the trade we do. The GPI (Genuine Progress Indicator) (Wikipedia)** is an alternative measure that captures this picture.

If GDP is accepted as a measure of wealth, or the standard of living of individuals in different countries, should it not also measure how well people live? We know that there are some societies in the world that are fairly poor but are very satisfied with their lives, and there are those that are very rich, yet live lives of stress and corruption. If we seek a more comprehensive view of national satisfaction, should we not therefore count the elements that contribute to sat-

isfaction but are not necessarily traded? For example, the abundance of housing, work, and education. Or the intangibles, such as civic engagement, freedom from tyranny, and a favourable level of work—life balance, trust, and safety. According to the *Better Life Index* compiled by the Organisation for Economic Co-operation and Development (OECD), "Canada ranks above the average in housing, subjective well-being, personal security, health status, social connections, environmental quality, jobs and earnings, education and skills" (OECD.org).[†] The *Better Life Index* provides a comprehensive overview of life in many countries, using alternative measures.

What does this mean for business? Well, GDP per capita is the most accepted index of a country's wealth, so when companies consider expansion, they look to where the best return on their investments might be realized, and that is generally where the highest per capita GDP exists. But in the future, this approach may actually limit a corporation's perspective and it might miss out on opportunities because what they're measuring is no longer as valid as it once was.

For example, let's assume that in the future more work is done by automation (capital) and less by labour. Let's also assume that artificial intelligence provides significantly higher levels of innovation than humans once did. If we're strictly measuring GDP, a lot of the work being done by capital is understated, simply because machines aren't paid and machines don't purchase goods and services. It's analogous to recognizing the work that a stay-at-home parent does but does not get paid for (thus it is not captured in GDP) versus paying a nanny to do the same work, which would be captured in GDP measures. Businesses will have to expand the elements they measure and also capture the values of what isn't measured to obtain a more accurate picture of a society's willingness and ability to pay for the goods and services offered. This requires a different type of analysis, using different data than is currently available.

If businesses concede that more advanced types of measurement are required, and if they believe that some of these societal components warrant weight in their decision-making process, then they have to accept, on some level,

---

*Ida Kubiszewski. 2014. "Beyond GDP: Are there better ways to measure well-being?" Australian National University, Newsroom, http://www.anu .edu.au/news/all-news/beyond-gdp-are-there-better-ways-to-measure-well-being.

**Wikipedia. 2018. *Genuine Progress Indicator*, https://en.wikipedia.org/ wiki/Genuine_progress_indicatorhttps://en.wikipedia.org/wiki/Genuine_ progress_indicator.

---

[†]OECD *Better Life Index*. "Create Your Better Life Index," http://www .oecdbetterlifeindex.org/#/11111111111.

that the drive for profits has run its course and that there are other considerations, as well as profit, that sound business decisions should include. This is a controversial topic for business owners and managers, as the foundation and measurement of their success, both personally and from a corporate view, are presently based on growth and profits. It will be difficult to change mindsets, as well as the infrastructure and systems that are now in use, to measure things other than those we've become so ingrained to measure.

So where do we start? Perhaps at the top, by adapting different matrixes for GDP to give us a better understanding of how countries and populations are actually doing as the foundations of our economies change.

1. Opponents to capturing the value of household or volunteer work argue that, since no money changed hands, such work should not be recognized as transactions. Is this a valid argument, or what arguments can you make that would be counter to this view?

2. President Donald Trump is advocating for more "Buy American" and less involvement in free trade pacts. One of his key arguments is that under current measures, the United States consistently has trade deficits with other countries. On the other hand, Prime Minister Justin Trudeau argues that nations should capture the value of unpaid work. Are these views consistent or in competition with each other? In what ways?

3. Based on your understanding of the chapter material and the comments in this Business Connection feature, how will Canada's GDP be affected by the legalization of marijuana?

## SECTION CHECK

- The expenditure approach to measuring GDP involves adding up the purchases of final goods and services by market participants. Four categories of spending are used in the GDP calculation: consumption ($C$), investment ($I$), government purchases ($G$), and net exports ($X - M$).
- Consumption includes spending on nondurable consumer goods—tangible items that are usually consumed in a short period of time; semi-durable goods—items that are used for an intermediate period of time; durable consumer goods—longer-lived consumer goods and services—intangible items of value.
- Fixed investment includes all spending on capital goods, such as machinery, tools, and buildings. Inventory investment includes the net expenditures by businesses to increase their inventories.
- Purchases of goods and services are the only part of government spending included in GDP. Transfer payments are not included in these calculations because that spending is not a payment for a newly produced good or service.
- Net exports are calculated by subtracting total imports from total exports.

# The Income Approach to Measuring GDP

- What is the income approach to measuring GDP?
- What do personal income and disposable income measure?

## WHAT IS THE INCOME APPROACH TO MEASURING GDP?

In the last section, we outlined the expenditure approach to GDP calculation. There is, however, an alternative method called the *income approach*. The **income approach** is a calculation of GDP based on the summation of incomes received by the owners of resources used in the production of goods and services.

**income approach**
*calculation of GDP based on the summation of incomes received by the owners of resources used in the production of goods and services*

When someone makes an expenditure for a good or service, that spending creates income for someone else. For example, if you spend $10 on groceries at the local supermarket, your $10 of spending creates $10 in income for the grocery store owner. The owner, then, must buy more goods to stock her shelves as a consequence of your consumer purchases; in addition, she must pay her employees, her electricity bill, and so on. Consequently, much of the $10 spent by you will eventually end up in the hands of someone other than the grocer. The basic point, however, is that someone (one person or many) receives the $10 you spent, and that receipt of funds is called *income*. Therefore, by adding up all of the incomes received by producers of goods and services, we can also calculate the GDP, because output creates income of equal value.

## Factor Payments

**factor payments**

*wages (salaries), rent, interest payments, and profits paid to the owners of productive resources*

**Factor payments** are the wages (salaries), rent, interest payments, and profits paid to the owners of productive resources; that is, the incomes received by people providing goods and services. National income accountants distinguish between three main categories of payments: compensation of employees, net operating surplus: corporations, and net mixed income.

**employee compensation**

*all compensation paid to employees, including wages and salaries and the employers' social contributions*

**Employee compensation** is defined as all compensation paid to employees, including wages and salaries and the employers' social contributions. Wages and salaries include regular remuneration, bonuses, directors' fees, commissions, gratuities, income in kind, taxable allowances, retroactive wage payments, and stock options. Employers' social contributions include employer contributions to pensions, Workers' Compensation, and Employment Insurance.

**net operating surplus: corporations**

*the income of corporations and government business enterprises resulting from the production of goods and services*

**Net operating surplus: corporations** refers to the income of corporations and government business enterprises (a government business that is operated for profit, similar to that of a private business) resulting from the production of goods and services.

**net mixed income**

*the income of unincorporated businesses generated from the production of goods and services*

**Net mixed income** is the income of unincorporated businesses generated from the production of goods and services. While the majority of this amount would typically be considered profit, a significant proportion is received in the form of remuneration to the owner for labour services.

Exhibit 1 presents the income approach to measuring GDP. Compensation of employees—the payment for labour services—totalled $1084 billion or 50.5 percent of GDP. Net operating surplus: corporations—corporate profits before taxes, subsidies, and depreciation—totalled $274 billion, or 12.8 percent of GDP. Net mixed income—the earnings of farmers and proprietors from their own businesses before taxes, subsidies, and depreciation—totalled $188 billion, or 8.8 percent of GDP. The sum of these three categories of income is called **net domestic income at factor cost**, which totalled $1546 billion in 2017.

**net domestic income at factor cost**

*a measure of income earned by the owners of factors of production*

We have to make two adjustments to net domestic income at factor cost to arrive at GDP. Net domestic income is the cost of the factor payments, but GDP is the value of the output at market prices. Therefore, the first adjustment we have to make to net domestic income is to add indirect taxes and subtract subsidies. An indirect tax is a tax paid by consumers when they buy goods and services (such as provincial/territorial sales taxes, the GST, and excise taxes). Because of indirect taxes, the market price of a product bought by consumers (e.g., $1 plus 7 percent tax = $1.07) is greater than the factor payments to the owners of the resources who produced the good ($1). A subsidy is a payment by the government to producers (such as payments to airplane manufacturers or grain farmers). Because of subsidies, the market price of a product bought by consumers is less than the cost of the factor payments.

| section 6.3 Exhibit 1 | 2017 Canadian GDP by Type of Income | |
|---|---|---|
| **Category** | **Amount (billions of current dollars)** | **Percentage of GDP** |
| Gross domestic product | $2145 | |
| Compensation of employees | 1084 | 50.5% |
| Net operating surplus: Corporations | 274 | 12.8 |
| Net mixed income | 188 | 8.8 |
| Indirect taxes less subsidies | 242 | 11.3 |
| Depreciation | 357 | 16.6 |

Note: This exhibit is the result of source data and author calculations.

SOURCE: Statistics Canada, CANSIM Table 380-0063. Gross domestic product, income-based.

The second adjustment to net domestic income is to add depreciation (or capital consumption allowances). When firms purchase capital equipment, the cost of such goods must be allocated over the time that the capital equipment will be used, possibly 10 to 20 years for some types of equipment. The cost allocated, which is called *depreciation,* is an estimate of the amount of the equipment being used up each year in production. Depreciation is a cost of production and is included in the market value of output, but it is not part of any factor's income and is not included in net domestic income.

Adding indirect taxes less subsidies, $242 billion, and depreciation, $357 billion, to net domestic income at factor cost brings us to GDP.

## WHAT DO PERSONAL INCOME AND DISPOSABLE INCOME MEASURE?

Often, we are interested in the income people *receive* rather than the income they *earn,* because the income received reflects the total amount available for spending before taxes. **Personal income** measures the amount of income received by households (including transfer payments) before income taxes. **Disposable income** is the personal income available after taxes. Disposable income can be used by households in two ways: consumption or saving.

**personal income**
*the amount of income received by households before taxes*

**disposable income**
*the personal income available after taxes*

## SECTION CHECK

- The income approach to measuring GDP involves adding together the incomes received by the producers of goods and services. These payments to the owners of productive resources are also known as *factor payments.* The income approach to GDP adds together compensation of employees, net operating surplus: corporations, and net mixed income to get net domestic income at factor cost. Adding indirect taxes less subsidies and depreciation to net domestic income gives us GDP.
- Personal income measures the amount of income received by households (including transfer payments) before taxes. Disposable income is the personal income available after taxes.

# Issues with Calculating an Accurate GDP

- What is the primary problem with GDP in measuring output?
- How is real GDP calculated?
- What is real GDP per capita?

## WHAT ARE THE PROBLEMS WITH GDP IN MEASURING OUTPUT?

The primary problem in calculating accurate GDP statistics becomes evident when attempts are made to compare the GDP over time. Between 1971 and 1976, a period of relatively high inflation, GDP in Canada rose over 100 percent. What great progress! Unfortunately, however, the measure used in adding together the values of different products, the Canadian dollar, also changed in value over this time period. A dollar in 1976, for example, would certainly not buy as much as a dollar in 1971, because the *overall* price level for goods and services increased.

One solution to this problem would be to use physical units of output—which, unlike the Canadian dollar, don't change in value from year to year—as our measure of total economic activity. The major problem with this approach is that different products have different units of measurement. How do you add together tonnes of steel, bushels of wheat, kilowatts of electricity, litres of paint, cubic metres of natural gas, kilometres of air passenger travel, number of games of bowling, and number of magazines sold? In order to compare GDP values over time, a common or standardized unit of measure, which only money can provide, must be used in the calculations.

The dollar, then, is the measure of value that we can use to correct the inflation-induced distortion of the GDP. We must adjust for the changing purchasing power of the dollar by constructing a price index. As we discussed in Chapter 5, a price index attempts to provide a measure of the trend in prices paid for a certain bundle of goods and services over time. The price index can be used to deflate the nominal or current dollar GDP values to a real GDP expressed in dollars of constant purchasing power.

There are many different types of price indices. In Chapter 5, we calculated the Consumer Price Index (CPI), which measures the trend in the prices of certain goods and services purchased for consumption purposes. The CPI may be the most relevant price index to households trying to evaluate their changing financial position over time. Another price index, the **GDP deflator**, corrects GDP statistics for changing prices. The GDP deflator is a price index that measures the average level of prices of all final goods and services produced in the economy.

**GDP deflator**
*a price index that helps to measure the average price level of all final goods and services produced in the economy*

## HOW IS REAL GDP CALCULATED?

To correct the nominal or current dollar GDP values for inflation, the appropriate price index to use is the GDP deflator. Once the GDP deflator has been calculated, the actual procedure for adjusting nominal, or current dollar, GDP to get real GDP is not complicated. Remember, real GDP gives us a measure of GDP in constant dollars that have been corrected for inflation.

The formula for converting any year's nominal GDP into real GDP (in constant dollars) is as follows:

$$\text{Real GDP} = \frac{\text{Nominal GDP}}{\text{GDP deflator}} \times 100$$

Exhibit 1 presents data on nominal GDP, real GDP, and the GDP deflator for the Canadian economy for the 2000 to 2017 period. The base year for the GDP deflator is 2007 (2007 = 100), so real GDP is expressed in billions of 2007 dollars; therefore, the GDP deflator for 2017 of 115.57 means that prices were 15.57 percent higher in 2017 than they were in 2007. Now, in order to correct the 2017 nominal GDP, we take the nominal GDP figure for 2017, $2144.4 billion, and divide it by the GDP deflator, 115.57, which results in a quotient of $18.554 billion. We then multiply this number by 100, giving us $1855.4 billion, which is the 2017 GDP in 2007 dollars (i.e., 2017 real GDP, in terms of a 2007 base year). Or to correct the 2003 nominal GDP into real GDP, take the nominal GDP figure for 2003, $1250.3 billion and divide it by the GDP deflator (88.54), which results in a quotient of $14.121 billion. We then multiply this number by 100, giving us $1412.1 billion, which would be the 2003 GDP in 2007 dollars (i.e., 2003 real GDP, in terms of the 2007 base year).

Notice that nominal GDP (in current dollars) increased from $1102.4 billion in 2000 to $1652.9 billion in 2008, an increase of 49.9 percent. However, over the same time period, the GDP deflator rose from 83.31 to 104.00, an increase of 24.8 percent. This means that the average price level of all the final goods and services produced in the economy increased by almost 25 percent, meaning the economy experienced almost 25 percent inflation over this eight-year period. This inflation was one of the factors that

| section 6.4 Exhibit 1 | Nominal GDP, Real GDP, and the GDP Deflator | | |
|---|---|---|---|
| Year | Nominal GDP (billions of current dollars) | GDP Deflator (2007 = 100) | Real GDP (billions of 2007 dollars) |
| 2000 | $1102.4 | 83.31 | $1323.2 |
| 2001 | 1140.5 | 84.69 | 1346.6 |
| 2002 | 1189.5 | 85.75 | 1387.1 |
| 2003 | 1250.3 | 88.54 | 1412.1 |
| 2004 | 1331.2 | 91.44 | 1455.7 |
| 2005 | 1417.0 | 94.32 | 1502.3 |
| 2006 | 1492.2 | 96.79 | 1541.7 |
| 2007 | 1573.5 | 100.00 | 1573.5 |
| 2008 | 1652.9 | 104.00 | 1589.3 |
| 2009 | 1567.4 | 101.62 | 1542.4 |
| 2010 | 1662.1 | 104.54 | 1590.0 |
| 2011 | 1769.9 | 107.93 | 1639.9 |
| 2012 | 1822.8 | 109.25 | 1668.5 |
| 2013 | 1897.5 | 110.98 | 1709.8 |
| 2014 | 1990.2 | 113.17 | 1758.6 |
| 2015 | 1994.9 | 112.31 | 1776.3 |
| 2016 | 2035.5 | 113.00 | 1801.4 |
| 2017 | 2144.4 | 115.57 | 1855.4 |

SOURCE: Statistics Canada, Table 380-0064—Gross domestic product, expenditure-based, annual (dollars unless otherwise noted). Plus author calculations.

led to the growth in nominal (current dollar) GDP. The other factor was growth in real GDP, or the economy's actual physical production of final goods and services. As we can see, real GDP (measured in 2007 dollars) increased from $1323.2 billion in 2000 to $1589.3 billion in 2008, an increase of 20.1 percent. This is the economy's "real" economic growth.

Finally, notice that during the years after the base year (2007), real GDP is less than nominal GDP. This means that the price level has risen since 2007 (2009 being an exception), lowering the purchasing power of the dollar. Prior to 2007, nominal GDP was less than real GDP; the purchasing power of the dollar was higher relative to the base year (2007). Also, notice that nominal GDP rises more rapidly than real GDP because inflation is included in the nominal GDP figures. When there is inflation, the adjustment of nominal (current dollar) GDP to real GDP (measured in constant dollars) will reduce the growth in GDP suggested by the nominal GDP figures. Thus, it is important when comparing GDP over time that we use real GDP as our measure of the economy's production of final goods and services, as this measure corrects nominal GDP for the distortions caused by inflation.

## Real GDP Has Not Always Been Less than Nominal GDP

In modern times, inflation has been prevalent. For many readers of this book, the price level (as measured by the Consumer Price Index) has risen in every year of their lifetime, because the last year with a negative price level was 1953. Therefore, the adjustment of nominal (money) GDP to real GDP will tend to reduce the growth in GDP suggested by nominal GDP figures. Given the distortions introduced by inflation, most news reports about GDP today speak of real GDP changes, although this distinction is not always made explicit.

### WHAT IS REAL GDP PER CAPITA?

**real gross domestic product per capita**
*real output of goods and services per person*

The measure of economic well-being, or standard of living, most often used is **real gross domestic product per capita**—real output of goods and services per person. We use a measure of real GDP for reasons already cited. To calculate real GDP per capita, we divide the real GDP by the total population to get the value of real output of final goods and services per person. *Ceteris paribus,* people prefer more goods to fewer, so a higher GDP per capita would seemingly make people better off, improving their standard of living. Economic growth, then, is usually considered to have occurred anytime the real GDP per capita has risen. In Exhibit 2, we see that in Canada, the real GDP per capita more than doubled between 1968 and 2012. However, the growth in real GDP per capita was not steady, as seen by the shaded areas that represent recessions in Exhibit 2. Falling real GDP per capita can bring on many human hardships, such as rising unemployment, lower profits, stock market losses, and bankruptcies. For example, the prolonged stagnation of the Canadian economy in the early 1990s saw real GDP per capita decline for three consecutive years. It took until 1994 for Canadians to enjoy the same level of real GDP per capita that they had enjoyed in 1989. In contrast, the relatively short economic downturn Canada experienced in 2008 resulted in two consecutive years of declining real GDP per capita. In this instance, Canadians had to wait only until 2011 for their real GDP per capita to return to the level it was at in 2007.

Because one purpose of using GDP is to relate output to human desires, we need to adjust for population change. If we do not take population growth into account, we can

**section 6.4**
Exhibit 2

**Canadian Real Gross Domestic Product per Capita, 1968–2017**

SOURCES: Nominal and real GDP data: Statistics Canada, Table 380-0064—Gross domestic product, expenditure-based, annual (dollars unless otherwise noted); population data: Statistics Canada, Table 051-0005—Estimates of population, Canada, provinces and territories, annual (persons).

be misled by changes in real GDP values. For example, in some less-developed countries in some time periods, real GDP has risen by perhaps 2 percent a year but the population has grown just as fast. In these cases, the real output of goods and services per person has remained virtually unchanged, but this would not be apparent in an examination of real GDP trends alone.

While real GDP per capita is therefore a superior indicator of how well-off individuals are in a given economy, as compared to just real GDP alone, it is important to recognize that it does not say anything about the distribution of output and income. For example, a country could have extraordinary growth in per capita output and yet the poor might experience little or no improvement in their standard of living. That is, it is possible that income group would make little or no gain.

## SECTION CHECK

- It is difficult to compare nominal GDP over time because of the changing value of money over time.
- The GDP deflator is a price index that measures the average level of prices of all final goods and services produced in the economy. It is used to convert nominal measures of GDP into equivalent real measures of GDP.
- Per capita real GDP is the real output of goods and services per person. In some cases, real GDP may increase but per capita real GDP may actually drop as a result of population growth.

# Problems with GDP as a Measure of Economic Welfare

● What are some of the deficiencies of GDP as a measure of economic welfare?

## WHAT ARE SOME OF THE DEFICIENCIES OF GDP AS A MEASURE OF ECONOMIC WELFARE?

As we noted earlier, real GDP is often used as a measure of the economic welfare of a nation. The accuracy of this measure for that purpose is, however, questionable because several important factors are excluded from its calculations. These factors include nonmarket transactions, the underground economy, leisure, externalities, and the quality of the goods purchased.

### Nonmarket Transactions

**Are her household production efforts included in GDP? If a family hires someone to clean the house, provide child care, mow the lawn, or cook, this is included in GDP; when members of the household provide these services, it is not. Neglecting household production in GDP distorts measurements of economic growth and leads to potential policy problems. Is it time to include household activities in GDP? An estimate of the value of these services could be obtained by calculating the cost to buy these services in the marketplace.**

Nonmarket transactions include the provision of goods and services outside of traditional markets for which no money is exchanged. We simply do not have reliable enough information on this output to include it in the GDP. The most important single nonmarket transaction omitted from the GDP is the work of housewives (or househusbands). These services are not sold in any market, so they are not entered into the GDP, but they are nonetheless performed. For example, if a single woman hires a tax accountant, those payments enter into the calculation of GDP. Suppose, though, that the woman marries her tax accountant. Now the woman no longer pays her husband for his accounting services. Reported GDP falls after the marriage, although output does not change.

In less-developed countries, where a significant amount of food and clothing output is produced in the home, the failure to include nonmarket economic activity in GDP is a serious deficiency. Even in Canada, homemade meals and clothing, housework, and the vegetables and flowers produced in home gardens are excluded, even though they clearly represent an output of goods and services.

### The Underground Economy

It is impossible to know for sure the magnitude of the underground economy, which includes unreported income from both legal and illegal sources. For example, illegal drug dealing and prostitution are not included in the GDP, leading to underreporting of an unknown dimension. The reason these activities are excluded, however, has nothing to do with the morality of the services performed, but rather results from the fact that the payments made for these services are not reported to governmental authorities. Likewise, cash payments made to employees "under the table" slip through the GDP net. The estimates of the size of the underground economy

MIXA next/Thinkstock

vary considerably. For example, one figure published by Statistics Canada estimated an upper limit for total underground activity in Canada of $35 billion for 2009. It also appears that a good portion of this unreported income comes from legal sources, such as self-employment.

## Measuring the Value of Leisure

The value that individuals place on leisure is omitted in calculating GDP. Many people could probably get part-time jobs if they wanted to, earning some additional money by working in the evening or on weekends. Yet they choose not to do so. Why? The opportunity cost is too high—they would have to forgo some leisure. If people work on Saturday nights, they cannot visit their friends, go to parties, see concerts, watch television, or go to the movies. The opportunity cost of the leisure is the income forgone by not working. For example, if people start taking more three-day weekends, GDP will surely fall, but can we necessarily say that the standard of living will fall? GDP will fall but economic well-being may rise.

Leisure, then, has a positive value that does not show up in the GDP accounts. To put leisure in the proper perspective, ask yourself if you would rather live in Country A, which has a per capita GDP of $25 000 a year and a 30-hour workweek, or Country B, with a $25 000 per capita GDP and a 50-hour workweek. Most would choose Country A. The problem that this omission in GDP poses can be fairly significant in international comparisons, or when one looks at one nation over time.

## GDP and Externalities

Economists have observed that side effects can accompany the production of some goods and services. These additional impacts (in the form of either benefits or costs) are referred to as *externalities*. As a result of these positive and negative externalities, the equilibrium prices of goods and services—the figures used in GDP calculations—do not reflect their true value to society (unless the externality has been internalized). For example, if a steel mill produces 100 000 more tonnes of steel, GDP increases; GDP does not, however, decrease to reflect damages from the air pollution that results from the production of that additional steel. Likewise, additional production of a vaccine would be reflected in the GDP, but the positive benefit to members of society—other than the purchaser—would not be included in the calculation. In other words, while GDP measures the goods and services produced, it does not adequately measure the "goods" and "bads" that result from the production processes.

In addition to the inability of GDP calculations to properly address the existence of externalities, there is the issue of sustainability. GDP is a measure of historical economic activity, not necessarily a projection of an economy's ability to sustain economic growth in the future. An economy that has been able to achieve GDP growth through unsustainable treatment of natural resources and misallocated investment would appear to be no different (in terms of its value of GDP) from an economy that accomplished its GDP growth through thoughtful natural resource management and investment strategies with a long-term planning horizon.

## Quality of Goods

GDP calculations can also miss important improvements in the *quality* of goods and services. For example, there is a huge difference between the quality of a computer bought today and one that was bought ten years ago, but it will not lead to an increase in measured GDP. The same is true of many goods, from cellular phones to automobiles to medical care.

## DEBATE

### SHOULD WE SWITCH TO ANOTHER MEANS OF MEASURING MACROECONOMIC PERFORMANCE THAT CAPTURES A MORE COMPREHENSIVE VIEW OF ECONOMIC WELL-BEING?

Just days before the turn of the twenty-first century, the U.S. Department of Commerce declared GDP as "one of the great inventions of the 20th century" (Landefeld).* The inspiration to use GDP to measure economic growth came about from the work of Simon Kuznets, an economist at the U.S. National Bureau of Economic Research, as the effects of the Great Depression were paralyzing the world's economies. His idea was to encapsulate all of the economic production of individuals, firms, and governments in a single measurement that could then be used as a comparator from year to year, or from nation to nation.

From Kuznets' original idea, GDP gained formal and permanent status as a gold standard measurement used when the Bretton Woods Conference of 1944 established the World Bank and the International Monetary Fund. Since that time virtually all of the countries in the world have used GDP as their foundational measure in assessing domestic economic performance.

### For:

As a well-established system for measuring a country's economy, GDP provides a comprehensive and historical comparison of its own economic performance. In addition, it also provides a means to compare itself to other countries that might be doing better or worse than itself, and to seek out reasons why and develop changes when deemed necessary. GDP provides reliable, well-tested indicators that are mostly objective in nature, as it measures transactions between the various stakeholders in an economy. The objective nature of the data comes from the market value that the goods were traded at—not a subjective value that might sometimes be employed when two different parties value the good or service differently.

Changing from GDP as an economy's measurement tool could prove to be a very expensive undertaking for any government and would develop a situation where the periods between transitions might become difficult or unreliable with which to compare data. Even if some countries decided to change from GDP measurement, there is no guarantee that others may follow (this would be a form of "network externality," where the usefulness of a product or service increases with the number of those using it).

### Against:

One of the major difficulties with GDP is that it doesn't capture all transactions—only those where money, or another financial instrument, is used. It does not capture the value of work that individuals or firms do for themselves, which is not traded (e.g., it does not capture the work of a stay-at-home parent but would capture that value if the family paid a nanny to do the work while they went off to their jobs). Similarly, it does not capture the work we do "in kind," such as volunteering, but if that work had to be paid for, it would be captured.

Since GDP captures only transactional situations, it would not capture the value that members of societies put on nontransactional attributes, such as political freedom, happiness, community, respect, trust, and the freedom to move or protest. There are limits to the GDP data, as well. For example, it does not measure per capita wealth well when there is a wide variance of income equality—a situation that is becoming a significant issue to many of the world's economies where the concentration of wealth is held by a few in a society. It is also vulnerable when higher rates of inflation are present—which makes comparisons to what policies may be best suited to combat these higher rates difficult and perhaps less effective.

GDP also doesn't account for costs to societies when choices are *not* undertaken (i.e., opportunity costs of decisions)—it measures only the outcomes of the various transactions occurring due to a course of action being taken. And because GDP is a transactional-based system, it reports more from a positive/fact-based perspective than a normative/subjective basis, which may provide significant benefit when comparing different economies.

Finally, situations such as disasters (wars, tsunamis, earthquakes) are represented in GDP as an economy rebuilds but it does not capture the more human costs and losses that might have a more devastating effect on the long-term health of a society.

### Questions:

1. How important to a society's general well-being is it to measure nontransactional items, such as political freedom, happiness, community, respect, trust, and the freedom to move or protest?
2. What ways could you suggest that GDP could be improved without moving away from the basic foundations of measurement it offers?
3. Explore some of the alternative ways to measure GDP (such as the OECD *Better Life Index* and others) and comment on whether you think they are better indicators of a society's well-being.

---

*J. Steven Landefeld, 2000, *Survey of Current Business*, "GDP: One of the Great Inventions of the 20th Century," https://apps.bea.gov/scb/account_articles/general/0100od/maintext.htm.

## Other Measures of Economic Well-Being

Even if we included some of these statistics that are difficult to measure, such as non-market transactions, the underground economy, leisure, externalities, and the quality of products, GDP would still not be a precise measure of economic well-being. Many other indices of well-being should be considered: life expectancies, infant mortality rates, education and environmental quality, levels of discrimination and fairness, health care, low crime rates, and minimum traffic congestion, to name just a few. One example of an index that attempts to incorporate these other indicators of well-being is the Human Development Index (HDI) first published by the United Nations Development Programme in 1990. The HDI, a composite measure of health, income, and education, has become the most widely cited and generally accepted measure of its kind. In closing, while GDP is solely a measure of economic production and not a measure of economic well-being, we must also remember that greater levels of GDP can lead to economic and social improvements because society would then be able to afford better education and health care and a cleaner, safer environment.

### SECTION CHECK

- Several factors make it difficult to use GDP as a welfare indicator, including nonmarket transactions, the underground economy, leisure, and externalities. Nonmarket transactions are the exchanges of goods and services that do not occur in traditional markets, so no money is exchanged. The underground economy is the unreported production and income that come from legal and illegal activities. The presence of positive and negative externalities also make it difficult to measure GDP accurately.

# For Your Review

## Section 6.1

1. Which of the following are included in Canadian GDP calculations?
   a. cleaning services performed by a cleaning company
   b. washing your own car
   c. drugs sold illegally on a local street corner
   d. prescription drugs manufactured in Canada and sold at a local pharmacy
   e. a rug woven by hand in Turkey
   f. air pollution that diminishes the quality of the air you breathe
   g. toxic waste cleanup performed by a local company
   h. car parts manufactured in Canada for assembly of a car in Mexico
   i. a purchase of 1000 shares in a Canadian-owned high-tech company
   j. a monthly Canada Pension Plan payment received by a retiree

2. Answer the following questions about GDP.

    a. What is the definition of GDP?

    b. Why does GDP measure only the final value of goods and services?

    c. Why does GDP measure only the value of goods and services produced within a country?

    d. How does GDP treat the sales of used goods?

    e. How does GDP treat sales of corporate shares from one shareholder to another?

3. Why do GDP statistics include real estate agents' commissions from selling existing homes and used-car dealers' profits from selling used cars, but not the value of existing homes or used cars when they are sold?

4. The expenditures on tires by the Ford Motor Company of Canada are not included directly in GDP statistics, whereas consumer expenditures on replacement tires are included. Why?

## Section 6.2

5. To which Canadian GDP expenditure category does each of the following correspond?

    a. Ministry of Transportation snow-clearing services

    b. automobiles exported to Europe

    c. a refrigerator

    d. a newly constructed four-bedroom house

    e. a restaurant meal

    f. additions to inventory at a furniture store

    g. purchases of new computers by Statistics Canada

    h. a new steel mill

6. Using any relevant information below, calculate GDP via the expenditure approach.

| | |
|---|---|
| Inventory investment | $ 50 billion |
| Fixed investment | 120 billion |
| Consumer durables | 420 billion |
| Consumer nondurables | 275 billion |
| Interest | 140 billion |
| Indirect business taxes | 45 billion |
| Government wages and salaries | 300 billion |
| Government purchases of goods and services | 110 billion |
| Imports | 80 billion |
| Exports | 40 billion |
| Consumer semi-durables | 185 billion |
| Profits | 320 billion |
| Consumer services | 600 billion |

7. Fill in the missing data for the following table (in millions).

| | |
|---|---:|
| Consumption | _____ |
| Consumption of durable goods | $1200 |
| Consumption of semi-durable goods | 1100 |
| Consumption of nondurable goods | 1800 |
| Consumption of services | 2400 |
| Investment | _____ |
| Fixed investment | 800 |
| Inventory investment | 600 |
| Government expenditures on goods and services | 1600 |
| Government transfer payments | 500 |
| Exports | 500 |
| Imports | 650 |
| Net exports | _____ |
| GDP | _____ |

8. Answer these questions about durable goods and GDP:

   a. Do consumer nondurable or durable goods tend to change more over the course of a business cycle?

   b. How are consumer durables like investments?

   c. Can either fixed investment or inventory be negative in a given year?

   d. Why isn't all of government spending part of GDP?

9. Why do you think economic forecasters focus so much on consumption purchases and their determinants?

## Section 6.3

10. What basic principle proves that the income approach to calculating GDP is valid?

11. Following is a list of national income figures for a given year. All figures are in millions. Using this data, determine GDP by both the expenditure and income approaches. The answer arrived at by each method should be the same.

| | |
|---|---:|
| Government current purchases of goods and services | $ 60 |
| Indirect taxes (less subsidies) | 35 |
| Compensation of employees | 210 |
| Corporation profits before taxes | 62 |
| Exports | 10 |
| Net mixed income | 21 |
| Gross investment | 100 |
| Undistributed corporate profits | 12 |
| Capital consumption allowances (depreciation) | 32 |
| Net investment | 68 |
| Imports | 20 |
| Personal consumption expenditures | 210 |

## Section 6.4

12. Nominal GDP in Nowhereland in 2017 and 2018 was as follows:

| Nominal GDP 2017 | Nominal GDP 2018 |
| --- | --- |
| $400 billion | $440 billion |

Can you say that the production of goods and services in Nowhereland increased between 2017 and 2018? Why or why not?

## Blueprint Problem

The following table contains partial National Income Accounting data for a hypothetical country,

| Year | Nominal GDP (in $billions) | GDP Deflator | Real GDP (in $billions) |
| --- | --- | --- | --- |
| 2012 |  | 93.8 | 956 |
| 2013 | 952 |  | 1000 |
| 2014 | 1005 | 97.5 |  |
| 2015 | 1158 |  | 1158 |
| 2016 |  | 101.5 | 1174 |
| 2017 | 1220 |  | 1171 |
| 2018 | 1321 | 106.7 |  |

a. Fill in the missing data in the above table.

b. What conclusion can be made regarding the economy's production of goods and services over the 2012 to 2018 time period?

## Blueprint Solution

a.

Use the following formula:

$$\text{Real GDP} = \left( \frac{\text{Nominal GDP}}{\text{GDP deflator}} \right) \times 100$$

Each year's amount of nominal GDP (current dollar output) has now been converted into real GDP (constant dollar output—output measured using 2015 prices).

| Year | Nominal GDP (in $millions) | GDP Deflator | Real GDP (in $millions) |
|------|---------------------------|--------------|-------------------------|
| 2012 | 897 | 93.8 | 956 |
| 2013 | 952 | 95.2 | 1000 |
| 2014 | 1005 | 97.5 | 1031 |
| 2015 | 1158 | 100 | 1158 |
| 2016 | 1192 | 101.5 | 1174 |
| 2017 | 1220 | 104.2 | 1171 |
| 2018 | 1321 | 106.7 | 1238 |

Use the following formula:

$$\text{Nominal GDP} = \left( \frac{\text{Real GDP} \times \text{GDP deflator}}{100} \right)$$

Each year's real GDP (constant dollar output—measured in 2015 prices) has now been converted into nominal GDP (current dollar output—measured in current prices).

Use the following formula:

$$\text{GDP deflator} = \left( \frac{\text{Nominal GDP}}{\text{Real GDP}} \right) \times 100$$

The GDP deflator is a price index (like the CPI). An increase in this value indicates a rise in the overall level of prices in the economy—that is, inflation.

b. When making any observation about the ability of an economy to produce goods and services over time, you must first look at the correct information. Real GDP has been adjusted to account for any distortions caused by price level changes. Therefore, it is each year's real GDP amount that must be interpreted as that year's true measure of production. With this distinction between nominal GDP and real GDP clear, we observe that real GDP increased from 2012 to 2016, then declined for 2017, returning to growth in 2018. Therefore we can conclude that our economy experienced economic growth for the majority of the time, with a short downturn in 2017.

It is important when comparing GDP over time that we use real GDP as our measure of the economy's production of final goods and services, as this measure corrects nominal GDP for the distortions caused by inflation.

13. Calculate real GDP for the years 2014 through 2018 using the following information:

| Year | Nominal GDP (in billions) | GDP Deflator | Real GDP |
|------|---------------------------|--------------|----------|
| 2014 | $720 | 100 | |
| 2015 | 750 | 102 | |
| 2016 | 800 | 110 | |
| 2017 | 900 | 114 | |
| 2018 | 960 | 120 | |

What was the real economic growth rate in 2018?

14. Fill in the missing data in the following table.

| Year | GDP Deflator | Nominal GDP (in billions) | Real GDP (in billions) |
|------|--------------|---------------------------|------------------------|
| 2014 | 90.9 | $ 700 | |
| 2015 | 100.0 | | $ 800 |
| 2016 | | 1000 | 800 |
| 2017 | 140.0 | 1400 | |
| 2018 | 150.0 | | 1200 |

15. The table below contains national income data for a hypothetical economy.

| Year | Nominal GDP (in millions ) | GDP Deflator | Real GDP (in millions) |
|------|----------------------------|--------------|------------------------|
| 2013 | $3237.0 | 93.3 | |
| 2014 | 3156.4 | | $3247.3 |
| 2015 | | 100 | 2995.3 |
| 2016 | 3376.2 | | 3271.5 |
| 2017 | 3517.6 | 101.4 | |
| 2018 | 3797.3 | | 3701.1 |

a. Fill in the missing data in the table.

b. Which year is the base year and what role does this year play in determining real GDP?

c. How would you describe the behaviour of production for this economy over the 2013 to 2018 time period?

16. Population and real GDP in Country A are as follows:

| Year | Population (in millions) | Real GDP (in millions) |
|------|--------------------------|------------------------|
| 1998 | 1.25 | $4000 |
| 2008 | 1.60 | 6750 |
| 2018 | 1.80 | 9000 |

Calculate real GDP per capita in 1998, 2008, and 2018. Does real output per person increase or decrease over time?

## Section 6.5

17. Answer these questions about GDP:
    a. Could next year's real GDP exceed next year's nominal GDP?
    b. Could real GDP grow at the same time that real GDP per capita falls?
    c. Could people's real consumption possibilities expand at the same time that real GDP per capita falls?
    d. How does changing the amount of leisure complicate comparisons of real well-being over time?

18. Evaluate the following statement: "Real GDP in the United States is higher than real GDP in Canada. Therefore, the standard of living in the United States must be higher than that in Canada."

19. As a matter of necessity, developing nations tend to rely more on custom and tradition, rather than market mechanisms, to make economic decisions. As a result, these economies tend to possess higher amounts of nonmarket activities than developed economies. How would the existence of these higher levels of nonmarket activities in developing nations impact real GDP comparisons between them and developed countries?

20. If we choose to decrease our hours worked because we value the additional leisure time more, will the resulting change in real GDP accurately reflect the change in our well-being? Why or why not?

# chapter
# 7

# Economic Growth in the Global Economy

# section
# 7.1

# Economic Growth

- How does economic growth differ from the business cycle?
- What is economic growth?
- What is the Rule of 70?

## HOW DOES ECONOMIC GROWTH DIFFER FROM THE BUSINESS CYCLE?

John Maynard Keynes, one of the most influential economic thinkers of all time, once said that "In the long run, we are all dead." Keynes said this because he was primarily concerned with explaining and reducing short-term fluctuations in the level of business activity. He wanted to smooth out the business cycle, largely because of the implications that cyclical fluctuations had for buyers and sellers in terms of unemployment and price instability. No one would deny that Keynes's concerns were important and legitimate.

At the same time, however, Keynes's flippant remark about the long run ignores the fact that human welfare is greatly influenced by long-term changes in a nation's capacity to produce goods and services. Emphasis on short-run economic fluctuations ignores the longer-term dynamic changes that affect output, leisure, real incomes, and lifestyles.

Economists distinguish between the short-run variations in economic activity that they call *business cycles* and long-run economic growth. In Chapter 5, we discussed the short-run economic fluctuations of business cycles. Here in Chapter 7, our focus will be on the long-run trend rate of growth—that is, economic growth. Exhibit 1 is provided to distinguish between short-run economic fluctuations and long-run economic growth.

What are the determinants of long-run economic growth? What are some of the consequences of rapid economic change? Why are some nations rich whereas others are poor? Does growth in output improve our economic welfare? These are a few questions that we need to explore.

## WHAT IS ECONOMIC GROWTH?

**Economic growth** refers to an upward trend in the real per capita output of goods and services (real GDP per capita). We focus on per capita because we want to isolate the effect of increased population on economic growth. That is, an increase in population, *ceteris paribus,* will lower the standard of living because more people will be sharing a fixed real GDP. For example, China's real GDP is much higher than less populated countries like Luxembourg and Switzerland. But Switzerland and Luxembourg both have real GDP per capita that is much higher than China's.

It is also important to note that our economic growth rate does not say anything about the distribution of output and income. For example, a country could have extraordinary growth in per capita output, yet the poor might experience little or no improvement in their standard of living. That is, it is possible that income group made little or no gain.

In Chapter 2, we introduced the production possibilities curve. Along the production possibilities curve, the economy is producing at its potential output. How much the economy will produce at its potential output, sometimes called its *natural rate of output,* depends on the quantity and quality of an economy's resources, including labour, capital (like factories, machinery, and tools), land (fish, lumber, and so on), and entrepreneurial activity. In addition, technology can increase the economy's production capabilities. As shown in Exhibit 2, improvements in and greater stocks of land, labour, capital, and entrepreneurial activity will shift the production possibilities curve outward. Another way of saying that economic growth has shifted the production possibilities curve outward is to say that it has increased potential output.

**economic growth**
*an upward trend in the real per capita output of goods and services*

| section 7.1 Exhibit 1 | Short-Run vs. Long-Run Economic Growth |
|---|---|

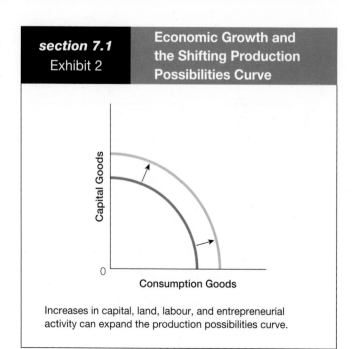

Short-run fluctuations in economic activity occur around the long-run trend rate of growth. It is this long-run trend rate that economists refer to when discussing economic growth.

## WHAT IS THE RULE OF 70?

If Nation A and Nation B start off with the same size of population and the same level of real GDP but grow at only slightly different rates over a long period of time, will it make much of a difference? Yes. In the first year or two, the differences will be small but even over a decade, the differences will be large and, after 50 to 100 years, the differences will be huge. The final impact will be a much higher standard of living in the nation with the greater economic growth, *ceteris paribus.*

A simple formula, called the *Rule of 70,* shows how long it will take a nation to double its output at various growth rates. If you take a nation's growth rate and divide it into 70, you will have the approximate time it will take to double the income level. For example, if a nation grows at 3.5 percent per year, then the economy will double every 20 years (70/3.5). However, if an economy grows at only 2 percent per year, then the economy will double every 35 years (70/2). And at a 1 percent annual

| section 7.1 Exhibit 2 | Economic Growth and the Shifting Production Possibilities Curve |
|---|---|

Increases in capital, land, labour, and entrepreneurial activity can expand the production possibilities curve.

growth rate, it will take 70 years to double income (70/1). So even a small change in the growth rate of a nation will have a large impact over a lengthy period.

In Exhibit 3, we see the growth in real GDP for Canada since 1968. The exhibit shows that Canadian real GDP per capita (measured in 2007 dollars) grew from $23 002.72 in 1968 to $50 615.46 in 2017. That is, Canadians today, on average, can purchase more than twice the amount of goods and services purchased nearly 50 years ago.

In Exhibit 4, we see a comparison of selected industrial countries. Because of differences in growth rates, some countries will become richer than others over time. With relatively slower economic growth, those countries that are rich now will not be the richest for very long. On the other hand, with even slight improvements in economic growth, the poorest countries now will not remain poor for long. Ireland, for example, once one of the poorest countries in western Europe, is now one of the richest. China and India have both experienced spectacular economic growth over the past 20 years. Because of this economic growth, much of the world is now poorer than these two heavily populated countries.

Because of past economic growth, the "richest" or "most-developed" countries today have many times the market output per person of the "poorest" or "least-developed" countries. Put differently, the most-developed countries produce and market more output per person per day than the least-developed countries do in a year. The international differences in income, output, and wealth are indeed striking and have caused a great deal of friction between developed and less-developed countries. Canada, the United States, Japan, and the nations of the European Union have had sizable increases in real output over the past two centuries, but even in 1800 most of these nations were better off in terms of real GDP per capita than impoverished countries such as Ethiopia, India, or Nepal are today.

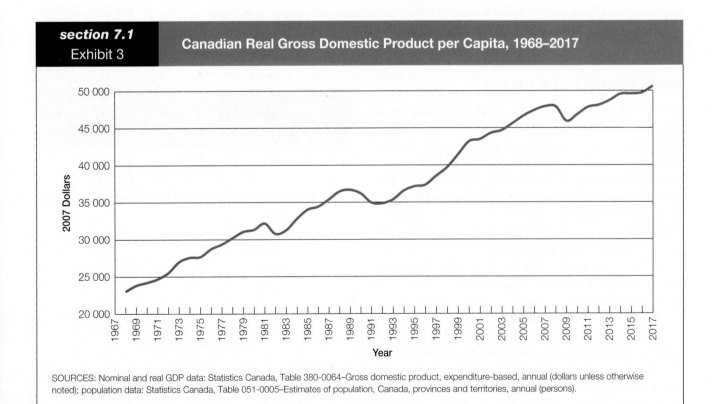

**section 7.1** Exhibit 3      **Canadian Real Gross Domestic Product per Capita, 1968–2017**

SOURCES: Nominal and real GDP data: Statistics Canada, Table 380-0064–Gross domestic product, expenditure-based, annual (dollars unless otherwise noted); population data: Statistics Canada, Table 051-0005–Estimates of population, Canada, provinces and territories, annual (persons).

| section 7.1 Exhibit 4 | Annual Growth Rates in Real GDP per Capita, Selected Countries |
|---|---|

| | Period Averages | |
|---|---|---|
| | **1996–2006** | **2007–17** |
| **Industrialized Economies** | | |
| Australia | 2.39% | 0.90% |
| Canada | 2.41 | 0.55 |
| France | 1.79 | 0.22 |
| Germany | 1.56 | 0.96 |
| Greece | 3.64 | –2.65 |
| Ireland | 5.50 | 3.51 |
| Italy | 1.28 | –0.91 |
| Japan | 0.81 | 0.59 |
| United Kingdom | 2.57 | 0.35 |
| United States | 2.24 | 0.63 |
| **Emerging Markets and Developing Economies** | | |
| Bangladesh | 3.84% | 5.17% |
| Brazil | 1.32 | 0.61 |
| Cameroon | 1.48 | 1.63 |
| China | 8.66 | 7.68 |
| Democratic Republic of the Congo | –2.70 | 2.97 |
| Haiti | –0.88 | 0.33 |
| India | 4.76 | 5.60 |
| Niger | 0.72 | 2.52 |
| Russia | 5.39 | 1.07 |
| South Africa | 2.07 | 0.28 |
| Thailand | 2.08 | 2.56 |

SOURCE: International Monetary Fund, World Economic Outlook Database, April 2018, http://www.imf.org/external/ns/cs.aspx?id=28; use the gross domestic product per capita, constant prices (national currency).

Both China and India have per capita real GDP levels that are far less than those found in Canada. The power of compound interest could well change this ranking in the future. The current rate of economic growth in these two countries will also change things in the future.

## SECTION CHECK

- *Economic growth* refers to the long-run trend rate of growth for an economy. *Business cycle* refers to the short-run fluctuation in economic activity around this trend rate of growth.
- Economic growth is usually measured by the annual percentage change in real output of goods and services per capita. Improvements in and greater stocks of land, labour, capital, and entrepreneurial activity will lead to greater economic growth and shift the production possibilities curve outward.
- According to the Rule of 70, if you take a nation's growth rate and divide it into 70, you have the approximate time it will take to double the income level.

# Determinants of Economic Growth

● What factors contribute to economic growth?

**productivity**
*the amount of goods and services a worker can produce per hour*

Will the standard of living in Canada rise, level off, or even decline over time? The answer depends on productivity growth. **Productivity** is the amount of goods and services a worker can produce per hour. Productivity is especially important because it determines a country's standard of living. For example, slow growth of capital investment can lead to lower labour productivity and, consequently, lower wages. On the other hand, increases in productivity and higher wages can occur as a result of carefully crafted economic policies, such as tax policies that stimulate investment or programs that encourage research and development.

The link between productivity and the standard of living can most easily be understood by recalling our circular flow model in Section 6.1. The circular flow model showed that aggregate expenditures are equal to aggregate income. In other words, the aggregate values of all final goods and services produced in the economy must equal the payments made to the factors of production—the wages and salaries paid to workers, the interest payment to capital, the profits, and so on. That is, the only way an economy can increase its rate of consumption in the long run is by increasing the amount it produces. But why are some countries so much better than others at producing goods and services? We will see the answer in this section as we examine the determinants of productivity—physical capital, quantity and quality of labour resources, natural resources, and technology.

## WHAT FACTORS CONTRIBUTE TO ECONOMIC GROWTH?

Four major factors contribute to growth in productivity: physical capital, human capital, natural resources, and technology. Today's workers generally produce more output than workers in the past. Of today's workers, those in some countries, like Canada, generally produce more output than do workers in most other countries. Workers with higher productivity usually have more physical capital like buildings and computers, are more educated than their counterparts, and have benefited from tremendous technological advancements.

Now that we know how productivity leads to long-run economic growth, let's look at the factors that lead to greater productivity.

### Physical Capital

Recall that physical capital includes goods such as tools, machinery, and factories that have already been produced and are now producing other goods and services. Combining workers with more capital makes workers more productive, so capital investment can lead to increases in labour productivity. Even in primitive economies, workers usually have some rudimentary tools to further their productive activity. Consider the farmer who needs to dig a ditch to improve drainage in his fields. If he used just his bare hands, it might take a lifetime to complete the job. If he used a shovel, he could dig the ditch in hours or days. But with a big earth-moving machine, he could do it in minutes. Most economists agree that capital formation has played a significant role in the economic development of nations. Physical capital increases labour productivity.

To better appreciate the impact of capital on labour consider the example of a small island economy that has only one industry, weaving. The following table shows production information for this economy in two different years.

| Year | Physical Capital | Labour Force | Labour Hours | Output |
|------|------------------|--------------|--------------|--------|
| 2016 | 20 looms | 20 workers | 2000 hours | 6000 rugs |
| 2017 | 30 looms | 20 workers | 2000 hours | 8000 rugs |

Based on this information, we can conclude the following characteristics about this economy:

| Year | Physical Capital per Worker | Labour Productivity |
|------|------------------------------|---------------------|
| 2016 | 1 loom per worker | 3 rugs per hour of labour |
| 2017 | 1.5 looms per worker | 4 rugs per hour of labour |

First, our simple economy had a capital labour ratio of 1 loom per worker in 2016 (20 looms/20 workers); this ratio increased to 1.5 looms per worker in 2017 (30 looms/20 workers). Second, in 2016, labour productivity in our island economy was 3 rugs per hour of labour (6000 rugs/2000 labour hours), this increased to 4 rugs per hour of labour in 2017 (8000 rugs/2000 labour hours).

The implication of this example is clear: The increase in physical capital per worker—as indicated by the higher capital labour ratio in 2017—is the driving force behind the increase in labour productivity. That is, when workers have larger quantities of capital assisting them in production, the more productive those workers tend to be.

**Per-Worker Production Function**   Since resources are scarce, in order to invest in new capital, society must sacrifice some current consumption. To save more now, we need to consume less now. Ultimately, this will allow society to consume more in the future. In Exhibit 1, we see how the amount of capital per worker influences the amount of output per worker. This positively sloped curve is called the *per-worker production function*. If the other determinants of output are held constant (human capital, natural resources, and technology), we see that moving up along the production function, when the quantity of capital per worker rises, so does the amount of output per worker, but at a diminishing rate—the curve eventually becomes flatter as more capital per worker is added. That is, capital is subject to diminishing marginal returns. If the economy has a very low level of capital, an extra unit of capital leads to a relatively large increase in output—a movement from point A to point B in Exhibit 1. If the economy already has a great deal of capital, an extra unit of capital leads to a relatively smaller increase in output—a movement from point C to point D in Exhibit 1.

Imagine that you owned a small company and you had ten employees and one computer. As you added more computers, output per worker rose, but only up to a point. What if you added 20 computers for your workforce of 10? Adding more computers (capital) still adds to output but by smaller and smaller additional amounts. This is what is called *diminishing marginal returns to capital*—in the long run, *ceteris paribus*, the benefits of a higher saving rate and additional capital stock become smaller and the rate of growth slows.

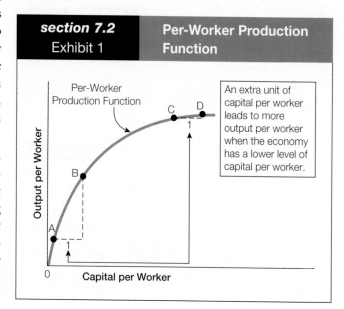

**section 7.2**
**Exhibit 1**

**Per-Worker Production Function**

Per-Worker Production Function

An extra unit of capital per worker leads to more output per worker when the economy has a lower level of capital per worker.

Output per Worker

Capital per Worker

Some economists believe diminishing marginal returns to capital can help explain the variation in growth rates between rich and poor countries. In poor countries, where there is little capital, small increases in capital investment can lead to relatively large increases in productivity. In rich countries, where workers already have large amounts of capital, increases in capital investment may have a very small additional effect on productivity. Economists call this the *catch-up effect*.

### Human Capital

We know that labour is needed in all forms of productive activity but, *ceteris paribus*, an increase in the quantity of labour inputs does not necessarily increase output per capita. For example, if the increase in the quantity of labour input is due to an increase in population, per capita growth might not occur because the increase in output could be offset by the increase in population. However, if a greater proportion of the population works (i.e., the labour force participation rate rises) or if workers put in longer hours, output per capita will increase—assuming that the additional work activity adds something to output.

When workers acquire qualitative improvements (learning new skills, for example), output increases. Workers with a large stock of human capital are more productive than those with small stocks of human capital. Indeed, it has become popular to view labour skills as human capital—the productive knowledge and skill that people receive from education and on-the-job training. Like physical capital, human capital must be produced, usually by means of teachers, apprenticeships, classrooms, libraries, computer labs, and time devoted to studying. Human capital may be more important than physical capital as a determinant of economic growth. It certainly can increase labour productivity. Human capital also includes improvements in health. Better health conditions allow workers to be more productive. Exhibit 2 shows Canadian labour productivity from 1997 to 2016. Measured in 2007 dollars per hour, Canadian labour productivity has increased each year (2008 and 2015 being the only two years when productivity declined), with an annual growth rate of 1.2 percent.

### Natural Resources

An abundance of natural resources, such as fertile soil, and other raw materials, such as timber and oil, can enhance output. Many scholars cite the abundance of natural resources in Canada as one reason for its historical success. Resources are, however, not the whole story; for example, Japan and Hong Kong have had tremendous economic success despite having relatively few natural resources. In addition, Kuwait and Saudi Arabia are rich because they sit on top of large pools of oil. On the other hand, Brazil has a large and varied natural resource base, yet its income per capita is relatively low compared with many developed countries. It appears that a natural resource base can affect the initial development process but sustained growth is influenced by other factors. However, most economists would agree that a limited resource base does pose an important obstacle to economic growth.

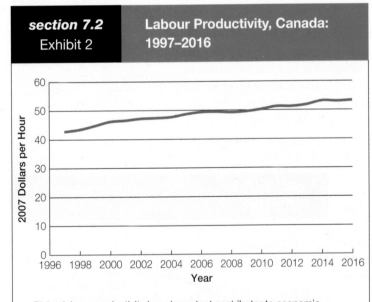

**section 7.2**
Exhibit 2

**Labour Productivity, Canada: 1997–2016**

Rising labour productivity is an important contributor to economic growth. The ability of Canadian labour to generate higher and higher rates of productivity has enabled the Canadian economy to achieve higher rates of economic growth. Together, these trends have had a positive impact on living standards in Canada.

SOURCE: Statistics Canada, Table 383-0033–Labour productivity and related measures by business sector industry and by non-commercial activity consistent with the industry accounts, provinces and territories, annual (jobs unless otherwise noted). Reproduced and distributed on an "as is" basis with the permission of Statistics Canada.

## Technology

Most economists believe that progress in technology drives productivity. It is technology that allows workers to produce more, even with the same amount of physical and human capital. Technological change can lead to better machinery and equipment, increases in capital, and better organization and production methods. Technological advances stem from human ingenuity and creativity in developing new ways of combining the factors of production to enhance the amount of output from a given quantity of resources. The process of technological advance involves invention and innovation. **Innovation** refers to the application of new knowledge that creates new products or improves existing products. For example, the invention and innovation of the combine machine in agriculture, the assembly line in manufacturing, and the railroad were important stimuli to economic growth. New technology, however, must be introduced into productive use by managers or entrepreneurs who must weigh the perceived estimates of benefits of the new technology against estimates of costs. So the entrepreneur is an important economic factor in the growth process.

© LAWRENCE LOWERY/PHOTODISC/GETTY IMAGES

Technological advance permits us to economize on one or more inputs used in the production process. It can permit savings of labour, such as when a new machine does the work of many workers. When this happens, technology is said to be embodied in capital and to be labour saving. Technology, however, can also save land (natural resource) or even capital. For example, nuclear fission has permitted us to build power plants that economize on the use of coal, a natural resource. The reduction in transportation time that accompanied the invention of the railroad allowed businesses to reduce the capital they needed for inventories. Because goods could be obtained more quickly, businesses could reduce the stock kept on their shelves.

Innovations can come in all sizes. Obviously, the semiconductor chip made a huge impact on productivity and growth, but so did the Post-it Note that was introduced in the early 1980s, the laptop computer, and bar-code scanners, which were first introduced in Walmart stores. We have also seen huge advances in communication (the Internet) and medicines.

In short, better methods of organization and production can lead to increases in labour productivity. When fewer workers are needed in a grocery store or a department store due to better methods of organization, or new machinery and equipment, labour productivity rises.

In Exhibit 3, we see that technological change can shift the per-worker production curve upward, producing more output per worker with the same amount of capital per worker. Technological change allows the economy to escape the full impact of diminishing marginal returns to capital. So, in the long run, *ceteris paribus*, an economy must experience technological advance in order to improve its standard of living and overcome the diminishing marginal returns to capital.

**Countries that do not keep up with technology will generally be unable to keep up their economic growth and standard of living. If a country is technologically backward, it will lose global competitiveness and often rely on a narrow range of exports that will eventually lose their profitability in the global economy. For example, a country that relies on exporting copper may lose its market as other countries around the world convert their phone and cable lines to fibre optics.**

**innovation**

*applications of new knowledge that create new products or improve existing products*

**section 7.2**
Exhibit 3

**Technological Change and the Per-Worker Production Function**

SECTION CHECK

SECTION CHECK

■ The factors that contribute to economic growth are the same factors that determine growth in productivity. They include physical capital, quantity and quality of labour, increased use of natural resources, and technology.

## section 7.3

# Public Policy and Economic Growth

● What policies can a nation pursue to increase economic growth?
● Can rates of economic growth between different economies converge?

## WHAT POLICIES CAN A NATION PURSUE TO INCREASE ECONOMIC GROWTH?

Economic growth means more than an increase in the real income (output) of the population. A number of other important changes accompany changes in output. Some have even claimed that economic growth stimulates political freedom or democracy, but the correlation here is far from conclusive. Although there are rich democratic societies and poor authoritarian ones, the opposite also holds. That is, some features of democracy, such as majority voting and special-interest groups, may actually be growth retarding. For example, if the majority decides to vote in large land reforms and wealth transfers, this will lead to higher taxes and market distortions that will reduce incentives for work, investment, and ultimately economic growth. In this section, we will investigate the major policies and institutional structures that help to promote economic growth.

### The Importance of Savings

One of the most important determinants of economic growth is the saving rate. In order to consume more in the future, we must save more now. Generally speaking, higher levels of saving will lead to higher rates of investment and capital formation and, therefore, to greater economic growth. Individuals can either consume or save their disposable income. If individuals choose to consume all of their disposable income, there will be nothing left for saving, which businesses could use for investment purposes to build new plants or replace worn-out or obsolete equipment. With little investment in capital stock, there will be little economic growth. Capital can also increase as a result of capital injections from abroad (foreign direct investments), but the role of national saving rates in economic growth is of particular importance. However, investment alone does not guarantee economic growth. Economic growth hinges on the quality and type of investment as well as on investments in human capital and improvements in technology.

### The Importance of Infrastructure

Infrastructure (e.g., highways, ports, bridges, power lines, airports, and information technology) is critical to economic coordination and activity. Some infrastructure is private and some is public. In the past several decades, the amount of government investment in Canadian infrastructure has fallen. Some economists argue that improvements in infrastructure could lead to higher productivity. Others argue that the causality runs in the other direction, that higher productivity leads to greater infrastructure. In addition, a special-interest problem concerns favoured jurisdictions with political clout that end up as the recipients of improved infrastructure—which may not be an efficient solution. Most would agree, however, that poor infrastructure is a major deterrent to economic growth.

## The Importance of Research and Development

Some scholars believe that the importance of research and development is understated. **Research and development (R&D)** are activities that are undertaken to create new products and processes that will lead to technological progress. The concept of R&D is broad indeed—it can include new products, management improvements, production innovations, or simply learning-by-doing. However, it is clear that investing in R&D and rewarding innovators with patents have paid big dividends in the past 50 to 60 years. Some would argue that even larger rewards for research and development would spur even more rapid economic growth. Some types of scientific research may have far-reaching benefits that cannot be captured by a private firm. Such a case presents a compelling argument for government support of basic research. GPS satellite systems in cars, for example, were originally designed for military purposes.

**research and development (R&D)**
*activities undertaken to create new products and processes that will lead to technological progress*

# Business *CONNECTION*

## SLOW(ER) GROWTH ECONOMY AHEAD

Over the past half-century, the economies of the developed world have hovered between 3 and 4 percent per annum. Put into perspective, those economies have doubled their output every generation, or every 20 years (World Bank).* It's no wonder that your parents and grandparents seemed to get ahead—perhaps it wasn't their industriousness but the very active economy. It appears that those days of heady prosperity are nearing an end, however, and we're moving toward a slower period that will affect both the micro and macro sides of our economy.

For Western economies, the biggest factor for slower growth is demographics—as the baby boomers age, retire, and die, there are fewer of them, and they were big spenders during their lives. At the same time, their offspring, the Gen Xers and Millennials, are having fewer children than their parents and grandparents did. This means that the number of consumers we had in the past is not being replenished. Compounding this, as the boomers approach retirement age, they are buying fewer big-ticket items and are not heavily in the market for things like cribs, linens, and tools. They're saving their money, as it has to last for 20 or 30 years of retirement.

Gen Xers and Millennials aren't buying much either, because there are fewer of them as a generation. Making it

worse, their real wages have been suppressed during the last few decades due to the oversupply of their elders in the workforce and the effects of the Great Recession. Structurally, our economy will experience slower growth rates for the foreseeable future. In addition to this, the continued introduction of automation and artificial intelligence into our economy will put further stress on people's incomes, their subsequent ability to spend, and by association, overall economic activity. These stresses will continue to grow unless we develop policies to address the problems of those who are displaced by these new technologies.

For business, one of the drivers of prosperity has been growth—producing more to meet the demand of the consumers. This has often meant not only growing the product lines to offer new goods and services, but also to produce greater quantities of those goods and services. In the past, by expanding growth and having the economies of scale that supported that growth, profits increased, which generated even higher levels of growth as those profits were reinvested into the economy. But that was yesterday. Today, higher profits driven by growth are harder to attain, and companies need to adjust their strategies in order to make the same profits. What changes in strategy should they consider?

If growth was a company's previous strategy, its options were either to grow the size of the market—increase the size of the pie—or try to take a larger slice of the pie. We'll likely see the "larger slice" strategy employed by larger companies

*World Bank, *GDP growth (annual %), 1961–2016*, https://data.worldbank.org/indicator/NY.GDP.MKTP.KD.ZG

*(continued)*

that have maintained lower costs by continued concentration of industries through mergers and acquisitions. Smaller to medium-sized companies will have to concentrate on building their business through marketing strategies of product, place, or promo—not price. This means changing product lines to ones that are unique and useful—it's not enough to just add features to existing products if customers aren't already buying them.

It also means that firms have to adapt to the "place" of purchase. By this we don't necessarily mean making the products widely available online. On the contrary, it means concentrating on the "experience" of the purchase as the deciding factor for the customer, as opposed to the product itself. It also means promoting the product—engaging in activities that communicate the product's features and benefits to the consumer and persuade the consumer to buy it.

Ideally, successful companies recognize they have to bring something truly different to the market, instead of trying to compete by building better versions of their existing products. This usually requires a significant investment in research and development—creative talent is far from inexpensive but is usually required if innovation is the company's goal.

Failure to recognize the changing dynamics in today's markets will ultimately lead to failure, often after disheartening experience with lower sales and higher costs in trying to compete, lower profits, disenchanted clientele, and a general feeling of defeat. Fortunately, Millennials often bring to their employers the innovative qualities that a modern economy needs, but in order to benefit from this energy, employers need to adapt more to the Millennial way. Millennials will not adapt to an outdated culture—they'll just leave. Which means trouble for older established firms.

1. Name some companies that you feel are adapting well to the changing marketplace, and provide examples of their product and/or activities that support your choices. Name some other companies that you feel might be heading for failure. Provide examples or observations that support your choice of these companies.

2. Do you think economies can change to expand expenditures and growth? Will this be achieved through organic changes, or will it require some government intervention? In what ways could government assist in achieving higher growth? What can corporations do?

3. What impact do you think automation and artificial intelligence will have on the economy other than affecting growth?

4. Are you optimistic or pessimistic about your future, and why?

---

**Free trade and a stable monetary environment are important to economic growth, but governance is important too. The government has to protect private property and individual rights and enforce contracts, otherwise globalization can lead to corruption and violence. Russians have high levels of education, but the failure of the legal system has led to a dismal economic performance.**

In addition, an important link exists between research and development and capital investment. As already noted, when capital depreciates over time, it is replaced with new equipment that embodies the latest technology. Consequently, R&D may work hand in hand with investment to improve growth and productivity. Lastly, there is the benefit of R&D to foreign countries to consider as they import goods and services from technologically advanced countries. Adoption or adaptation of some of these advances might make their firms more efficient.

## Importance of Property Rights and Political Stability

Economic growth rates tend to be higher in countries where the government enforces property rights. Property rights give owners the legal right to keep or sell their property—land, labour, or capital. In addition, intellectual property (IP) rights are the legal rights that result from intellectual activity in the industrial, scientific, literary, and artistic fields. IP rights protection can take many forms: patents, copyrights, and trademarks are some examples. Without property and IP rights, life would be a huge free-for-all, where people could take whatever they wanted. Economists call the government's ability to protect private property and IP rights and to enforce contracts the *rule of law*.

People living in developed countries take property and IP rights for granted, but those living in developing countries know the difficulties associated with a lack of property and IP rights. In most developed countries, property and IP rights are effectively protected by the government. However, in developing

Cayuwe Kulzer/iStockphoto.com

countries, such protection is not usually the case. If the government is not enforcing these rights, the private sector must respond in costly ways that stifle economic growth. For example, an oil company will not undertake the significant investment of setting up a drilling operation if it expects that the oil it extracts will be stolen. Nor will the company undertake an investment if it cannot receive at least some assurance that the buyer will fulfill its part of the contract.

The effective operation of the market system relies on both buyers and sellers being held accountable. An unreliable judiciary system means that entrepreneurs are often forced to rely on informal agreements that are difficult to enforce. As a result, they may have to pay bribes to get things done, and even then, they may not receive the promised services. Individuals sometimes have to obtain private security or pay organized crime for protection against crime and corruption.

Political instability represents another significant threat to property rights. If land owners and business owners are fearful of coups or takeovers from a new government, a government that might confiscate their property entirely, not only will domestic saving and investment be discouraged, but foreign investment and saving will also be negatively affected.

In short, if government does not adequately protect property rights, the incentive to invest will be hindered, and political instability, corruption, and lower rates of economic growth will be likely. However, it may very well be a two-way street. In the words of former U.N. Secretary-General Kofi Annan, "we will not enjoy development without security, or security without development."

## The Importance of Free Trade

Allowing free trade can also lead to greater output because of the principle of comparative advantage. Essentially, the principle of comparative advantage suggests that if two nations or individuals with different resource endowments and production capabilities specialize in producing a smaller amount of goods and services and engage in trade, both parties will benefit. Total output and consumption will rise. This will be discussed in greater detail in Chapter 14. However, it is important to note that for a country like Canada, which is a significantly open economy that trades considerably with the rest of the world, international trade has played a central role in its economic growth over the last half-century.

## The Importance of Education

Education, an investment in human capital, may be just as important as improvements in physical capital. At any given time, an individual has a choice between current work and investment activities like education that can increase future earning power. People accept reductions in current income to devote current effort to education and training. In turn, a certain return on the investment is expected, because in later years they will earn a higher wage rate (the amount of the increase depending on the nature of the education and training as well as individual natural ability). For example, in Canada, a person with a college or university degree can be expected to earn almost twice as much per year as a high-school graduate.

One argument for government subsidizing education is that this investment can increase the skill level of the population and raise the standard of living. However, even if the individual does not

**Better education is a relatively inexpensive method to enrich the lives of those in poorer countries. Education allows these countries to produce more advanced goods and services and enjoy the wealth created from trading in the global economy. Taiwan, India, and Korea are now all part of the high-tech global economy, but most of Africa, with the lowest levels of education, has been left behind.**

BIRUTE VIJEIKIENE/Shutterstock.com

benefit financially from increased education, society may benefit socially and in other respects from having its members highly educated. For example, more education may lead to lower crime rates, new ideas that may benefit the society at large, and more informed voters.

With economic growth, illiteracy rates fall and formal education grows. Improvements in literacy stimulate economic growth by reducing barriers to the flow of information; when information costs are high, ignorance often results in many resources flowing to or remaining in uses that are rather unproductive. Moreover, education imparts skills that are directly useful in raising labour productivity, whether it is mathematics taught to a sales clerk, engineering techniques taught to a college or university graduate, or just good ideas that facilitate production and design.

Many economists believe that the tremendous growth in East Asia (South Korea, Taiwan, Hong Kong, and Singapore) in the last half of the twentieth century was a result of good basic education for many of the countries' citizens. This reason was one of many factors that contributed to growth, including high rates of saving and a large increase in labour force participation.

However, in developing poor countries, the higher opportunity costs of education present an obstacle. Children in developing countries are an important part of the labour force starting at a young age. But children who are attending school cannot help in the field—planting, harvesting, fence building, and many other tasks that are so important in the rural areas of developing countries. A child's labour contribution to the family is far less important in a developed country. Thus, the higher opportunity cost of an education in developing countries is one of the reasons that school enrolments are lower.

Education may also be a consequence of economic growth, because as incomes rise, people's tendency to consume education increases. People increasingly look to education for more than the acquisition of immediately applicable skills. Education becomes a consumption good as well as a means of investing in human capital.

There are also a number of factors that can lead to slower economic growth. Countries that fail to enforce the rule of law, experience wars and revolutions, have poor education and health systems and low rates of saving and investment are not likely to grow very rapidly.

## CAN RATES OF ECONOMIC GROWTH BETWEEN DIFFERENT ECONOMIES CONVERGE?

Many economists believe that, holding other things equal, countries with lower real GDP per capita will grow faster than countries with higher real GDP per capita. However, other things, including infrastructure, the extent to which the rule of law is followed, and the level of education are not equal. Adjusting for such additional variables, there is a tendency for poorer countries to grow faster. This has certainly been true of South Korea, Taiwan, and Singapore, which have invested in technology and human resources, but many poor countries in Africa and Latin America continue to be poor. So, there is no guarantee that being poorer leads to greater economic growth.

What are some of the factors that impact the ability of developing nations to achieve economic growth? First, they can adopt existing technology from developed countries. Second, developed economies may be subject to diminishing marginal returns to capital—a concept we discussed earlier in the chapter. Third, population growth is higher in developing counties, leading to lower levels of per capita consumption for a given level of economic output. For example, in western Europe and Canada, population growth rates are currently roughly 1 percent per year, while in some of the poorer African countries, they can approach 3 percent per year or more. Finally, while technology is portable, the ability to use that technology is not. With low literacy rates and educational attainment, as in sub-Saharan African nations, countries can lack the human capital to adopt and use the new technology.

In summary then, the issue of economic growth in the developing world is both complex and conflicting—its difficulty evidenced by the sheer number of countries that struggle with finding a winning recipe for success.

---

## SECTION CHECK

- Generally speaking, greater economic growth is fostered by those policies and institutional structures that promote higher levels of saving, more research and development, better protection of private property rights, freer trade, and more education.
- While certain factors such as the ability to adopt existing technology would seem to allow developing nations to grow faster than developed nations, population growth and low literacy rates tend to have the opposite effect. Therefore, there seems to be no clear indication that rates of economic growth between economies will converge.

---

**section**
**7.4**

# Population and Economic Growth

- What is the effect of population growth on per capita economic growth?
- What is the Malthusian prediction?

## WHAT IS THE EFFECT OF POPULATION GROWTH ON PER CAPITA ECONOMIC GROWTH?

At the beginning of the English Industrial Revolution (c. 1750), the world's population was perhaps 700 million. It took 150 years (to 1900) for that population to slightly more than double to 1.6 billion. Just 64 years later (in 1964), it had doubled again to 3.2 billion.

After another 41 years (in 2005), the population doubled yet again to more than 6.4 billion. At the end of October 2011, the United Nations Population Fund announced that the world's population had reached 7 billion. According to United Nations estimates, world population should reach approximately 9 billion by 2050 and then level off. Most of this population growth will occur in developing countries—industrialized countries will see very little growth in population. Economic development occurred amid all of the past growth in population, but what role does population play in economic growth?

The effect of population growth on per capita economic growth is far from obvious. If population was to expand faster than output, per capita output would fall; population growth would inhibit growth. With a larger population, however, comes a larger labour force. Also, economies of large-scale production may exist in some forms of production, so larger markets associated with greater populations lead to more efficient-sized production units.

The general feeling, however, is that in many of the developing countries today, rapid population growth threatens the possibility of attaining sustained economic growth. These countries are predominantly agricultural with modest natural resources, especially land. The land–labour ratio is low. Why is population growth a threat in these countries? One answer was provided nearly two centuries ago by an English economist, the Reverend Thomas Malthus.

## WHAT IS THE MALTHUSIAN PREDICTION?

Malthus formulated a theoretical model that predicted that per capita economic growth would eventually become negative and that wages would ultimately reach equilibrium at a subsistence level, or just large enough to provide enough income to stay alive. To create this model, Malthus made three assumptions: (1) the economy was agricultural, with goods produced by two inputs, land and labour; (2) the supply of land was fixed; and (3) human sexual desires worked to increase population.

### The Law of Diminishing Returns

As population increases, the number of workers increases, and with greater labour inputs available, output also goes up. At some point, however, output will increase by diminishing amounts because of the law of diminishing returns, which states that if you add variable amounts of one input (in this case, labour) to fixed quantities of another input (in this case, land), output will rise but by diminishing amounts (because as the land–labour ratio falls, less land is available per worker). For example, a rapid growth in the labour force might make it more difficult to equip each worker with sufficient capital, and lower amounts of capital per worker lead to lower productivity and a lower real GDP per capita. In short, the increase in the one factor of production, labour, might cause the other factors of production to be spread too thinly.

### Avoiding Malthus's Prediction

Fortunately, Malthus's theory proved spectacularly wrong for much of the world. Although the law of diminishing returns is a valid concept, Malthus's other assumptions were unrealistic. The quantity or quality of tillable land is not completely fixed. Irrigation, fertilizer, and conservation techniques effectively increase arable land. More important, Malthus implicitly neglected the potential for technological advances and ignored the real possibility that improved technology, often embodied in capital, could overcome the impact of the law of diminishing returns.

Malthus did not envision a world of greater agricultural productivity through fertilizers, pesticides, and mechanization of farm equipment. A world where fewer farmers could produce more food. Furthermore, the Malthusian assumption that sexual desire would necessarily lead to population increase is not accurate. True, sexual desire will always be with us, but the number of births can be reduced by birth control techniques.

Alternatively, some economists believe that population growth can lead to greater economic growth. In some countries, a larger population may lead to more entrepreneurs, engineers, and scientists who will contribute to even greater economic growth through technological progress. Furthermore, a larger labour force is created by a larger population. A larger labour force can produce more goods and services. However, that does not necessarily mean a higher standard of living for the typical citizen, which requires that real output must grow faster than the population. One size does not fit all: Countries with small populations and countries with large populations can experience high standards of living. These factors turn Malthus's theory on its head; instead of population being the villain, it could actually turn out to be the hero.

### Economic Growth and Fertility

Economists have also found that as countries become richer, family sizes tend to become smaller. This has been the case in Canada, western Europe, and the United States. As a nation becomes richer, families have access to better medical care and do not require as many children to provide for them as they age. Another reason that birth rates fall as nations become richer is that, as women achieve better access to education and jobs, their opportunity costs of raising children rise and fertility rates fall. So one possible policy approach for developing countries struggling with an exploding population is to provide more equal treatment for women.

# DEBATE

## SHOULD SUSTAINABLE GROWTH BE THE GOAL OR MAXIMUM GROWTH?

Over the last century, our modern industrialized economies have attained levels of economic growth the world has never previously experienced. And since this period of long-term growth has endured within ranges of 3 to 4 percent per year, our economies have essentially doubled every generation.

For most of us, this has been the norm for all of our lives, and for those of our parents and grandparents. We've come to think that this long-term growth rate will remain the norm and that it is sustainable over the long term. But we'd be in for a surprise, because the average rate of economic growth for human beings since primitive hunter-gatherer societies – early/primitive social systems has been less than 0.5 percent per year. This means our standard of living barely changed every 200 years, and it wasn't until just over a thousand years ago that there was any significant change in growth rates since primitive days.

As we evolved into the modern beings that we are today, there were periods when our economic growth rates increased dramatically, but this was always due to significant changes in tools and technology. And during those periods, we could always benefit from growth, as the Earth and our economies always provided more than we consumed. But then, in the last half of the last century, we hit a wall and can no longer sustain unlimited or maximum growth—we are now confronted with the concept of sustainable growth.

Sustainability, as it is commonly defined, is meeting the needs of those who are present without compromising the ability of future generations to meet their needs. Ideally, for all economies, growth offers the benefits of rising wealth for all and higher standards of living for those living within the economy. Growth fuels the benefits we all enjoy as a complex, integrated society. Without growth, our standard of living would be compromised and we would have fewer benefits.

So, central to this debate is not whether growth is needed, but is it sustainable? Should we continue under the economic goals of maximizing growth, or should we reset and look at sustainable growth? The argument is set up under the premise that sustainable growth is preferable over maximum growth.

## For:

Just on a purely physical basis, maximum growth is unsustainable, as it requires the planet to provide unlimited physical resources for all societies. It also suggests that our populations are challenging the ability of the planet to feed itself. These environmental resources are not universally available to all, and as some resources are depleted in certain areas, it puts pressure on populations and governments to provide resources by other means. Sometimes those means are by war or forced possession, other times it might be by the movement of populations going to where the resources are.

Increasing growth puts a strain on what the planet can provide, and those who are often most affected are those who can least afford the costs associated with increasing scarcity. Poorer people pay a higher percentage of their limited incomes on acquiring the basics of life, whereas those who are more affluent can absorb the higher costs of scarcity.

The environmental aspects of growth have been manifested not only in the consumption of the available resources that the planet can provide, but also in the effects of the externalities of this rising consumption. As we moved into carbon-based fuels, we never imagined the harm that rising $CO_2$ levels would inflict on the planet, yet we're now faced with melting ice caps, rising tides, warmer and more severe weather, and the inability to respond to it all in a timely manner.

We are already seeing some of the rising costs of these outcomes as we observe some of the world's port cities experiencing the challenges and costs of keeping the sea at bay. These are costs that our economies never planned for, and the speed and magnitude in which they have to address these issues will put a damper on future growth rates.

While there are environmental limits to growth, so too are there limits to growth of employment. Increasing growth in a modern economy relies more on investment in capital and automation to replace the relatively higher costs of labour, but this automation may not benefit individuals or consumers, since it puts them out of work. As corporations have been driven to higher productive levels, it is often at the cost of the workers—the same people who are expected to purchase the goods and services that these companies make. When corporations transfer production from labour to capital, the net effect is to transfer the benefits of automation from the lower and middle economic classes to those who own capital, usually the upper-middle class and the wealthy.

There is an urgent need for sustainable growth, and this must be understood and accepted by the populations of the world before it is too late. Sustainability will not be determined by allocative efficiencies (how resources are allocated in a market economy), but should be a social decision based on ecological and productive limits. In other words, we may not be in the position to find the best or least-cost solution, but we need to act now.

This moves us away from the classic circular flow model of a market economy, where decisions are primarily made by individuals and firms, with governments (society) taking a supportive role, to one where governments take on a more proactive and significant role in the decisions that affect our economies. We will soon find that the marginal benefits of unbounded growth will eventually be offset by the marginal cost of consumption. Perhaps it's

*(continued)*

a decision to choose unbounded growth based on materialism versus the intrinsic happiness that sustainable growth may provide.

## Against:

Growth is the engine that fuels the market economy and the well-being of the populations. Compromising on growth ultimately means compromising on one's wealth and standard of living. Those who are aspiring to a better life for themselves and their families will have a hard time accepting a lower standard of living. The nobility and morality of work have been ingrained in us—the more work we do, the more we consume, and the higher reward (level of consumption) we expect. To accept otherwise is a refutation of our upbringing.

Sustainability is a fantasy. Not that it's not possible, but society won't allow us to get there. Humans are selfish and self-serving, which means they will almost always choose what's better for themselves than what is better for society as a whole. This again is the paradox that what is good for individuals is not necessarily good for the masses. It's not that we don't believe it is in our best interest to change—we generally do, but it's often the method of how we get there that proves to be the biggest challenge. Unfortunately, these are problems much bigger

than any one individual can take on and solve, perhaps even bigger than one individual can motivate a population to take on.

So as we find ourselves challenged in finding a solution to these problems, we find ourselves with bigger problems. This is not a situation where public policy will be successful: The most successful changes within society come from the power of consumer spending. If, and only if, consumers make the choice that cleaner air is preferable will they accept carbon tax as the cost of that clean air. But unfortunately, as history has shown, individuals usually choose individual well-being over that of society's well-being.

## Questions:

1. If we choose to measure growth differently than by GDP (since it captures only transactions), do you think it might make a difference in attaining sustainable growth?

2. Can you think of ways that you could convince individuals to reset their expectations and accept the lower levels of wealth that declining growth would bring?

3. Can sustainability be achieved politically, through policies and regulations? Do you see a way in which people would make different choices through an economic model?

## Developing Countries and Malthus's Prediction

Unfortunately, however, the Malthusian assumptions don't vary widely from reality for several developing countries. Some developing nations of the world are having substantial population increases, with a virtually fixed supply of land, slow capital growth, and few technological advances. For example, in some African nations, the population growth rate is 3 percent per year, whereas food output is growing at only 2 percent per year. In these cases, population growth causes a negative effect on per capita output because the added output derived from having more workers on the land is small.

In fact, some developing countries have tried to reduce the rate of population growth to achieve greater economic growth per capita and higher standards of living. For example, China tried to reduce its population growth rate through laws regulating the number of children a family may have. It is true that in many poor countries, the population growth rate is much higher, nearly 3 percent per year, than in richer countries, about 1 percent per year. High population growth rates may be one explanation for lower standards of living, but many non-Malthusian explanations help explain the recurring poverty that exists in developing countries today, such as political instability, the lack of defined and enforceable property rights, and inadequate investment in human capital.

## SECTION CHECK

- Population growth may increase per capita output in resource-rich countries such as Canada, the United States, Australia, and Saudi Arabia, because these countries have more resources for production use by each labourer. Such countries are more likely to be able to take advantage of economies of large-scale production and are also more likely to have rapidly expanding technology.
- The Malthusian prediction was that, due to limited productive resources and rapid population growth, eventually per capita economic growth would become negative.

# For Your Review

## Section 7.1

1. Answer the following questions.

   a. According to the Rule of 70, how many years would it take a country to double its output at each of the following annual growth rates?

      0.5 percent: _____ years

      1.0 percent: _____ years

      1.4 percent: _____ years

      2.0 percent: _____ years

      2.8 percent: _____ years

      3.5 percent: _____ years

      7.0 percent: _____ years

   b. If a country had $100 billion of real GDP today, what would its real GDP be in 50 years if it grew at an annual growth rate of

      1.4 percent? _____

      2.8 percent? _____

      7.0 percent? _____

2. Explain how choosing between consumer goods and capital goods in the current period can impact the availability of choices between present and future consumption.

3. Answer the following questions about real GDP per capita:

   a. If Country A had four times the initial level of real GDP per capita of Country B and it was growing at 1.4 percent a year, while real GDP was growing at 2.8 percent in Country B, how long would it take before the two countries had the same level of real GDP per capita?

   b. If two countries had the same initial level of real GDP per capita and Country A grew at 2.8 percent while Country B grew at 3.5 percent, how would their real per capita GDP levels compare over the span of a century?

4. Suppose that two poor countries experience different growth rates over time. Country A's real GDP per capita grows at a rate of 7 percent per year on average, while Country B's real GDP per capita grows at a rate of only 3 percent per annum. Predict how the standard of living will vary between these two countries over time as a result of divergent growth rates.

5. When the Dutch "created" new land with their system of dikes, what did it do to their production possibilities curve? Why?

6. Which of the following will shift the Canadian production possibilities curve outward?

   a. the discovery of new oil reserves

   b. increased immigration of scientists and engineers to Canada

   c. a nuclear war that destroys both people and structures

   d. producing fewer pizzas in order to produce more tractors

   e. producing fewer strawberries in order to produce more corn

## Section 7.2

7. Would a shift from investment in capital goods to investment in education increase or decrease the growth rate of real GDP per capita?

8. What is the difference between "labour" and "human capital"? How is human capital increased?

9. Which of the following are likely to improve the productivity of labour and thereby lead to economic growth?

   a. on-the-job experience

   b. college education

   c. a decrease in the amount of capital per worker

   d. improvements in management of resources

10. How is Hong Kong a dramatic example of why abundant natural resources are not necessary for rapid economic growth?

## Sections 7.2 and 7.3

11. Which direction would the following changes alter GDP growth and per capita GDP growth in a country (increase, decrease, or indeterminate), other things being equal?

| | Real GDP Growth | Real GDP Growth per Capita |
|---|---|---|
| An increase in population | _____ | _____ |
| An increase in labour force participation | _____ | _____ |
| An increase in population and labour force participation | _____ | _____ |
| An increase in current consumption | _____ | _____ |
| An increase in technology | _____ | _____ |
| An increase in illiteracy | _____ | _____ |
| An increase in tax rates | _____ | _____ |
| An increase in productivity | _____ | _____ |
| An increase in tariffs on imported goods | _____ | _____ |
| An earlier retirement age in the country | _____ | _____ |
| An increase in technology and a decrease in labour force participation | _____ | _____ |
| An earlier retirement age and an increase in the capital stock | _____ | _____ |

## Section 7.3

12. What is the implication for an economic system with weak enforcement of patent and copyright laws? Why does weak property right enforcement create an incentive problem?

13. How could permanently lower marginal tax rates increase the capital stock, the level of education, the level of technology, and the amount of developed natural resources over time?

14. Why is the effective use of land, labour, capital, and entrepreneurial activities dependent on the protection of property rights and the rule of law?

## Section 7.4

15. Answer these questions about GDP:

    a. How could real GDP grow, while, over the same period, real GDP per capita falls?

    b. If Country A has a 4 percent annual growth rate of real GDP and a 2 percent annual rate of population growth, while Country B has a 6 percent annual growth rate of real GDP and a 5 percent annual rate of population growth, which country will have a higher growth rate of real GDP per capita?

16. Could a country experience a fall in population and a rise in real GDP at the same time? Could an increase in labour force participation allow that?

17. Why is population control a particularly important issue in countries with very low levels of per capita income?

# chapter
# 8

# Aggregate Demand

## section 8.1

# The Determinants of Aggregate Demand

- What is aggregate demand?
- What is consumption?
- What is investment?
- What are government purchases?
- What are net exports?

### WHAT IS AGGREGATE DEMAND?

**aggregate demand (AD)**
*the total demand for all final goods and services in the economy*

**Aggregate demand (AD)** is the total demand for all final goods and services in the economy. It can also be seen as the quantity of real GDP demanded at different price levels. The four major components of aggregate demand are consumption ($C$), investment ($I$), government purchases ($G$), and net exports ($X - M$). Aggregate demand, then, is equal to $C + I + G + (X - M)$.

### WHAT IS CONSUMPTION?

Consumption ($C$) is by far the largest component in aggregate demand. Expenditures for consumer goods and services typically absorb almost 60 percent of total economic activity, as measured by GDP. Understanding the determinants of consumption, then, is critical to an understanding of the forces leading to changes in aggregate demand, which in turn, change total output and income.

### The Impact of Higher Income on Consumption

The notion that the higher a nation's income, the more it spends on consumer items, has been validated empirically. At the level of individuals, most of us spend more money when we have higher incomes. But what matters most to us is not our total income but our after-tax or *disposable income.* Moreover, other factors might explain consumption.

## DEBATE

### SHOULD THERE BE A GUARANTEED ANNUAL INCOME BENEFIT?

Since the start of the Great Recession, many developed economies have experienced an increase in growth and the beginning of increases in inflation that would indicate the economies are approaching near long-term capacity. At or near this point, we should also see lowering unemployment rates—which we do. Unfortunately, while the unemployment rates are decreasing, the labour participation rates are decreasing, as well as the employed population ratio. This suggests that a higher number of workers are leaving the workforce, many of whom have been displaced through automation or off-shoring of their jobs. This has led many jurisdictions to explore the concept of a guaranteed annual income (GAI) supplement, which provides financial assistance for low-income earners.

GAI was first tested in a five-year pilot program in Dauphin, Manitoba, in the mid- to late 1970s. The project provided a basic annual income to 1000 of the poorest residents, including seniors and the disabled, to raise their incomes to the livable wage level. At the end of the five years, the program simply ended. Not even a report was prepared.

### For:

The net effect of a GAI program to the economy would be to increase the rate (or more accurately, lower the rate of decline) of *AD* demand during periods of slow or declining growth. Many benefits come from ensuring individuals have an adequate livable wage; they tend to lead a healthier life style and consume higher-quality calories, which actually decreases their draw on public health care. Allowing individuals to acquire an education while receiving GAI increases the productivity and the marginal value it creates in the economy. More highly developed skills mean higher-paid jobs, which increase the government tax revenues and decrease the costs to governments; the amount of GAI provided is reduced by the amount of any other income received. As families are able to support themselves, earning an amount above the GAI allowance, the social cost of supporting these families decreases.

It's possible that a GAI program would lead to lower crime rates, which would mean lower costs for legal aid and court systems, as well as for police services. Finally, the GAI provides assurances and hope to individuals who will become displaced due to automation and artificial intelligence. The economy works because people get paid to create the products and services they ultimately purchase. If machines and artificial intelligence replace workers, then who is left to purchase these goods? A GAI program affords the economy the opportunity to benefit from an equitable distribution of income, which provides stability to both the political and economic systems.

### Against:

One of the most compelling arguments for not instituting a GAI program is that it serves as a disincentive to work. According to this argument, GAI programs result in lost revenue because if people are receiving a basic living income from the government, they are likely to work less and pay less in taxes.

Another argument against a GAI program is that many people feel that not working for your income is immoral. This has its basis in the Protestant work ethic; it also is a contributing factor to how we judge each other based on the work we do.

The moral debate over GAI programs is more a debate over the values people hold than a discussion on facts and figures—a dilemma that must be overcome if we are to successfully address upcoming periods of higher unemployment and capital productivity.

### Questions:

1. If we continue to use automation to increase our productivity, should we ultimately have to help financially support people who lose their jobs as a result of automation?
2. Do you feel that not working for an income is immoral? Why or why not?
3. Suggest other arguments for or against GAI programs.

Some consumer goods are "lumpy"; that is, the expenditures for these goods must come in big amounts rather than in small dribbles. So, in years in which a consumer buys a new car, takes the family on a European trip, or goes to college or university, consumption may be much greater in relation to income than in years in which the consumer does not buy such high-cost consumer goods or services. Interest rates also affect consumption because they affect savings. At higher real interest rates, people save more and consume less. At lower real interest rates, people save less and consume more.

## The Average and Marginal Propensity to Consume

Households typically spend a large portion of their disposable income and save the rest. The fraction of their total disposable income that households spend on consumption is called the **average propensity to consume (*APC*)**. For example, a household

**average propensity to consume (*APC*)**
*the fraction of total disposable income that households spend on consumption*

that consumes $450 out of $500 disposable income has an *APC* of 0.9 ($450/$500). However, households tend to behave differently with additional income than with their income as a whole. How much increased consumption results from an increase in income? That depends on the **marginal propensity to consume (*MPC*)**, which is the additional consumption resulting from an additional dollar of disposable income. If consumption goes from $450 to $600 when disposable income goes from $500 to $700, what is the marginal propensity to consume out of disposable income? First, we calculate the change in consumption: $600 − $450 = $150. Next, we calculate the change in income: $700 − $500 = $200. The marginal propensity to consume, then, equals change in consumption divided by change in disposable income. In this example,

**marginal propensity to consume (*MPC*)**
*the additional consumption resulting from an additional dollar of disposable income*

$$MPC = \frac{\text{Change in consumption}}{\text{Change in disposable income}} = \frac{150}{200} = \frac{3}{4} = 0.75$$

For each additional dollar in after-tax income over this range, this household consumes three-fourths of the addition, or 75 cents.

## WHAT IS INVESTMENT?

Because investment (*I*) spending (purchases of investment goods) is an important component of aggregate demand, which in turn is a determinant of the level of GDP, changes in investment spending are often responsible for changes in the level of economic activity. If consumption is determined largely by the level of disposable income, what determines the level of investment expenditures? As you may recall, investment expenditure is the most unstable category of GDP; it is sensitive to changes in economic, social, and political variables. In 2017, investment was very nearly 20 percent of GDP.

Many factors are important in determining the level of investment. Good business conditions "induce" firms to invest because a healthy growth in demand for products in the future is likely based on current experience. In the next section, we will consider the key variables that influence investment spending.

## WHAT ARE GOVERNMENT PURCHASES?

**If firms expect higher sales and profits, they will increase investment spending on capital goods, such as factories, machinery, and equipment.**

Government purchases (*G*), another component of aggregate demand, are purchases by federal, provincial and territorial, and local governments of new goods and services produced. Government purchases include expenditures on health, education, highways, and police protection. In 2017, government purchases accounted for 25 percent of total spending. Although dramatic shifts in government purchases are less frequent and volatile than shifts in investment spending, they do occasionally occur, most recently in response to the global financial crisis.

iStockPhoto/Thinkstock

## WHAT ARE NET EXPORTS?

The interaction of the Canadian economy with the rest of the world is becoming increasingly important. Models that include international trade effects are called **open economy** models.

Remember, exports are Canadian-made goods and services that we sell to foreign customers, like lumber, wheat, and telecommunications equipment; imports are goods and services that we buy from foreign companies, like BMWs, French wine, and Sony TVs. Exports and imports can alter aggregate demand.

The difference between the value of total exports and the value of total imports is what we call **net exports** ($X - M$ = Net exports). If exports are greater than imports, we have positive net exports ($X > M$). If imports are greater than exports, net exports are negative ($X < M$).

The impact that net exports have on aggregate demand is similar to the impact that government purchases have on aggregate demand. Suppose that Canada has no trade surplus and no trade deficit—zero net exports. Now say that foreign consumers start buying more Canadian goods and services whereas Canadian consumers continue to buy imports at roughly the same rate. This will lead to *positive net exports* ($X > M$) and result in greater demand for Canadian goods and services, a higher level of aggregate demand. From a policy standpoint, this might explain why countries that are currently in a recession might like to run a trade surplus by increasing exports.

Of course, it is also possible that a country could run a trade deficit. Again let us assume that the economy was initially in a position with zero net exports. A trade deficit, or *negative net exports* ($X < M$), *ceteris paribus,* would lower Canadian aggregate demand.

**open economy**
*a type of model that includes international trade effects*

**net exports ($X - M$)**
*the value of total exports minus total imports*

## SECTION CHECK

- Aggregate demand is the sum of the demand for all final goods and services in the economy. It can also be seen as the quantity of real GDP demanded at different price levels.
- Consumption—the purchases of consumer goods and services by households—is the largest component of aggregate demand. Empirical evidence suggests that consumption increases directly with any increase in income.
- Investment spending refers to the purchases of investment goods such as machinery and equipment. Changes in investment spending are often responsible for changes in the level of economic activity.
- Government purchases are made up of federal, provincial/territorial, and local purchases of goods and services.
- Net exports are the difference between the total value of exports and the total value of imports. Trade deficits lower aggregate demand, other things equal; trade surpluses increase aggregate demand, other things equal.

**section**
**8.2**

# The Investment and Saving Market

- What is the investment demand curve?
- What is the saving supply curve?
- How is equilibrium determined in the investment and saving market?
- What effect do budget surpluses and budget deficits have on the investment and saving market?

Exhibit 1 shows the behaviour of total investment along with three important components of aggregate investment expenditure since 1981. The significant variability exhibited by investment, as well as the variability among the selected components

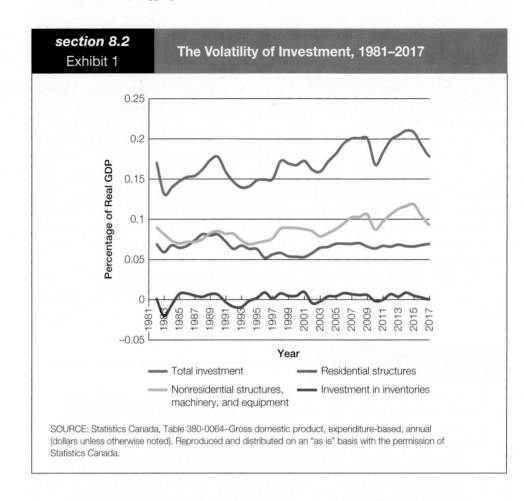

**section 8.2**
Exhibit 1

**The Volatility of Investment, 1981–2017**

SOURCE: Statistics Canada, Table 380-0064–Gross domestic product, expenditure-based, annual (dollars unless otherwise noted). Reproduced and distributed on an "as is" basis with the permission of Statistics Canada.

of aggregate investment and the sizable contribution of investment spending to total GDP, necessitate that we take a closer look at the investment and saving market.

## WHAT IS THE INVESTMENT DEMAND CURVE?

If we put the investment demand for the whole economy and national savings together, we can establish the real interest rate in the saving and investment market. We begin by revisiting investment, and then follow with the introduction of the saving supply curve and equilibrium.

Exhibit 2 shows the investment demand curve for all the firms in the whole economy. The investment demand (*ID*) curve is downward sloping, reflecting the fact that investment spending varies inversely with the real interest rate—the amount borrowers pay for their loans. At higher real interest rates, firms will pursue only those few investment activities with even higher expected rates of return, causing the quantity of investment demand to fall—a movement from point A to point B in Exhibit 2. As the real interest rate falls, additional projects with lower expected rates of return become profitable for firms, and the quantity of investment demanded rises—a movement from point A to point C in Exhibit 2. In other words, the investment demand curve shows the dollar amount of investment forthcoming at different real interest rates. Because lower interest rates stimulate the quantity of investment demanded, governments often try to combat recessions by lowering interest rates.

## Shifting the Investment Demand Curve

Several other determinants will shift the investment demand curve. If firms expect higher rates of return on their investments, for a given interest rate, the *ID* curve will shift to the right, from point A to point B, as seen in Exhibit 3. If firms expect lower rates of return on their investments, for a given interest rate, the *ID* curve will shift to the left, from point A to point C, also seen in Exhibit 3. Possible investment demand curve shifters include changes in technology, inventories, expectations, and business taxes.

**Technology**    Product and process innovation can cause the *ID* curve to shift rightward. For example, the development of new machines that can improve the quality and the quantity of products or lower the costs of production will increase the rate of return on investment, independent of the interest rate. The same is true for new products like hand-held computers, the Internet, genetic applications in medicine, or HDTV. Imagine how many different firms increased their investment demand during the computer revolution.

**Inventories**    When inventories are high and goods are stockpiled in warehouses all over the country, there is a lower expected rate of return on new investment—*ID* shifts to the left. Firms with excess inventories of finished goods have very little incentive to invest in new capital. Alternatively, if inventories are depleted below the levels desired by firms, the expected rate of return on new investment increases, as firms look to replenish their shelves to meet the growing demand—*ID* shifts to the right.

**Expectations**    If sales and profit rates are expected to be higher in the future, firms will invest more in plant and equipment now, causing the *ID* curve to shift to the right—more investment will be desired at a given interest rate. If lower sales and profits are forecast, the *ID* curve shifts to the left—fewer investments will be desired at a given interest rate.

**Business Taxes**    If business taxes are lowered—such as with an investment tax credit—potential after-tax profits on investment projects will increase and shift the *ID* curve to the right. Higher business taxes will lead to lower potential after-tax profits on investment projects and shift the *ID* curve to the left.

**section 8.2** Exhibit 2 — **The Investment Demand Curve**

There is an inverse relationship between the real interest rate and the quantity of investment demanded. As the real interest rate rises, the quantity of investment demanded falls, and as the real interest rate falls, the quantity of investment demanded rises.

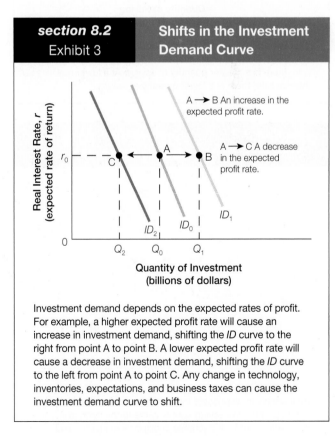

**section 8.2** Exhibit 3 — **Shifts in the Investment Demand Curve**

Investment demand depends on the expected rates of profit. For example, a higher expected profit rate will cause an increase in investment demand, shifting the *ID* curve to the right from point A to point B. A lower expected profit rate will cause a decrease in investment demand, shifting the *ID* curve to the left from point A to point C. Any change in technology, inventories, expectations, and business taxes can cause the investment demand curve to shift.

**private saving**
*the amount of income that households have left over after consumption and taxes*

**public saving**
*the amount of income that the government has left over after paying for its spending*

**national saving**
*the sum of both private and public saving*

## WHAT IS THE SAVING SUPPLY CURVE?

There are two types of saving—private and public. **Private saving** is the amount of income that households have left over after consumption and taxes. So private savings ($S_{private}$) is equal to the amount of total income (GDP) that remains after people have paid for consumption ($C$) and taxes ($T$):

$$S_{private} = \text{GDP} - C - T$$

**Public saving** is the amount of income the government has left over after paying for its spending. Therefore, public saving ($S_{public}$) is equal to the amount of tax revenues ($T$) that the government has left over after paying for government purchases ($G$):

$$S_{public} = T - G$$

**National saving** in an economy is the sum of both private and public saving:

$$S = (\text{GDP} - C - T) + (T - G)$$

Most people are familiar with the idea that households and firms can save but are less familiar with the idea that the government can also save. If the government collects more in taxes than it spends ($G > T$), it runs a surplus and public saving is positive. If the government spends more than it collects in taxes ($G < T$), it runs a deficit and public saving is negative. In the next section, we use the tools of supply and demand to examine how budget surpluses and budget deficits affect the real interest rate, national saving, and investment.

The supply curve of savings, as seen in Exhibit 4, is upward sloping, indicating a positive relationship between the real interest rate and the quantity of saving supplied. At a higher real interest rate, a greater quantity of savings is supplied—the movement from point A to point B in Exhibit 4. At a lower real interest rate, a lower quantity of saving is supplied—the movement from point A to point C in Exhibit 4. Think of the interest rate as the reward for saving and supplying funds to financial markets.

### Shifting the Saving Supply Curve

As with the investment demand curve, there are noninterest determinants of the saving supply curve. Two such saving supply curve shifters are disposable (after-tax) income and future expected earnings.

**Disposable Income**   If taxes are lowered—allowing disposable income to increase—the supply of saving would shift to the right, from point A to point B in Exhibit 5—more saving would occur at any given interest rate. If taxes increased, causing disposable income to decline, there would be less saving at any given interest rate and the supply of saving would shift to the left, from point A to point C in Exhibit 5.

---

**section 8.2**
Exhibit 4    **Saving Supply Curve**

There is a positive relationship between the real interest rate and the quantity of saving supplied. At a higher real interest rate, there is a greater quantity of saving. At a lower real interest rate, there is a lower quantity of saving.

---

**section 8.2**
Exhibit 5    **Shifts in the Saving Supply Curve**

An increase in disposable income or lower expected future earnings shifts the saving supply curve to the right, from point A to point B. A decrease in disposable income and higher expected future earnings will shift the saving supply curve to the left, from point A to point C.

**Earnings Expectation**  If you expected lower future earnings, you would tend to save more now at any given interest rate—shifting the saving supply curve to the right, from point A to point B. If you expected higher future earnings, you would tend to consume more and save less now, knowing that more income is right around the corner—shifting the saving supply curve to the left, from point A to point C in Exhibit 5.

## HOW IS EQUILIBRIUM DETERMINED IN THE INVESTMENT AND SAVING MARKET?

In equilibrium, desired investment equals desired national saving at the intersection of the investment demand curve and the saving supply curve. The real equilibrium interest rate is shown by the intersection of these two curves, as seen in Exhibit 6. If the real interest rate, $r_1$, is above the equilibrium real interest rate, $r_E$, forces within the economy would tend to restore the equilibrium. At a higher-than-real equilibrium interest rate, the quantity of savings supplied would be greater than the quantity of investment demanded—there would be a surplus of savings at this real interest rate. As savers (lenders) compete against each other to attract investment demanders (borrowers), the real interest rate falls. Alternatively if the real interest rate, $r_2$, is below the equilibrium real interest rate, $r_E$, the quantity of investment demanded is greater than the quantity of saving supplied at that interest rate—a shortage of saving occurs. As investment demanders (borrowers) compete against each other for the available saving, the real interest rate is bid up to $r_E$.

## WHAT EFFECT DO BUDGET SURPLUSES AND BUDGET DEFICITS HAVE ON THE INVESTMENT AND SAVING MARKET?

First, let's see how a budget surplus affects the real interest rate and the amount of saving and investment. In Exhibit 7, suppose that the government has a balanced budget, the saving supply curve is $SS_0$, and the investment demand curve is $ID$, resulting in an equilibrium real interest rate equal to $r_0$ and an equilibrium quantity of saving and investment equal to $Q_0$. If the government now runs a budget surplus—the government receives more in tax revenues than it spends—there is an increase in public saving, assuming that private saving is unchanged. Because national saving is the sum of private saving and public saving, national saving increases, shifting the saving supply curve from $SS_0$ to $SS_1$.

**section 8.2**
Exhibit 6

**Equilibrium in the Saving and Investment Market**

Quantity of Saving and Investment

Desired investment equals desired national saving at the intersection of the investment demand curve and the saving supply curve, the equilibrium in the saving and investment market. The intersection of these two curves shows the real equilibrium interest rate. If the real interest rate, $r_1$, is above the equilibrium real interest rate, $r_E$, a surplus of savings occurs. If the real interest rate, $r_2$, is below the equilibrium real interest rate, $r_E$, a shortage of saving occurs.

**section 8.2**
Exhibit 7

**Effects of a Government Budget Surplus**

Quantity of Saving and Investment

When the government runs a budget surplus, public saving is positive. This increases national saving and causes the saving supply curve to shift rightward from $SS_0$ to $SS_1$. This leads to a decrease in the real interest rate to $r_1$ and an increase in equilibrium saving and investment from $Q_0$ to $Q_1$.

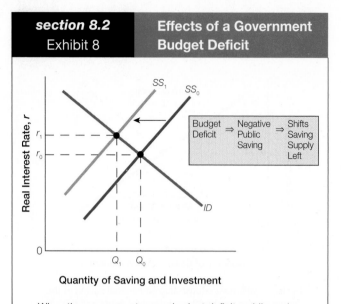

**section 8.2**
Exhibit 8

**Effects of a Government Budget Deficit**

Budget Deficit ⇒ Negative Public Saving ⇒ Shifts Saving Supply Left

Quantity of Saving and Investment

When the government runs a budget deficit, public saving is negative. This lowers the supply of national saving, shifting the saving supply curve leftward from $SS_0$ to $SS_1$. At the new equilibrium, there is a higher real interest rate and a lower amount of saving and investment.

**dissaving**

*consuming more than total available income*

What impact does this budget surplus (government saving) have on the real interest rate, saving, and investment? The increase in the saving supply from $SS_0$ to $SS_1$ leads to a decrease in the real interest rate to $r_1$ and an increase in equilibrium saving and investment from $Q_0$ to $Q_1$, as shown in Exhibit 7. The budget surplus leads to an increase in the saving supply, a lower real interest rate, and a larger amount of saving and investment. This increase in capital formation will tend to increase long-term economic growth.

When the government spends more than it receives in tax revenues, it experiences a budget deficit; the government is actually **dissaving**—consuming more than total available income. This negative saving or borrowing will cause national saving to decrease. That is, the budget deficit reduces the national supply of saving, shifting the saving supply curve leftward from $SS_0$ to $SS_1$ in Exhibit 8. At the new equilibrium, there is a higher real interest rate and a lower amount of saving and investment.

When the real interest rate rises because of the government budget deficit, private investment decreases. Economists call this the *crowding-out effect,* a topic we will expand on in Chapter 10, "Fiscal Policy." In sum, when the government runs a budget deficit, it reduces national saving, which leads to a higher real interest rate and lower investment. Because investment is critical for capital formation, long-term economic growth is reduced by budget deficits.

## SECTION CHECK

- The investment demand curve is downward sloping, reflecting the fact that the quantity of investment demanded varies inversely with the real interest rate. Technology, inventories, expectations, and business taxes can shift the investment demand curve at a given real interest rate.
- The supply of national saving is composed of both private saving and public saving. The supply curve of saving is upward sloping, reflecting the fact that the quantity of savings is positively related to the real interest rate. Two noninterest determinants of the saving supply curve are disposable (after-tax) income and expected future earnings.
- In equilibrium, desired investment equals desired national saving at the intersection of the investment demand curve and the saving supply curve. A surplus of saving will occur at real interest rates above equilibrium and shortages of saving will occur at real interest rates below equilibrium.
- Budget surpluses lead to an increase in national saving, a lowering of the real interest rate, and an increase in the quantity of saving and investment. Budget deficits reduce national saving, increase the real interest rate, and lower the quantity of saving and investment.

# The Aggregate Demand Curve

- How is the quantity of real GDP demanded affected by the price level?
- Why is the aggregate demand curve negatively sloped?

The aggregate demand curve reflects the total amount of real goods and services that all groups together want to purchase in a given time period. In other words, it indicates the quantities of real gross domestic product (RGDP) demanded at different price levels. Note that this is different from the demand curve for a particular good presented in Chapter 3, which looked at the relationship between the relative price of a good and the quantity demanded. Because we are dealing with the economy as a whole, we need an explanation for why the aggregate demand curve is downward sloping and why the short-run aggregate supply curve is upward sloping.

## HOW IS THE QUANTITY OF REAL GDP DEMANDED AFFECTED BY THE PRICE LEVEL?

The **aggregate demand curve** is a graphical representation that shows the inverse (or opposite) relationship between the price level and real gross domestic product demanded. Exhibit 1 illustrates this relationship, where the quantity of RGDP demanded is measured on the horizontal axis and the overall price level is measured on the vertical axis. As we move from point A to point B on the aggregate demand curve, we see that an increase in the price level causes RGDP demanded to fall. Conversely, if there is a reduction in the price level, a movement from point B to point A, quantity demanded of RGDP increases. Why do purchasers in the economy demand less real output when the price level rises, and more real output when the price level falls?

**aggregate demand curve**
*a graphical representation that shows the inverse relationship between the price level and RGDP demanded*

## WHY IS THE AGGREGATE DEMAND CURVE NEGATIVELY SLOPED?

Three complementary explanations exist for the negative slope of the aggregate demand curve: the real wealth effect, the interest rate effect, and the open economy effect.

### The Real Wealth Effect: Changes in Consumer Spending

If you had $1000 in cash stashed under your bed while the economy suffered a serious bout of inflation, the purchasing power of your cash would be eroded by the extent of the inflation. That is, an increase in the price level reduces real wealth and would consequently decrease your planned purchases of goods and services, lowering the quantity of RGDP demanded.

**section 8.3**
**Exhibit 1**

**The Aggregate Demand Curve**

The aggregate demand curve slopes downward, reflecting an inverse relationship between the overall price level and the quantity of real GDP demanded. When the price level increases, the quantity of RGDP demanded decreases; when the price level decreases, the quantity of RGDP demanded increases.

In the event that the price level falls, the reverse would hold true. A falling price level would increase the real value of your cash assets, increasing your purchasing power and increasing RGDP. The connection can be summarized as follows:

$$\uparrow \text{Price level} \Rightarrow \downarrow \text{Real wealth} \Rightarrow \downarrow \text{Purchasing power} \Rightarrow \downarrow \text{RGDP demanded}$$

and

$$\downarrow \text{Price level} \Rightarrow \uparrow \text{Real wealth} \Rightarrow \uparrow \text{Purchasing power} \Rightarrow \uparrow \text{RGDP demanded}$$

## The Interest Rate Effect: A Change in Investment

If the price level falls, households and firms will need to hold less money to conduct their day-to-day activities. Firms will need to hold less money for such inputs as wages and taxes; households will need to hold less money for such purchases as food, rent, and clothing. At a lower price level, households and firms will shift their "excess" money into interest-earning assets such as bonds or savings accounts. This will increase the supply of funds to the loanable funds market, leading to lower interest rates. As interest rates fall, households and firms will borrow more and buy more goods and services, so the quantity of RGDP demanded will increase.

If the price level rises, households and firms will need to hold more money to buy goods and services and conduct their daily activities. Households and firms will need to borrow money, and this increased demand for loanable funds will result in higher interest rates. At higher interest rates, consumers may give up plans to buy new cars or houses, and firms may delay investments in plant and equipment. We can summarize this process as follows:

$$\uparrow \text{Price level} \Rightarrow \uparrow \text{Interest rate} \Rightarrow \downarrow \text{Investment} \Rightarrow \downarrow \text{RGDP demanded}$$

and

$$\downarrow \text{Price level} \Rightarrow \downarrow \text{Interest rate} \Rightarrow \uparrow \text{Investment} \Rightarrow \uparrow \text{RGDP demanded}$$

## The Open Economy Effect: Changes in Net Exports

Many goods and services are bought and sold in global markets. If the price level in Canada rises relative to the price level in other countries, Canadian exports will become relatively more expensive and foreign imports will become relatively less expensive. As a result, some Canadian consumers will shift from buying domestic goods to buying foreign goods (imports) and some foreign consumers will stop buying Canadian goods. Canadian exports will fall and Canadian imports will rise. This means that net exports will fall, reducing the amount of RGDP purchased in Canada. A lower price level makes Canadian exports less expensive and foreign imports more expensive. So Canadian consumers will buy more domestic goods, and foreign consumers will buy more Canadian goods. This will increase net exports, increasing the amount of RGDP purchased in Canada. This relationship can be shown as follows:

$$\uparrow \text{Price level} \Rightarrow \downarrow \text{Demand for domestic goods} \Rightarrow \downarrow \text{RGDP demanded}$$

and

$$\downarrow \text{Price level} \Rightarrow \uparrow \text{Demand for domestic goods} \Rightarrow \uparrow \text{RGDP demanded}$$

# Shifts in the Aggregate Demand Curve

**section 8.4**

● What variables cause the aggregate demand curve to shift?
● Can we review the determinants that change aggregate demand?

As with the supply and demand curves in microeconomics (see Chapter 3), there can be both shifts in and movements along the aggregate demand curve. In the previous section, we discussed three factors—the real wealth effect, the interest rate effect, and the open economy effect—that result in the downward slope of the aggregate demand curve. Each of these factors, then, generates a movement *along* the aggregate demand curve because the general price level changed. In this section, we will discuss some of the many factors that can cause the aggregate demand curve to shift to the right or left.

## WHAT VARIABLES CAUSE THE AGGREGATE DEMAND CURVE TO SHIFT?

The whole aggregate demand curve can shift to the right or left, as seen in Exhibit 1. Put simply, if some nonprice-level determinant causes total spending to increase, then the aggregate demand curve will shift to the right. If a nonprice-level determinant causes the level of total spending to decline, then the aggregate demand curve will shift to the left. More specifically, an increase in any component of GDP ($C$, $I$, $G$, or $X - M$) can cause the aggregate demand curve to shift rightward. Conversely, decreases in $C$, $I$, $G$, or ($X - M$) will shift aggregate demand leftward. Now let's look at some specific factors that could cause the aggregate demand curve to shift.

## Changing Consumption

A whole host of changes could alter consumption ($C$) patterns. For example, an increase in consumer confidence, an increase in wealth, or a tax cut can each

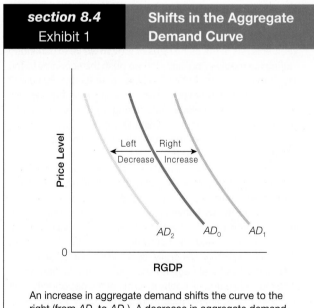

**section 8.4**
Exhibit 1

**Shifts in the Aggregate Demand Curve**

An increase in aggregate demand shifts the curve to the right (from $AD_0$ to $AD_1$). A decrease in aggregate demand shifts the curve to the left (from $AD_0$ to $AD_2$).

increase consumption and shift the aggregate demand curve to the right. An increase in population will also increase the aggregate demand because more consumers will be spending more money on goods and services. A lower interest rate can also spur consumption spending.

Of course, the aggregate demand curve could shift to the left due to decreases in consumption demand. For example, if consumers sensed that the economy was headed for a recession or if the government imposed a tax increase, this would result in a left-ward shift of the aggregate demand curve. Because consuming less is saving more, an increase in saving, *ceteris paribus,* will shift aggregate demand to the left. High levels of accumulated consumer debt may also be a reason that some consumers might put off additional spending.

## Changing Investment

Investment ($I$) is also an important determinant of aggregate demand. Increases in the demand for investment goods occur for a variety of reasons. For example, if business confidence increases or real interest rates fall, business investment will increase and aggregate demand will shift to the right. A reduction in business taxes would also shift the aggregate demand curve to the right because businesses would now retain more of their profits to invest. However, if interest rates or business taxes rise, we would expect to see a leftward shift in aggregate demand.

# Business *CONNECTION*

## CHANGES IN GDP: THE LONG AND THE SHORT OF IT

Since the depths of the Great Recession of 2008 to 2009, we've experienced growth during the recovery phase— aggregate demand has shifted right. But this has been in the short term, as we're recovering from a point we were at before. The question now is whether this growth can be sustained in the long term. Can we push the economy to greater levels at the same rates of growth we've experienced during the recovery phase? Can we push the economy to the levels of expansion that we have had over the last 50 years?

During the recovery phase, consumers, businesses, and all levels of governments, along with foreign buyers, increase their demand for Canadian goods and services. While we are experiencing growth we are still not at our level of long-run potential output.

In expansionary phases, businesses experience increases in sales revenues and are encouraged to make capital expenditures to increase operating capacity and output, and do so knowing that investment is required to meet the growing demand. But they also know that they must not overproduce and create unwarranted levels of inventory. Too little inventory generally costs firms sales, or if they attempt to meet that demand, increases in production costs. Too much inventory is costly in terms of the opportunity cost it represents as limited resources are not used wisely. Being forced to lower prices to clear inventory means lost profit. Having just a small amount of inventory less than demand helps firms maintain higher price levels and reduces the possibility of losses due to unsold or reduced-price goods. This is why changes in aggregate supply lag slightly behind changes in aggregate demand.

Business operators need to understand the nature and implications of expansionary phases of the economy if they want to benefit most from the growth. But they also need to be aware of the limits of expansionary phase benefits, and not be fooled into thinking the same levels of growth will continue throughout the longer term. The key is to monitor several leading indicators in such expansion. Expansion often starts with the consumer sector, which accounts for approximately 58 percent of economic growth in Canada and about 70 percent in the United States. We know that the consumer drives the economy, much more than producers, governments, or net exports. The axiom "As goes consumer spending, so goes the economy" is true.

There is a mixed message for businesses in the recovery stage. In the beginning, they take advantage of the impending growth in consumer demand for goods and services by hiring and training workers, purchasing new capital equipment, or adapting to new processes. This higher growth period is a reality in the short term as all sectors of the economy recover to near full capacity (or full employment). But as we near full-employment levels, the energy starts to wane and businesses must take the necessary steps for transition into long-term success.

Growing into the long term requires firms to innovate and present something truly different to the markets. Most firms believe they are growing because their revenues and profits grow. But that is short-term thinking—firms need to understand that sustainability is not providing the market with a different version of something already there, but providing a truly unique and different product or service.

Firms that focus on longer-term objectives will invest significant funds into R&D, based on revenue, rather than on profits. Basing R&D investment on profit levels is tenuous at best, as profits can be eroded quickly, often for reasons the business cannot control, whereas R&D investment based on revenue helps to ensure that funds returned to the corporation act as a "renewal" fee. The one major caveat however is that firms must maintain higher margins on the goods and services they produce in order to sustain these R&D costs. We've seen numerous examples of even some of the largest firms falling prey to underfunding this vital process of revitalizing and reinventing their businesses—think Kodak, IBM, Sears—certainly the captains of industry during these times could never have envisioned their demise. They were great in what they did, the problem was they were great in doing something that was getting stale and they didn't adapt, or when they did, it was too late and they became followers rather than the leaders they once were.

So business leaders not only have to pay attention to the microeconomic decisions of running a company, they also need to be aware at the macro level. They know they can't change the macro level indicators and have to work within the indicators, but the question is how to do that. If a firm's long-term goal is to stay in business and compete, owners, boards, and managers must think and adapt and be prepared to finance for change. If not, then they need to recognize their limits and prepare for a profitable exit strategy, rather than being forced into an unprofitable one by their competition.

1. Can you think of a firm that didn't innovate for long-term sustainability? What products or services became uncompetitive and which products leapfrogged them? Do you think they could have been successful in the long term? Why or why not?

2. What do you think are the benefits and costs of firms that concentrate on the short term versus the long term? What about those that do the opposite—concentrate on the long term over the short term?

3. Can you think of countries that prefer short-term objectives over those that value long-term objectives? (And, just out of curiosity, what do you think a country's long-term perspective might be in terms of years?)

## Changing Government Purchases

Government purchases ($G$) are also part of total spending and therefore must impact aggregate demand. An increase in government purchases, other things equal, shifts the aggregate demand curve to the right, whereas a reduction shifts aggregate demand to the left. For example, a decision by the federal government to start building new highways would lead to an increase in government expenditure and a rightward shift in aggregate demand.

## Changing Net Exports

Global markets are also important in a domestic economy. For example, in 2008, when Canada's major trading partner, the United States, fell into a major recession, Canadian exports of goods and services to the United States fell by nearly 27 percent in 2009, causing overall Canadian exports to decline by close to 25 percent. This dramatic reduction in exports was the leading cause of net exports ($X - M$) falling by more than $50 billion in 2009, shifting the aggregate demand curve for Canada to the left. Alternatively, an economic boom in the U.S. economy might lead to an increase in our exports to the United States, causing net exports ($X - M$) to rise and aggregate demand to increase.

Another factor that has an important effect on net exports is the exchange rate. The exchange rate is the price of one unit of a country's currency in terms of another country's currency. For example, if it takes US$0.96 to buy one Canadian dollar (as was the case on December 14, 2011), then the exchange rate is US$0.96 per Canadian dollar. When the Canadian dollar appreciates in value (to, say, US$1.02 per Canadian dollar—as was the case on January 15, 2013), it is more expensive for foreigners to buy Canadian dollars, and therefore more expensive for foreigners to buy Canadian goods and services (which are priced in Canadian dollars). At the same time, it becomes less expensive for

Canadians to buy U.S. dollars, and therefore less expensive for Canadians to buy U.S. goods and services (which are priced in U.S. dollars). As a result, Canadian exports decline and Canadian imports increase. Therefore, an appreciation of the Canadian dollar decreases Canadian net exports and shifts the aggregate demand curve to the left. On the other hand, when the Canadian dollar depreciates in value (to, say, US\$0.75 per Canadian dollar, as was the case on March 15, 2016), Canadian net exports increase, and the aggregate demand curve shifts to the right.

## CAN WE REVIEW THE DETERMINANTS THAT CHANGE AGGREGATE DEMAND?

Any aggregate demand category that has the ability to change total purchases in the economy will shift the aggregate demand curve. That is, changes in consumption purchases, investment purchases, government purchases, or net export purchases shift the aggregate demand curve. The effects of some of the determinants that cause a change in aggregate demand (shifters) are reviewed in Exhibit 2.

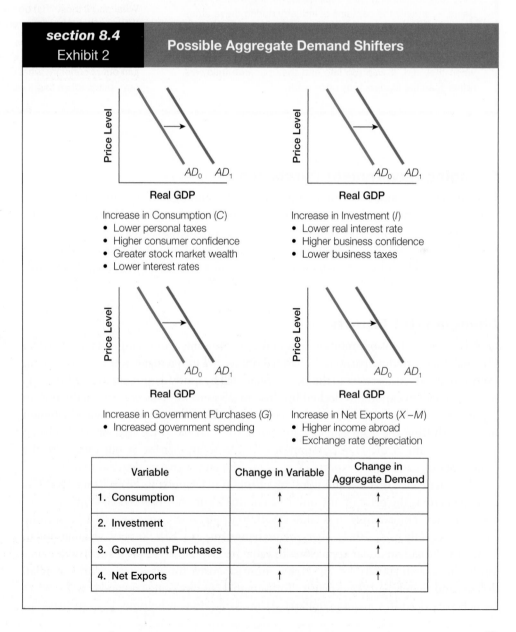

**section 8.4**
Exhibit 2     **Possible Aggregate Demand Shifters**

Increase in Consumption ($C$)
- Lower personal taxes
- Higher consumer confidence
- Greater stock market wealth
- Lower interest rates

Increase in Investment ($I$)
- Lower real interest rate
- Higher business confidence
- Lower business taxes

Increase in Government Purchases ($G$)
- Increased government spending

Increase in Net Exports ($X-M$)
- Higher income abroad
- Exchange rate depreciation

| Variable | Change in Variable | Change in Aggregate Demand |
|---|---|---|
| 1. Consumption | ↑ | ↑ |
| 2. Investment | ↑ | ↑ |
| 3. Government Purchases | ↑ | ↑ |
| 4. Net Exports | ↑ | ↑ |

## SECTION CHECK

■ A change in the price level causes a movement along the aggregate demand curve, not a shift in the aggregate demand curve. Aggregate demand is made up of total spending, or $C + I + G + (X − M)$. Any change in these factors will cause the aggregate demand curve to shift.

| Variable | Change in Variable | Change in Aggregate Demand |
|---|---|---|
| 1. Consumption (C) | ↑ | ↑ |
| 2. Investment (I) | ↑ | ↑ |
| 3. Government purchases (G) | ↑ | ↑ |
| 4. Exports (X) | ↑ | ↑ |
| 5. Imports (M) | ↑ | ↓ |
| 6. Net exports (X − M) | ↑ | ↑ |

# For Your Review

## Section 8.1

1. Assume that Melanie had $200 000 of disposable income and spent $180 000 on consumption in 2012, and had $300 000 of disposable income and spent $240 000 on consumption in 2013.

   a. What was Melanie's average propensity to consume in 2012?

   b. What was Melanie's average propensity to consume in 2013?

   c. What was Melanie's marginal propensity to consume?

   d. If Melanie's income went up to $400 000 in 2014, how much would she be likely to spend on consumption that year? What would be her average propensity to consume?

   e. If Melanie's income went down to $100 000 in 2014, how much would she be likely to spend on consumption that year? What would be her average propensity to consume?

2. How does a higher price level in the Canada economy affect purchases of imported goods? Explain.

## Section 8.2

3. In the saving and investment market,

   a. what happens to the investment demand curve when the real interest rate declines?

   b. what happens to the investment demand curve when firms' inventories are rising above what the firms desire?

c. what happens to the investment demand curve when technological advances give rise to popular new products?

d. what happens to the saving supply curve when the real interest rate increases?

e. what happens to the saving supply curve when disposable income increases?

4.

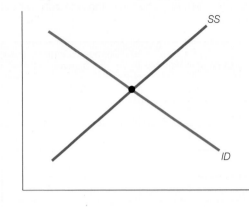

Label the axes for the saving and investment market. Then explain and illustrate what would happen in the saving and investment market if

a. businesses became more optimistic about future business conditions.

b. individuals became less optimistic about their future incomes.

c. business taxes increased.

d. individuals' disposable incomes increased.

5. What would happen to the saving supply curve if there was both an increase in current disposable income and a decrease in new technologies creating investment opportunities?

6. Other things equal, in which direction will a budget deficit change the equilibrium interest rate, the saving supply curve, the level of saving and investment in the economy, and the likely rate of economic growth, other things equal?

7. Why does GDP $- C - G = S$ in a simple, closed economy?

8. If net personal taxes rise, what happens to private saving? To public saving?

## Blueprint Problem

The following graph depicts the market for saving and investment.

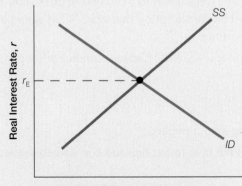

Initially, the government budget is balanced. Suppose the government significantly reduces spending on health care without changing taxes.

a. How will this change impact the market for saving and investment?

b. Will such a change to government spending prove to be beneficial to the economy?

## Blueprint Solution

a. Initially:
$$G = T$$

> When the government is running a balanced budget, government expenditures ($G$) are equal to taxes ($T$).

Proposed:
$$G < T$$

> The decrease in spending on health care will result in a reduction in $G$ (while leaving $T$ constant). This will create a budget surplus.

Recall
$$\text{National Saving} = \text{Private Saving} + \text{Public Saving}$$
$$S = (\text{GDP} - C - T) + (T - G)$$

If the government is running a budget surplus, *ceteris paribus*, public saving ($T - G$) will increase and therefore national saving ($S$) will increase.

**Quantity of Saving and Investment**

> The reduction in health care spending increased public saving, shifting the saving supply curve to the right. As a result, the real interest rate declined and the equilibrium quantity of saving and investment increased.

b. The lower real interest rate and higher quantity of saving and investment is generally seen as a positive economic indicator. Lower real borrowing costs and greater capital formation would generally be seen as conducive to higher rates of future economic growth. One negative implication of this change in government expenditure is that the budget surplus has come at the expense of less publically funded health care.

## Section 8.3

9. According to the aggregate demand (*AD*) curve, what is the relationship between different prices and the level of real GDP demanded in the economy?

10. Evaluate the following statement: A higher price level decreases the purchasing power of the dollar and reduces RGDP.

11. What is the wealth effect, and how does it imply a downward-sloping aggregate demand curve?

12. What is the interest rate effect, and how does it imply a downward-sloping aggregate demand curve?

13. What is the open economy effect, and how does it imply a downward-sloping aggregate demand curve?

## Section 8.4

14. Describe what the effect on aggregate demand would be, other things being equal, if
    a. exports increase.
    b. both imports and exports decrease.
    c. consumption decreases.
    d. investment increases.
    e. investment decreases and government purchases increase.
    f. the price level increases.
    g. the price level decreases.

15. Suppose retailers like Canadian Tire and Walmart find that their inventories are being depleted. What type of change in aggregate demand (a rightward or leftward shift) could be seen as responsible? What are the likely consequences for output and investment of this type of change in aggregate demand?

16. Which of the following both decreases consumption and shifts the aggregate demand curve to the left?
    a. an increase in financial wealth
    b. an increase in personal income taxes
    c. an increase in the price level
    d. a decrease in interest rates

17. Predict how each of the following would impact investment expenditures.
    a. Inventory levels are depleted.
    b. Banks scrutinize borrower credit more carefully and interest rates rise.
    c. Profit rates have decreased over the past few quarters.
    d. Factories operate at 60 percent capacity, down from 80 percent.

18. Identify which expenditure category each of the following will directly impact, and also in which direction the Canadian aggregate demand curve will shift as a result.
    a. Income increases abroad.
    b. There is a decrease in interest rates.
    c. Parliament passes permanent tax cuts for both households and businesses.
    d. Firms become more optimistic about the outlook for the economy.
    e. Stocks traded on the Toronto Stock Exchange lose 40 percent of their value in one month's time.

19. Explain how the most recent recession in the United States affected aggregate demand in the Canadian economy.

# Aggregate Supply and Macroeconomic Equilibrium

# The Aggregate Supply Curve

- What is the aggregate supply curve?
- Why is the short-run aggregate supply curve positively sloped?
- Why is the long-run aggregate supply curve vertical at the natural rate of output?

## WHAT IS THE AGGREGATE SUPPLY CURVE?

The **aggregate supply (AS) curve** is a graphical representation that shows the positive relationship between the price level and real gross domestic product supplied. It illustrates the relationship between the overall price level and the total quantity of final goods and services that suppliers are *willing* and *able* to produce. In fact, there are two aggregate supply curves—a short-run aggregate supply curve and a long-run aggregate supply curve. The **short-run aggregate supply (SRAS) curve** is the graphical relationship between *RGDP* and the price level when output prices can change but input prices are unable to adjust. For example, nominal wages are assumed to adjust slowly in the short run. The **long-run aggregate supply (LRAS) curve** is the graphical relationship between *RGDP* and the price level when output prices and input prices can fully adjust to economic changes.

## WHY IS THE SHORT-RUN AGGREGATE SUPPLY CURVE POSITIVELY SLOPED?

In the short run, the aggregate supply curve is upward sloping, as shown in Exhibit 1. This means that at a higher price level, producers are willing to supply more real output, and at lower price levels, they are willing to supply less real output. Why would producers be willing to supply more output just because the price level increases? There are two possible explanations: the profit effect and the misperception effect.

### The Profit Effect

To many firms, input costs—like wages and rents—are relatively constant in the short run. Workers and other material input suppliers often enter into long-term contracts with firms at prearranged prices. Thus, the slow adjustments of input prices are due to

**aggregate supply (AS) curve**
*a graphical representation that shows the positive relationship between the price level and real gross domestic product supplied*

**short-run aggregate supply (SRAS) curve**
*the graphical relationship between RGDP and the price level when output prices can change but input prices are unable to adjust*

**long-run aggregate supply (LRAS) curve**
*the graphical relationship between RGDP and the price level when output prices and input prices can fully adjust to economic changes*

The short-run aggregate supply (*SRAS*) curve is upward sloping. Suppliers are willing to supply more RGDP at higher price levels and less at lower price levels, other things equal.

contracts that do not adjust quickly to output price level changes. So when the price level rises, output prices rise relative to input prices (costs), raising producers' short-run profit margins. That is, a higher price level leads to a higher profit per unit of output and higher RGDP supplied because wages and other input prices can be slow to adjust in the short run. With this short-run profit effect, the increased profit margins make it in the producers' self-interest to expand production and sales at higher price levels.

If the price level falls, output prices fall and producers' profits tend to fall. That is, a lower price level leads to a lower profit per unit of output and lower RGDP supplied because wages and other input prices can be slow to adjust in the short run. Again, this is because many input costs, such as wages and other contracted costs, are relatively constant in the short run. When output price levels fall, producers find it more difficult to cover their input costs and, consequently, reduce their level of output.

## The Misperception Effect

The second explanation of the upward-sloping short-run aggregate supply curve is that producers can be fooled by price changes in the short run. That is, changes in the overall price level can temporarily mislead producers about what is taking place in their particular market. For example, say a wheat farmer sees the price of wheat rising. Thinking that the *relative price* of his wheat is rising (i.e., that wheat is becoming more valuable in real terms), the wheat farmer supplies more. Suppose, however, that wheat was not the only thing for which prices were rising. What if the prices of many other goods and services were rising at the same time as a result of an increase in the price level? The relative price of wheat, then, was not actually rising, although it appeared so in the short run. In this case, the producer was fooled into supplying more based on the *short-run misperception* of relative prices. In other words, producers may be fooled into thinking that the relative price of the item they are producing is rising, so they increase production. Similarly, if the overall price level falls, many wheat farmers may mistakenly believe that the relative price of wheat has fallen. This could fool these farmers into temporarily producing less wheat.

Workers can also be fooled. If the price level is rising, the first thing they may notice is that their nominal wages—expressed in current dollars—are rising. So they may mistakenly believe that the reward for working has risen and increase the quantity of labour they supply. Only later do they realize that the prices of the goods and services they buy are also rising; that is, their real wages (wages that are adjusted for inflation) have not risen. They have been fooled into supplying more of their labour into the market. The key in all of these cases is that short-run misperceptions about relative prices temporarily fool the supplier into producing more as the overall price level rises and producing less as the overall price level falls. This leads to an upward-sloping short-run aggregate supply curve.

## WHY IS THE LONG-RUN AGGREGATE SUPPLY CURVE VERTICAL AT THE NATURAL RATE OF OUTPUT?

Along the short-run aggregate supply curve, we assume that wages and other input prices are constant. This is not the case in the long run, which is a period long enough for the price of all inputs to fully adjust to changes in the economy. When we move along the long-run aggregate supply curve, we are then looking at the relationship between RGDP produced and the price level, once input prices have been able to respond to changes in output prices. Along the long-run aggregate supply (*LRAS*) curve, two sets of prices are changing—the price of outputs and the price of inputs. That is, along the *LRAS* curve, a 10 percent increase in the price of goods and services is matched by a 10 percent increase in the price of inputs. The long-run aggregate supply curve, then, is insensitive to the price level. As you can see in Exhibit 2, the *LRAS* curve is drawn as perfectly vertical, reflecting the fact that the level of RGDP producers are willing to supply is not affected by changes in the price level. Note that the vertical long-run aggregate supply curve will always be positioned at the natural rate of output, where all resources are fully employed ($RGDP_{NR}$). That is, in the long run, firms will always produce at the maximum level allowed by their capital, land, labour, and technology, regardless of the price level.

Since the *LRAS* represents the level of output an economy can achieve with a base of resources and technology that are being fully employed, we can establish a link between the positioning of the *LRAS* curve and the positioning of an economy's production possibilities curve (PPC). Recall that an economy's stock of resources and its level of technology define the position of its PPC, as shown in Exhibit 2(a). These same conditions also determine the amount of RGDP a nation can produce in the long run and therefore the positioning of the *LRAS* curve, as shown in Exhibit 2(b).

The long-run equilibrium level is where the economy will settle when undisturbed and when all resources are fully employed. Remember that the economy will always be at the intersection of short-run aggregate supply and aggregate demand, but that will not always be at the natural rate of output, $RGDP_{NR}$. Long-run equilibrium will occur only where the short-run aggregate supply and aggregate demand curves intersect along the long-run aggregate supply curve at the natural, or potential, rate of output.

| section 9.1 Exhibit 2 | The Long-Run Aggregate Supply Curve |
|---|---|

An economy's stock of resources and level of technology define the position of its production possibilities curve (PPC), as illustrated in part (a). Similarly, along the long-run aggregate supply curve, the level of RGDP does not change with the price level. The position of the *LRAS* curve is determined by the natural rate of output, $RGDP_{NR}$, which reflects the levels of capital, land, labour, entrepreneurship and technology in the economy, as illustrated in part (b).

## SECTION CHECK

- The aggregate supply curve is the relationship between the overall price level and the total quantity of final goods and services that suppliers are *able* and *willing* to produce.
- The short-run aggregate supply curve measures how much RGDP suppliers are willing to produce at different price levels when input prices are unable to adjust. For this reason, producers can make a profit by expanding production when the price level rises. Producers also may be fooled into thinking that the relative price of the item they are producing is rising, so they increase production.
- In the long run, the aggregate supply curve is vertical. In the long run, input prices change proportionally with output prices. The position of the *LRAS* curve is determined by the level of capital, land, labour, and technology at the natural rate of output, $RGDP_{NR}$.

**section**
**9.2**

# Shifts in the Aggregate Supply Curve

- What factors of production affect the short-run and the long-run aggregate supply curves?
- What factors exclusively shift the short-run aggregate supply curve?
- Can we review the determinants that change aggregate supply?

## WHAT FACTORS OF PRODUCTION AFFECT THE SHORT-RUN AND LONG-RUN AGGREGATE SUPPLY CURVES?

We will now examine the determinants that can shift the short-run and the long-run aggregate supply curves to the right or left, as shown in Exhibit 1. Any change in the quantity of any factor of production available—capital, land, labour, or entrepreneurship—can cause a shift in both the long-run and short-run aggregate supply curves. We will now see how these factors can change the position of both types of aggregate supply curves.

### How Capital Affects Aggregate Supply

Changes in the stock of capital—the amount of equipment and structures to aid production—will alter the amount of goods and services the economy can produce. Investing in capital improves the quantity and quality of the capital stock, which lowers the cost of production in the short run. This in turn shifts the short-run aggregate supply curve rightward, and allows output to be permanently greater than before, shifting the long-run aggregate supply curve rightward, *ceteris paribus*.

Changes in human capital can also alter the aggregate supply curve. Investments in human capital may include educational or vocational programs and/or on-the-job training. All of these investments in human capital cause productivity to rise. As a result, the short-run aggregate supply curve shifts to the right because a more skilled workforce lowers the cost of production; in turn, the *LRAS* curve shifts to the right because greater output is achievable on a permanent, or sustainable, basis, *ceteris paribus*.

### Land (Natural Resources)

Remember that, in economics, *land* is an all-encompassing definition that includes all natural resources. An increase in natural resources, such as successful oil exploration in Alberta, would presumably lower the costs of production and expand the economy's sustainable rate of output, shifting both the short-run and long-run aggregate supply curves to the right. Likewise, a decrease in natural resources available would result in a leftward shift of both the short-run and long-run aggregate supply curves.

### The Labour Force

The addition of workers to the labour force, *ceteris paribus*, can increase aggregate supply. For example, during the 1960s and 1970s, women and baby boomers entered the labour force in large numbers. More recently, however, immigrants have become a major contributor to Canada's labour force—accounting for over 20 percent of Canada's

| *section 9.2* Exhibit 1 | **Shifts in Both Short-Run and Long-Run Aggregate Supply** |
|---|---|

Increases in technology or any of the factors of production—capital, land, labour, or entrepreneurship—can shift both the *LRAS* and *SRAS* curves to the right. Decreases in any of the factors of production can shift both the *SRAS* and *LRAS* curves to the left.

labour force. This increase tended to depress wages and increase short-run aggregate supply, *ceteris paribus*. The expanded labour force also increased the economy's potential output, increasing long-run aggregate supply. Japan's aging population is causing a decrease in the labour force in recent years—a leftward shift in the short-run and long-run aggregate supply curves, *ceteris paribus*.

## Entrepreneurship and Technology

The online *Business Dictionary* defines entrepreneurship as "the capacity and willingness to develop, organize, and manage a business venture along with any of its risks in order to make a profit." Combining entrepreneurship with the other factors of production (capital, land, and labour) and adding technology can lead to significant rewards, as in the cases of Bill Gates of Microsoft, Elon Musk of SpaceX and Tesla Motors, and Joseph-Armand Bombardier of Bombardier Inc. Their innovative technological developments, such as computers and specialized software, space and Earth vehicles, and peace and wartime transportation systems, have led to a variety of cost savings for all types of businesses—3D printing, nanotechnology, Cloud computing, and increased productivity across the board. These activities shift both the short-run and long-run aggregate supply curves outward by lowering costs and expanding real output possibilities.

## Government Regulations

Increases in government regulations can increase production costs, resulting in a leftward shift of the short-run aggregate supply curve; a reduction in society's potential output shifts the long-run aggregate supply curve to the left as well. Likewise, a reduction in government regulations on businesses would lower the costs of production and expand potential real output, causing both the *SRAS* and *LRAS* curves to shift to the right.

## WHAT FACTORS EXCLUSIVELY SHIFT THE SHORT-RUN AGGREGATE SUPPLY CURVE?

Some factors shift the short-run aggregate supply curve but do not impact the long-run aggregate supply curve. The most important of these factors are changes in wages and other input prices, productivity, and unexpected supply shocks. Exhibit 2 illustrates the impact of these factors on short-run aggregate supply.

## Wages and Other Input Prices

The price of factors, or inputs, that go into producing outputs will affect only the short-run aggregate supply curve if they don't reflect permanent changes in the supplies of some factors of production. For example, if money or nominal wages increase without a corresponding increase in labour productivity, then it will become more costly for suppliers to produce goods and services at every price level, causing the *SRAS* curve to shift to the left. Long-run aggregate supply will not shift because with the same supply of labour as before, potential output does not change. If the price of steel rises, automobile producers will find it more expensive to do business because their production costs will rise, again resulting in a leftward shift in the short-run aggregate supply curve. The *LRAS* curve will not shift, however, as long as the capacity to make steel has not been reduced.

**section 9.2** Exhibit 2 — **Shifts in Short-Run Aggregate Supply but Not Long-Run Aggregate Supply**

A change in input prices that does not reflect a permanent change in the supply of those inputs will shift the *SRAS* curve but not the *LRAS* curve. Likewise, adverse supply shocks, such as those caused by natural disasters, may cause a temporary change that will impact only short-run aggregate supply.

Temporary natural disasters
like droughts can destroy
crops and leave the land
parched. This may shift the
*SRAS* curve but not the *LRAS*
curve.

### Temporary Supply Shocks

*Supply shocks* are unexpected temporary events that can either increase or
decrease aggregate supply. For example, negative supply shocks like major
widespread flooding, earthquakes, droughts, and other natural disasters can
increase the costs of production, causing the short-run aggregate supply curve
to shift to the left, *ceteris paribus*. However, once the temporary effects of
these disasters have been felt, no appreciable change in the economy's productive capacity has occurred, so the long-run aggregate supply doesn't shift
as a result. Other temporary supply shocks, such as disruptions in trade due
to war, electric power blackouts, or labour strikes, will have similar effects on
short-run aggregate supply. However, positive supply shocks such as favourable weather conditions or temporary price reductions of imported resources
like oil can shift the short-run aggregate supply curve rightward.

### CAN WE REVIEW THE DETERMINANTS THAT CHANGE AGGREGATE SUPPLY?

The factors detailed in Exhibit 3 can shift the short-run aggregate supply curve, the
long-run aggregate supply curve, or both, depending on whether the effects are temporary or permanent.

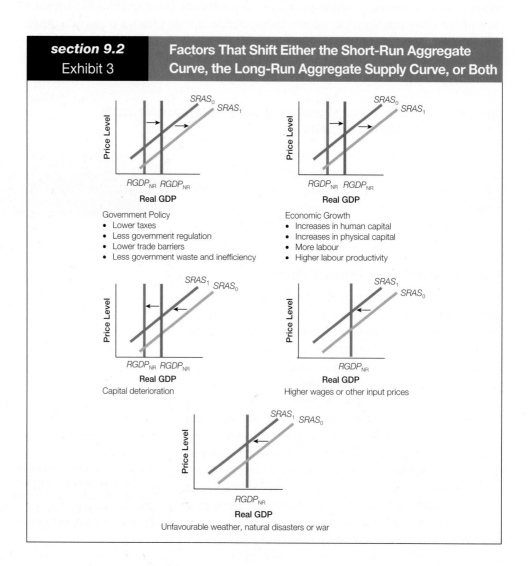

| **section 9.2** Exhibit 3 | **Factors That Shift Either the Short-Run Aggregate Curve, the Long-Run Aggregate Supply Curve, or Both** |

Government Policy
• Lower taxes
• Less government regulation
• Lower trade barriers
• Less government waste and inefficiency

Economic Growth
• Increases in human capital
• Increases in physical capital
• More labour
• Higher labour productivity

Capital deterioration

Higher wages or other input prices

Unfavourable weather, natural disasters or war

## SECTION CHECK

- Any increase in technology or the quantity of any of the available factors of production—capital, land, labour, or entrepreneurship—will cause both the long-run and short-run aggregate supply curves to shift to the right. A decrease in any of these factors will shift both of the aggregate supply curves to the left.
- Changes in wages and other input price, productivity, and temporary supply shocks shift the short-run aggregate supply curve but do not affect the long-run aggregate supply curve.

| Variable | Change in Variable | Change in *SRAS* | Change in *LRAS* |
|---|---|---|---|
| **1. Costs** | | | |
| • Wages | ↑ | ↓ | n/c* |
| • Other input prices | ↑ | ↓ | n/c* |
| **2. Government policy** | | | |
| • Taxes | ↑ | ↓ | ↓ |
| • Regulatory framework | ↑ | ↓ | ↓ |
| • Trade barriers | ↑ | ↓ | ↓ |
| • Waste and inefficiency | ↑ | ↓ | ↓ |
| **3. Economic growth** | | | |
| • Quantity of human capital | ↑ | ↑ | ↑ |
| • Quantity of physical capital | ↑ | ↑ | ↑ |
| • Technology and entrepreneurship | ↑ | ↑ | ↑ |
| • Labour productivity | ↑ | ↑ | ↑ |
| **4. Other** | | | |
| • Unfavourable weather | ↑ | ↓ | n/c* |
| • Natural disasters, war | ↑ | ↓ | n/c* |

n/c*—The curve does not shift unless the variable change is permanent.

**section**

**9.3**

# Macroeconomic Equilibrium

- How is macroeconomic equilibrium determined?
- What are recessionary and inflationary gaps?
- How can the economy self-correct to a recessionary gap?
- How can the economy self-correct to an inflationary gap?

### HOW IS MACROECONOMIC EQUILIBRIUM DETERMINED?

The *short-run* equilibrium level of real output and the price level are given by the intersection of the aggregate demand curve and the short-run aggregate supply curve. When this equilibrium occurs on the long-run aggregate supply curve, as seen in Exhibit 1, the *long-run* equilibrium level of real output and the price level is achieved. At the long-run equilibrium, the economy is operating at its full-employment level of RGDP. That is, when the short-run equilibrium occurs on the long-run aggregate supply curve, the economy is at its potential, or natural, rate of output ($RGDP_{NR}$). Only a short-run equilibrium that is at potential output is also a long-run equilibrium.

| section 9.3 | Long-Run Macroeconomic |
| Exhibit 1 | Equilibrium |

Long-run macroeconomic equilibrium occurs at the level where short-run aggregate supply and aggregate demand intersect at a point on the long-run aggregate supply curve. At this level, real GDP will equal potential GDP at full employment ($RGDP_{NR}$).

Short-run equilibrium can change when the aggregate demand curve or the short-run aggregate supply curve shifts rightward or leftward, but the long-run equilibrium level of RGDP changes only when the *LRAS* curve shifts. Sometimes, these supply or demand changes are anticipated; at other times, however, the shifts occur unexpectedly. Economists call these unexpected aggregate supply or aggregate demand changes **shocks**.

The economy can be either at a point where actual and potential RGDP are equal at $RGDP_{NR}$ or the economy can be at a point where the potential RGDP and actual RGDP are not equal. In Exhibit 2, we see that it is rare that actual and potential RGDP are equal. In other words, the economy can be in a boom, where actual RGDP is greater than potential RGDP (point A), or in a recession, where actual RGDP is less than potential RGDP (point B). However, notice that the economy does not often stray too far from potential RGDP—of course, the recent exception is the financial crisis of 2008.

**shocks**

*unexpected aggregate supply or aggregate demand changes*

## WHAT ARE RECESSIONARY AND INFLATIONARY GAPS?

As we just discussed, equilibrium will not always occur at full employment. In fact, equilibrium can occur at less than the potential output of the economy, $RGDP_{NR}$, temporarily beyond $RGDP_{NR}$, or at potential GDP. Exhibit 3 shows these three possibilities.

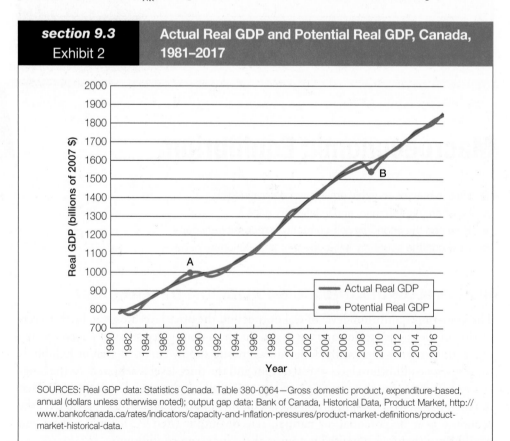

| section 9.3 | Actual Real GDP and Potential Real GDP, Canada, |
| Exhibit 2 | 1981–2017 |

SOURCES: Real GDP data: Statistics Canada. Table 380-0064—Gross domestic product, expenditure-based, annual (dollars unless otherwise noted); output gap data: Bank of Canada, Historical Data, Product Market, http://www.bankofcanada.ca/rates/indicators/capacity-and-inflation-pressures/product-market-definitions/product-market-historical-data.

**section 9.3**
Exhibit 3        **Recessionary and Inflationary Gaps**

In Exhibit 3(a), the economy is currently in short-run equilibrium at $E_{SR}$. At this point, $RGDP_0$ is less than $RGDP_{NR}$; that is, the economy is producing less than its potential output and the economy is in a recessionary gap. In Exhibit 3(c), the economy is currently in short-run equilibrium at $E_{SR}$. At this point, $RGDP_2$ is greater than $RGDP_{NR}$. The economy is temporarily producing more than its potential output and we have an inflationary gap. In Exhibit 3(b) the economy is producing its potential output at the $RGDP_{NR}$. At this point, the economy is in long-run equilibrium and is not experiencing an inflationary or recessionary gap.

In Exhibit 3(a) we have a recessionary gap at the short-run equilibrium, $E_{SR}$, at $RGDP_0$. An output gap that occurs when actual output ($RGDP$) is less than potential output ($RGDP_{NR}$) is a **recessionary gap**—aggregate demand is insufficient to fully employ all of society's resources, so unemployment will be above the natural rate. In Exhibit 3(c) we have an inflationary gap at the short-run equilibrium, $E_{SR}$, at $RGDP_2$. An output gap that occurs when the actual output (RGDP) is greater than the potential output ($RGDP_{NR}$) is an **inflationary gap**. In this case, aggregate demand is so high that the economy is temporarily operating beyond full capacity ($RGDP_{NR}$), which will usually lead to inflationary pressure, so unemployment will be below the natural rate. In Exhibit 3(b) the economy is just right, where $AD_1$ and $SRAS$ intersect at $RGDP_{NR}$—the long-run equilibrium position.

**recessionary gap**
*an output gap that occurs when the actual output is less than the potential output*

**inflationary gap**
*an output gap that occurs when the actual output is greater than the potential output*

## Demand-Pull Inflation

**Demand-pull inflation** occurs when the price level increases due to an increase in aggregate demand. Consider the case in which an increase in consumer optimism results in a corresponding increase in aggregate demand. Exhibit 4 shows that an increase in aggregate demand causes an increase in the price level and an increase in real output. The movement is along *SRAS* from point $E_0$ to point $E_1$. This causes an inflationary gap. Recall that there is an increase in output as a result of the increase in the price level in the short run because firms have an incentive to increase real output when the prices of the goods they are selling are rising faster than the costs of the inputs they use in production.

Note that $E_1$ in Exhibit 4 is positioned beyond $RGDP_{NR}$—an inflationary gap. It seems peculiar that the economy can operate beyond its potential, but this is possible, temporarily, as firms encourage workers to work overtime, extend the hours of part-time workers, hire recently retired employees, reduce frictional unemployment through more extensive searches for employees, and so on. However, this level of output and employment *cannot* be sustained in the long run.

**demand-pull inflation**
*a price level increase due to an increase in aggregate demand*

**section 9.3**
Exhibit 4

**Demand-Pull Inflation**

Demand-pull inflation occurs when the aggregate demand curve shifts to the right along the short-run aggregate supply curve.

**section 9.3**
Exhibit 5

**Cost-Push Inflation**

Cost-push inflation is caused by a leftward shift in the short-run aggregate supply curve, from $SRAS_0$ to $SRAS_1$.

## Cost-Push Inflation

**stagflation**

*a situation in which lower growth and higher prices occur together*

**cost-push inflation**

*a price level increase due to a negative supply shock or increase in input prices*

The mid-1970s to early 1980s witnessed a phenomenon known as **stagflation**, a situation in which lower growth and higher prices occurred together. Some economists believe that this was caused by a leftward shift in the short-run aggregate supply curve, as seen in Exhibit 5. If the aggregate demand curve did not increase considerably but the price level increased significantly, then the inflation was caused by supply-side forces. This is called **cost-push inflation**—a price level increase due to a negative supply shock or increase in input prices.

The increase in oil prices was the primary culprit responsible for the leftward shift in the aggregate supply curve. As we discussed in the last section, an increase in input prices can cause the short-run aggregate supply curve to shift to the left, and this spelled big trouble for the Canadian economy—higher price levels, lower output, and higher rates of unemployment. The impact of cost-push inflation is illustrated in Exhibit 5.

In Exhibit 5, we see that the economy is initially at full-employment equilibrium at point $E_0$. Now suppose there is a sudden increase in input prices, such as the increase in the price of oil. This increase would shift the *SRAS* curve to the left—from $SRAS_0$ to $SRAS_1$. As a result of the shift in short-run aggregate supply, the price level rises to $PL_1$ and real output falls from $RGDP_{NR}$ to $RGDP_1$ (point $E_1$). Now firms demand fewer workers as a result of the higher input costs that cannot be passed on to the consumers. The result is higher prices, lower real output, and more unemployment—and it leads to a recessionary gap. These supply shocks can change RGDP significantly, but temporarily, away from potential aggregate output at $RGDP_{NR}$. In 2007–08, the price of many raw materials shot up globally—a global negative supply shock. Many countries around the world, including Canada, felt the effects of the negative supply shock.

## A Decrease in Aggregate Demand and Recessions

Just as cost-push inflation can cause a recessionary gap, so can a decrease in aggregate demand. For example, consider the case in which consumer confidence plunges and the stock market crashes. As a result, aggregate demand would fall, shown in Exhibit 6 as the shift from $AD_0$ to $AD_1$, and the economy would be in a new short-run equilibrium at point $E_1$. Now, households are buying fewer goods and services at every price level. In response to this drop in demand, output would fall from $RGDP_{NR}$ to $RGDP_1$, and the price level would fall from $PL_0$ to $PL_1$. So in the short run, this fall in aggregate demand causes higher unemployment and a reduction in output—and it too can lead to a recessionary gap.

Most of the post-war recessions have been caused by negative demand shocks. Negative supply shocks have been relatively few but quite severe in terms of unemployment rates. The 2008 to 2009 recession appears to have been the product of both negative demand and supply shocks. During the financial crisis of 2008, both consumers and firms reduced their spending and this caused the aggregate demand curve to shift to the left, in turn leading to a recessionary gap. In short, financial market wealth decreased and precautionary saving by consumers increased as confidence fell, obtaining credit became more difficult, and both households and firms adopted a "wait and see" attitude. The rate of inflation slowed and GDP fell by nearly 3 percent in a year.

In an attempt to stave off what some feared was the onset of the next great depression, the Bank of Canada increased the money supply and lowered interest rates. In addition, the Canadian government enacted a number of extraordinary measures to stimulate consumption, investment, and government spending. This helped to shift the aggregate demand curve to the right and RGDP and the price level rose by the end of 2009. We will discuss this in much more detail in our chapters on fiscal policy and monetary policy.

## HOW CAN THE ECONOMY SELF-CORRECT TO A RECESSIONARY GAP?

Many recoveries from a recessionary gap occur because of increases in aggregate demand—perhaps consumer and business confidence picks up or the government lowers taxes and/or lowers interest rates to stimulate the economy. That is, there is eventually a rightward shift in the aggregate demand curve that takes the economy back to potential output—$RGDP_{NR}$.

However, it is possible that the economy could *self-correct* through declining wages and prices. In Exhibit 7, at point $E_1$, the intersection of $PL_1$ and $RGDP_1$, the economy is in a recessionary gap—the economy is producing less than its potential output. At this lower level of output, recessionary pressures will begin to force firms to lay off workers to avoid inventory accumulation. In addition, firms may cut prices in an attempt to increase sales for their products. Unemployed workers and other input suppliers may also bid down wages and prices in an attempt to increase the demand for their goods and services. That is, in a recession, labourers and other input suppliers are now willing to accept lower wages and prices for the use of their resources, and the resulting reduction in production costs shifts the short-run supply curve from $SRAS_0$ to $SRAS_1$. Eventually, the economy returns to a long-run equilibrium at $E_2$ at $RGDP_{NR}$ and a lower price level, $PL_2$.

**section 9.3**
**Exhibit 6**

**Short-Run Decrease in Aggregate Demand**

A fall in aggregate demand from a drop in consumer confidence can cause a short-run change in the economy. The decrease in aggregate demand (shown in the movement from point $E_0$ to $E_1$) causes lower output and higher unemployment in the short run.

**section 9.3**
**Exhibit 7**

**Self-Correcting to a Recessionary Gap**

At point $E_1$, the economy is in a recessionary gap. However, the economy may self-correct as labourers and other input suppliers are now willing to accept lower wages and prices for the use of their resources. This results in a reduction in production costs that shifts the short-run supply curve from $SRAS_0$ to $SRAS_1$. Eventually, the economy returns to a long-run equilibrium at point $E_2$, at $RGDP_{NR}$, and a lower price level, $PL_2$.

For example, in the 1980s, OPEC had lost some of its clout due to internal problems and the increased production of many non-OPEC oil producers. The net result in the short run was a rightward shift in the aggregate supply curve. Holding aggregate demand constant, this rightward shift in the aggregate supply curve leads to a lower price level, greater output, and lower unemployment—moving the economy back toward long-run potential as illustrated in Exhibit 7.

## Self-Correction to a Recessionary Gap Can Be Slow

Many economists believe that wages and prices may be slow to adjust, especially downward. The tendency for prices and wages to only adjust slowly downward to changes in the economy is referred to as **wage and price inflexibility**. The significance of this inflexibility is that it may lead to prolonged periods of a recessionary gap.

For example, in Exhibit 7 we see that the economy is in a recession at $E_1$ at $RGDP_1$. The economy will eventually self-correct to $RGDP_{NR}$ at $E_2$, as workers and other input owners accept lower wages and prices for their inputs, shifting the $SRAS$ curve to the right from $SRAS_0$ to $SRAS_1$. However, if wages and other input prices are sticky, the economy's adjustment mechanism might take many months, or even a few years, to totally self-correct.

Japan witnessed several recessionary gaps in the 1990s and even experienced deflation as the self-adjustment mechanism predicts. However, the adjustment out of the recessionary gap was slow and painful.

Empirical evidence supports several reasons for the downward stickiness of wages and prices. Firms may not be able to legally cut wages because of long-term labour contracts (particularly with union workers) or a legal minimum wage. Efficiency wages may also limit a firm's ability to lower wage rates. Menu costs may cause price inflexibility as well.

**Efficiency Wages**    In economics, it is generally assumed that as productivity rises, wages will rise, and that workers can raise their productivity through investments in human capital like education and on-the-job training. However, some economists believe that in some cases, *higher wages will lead to greater productivity.*

In the efficiency wage model, employers pay their employees more than the equilibrium wage as a means to increase efficiency. Proponents of this theory suggest that higher-than-equilibrium wages may attract the most productive workers, lower job turnover and training costs, and improve morale. Because the efficiency wage rate is greater than the equilibrium wage rate, the quantity of labour that would be willingly supplied is greater than the quantity of labour demanded, resulting in greater amounts of unemployment.

However, aside from creating some additional unemployment, it may also cause wages to be inflexible downward. For example, in the event that there is a decrease in aggregate demand, firms that pay efficiency wages may be reluctant to cut wages for fear that it could lead to lower morale, greater absenteeism, and general productivity losses. In short, if firms are paying efficiency wages, they may be reluctant to lower wages in a recession, leading to downward wage inflexibility.

**Menu Costs**    As we explained in Chapter 5, there is a cost to changing prices in an inflationary environment. But the higher price level in an inflationary environment is often reflected slowly, as restaurants, mail-order houses, and department stores change their prices gradually so that they incur fewer *menu costs* (the costs of changing posted prices) in printing new menus, new catalogues, new mailers, new advertisements, and so on. Since businesses are not likely to change these prices instantly, we can say that some prices are sticky, or slow to change. For example, many outputs, like steel, are inputs in the production of other products, like automobiles. As a result, these prices are slow to change.

**wage and price inflexibility**

*the tendency for prices and wages to only adjust slowly downward to changes in the economy*

Suppose that there was an unexpected reduction in the money supply that led to a decrease in aggregate demand. This could lower the price level. Although some firms may adjust to the change quickly, others may move more slowly because of menu costs. The potential result is that their prices may become too high (above equilibrium); sales and output will fall, causing a potential recession.

If some firms are not responding quickly to changes in demand, there must be a reason, and to some economists, menu costs are at least part of that reason.

## HOW CAN THE ECONOMY SELF-CORRECT TO AN INFLATIONARY GAP?

In Exhibit 8, the economy is currently in an inflationary gap at $E_1$, where $RGDP_0$ is greater than $RGDP_{NR}$. Workers were anticipating price level $PL_0$, but because the price level is now higher, at $PL_1$, workers become disgruntled with wages that have not yet adjusted. Remember that your real wage—the purchasing power of your income—falls when prices rise by more than your nominal wage—your money income. Recall also that along the *SRAS* curve, wages and other input prices are assumed to be constant. Therefore, workers' and input suppliers' purchasing power falls as output prices rise. Real (adjusted for inflation) wages have fallen. Consequently, workers and other suppliers demand higher prices, to be willing to supply their inputs. As input prices respond to the higher level of output prices, the short-run aggregate supply curve shifts to the left, from $SRAS_0$ to $SRAS_1$. Suppliers will continually seek higher prices for their inputs until they reach the long-run equilibrium, at point $E_2$ in Exhibit 8. At point $E_2$, input suppliers' purchasing power is now restored at the long-run equilibrium, at $RGDP_{NR}$, and a new higher price level, $PL_2$.

## PRICE LEVEL AND RGDP OVER TIME

In Exhibit 9, we trace the pattern of RGDP versus the price level from 1981 to 2017. According to Statistics Canada, both the price level and RGDP have been trending upward for nearly 40 years. So what is responsible for the changes? The answer is both aggregate demand and aggregate supply. Aggregate demand has risen because of growing population (which impacts consumption and investment spending), rising income, increases in government purchases, and increases in the money supply. Aggregate supply has generally been increasing as well, including increases in the labour force and improvements in labour productivity and technology.

**section 9.3** Exhibit 8 — **Self-Correction to an Inflationary Gap**

The economy is currently in an inflationary gap at $E_1$, where $RGDP_0$ is greater than $RGDP_{NR}$. Because the price level is now higher than workers anticipated (i.e., it is $PL_1$ rather than $PL_0$), workers and other suppliers demand higher prices. As input prices respond to the higher level of output prices, the short-run aggregate supply curve shifts to the left, from $SRAS_0$ to $SRAS_1$. Suppliers will continually seek higher prices for their inputs until they reach the long-run equilibrium, at point $E_2$. At point $E_2$, input suppliers' purchasing power is now restored at the natural rate, $RGDP_{NR}$, at a new higher price level, $PL_2$.

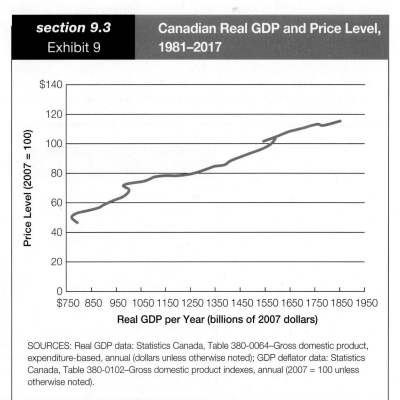

**section 9.3** Exhibit 9 — **Canadian Real GDP and Price Level, 1981–2017**

SOURCES: Real GDP data: Statistics Canada, Table 380-0064–Gross domestic product, expenditure-based, annual (dollars unless otherwise noted); GDP deflator data: Statistics Canada, Table 380-0102–Gross domestic product indexes, annual (2007 = 100 unless otherwise noted).

# Business **CONNECTION**

## FACING THE STORM CLOUDS: LOW INFLATION AND DEFLATION

Recent economic history has always addressed fears of higher rates of inflation. There are two sources of inflation: (1) *demand-pull inflation*, or inflation fuelled by aggregate demand, which occurs when the price level for goods and services in the economy increases because aggregate demand is growing at a greater rate than aggregate supply, and (2) *cost-push inflation*, which usually occurs when input costs for the factors of production increase, which in turn feed into the costs of a host of basic goods and services. This type of inflation forces suppliers in the affected industries to increase prices or, at worst, to leave the industry entirely, resulting in a reduction in aggregate supply.

Inflation usually occurs during high periods of growth in the economy, but what happens when the economy is experiencing a recession or a period of prolonged stagnant growth? This situation, triggered by either a fall in wages or a depression in consumer demand, may actually cause prices to contract—a condition that economists call *deflation*. For business, low inflation or deflation ultimately means losses in revenues and profits that many firms will not survive.

Firms need to recognize that they may not be able to do much when demand is greatly influenced by demographic issues. These are challenges to the economy as a whole and there isn't much opportunity to change that at the micro level. Still, firms can look at their product mix and decide whether changes in demographics would adversely affect their products. For example, a firm producing baby diapers might consider changing to adult diapers.

Firms will also have to pay particular attention to their inventory levels. They need to recognize that falling prices send a message to consumers to wait to buy, because prices will be lower in the future. For inventories that are perishable or could be a challenge to sell once they're outdated, it's imperative that firms reduce their inventories and order smaller quantities—more frequently too. They can reduce their input costs by being proactive in their ordering patterns.

Firms will also need to look at all of their operating costs to find any specific reductions they can make to help reduce their product or service costs. This might mean looking into longer-term contracts that have favourable prices and becoming more flexible on contracts for inputs that tend to be commodities. If firms are successful, they can still be profitable if they are forced to lower prices in the market.

When there's downward pressure on prices, firms need to find ways to compete on anything but price. This means increasing the value-added on their products and avoiding competition in markets where their products are viewed as commodities. This might mean investing more in R&D. Firms should recognize that they will get great value from these investments because individuals will likely be willing to work for less (or produce more) just to keep their jobs or contracts. It also helps firms to invest in technology that was too expensive in an expanding market—suppliers are just as anxious to pare down their inventories during deflationary periods, which can mean considerable access and savings to a firm that is trying to increase productivity.

All in all, competing in periods of low inflation or deflation poses extreme challenges to firms, but a careful and well-managed firm will find opportunities while others will fall by the wayside.

1. As a business manager, which is more volatile for your business: demand-pull inflation or cost-push inflation?

2. In a period of "lowflation" or deflation, do you think a business manager would care whether the cause is lower prices or lower demand? What could the manager do differently if the cause of the lowflation was lower prices as opposed to lower demand?

3. When growth starts to slow and inflation lags, many firms' first response is to lay off high-cost sales personnel. In your opinion, is this a good strategy, and why?

## SECTION CHECK

- Short-run macroeconomic equilibrium is shown by the intersection of the aggregate demand curve and the short-run aggregate supply curve. A short-run equilibrium is also a long-run equilibrium only if it is at potential output on the long-run aggregate supply curve.
- If short-run equilibrium occurs at less than the potential output of the economy, $RGDP_{NR}$, there is a recessionary gap. If short-run equilibrium temporarily occurs beyond $RGDP_{NR}$, there is an inflationary gap.
- It is possible for the economy to self-correct from a recessionary gap through declining wages and prices. The short-run aggregate supply curve eventually increases, returning the economy to the long-run equilibrium, at $RGDP_{NR}$, at a lower price level.
- It is possible for the economy to self-correct from an inflationary gap through increasing wages and prices. The short-run aggregate supply curve ultimately decreases, returning the economy to the long-run equilibrium, at $RGDP_{NR}$, at a higher price level.

# For Your Review

## Section 9.1

1. You operate a business manufacturing furniture. You are able to increase your furniture prices by 5 percent this quarter. You assume that the demand for your furniture has increased and begin increasing furniture production. Only later do you realize that prices in the macroeconomy are rising generally at a rate of 5 percent per quarter. This is an example of what effect? What does it imply about the slope of the short-run aggregate supply curve?

2. Why is the short-run aggregate supply curve upward sloping, while the long-run aggregate supply curve is vertical at the natural rate of output?

3. Why is focusing on producers' profit margins helpful in understanding the logic of the short-run aggregate supply curve?

## Section 9.2

4. How will each of the following changes alter aggregate supply?

| Change | Short-Run Aggregate Supply | Long-Run Aggregate Supply |
|---|---|---|
| An increase in aggregate demand | _____ | _____ |
| A decrease in aggregate demand | _____ | _____ |
| An increase in the stock of capital | _____ | _____ |
| A reduction in the size of the labour force | _____ | _____ |
| An increase in input prices (that does not reflect permanent changes in a firm's supplies) | _____ | _____ |
| A decrease in input prices (that does reflect permanent changes in a firm's supplies) | _____ | _____ |
| An increase in usable natural resources | _____ | _____ |
| A temporary adverse supply shock | _____ | _____ |
| Increases in the cost of government regulations | _____ | _____ |

5. What would each of the following do to the short-run aggregate supply curve?

   a. a decrease in wage rates

   b. passage of more stringent environmental and safety regulations affecting businesses

   c. technological progress

   d. an increase in consumer optimism

   e. an electric power blackout in Ontario

6. What would each of the following do to the long-run aggregate supply curve?

    a.  advances in medical technologies

    b.  increased immigration of skilled workers

    c.  an increase in wage rates

    d.  an epidemic involving a new strain of the flu that kills hundreds of thousands of people

7. Indicate whether the following events affect short-run aggregate supply or long-run aggregate supply. Identify the direction of impact.

    a.  Unusually cold weather in Saskatchewan reduces the wheat crop.

    b.  A devastating earthquake in British Columbia destroys hundreds of buildings and kills thousands of people.

    c.  Economy-wide wage increases are made.

    d.  Advances in computers and wireless technologies improve the efficiency of production.

8. How can a change in input prices change the short-run aggregate supply curve but not the long-run aggregate supply curve? How could it change both long-run and short-run aggregate supply?

## Section 9.3

### Blueprint Problem

Use the following diagram to answer questions (a) and (b).

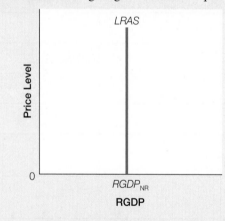

a.  On the diagram provided, illustrate the short-run effects of a decrease in aggregate demand. What happens to the price level, real output, employment, and unemployment?

b.  On the diagram provided, illustrate the long-run effects of a decrease in aggregate demand. What happens to the price level, real output, employment, and unemployment?

## Blueprint Solution

a.

Use the same three-step procedure used to perform demand/supply analysis in Chapter 4.

Step 1: Establish model in long-run equilibrium ($E_0$). Note: Whenever doing this type of *AD/AS* analysis, remember to always start from a position of long-run equilibrium.

Step 2: Decrease aggregate demand (leftward shift).

Step 3: Re-establish model in the temporary short-run equilibrium $E_1$. This equilibrium is considered short-run since it is achieved by the intersection of the *AD* and the *SRAS* curves. The assumption is that, at this point, the economy has not had sufficient time to self-correct to the decrease in aggregate demand (i.e., the short run).

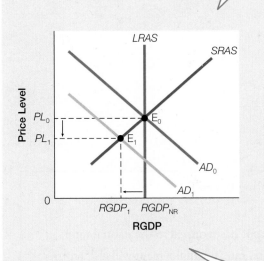

Short-Run Impact Analysis (Comparing $E_0$ and $E_1$)

a. Price level is lower ($PL_1 < PL_0$).

b. Real GDP is lower (now below $RGDP_{NR}$), therefore economy is experiencing a recessionary gap ($RGDP_{NR} - RGDP_1$).

c. Some of the decrease in real GDP will come from the existing employed working fewer hours (therefore no impact on employment or unemployment rates). However, at least some of the decrease would presumably come from job loss—an increase in cyclical unemployment (therefore a rise in unemployment and reduction in employment).

b.

> What distinguishes this analysis from that done in part (a) is that this question is looking for the impact of the decrease in *AD*, assuming that the economy has had sufficient time to adjust (i.e., the long run).
>
>     Because the initial decrease in *AD* lowered RGDP below the natural rate of output, the economy is now experiencing a recessionary gap. In response to the resulting recessionary pressures, both labour and other input suppliers will *eventually* accept lower wages and prices for the use of their resources. These lower prices will have the effect of shifting the *SRAS* curve rightward—restoring the economy back to long-run equilibrium ($RGDP_{NR}$) at a lower price level ($PL_2$).

> Long-Run Impact Analysis (Comparing $E_1$ and $E_2$)
>
> a. Price level is lower ($PL_2 < PL_1$).
> b. Real GDP has increased (real output has returned to the natural rate).
> c. As real output returns to its natural rate, unemployment will also return to its natural rate—necessarily causing the unemployment rate to decrease back to the natural rate (the rate of employment increasing as a result).

9. Use the following diagram to answer questions (a) and (b).

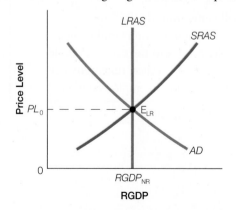

   a. On the diagram provided, illustrate the short-run effects of an increase in consumer confidence. What happens to the price level, real output, employment, and unemployment?

b. On the diagram provided, illustrate the long-run effects of an increase in consumer confidence. What happens to the price level, real output, employment, and unemployment?

10. Use the following diagram to answer questions (a) and (b).

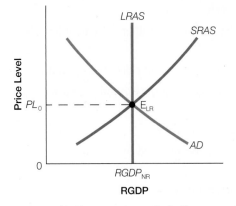

a. On the diagram provided, illustrate the short-run effects of a decrease in government purchases. What happens to the price level, real output, employment, and unemployment?

b. On the diagram provided, illustrate the long-run effects of a decrease in government purchases. What happens to the price level, real output, employment, and unemployment?

11. Use the following diagram to answer questions (a) and (b).

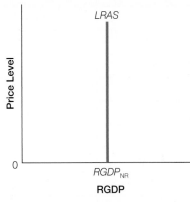

a. Illustrate a recessionary gap on the diagram provided.

b. Given the illustration in (a), illustrate and explain the eventual long-run equilibrium in this case.

12. Use the following diagram to answer questions (a) and (b).

a. Illustrate an inflationary gap on the diagram provided.

b. Given the illustration in (a), illustrate and explain the eventual long-run equilibrium in this case.

13. Distinguish cost-push from demand-pull inflation. Provide an example of an event or shock to the economy that would cause each.

14. Is it ever possible for an economy to operate above the full-employment level in the short term? Explain.

15. What do economists mean when they refer to wages and prices being "sticky"?

16. Which of the following leads to stagflation, assuming the economy is currently operating at full employment?

a. an increase in government spending on education

b. large nominal wage increases demanded and received by striking workers

c. a decrease in federal spending on national defence

d. a temporary increase in oil production from the Organization of the Petroleum Exporting Countries (OPEC)

e. a temporary decrease in OPEC oil production

17. The following table shows the initial level of aggregate demand ($AD_0$) and aggregate supply ($AS_0$) for the economy of Adanac. The full-employment level of output is $500 billion.

| Price Index | $AD_0$ (billions) | $AS_0$ (billions) | $AD_1$ (billions) |
|---|---|---|---|
| 60 | $875 | $250 | $ |
| 70 | 800 | 300 | |
| 80 | 725 | 350 | |
| 90 | 650 | 400 | |
| 100 | 575 | 450 | |
| 110 | 500 | 500 | |
| 120 | 425 | 550 | |
| 130 | 350 | 600 | |
| 140 | 275 | 650 | |

a. Draw the corresponding initial aggregate demand and aggregate supply curves ($AD_0$ and $AS_0$).

b. What is the initial equilibrium price level and level of real GDP?

c. At this initial equilibrium ($AD_0$ and $AS_0$), is Adanac experiencing either a recessionary or inflationary gap? If so, how large a gap exists?

d. Suppose the aggregate demand in Adanac declines for $125 billion at every price level. In the above table, compute the new quantity of aggregate demand in the column labelled $AD_1$. Add $AD_1$ to the diagram from part (a). What is the new equilibrium price level and quantity of real GDP?

e. At the new equilibrium ($AD_1$ and $AS_0$) is Adanac experiencing either a recessionary or inflationary gap? If so, how large a gap exists?

# Appendix

## THE SIMPLE KEYNESIAN AGGREGATE EXPENDITURE MODEL

The Keynesian aggregate expenditure model is based on the condition that the components of aggregate demand (consumption, investment, government spending, and net exports) must equal total output. Recall from Chapter 7 that Keynes was concerned with explaining and reducing short-term fluctuations in the economy. Keynes believed that total spending was a critical determinant of the overall level of economic activity. When total spending increases, firms increase their output and hire more workers. Even though Keynes ignored an important economic component—aggregate supply—his model still provides a great deal of information about aggregate demand.

### Why Do We Assume the Price Level Is Fixed?

Keynes believed wages and prices were inflexible in the short run, so in this appendix we will assume that the price level is fixed or constant. If the price level is fixed, then changes in nominal income will be equivalent to changes in real income. That is, when we assume the price level is fixed, we do not have to distinguish real variable changes from nominal variable changes. Keynes believed that prices and wages were rigid or fixed until full employment is reached. But let us begin by looking at the most important aggregate demand determinant—consumption spending.

### The Simplest Aggregate Expenditure Model: Autonomous Consumption Only

It is useful to begin by considering consumption spending by households. Household spending on goods and services is the largest single component of the demand for final goods, accounting for nearly 60 percent of GDP.

Numerous economic variables influence aggregate demand for consumer goods and services and, therefore, aggregate consumption expenditures. Using you or your family as an example, you know that such things as disposable income (after-tax income), credit conditions, the level of debt outstanding, the amount of financial assets, and expectations are important determinants of consumption purchases. Most economists believe that disposable income is one of the dominant factors.

To simplify things bit, imagine an economy in which only consumption spending exists (no investment, government purchases, or net exports; later, we'll add in these other sectors). To begin with the simplest situation possible, let's suppose that each household has the same level of disposable income. This kind of analysis relies on averages and is called representative household analysis. On a graph of consumption spending (vertical axis) for our representative household and the household's representative disposable income (horizontal axis), we could represent average consumption of disposable income at point A in Exhibit 1. From point A, a horizontal dotted line to the vertical axis permits us to read the value of average consumption spending, $C_0$.

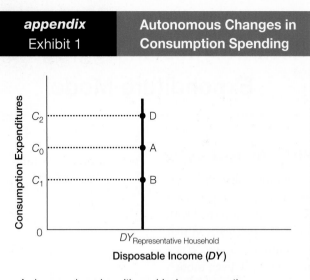

**appendix Exhibit 1**

**Autonomous Changes in Consumption Spending**

An increase in real wealth would raise consumption spending to $C_2$, at point D. A decrease in real wealth would tend to lower the level of consumption spending to $C_1$, at point B. A higher interest rate tends to cause a decrease in consumption spending from point A to point B. As household debt increases, other things equal, consumption spending would fall from point A to point B. In general, an increase in consumer confidence would act to increase household spending (a movement from point A to point D) and a decrease in consumer confidence would act to decrease household spending (a movement from point A to point B).

## What Are the Autonomous Factors That Influence Consumption Spending?

Even though income is given for the representative household, other economic factors that influence consumption spending are not. When consumption (or any of the other components of spending, such as investment) does not depend on income, we call it *autonomous* (or independent). Let's look at some of these other autonomous factors and see how they would change consumption spending.

**Real Wealth**   The larger the value of a household's real wealth (the money value of wealth divided by the price level, which indicates the amount of consumption goods that the wealth could buy), the larger the amount of consumption spending, other things being equal. Thus, in Exhibit 1, an increase in real wealth would raise consumption to $C_2$, at point D, for a given level of current income. Similarly, something that would lower the value of real wealth, such as a decline in property values or a stock market decline would tend to lower the level of consumption to $C_1$, at point B in Exhibit 1.

**Interest Rate**   A higher interest rate tends to make the consumption items that we buy on credit more expensive, which reduces expenditures on those items. An increase in the interest rate increases the monthly payments made to buy such things as automobiles, furniture, and major appliances and reduces our ability to spend out of a given income. This shift is shown as a decrease in consumption from point A to point B in Exhibit 1. Moreover, an increase in the interest rate provides a higher future return from reducing current spending, which motivates increasing savings. Thus, a higher interest rate in the current period would likely motivate an increase in savings today, which would permit households to consume more goods and services at some future date.

**Household Debt**   Remember when that friend of yours ran up his credit card obligations so high that he stopped buying goods except the basic necessities? Well, our average household might find itself in the same situation if its outstanding debt exceeds some reasonable level relative to its income. So, as debt increases, other things being equal, consumption expenditure would fall from point A to point B in Exhibit 1.

**Expectations**   Just as in microeconomics, decisions to spend may be influenced by a person's expectations of future disposable income, employment, or certain world events. Based on monthly surveys conducted that attempt to measure consumer confidence, an increase in consumer confidence generally acts to increase household spending (a movement from point A to point D in Exhibit 1) and a decrease in consumer confidence would act to decrease spending (a movement from point A to point B in Exhibit 1).

**Tastes and Preferences**  Of course, each household is different. Some are young and beginning a working career; some are without children; others have families; still others are older and perhaps retired from the workforce. Some households like to save, putting dollars away for later spending, whereas others spend all their income, or even borrow to spend more than their current disposable income. These saving and spending decisions often vary over a household's life cycle.

As you can see, many economic factors affect consumption expenditures. The factors already listed represent some of the most important. All of these factors are considered **autonomous determinants of consumption expenditures**; that is, those expenditures that are not dependent on the level of current disposable income.

*autonomous determinants of consumption expenditures*
*expenditures not dependent on the level of current disposable income*

## CONSUMPTION IN THE KEYNESIAN MODEL

In our first model, we looked at the economic variables that affected consumption expenditures when disposable income was fixed. This assumption is clearly unrealistic, but it allows us to develop some of the basic building blocks of the Keynesian expenditure model. Now we'll look at a slightly more complicated model in which consumption also depends on disposable income.

If you think about what determines your own current consumption spending, you know that it depends on many factors previously discussed, such as your age, family size, interest rates, expected future disposable income, wealth, and, most importantly, your current disposable income. Recall from earlier chapters, disposable income is your after-tax income. Your personal consumption spending depends primarily on your current disposable income. In fact, empirical studies confirm that most people's consumption spending is closely tied to their disposable income.

### Revisiting Marginal Propensity to Consume and Save

What happens to current consumption spending when a person earns some additional disposable income? Most people will spend some of their extra income and save some of it. The additional consumption resulting from an additional dollar of disposable income is what economists call your **marginal propensity to consume (*MPC*)**. That is, *MPC* is equal to the *change* in consumption spending ($\Delta C$) divided by the *change* in disposable income ($\Delta DY$):

$$MPC = \Delta C/\Delta DY$$

*marginal propensity to consume (MPC)*
*the additional consumption resulting from an additional dollar of disposable income*

For example, suppose you won a lottery prize of $1000. You might decide to spend $750 of your winnings today and save $250. In this example, your marginal propensity to consume is 0.75 (or 75 percent) because out of the extra $1000, you decided to spend 75 percent of it (0.75 × $1000 = $750).

The term *marginal propensity to consume* has two parts: (1) *marginal* refers to the fact that you received an extra amount of disposable income—in addition to your income, not your total income; and (2) *propensity to consume* refers to how much you tend to spend on consumer goods and services out of your additional income.

The flip side of the marginal propensity to consume is the **marginal propensity to save (*MPS*)**—the additional saving that results from an additional dollar of disposable income. That is, *MPS* is equal to the *change* in savings ($\Delta S$) divided by the change in disposable income ($\Delta DY$):

$$MPS = \Delta S/\Delta DY$$

*marginal propensity to save (MPS)*
*the additional saving that results from an additional dollar of income*

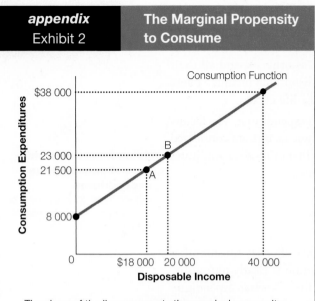

**appendix**
Exhibit 2

**The Marginal Propensity to Consume**

The slope of the line represents the marginal propensity to consume. At a disposable income of $18 000, you spend $8000 plus 75 percent of $18 000 (which is $13 500), for total spending of $21 500. If your disposable income rises to $20 000, you spend $8000 plus 75 percent of $20 000 (which is $15 000), for total spending of $23 000. So when your disposable income rises by $2000 (from $18 000 to $20 000), your spending goes up by $1500 (from $21 500 to $23 000). Your marginal propensity to consume is $1500 (the increase in spending) divided by $2000 (the increase in disposable income), which equals 0.75, or 75 percent. But notice that this *MPC* calculation is also the calculation of the slope of the line from point A to point B.

In the earlier lottery example, your marginal propensity to save is 0.25, or 25 percent, because you decided to save 25 percent of your additional disposable income (0.25 × $1000 = $250). Because your additional disposable income must be either consumed or saved, the marginal propensity to consume plus the marginal propensity to save must add up to 1, or 100 percent.

Let's illustrate the marginal propensity to consume in Exhibit 2. Suppose you estimated that you had to spend $8000 a year, even if you earned no income for the year, for necessities such as food, clothing, and shelter. And suppose for every $1000 of added disposable income you earn, you spend 75 percent of it and save 25 percent of it. So if your disposable income is $0, you spend $8000 (that means you have to borrow or reduce your existing savings just to survive). If your disposable income is $20 000, you'll spend $8000 plus 75 percent of $20 000 (which equals $15 000), for total spending of $23 000. If your disposable income is $40 000, you'll spend $8000 plus 75 percent of $40 000 (which equals $30 000), for total spending of $38 000.

What's your marginal propensity to consume? In this case, if you spend 75 percent of every additional $1000 you earn, your marginal propensity to consume is 0.75 or 75 percent. And if you save 25 percent of every additional $1000 you earn, your marginal propensity to save is 0.25.

In Exhibit 2, the slope of the line represents the marginal propensity to consume. To better understand this concept, look at what happens when your disposable income rises from $18 000 to $20 000. At a disposable income of $18 000, you spend $8000 plus 75 percent of $18 000 (which is $13 500), for total spending of $21 500. If your disposable income rises to $20 000, you spend $8000 plus 75 percent of $20 000 (which is $15 000), for total spending of $23 000. So when your disposable income rises by $2000 (from $18 000 to $20 000), your spending goes up by $1500 (from $21 500 to $23 000). Your marginal propensity to consume is $1500 (the increase in spending) divided by $2000 (the increase in disposable income), which equals 0.75, or 75 percent. But notice that this calculation is also the calculation of the slope of the line from point A to point B in the exhibit. Recall that the slope of the line is the rise (the change on the vertical axis) over the run (the change on the horizontal axis). In this case, that's $1500 divided by $2000, which makes 0.75 the marginal propensity to consume. So the marginal propensity to consume is the same as the slope of the line in our graph of consumption and disposable income.

Now, let's take this same logic and apply it to the economy as a whole. If we add up, or aggregate, everyone's consumption and everyone's income, we'll get a line that looks like the one in Exhibit 2, but that applies to the entire economy. This line or functional relationship is called a *consumption function*. Let's suppose consumption spending in the economy is $1 billion plus 75 percent of income.

Now, with consumption equal to $1 billion plus 75 percent of income, consumption is partly autonomous (the $1 billion part, which people would spend no matter what their income, which depends on the current interest rate, real wealth, debt, and expectations), and partly *induced*, which means it depends on income. The induced consumption is the portion that's equal to 75 percent of income.

What is the total amount of expenditure in this economy? Because we've assumed that investment, government purchases, and net exports are zero, aggregate expenditure is just equal to the amount of consumption spending represented by our consumption function.

## EQUILIBRIUM IN THE KEYNESIAN MODEL

The next part of the Keynesian aggregate expenditure model is to examine what conditions are needed for the economy to be in equilibrium. This discussion also tells us why the Keynesian expenditure model is sometimes called a *Keynesian-cross model.* In order to determine equilibrium, we need to show (1) that income equals output in the economy and (2) that in equilibrium, aggregate expenditure (or consumption in this example) equals output. First, income equals output because people earn income by producing goods and services. For example, workers earn wages because they produce some product that is then sold on the market, and owners of firms earn profits because the products they sell provide more income than the cost of producing them. So any income that is earned by anyone in the economy arises from the production of output in the economy. From now on, we'll use this idea and say that income equals output; we'll use the terms *income* and *output* interchangeably.

The second condition needed for equilibrium (aggregate expenditure in the economy equals output) is the distinctive feature of the Keynesian expenditure model. Just as income must equal output (because income comes from selling goods and services), aggregate expenditure equals output because people can't earn income until the products they produce are sold to someone. Every good or service that is produced in the economy must be purchased by someone or added to inventories. Exhibit 3 plots aggregate expenditure against output. As you can see, it's a 45-degree line (slope = 1). The 45-degree line shows that the number on the horizontal axis, representing the amount of output in the economy, real GDP ($Y$), is equal to the number on the vertical axis, representing the amount of real aggregate expenditure ($AE$) in the economy. If output is $5 billion, then in equilibrium, aggregate expenditure must equal $5 billion. All points of macroeconomic equilibrium lie on the 45-degree line.

## DISEQUILIBRIUM IN THE KEYNESIAN MODEL

What would happen if, for some reason, output was lower than its equilibrium level, as would be the case if output was $Y_1$ in Exhibit 4?

Looking at the vertical dotted line, we see that when output is $Y_1$, aggregate expenditure (shown by the consumption function) is greater than output (shown by the 45-degree line). This amount is labelled the distance AB on the graph. So, people would be trying to buy more goods and services (A) than were being produced (B), which would cause producers to increase the amount of production, which would increase output in the economy. This process would continue until output reached its equilibrium level, where the two lines intersect. Another way to think about this disequilibrium is that consumers would be buying more than is currently produced, causing a decrease in inventories on shelves and in warehouses from their desired levels. Clearly, profit-seeking businesspeople would increase production to bring their inventory stocks back up to the desired levels. In doing so, they would move production to the equilibrium level.

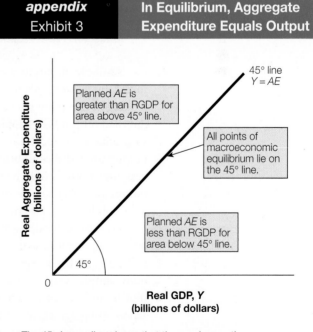

**appendix**
Exhibit 3

**In Equilibrium, Aggregate Expenditure Equals Output**

Planned *AE* is greater than RGDP for area above 45° line.

All points of macroeconomic equilibrium lie on the 45° line.

Planned *AE* is less than RGDP for area below 45° line.

45° line
$Y = AE$

45°

Real Aggregate Expenditure (billions of dollars)

Real GDP, *Y* (billions of dollars)

The 45-degree line shows that the number on the horizontal axis, representing the amount of output in the economy, is equal to the number on the vertical axis, representing the amount of aggregate expenditure in the economy. If output is $5 billion, then in equilibrium, aggregate expenditure must equal $5 billion.

**appendix**
Exhibit 4

## Disequilibrium and Equilibrium in the Keynesian Model

When RGDP is $Y_1$, aggregate expenditure is greater than output—distance AB on the graph. Consumers are trying to buy more goods and services (A) than are being produced (B), which causes producers to increase the amount of production, increasing output in the economy. This process continues until output reaches its equilibrium level, where the two lines intersect. If RGDP is at $Y_2$, aggregate expenditure (D) is less than output (C). Consumers wouldn't want to buy all the output that is being produced, so producers would want to reduce their production. They would keep reducing their output until the equilibrium level of output was reached. The only point for which consumption spending equals real aggregate planned expenditure equals output is the point where those two lines intersect. Because these points are on the 45-degree line, equilibrium output equals equilibrium aggregate expenditure.

Similarly, if output was above its equilibrium level, as would occur if output was $Y_2$ in Exhibit 4, economic forces would act to reduce output. At this point, as you can see by looking at the graph above point $Y_2$ on the horizontal axis, aggregate expenditure (D) is less than output (C). People wouldn't want to buy all the output that is being produced, so producers would want to reduce their production. They would keep reducing their output until the equilibrium level was reached. Using the inventory adjustment process, inventories would be bulging from shelves and warehouses and firms would reduce output and production until inventory stocks returned to the desired level. For example, automobile companies might close plants to reduce inventories.

This basic model—in which we've assumed that consumption spending is the only component of aggregate expenditure (i.e., we've ignored investment, government spending, and net exports) and that some consumption spending is autonomous—is quite simple, yet it is the essence of the Keynesian-cross model. Equilibrium in this model, and in more complicated versions of the model, always occurs where one line representing aggregate expenditure crosses another line that represents the equilibrium condition where aggregate expenditure equals output (the 45-degree line).

Now let's put Exhibits 2 and 3 together to find the equilibrium in the economy, shown in Exhibit 4. As you might guess, the point where the two lines cross is the equilibrium point. Why? Because it is only at this point that aggregate expenditure is equal to output. Aggregate expenditure is shown by the flatter line (Aggregate expenditure = Consumption). The equilibrium condition is shown by the 45-degree line ($Y = AE$). The only point for which consumption spending equals aggregate expenditure equals output is the point where those two lines intersect, labelled "Equilibrium." Because these points are on the 45-degree line, equilibrium output equals equilibrium aggregate expenditure.

## ADDING INVESTMENT, GOVERNMENT PURCHASES, AND NET EXPORTS

Now we can complicate our model in another important way by adding in the other three major components of expenditure in the economy: investment, government purchases, and net exports. We'll add these components to the model but assume that they are autonomous, that is, they don't depend on the level of income or output in the economy.

Suppose that consumption depends on the level of income or output in the economy, but investment, government purchases, and net exports don't; instead, they depend on other things in the economy, such as interest rates, political considerations, or the condition of foreign economies. Now, aggregate expenditure ($AE$) consists of consumption ($C$) plus investment ($I$) plus government purchases ($G$) plus net exports ($NX$):

$$AE \equiv C + I + G + NX$$

This equation is nothing more than a definition (indicated by the $\equiv$ rather than $=$): Aggregate expenditure equals the sum of its components.

When we add up all the components of aggregate expenditure, we'll get an upward-sloping line, as we did in the previous section because consumption increases as income increases. But because we're now allowing for investment, government purchases, and net exports, the autonomous portion of aggregate expenditure is larger. Thus, the intercept of the aggregate expenditure line is higher, as shown in Exhibit 5.

**appendix** Exhibit 5 — **Adding Investment, Government Purchases, and Net Exports to Aggregate Expenditures**

Adding $I + G + NX$ leads to a larger intercept of the aggregate expenditure line. Because consumption is the only component of aggregate expenditure that depends on income, the slope of the line is the same as the slope of the line in Exhibit 4. The new equilibrium occurs where the two lines cross, where the aggregate expenditure line, which has a slope of 0.75, intersects the equilibrium line, which is the 45-degree line.

What is the new equilibrium? As before, the equilibrium occurs where the two lines cross, that is, where the aggregate expenditure line intersects the equilibrium line, which is the 45-degree line.

Now that we've added in the other components of spending, especially investment spending, we can begin to discuss some of the more realistic factors related to the business cycle. This discussion of what happens to the economy during business cycles is a major element of Keynesian theory, which was designed to explain what happens in recessions.

If you look at historical economic data, you'll see that investment spending fluctuates much more than overall output in the economy. In recessions, output declines, and a major portion of the decline occurs because investment falls sharply. In expansions, investment is the major contributor to economic growth. The two major explanations for the volatile movement of investment over the business cycle involve planned investment and unplanned investment.

The first explanation for investment's strong business cycle movement is that *planned* investment responds dramatically to perceptions of future changes in economic activity. If firms think that the economy will be good in the future, they'll build new factories, buy more computers, and hire more workers today, in anticipation of being able to sell more goods in the future. On the other hand, if firms think the economy will be weak in the future, they'll cut back on both investment and hiring. Economists find that planned investment is extremely sensitive to firms' perceptions about the future. And if firms desire to invest more today, it generates ripple effects that make the economy grow even faster.

**unplanned inventory investment**

*collection of inventory that results when people do not buy the products firms are producing*

The second explanation for investment's movement over the business cycle is that businesses encounter *unplanned* changes in investment as well. The idea here is that recessions, to some extent, occur as the economy is making a transition, before it reaches equilibrium. We'll use Exhibit 6 to illustrate this idea. In the exhibit, equilibrium occurs at output of $Y^*$. Now, consider what would happen if, for some reason, firms produced too many goods, bringing the economy to output level $Y_2$. At output level $Y_2$, aggregate expenditure is less than output because the aggregate expenditure line is below the 45-degree line at that point. When people aren't buying all the products that firms are producing, unsold goods begin piling up. In the national income accounts, unsold goods in firms' inventories are counted in a subcategory of investment—inventory investment. The firms didn't plan for this to happen, so the piling up of inventories reflects **unplanned inventory investment**. Of course, once firms realize that inventories are rising because they've produced too much, they cut back on production, reducing output below $Y_2$. This process continues until firms' inventories are restored to normal levels and output returns to $Y^*$.

Now let's look at what would happen if firms produced too few goods, as occurs when output is at $Y_1$. At output level $Y_1$, aggregate expenditure is greater than output because the aggregate expenditure line is above the 45-degree line at that point. People want to buy more goods than firms are producing, so firms' inventories begin to decline or become depleted. Again, this change in inventories shows up in the national income accounts, this time

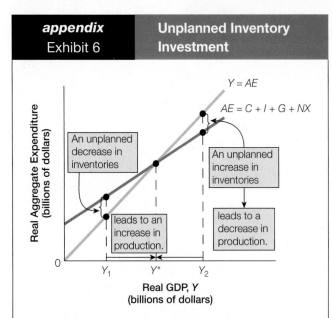

**appendix**
Exhibit 6

**Unplanned Inventory Investment**

At $Y_2$, *AE* is less than output and unsold goods pile up. As unplanned inventory investment builds up, firms cut back on production until equilibrium output is restored at $Y^*$. At $Y_1$, *AE* is greater than output: Consumers want to buy more than firms are producing. Inventories become depleted and firms increase production until inventories are restored and output returns to equilibrium at $Y^*$.

as a decline in firms' inventories and thus a decline in investment. Again, the firms didn't plan for this situation, so once they realize that inventories are declining because they haven't produced enough, they'll increase production beyond $Y_1$. Equilibrium is reached when firms' inventories are restored to normal levels and output returns to $Y^*$. So, our Keynesian aggregate expenditure model helps to explain the process of the business cycle, working through investment.

## Shifts in Aggregate Expenditure and the Multiplier

What happens if one of the components of aggregate expenditure increases for reasons other than an increase in income? Remember that we called these components or parts *autonomous*. Households' expectations might become more optimistic, or households may find credit conditions easier as interest rates decline, or their real wealth might increase as the stock market rises. All of these factors increase autonomous consumption, so total consumption at every level of income increases. Firms might increase their investment (especially if their productivity rises or the interest rate declines), government might increase its spending, or net exports could rise as foreign economies improve their economic health. Any of these things would increase aggregate expenditure for any given level of income, shifting the aggregate expenditure curve up, as shown in Exhibit 7.

Suppose that firms optimistic about their future profitability increase their planned investment spending on plants, factories, and machines by $100 million. In Exhibit 7, we see that the increase in planned investment spending shifts the aggregate expenditure curve upward and results in a $400 million gain in equilibrium real GDP, the difference between the equilibrium real GDP at point A and the equilibrium real GDP at point Z. How did the $100 million increase in autonomous investment raise real GDP demanded by $400 million? This result might seem amazing—that an increase in planned investment spending of a $100 billion can result in a $400 million increase in real GDP—but it merely reflects a well-understood process, known as the **expenditure multiplier**—the multiplier that considers only the impact of consumption changes on aggregate expenditures.

A caution here: Do not assume that the multiplier applies only to changes in planned investment spending. Multipliers apply to any increase in autonomous expenditure. As an example, if the stock market went up to increase the amount of autonomous household spending by $100 million, the level of output would go up the same $400 million as found in the preceding example. The idea of the multiplier is that permanent increases in spending in one part of the economy lead to increased spending by others in the economy as well. When firms increase investment spending, private resource owners earn more wages, interest, rents, and profits, so they spend more. The higher level of economic activity encourages even more spending, until a new equilibrium with higher output is reached, $Y_1$ rather than $Y_0$. In this example, the increase in output is four times as large as the initial increase in investment spending that started the cycle. Let's see how this process works in more detail.

**expenditure multiplier**
*the multiplier that considers only the impact of consumption changes on aggregate expenditures*

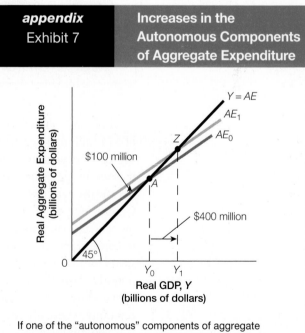

*appendix*
Exhibit 7

**Increases in the Autonomous Components of Aggregate Expenditure**

If one of the "autonomous" components of aggregate expenditure increases for reasons other than an increase in income (such as optimistic consumer or business expectations, a decrease in the interest rate, real wealth increases, government spending increases, or an increase in net exports), aggregate expenditure will increase for any given level of income, shifting the aggregate expenditure curve up, as shown in this exhibit.

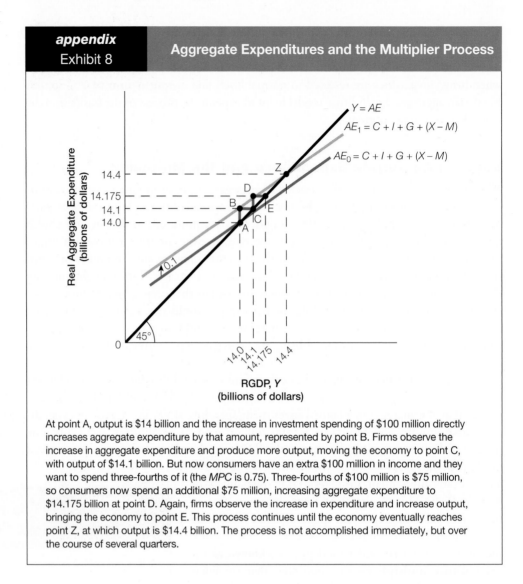

**appendix**
Exhibit 8

**Aggregate Expenditures and the Multiplier Process**

At point A, output is $14 billion and the increase in investment spending of $100 million directly increases aggregate expenditure by that amount, represented by point B. Firms observe the increase in aggregate expenditure and produce more output, moving the economy to point C, with output of $14.1 billion. But now consumers have an extra $100 million in income and they want to spend three-fourths of it (the *MPC* is 0.75). Three-fourths of $100 million is $75 million, so consumers now spend an additional $75 million, increasing aggregate expenditure to $14.175 billion at point D. Again, firms observe the increase in expenditure and increase output, bringing the economy to point E. This process continues until the economy eventually reaches point Z, at which output is $14.4 billion. The process is not accomplished immediately, but over the course of several quarters.

Exhibit 8 shows what happens along the way. We begin at point A, with output of $14 billion. The increase in investment spending of $100 million directly increases aggregate expenditure by that amount, represented by point B. Firms observe the increase in aggregate expenditure (perhaps because they see their inventories declining), so over the next few months, they produce more output, moving the economy to point C, with output of $14.1 billion. But now consumers have an extra $100 million in income and they want to spend three-fourths of it (because the marginal propensity to consume is 0.75). Three-fourths of $100 million is $75 million, so consumers now spend an additional $75 million, increasing aggregate expenditure to $14.175 billion at point D. Again, firms observe the increase in expenditure, so over the next few months, they increase output, bringing the economy to point E. This process continues until the economy eventually reaches point Z, at which output is $14.4 billion.

You can see on the graph how the economy reaches its new equilibrium at point Z. We can also calculate it numerically by adding up an infinite series of numbers in the following way. The first increase in output was $100 million, which comes directly from the increase in investment spending. Then consumers, with higher incomes of $100 million, want to spend three-fourths of it, so they increase spending: $100 million × 3/4 = $75 million. Now, with incomes higher by $75 million, consumers want to spend an additional three-fourths of it: $75 million × 3/4 = $56 million. Again, incomes are higher, so consumers will spend more, this time in the amount $56 million × 3/4 = $42 million. The process continues indefinitely. To find the total increase in output (or income), we simply need to add up all these amounts. It turns out that an infinite sum with this pattern is exactly $100 million/(1 − 3/4) = $400 million. So output increases by $400 million from $14 billion to $14.4 billion.

This calculation of the sum of all of the increases to output can be written in a convenient way. As you saw in this example, the multiplier depends on how much consumers spend out of any additions to their income. So in this model in which consumption spending is the only component of aggregate expenditure that depends on income, the multiplier is equal to $1/(1 − MPC)$, where $MPC$ is the marginal propensity to consume. In the previous example, $MPC$ = 3/4, so the multiplier is $1/(1 − 3/4)$ = 4. The same multiplier holds whether the increase in aggregate expenditures arises from an increase in investment spending, as in the example, or from an increase in other autonomous elements of spending, such as government purchases, net exports, or the autonomous portion of consumption spending. The larger (smaller) the $MPC$ the larger (smaller) the multiplier. For example, if the $MPC$ is 0.8 ($1/[1 − 0.8]$ or $1/0.2$ = 5) then the multiplier would be 5. If the $MPC$ is 0.5 ($1/[1 − 0.5]$ or $1/0.5$ = 2), then the multiplier would be reduced to 2. The true multiplier is usually smaller because of complications that we will discuss in the chapter on fiscal policy.

The multiplier can operate in both directions. During the Great Depression, both consumption spending and planned investment fell, causing a decrease in aggregate expenditure. As sales fell, workers were laid off and falling levels of production and income led to further declines in consumption spending as the economy fell into a downward spiral. The downturn can also start in a certain sector and then spread via the multiplier to other sectors of the economy. Recall, the information technology recession of 2001. The initial impact of the decline in investment spending was felt in the computer and telecommunications industries, but eventually the declines in production, income, and spending spread into other industries, such as those for automobiles, furniture, appliances, airlines, and restaurants. And the financial crisis of 2008 started in the U.S. housing and financial sectors and was quickly felt throughout the Canadian economy.

# For Your Review   (Chapter 9 Appendix)

1. Which of the following are likely to cause a reduction in consumption?
    a.  an increase in interest rates
    b.  an increase in the value of stock market portfolios
    c.  a decrease in disposable income
    d.  an increase in income taxes
    e.  deflation

2. Identify the most volatile component of aggregate expenditure. Identify its largest component.

3. Which of the following will cause the aggregate expenditure schedule to increase?

    a. an increase in consumer optimism

    b. an increase in the purchase of imports

    c. an increase in the sale of exports

    d. pessimism by business owners about the outlook of the economy

    e. an increase in government spending due to the outbreak of war

4. What would happen to autonomous consumption if household debt fell and the interest rate rose over the same time period?

5. What would happen to autonomous consumption if real wealth increased and expectations of the future became more optimistic?

6. Consumption equals $32 000 when disposable income equals $40 000. Consumption increases to $38 000 when disposable income increases to $50 000. What is the marginal propensity to consume? The marginal propensity to save? What is the value of the spending multiplier?

7. What would happen to autonomous consumption expenditures if the value of a consumer's stock market investments rose and that person's household debt rose at the same time?

8. If *MPC* was equal to 0.5, would doubling your income double your consumption spending?

9. Why can't an economy with an *MPC* greater than 1 reach a stable equilibrium in the aggregate expenditure model?

10. Why are unplanned inventory changes the key to predicting future changes in real GDP in the aggregate expenditure model?

11. Why would an increase in planned investment increase real GDP, but an unplanned increase in inventory investment decrease real GDP, in the aggregate expenditure model?

12. If net exports are negative, what happens to the aggregate expenditures line, other things being equal? What will happen to equilibrium income?

13. Why are planned and unplanned investment unlikely to both increase over the same period of time?

14. If the marginal propensity to consume was 0.75, what would happen to equilibrium income if government purchases increased by $500 million and investment fell by $500 million at the same time? What if government purchases increased by $500 million and investment fell by $400 million at the same time?

15. What would happen to equilibrium income if, other things being equal, imports increased by $100 million and the marginal propensity to consume was 0.9?

# 10

# Fiscal Policy

# Fiscal Policy

**section**

**10.1**

- What is fiscal policy?
- How does fiscal policy affect the government's budget?

## WHAT IS FISCAL POLICY?

**Fiscal policy** is the use of government spending and/or taxes to alter RGDP and the price level. Sometimes it is necessary for the government to use fiscal policy to stimulate the economy during a contraction (or recession) or to try to curb an expansion in order to bring inflation under control. In the early 1980s, the U.S. government implemented large tax cuts, which helped the U.S. economy out of a recession. In 2001 and 2003, tax cuts were again implemented to combat an economic slowdown and promote long-term economic growth. In the 1990s, Japan used large government spending programs to help pull itself out of a recessionary slump.

Beginning in the early 2000s, the federal government in Canada began cutting income taxes to promote long-term economic growth, a policy objective it continued in subsequent budgets. The 2009 budget, however, marked a dramatic departure from the fiscal restraint illustrated in earlier budgets, as the government began to deal with the global economic crisis. The first year of Canada's Economic Action Plan saw the government provide almost $30 billion in support of the Canadian economy. In total, this was equivalent to 1.9 percent of total spending in the Canadian economy in 2009. The 2010 budget confirmed an additional $19 billion in new federal spending under year 2 of Canada's Economic Action Plan, stimulus that was accompanied by additional tax relief measures designed to augment the already substantial tax relief provided by the government since 2006. The tax relief provided to individuals and families was estimated to be about $160 billion throughout 2008 to 2009 and the following five fiscal years.

**fiscal policy**

*use of government spending and/or taxes to alter RGDP and the price level*

With the 2011 budget, as planned, the vast majority of initiatives first announced in the 2009 budget were concluded. The conclusion of this first phase of Canada's Economic Action Plan—the stimulus phase—marked the commencement of the second phase of the plan—the low-tax plan for jobs and growth phase. This second phase would see the government return to the sustainable low-tax environment and growth-friendly policies it had first introduced in 2006. In the 2012 and 2013 versions of Canada's Economic Action Plan, the government maintained its focus on low-tax fiscal policies, emphasizing a return to balanced budgets, job creation, growth, and long-term prosperity.

The importance of job creation and economic growth continued to be emphasised in both the 2014 and 2015 editions of Canada's Economic Action Plan, as the global economic environment continued to exhibit uncertainty. In October of 2015, the new Liberal government was elected on a promise to launch major new infrastructure spending. Budget 2016 focused on job creation, economic growth, and strengthening the middle class. Renewed infrastructure spending along with a sizable tax cut for middle-income earners were at the centre of this first Liberal budget. With Budget 2017, the Liberal governments focus turned decidedly toward long-term economic planning. Additional infrastructure spending—with a focus on innovation— was promised, along with continued support to grow and strengthen the middle class.

When should the government use such policies? How well do they work? These are just a couple of the questions we will answer in this chapter.

When government spending (for purchases of goods and services and for transfer payments to individuals, like EI benefits) exceeds tax revenues for a given fiscal year, there is a **budget deficit**. When tax revenues are greater than government spending for a given fiscal year, a **budget surplus** exists. A balanced budget, where government expenditures equal tax revenues, may seldom occur unless efforts are made to deliberately balance the budget as a matter of public policy.

## HOW DOES FISCAL POLICY AFFECT THE GOVERNMENT'S BUDGET?

When the government wants to stimulate the economy by increasing aggregate demand, it will use **expansionary fiscal policy** and increase government spending on goods and services, lower taxes, or use some combination of these approaches. Any of those options will increase a budget deficit (or reduce a budget surplus). Thus, expansionary fiscal policy is associated with increased government budget deficits. Likewise, if the government wants to dampen a boom in the economy by reducing aggregate demand, it will use **contractionary fiscal policy** and reduce its spending on goods and services, increase taxes, or use some combination of these approaches. Thus, contractionary fiscal policy will tend to increase a budget surplus (or reduce a budget deficit).

**budget deficit**
*Government spending exceeds tax revenues for a given fiscal year.*

**budget surplus**
*Tax revenues are greater than government expenditures for a given fiscal year.*

**expansionary fiscal policy**
*use of fiscal policy tools to foster increased output by increasing government spending and/or lowering taxes*

**contractionary fiscal policy**
*use of fiscal policy tools to reduce output by decreasing government spending and/or increasing taxes*

### SECTION CHECK

- Fiscal policy is the use of government spending on goods and services and/or taxes to affect aggregate demand and to alter RGDP and the price level.
- Expansionary fiscal policies will increase a budget deficit (or reduce a budget surplus) through greater government spending, lower taxes, or both. Contractionary fiscal policies will increase a budget surplus (or reduce a budget deficit) through reduced government spending, higher taxes, or both.

# Government: Spending and Taxation

- What are the major categories of government spending?
- What are the major sources of government revenue?

## WHAT ARE THE MAJOR CATEGORIES OF GOVERNMENT SPENDING?

In 2016 to 2017, the federal government spent $296.4 billion on goods and services and on transfer payments to individuals. According to Exhibit 1(a), 29 percent of federal government spending in 2016 to 2017 was accounted for under major transfers to persons, including Employment Insurance and Old Age Security programs. Transfers of money from the federal government to other levels of government (for spending on postsecondary education and health care) amounted to 22 percent of federal government expenditure. Interest payments that the federal government made on its outstanding debt accounted for 8 percent of total spending, and national defence also accounted for 8 percent. Expenses associated with the operation of Crown corporations and other federal departments and agencies accounted for 3 percent and 17 percent of total spending, respectively. The remaining 13 percent of federal government spending (other transfers) included foreign affairs and international aid, the environment, recreation and culture, resource conservation, and industrial development.

**section 10.2**
Exhibit 1          **Federal Government Expenditures and Revenues**

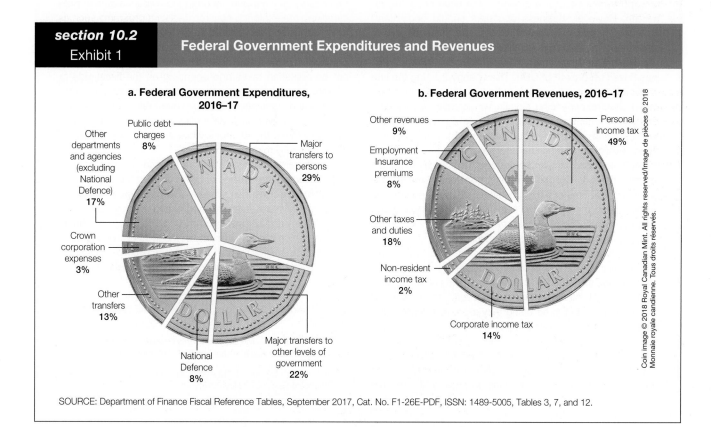

**a. Federal Government Expenditures, 2016–17**

Other departments and agencies (excluding National Defence) 17%

Public debt charges 8%

Major transfers to persons 29%

Crown corporation expenses 3%

Other transfers 13%

National Defence 8%

Major transfers to other levels of government 22%

**b. Federal Government Revenues, 2016–17**

Other revenues 9%

Employment Insurance premiums 8%

Other taxes and duties 18%

Non-resident income tax 2%

Personal income tax 49%

Corporate income tax 14%

SOURCE: Department of Finance Fiscal Reference Tables, September 2017, Cat. No. F1-26E-PDF, ISSN: 1489-5005, Tables 3, 7, and 12.

# Business *CONNECTION*

## CORPORATE NAVIGATION FOR A CHANGE IN LONG-TERM FISCAL GOALS

There's no question that one of the main roles of government is to help increase real GDP. Only with increases in economic growth can a country improve its standard of living, characterized and measured by per capita real GDP. The ability to increase real GDP depends on the four engines of the economy: consumer spending (*C*); business investment (*I*) spending; government spending and taxation (G); and net exports, or exports less imports (*X* – *M*).

Generally speaking, consumers and business drive the economy, and government involvement should be limited to stabilization and stimulation. Many consumers and businesses feel that the less government involvement in the economy, the better—but we rarely hear those sentiments in recessionary periods, when consumers aren't spending and business isn't investing due to consumer lethargy. It's left to governments to stimulate their economies when the other engines can't or won't contribute. While government involvement has traditionally been limited to the short-term to medium-term decisions of either stimulating or suppressing excessive growth, with the introduction of increased automation and AI to the economy, some longer term fiscal decisions will have to be made—and they are decisions that will likely impact a corporation's taxes and corporate participation/contribution within and for society. This becomes more significant as the move to this new digital/information-based economy increases.

How we accomplish the goals of either stimulating or suppressing excessive growth in the economy is up for debate. However, business operators should understand how government involvement affects their revenues, costs, and net profits, in both the short and long terms.

Historically, the primary target in adjusting the economy was based on growth of GDP. This changed during the late 1970s when, through a variety of factors, the economy stagnated while experiencing significant increases in inflation. Both governments and central banking agencies realized that targeting inflation, rather than growth, could provide better outcomes during the short and long terms. This is where both consumers and producers have been during this last half-century. But the one thing constant in macroeconomics is that time and circumstances change and now, as we approach the end of the first quarter of the twenty-first century, society needs to take a hard look at our new realities and be prepared to change for sustainability.

The two biggest drivers of change affecting businesses (and consumers) are environmental issues (such as global warming and its impact on business) and the effects of automation and AI. All stakeholders can debate the realities of these changes, but in so doing they are squandering valuable time and resources in clinging to old standards while the new realities challenge their business existence.

One of the most profound changes that business will have to consider is the effect of automation and AI on their customer base and overall demand. In this era of customer convenience, businesses are investing significant resources in order to lower their costs. We only have to visit a local fast-food restaurant to see how order-takers and cooks have been replaced by machines. In essence, the necessity to convert to such conveniences is resulting in the increased cost of running a business being passed on to consumers.

"(This) self-service revolution is reversing the division of labour… . In previous eras, workers who were rendered surplus to requirements by technological advances were redeployed to more productive activities. Today they are being deployed to less productive ones" (Wooldridge).* Peter Fleming makes a similar observation, "In the decade since the financial crisis of 2008, we've seen the decline and fall of good-paying jobs with benefits and the rise of inequality and the precariat. Now we're being warned about a future without jobs as we have come to know and depend upon them" (Fleming).**

Many businesses will experience increased profits by lowering their labour costs over the short term; this period will be short-lived for two reasons: (1) businesses will experience lower demand for their products as their customer base declines (remember, people buy products, not machines!), and (2) governments will enact changes in fiscal policies that will extract higher corporate taxes as a way to pay for the draws that the unemployed and underemployed will make on the social systems. Business cannot be blind to the ways that change will happen, ignoring the evidence of how policymakers are exploring new realities with programs such as living wages and guaranteed incomes.

So it can be argued that in the next half-century, the primary ways for adjusting to a slower growth economy will not be adjusting taxes and spending on the fiscal side or interest rates on the monetary side, but rather targeting reasonable and sustainable unemployment rates. Business has been less involved in fiscal policymaking, leaving governments to make the changes while they adjust and critique these relatively minor adjustments.

Some argue that the state will impose changes on business based on the realities of how business has imposed its costs onto the consumer/worker. "Why not instead challenge those employment models—bogus self-employment in the gig economy and an over-reliance on agency and zero-hours labour—which create insecurity in the lives of working families, rather than give the state a mere reactive role of cleaning up the human wreckage caused by those models" (Field).†

---

*Adrian Wooldridge, *The Economist*, "Trapped in self-service hell," June/July 2018.

**Peter Fleming, 2017, *The Death of* Homo Economicus: *Work, Debt and the Myth of Endless Accumulation,* London, UK: Pluto Press.

†Frank Field, *The Economist*, "Universal basic income won't fix problems but will create new ones." May 2018.

Starting yesterday, prudent owners and managers should be looking for ways to have a *real* impact on government policy that will affect their very survival, all the while bearing in mind that the time of maximizing profits may be coming to an end.

Let's think about the relationship between government fiscal policy and how it affects business:

1. If you were a business owner, what advice would you offer governments that will experience declining tax revenues and higher unemployment due to automation and artificial intelligence?

2. As a business owner/manager, what actions would you consider necessary within your own business to face the new economic realities of lower growth?

3. Which do you think should be more of a priority in today's economy: profits or jobs? Do you think businesses should be made to shoulder more of society's costs?

## WHAT ARE THE MAJOR SOURCES OF GOVERNMENT REVENUE?

Governments have to pay their bills like any person or institution that spends money. But how do they obtain revenue? Two major avenues are taxation and borrowing. When the government runs a budget deficit, spending exceeds tax revenue and therefore part of the spending must be financed by borrowing. When the budget is balanced, all spending is financed by tax revenue and there is no necessity to borrow.

In 2016 to 2017, the federal government made $293.5 billion in revenue. Exhibit 1(b) shows the revenue sources for the federal government. At the federal level, the majority of revenue, 65 percent, comes in the form of income taxes on individuals, corporations, and nonresidents. Consumption taxes, such as the GST and federal excise taxes on gasoline, alcohol, and tobacco products, account for 18 percent of federal revenue. Social security contributions, like Employment Insurance premiums paid by both employees and employers, amount to 8 percent of federal government revenue. Other revenue, at 9 percent, comes largely from investment income and sales of goods and services.

### A Progressive Tax

One impact of substantial taxes on personal income is that the effective take-home income of Canadians is significantly altered by the tax system. A **progressive tax** is designed so that the amount of an individual's tax rises as a proportion of income, as the person's income rises. With progressive taxes, of which the federal personal income tax is one example, those with higher incomes pay a greater proportion of their income in taxes. A progressive tax is one tool that the government can use to redistribute income.

Another way of identifying a tax as being progressive is if its marginal tax rate (the amount of tax paid on an additional dollar of taxable income) is greater than its average tax rate (the average amount of tax paid out of your total taxable income). For example, suppose you have $55 000 in taxable income, with the first $10 000 taxed at 10 percent, the next $15 000 taxed at 15 percent, and the remainder taxed at 20 percent. The marginal tax rate would be determined by the third tax bracket (in this example, 20 percent), since your total taxable income exceeds the upper limits of both the first and second brackets ($10 000 and $25 000, respectively).

To determine the average tax rate, we first need to calculate your total tax liability, remembering that each tax rate applies to only a proportion of your taxable income. In this example, the total tax liability is determined as follows: the 10 percent tax rate applies to the first $10 000 of taxable income—generating $1000 of tax liability ($10 000 × 10 percent); the 15 percent tax rate applies to the next $15 000 of taxable income—generating $2250 of tax liability ($15 000 × 15 percent); finally, the 20 percent tax rate applies to the remaining amount of taxable income ($30 000 in

**progressive tax**

*The amount of an individual's tax rises, as a proportion of income, as the person's income rises.*

this example)—generating a tax liability of $6000 ($30 000 × 20 percent). Adding together the tax liabilities from each tax bracket generates a total tax liability of $9250 ($1000 + $2250 + $6000). Once we know our total tax liability, the average tax rate can be calculated by determining what percentage of your total taxable income that your total tax liability represents. For this example, the average tax rate is 16.8 percent ($9250/$55 000). Therefore, since the marginal tax rate, 20 percent, is greater than the average tax rate, 16.8 percent, the tax is confirmed as progressive.

## A Regressive Tax

**excise tax**

*a sales tax on individual products such as alcohol, tobacco, and gasoline*

**regressive tax**

*The amount of an individual's tax falls, as a proportion of income, as the person's income rises.*

Some people consider an **excise tax**—a sales tax on individual products such as alcohol, tobacco, and gasoline—to be the most unfair type of tax because it is generally the most regressive. A **regressive tax** is designed so that the amount of an individual's tax falls as a proportion of income, as the person's income rises. A regressive tax takes a greater proportion of the income of lower-income groups than of higher-income groups. This type of tax on specific items will impose a far greater burden, as a percentage of income, on the poor and middle class than on the wealthy, because low-income families pay a greater proportion of their income on these taxes than do high-income families.

In addition, excise taxes may lead to economic inefficiencies. By isolating a few products and subjecting them to discriminatory taxation, consumption taxes expose economic choices to political manipulation and lead to inefficiency. Regressive taxes can also be described as a tax where the marginal tax rate is less than the average tax rate.

## Proportional Tax

**proportional tax**

*designed so that all taxpayers are subject to the tax rate, regardless of earnings*

Sometimes referred to as a *flat tax*, a **proportional tax** is designed so that all tax payers are subject to the tax rate regardless of earnings. In the case of a proportional tax system, marginal and average tax rates would be equal. From 1998 until 2014, the province of Alberta set a singular tax rate for all taxpayers. At that time, it was equal to 10 percent of taxable income.

# DEBATE

## SHOULD CANADA RAISE CORPORATE TAXES?

### For:

Western economies have been rebounding slowly since the end of the Great Recession, although below target levels of growth, inflation, and unemployment. Raising corporate taxes would go against conventional wisdom, which favours lowering taxes to try to stimulate the economy. Consistently, governments have lowered corporate tax rates in the belief that raising these taxes would stifle growth and cause unemployment rates to be above targets: Why would firms invest in employees if they had to pay higher taxes?

There are those who would argue that the benefits of low tax rates have actually intensified lower rates of corporate investment. They say that if corporations don't use the high amounts of capital they are sitting on, the government may as well tax corporations at a higher level

to entice them to use this capital. If it is still left idle, tax those funds and use the proceeds to invest back into the economy through infrastructure investment or other public uses. Since this theoretical model supports raising corporate taxes, surely that is what Canada should do for the benefit of the economy.

### Against:

The foundations of fiscal policy are based on government's use of spending, taxation, and transfer payments. Since Ronald Regan's term of office as U.S. president, politicians have commonly believed that lowering tax rates benefits the economy in two ways: (1) more total revenues are actually generated for governments (a relationship known as the *Laffer curve*—see the Chapter 1 Appendix) and (2) there is a *trickle-down effect*, which is best explained by the author of the phrase, humourist Will Rogers, who during the Depression stated that "money was all appropriated for the top in hopes that it would trickle down to the needy."

If governments subscribe to these theories, the premise in developing fiscal policy would be to lower corporate taxes. In the current economic climate, where the economy demands to be stimulated, there can be no reason to raise corporate taxes—that would lead to lower investment by corporations and ultimately lower employment and lower profits.

Even the most conservative economists recognize that stimulation requires lower taxes and higher spending until the economy shows evidence of consistent growth and lowering unemployment. Then and only then will raising corporate taxes be justified, to help pay back the deficits that will have developed.

**Questions:**
1. Can you think of other arguments that you could use to defend the economic benefits of raising corporate taxes?
2. Can you think of any other reasons why raising corporate taxes during the recovery stage would be detrimental to the Canadian economy?

## SECTION CHECK

- Major transfers to persons, such as Employment Insurance and Old Age Security programs, account for 29 percent of federal government spending. Other major expenditures are transfers to other levels of government (22 percent) and expenditures associated with the operation of other departments and agencies (17 percent).
- The largest source of federal revenue is income taxes on individuals and corporations (49 percent and 14 percent, respectively). Other taxes and duties collected by the federal government account for 18 percent of revenue.

**section**

**10.3**

# The Multiplier Effect

- What is the multiplier effect?
- What impact does the multiplier effect have on the aggregate demand curve?
- What impact does the multiplier effect have on tax cuts?
- What factors can potentially reduce the size of the multiplier?

Recall from our earlier discussion that any one of the major spending components of aggregate demand ($C$, $I$, $G$, or $X - M$) can initiate changes in aggregate demand, thereby producing a new short-run equilibrium. If policymakers are unhappy with the present short-run equilibrium GDP, perhaps they consider unemployment too high because of a current aggregate demand shortfall. If government increased its purchases of jet fighters, highways, and schools, this increased spending would lead to an increase in aggregate demand. That is, governments can deliberately manipulate the level of their purchases to obtain a new short-run equilibrium value. But how much new additional government purchasing is necessary?

## WHAT IS THE MULTIPLIER EFFECT?

Usually when an initial increase in purchases of goods or services occurs, the ultimate increase in total purchases will tend to be greater than the initial increase; this chain reaction of additional income and purchases that result in total purchases that

**multiplier effect**

*a chain reaction of additional income and purchases that results in total purchases that are greater than the initial increase in purchases*

are greater than the initial increase in purchases is called the **multiplier effect**. But how does this effect work? Suppose the federal government increases its Department of National Defence budget by $100 million to buy new search-and-rescue helicopters. When the government purchases the helicopters, not only does it add to the total demand for goods and services directly, it also provides $100 million in added income to the companies that actually construct the helicopters. Those companies will then hire more workers and buy more capital equipment and other inputs in order to produce the new output. The owners of these inputs therefore receive more income because of the increase in government purchases. And what will they do with this additional income? Although behaviour will vary somewhat among individuals, collectively they will probably spend a substantial part of the additional income on additional consumption purchases, pay some additional taxes incurred because of the income, and save a bit of it as well. The marginal propensity to consume (*MPC*) is the fraction of additional disposable income that a household consumes rather than saves.

## The Multiplier Effect at Work

Suppose that out of every dollar in *added* disposable income generated by increased government purchases, individuals collectively spend 75 cents on consumption purchases. In other words, the *MPC* is 0.75. The initial $100 million increase in government purchases causes both a $100 million increase in aggregate demand and an income increase of $100 million to suppliers of the inputs used to produce helicopters; the owners of those inputs, in turn, will spend an additional $75 million (75 percent of $100 million) on additional consumption purchases.

As Exhibit 1 illustrates, a chain reaction has been started with each new round of purchases providing income to a new group of people who in turn increase their purchases. As successive changes in consumption purchases occur, the feedback becomes smaller and smaller. The added income generated and the number of resulting consumer purchases become smaller because some of the increase in income goes to savings and tax payments that do not immediately flow into greater investment or government expenditure. For example, as Exhibit 1 indicates, the fifth change in consumption purchases is indeed much smaller than the first change in consumption purchases. What is the total impact of the initial increase in purchases on additional purchases and income? We can find that out using the multiplier formula, calculated as follows:

$$\text{Multiplier} = \frac{1}{1 - MPC}$$

---

**section 10.3**
Exhibit 1                **The Multiplier Process**

| | |
|---|---|
| Change in government purchases | $100 million—direct effect on *AD* |
| First change in consumption purchases | 75 million (0.75 of 100) |
| Second change in consumption purchases | 56.25 million (0.75 of 75) |
| Third change in consumption purchases | 42.19 million (0.75 of 56.25) |
| Fourth change in consumption purchases | 31.64 million (0.75 of 42.19) |
| Fifth change in consumption purchases | 23.73 million (0.75 of 31.64) |

The sum of the indirect effect on *AD*, through induced additional consumption purchases, is equal to $300 million.

...

$400 million = Total effect on purchases (*AD*)

In this case,

$$\text{Multiplier} = 1/(1 - 0.75) = 1/(0.25) = 4$$

An initial increase in purchases of goods or services of $100 million will increase total purchases by $400 million ($100 million × 4), as the initial $100 million in government purchases also generates an additional $300 million in consumption purchases.

## Changes in the *MPC* Affect the Multiplier Process

Note that the larger the marginal propensity to consume, the larger the multiplier effect, because relatively more additional consumption purchases out of any given income increase generate relatively larger secondary and tertiary income effects in successive rounds of the process. For example, if the *MPC* is 0.80, the multiplier is 5:

$$\text{Multiplier} = 1/(1 - 0.8) = 1/(0.2) = 5$$

If the *MPC* is only 0.50, however, the multiplier is 2:

$$\text{Multiplier} = 1/(1 - 0.50) = 1/(0.50) = 2$$

## WHAT IMPACT DOES THE MULTIPLIER EFFECT HAVE ON THE AGGREGATE DEMAND CURVE?

As we discussed earlier, when the Department of National Defence decides to buy additional helicopters, it increases aggregate demand. The initial effect is that it increases the incomes of owners of inputs used to make the helicopters, including profits that go to owners of the firms involved. The secondary effect, the greater income that results, will lead to increased consumer purchases. So the initial effect of the government's purchases will tend to have a multiplier effect on the economy. In Exhibit 2, we see that the initial impact of a $100 million additional purchase by the government directly shifts the aggregate demand curve from $AD_0$ to $AD_1$. The multiplier effect then causes the aggregate demand to shift out $300 million further, to $AD_2$. The total effect on aggregate demand of a $100 million increase in government purchases is therefore $400 million, if the marginal propensity to consume equals 0.75.

## WHAT IMPACT DOES THE MULTIPLIER EFFECT HAVE ON TAX CUTS?

If the government finds that it needs to use fiscal stimulus to move the economy to the natural rate, increased government spending is only one alternative. The government can also stimulate business and consumer spending through tax cuts. Both Canada (2000, 2003, and again in 2008–09) and the United States (2001, 2003, and 2012) have employed tax cuts to stimulate their economies.

How much of an *AD* shift do we get from a change in taxes? As in the case of government spending, it depends

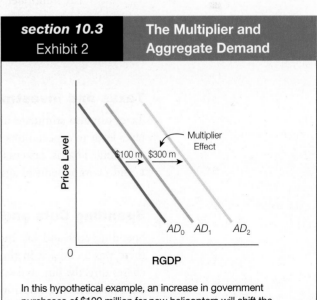

**section 10.3**
Exhibit 2

**The Multiplier and Aggregate Demand**

In this hypothetical example, an increase in government purchases of $100 million for new helicopters will shift the aggregate demand curve to the right by more than the $100 million initial purchase, other things being equal. It will shift aggregate demand by a total of $400 million, to $AD_2$.

on the marginal propensity to consume. However, the tax multiplier is smaller than the government spending multiplier because government spending has a direct impact on aggregate demand, whereas a tax cut has only an indirect impact on aggregate demand. Why? Because consumers will save some of their income from the tax cut. So if the *MPC* is 0.60, then when their disposable income rises by $1000, households will increase their consumption by $600 ($1000 × 0.60) while saving $400 of the added income.

To compare the multiplier effect of a tax cut with an increase in government purchases, suppose there was a $100 million tax cut and that the *MPC* was 0.75. The initial increase in consumption spending from the tax cut would be 0.75 × 100 million (*MPC* − tax cut) = $75 million. Because in this case people would save 25 percent of their tax-cut income, the effect on aggregate demand of the change in taxes would be smaller than that of a change of equal size in government spending. The cumulative change in spending (the increase in *AD*) due to the $100 million tax cut can be found by plugging the initial effect of the changed consumption spending into our earlier formula: 1/(1 − *MPC*) × $75 million, which is 4 × $75 = $300 million. So the initial tax cut of $100 million leads to a stimulus of $200 million in consumer spending. Although this is less than the $400 million from government spending, it is easy to see why tax cuts and government spending are both attractive policy prescriptions for a slow economy.

An alternative technique for determining the cumulative change in spending due to a tax cut is to use the *tax multiplier* formula, calculated as follows:

$$\text{Tax multiplier} = -\frac{MPC}{1 - MPC}$$

Notice that the tax multiplier is displayed as a negative value. This is due to the inverse relationship that exists between taxes and expenditure. That is, the tax multiplier is negative because a change in taxes will always have the opposite effect on aggregate expenditure.

Returning to our earlier example, if the *MPC* is 0.75, the tax multiplier is −3:

$$\text{Tax multiplier} = -\frac{MPC}{1 - MPC} = -\frac{0.75}{1 - 0.75} = -\frac{0.75}{0.25} = -3$$

An initial tax cut of $100 million will increase total purchases by $300 million (−$100 million × −3).

## Taxes and Investment Spending

Taxes can also stimulate investment spending. For example, if a cut in corporate profit taxes leads to expectations of greater after-tax profits, it could fuel additional investment spending. That is, tax cuts designed for consumers and investors can stimulate both the *C* and *I* components of aggregate demand.

## Spending Cuts and Tax Increases

Spending cuts and tax increases are magnified by the multiplier effect, too. Suppose there was a cutback in the public sector. Not only would it decrease government purchases directly, but civil servants would be laid off and unemployed workers would cut back on their consumption spending; this would have a multiplier effect throughout the economy, leading to an even greater reduction in aggregate demand. Similarly, tax hikes would leave consumers with less disposable income, so they would cut back on their consumption. This would lower aggregate demand and set off the multiplier process, leading to an even larger cumulative effect on aggregate demand.

## WHAT FACTORS CAN POTENTIALLY REDUCE THE SIZE OF THE MULTIPLIER?

The multiplier process is not instantaneous. If you get an additional $100 in income today, you may spend two-thirds of that on consumption purchases eventually, but you may wait six months or even longer to do it. Such time lags mean that the ultimate increase in purchases resulting from an initial increase in purchases may not be achieved for a year or more. The extent of the multiplier effect evident within a short time period will be less than the total effect indicated by the multiplier formula. In addition, saving, taxes, and money spent on import goods (which are not part of aggregate demand for domestically produced goods and services) will reduce the size of the multiplier because each of them reduces the fraction of a given increase in income that will go to additional purchases of domestically produced consumption goods.

It is also important to note that the multiplier effect is not restricted to changes in government purchases. The multiplier effect can apply to changes that alter spending in any of the components of aggregate demand: consumption, investment, government purchases, or net exports.

It is important to note that the multiplier is most effective when it brings idle resources into production. If all resources are already fully employed, the expansion in demand and the multiplier effect will lead to a higher price level, not increases in employment and RGDP.

### SECTION CHECK

- The multiplier effect is a chain reaction of additional income and purchases that results in a final increase in total purchases that is greater than the initial increase in purchases.
- Initially, the *AD* curve shifts rightward by the amount of the original increase in expenditure. The multiplier effect has the effect of shifting the *AD* curve farther rightward.
- Because taxes have only an indirect impact on aggregate demand, the tax multiplier is smaller than the government spending multiplier.
- Because of a time lag, the full impact of the multiplier effect on GDP may not be felt until a year or more after the initial purchase. Also, the ultimate size of the multiplier may be reduced by increases in saving rates, taxes, and money spent on imported goods.

# Fiscal Policy and the *AD/AS* Model

**section 10.4**

- How can fiscal policy alleviate a recessionary gap?
- How can fiscal policy alleviate an inflationary gap?

## HOW CAN FISCAL POLICY ALLEVIATE A RECESSIONARY GAP?

The primary tools of fiscal policy, government spending and taxes, can be presented in the context of the aggregate supply and demand model. In Exhibit 1, we have used the *AD/AS* model to show how the government can use fiscal policy as an expansionary tool to help control the economy.

**section 10.4**
**Exhibit 1**

**Expansionary Fiscal Policy in a Recessionary Gap**

The increase in government spending or tax decrease causes an increase in aggregate demand from $AD_0$ to $AD_1$. This triggers the multiplier effect ($AD_1$ to $AD_2$) and the result is a new equilibrium at $E_2$, reflecting a higher price level and an increase in $RGDP$ from $RGDP_0$ to $RGDP_{NR}$. Because this result is on the *LRAS* curve, it is a long-run, sustainable equilibrium.

## Budget Deficits and Fiscal Policy

As we discussed earlier, when the government spends more and/or taxes less, the size of the government's budget deficit will grow, or the size of the budget surplus will fall. Although budget deficits are often thought to be bad, a case can be made for using budget deficits to stimulate the economy when it is operating at less than full capacity. Such expansionary fiscal policy may have the potential to move an economy out of a contraction (or a recession) and closer to full employment.

**Expansionary Fiscal Policy at Less than Full Employment** If the government decides to spend more and/or cut taxes, other things constant, total purchases will rise. That is, increased government spending and tax cuts can increase consumption, investment, and government purchases, shifting the aggregate demand curve to the right. The effect of this increase in aggregate demand depends on the position of the macroeconomic equilibrium prior to the government stimulus. For example, in Exhibit 1, the initial equilibrium is at $E_0$, a recession scenario, with real output below potential RGDP. Starting at this point and moving along the short-run aggregate supply curve, an increase in government spending and/or a tax cut would increase the size of the budget deficit and lead to an increase in aggregate demand, ideally from $AD_0$ to $AD_2$. The result of such a change would be an increase in the price level, from $PL_0$ to $PL_2$, and an increase in RGDP, from $RGDP_0$ to $RGDP_{NR}$. We must remember, of course, that some of this increase in aggregate demand is caused by the multiplier process (from $AD_1$ to $AD_2$), so the magnitude of the change in aggregate demand will be larger than the magnitude of the stimulus package of tax cuts and/or government spending (from $AD_0$ to $AD_1$). If the policy change is of the right magnitude and timed appropriately, the expansionary fiscal policy might stimulate the economy, pull it out of the contraction and/or recession, and result in full employment at $RGDP_{NR}$. The recessionary gap is then closed and rising production will lead to increasing employment and a lower unemployment rate.

**The 2008 to 2009 Recession** Referred to by some economists as the Great Recession, the general economic downturn during the late 2000s and early 2010s was the worst global recession since World War II. For Canada, the 2008 to 2009 recession was not the worst recession on record, but it did trigger an unprecedented fiscal expansion. In January 2009, the federal government introduced Canada's Economic Action Plan in response to the global financial crisis. Among other stimulus measures, the plan contained significant tax relief—$20 billion in personal income tax relief over 2008 to 2009 and the next five fiscal years—in addition to unprecedented government spending initiatives—$12 billion in new infrastructure stimulus funding over two years. In addition to this, the government provided up to $200 billion through the Extraordinary Financing Framework to improve access to credit for Canadian consumers and businesses. Many other countries around the world, most notably the United States, also increased the size of their budget deficits by cutting taxes and increasing government spending in response to the financial crisis.

In terms of the *AD/AS* model, the impact of this type of expansionary fiscal policy is clear: a rightward shift of the aggregate demand curve from $AD_0$ to $AD_1$ as shown in Exhibit 1. There is, however, debate among economists as to the effectiveness of fiscal policy to stimulate the economy, and much of that debate depends on the size of the multiplier. A multiplier of 1 means that an increase in government purchases of $100 million would increase aggregate demand and lead to an increase of $100 million in RGDP. The economy could now have new highways, bridges, public arenas, and fighter jets without sacrificing other components of aggregate demand, like private consumption and investment. How is this possible? The answer is that these are idle resources that are now being put to use. If a multiplier is greater than 1, it is even more magical: RGDP rises by more than the increase in government spending.

Despite a lack of uniform agreement on the size of the expenditure multiplier, economists do agree that the multiplier is very small—close to zero—when the economy is at or near full employment and that the effectiveness of fiscal policy depends on the type of action taken. For example, the short-run effect of government spending on infrastructure like highways and bridges tends to be greater than, say, that of a tax cut where individuals will save a large portion of their tax windfall. Tax cuts for poorer people may be more effective than those for richer people because the poor tend to spend a larger proportion of their additional (marginal) incomes. Economists also agree that tax multipliers are much higher when taxes are permanent than when they are temporary and that fiscal multipliers will be lower in heavily indebted economies than in prudent ones.

## HOW CAN FISCAL POLICY ALLEVIATE AN INFLATIONARY GAP?

When the government spends less and/or taxes more, the size of the government's budget deficit will fall or the size of the budget surplus will rise, other things being equal. Sometimes such a change in fiscal policy may help "cool off" the economy when it has overheated and inflation has become a serious problem. Then, contractionary fiscal policy has the potential to offset an overheated, inflationary boom.

### Contractionary Fiscal Policy beyond Full Employment

Suppose that the price level is at $PL_0$ and that short-run equilibrium is at $E_0$, as shown in Exhibit 2. Say that the government decides to reduce its spending and increase taxes. A government spending change may directly affect aggregate demand. A tax increase on consumers will reduce households' disposable incomes, thus reducing purchases of consumption goods and services, and higher business taxes will reduce investment purchases. The reductions in consumption, investment, and/or government spending will shift the aggregate demand curve leftward, ideally from $AD_0$ to $AD_2$. This lowers the price level from $PL_0$ to $PL_2$ and brings RGDP back to the full-employment level at $RGDP_{NR}$, resulting in a new short- and long-run equilibrium at $E_2$, and the inflationary gap is closed.

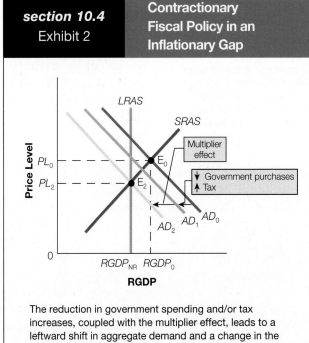

**section 10.4** Exhibit 2

**Contractionary Fiscal Policy in an Inflationary Gap**

The reduction in government spending and/or tax increases, coupled with the multiplier effect, leads to a leftward shift in aggregate demand and a change in the short-run equilibrium from $E_0$ to $E_2$, reflecting a lower price level and a return to full-employment RGDP ($RGDP_{NR}$).

## section 10.5

# Automatic Stabilizers

● What are automatic stabilizers?
● How does the tax system stabilize the economy?

### WHAT ARE AUTOMATIC STABILIZERS?

Some changes in government spending and taxes take place automatically as business cycle conditions change, without deliberations in Parliament. Changes in government spending or tax collections that automatically help counter business cycle fluctuations are called **automatic stabilizers**.

**automatic stabilizers**
*changes in government spending or tax collections that automatically help counter business cycle fluctuations*

### HOW DOES THE TAX SYSTEM STABILIZE THE ECONOMY?

The most important automatic stabilizer is the tax system. For example, with the personal income tax, as incomes rise, tax liabilities also increase automatically. Progressive personal income taxes vary directly in amount with income and, in fact, rise or fall by greater percentage terms than income itself. Big increases and big decreases in RGDP are both lessened by automatic changes in income tax receipts. In addition, there is the corporate profit tax. Because incomes, earnings, and profits all fall during a recession, the government collects less in taxes. This reduced tax burden partially offsets the magnitude of the recession.

**Automatic stabilizers work without legislative action. The stabilizers serve as a shock absorber to the economy. But the key is that they do it quickly.**

BRIGITTE BOUVIER, PMO

Beyond this, the Employment Insurance program is another example of an automatic stabilizer. During recessions, unemployment is usually high and Employment Insurance benefits increase, providing income that will be consumed by recipients. During boom periods, such benefit payments will fall as the number of unemployed declines. The system of social assistance (welfare) payments tends to be another important automatic stabilizer because the number of low-income persons eligible for some form of social assistance grows during recessions (stimulating aggregate demand) and declines during booms (reducing aggregate demand).

Perhaps the Great Depression would not have been so "great" if automatic stabilizers had been in place. Many had to dig into their savings and cut back on their spending, which made matters worse. Automatic stabilizers are not strong enough to completely offset a serious recession. However, they certainly reduce the severity of a recession, without the problems associated with lags that were discussed in the last section.

Despite the shortcomings of traditional fiscal policy, it provides policymakers with another option in the event of a severe downturn. The use of fiscal policy can reassure investors and consumers that the government realizes it has the potential to make up for insufficient demand, especially if the economy is far from its potential output.

## SECTION CHECK

- Automatic stabilizers are changes in government transfer payments or tax collections that happen automatically and with effects that vary inversely with business cycles.
- The tax system is the most important automatic stabilizer; it has the greatest ability to smooth out swings in RGDP during business cycles. Other automatic stabilizers are Employment Insurance and social assistance payments.

# Possible Obstacles to Effective Fiscal Policy

- How does the crowding-out effect limit the economic impact of expansionary fiscal policy?
- How do time lags in fiscal policy implementation affect policy effectiveness?

## HOW DOES THE CROWDING-OUT EFFECT LIMIT THE ECONOMIC IMPACT OF EXPANSIONARY FISCAL POLICY?

The multiplier effect of an increase in government purchases implies that the increase in aggregate demand will tend to be greater than the initial fiscal stimulus, other things being equal. However, because all other things will not tend to stay equal in this case, the multiplier effect may not hold true. For example, when an increase in government purchases stimulates aggregate demand, it also drives up the interest rate. In particular, when the federal government's borrowing competes with private borrowers for available savings, it drives up interest rates. As a result of the higher interest rate, consumers may decide against buying a car, a home, or other interest-sensitive goods, and businesses may cancel or scale back plans to expand or buy new capital equipment. In short, the higher interest rate will choke off private investment spending, and as a result, the impact of the increase in government purchases may be smaller than we first assumed. Economists call the theory that government borrowing drives up the interest

**crowding-out effect**

*theory that government borrowing drives up the interest rate, lowering consumption by households and investment spending by firms*

rate, lowering consumption by households and investment spending by firms, the **crowding-out effect**. The crowding-out effect happened in Canada in the late 1980s and early 1990s, when record levels of government borrowing contributed, in part, to interest rates rising above 12 percent.

In Exhibit 1, suppose there was an initial $100 million increase in government purchases. This by itself would shift aggregate demand right by $100 million times the multiplier, from $AD_0$ to $AD_1$. However, when the government borrows in the money market to pay for increases in government purchases, the interest rate increases. The higher interest rate crowds out investment spending. This causes the aggregate demand curve to shift left, from $AD_1$ to $AD_2$. Because both of these processes are taking place at the same time, the net effect is an increase in aggregate demand from $AD_0$ to $AD_2$ rather than $AD_0$ to $AD_1$.

The multiplier and crowding-out effect can also impact the size of the shift in aggregate demand from a tax change. Recall that when tax cuts stimulate consumer spending, earnings and profits rise, which further stimulates consumer spending—the multiplier effect. But the higher income leads to an increase in the demand for money, which tends to lead to higher interest rates. The higher interest rates make borrowing more costly and reduce investment spending—the crowding-out effect. Also, remember that if households view tax cuts as permanent, they are more likely to increase spending by a larger amount than if they viewed the tax cuts as temporary.

## Critics of the Crowding-Out Effect

Critics of the crowding-out effect argue that the increase in government spending, particularly if the economy is in a severe recession, could actually improve consumer and business expectations and actually encourage private investment spending. It is also possible that the monetary authorities could actually increase the money supply to offset the higher interest rates from the crowding-out effect.

**section 10.6**
Exhibit 1

**The Crowding-Out Effect**

Government borrowing to finance a budget deficit leads to a higher interest rate and lower levels of private investment spending. The lower levels of private spending can crowd out the fiscal policy effect, shifting aggregate demand to the left from $AD_1$ to $AD_2$; the net effect of the fiscal policy is $AD_0$ to $AD_2$, not the larger increase, $AD_0$ to $AD_1$.

## The Crowding-Out Effect in the Open Economy

Another form of crowding out can take place in international markets. For example, when the government increases purchases, it tends to drive up interest rates (assuming the money supply is unchanged). This is the basic crowding-out effect. However, the higher Canadian interest rate will attract funds from abroad. In order to invest in the Canadian economy, foreigners will have to first convert their currencies into Canadian dollars. The increase in the demand for dollars relative to other currencies will cause the dollar to appreciate in value. This will cause net exports $(X - M)$ to fall for two reasons. One, because of the higher relative price of the Canadian dollar, imports become cheaper for those in Canada, and imports will increase. Two, because of the higher relative price of the dollar, Canadian-made goods become more expensive to foreigners, so exports fall. The increase in imports and the decrease in exports cause a reduction in net exports and a fall in aggregate demand. The net effect is that to the extent net exports are crowded out, fiscal policy has a smaller effect on aggregate demand than it would otherwise.

## HOW DO TIME LAGS IN FISCAL POLICY IMPLEMENTATION AFFECT POLICY EFFECTIVENESS?

It is important to recognize that in a democratic country, fiscal policy is implemented through the political process, and that process takes time. Often, the lag between the time that a fiscal response is desired and the time an appropriate policy is implemented and its effects felt are considerable. Sometimes a fiscal policy designed to deal with a contracting economy may actually take effect during a period of economic expansion, or vice versa, resulting in a stabilization policy that actually destabilizes the economy.

### The Recognition Lag

Suppose the economy is beginning a downturn. It may take from three to six months before enough data are gathered to indicate the actual presence of a downturn. This is called the *recognition lag*. Sometimes a future downturn can be forecast through econometric models or by looking at the index of leading indicators, but usually decision makers are hesitant to plan policy on the basis of forecasts that are not always accurate.

### The Implementation Lag

At some point, however, policymakers may decide that some policy change is necessary. If, for example, a tax cut is recommended, what form should the cut take and how large should it be? Across-the-board income tax reductions? Reductions in corporate taxes? More generous exemptions and deductions from the income tax (e.g., for child care, education)? In other words, who should receive the benefits of lower taxes? Likewise, if the decision is made to increase government expenditures, which programs should be expanded or initiated and by how much? These are questions with profound political consequences, so reaching a decision is not always easy and usually involves much compromise and a great deal of time.

Finally, once the budget is formulated by the staff at the Department of Finance, the finance minister presents the budget to Parliament, which must eventually give approval to the budget. This is all part of what is called the *implementation lag*.

In recognition of this lag, the federal government, through Canada's Economic Action Plan, streamlined the federal approval processes so that more provincial, territorial, and municipal projects under the Building Canada Plan could start in 2009 and 2010. Prior to these changes, the infrastructure approval process was subject to significant duplication and administrative inefficiencies, leading to unnecessary project delays. With changes now in place, the time needed to provide federal approvals for major projects was shortened by up to 12 months, allowing construction to begin more quickly.

### The Impact Lag

Even after legislation is passed, it takes time to bring about the actual fiscal stimulus desired. If the legislation provides for a reduction in income taxes, for example, it might

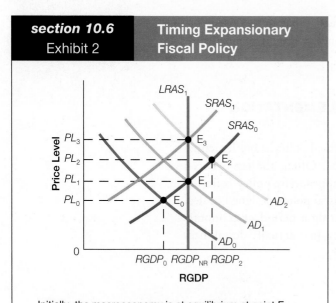

**section 10.6**
**Exhibit 2**

**Timing Expansionary Fiscal Policy**

Initially, the macroeconomy is at equilibrium at point $E_0$. With high unemployment (at $RGDP_0$), the government decides to increase government purchases and cut taxes to stimulate the economy. This shifts aggregate demand from $AD_0$ to $AD_1$ over time, perhaps 12 to 16 months. In the meantime, if consumer confidence increases, the aggregate demand curve might shift to $AD_2$, leading to much higher prices ($PL_3$) in the long run, rather than at the target level, $E_1$, at price level $PL_1$.

take a few months before the changes actually show up in workers' paycheques. With respect to changes in government purchases, the delay is usually much longer. If the government increases spending for public works projects like sewer systems, new highways, or urban transit systems, it takes time to draw up plans and get permissions, to advertise for bids from contractors, to get contracts, and then to begin work. And there may be further delays because of government regulations. For example, an environmental impact assessment must be completed before most public works projects can begin, a process that often takes many months or even years. This is called the *impact lag*.

### Timing Is Critical

The timing of fiscal policy is crucial. Because of the significant lags before the fiscal policy has its impact, the increase in aggregate demand may occur at the wrong time. For example, imagine that we are initially at $E_0$ in Exhibit 2. The economy is currently suffering from low levels of output and high rates of unemployment. In response, policymakers decide to increase government purchases and implement a tax cut (shifting the $AD$ curve from $AD_0$ to $AD_1$). But from the time when the policymakers recognized the problem to the time when the policies had a chance to work themselves through the economy, business and consumer confidence increased, shifting the aggregate demand curve rightward—increasing RGDP and employment. Now when the fiscal policy takes effect, the policies will have the undesired effect of causing inflation, with little permanent effect on output and employment. This is seen in Exhibit 2, as the aggregate demand curve shifts from $AD_1$ to $AD_2$. At $E_2$, input owners will require higher input prices, shifting the $SRAS$ leftward from $SRAS_0$ to $SRAS_1$ to the new long-run equilibrium at $E_3$.

## SECTION CHECK

- The crowding-out effect states that as the government borrows to finance the budget deficit, it drives up the interest rates and crowds out private investment spending. If crowding out causes a higher Canadian interest rate, it will attract foreign funds. In order to invest in the Canadian economy, foreigners will have to first convert their currencies into Canadian dollars. The increase in the demand for dollars relative to other currencies will cause the dollar to appreciate in value, making imports relatively cheaper in Canada and Canadian exports relatively more expensive in other countries. This will cause net exports ($X - M$) to fall. This is the crowding-out effect in the open economy.
- The lag time between when a fiscal policy may be needed and when it eventually affects the economy is considerable. Time lags are generally grouped in three classifications: recognition lags, implementation lags, and impact lags.

# The Federal Government Debt

- How is the budget deficit financed?
- What has happened to the federal budget balance?
- What is the impact of reducing a budget deficit?
- How much is the burden of government debt in Canada?

## HOW IS THE BUDGET DEFICIT FINANCED?

For many years, the Canadian government ran budget deficits and built up a large federal debt. How did it finance those budget deficits? After all, it has to have some means of paying out the funds necessary to support government expenditures that are in excess of the funds derived from tax payments. One thing the federal government can do is simply print money. However, printing money to finance activities is highly inflationary and also undermines confidence in the government. Typically, the budget deficit is financed by issuing debt. The federal government in effect borrows an amount necessary to cover the deficit by issuing bonds, or IOUs, payable typically at some maturity date. The sum total of the values of all bonds outstanding constitutes the federal government debt.

## WHAT HAS HAPPENED TO THE FEDERAL BUDGET BALANCE?

Exhibit 1 shows the evolution of budget balances in Canada since the late 1960s. As illustrated in the exhibit, the early to mid-1970s were generally characterized by the federal government running balanced budgets. However, this began to change by the late 1970s when the federal government started to spend more in government expenditures than it collected in tax revenue. Throughout the 1980s and into the 1990s, the federal government incurred growing budget deficits, reaching a height of $40 billion in both 1993 and 1994; as a result, public debt soared. This is illustrated by the negative budget balances in Exhibit 1. Mounting public debt led to growing public pressure on the government to change its budgetary philosophy. In 1998, the government ran its first budget surplus in almost 25 years, and succeeded in posting annual budget surpluses for the next 12 years.

This period of fiscal prosperity ended dramatically in 2009, when the government was plunged back into deficit as a result of the Canadian economy beginning to experience the impact of the global financial crisis. In response to these events, the Canadian government again began to run deficits as tax revenues declined and expenditures skyrocketed.

The government launched its Economic Action Plan in 2009, a plan that consisted largely of pumping billions of dollars of stimulus into the economy. As a result of these efforts to stave off the ever-worsening global recession, the federal government posted its largest budget deficit ever in 2009 to 2010: $55.4 billion.

Following this unprecedented period of fiscal policy, the government began to undertake significant efforts to return to a more balanced budget situation—as evidenced by the dramatically lower budget deficits in both 2010 to 2011 and 2011 to 2012. Unfortunately, despite government projections of a return to responsible fiscal management (the then governing Conservative government in its 2015 budget had

SOURCE: Department of Finance Fiscal Reference Tables, September 2017, Cat. No.: F1-26E-PDF ISSN: 1489-5005, Table 15.

projected a surplus of $1.4 billion by 2015–16) the continued weakness in global economic performance slowed Canada's recovery as well as its return to a balanced budget.

In addition to the slower than expected economic recovery, a change in government (a Liberal government was elected in October 2015) brought with it another change in budget philosophy. The newly elected Liberals made good on their promises of improved infrastructure spending and tax reform. The net result fiscally was a return to budget deficits.

## WHAT IS THE IMPACT OF REDUCING A BUDGET DEFICIT?

Budget deficits can be important because they provide the federal government with the flexibility to respond appropriately to changing economic circumstances. For example, the government may run deficits in times of special emergencies like military involvement, earthquakes, fires, or floods. The government may also use a budget deficit to avert an economic downturn.

Historically, the largest budget deficits and a growing government debt occur during war years when defence spending escalates and taxes typically do not rise as rapidly as spending. For example, during World War II, the federal government debt increased by over 300 percent between 1940 and 1946. The federal government will also typically run budget deficits during recessions as tax revenue falls and government spending increases.

Recall that when the government borrows to finance a budget deficit, it causes the interest rate to rise. The higher interest rate will crowd out private investment by households and firms. But we know that higher private investment and increases in capital formation are critical in a growing economy. So what would happen if the government reduced the budget deficit? In the short run, deficit reduction is the same as running contractionary fiscal policy; either tax increases and/or a reduction in government purchases will shift the aggregate demand curve to the left from $AD_0$ to $AD_1$, as seen in Exhibit 2. Unless this is offset by expansionary monetary policy (see Chapter 13), this will lead to a lower price level and lower RGDP. That is, in the short run an aggressive program of deficit reduction can lead to a recession.

**section 10.7** Exhibit 2 — Reducing a Budget Deficit—The Short-Run Effects

In the short run, a reduction in the budget deficit (higher taxes and/or a reduction in government purchases) will lead to a reduction in aggregate demand. The leftward shift of aggregate demand from $AD_0$ to $AD_1$ leads to a lower price level and a lower level of RGDP.

**section 10.7** Exhibit 3 — Reducing a Budget Deficit—The Long-Run Effects

A smaller budget deficit, or a larger budget surplus, lowers the interest rate and stimulates private investment and capital formation, leading to an increase in RGDP from $RGDP_{NR}$ to $RGDP'_{NR}$. Even with an increase in aggregate demand, the price level would be lower than it would have been without the shift in the SRAS and LRAS curves.

In the long run, however, the story is different. Lowering the budget deficit, or running a larger budget surplus, leads to lower interest rates, which increase private investment and stimulate higher growth in capital formation and economic growth. In fact, this is what happened in the late 1990s as the budget deficit was reduced and finally turned into a budget surplus. The reduction in the deficit increased the natural rate of output, shifting the *SRAS* and *LRAS* curves rightward in Exhibit 3. The final effect was a higher RGDP and a lower price level than would have otherwise prevailed. Both investment and RGDP grew as the budget deficit shrank. The long-run effects of the deficit reduction are greater economic growth and a lower price level, *ceteris paribus*. The short-run recessionary effects of a budget deficit reduction can be avoided through the appropriate monetary policy, as we will explore in Chapter 13.

## What to Do with a Budget Surplus

When Canada has a budget surplus, policymakers have to decide what to do with it. Some favour paying down the government debt, arguing this might drive interest rates down further and stimulate private investment and economic growth. Others think that we should cut taxes since economic theory indicates that taxes can lead to a misallocation of resources. Still others believe the surplus should be used for improvements in education, health care, and research and development that will lead to greater economic growth.

## HOW MUCH IS THE BURDEN OF GOVERNMENT DEBT IN CANADA?

The burden of the federal government debt is a topic that has long interested economists, particularly whether the debt falls on present or future generations. Exhibit 4 shows the level of the outstanding federal government debt and the debt expressed as a percentage

| section 10.7 Exhibit 4 | Federal Government Debt, Selected Years |
| --- | --- |

| Year | Debt (billions of dollars) | Debt as a Percentage of GDP |
| --- | --- | --- |
| 1930 | $ 2.2 | 39% |
| 1940 | 3.3 | 49 |
| 1950 | 11.6 | 63 |
| 1960 | 12.0 | 31 |
| 1970 | 18.1 | 20 |
| 1980 | 72.6 | 23 |
| 1990 | 378.8 | 54 |
| 2000 | 590.1 | 54 |
| 2001 | 571.7 | 50 |
| 2002 | 565.3 | 48 |
| 2003 | 559.6 | 45 |
| 2004 | 551.0 | 41 |
| 2005 | 549.6 | 39 |
| 2006 | 536.9 | 36 |
| 2007 | 523.9 | 33 |
| 2008 | 516.3 | 31 |
| 2009 | 525.2 | 34 |
| 2010 | 582.5 | 35 |
| 2011 | 616.9 | 35 |
| 2012 | 651.5 | 36 |
| 2013 | 678.3 | 36 |
| 2014 | 682.3 | 34 |
| 2015 | 687.0 | 34 |
| 2016 | 693.8 | 34 |
| 2017 | 714.5 | 33 |

SOURCES: Adapted from Statistics Canada, NGDP data: Statistics Canada, Table 380-0064-Gross domestic product, expenditure-based, annual (dollars unless otherwise noted): net debt data: Department of Finance Fiscal Reference Tables, October 2016, Cat. No. F1-26E-PDF ISSN: 1489-5005, Table 15.

of GDP for selected years from 1930 to 2017. The debt–GDP ratio measures the size of the debt in relation to the size of our national income. The lower the debt–GDP ratio, the smaller the burden of the debt, because less of our national income goes to the federal government in taxes so that the government can service the debt (i.e., make interest payments to the bondholders). Conversely, the higher the debt–GDP ratio, the greater the burden of the debt, because more of our national income goes to the federal government in taxes so that the government can service the debt.

It is interesting to note that between 1930 and 1950, the debt–GDP ratio increased sharply from 39 to 63 percent, as the growth in the debt (caused largely by the Great Depression in the 1930s and World War II in the 1940s) far exceeded the growth in GDP. Although the debt continued to rise to $73 billion in 1980, the debt–GDP ratio fell to 23 percent as strong economic growth reduced the debt in relation to the size of the economy. Between 1980 and 2000, large budget deficits added almost $500 billion in additional debt, bringing the debt to $590 billion and the debt–GDP ratio up to a burdensome 54 percent. The debt–GDP ratio peaked, in fact, in 1996 at 70 percent.

On a more positive note, the budget surpluses that the federal government was able to post between 2000 and 2008 were, at least in part, used to pay down some of the debt. This in combination with good economic growth over this same period of time enabled the government to lower the debt–GDP ratio to 31 percent by 2008. This trend has since reversed somewhat as the Canadian economy struggles to recover from the recent global economic crisis. The most recent data show Canada's debt–GDP ratio at 33 percent.

Arguments can be made that the generation of taxpayers living at the time that the debt is issued shoulders the true cost of the debt, because the debt permits the government to take command of resources that might be available for other, private uses. In a sense, the resources it takes to purchase government bonds might take away from private activities, such as private investment financed by private debt. There is no denying, however, that the issuance of debt does involve some intergenerational transfer of incomes. Long after federal debt is issued, a new generation of taxpayers is making interest payments to people of the generation that bought the bonds issued to finance that debt. If public debt is created intelligently, however, the burden of the debt should be less than the benefits derived from the resources acquired as a result; this is particularly true when the debt allows for an expansion in real economic activity or for the development of vital infrastructure for the future. The opportunity cost of expanded public activity may be very small in terms of private activity that must be forgone to finance the public activity, if unemployed resources are put to work. The real issue of importance is whether the government's activities have benefits that are greater than costs; whether taxes are raised, money is printed, or deficits are run are for the most part financing issues.

Parents can offset some of the intergenerational debt by leaving larger bequests. In addition, if the parents save now to bear the cost of the burden of future taxes, the reduced consumption and increased savings will lower interest rates or, more precisely, offset the higher interest rate caused by the budget deficit. Many parents might not respond that way, but some might.

It is possible that if the budget deficits led people to believe there would be higher future taxes, a budget surplus might lead them to think there would be lower future taxes—and perhaps they would save less and consume more. So do we pay down the debt or cut taxes? They may be equivalent policy prescriptions since each tends to lead to increases in consumption spending.

A look internationally at federal, or central, government indebtedness shows us that Canada's situation is by no means an exception—see Exhibit 5. The reality of public finances around the world is that all central governments are to some extent in debt; the issue is the *amount* of government debt. The recent global economic crisis has increased the debt–GDP ratios of virtually every economy in the world. The central concern now is that, for those economies that already had significant ratios of debt to GDP, recent events have pushed them dangerously higher.

| section 10.7 Exhibit 5 | Net Government Debt as a Percentage of GDP, Selected Countries, 2017 |
|---|---|

| Country | Central Government Debt as a Percentage of GDP |
|---|---|
| Australia | 11.0 |
| Switzerland | 20.2 |
| Norway | 26.1 |
| Mexico | 27.5 |
| **Canada** | **36.1** |
| Germany | 44.4 |
| Ireland | 60.7 |
| United States | 61.3 |
| France | 67.4 |
| United Kingdom | 85.5 |
| Italy | 109.0 |
| Greece | 147.8 |

A comparison of net debt–GDP ratios as a percentage of GDP for major advanced economies reveals that Canada has the lowest net debt–GDP ratio of any G7 country.

SOURCE: International Monetary Fund, *Fiscal Monitor*, April 2017.

## SECTION CHECK

- The budget deficit is financed by issuing debt.
- Improvement in the federal budget balance since the mid-1990s resulted from economic growth, increased tax revenues, and the efforts of the federal government to control the growth of government spending.
- In the short run, reducing a budget deficit can lead to a recession if not offset by expansionary monetary policy. In the long run, however, deficit reduction increases economic growth and lowers the price level.
- With greater fiscal responsibility and increased economic growth, Canada has managed to lower its debt–GDP ratio (the international measure of debt burden).

# For Your Review

## Section 10.1

1. Answer the following questions.
   a. If there is currently a budget surplus, what would an increase in government purchases do to it?
   b. What would that increase in government purchases do to aggregate demand?
   c. When would an increase in government purchases be an appropriate fiscal policy?

2. Are increases in both government purchases and net taxes at the same time expansionary or contractionary? Would both changes together increase or decrease the federal government deficit?

3. Answer the following questions.
   a. If there is currently a budget deficit, what would an increase in taxes do to it?
   b. What would that increase in taxes do to aggregate demand?
   c. When would an increase in taxes be an appropriate fiscal policy?

4. Why are federal government actions that increase deficits considered expansionary fiscal policy and those that decrease deficits considered contractionary fiscal policy?

## Section 10.2

5. Excise taxes make up the bulk of the retail price of cigarettes and alcohol in Canada. Explain how excise taxes such as these are regressive and unfairly target lower-income individuals.

6. How does Canada's federal government make money?

## Section 10.3

7. What would the multiplier be if the marginal propensity to consume was 0.25, 0.5, and 0.75? How would the value for the tax multiplier differ?

8. If there was a $2 billion increase in government spending, other things being equal, what would be the resulting change in aggregate demand, and how much of the change would be a change in consumption, if the *MPC* was
   a. 0.20?
   b. 0.5?
   c. 2/3?
   d. 0.75?
   e. 0.8?

9. Why does the multiplier effect get larger as the marginal propensity to consume gets larger?

10. Why does it take a larger reduction in taxes to create the same increase in *AD* as a given increase in government purchases?

## Section 10.4

### Blueprint Problem

An economy with an $MPC = 0.75$ is experiencing an inflationary gap of $90 million.

   a. What change in government spending would be necessary to bring the economy back to full employment?
   b. What change in taxation would be necessary to bring the economy back to full employment?

### Blueprint Solution

a.

> The first step in solving this problem is to calculate the size of the expenditure multiplier.

$$\text{Expenditure multiplier} = \frac{1}{1 - MPC} = \frac{1}{1 - 0.75} = 4$$

> Next, recall the operation of the multiplier effect; an initial change in spending has a magnified (or multiplied) effect on the overall amount of economic activity. In terms of a formula, this effect can be expressed as follows:
>
> Aggregate economic activity = Initial change in spending × Expenditure multiplier
>
> Note that the "Aggregate economic activity" is represented as a negative value, indicating that the gap is inflationary and aggregate economic activity needs to be reduced by the size of the output gap.
>
> Now enter the given information in the question into this formula.

−$90 million = Initial change in spending × 4

> Solving for the "Initial change in spending" reveals that a $22.5 million reduction in government spending would be the necessary catalyst to trigger a $67.5 million multiplier effect. Together, the initial injection and multiplier effect would be sufficient to close the $90 million inflationary gap.

Initial change in spending = $22.5 million

b.

> As with the first part of this question, the first step in the solution is to determine the relevant multiplier—in this case, the tax multiplier.

$$\text{Tax multiplier} = -\frac{MPC}{1-MPC} = -\frac{0.75}{1-0.75} = -3$$

> Next, substitute the given information in the question into the multiplier identity, solving for the necessary "Change in taxes."

$$-\$90 \text{ million} = \text{Change in taxes} \times -3$$

$$\text{Change in taxes} = \$30 \text{ million}$$

> The final solution reveals that the government will need to increase taxes by $30 million to close the $90 million inflationary gap.

11. Predict the potential impact on real GDP of each of the following events.

    a. an increase in government spending of $5 billion in order to build new highways

    b. a decrease in federal spending of $1 billion due to peacetime military cutbacks

    c. consumer optimism leading to an $8 billion spending increase

    d. gloomy business forecasts leading to a $12 billion decline in investment spending

12. The economy is experiencing a recessionary gap of $30 billion. If the $MPC = 0.75$, what government spending stimulus would you recommend to move the economy back to full employment? If the $MPC = 0.66$?

13. Review the information in question 12. Suppose that instead of using government spending to close the recessionary gap, the government decided to reduce taxes. What amount of tax reduction would be recommended to move the economy back to full employment, if the $MPC = 0.75$? If the $MPC = 0.66$?

14. The economy is experiencing a $225 million inflationary gap. If the government decided to solve this macroeconomic disequilibrium using a change in taxes, would you recommend an increase or decrease in taxes? If the $MPC = 0.9$, what magnitude of tax change would be appropriate?

15. The economy is experiencing a $25 billion inflationary gap. Absent government intervention, what can you predict will happen to the economy in the long run? (Use aggregate demand–aggregate supply analysis in your answer.) If the government decides to intervene using changes in spending, would you recommend a spending increase or decrease? Of what magnitude?

16. Illustrate the impact of a tax cut using aggregate demand–aggregate supply analysis when the economy is operating above full employment. Is this a wise policy? Why or why not?

17. Use the following diagram to answer questions (a) through (f).

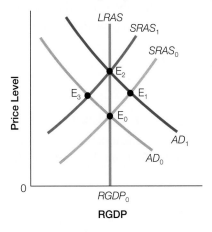

a. At what short-run equilibrium point might expansionary fiscal policy make sense to help stabilize the economy?

b. What would be the result of appropriate fiscal policy in that case?

c. What would be the long-run result if no fiscal policy action was taken in that case?

d. At what short-run equilibrium point might contractionary fiscal policy make sense to help stabilize the economy?

e. What would be the result of appropriate fiscal policy in that case?

f. What would be the long-run result if no fiscal policy action was taken in that case?

## Section 10.5

18. How do automatic stabilizers affect budget deficits and surpluses? How would automatic stabilizers be affected by an annually balanced budget rule?

19. Why do automatic stabilizers minimize the lag problems with fiscal policy?

20. What happens to the following variables during an expansion?

a. Employment Insurance benefits

b. welfare payments

c. income tax receipts

d. government budget deficit (surplus)

21. How does the tax system act as an automatic stabilizer? Why would transfer payments such as Employment Insurance also serve as an effective automatic stabilizer?

## Section 10.6

22. Can government spending that causes crowding out be detrimental to long-run economic growth? Explain.

23. Answer the following questions:

    a. Describe the crowding-out effect of an increase in government purchases.

    b. Why does the magnitude of the crowding-out effect depend on how responsive interest rates are to increase government borrowing and how responsive investment is to changes in interest rates?

    c. How would the size of the crowding-out effect affect the size of the change in aggregate demand that would result from a given increase in government purchases?

24. How do time lags affect the effectiveness of fiscal policy?

## Section 10.7

25. Illustrate diagrammatically the short-run effects of government deficit reduction.

26. Illustrate diagrammatically the long-run effects of government deficit reduction. Describe the mechanism that makes these effects different from the short-run effects described in question 25.

27. What are the intergenerational effects of government debt?

# chapter

# 11

# Money and the Banking System

## What Is Money?

- What is money?
- What are the four functions of money?

## WHAT IS MONEY?

**Money** is anything that is generally accepted in exchange for goods or services. Hundreds of years ago, commodities such as tobacco and furs were sometimes used as money. At some times and in some places, even cigarettes and playing cards have been used as money. But commodities have several disadvantages when used as money, the most important of which is that many commodities deteriorate easily after a few trades. Precious metal coins were used for money for millennia, partly because of their durability.

**money**
*anything generally accepted in exchange for goods or services*

## WHAT ARE THE FOUR FUNCTIONS OF MONEY?

Money has four important functions in the economy: as a medium of exchange, a store of value, a unit of account, and a means of deferred payment. Let's examine the four important functions of money to see how they are different from the functions of other assets in the economy, such as stocks, bonds, art, real estate, and comic book collections.

### 1. Money as a Medium of Exchange

The primary function of money is to serve as a **medium of exchange**, to facilitate transactions, and to lower transactions costs; that is, sellers will accept it as payment in a transaction. However, money is not the only medium of exchange; rather, it is the only medium that is generally accepted for most transactions. How would people trade with one another in the absence of money? They would **barter** for goods and services they desire, that is, transactions would involve the direct exchange of goods and services without the use of money.

**medium of exchange**
*the primary function of money, which is to facilitate transactions and lower transactions costs*

**barter**
*direct exchange of goods and services without the use of money*

**The Barter System Is Inefficient**   Under a barter system, individuals pay for goods or services by offering other goods and services in exchange. Suppose you are a farmer who needs some salt. You go to the merchant selling salt and offer her 30 kilograms of

SuperStock/Glow Images

**In the seventeenth century, in the absence of coinage, British and French colonists used individual pieces of wampum (polished shells) as lawful money. Tobacco was once used as money in colonial America and the ancient Chinese used chisels for money. Still other societies have used fish and cattle and, of course, gold coins as money. Pictured here are Iroquois wampum belts.**

**measure of value**

*money as a common "ruler" of worth, allowing for the comparison of diverse goods and services*

**store of value**

*Money provides a means of saving or accumulating purchasing power from the present and transferring it to the future.*

wheat for 2 kilograms of salt. The wheat that you use to buy the salt is not money and the salt merchant may not want wheat and therefore may not accept it as payment. That is one of the major disadvantages of the barter system: The buyer may not have appropriate items of value to the seller. The salt merchant may reluctantly take the wheat that she does not want, later bartering it away to another customer for something that she does want. In any case, bartering is inefficient because several trades may be necessary in order to receive the desired goods.

Moreover, bartering is extremely expensive over long distances. What would it cost a customer living in Saskatchewan to send a large quantity of wheat to Toronto in return for an item in the Sears catalogue? It is much cheaper to mail a cheque. Finally, bartering is time-consuming because of difficulties in evaluating the value of the product that is being offered for barter. For example, the person who is selling the salt may want to inspect the wheat first to make sure that it is pure and not filled with dirt or other unwanted items.

Barter, in short, is expensive, inefficient, and generally prevails only where limited trade is carried out over short distances, which generally means in relatively primitive economies. The more complex the economy (e.g., the higher the real per capita GDP), the greater the economic interactions between people, and consequently, the greater the need for one or more universally accepted asset serving as money. Only in a Robinson Crusoe economy, where people live in isolated settlements and are generally self-sufficient, is the use of money unnecessary.

## 2. Money as a Measure of Value

Besides serving as a medium of exchange, money is also a **measure of value**—a common "ruler" of worth allowing for the comparison of diverse goods and services. With a barter system, one does not know precisely what 30 kilograms of wheat are worth relative to 2 kilograms of salt. With money, a common "ruler" exists so that the values of diverse goods and services can be very precisely compared. So if wheat costs 50 cents a kilogram and salt costs $1 a kilogram, we can say that a kilogram of salt is valued precisely two times as much as a kilogram of wheat ($1 divided by 50 cents = 2). By providing a universally understood measure of value, money serves to lower the information costs involved in making transactions. Without money, a person might not know what a good price for salt is, because so many different commodities can be bartered for it. With money, there is but one price for salt, and that price is readily available as information to the potential consumer.

## 3. Money as a Store of Value

Money also serves as a **store of value**; that is, money provides a means of saving or accumulating purchasing power from the present and transferring it to the future. The farmer in a barter society who wants to save for retirement might accumulate enormous inventories of wheat, which he would then gradually trade away for other goods in his old age. This is a terribly inefficient way to save. Storage buildings would have to be constructed to hold all of the wheat, and the interest payments that the farmer would earn on the wheat would actually be negative, as rats will eat part of the wheat or it will otherwise deteriorate. Most important, physical goods of value would be tied up in unproductive use for many years. With money, the farmer saves pieces of paper that can be used to purchase goods and services after retirement. It is both cheaper and safer to store paper rather than wheat.

## 4. Money as a Means of Deferred Payment

Finally, the attribute of money that makes it easier to borrow and to repay loans is money as a **means of deferred payment**. With barter, lending is cumbersome and subject to an added problem. What if a wheat farmer borrows some wheat and agrees to pay it back in wheat next year, but the value of wheat soars because of a poor crop resulting from drought? The debt will be paid back in wheat that is far more valuable than that borrowed, causing a problem for the borrower. Of course, fluctuations in the value of money can also occur, and indeed, inflation has been a major problem in our recent past and continues to be a problem in many countries. But the value of money fluctuates far less than the value of many individual commodities, so lending money poses fewer risks to buyers and sellers than lending commodities.

**means of deferred payment**
*the attribute of money that makes it easier to borrow and to repay loans*

### SECTION CHECK

- Money is anything that is generally accepted in exchange for goods or services.
- The four important functions of money are money as a medium of exchange, money as a measure of value, money as a store of value, and money as a means of deferred payment.

# Measuring Money

**section**
**11.2**

- What is currency?
- What are demand and savings deposits?
- What is liquidity?
- How is the money supply measured?
- What backs the money supply?

## WHAT IS CURRENCY?

**Currency** consists of coins and banknotes that an institution or government has created to be used in the trading of goods and services and the payment of debts. Currency in the form of metal coins is still used as money throughout the world today but metal currency has a disadvantage: It is bulky. Also, certain types of metals traditionally used in coins, like gold and silver, are not available in sufficient quantities to meet our demands for a monetary instrument. For these reasons, metal coins were supplemented first by paper currency and now by polymer currency. In Canada, the Bank of Canada issues Bank of Canada notes in various denominations, and this polymer currency, along with coins, provides the basis for most transactions of relatively modest size in Canada today.

**currency**
*coins and banknotes that an institution or government has created to be used in the trading of goods and services and the payment of debts*

## Currency as Legal Tender

In Canada and in most other nations of the world, metal coins and banknotes are the only forms of legal tender. **Legal tender** refers to coins and banknotes officially declared to be acceptable for the settlement of debts incurred in financial transactions.

**legal tender**
*coins and banknotes officially declared to be acceptable for the settlement of debts incurred in financial transactions*

**fiat money**
*a means of exchange established by government declaration*

In effect, the government says, "We declare these instruments to be money, and citizens are expected to accept them as a medium of exchange." Legal tender is **fiat money**—a means of exchange that has been established not by custom and tradition or because of the value of the metal in a coin, but by government fiat, or declaration.

## WHAT ARE DEMAND AND SAVINGS DEPOSITS?

Most of the money that we use for day-to-day transactions, however, is not official legal tender. Rather, it is a monetary instrument that has become generally accepted in exchange over the years and has now, by custom and tradition, become money. What is this instrument? It is balances in chequing accounts in financial institutions, more formally called *demand deposits*. **Demand deposits** are defined as balances in financial institution accounts that depositors can access on demand by simply writing a cheque or using a debit card. That is, demand deposits are convertible to currency on demand. Some other forms of accounts in financial institutions also have virtually all of the attributes of demand deposits. For example, other chequable deposits earn interest but have some restrictions, such as higher monthly fees or minimum balance requirements. Practically speaking, funds in these accounts are the equivalent of demand deposits and have become an important component in the supply of money.

**demand deposits**
*balances in bank accounts that depositors can access on demand*

### The Popularity of Demand Deposits

Demand deposits have replaced banknotes and metal currency as the major source of money used for larger transactions in Canada and in most other relatively well-developed nations for several reasons, including ease and safety of transactions, lower transaction costs, and convenient transaction records.

Why are financial institution balances that depositors have access to by writing cheques or using debit cards the most popular form of money in Canada, as well as in most other well-developed nations? The answer is simple really: Demand deposits offer all the benefits of coins and banknotes in terms of liquidity without the danger and inconvenience of having to carry around large sums of money to facilitate daily transactions.

**Ease and Safety of Transactions**    Paying for goods and services with a cheque is less risky than paying with banknotes, which are readily transferable: If someone takes a $20 bill from you, it is gone and the thief can use it to buy goods with no difficulty. If, however, someone steals a cheque that you have written to the telephone company to pay a monthly bill, that person probably will have great difficulty using it to buy goods and services, because the individual has to be able to identify himself as a representative of the telephone company. If your chequebook is stolen, a person can use your cheques as money only if she can successfully forge your signature and provide some identification. Hence, transacting business by cheque is much less risky than using legal tender; an element of insurance or safety exists in the use of demand deposits instead of currency.

MIKA Images/Alamy Stock Photo

**Lower Transaction Costs**    Suppose you decide that you want to buy a compact disc player that costs $81.25 from a mail-order catalogue. It is much cheaper, easier, and safer for you to send a cheque for $81.25 rather than four $20 bills, a $1 coin, and a quarter. Demand deposits are popular precisely because they lower transaction costs compared with the use of metal or polymer currency. In very small transactions, the gains in safety and convenience of cheques are outweighed by the time and cost required to write and process them; in these cases, transaction costs are lower with banknotes and metal currency. For this reason, it is unlikely that the use of banknotes or metal currency will disappear entirely.

**Transaction Record**   Another useful feature of demand deposits is that they provide a record of financial transactions. Each month, the financial institution provides the depositor with a statement recording the deposit and withdrawal of funds. In an age where detailed records are often necessary for tax purposes, this is a useful feature. Of course, this feature of transaction records could be a negative for some types of business activities, whose participants might prefer that no records exist. In these cases, banknote transactions could be preferred because they do not leave a paper trail for the government or authorities to follow.

## Credit Cards and Debit Cards

A credit card is generally acceptable in exchange for goods and services. At the same time, however, a credit card payment is actually a guaranteed loan available on demand to the cardholder, which merely defers the cardholder's payment for a transaction using a demand deposit. After all, the word "credit" means you are receiving money today with a promise to pay it back in the future—it really is a short-term loan. Ultimately, an item purchased with a credit card must be paid for online or with a cheque; monthly payments on a credit card account are required for continued use of the card. A credit card, then, is not money but rather a convenient tool for carrying out transactions that minimize the physical transfer of cheques or currency. In this sense, it is a substitute for the use of money and allows cardholders to use any given amount of money in future exchanges.

A debit card lets you access the money in your chequing account, but the card is not money. They are called *debit cards* because they debit your bank account directly when you use them. People often prefer to use debit cards to writing a cheque because it is more convenient—no chequebook is required. It may be safer than a credit card, too, because debit cards require a personal identification number (PIN) for their use. However, there is no grace period, and the transaction immediately reduces the amount of money in your bank account. Consequently, consumers have less leverage if disputing a purchase; with a cheque, you can stop payment and with a credit card you have a grace period between purchase and payment.

## Electronic Payment

Advancements in technology and the spread of the Internet have impacted not only how people buy things, but how they pay for their purchases as well. Electronic banking services, widely available throughout Canada and the United States, now enable people to pay bills and transfer funds with a few clicks of the computer mouse. No longer do you have to mail a cheque or line up at an ATM to pay your bills; financial institutions now provide online services that allow you to transmit your payments electronically. The simplicity and security associated with electronic payment systems has made them increasingly popular with consumers.

## Savings Deposits

Coins, banknotes, and demand deposits are certainly forms of money, because all are accepted as direct means of payment for goods and services. Money also includes **savings deposits**, which are financial institution accounts containing funds that cannot be used directly for payment, such as by writing cheques. If these funds cannot be used

**savings deposits**
*financial institution accounts containing funds that cannot be used directly for payment*

directly as a means of payment, then why do people hold such accounts? People use these accounts primarily because they generally pay higher interest rates than demand deposits.

## Money Market Mutual Funds

Money market mutual funds are interest-earning accounts provided by brokers who pool funds into investments such as Treasury bills. These funds are invested in short-term securities, and depositors are allowed to write cheques against their accounts subject to certain limitations. This type of fund experienced tremendous growth over the last 20 years. Money market mutual funds are highly liquid assets. While not technically considered money, these funds are important because they are relatively easy to convert into money for the purchase of goods and services.

## Stocks and Bonds

Virtually everyone agrees that many other forms of financial assets, such as stocks and bonds, are not money. Suppose you buy 1000 shares of common stock in Microsoft at $100 per share, for a total of $100 000. The stock is traded daily on the Toronto Stock Exchange and elsewhere; you can readily sell the stock and get paid in legal tender or a demand deposit. Why, then, is this stock not considered money? First, it will take a few days for you to receive payment for the sale of stock; you cannot turn the asset into cash as you can a savings deposit in a financial institution. Second, and more importantly, the value of the stock fluctuates over time, and as an owner of the asset, you have no guarantee that you will be able to obtain its original nominal value at any time. Thus, stocks and bonds are not generally considered to be money.

## WHAT IS LIQUIDITY?

**liquidity**
*the ease with which one asset can be converted into another asset or into goods and services*

Money is an asset that we generally use to buy goods or services. In fact, it is so easy to convert money into goods and services that we say it is the most liquid of assets. When we speak of **liquidity**, we are speaking about the ease with which one asset can be converted into another asset or into goods and services. For example, to convert a stock or bond into goods and services would prove to be somewhat more difficult—contacting your broker or going online, determining at what price to sell your stock, paying the commission, and waiting for the completion of the transaction. Clearly, stocks and bonds are not as liquid an asset as money. But other assets are even less liquid, like converting your oil paintings or your hockey card collection into other goods and services.

## HOW IS THE MONEY SUPPLY MEASURED?

**M2**
*currency outside chartered banks plus demand and savings deposits at chartered banks*

**M2+**
*M2 plus demand and savings deposits at trust companies, mortgage loan companies, credit unions, caisses populaires, and other financial institutions*

There is no unique official measure of the Canadian money supply. The most common definition of the money supply is called **M2**, which consists of currency held outside chartered banks plus demand and savings deposits at chartered banks. Exhibit 1 shows that in February 2018, the M2 measure of the money supply in Canada was 1588.4 billion, comprising $83.4 billion of currency held outside chartered banks plus 1505.0 billion of demand deposits and savings deposits at the chartered banks. A broader definition of the money supply is called **M2+**, which consists of M2 plus demand and savings deposits at trust companies, mortgage loan companies, credit unions, caisses populaires, and other financial institutions. M2+ totalled $1994.1 billion in February 2018. Of these two different definitions of the money supply, it is the M2 measurement that is more commonly used as the official money supply.

| section 11.2 Exhibit 1 | Two Definitions of the Money Supply: M2 and M2+ |
| --- | --- |

| | |
| --- | --- |
| Currency held outside chartered banks | $ 83.4 billion |
| Demand deposits and savings deposits at chartered banks | 1505.0 billion |
| M2 | $1588.4 billion |
| Deposits at other financial institutions | 405.7 billion |
| M2+ | $1994.1 billion |

SOURCE: Bank of Canada, *Banking Financial Statistics*, April 26, 2018 (data as of February 2018).

Exhibit 2 illustrates the growth of currency outside the banking system as well as the two most common monetary aggregates, M2 and M2+, from 1968 to 2017. As seen in the exhibit, currency held by the Canadian public has experienced only slight growth over the last 45 years, indicating that while the majority of transactions are performed using other forms of money, some transactions are still cash-based. However, the dramatic growth of both M2 and M2+ is evidence of the extent to which the Canadian public prefers to keep its liquid assets in the form of savings and chequing accounts of various kinds. The popularity of savings and chequing accounts has placed financial intermediaries, of which banks are the predominant form in Canada, at the centre of the Canadian financial system and of particular importance to the Canadian economy.

| section 11.2 Exhibit 2 | Currency and Selected Monetary Aggregates, Canada, 1968–2017 |
| --- | --- |

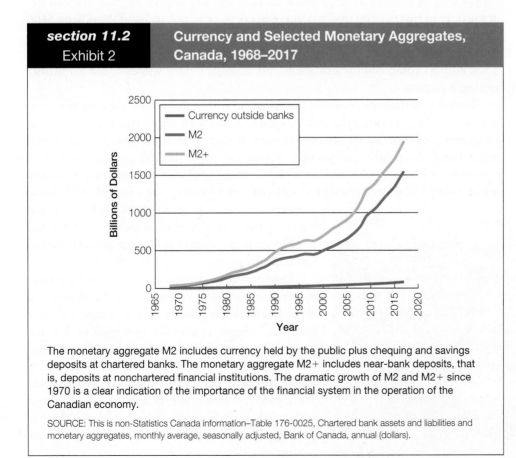

The monetary aggregate M2 includes currency held by the public plus chequing and savings deposits at chartered banks. The monetary aggregate M2+ includes near-bank deposits, that is, deposits at nonchartered financial institutions. The dramatic growth of M2 and M2+ since 1970 is a clear indication of the importance of the financial system in the operation of the Canadian economy.

SOURCE: This is non-Statistics Canada information–Table 176-0025, Chartered bank assets and liabilities and monetary aggregates, monthly average, seasonally adjusted, Bank of Canada, annual (dollars).

## WHAT BACKS THE MONEY SUPPLY?

Until fairly recently, coins in most nations were largely made from precious metals, usually gold or silver. These metals had considerable intrinsic worth: If the coins were melted down, the metal would be valuable for use in jewellery, industrial applications, dentistry, and so forth. Until 1929 (with the exception of the World War I period of 1914–26), Canada was on an internal **gold standard**, a monetary system that defined the value of the dollar as equivalent in value to a certain amount of gold, thereby allowing direct convertibility from currency to gold. Under this system, the quantity of gold purchased by the government determines the monetary reserves and therefore the supply of money in the economy.

In 1929, Canada effectively went off the gold standard. Excessive monetary expansion in the 1920s, which lowered the ratio of gold reserves to government-issued notes, in addition to a reluctance by Canadian authorities to accept the constraints on the gold standard, were seen as major contributing factors leading to this decision.

**gold standard**

*a monetary system that defines the value of the dollar as equivalent in value to a certain amount of gold, thereby allowing direct convertibility from currency to gold*

### What Backs Our Money Has Changed

Canadian dollars are no longer convertible into gold, so today no meaningful precious metal gives our money value. Why, then, do people accept currency in exchange for goods? After all, a $20 bill is just a piece of polymer with virtually no inherent utility or worth. Do we accept these bills because it states on the front of the bills that "This note is legal tender"? Perhaps, but we accept demand deposits without that statement.

The true backing behind money in Canada is faith that people will take it in exchange for goods and services. People accept with great eagerness these pieces of coloured polymer simply because we believe that they will be exchangeable for goods and services with an intrinsic value. If you were to drop two pieces of polymer of equal size on the floor in front of 100 students, one a blank piece of polymer and the other a $100 bill and then leave the room, the group would probably start fighting for the $100 bill while the blank piece of polymer would be ignored. As long as people have confidence in something's convertibility into goods and services, money will exist and no further backing is necessary.

Because governments represent the collective will of the people, they are the institutional force that traditionally defines money in the legal sense. People are willing to accept pieces of paper as money only because of their faith in the government. When people lose faith in the exchangeability of pieces of paper that the government decrees as money, even legal tender loses its status as meaningful money. Something is money only if people will generally accept it. Although governments play a key role in defining money, much of it is actually created by chartered banks. A majority of Canadian money, whether M2 or M2+, is in the form of deposits at privately owned financial institutions.

People who hold money, then, must have faith not only in their government, but also in banks and other financial institutions. If you accept a cheque drawn on a bank, you believe that bank or, for that matter, any financial institution will be willing to convert that cheque into legal tender (currency), enabling you to buy goods or services that you want to have. Thus, you have faith in the bank as well. In short, our money is money because of the confidence that we have in private financial institutions as well as in our government.

**What makes this money valuable? Banknotes are valuable if they are acceptable to people who want to sell goods and services. Sellers must be confident that the money they accept is also acceptable at the place where they want to buy goods and services. Imagine if money in Alberta was not accepted as money in Ontario or Nova Scotia. It would certainly make it more difficult to carry out transactions.**

iStock/Thinkstock, bank notes images used with the permission of the Bank of Canada.

# How Banks Create Money

- What types of financial institutions exist in Canada?
- How do banks create money?
- What does a bank balance sheet look like?
- What is a desired reserve ratio?

## WHAT TYPES OF FINANCIAL INSTITUTIONS EXIST IN CANADA?

Financial institutions in Canada can be classified into three general categories: depository institutions, contractual savings institutions, and investment intermediaries. Each type of institution is unique in terms of where it obtains its funds (primary liability) and how it uses those funds (primary asset). For example, customer deposits are a depository institution's largest liability (use of funds), while the loans and mortgages it grants to its customers are its largest asset (source of funds). Alternatively, consider pension plans that are established by an employer for the purpose of organizing employee retirement contributions (source of funds). Since most companies do not administer their own pension plans, financial institutions receive this money and invest it in corporate stocks and bonds (use of funds).

Exhibit 1 shows the relative size of the major types of financial institutions in Canada in terms of total financial assets. *Deposit-taking institutions,* a category that includes chartered banks, control over 75 percent of all financial assets in Canada.

## Canada's Banking System

Canada's banking system is widely considered to be the most efficient and safest in the world. The biggest players in the Canadian banking industry are its six large **chartered banks**, financial institutions that accept deposits and make loans. The

**chartered banks**
*financial institutions that accept deposits and make loans*

"Big Six" includes the Bank of Montreal, Bank of Nova Scotia, Canadian Imperial Bank of Commerce, National Bank of Canada, Royal Bank of Canada, and Toronto-Dominion Bank. These banks account for approximately 90 percent of total assets among Canada's federally regulated deposit-taking institutions and approximately 70 percent of the total domestic assets held by the financial services sector. While chartered banks dominate the financial landscape, there are thousands of other financial institutions offering a variety of financial services in Canada.

By comparison, the structure of Canada's banking industry is dramatically different than that used in the United States. While Canada had a total of 86 banks as of August 2018, the United States had over 7000 commercial banks, far more than any other country in the world. In addition to the extraordinary number of banks, another distinguishing feature of the U.S. banking industry is the fact that the majority of the banks are small: 90 percent have assets under $1 billion and 30 percent have assets under $100 million.

## The Functions of Banks

Banks offer a large number of financial functions. For example, they often will pay an individual's monthly bills by automatic withdrawals, provide financial planning services, rent safe-deposit boxes, and so on. Most important, though, they accept demand deposits and savings deposits from individuals and firms. They can create money by making loans. In making loans, financial institutions act as intermediaries (the middle persons) between savers, who supply funds, and borrowers, who demand funds.

## HOW DO BANKS CREATE MONEY?

As we have already learned, most money, narrowly defined, is in the form of demand deposits, assets that can be directly used to buy goods and services. But how did the balance in, say, a chequing account get there in the first place? Perhaps it was through a loan made by a chartered bank. When a bank lends to a person, it does not typically give the borrower cash (banknotes and metal currency). Rather, it gives the person the funds by a cheque or by adding funds to an existing chequing account of the borrower. If you go into a bank and borrow $1000, the bank probably will simply add $1000 to your chequing account at the bank. In doing so, a new demand deposit—money—is created.

| *section 11.3*<br>Exhibit 1 | **Relative Shares of Financial Institutions in Canada (as of Q4, 2017)** | | |
|---|---|---|---|
| **Type of Institution** | **Number** | **Total Assets (in billions)** | **Percentage (%)** |
| Deposit-taking institutions | 148 | $ 5721 | 76.3 |
| Life insurance companies | 80 | 1444 | 19.3 |
| Property and casualty companies | 153 | 125 | 1.7 |
| Federally regulated private pension plans | 1230 | 206 | 2.7 |
| **Total** | **1611** | **$7496** | **100.0** |

SOURCE: To come from permissions

## Bank Profits

Banks make loans and create demand deposits in order to make a profit. How do they make their profit? By collecting higher interest payments on the loans, they make than the interest they pay their depositors for those funds. If you borrow $1000 from Loans R Us National Bank, the interest payment you make, less the expenses the bank incurs in making the loan, including its costs of acquiring the funds, represents profit to the bank.

## Fractional Reserve System

Because the way to make more profit is to make more loans, banks want to make a large volume of loans. Shareholders, or owners, of banks want the largest profits possible, so what keeps banks from making nearly infinite quantities of loans? A prudent bank would put some limit on its loan (and therefore deposit) volume. For people to accept demand deposits as money, the cheques written must be generally accepted in exchange for goods and services. People will accept cheques only if they know that they are quickly convertible at par (face value) into legal tender. For this reason, banks must have adequate cash reserves on hand to meet the needs of customers who wish to convert their demand deposits into currency.

Our banking system is sometimes called a **fractional reserve system** because banks hold reserves equal to some fraction of their demand deposits. If a bank were to create $100 in demand deposits for every $1 in cash reserves that it had, the bank might well find itself in difficulty before too long. Why? Consider a bank with $10 000 000 in demand deposits and $100 000 in cash reserves. Suppose a couple of large companies with big accounts decide to withdraw $120 000 in cash on the same day. The bank would be unable to convert into legal tender all of the funds requested. The word would then spread that the bank's deposits are not convertible into lawful money. This would cause a so-called "run on the bank." The bank would have to quickly convert some of its other assets into currency, or it would be unable to meet its obligations to convert its demand deposits into currency, and it would have to close.

Therefore, few banks would risk maintaining fewer reserves on hand than they thought prudent for their amount of deposits (particularly demand deposits). Although banks must maintain a prudent level of reserves, they do not want to keep any more of their funds as additional reserves than necessary for safety, because cash reserves do not earn any interest for the bank.

In Canada, if a financial institution should fail, depositors are insured against financial loss by the federal government. The Canadian Deposit Insurance Corporation (CDIC), a federal Crown corporation, is the most important government agency that provides this type of insurance. Specifically, deposits at member deposit-taking financial institutions are insured up to $100 000 per account. CDIC members are required to make contributions into the CDIC fund, which is then used to reimburse depositors in the case of a member bank's failure. With some exceptions, virtually all deposit-accepting financial institutions in Canada are members of the CDIC.

## WHAT DOES A BANK BALANCE SHEET LOOK LIKE?

Earlier in this chapter, we learned that money is created when banks make loans. We will now look more closely at the process of bank lending and its impact on the stock of money. In doing so, we will take a closer look at the structure and behaviour of our hypothetical bank, the Loans R Us National Bank. To get a good picture of the size of the bank, what it owns, and what it owes, we look at its **balance sheet**, which is sort of a financial photograph of the bank at a single moment in time. Exhibit 2 presents a balance sheet for the Loans R Us National Bank.

**fractional reserve system**
*a system in which banks hold reserves equal to some fraction of their demand deposits*

**balance sheet**
*a financial record that indicates the balance between a bank's assets and its liabilities plus capital*

## Assets

The assets of a bank are those things of value that the bank owns (e.g., cash reserves, bonds, and its buildings), including contractual obligations of individuals and firms to pay funds to the bank (loans). The largest asset item for most banks is loans. Banks maintain most of their assets in the form of loans because interest payments on loans are the primary means by which they earn revenue. Some assets are kept in the form of noninterest-bearing cash reserves, to meet the cash demands of customers. Banks also keep some assets in the form of bonds (usually Government of Canada bonds) that are quickly convertible into cash if necessary, but also earn interest revenue.

## Liabilities

All banks have substantial liabilities, which are financial obligations that the bank has to other people. The predominant liability of virtually all banks is deposits. If you have money in a demand deposit account, you have the right to demand cash for that deposit at any time. Basically, the bank owes you the amount in your chequing account. Savings deposits similarly constitute a liability of banks.

## Capital

For a bank to be healthy and solvent, its assets, or what it owns, must exceed its liabilities, or what it owes to others. In other words, if the bank was liquidated and all the assets converted into cash and all the obligations to others (liabilities) paid off, there would still be some cash left to distribute to the owners of the bank, its shareholders. This difference between a bank's assets and its liabilities constitutes the bank's capital. Note that this definition of capital differs from the earlier definition, which described capital as goods used to further production of other goods (machines, structures, tools, etc.). As you can see in Exhibit 2, capital is included on the right side of the balance sheet so that both sides (assets and liabilities plus capital) are equal in amount. Anytime the aggregate amount of bank assets changes, the aggregate amount of liabilities and capital also must change by the same amount, by definition.

## WHAT IS A DESIRED RESERVE RATIO?

Suppose for simplicity that the Loans R Us National Bank wants to hold cash reserves equal to 10 percent of its deposits. That percentage of deposits that a bank chooses to

| section 11.3 Exhibit 2 | Balance Sheet, Loans R Us National Bank | | |
|---|---|---|---|
| **Assets** | | **Liabilities and Capital** | |
| Cash reserves | $ 900 000 | Demand deposits | $ 5 000 000 |
| Loans | 7 200 000 | Savings deposits | 4 000 000 |
| Bonds | 1 500 000 | Total Liabilities | $ 9 000 000 |
| | | Capital | 1 000 000 |
| Bank building, equipment, fixtures | 400 000 | | |
| **Total Assets** | **$10 000 000** | **Total Liabilities and Capital** | **$10 000 000** |

hold as cash reserves is often called the **desired reserve ratio**. But what does a desired reserve ratio of 10 percent mean? This means that the bank *wants to* keep cash on hand equal to one-tenth (10 percent) of its deposits. For example, if the desired reserve ratio was 10 percent, banks would want to hold $100 000 in reserves for every $1 million in deposits. The remaining 90 percent of cash, the cash reserves that are in excess of desired reserves, is called **excess reserves**.

In Canada, the section of the Bank of Canada Act that required banks to hold a specified amount of cash reserves has since been repealed. In June of 1994, banks in Canada were allowed to determine their own reserve requirements, that is, their reserves were subject to a desired reserve ratio. Canadian banks typically keep about 4.5 percent reserves.

Reserves in the form of vault cash earn no revenue for the bank. Whenever excess reserves appear, banks will invest the excess reserves in interest-earning assets, sometimes bonds but usually loans.

## Loaning Excess Reserves

Let's see what happens when someone deposits $100 000 at the Loans R Us National Bank. We will continue to assume that the desired reserve ratio is 10 percent. That is, the bank wants to hold $10 000 in reserves for this new deposit of $100 000. The remaining 90 percent, or $90 000, becomes excess reserves, and most of this will likely become available for loans for individuals and businesses. Notice that at this point, the money supply (M2) is unchanged. Demand deposits have increased by $100 000 while currency outside the chartered banks has decreased by $100 000, as the currency is now stored in the bank's vault.

However, this is not the end of the story. Let us say that the bank loans all of its new excess reserves of $90 000 to an individual who is remodelling her home. At the time that the loan is made, the money supply will increase by $90 000. Specifically, no one has less money—the original depositor still has $100 000 and the bank now adds $90 000 to the borrower's chequing account (demand deposit). A new demand deposit, or chequing account, of $90 000 has been created. *Since demand deposits are money, the issuers of the new loan have created money.*

Furthermore, borrowers are not likely to keep the money in their chequing accounts for long, since you usually take out a loan to buy something. If that loan is used for remodelling, then the borrower pays the construction company, whose owner will likely deposit the money into his account, perhaps at another bank, to add even more funds for additional money expansion. This whole process is summarized in Exhibit 3.

## Money Creation Is Not Wealth Creation

When banks create more money by putting their excess reserves to work, they make the economy more liquid. There is clearly more money in the economy after the loan, but is the borrower any wealthier? The answer is no. Although borrowers have more money to buy goods and services, they are not any richer because the new liability, the loan, has to be repaid.

In short, banks create money when they increase demand deposits through the process of creating loans. However, the process does not stop here. In the next section, we will see how the process of loans and deposits has a multiplying effect throughout the banking industry.

## Leverage and the 2008 to 2009 Financial Crisis

To what extent, if any, are financial institutions regulated in their ability to generate loans? To best answer this question, we first need to understand the concept of **leverage**—the use of borrowed money for the purpose of investing. As a business practice, leverage

**desired reserve ratio**
*the percentage of deposits that a bank chooses to hold as cash reserves*

**excess reserves**
*cash reserves that are in excess of desired reserves*

**leverage**
*the use of borrowed money for the purpose of investing*

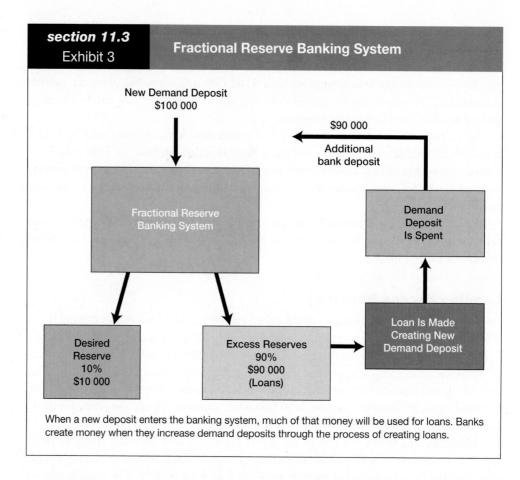

**section 11.3**
Exhibit 3

**Fractional Reserve Banking System**

When a new deposit enters the banking system, much of that money will be used for loans. Banks create money when they increase demand deposits through the process of creating loans.

is a common way in which enterprises finance investment projects; that is, it is not uncommon to see businesses finance an investment using debt as opposed to their own capital. For banks, leverage is central to their ability to operate successfully since their business centres around the actions of borrowing and lending funds.

In banking, the ratio of total assets (recall that for a bank, assets consist primarily of loans) to bank capital—referred to as the **leverage ratio**—is a common measurement of the degree to which an institution is leveraged. For example, looking back at Exhibit 2, Loans R Us National Bank has a leverage ratio of 10 ($10 000 000/$1 000 000), meaning that for every dollar of capital supplied by the bank owners, the bank has $10 of assets.

To help appreciate the impact of leverage on banking operations, let us continue with the example from Exhibit 2 and consider what happens to bank capital when the value of total assets increases by 10 percent. A 10 percent increase in total assets increases their value to $11 000 000, and since total liabilities remain unchanged, bank capital increases to $2 000 000. That is, since Loans R Us National Bank has a leverage ratio of 10, the 10 percent increase in total assets generates a 100 percent increase in bank capital. Alternatively, if total assets decrease in value by 10 percent, total assets would fall by $1 000 000 (to $9 000 000) and bank capital would be reduced by 100 percent to a value of zero!

In summary, when a bank has total assets that far exceed its capital, its leverage ratio is high, an indication of not only the bank's aggressive business model, but also an indication of the potential risk of failure of the bank. The multiple of assets to capital, that is the degree of leverage that Canadian financial institutions can pursue, is regulated by the Office of the Superintendent of Financial Institutions (OSFI). By restricting how much debt securities a bank can issue, the OSFI effectively controls how much leverage a financial institution can take on.

**leverage ratio**
*the ratio of total assets to bank capital*

Beginning in the early 1960s until 1980, the average leverage ratios of major Canadian banks steadily increased from around 20 to a high of over 40. That is, over a 20-year period, Canadian banks went from having $20 of total assets (primarily loans) for each dollar of bank capital to over $40 of total assets (primarily loans) to each dollar of bank capital. In response to this rise in leverage (and the related financial risk it placed on the banking system), a regulatory limit of 30 was imposed on the leverage ratios of large banks beginning in 1982 until 1991. This regulatory limit was further reduced to 20 in 1991 where it remained until 2000. Presently, banks that meet specific preconditions are eligible for a maximum leverage ratio of 23. These lower leverage ratios and the higher capital reserves they generated have been seen as a major reason why Canadian banks weathered the 2008 to 2009 financial crisis so successfully. U.S. and European banks were widely viewed as being dangerously over-leveraged in the years leading up to the global financial crisis—a position that is being cited as a major contributing factor to the global financial crisis of 2008.

From an international perspective, it is important to note that few countries have formal leverage constraints. In response to this and the global financial crisis, the Third Basel Accord (*Basel III*) was negotiated in 2010 to 2011 and was scheduled to be introduced from 2013 to 2015; however, changes have extended this implementation until 2019. It will require central banks to impose lower leverage ratios on their national banks. The impact of *Basel III* on Canadian financial institutions is expected to be minimal, as the new requirements are largely in line with current OSFI regulations. For the United States and Europe, adherence to the tighter regulations will be considerably more difficult.

## Business *CONNECTION*

### DANCING WITH DEBT AND THE MONEY SUPPLY

In reality, business has little impact on money and the banking system (unless of course the business is banking!). But it's useful for business owners to understand the relationship of business, the money supply, and debt.

Many consumers believe that the money supply is literally a creation of the government's print shop, while business owners appreciate that, in fact, the vast amount of money created stems from the fractional reserves and creation of loans within the banking system. Businesses outside the financial sector have little impact on the money supply, but they do have an indirect effect through the financing of their products. Consider the following example.

About 20 years ago, North American companies started losing some of their share of the car market. Consumers were turning away from domestic cars in favour of foreign ones that were of higher quality and had more features. In an attempt to keep market share, the domestic auto industry started to address product issues, but that required major investment of capital and time. In the meantime, the domestic industry turned to the financial markets for assistance. Specifically, the car companies began to subsidize the cost of loans to consumers by "buying down" interest rates and taking greater equity positions (or investments) in car leases. In any event, this resulted in more vehicles being sold and more loans to consumers.

As you've learned, the more loans that banks make, the greater the creation of the money supply, so in offering financial

incentives to consumers to buy cars, the industry was contributing to inflation. At the same time the industry was contributing to various debt levels within the economy. The auto industry took on significant debt to finance its retooling and to finance the consumer incentives. Consumers took on extra debt by buying cars they might have not been able or willing to buy without taking on debt. Over the short and medium term, this had little effect on the economy—especially when the economy was growing. (Growth hides demons within the economy!)

The net effect of this growing debt is that it has produced unparalleled levels of consumption—this has been a perceived benefit for business and consumers (and business and governments). This increase in growth and consumption has in turn put upward pressure on inflation rates. But, since the start of the Great Recession of 2008, growth has been hampered by this unsustainable level of debt and inflation has been reduced to near-record low levels—to the point where deflation is a major concern. All levels of the economy have been burdened by debt, which has to be paid before further demand for products and services can recover. Until debt levels are reduced, inflation rates will struggle to get to healthy levels.

So, while business has not been directly responsible for the increases in debt and the money supply, it has contributed to them. Sensible business owners need to be aware of the dance among themselves, the money supply, inflation, and debt—these are short-term decisions affecting the health of the economy in the longer term.

*(continued)*

1. As a business owner, do you think the level of consumer debt is an issue for business? For the economy at large? Why or why not?

2. As a business owner, do you think the level of government debt is an issue for business? For the economy at large? Why or why not?

3. One of the concerns of governments is that the business sector is sitting on a tremendous amount of cash that is not being reinvested into the economy. One suggested solution is to tax corporations that are not investing that cash. As a business owner, what is your opinion about such a policy?

## SECTION CHECK

- While a variety of financial institutions exist in the Canadian financial system, the sector is dominated by deposit-accepting institutions—banks. The Canadian banking industry itself is dominated by six large chartered banks. The "Big Six" hold the majority of the financial assets in the banking industry.
- Money is created when banks make loans. Borrowers receive newly created demand deposits.
- A balance sheet is a financial record that indicates the balance between a bank's assets and its liabilities plus capital. A bank's largest asset is loans and its largest liability is deposits.
- A desired reserve ratio is the percentage of deposits a bank chooses to keep on hand in the form of cash reserves.

## section 11.4

# The Money Multiplier

- How does the multiple expansion of the money supply process work?
- What is the money multiplier?
- Why is it only "potential" money creation?

### HOW DOES THE MULTIPLE EXPANSION OF THE MONEY SUPPLY PROCESS WORK?

We have just learned that banks can create money (demand deposits) by making loans and that the monetary expansion of an individual bank is limited to its excess reserves. Although this is true, it ignores the further effects of a new loan and the accompanying expansion in the money supply. New loans create new money directly, but they also create excess reserves in other banks, which leads to still further increases in both loans and the money supply. There is a multiple expansion effect, where a given volume of bank reserves creates a multiplied amount of money.

### New Loans and Multiple Expansions

To see how the process of multiple expansion works, let us extend our earlier example. Say Loans R Us National Bank receives a new cash deposit of $100 000. For convenience, say the bank wants to keep new cash reserves equal to one-tenth (10 percent) of new deposits. With that, Loans R Us National Bank chooses to hold $10 000 of the $100 000 deposit for reserves. Thus, Loans R Us now has $90 000 in excess reserves as a consequence of the new cash deposit.

The Loans R Us National Bank, being a profit maximizer, will probably put its newly acquired excess reserves to work in some fashion, earning income in the form of interest. Most likely, it will make one or more new loans totalling $90 000.

When the borrowers from Loans R Us National Bank get their loans, the borrowed money will almost certainly be spent on something—such as new machinery, a new house, a new car, or larger store inventories. The new money will lead to new spending.

The $90 000 spent by people borrowing from Loans R Us National Bank likely will end up in bank accounts in still other banks, such as Bank A shown in Exhibit 1. Bank A now has a new deposit of $90 000 with which to make more loans and create still more money. So Bank A's T-account now looks like this:

**Bank A**

| Assets | | Liabilities | |
|---|---|---|---|
| Reserves | $9000 | Chequing deposits | $90 000 |
| Loans | $81 000 | | |

After the deposits, Bank A has liabilities of $90 000. So, Bank A creates $81 000 of money. Now if the money deposited in Bank A is made available for a loan and is then deposited in Bank B, the T-account for Bank B will be

**Bank B**

| Assets | | Liabilities | |
|---|---|---|---|
| Reserves | $8100 | Chequing deposits | $81 000 |
| Loans | $72 900 | | |

This process continues with Bank C, Bank D, Bank E, and others. Loans R Us National Bank's initial cash deposit, then, has a chain-reaction impact that ultimately involves many banks and a total monetary impact that is far greater than suggested by the size of the original deposit of $100 000; that is, every new loan gives rise to excess reserves, which lead to still further lending and deposit creation. Of course, each round of lending is smaller than the preceding one because some (we are assuming 10 percent) of the new money created will be kept as desired reserves.

## WHAT IS THE MONEY MULTIPLIER?

The **money multiplier** measures the potential amount of demand deposit money that the banking system generates with each dollar of reserves. To determine the size of the money multiplier we simply divide 1 by the desired reserve ratio, as indicated by the following formula:

$$\text{Money multiplier} = \frac{1}{\text{Desired reserve ratio}}$$

**money multiplier**
*measures the potential amount of demand deposit money that the banking system generates with each dollar of reserves*

The larger the desired reserve ratio, the smaller the money multiplier. Thus, a desired reserve ratio of 25 percent means a money multiplier of 4. Likewise, a desired reserve ratio of 10 percent means a money multiplier of 10.

The next formula can be used to measure the potential impact on demand deposits of an initial change in reserves:

$$\text{Potential deposit creation} = \text{Excess reserves} \times \text{Money multiplier}$$

In the example in Exhibit 1, where Loans R Us National Bank (with a 10 percent desired reserve ratio) receives a new $100 000 cash deposit, the initial deposit equals

$100 000. Potential demand deposit creation, then, equals $90 000 (excess reserves) multiplied by 10 (the money multiplier), or $900 000. Using the money multiplier, we can calculate that the total potential impact of the initial $100 000 deposit is $900 000 in demand deposit money being created. What is the final impact on the money supply (M2)? Demand deposits at the chartered banks are up by $1 000 000 ($900 000 deposit creation + $100 000 initial deposit), but currency outside the chartered banks is down by $100 000 (as the initial deposit is in the banks' vaults), so the money supply has increased by $900 000.

## WHY IS IT ONLY "POTENTIAL" DEPOSIT CREATION?

Note that the expression "potential" deposit creation was used in describing the impact of creating loans and deposits out of excess reserves. Why "potential"? Because it is possible that some banks will choose not to lend all of their excess reserves. Some banks may simply be extremely conservative and keep some extra newly acquired cash assets in that form. When that happens, the chain-reaction effect is reduced by the amount of excess reserves not loaned out.

Moreover, some borrowers may not spend all of their newly acquired bank deposits, or they may wait a considerable period of time before doing so. Others may choose to keep some of their loans as currency in their pockets. Such leakages and time lags in

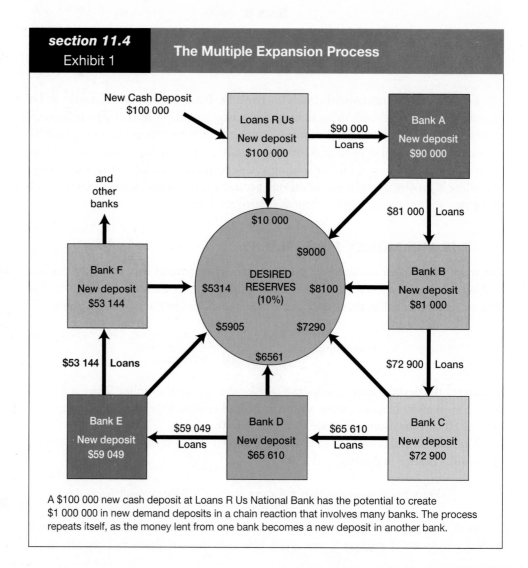

**section 11.4**
Exhibit 1

**The Multiple Expansion Process**

A $100 000 new cash deposit at Loans R Us National Bank has the potential to create $1 000 000 in new demand deposits in a chain reaction that involves many banks. The process repeats itself, as the money lent from one bank becomes a new deposit in another bank.

the bank money expansion process usually mean that the actual monetary impact of an initial deposit created out of excess reserves within a short time period is less than indicated by the money multiplier. Still, the multiplier principle does work, and a multiple expansion of deposits will generally occur in a fractional reserve banking system.

## DEBATE

### SHOULD CANADA BECOME A CASHLESS SOCIETY?

Canadian consumers purchase most of their goods and services today using either credit cards or debit cards, lessening the need for hard currency. As the demand for cash has decreased significantly with the advent of a number of different payment options/applications offered by banks and nonbank entities, consumers rely less on keeping cash in their wallets. In addition to this, producers and firms are finding it increasingly expensive to facilitate cash-based transactions, especially given the reduced number of purchases that are actually settled on a cash basis. This has led some countries, such as Sweden, to formally move toward being a totally cashless society. Should Canada follow suit?

### For:

Becoming a cashless society would provide a number of benefits to the consumers and to the producers. Consumers would always have readily available funds to spend without having to physically carry those funds. Some individuals already carry only a smartphone and a payment card in their phone case.

In addition to convenience, there's a security factor: if they lose the card, they haven't necessarily lost any money. A PIN is usually required to access funds with a debit card, and if a card is lost or stolen, most credit card companies and financial institutions have a system in place to protect their customers. Once notified of a loss or theft, they usually remove any unauthorized charges on the user's account.

Keeping track of debits and credits is easy, as each transaction is documented. This also makes income and corporate tax preparation more efficient.

### Against:

People who grew up using cash sometimes have an emotional and personal attachment to it. It provides them with a sense of security and is tangible evidence of how much they have available to make transactions. Those who do not trust governments or the banking system prefer to transact with cash.

Many also believe that cash provides more security in that it is less subject to fraud or theft through automated processes. Thieves and fraudsters actually have to get their hands on the cash instead of diverting the amounts out of online accounts. In addition, because every transaction is recorded, there is the possibility that someone could get access to another's transaction history and use it against them. For example, there would be a record of cigarette purchases that a health insurance company could access and likely use when handling claims.

A cashless system would result in an increase in certain transactional costs. When we pay by cash, there is no fee to process the payment or move the funds from one individual's account to another—it happens in real time with real money, not virtually. Performing the same transaction using a debit or credit card would involve processing fees that are usually on a set fee per transaction basis, so paying for something that is relatively inexpensive can increase dramatically in price just because of the fees.

Also, fees are set by the institutions, and they make much of their revenues on fees, which means they are highly motivated to increase fees as much as they can. If they constitute a monopoly, or near monopoly, then the consumer has very little opportunity to avoid these fees. Having a cash option provides competition and a valuable alternative for both producers and consumers.

Credit and debit cards are useless when there are power outages. Many in North America will remember a number of years back when the whole of the eastern side of the continent's power grid failed and it was days before power was restored. During those days, only those with cash could purchase goods, and while some vendors took IOUs as payment, they did this for only some trusted customers. Central bankers and senior government officials also are concerned when there are power failures. These disruptions could be accidental but they also could be deliberate criminal action.

One of the biggest arguments against going to a cashless society is that many seniors do not want to use electronic devices. Also, some people cannot afford the hardware and Internet access, although they could be serviced by the distribution and reloading of debit cards.

### Questions:

1. Would you be comfortable living in a cashless society? If your answer is yes, might your position change if you experienced a major power outage that lasted for days?
2. How can you prepare for such a situation?
3. Who do you think would gain most from having a cashless society: consumers or financial institutions? Explain your answer.

## SECTION CHECK

- New loans mean new money (demand deposits), which can increase spending as well as the money supply.
- The money multiplier is equal to 1 divided by the desired reserve ratio.
- The banking system as a whole can potentially create new money equal to several times the amount of new reserves—as determined by the money multiplier. However, due to various leakages and time lags, the actual monetary impact of an initial deposit created out of excess reserves within a short period of time will be less than that calculated by the money multiplier.

# For Your Review

## Section 11.1

1. Explain the difficulties that an economics professor might face in purchasing a new car using the barter system.

2. Why do people who live in countries experiencing rapid inflation often prefer to hold another country's currency (e.g., U.S. dollars) rather than their own country's currency? Explain.

3. Why do virtually all societies designate something to function as money?

## Section 11.2

4. Which one of each of the following pairs of assets is most liquid?
   a. Air Canada shares or a savings deposit
   b. a 30-year bond or a six-month Treasury bill
   c. a term deposit or a demand deposit
   d. a savings account or residential real estate

5. Why have ATMs and online banking made savings accounts more liquid than they used to be?

6. What would each of the following changes do to M2 and M2+?

| Change | M2 | M2+ |
|---|---|---|
| An increase in currency in circulation | | |
| An increase in demand deposits | | |
| An increase in savings deposits | | |
| An increase in credit card balances | | |
| A transfer of demand deposit balances from credit unions to chartered banks | | |

7. Are credit cards money?

## Section 11.3

8. Indicate whether each of the following belongs on the asset or liability side of a bank's balance sheet.

   a. loans

   b. holdings of government bonds

   c. demand deposits

   d. vault cash

   e. savings deposits

   f. bank buildings

   g. term deposits

9. In what way is it true that "Banks make money by making money"?

10. If the Bank of Canada paid interest for bank reserves held at the Bank of Canada, would banks still want to avoid holding excess reserves?

11. Suppose you found $10 000 while digging in your backyard and you deposited it in the bank. How would your new demand deposit account create a situation of excess reserves at your bank?

## Section 11.4

12. Assume there was a new $100 000 deposit into a demand deposit at a bank.

   a. What would be the resulting excess reserves created by that deposit if banks faced a desired reserve ratio of 10 percent, 20 percent, 25 percent, and 50 percent? Display using a T-account.

   b. How many additional dollars could that bank lend out as a result of that deposit if banks faced a desired reserve ratio of 10 percent, 20 percent, 25 percent, and 50 percent? Display using a T-account.

   c. How many additional dollars of demand deposit money could the banking system as a whole create in response to such a new deposit if banks faced a desired reserve ratio of 10 percent, 20 percent, 25 percent, and 50 percent?

13. Answer the following questions.

   a. If a bank had reserves of $30 000 and demand deposits of $200 000 (and no other deposits), how much could it lend out if it had a desired reserve ratio of

   10 percent?     _____

   15 percent?     _____

   20 percent?     _____

   b. If the bank then received a new $40 000 deposit in a customer's demand deposit account, how much could it now lend out (including the amount in question [a]) if it had a desired reserve ratio of

   10 percent?     _____

   15 percent?     _____

   20 percent?     _____

14. Calculate the money multiplier when the desired reserve ratio is
    a. 10 percent.
    b. 2 percent.
    c. 20 percent.
    d. 8 percent.

15. If the desired reserve ratio is 10 percent, calculate the potential change in demand deposits in the banking system under the following circumstances.
    a. You take $5000 from under your mattress and deposit it in your bank.
    b. You withdraw $50 from the bank and leave it in your wallet for emergencies.
    c. You write a cheque for $2500 drawn on your bank (CIBC) to an auto mechanic, who deposits the funds in his bank (TD Bank).

16. Calculate the magnitude of the money multiplier if banks were to hold 100 percent of deposits in reserve. Would banks be able to create money in such a case? Explain.

## Blueprint Problem

Examine the balance sheet for a banking system:

| Banking System Balance Sheet (original) | | | |
|---|---|---|---|
| **Assets** | | **Liabilities** | |
| Reserves | $  600 000 | Demand deposits | $6 000 000 |
| Loans | 5 400 000 | | |
| Buildings | 2 000 000 | Capital | 2 000 000 |
| **Total Assets** | **$8 000 000** | **Total Liabilities and Capital** | **$8 000 000** |

a. If all of the banks in this banking system have the same desired reserve ratio and are fully loaned up, what is the desired reserve ratio?

b. Suppose bank customers deposit an additional $100 000 into the banking system. What would be the initial impact of this deposit?

c. Redesign the balance sheet to reflect the ultimate impact of this deposit on the banking system, once all possible lending has taken place (for simplicity, assume all excess reserves are lent out and the public holds no cash, choosing to deposit all of their money in the banking system).

## Blueprint Solution

a. The desired reserve ratio implied by the banking system balance sheet is 10 percent.

By definition, in a fractional reserve banking system, the institutions have only a fraction of the money they are responsible for (their depositors' demand deposits) on hand in the form of reserves. To determine the desired reserve ratio, calculate what percentage of current demand deposits the banks are holding as reserves:

$$\text{Desired reserve ratio} = \frac{\text{Total reserves}}{\text{Total demand deposits}} = \frac{600\ 000}{6\ 000\ 000} = 0.1 = 10\%$$

b. The initial impact of the $100 000 deposit would be that demand deposits and reserves both increase by $100 000. The balance sheet would reflect these changes.

| Banking System Balance Sheet (initial) | | | |
|---|---|---|---|
| **Assets** | | **Liabilities** | |
| Reserves | $ 600 000 | Demand deposits | $ 6 000 000 |
| Reserves (new) | 100 000 | Demand deposits (new) | 100 000 |
| Loans | 5 400 000 | | |
| Buildings | 2 000 000 | Capital | 2 000 000 |
| **Total Assets** | **$8 100 000** | **Total Liabilities and Capital** | **$8 100 000** |

When accounting for the additional $100 000 in customer deposits, remember that this money (in the form of a deposit) represents an additional liability to the banking system (as this money belongs to the bank's customers), while at the same time an additional asset (in the form of reserves). Also, it is important to remember that the banks in our banking system will not need to hold in reserve all of these additional deposits—as represented by the desired reserve ratio, only 10 percent will need to be held in reserve (to act as the necessary insurance against the possibility of customer withdrawal). This means that the new $100 000 in reserve comprises $10 000 of desired reserves and $90 000 of excess reserves.

c.

The first step to solving this problem is to calculate the size of the money multiplier.

$$\text{Money multiplier} = \frac{1}{\text{Desired reserve requirement}} = \frac{1}{0.1} = 10$$

Next, recall the operation of the money multiplier process; when banks have excess reserves this enables them to generate loans. When these are re-deposited, additional excess reserves are created and additional lending results. In terms of a formula, this effect can be expressed as follows:

Potential deposit creation = Excess reserves × Money multiplier

Now enter the given information in the question into this formula.

Potential deposit creation = $90 000 × 10

Solving for "Potential deposit creation" reveals that from the initial $90 000 in initial excess reserves present in the banking system, $900 000 in potential deposit creation would be possible.

Potential deposit creation = $900 000

Finally, revisit the banking system's balance sheet and make the necessary updates to reflect this potential deposit creation. Remember, when a bank makes a loan available, it does so by creating a deposit equal to the loan amount. Therefore, when our system creates the $900 000 in loans, this is done through the creation of $900 000 in demand deposits.

| Banking System Balance Sheet (redesigned) | | | |
|---|---|---|---|
| **Assets** | | **Liabilities** | |
| Reserves | $ 700 000 | Demand deposits<br>Demand Deposits (new) | $ 6 100 000<br>900 000 |
| Loans<br>Loans (new) | 5 400 000<br>900 000 | | |
| Buildings | 2 000 000 | Capital | 2 000 000 |
| **Total Assets** | **$9 000 000** | **Total Liabilities and Capital** | **$9 000 000** |

The redesigned banking system balance sheet shows the system after it has fully adjusted to the initial $100 000 in deposits. Notice that the new total of reserves held by the banking system is $700 000, which is 10 percent of the demand deposits for which the banking system is responsible ($7 million × 10% = $700 000).

17. Suppose the simplified balance sheet shown below is for the entire banking system.

| Bank Balance Sheet | | | |
|---|---|---|---|
| **Assets** | | **Liabilities** | |
| Reserves | $ 500 000 | Demand deposits | $2 000 000 |
| Loans | 1 600 000 | | |
| Buildings | 1 200 000 | Capital | 1 300 000 |
| **Total Assets** | **$3 300 000** | **Total Liabilities and Capital** | **$3 300 000** |

If the desired reserve ratio is 10 percent, how much in excess reserves does the banking system have? If the banking system was to loan out those excess reserves, what is the potential expansion in demand deposits? Redesign the above balance sheet to show how it would look after this amount has been loaned.

18. Suppose the simplified balance sheet shown below is for the entire banking system.

| Bank Balance Sheet | | | |
|---|---|---|---|
| **Assets** | | **Liabilities** | |
| Reserves | $ 300 000 | Demand deposits | $1 500 000 |
| Loans | 1 200 000 | | |
| Buildings | 500 000 | Capital | 500 000 |
| **Total Assets** | **$2 000 000** | **Total Liabilities and Capital** | **$2 000 000** |

If the desired reserve ratio is 15 percent, how much in excess reserves does the banking system have? If the banking system was to loan out those excess reserves, what is the potential expansion in demand deposits? Redesign the above balance sheet to show how it would look after this amount has been loaned.

19. Suppose the simplified balance sheet shown below is for the entire banking system.

| Bank Balance Sheet | | | |
|---|---|---|---|
| **Assets** | | **Liabilities** | |
| Reserves | $ 750 000 | Demand deposits | $3 500 000 |
| Loans | 2 500 000 | | |
| Buildings | 1 250 000 | Capital | 1 000 000 |
| **Total Assets** | **$4 500 000** | **Total Liabilities and Capital** | **$4 500 000** |

If the desired reserve ratio is 20 percent, how much in excess reserves does the banking system have? If the banking system was to loan out those excess reserves, what is the potential expansion in demand deposits? Redesign the above balance sheet to show how it would look after this amount has been loaned.

section

## 12.1    The Bank of Canada

- What is the Bank of Canada?
- What are the main responsibilities of the Bank of Canada?

### WHAT IS THE BANK OF CANADA?

In most countries of the world, the job of controlling the supply of money belongs to the central bank. The Bank of Canada is Canada's central bank. It was established in 1935, largely as a result of the economic problems of the Great Depression and the need for better control of the money supply. Chartered banks' goal, remember, is to maximize profits for their shareholders. However, the banks' behaviour can have adverse effects on the nation's money supply. For example, during a period of economic recession, banks may have increasing concerns about the ability of new borrowers to repay their loans, or they may find that their customers are withdrawing more cash due to fears that the banks may fail. As a result, the banks may choose to hold more excess reserves for safety and liquidity, rather than loaning those excess reserves out. Thus, during a period of economic recession, there is a tendency for the money supply to decrease, which further destabilizes the economy. A central bank, however, can use certain tools to adjust the money supply in order to help stabilize the economy.

The Bank of Canada is owned by the federal government. It is controlled by a board of directors, which is appointed by the government. The governor of the Bank of Canada, who is the chief executive, is appointed for a seven-year term. The current governor, Stephen Poloz, was appointed in 2013. Although the government has final responsibility for the Bank of Canada's actions, the governor has considerable independence in the day-to-day operations of the Bank of Canada. This operational independence is important, as studies have shown that central banks with greater degrees of independence appear to have a lower annual inflation rate. If there was a very significant disagreement between the governor and the government, the government could issue a written directive to the governor, forcing him or her to either comply with the directive or resign.

The objectives of the Bank of Canada are outlined in the Bank of Canada Act, which starts out:

Whereas it is desirable to establish a central bank in Canada to regulate credit and currency in the best interests of the economic life of the nation, to control and protect the external value of the national monetary unit and to mitigate by its influence fluctuations in the general level of production, trade, prices and employment, so far as may be possible within the scope of monetary action, and generally to promote the economic and financial welfare of Canada....

Inflation control is how the Bank of Canada contributes to improved economic performance. Low inflation allows the economy to function more efficiently, resulting in better economic growth over time and reduced short-run cyclical fluctuations in output and employment. In 1991, the Bank of Canada and the federal government jointly announced inflation targets. The current inflation target aims to keep the annual inflation rate within a target range of 1 to 3 percent.

## The Federal Reserve System

In Canada, as in most countries, the central bank is a single bank. In the United States, however, the central bank is 12 institutions, closely tied together and collectively called the *Federal Reserve System*. The Federal Reserve System, or "the Fed," as it is nicknamed, comprises separate banks in Boston, New York, Philadelphia, Richmond, Atlanta, Dallas, Cleveland, Chicago, St. Louis, Minneapolis–St. Paul, Kansas City, and San Francisco. As Exhibit 1 shows, while these banks and their branches are spread all over the country, they are most heavily concentrated in the eastern states.

Each Federal Reserve Bank has its own board of directors and, to a limited extent, can set its own policies. Effectively, however, the 12 banks act in unison on major policy issues, with control of major policy decisions resting with the Board of Governors and the Federal Open Market Committee (FOMC), headquartered in Washington, DC. The chairperson of the Federal Reserve Board of Governors, currently Jerome Hayden "Jay" Powell, is generally regarded as one of the most important and powerful economic policymakers in the United States.

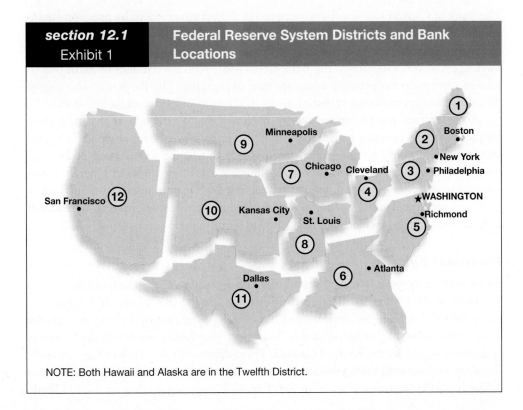

| section 12.1 Exhibit 1 | Federal Reserve System Districts and Bank Locations |
|---|---|

NOTE: Both Hawaii and Alaska are in the Twelfth District.

Created in 1913, the Federal Reserve System is privately owned by the banks that "belong" to it. This private ownership, however, is essentially meaningless, as the Federal Reserve Board of Governors, which controls major policy decisions, is appointed by the president of the United States, not by the shareholders. The owners of the Fed have relatively little control over its operations and receive only small fixed dividends on their modest financial stake in the system. The feature of private ownership but public control is a compromise made to appease commercial banks opposed to direct public (government) regulation.

## WHAT ARE THE MAIN RESPONSIBILITIES OF THE BANK OF CANADA?

According to the Bank of Canada's website, in its role as Canada's central bank, the Bank of Canada has four main areas of responsibility:

- Currency
- Funds management
- Financial system
- Monetary policy

### Currency

The Bank of Canada has monopoly power over issuing legal tender in the form of Bank of Canada banknotes. The Bank of Canada is responsible for note design, for overseeing the printing and distribution of banknotes, and for replacing worn-out currency. Included as part of this currency function is the role the Bank of Canada plays in counterfeit prevention. A considerable amount of Bank resources have been used to research and develop banknotes that are durable, easy to verify, and difficult to counterfeit. Directly related to this objective is the polymer series of banknotes first issued by the Bank of Canada in 2011.

### Funds Management

The Bank of Canada acts as a fiscal agent to the federal government by providing debt-management services, such as policy advice on new debt offerings and the servicing of existing debt. In addition to this, the Bank also manages the government's foreign exchange reserves. Specifically, the Bank assists the federal government in managing its foreign reserves to maintain an adequate level of liquidity. The Bank may also engage directly in foreign exchange transactions in an effort to influence exchange rates.

A second function performed by the Bank of Canada as it acts as the fiscal agent for the federal government has to do with its role in managing the government's foreign exchange reserves held by the Exchange Fund Account of the Department of Finance. Specifically, the Bank of Canada, working alongside the Department of Finance, maintains adequate levels of foreign reserves as well as invests foreign reserves. In addition to these activities, the Bank of Canada is also involved in international financial transactions designed to influence exchange rates, as directed by the federal government.

### Financial System

As a central participant in Canada's national payments system, the Bank of Canada acts as a bank to the various financial institutions that operate in Canada. In Chapter 11, we explained that financial institutions hold a small proportion of their reserves as currency in their vaults. In addition to this "vault cash" they hold a portion of their reserves as demand deposit at the Bank of Canada. These deposits at the Bank of Canada allow financial institution to make payments to each other. For example, let's say you pay your monthly rent by writing a cheque for $800 on your chequing account at the TD Bank.

Your landlord deposits the cheque in her chequing account at the Royal Bank. The Royal Bank will credit your landlord's chequing account for $800. But the Royal Bank will want payment of $800 from the TD Bank. Therefore, as the cheque clears, $800 will be deducted from the TD Bank's reserve account at the Bank of Canada and transferred to the Royal Bank's reserve account at the Bank of Canada. Of course, once the cheque clears, the TD Bank will deduct $800 from your chequing account.

## DEBATE

### SHOULD CANADA, THE UNITED STATES, AND MEXICO SHARE A COMMON CURRENCY?

**For:**

Money is central to a national government's economy, but it's also a medium of exchange. In recent years, some governments have gone beyond just thinking about sharing a currency with their neighbours—the euro is an example of this. As a common currency, the euro provides a number of benefits in trading goods and services between countries, while getting rid of the risks and transaction costs involved with currency exchanges.

Because the North American economy is so entwined, it seems natural for Canada, the United States, and Mexico to move closer to a common currency too. Many of the barriers to trade exist not because of a lack of markets or customers, but because there are major barriers to getting products to market at competitive prices. Transaction costs are significant for companies—not only the straight exchange costs, but also the cost of converting, paying, and hedging funds just to pay for the goods and services.

Having a common currency means that many of those transaction costs disappear and the savings can be reinvested back into firms' productivity and innovation. Basically, useless costs turn into productive costs—with longer-term benefits to the whole economy. By unifying some of the currencies, whole economies benefit and grow more than they would as independents. So a common currency provides for a strong economic foundation that all can benefit from.

It's argued that Canada and the United States are so strikingly similar that the differences in our currencies are minor. While the two nations' people live in different regions, they still maintain their cultural differences. This is true at present in the United States, where the folks in the Midwest are regarded as different from those in New England or California. And it's true in Canada: People living in Quebec have retained their culture even as they share one currency and one federal government with the other provinces and the territories.

The strength of culture is what will endure—it's not based on the independent currencies. So, what a country loses in autonomy of monetary policy when it switches to a common currency, it gains in added trade, wealth, and employment. Surely it's clear that Canada, the United States, and Mexico should adopt a common currency.

**Against:**

Economic freedom is not the same as political freedom, and moving toward a common currency usually ends up with one country dominating the others, both politically and economically. This is evident in the current European Union, where Germany's policies end up holding more weight than the policies of the other nations.

The way those policies are carried out and received by the other nations is not always harmonious. In the EU, how Germany wants to move is how the rest of the union moves. This would be similar in North America, because the United States is the dominant nation and whatever policies it favoured would likely be imposed on the other two countries.

Having different monetary policies can also be an advantage that countries are unwilling to lose. For example, during the lead-up to the Great Recession of 2008–09, Canada and the United States had significantly different monetary policies: While the United States was more liberal in regulating the economy, Canada was more conservative. At the end of the day, it was the conservative nature of our policies that best helped us through the recession—the same can't be said for U.S. citizens.

Keeping independent currencies allows for a nation to have its own monetary policy, which is one of the main reasons why Britain didn't rush to join the EU—it valued its own ability to regulate the economy through currency adjustments and monetary policy.

Trade benefits from freeing up access, and there is no question that the allure of a common currency is attractive to the business community. But there are significant losses to a country, and not all of those losses have to do with its currency. As countries break down barriers, they become culturally more integrated. Money as well as monetary policy allows countries to keep their character and uniqueness. Surely these are strong reasons to avoid a common currency in North America.

**Questions:**

1. What other arguments could you make to justify a common North American currency?
2. What are some of the other reasons countries might argue against a common currency?
3. If approved, should the common currency be one of the existing ones or should a new currency be introduced?

The Bank of Canada also serves as a "lender of last resort." When a deposit-taking financial institution finds itself in financial distress because it is short of reserves and cannot meet the withdrawal demands of its customers, the Bank of Canada may act as a lender of last resort and lend reserves to the bank in order to help maintain stability in the financial system.

Finally, the Bank of Canada acts as a banker to the federal government. The federal government has a demand deposit account at the Bank of Canada and at the chartered banks as well. The Bank of Canada manages the government's bank accounts in these different financial institutions.

## Monetary Policy

**monetary policy**
*the policy decisions that the Bank of Canada makes in managing the money supply and interest rates, consistent with its inflation-control objective*

The Bank of Canada's most important responsibility is **monetary policy**, that is, the policy decisions that the Bank of Canada makes in managing the money supply and interest rates, consistent with its inflation-control objective. Currently, the Bank of Canada inflation-control target range is between 1 and 3 percent, with a policy aim of keeping inflation at a midpoint amount of 2 percent.

### SECTION CHECK

- The Bank of Canada is Canada's central bank. It is owned by the federal government, which has the final responsibility for the Bank of Canada's policies. Despite goal dependence, the governor of the Bank of Canada has considerable independence in formulating the Bank of Canada's monetary policy.
- The Bank has four main responsibilities: currency, funds management, the financial system, and monetary policy. Of the four main responsibilities of a central bank, the most important is its role in monetary policy.

## section 12.2

# Tools of the Bank of Canada

- What are the tools of the Bank of Canada?
- What is the Bank of Canada's approach to monetary policy?

### WHAT ARE THE TOOLS OF THE BANK OF CANADA?

As noted previously, the most important responsibility of the Bank of Canada is monetary policy. The Bank of Canada decides whether to lower interest rates (expand the money supply) or to raise interest rates (contract the money supply), based on how the economy is performing relative to its inflation-control objective. The Bank of Canada has two primary methods that it can use to enact monetary policy: It can alter its target for the overnight interest rate or it can engage in open market operations.

### The Target for the Overnight Interest Rate

**overnight interest rate**
*the interest rate that major financial institutions charge each other for one-day loans*

The Bank of Canada's main tool for executing monetary policy is raising and lowering the target for the **overnight interest rate**, the interest rate that major financial institutions charge each other for one-day loans. Under normal economic circumstances, the Bank of Canada operates a system that has the overnight interest rate fluctuating within a one-half of a percentage point (50 basis points) operating band.

The top of the band is the **bank rate**, the interest rate that the Bank of Canada charges major financial institutions on the loans it extends to them. The bottom of the band is the **bankers' deposit rate**, the interest rate that Bank of Canada pays major financial institutions on surplus funds deposited at the Bank of Canada.

For example, say the Bank of Canada sets a target of 3 percent for the overnight interest rate. That means that major financial institutions can borrow funds from each other at an interest rate of 3 percent. To achieve this, the Bank of Canada establishes an operating band around the target overnight interest rate. The operating band is the target overnight interest rate plus or minus one-quarter of a percentage point. The upper limit of the band (one-quarter of a percentage point above the target overnight interest rate) is the bank rate and the lower limit (one-quarter of a percentage point below the target overnight interest rate) is the bankers' deposit rate. In this case, the bank rate would be 3.25 percent and the banker's deposit rate would be 2.75 percent. We can now see that if one financial institution needed to borrow reserves overnight (because its actual reserves were less than its desired reserves), it would first try to borrow those reserves from a second bank that had some excess reserves. What overnight interest rate might those two banks find it beneficial to agree to?

The actual overnight interest rate will fall somewhere between 2.75 percent and 3.25 percent. The first bank will not borrow reserves from the second bank for more than 3.25 percent, since it can borrow reserves from the Bank of Canada at that interest rate. Likewise, the second bank will not lend reserves to the first bank for less than 2.75 percent, since it can earn that rate of interest by holding its excess reserves at the Bank of Canada. Thus, an overnight interest rate of, say, 3 percent would benefit the chartered bank trying to borrow reserves overnight as well as the chartered bank trying to lend excess reserves overnight. In practice, the actual overnight rate does in fact remain very close to the middle of the operating band established by the bank rate and bankers' deposit rate.

If the Bank of Canada raises the target for the overnight interest rate, it makes it more costly for banks to borrow funds to increase their reserves. The higher the interest rate that banks have to pay on the borrowed funds, the lower the potential profit from any new loans made from borrowed reserves, so fewer new loans will be made and less money created. Conversely, if the Bank of Canada lowers the target for the overnight interest rate, it makes it less costly for banks to borrow funds to increase their reserves. This lower interest rate will raise the potential profit from any new loans made from these borrowed reserves, so more new loans will be made and more money created.

## Open Market Operations

**Open market operations** involve the purchase and sale of Government of Canada securities (bonds and Treasury bills) by the Bank of Canada. When the Bank of Canada purchases Government of Canada bonds from the nonbank public, an investment dealer, for example, the Bank of Canada pays for the bonds with a cheque drawn on itself. The investment dealer receiving the payment will likely deposit the cheque in its chequing account at its chartered bank, thereby increasing the money supply in the form of a demand deposit. More important, the chartered bank will collect payment of this cheque from the Bank of Canada. The Bank of Canada will credit the chartered bank's reserve account at the Bank of Canada. Therefore, the chartered bank, in return for crediting the chequing account of the investment dealer with a new deposit, gets a credit in its reserve account at the Bank of Canada.

For example, suppose the Loans R Us National Bank has no excess reserves and that one of its customers, an investment dealer, sells a bond for $10 000 to the Bank of Canada.

**bank rate**
*the interest rate that the Bank of Canada charges major financial institutions on the loans it extends to them*

**bankers' deposit rate**
*the interest rate that the Bank of Canada pays major financial institutions on surplus funds deposited at the Bank of Canada*

**open market operations**
*purchase and sale of government securities by the Bank of Canada*

The customer deposits the cheque from the Bank of Canada for $10 000 into its account, and the Bank of Canada credits the Loans R Us National Bank with $10 000 in reserves. Suppose the desired reserve ratio is 10 percent. The Loans R Us National Bank, then, needs new reserves of only $1000 ($10 000 × 0.10) to support the $10 000 demand deposit, meaning that it has acquired $9000 in new excess reserves ($10 000 new actual reserves minus $1000 in new desired reserves). Loans R Us National Bank can, and probably will, lend out its excess reserves of $9000, creating $9000 in new deposits in the process. The recipients of the loans, in turn, will likely spend the money, leading to still more new deposits and excess reserves in other banks, as discussed in Chapter 11. This series of transactions is illustrated in Exhibit 1.

In other words, the Bank of Canada's purchase of the bond directly creates $10 000 in money in the form of demand deposits, and indirectly permits up to $90 000 in additional money to be created through the multiple expansion in bank deposits. (The money multiplier is 1/0.10, or 10; 10 × $9000 = $90 000.) Thus, if the desired reserve ratio is 10 percent, a potential total of up to $100 000 in new money is created by the purchase of one $10 000 bond by the Bank of Canada.

---

| *section 12.2* Exhibit 1 | Open Market Operations: Bank of Canada Buys Securities from Investment Dealer |
| --- | --- |

**a. Investment Dealer (nonbank public)**

| Assets | | Liabilities |
| --- | --- | --- |
| Securities | –$10 000 | |
| Demand deposits | +$10 000 | |

**b. Loans R Us National Bank**

| Assets | | Liabilities | |
| --- | --- | --- | --- |
| Reserves | +$10 000 | Demand deposits | +$10 000 |

10 percent desired reserve ratio

**c. Bank of Canada**

| Assets | | Liabilities | |
| --- | --- | --- | --- |
| Securities | +$10 000 | Reserves of Loans R Us Bank | +$10 000 |

**d. Loans R Us National Bank**

| Assets | | Liabilities | |
| --- | --- | --- | --- |
| Reserves | $1000 | Demand deposits | $10 000 |
| Loans | $9000 | | |

When the Bank of Canada buys securities from the nonbank public in the open market, it creates reserves. The nonbank public exchanges its securities for deposits, as seen in Exhibit 1(a). These additional deposits increase bank reserves, as seen in Exhibit 1(b). The additional bank reserves, along with the original purchase of securities, increase both assets and liabilities at the Bank of Canada, as seen in Exhibit 1(c). The increase in bank reserves will likely trigger additional lending and therefore money creation, as seen in Exhibit 1(d).

The process works in reverse when the Bank of Canada sells a bond. The investment dealer purchasing the bond will pay the Bank of Canada by cheque, lowering demand deposits in the banking system. Reserves of the bank where the investment dealer has a bank account will likewise fall. If the bank had zero excess reserves at the beginning of the process, it will now be short of reserves. The bank will likely reduce its volume of loans, which will lead to a further reduction of demand deposits. A multiple contraction of deposits, and money, will begin.

## WHAT IS THE BANK OF CANADA'S APPROACH TO MONETARY POLICY?

The process that the Bank of Canada follows in implementing monetary policy is directly linked to its objective of inflation-rate control. As we identified earlier, the joint Bank of Canada/Government of Canada inflation-control agreement targets a range of inflation between 1 and 3 percent, with a policy aim of keeping inflation at the midpoint amount of 2 percent. The Bank of Canada accomplishes monetary policy by changing the target for the overnight rate, which in turn causes changes to

## Business CONNECTION

### WHEN THE BANK RATE INCREASES, BEWARE!

One of the Bank of Canada's most important responsibilities is monetary policy. Generally speaking, there are two ways in which the central bank can put its monetary policy into effect: (1) by raising or lowering its target for the overnight interest rate via changes to the bank rate, which increases or decreases the money supply, respectively, or (2) by buying or selling bonds, which again has the effect of increasing or decreasing the money supply, respectively.

The Bank of Canada changes the bank rate mainly to adjust the money supply. A change in the money supply may not readily affect a business, but a change in the bank rate will often directly and immediately start having a negative effect on the profitability of most businesses—particularly those that have either outstanding short-term bank loans or funds deposited in short-term bank securities. This occurs because the rate that the Canadian chartered banks charge their business customers is tied to the *prime rate,* an index rate that in turn is tied to the Bank of Canada bank rate.

An increase in a company's bank loan rate is just one of several concerns. When a company experiences an increase in its bank loan rate, the interest expense charges it must pay to the bank will also rise. Without any other changes, increases in loan interest expenses will reduce the company's profits. Faced with the reality of higher interest rates, many consumers and businesses that use credit to finance their purchases will refrain from taking out loans and will accordingly reduce their expenditures. The net effect is that for most businesses, revenue growth will be constrained. Also, when the Bank of Canada causes an increase in loan interest rates, there is usually concern that the economy is overheating and should be restrained. As the Bank of Canada tries to restrain the economy, the Government of Canada may simultaneously be taking fiscal policy steps to cool the economy. If governments put into effect fiscal policies that lead to higher tax rates on profit, business will also find that after-tax profits are reduced.

So when the Bank of Canada causes an increase in interest rates, companies must be aware of three developments:

1. Those with debt will in the first instance see profits eroded due to higher interest expense.
2. Revenue growth may come under pressure.
3. Possible fiscal policies such as higher tax rates may reduce after-tax profits.

These three developments can have a major negative impact on a company's overall profitability. As a result, the typical business with some debt can't afford to be unaware of the actions of the Bank of Canada with respect to immediate and long-term plans for the overnight interest rate target.

1. What are some of the tactics that a business can use to hedge its bets when interest rates increase? Are your suggestions practical in the short term or over the long term?
2. What strategies can a business use when interest rates decrease? Are your suggestions practical in the short term or over the long term?
3. As a business owner, if you had to choose between deflation or hyperinflation, which would be your choice and why?

other commercial interest rates, the exchange rate, and ultimately the overall level of economic activity.

Suppose the Bank of Canada expects the rate of inflation to rise and persist above the 2 percent control target (caused by overall demand in the economy exceeding overall supply in the economy—a positive output gap). To address this issue, the Bank of Canada would typically raise the target for the overnight interest rate, which would raise other commercial interest rates as well as the exchange rate of the Canadian dollar. The higher cost of borrowing will have the effect of lowering consumption and investment, while the higher exchange rate of the Canadian dollar will lower Canadian exports. The ultimate impact of these changes will be a reduction in the overall demand for goods and services in the economy. As overall demand begins to align with overall supply, the rate of inflation will begin to fall back toward the desired 2 percent target rate.

Conversely, if the Bank of Canada expects the rate on inflation to fall and persist below the 2 percent control target, it lowers the target for the overnight interest rate. The resulting lower commercial interest rates and lower exchange rate of the Canadian dollar will have the effect of raising overall demand. As overall demand and overall supply begin to align, the rate of inflation will begin to increase back up to the target 2 percent level.

## SECTION CHECK

- The two major tools of the Bank of Canada are open market operations and changing the target for the overnight interest rate.
- The Bank of Canada will raise the target for the overnight interest rate in response to an expectation of inflation above the 2 percent control target. A higher target for the overnight interest rate will raise other commercial interest rates and the exchange rate for the Canadian dollar, thus lowering overall economic demand. This reduction in overall demand will have the effect of returning the rate of inflation back to its 2 percent target. If the Bank of Canada expects the rate of inflation to fall below its 2 percent control target, it will lower the target for the overnight interest rate. The resulting lower commercial interest rates and exchange rate for the Canadian dollar will lead to greater overall demand in the economy, thus increasing the inflation rate back toward the 2 percent target.

## section 12.3  Money and Inflation

- What is the equation of exchange?
- What is the quantity theory of money and prices?

For many centuries, scholars have known that there is a positive relationship among the money supply, the price level, the growth in the money supply, and the inflation rate. In the 1500s, a huge influx of gold and silver into Europe followed the Spanish conquest in the New World. The influx of precious metals almost tripled the money supply of Europe—too many coins were chasing what goods were available and prices rose steadily.

One of the major reasons that the control of the money supply is so important is that, in the long run, the amount of money in circulation and the overall price level are closely linked. It is virtually impossible for a country to have sustained inflation without a rapid growth in the money supply. The inflation rate tends to be greater in periods of rapid monetary expansion than in periods of slower growth in the money supply. The relationship between inflation and money supply growth in selected countries around the world is illustrated in Exhibit 1.

## WHAT IS THE EQUATION OF EXCHANGE?

The role that money plays in determining equilibrium GDP, the level of prices, and real output of goods and services has attracted the attention of economists for generations. The equation of exchange is a useful relationship that can help us to understand the role of money in the national economy. The equation of exchange (or quantity equation) can be presented as follows:

$$M \times V = P \times Q$$

where $M$ is the money supply, however defined (usually M2 or M2+); $V$ is the velocity of money; $P$ is the average level of prices of final goods and services; and $Q$ is the physical quantity of final goods and services produced in a given period (usually one year).

The expression $P \times Q$ represents the dollar value of all final goods and services sold in a country in a given year. Does that sound familiar? It should, because that is the definition of nominal gross domestic product (GDP). Thus, for our purposes, we may

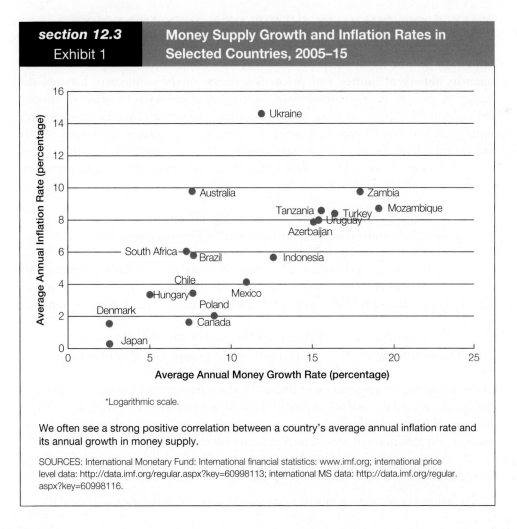

| **section 12.3** Exhibit 1 | **Money Supply Growth and Inflation Rates in Selected Countries, 2005–15** |

*Logarithmic scale.

We often see a strong positive correlation between a country's average annual inflation rate and its annual growth in money supply.

SOURCES: International Monetary Fund: International financial statistics: www.imf.org; international price level data: http://data.imf.org/regular.aspx?key=60998113; international MS data: http://data.imf.org/regular.aspx?key=60998116.

consider the average level of prices ($P$) times the physical quantity of final goods and services in a given time period ($Q$) to be equal to nominal GDP.

The **velocity of money** ($V$), represents the average number of times that a dollar is used in purchasing final goods or services in a one-year period. So if individuals are hoarding their money, velocity will be low; if individuals are writing lots of cheques on their chequing accounts and spending currency as fast as they receive it, *velocity* will tend to be high. Velocity is defined as the nominal or current dollar value of output divided by the money supply, or

$$V = \frac{P \times Q}{M}$$

Suppose we have a simple economy that produces only frozen yogurt. The economy produces 200 litres of frozen yogurt per year. The frozen yogurt sells for $5 a litre and the quantity of money in the economy is $100. Plugging the number into our equation for velocity, we get

$$V = \frac{P \times Q}{M} = \frac{\$5 \times 200}{\$100} = 10$$

That is, the people in the economy spend $1000 per year on frozen yogurt. If there is only $100 of money in the economy, each dollar must change hands on average 10 times per year. Thus, the velocity is 10.

## WHAT IS THE QUANTITY THEORY OF MONEY AND PRICES?

If we make certain assumptions about the variables in the equation of exchange, we can clearly see the relationship between the money supply and the price level. The **quantity theory of money and prices** is a theory of the connection between the money supply and the price level when the velocity of money is constant. If velocity ($V$) and real GDP ($Q$) both remain constant, then a 10 percent increase in the money supply will lead to a 10 percent increase in the price level—that is, the money supply and the price level change in the same proportion. We can extend this equation to link the growth rates of these four variables. Using the *growth version of the quantity equation,* we can transform $M \times V = P = Q$ into

> Growth rate of the money supply + Growth rate of velocity =
> Growth rate of the price level (inflation rate) + Growth rate of real output

This makes it easier to see the effects of the money supply on the inflation rate. Suppose money growth is 5 percent per year, the growth of real output is 3 percent per year, and velocity has not changed at all—its growth rate is 0 percent. What is the inflation rate?

> The growth rate of $M$ (5 percent) + The growth rate of $V$ (0 percent) =
> The growth rate of $P$ (_____ percent) + The growth rate of $Q$ (3 percent)

In this situation, the growth rate of prices ($P$), the inflation rate, is equal to 2 percent. We can also extend the analysis to predict the inflation rate when real GDP and velocity also vary. For example, if velocity grew at 1 percent annually rather than zero as in our example, the inflation rate would be 3 percent rather than 2 percent.

If velocity remains constant, the growth rate of velocity (the percentage change from one year to the next) will be zero. Then we can simplify our equation once more:

> Inflation rate = Growth rate of the money supply − Growth rate of real GDP

**velocity of money (V)**
*the average number of times that a dollar is used in purchasing final goods or services in a one-year period*

**quantity theory of money and prices**
*a theory of the connection between the money supply and the price level when the velocity of money is constant*

If this is the case, there are three possible scenarios:

1. If the money supply grows at a faster rate than real GDP, there will be inflation.
2. If the money supply grows at a slower rate than real GDP, there will be deflation.
3. If the money supply grows at the same rate as real GDP, the price level will be stable.

Economists once expected that they could treat the velocity of money as a given because the determinants of velocity they focused on would change very slowly. We now know that velocity is not constant but often moves in a fairly predictable pattern. Historically, the velocity of money has been quite stable over a long period of time, particularly when using the M2 definition of money. Thus, the connection between money supply and the price level is still fairly predictable, especially during periods of high inflation.

If an increase in the money supply leads to inflation in the long run, why do countries allow the growth rate of their money supply to increase so rapidly? There are several possible reasons. For instance, due to war or political instability, countries' spending may exceed what they can raise through borrowing from the public or by taxation, so they create more money to pay their bills. The more money these countries create, the larger amount of inflation they will experience.

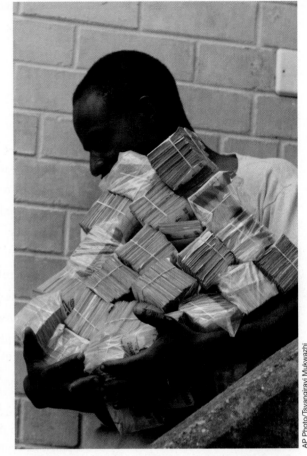

A man carries an armful of cash in Zimbabwe in order to make his daily purchases. During the 2004 to 2009 hyperinflation in Zimbabwe, the *monthly* rate of inflation reached an estimated 79 600 000 000 percent, ultimately leading to an abandonment of the domestic currency.

## Hyperinflation

The relationship between the growth rate of the money supply and the inflation rate is particularly strong when there is very rapid inflation, called *hyperinflation*. One of the most famous cases of hyperinflation was in Germany in the 1920s—inflation rose to roughly 300 percent *per month* for over a year. The German government had incurred large amounts of debt as a result of World War I and could not raise enough money to pay its expenses, so it printed huge amounts of money. The inflation rate became so rapid that store owners would change their prices in the middle of the day, firms had to pay workers several times a week, and many resorted to barter. Brazil and Argentina in the early 1990s and, more recently, Zimbabwe have experienced hyperinflation. The cause of hyperinflation is simply excessive money growth.

## SECTION CHECK

- The equation of exchange is expressed as $M \times V = P \times Q$, where $M$ is the money supply, $V$ is the velocity of money, $P$ is the average level of prices of final goods and services, and $Q$ is the physical quantity of final goods and services produced in a given period.
- The theory that draws a connection between the money supply and the price level when the velocity of money is constant is referred to as the *quantity theory of money and prices*.

# For Your Review

## Section 12.1

1. Which of the following are functions of the Bank of Canada?
    a.  provide loans to developing economies
    b.  lender of last resort
    c.  back the Canadian dollar with gold
    d.  issue currency
    e.  regulate the money supply
    f.  loan reserves to banks
    g.  act as the bank for the Canadian government
    h.  set interest rates on mortgages

2. How is central bank independence related to average inflation rates across countries? How is the Bank of Canada insulated from federal government pressures?

## Section 12.2

3. If the Bank of Canada purchases from the nonbank public $10 million worth of government bonds in the open market when the desired reserve ratio is 5 percent, what is the potential change in the money supply? If the desired reserve ratio is 25 percent? Using T-accounts, show the impact of this transaction on the nonbank public, the banking system, and the Bank of Canada.

4. Answer question 3 again but this time have the Bank of Canada purchase the bonds directly from a bank within the banking system (as opposed to the nonbank public). Using T-accounts, show the impact of this transaction on the banking system and the Bank of Canada.

5. If the Bank of Canada buys a $50 000 bond from an investor, what is the potential change in the money supply if the desired reserve ratio is 20 percent?

6. The following table shows the balance sheet for the Loans R Us National Bank. If the desired reserve ratio decreases from 10 to 5 percent, what happens to the "Reserves" and "Excess Reserves" on the bank's balance sheet? What is the potential change in the money supply?

| Loans R Us National Bank | | | |
|---|---|---|---|
| **Assets** | | **Liabilities** | |
| Reserves | $100 000 | Demand Deposits | $1 000 000 |
| Excess Reserves | 0 | Equity Capital | 50 000 |
| Loans | 700 000 | | |
| Securities | 250 000 | | |

7. Answer question 6 again for the situation in which the bank increases the desired reserve ratio from 10 to 12.5 percent. Where can the bank acquire the additional funds necessary to cover the desired reserves?

8. In which direction would the money supply change if the Bank of Canada

   a. raised the target on the overnight interest rate?

   b. conducted an open market sale of government bonds?

   c. lowered the target on the overnight interest rate?

   d. conducted an open market sale of government bonds and raised the target on the overnight interest rate?

   e. conducted an open market purchase of government bonds and raised the target on the overnight interest rate?

9. How does an open market purchase by the Bank of Canada increase bank reserves? How does it increase the money supply?

10. Why would the Bank of Canada seldom do an open market purchase of government securities at the same time that it raises the target on the overnight interest rate?

## Section 12.3

11. Answer the following questions.

    a. What is the equation of exchange?

    b. In the equation of exchange, if $V$ doubled, what would happen to nominal GDP as a result?

    c. In the equation of exchange, if $V$ doubled and $Q$ remained unchanged, what would happen to the price level as a result?

    d. In the equation of exchange, if $M$ doubled and $V$ remained unchanged, what would happen to nominal GDP as a result?

    e. In the equation of exchange, if $M$ doubled and $V$ fell by half, what would happen to nominal GDP as a result?

12. Suppose that velocity and the money supply remain constant. If real GDP grows at an annual rate of 5 percent, what can you predict will happen to the price level using the equation of exchange? If real GDP falls by 2 percent?

13. If the money supply (e.g., M2) is $50 billion and velocity is 2, what is the product of the price level and real output (nominal GDP)? If the price level is 10, what does real GDP equal?

14. If nominal GDP is $200 billion and the money supply is $50 billion, what must velocity be?

## section

## 13.1

# Money, Interest Rates, and Aggregate Demand

- What determines the money market?
- How does the Bank of Canada affect RGDP in the short run?
- Does the Bank of Canada target the money supply or the interest rate?
- Which interest rate does the Bank of Canada target?
- Does the Bank of Canada influence the real interest rate in the short run?

### WHAT DETERMINES THE MONEY MARKET?

The Bank of Canada's policies with respect to the money supply have a direct impact on short-run real interest rates and accordingly, on the components of aggregate demand. The **money market** is the market in which money demand and money supply determine the equilibrium *nominal* interest rate. When the Bank of Canada acts to change the money supply, it alters the money market equilibrium.

**money market**
*market in which money demand and money supply determine the equilibrium nominal interest rate*

### The Demand for Money

Money has several functions, but why would people hold money instead of other financial assets? That is, what is responsible for the demand for money? Transaction purposes, precautionary reasons, and asset purposes are at least three determinants of the demand for money.

**Transaction Purposes** First, the primary reason that money is demanded is for transaction purposes—to facilitate exchange. The higher one's income, the more transactions a person will make (because consumption is income-related), the greater GDP will be, and the greater the demand for money for transaction purposes will be, other things being equal.

**Precautionary Reasons**  Second, people like to have money on hand for precautionary reasons. If unexpected expenses require an unusual outlay of cash, people like to be prepared. The extent to which people demand cash for precautionary reasons depends partly on an individual's income and partly on the opportunity cost of holding money, which is determined by market rates of interest. The higher market interest rates, the higher the opportunity cost of holding money, and people will hold less of their financial wealth as money.

**Asset Purposes**  Third, money has a trait (liquidity) that makes it a desirable asset. Other things equal, people prefer more-liquid assets to less-liquid assets. That is, they would like to easily convert some of their assets into goods and services. For this reason, most people choose to have some of their portfolio in money form. At higher interest rates on other assets, the amount of money desired for this purpose will be smaller because the opportunity cost of holding money will have risen.

## The Demand for Money and the Nominal Interest Rate

The quantity of money demanded varies inversely with the nominal interest rate. When interest rates are higher, the opportunity cost—in terms of the interest income on alternative assets—of holding monetary assets is higher, and people will want to hold less money. At the same time, the demand for money, particularly for transaction purposes, is highly dependent on income levels, because the transaction volume varies directly with income. And lastly, the demand for money depends on the price level. If the price level increases, buyers will need more money to purchase goods and services. Or if the price level falls, buyers will need less money to purchase goods and services.

The demand curve for money is presented in Exhibit 1. At lower interest rates, the quantity of money demanded is greater, a movement from A to B in Exhibit 1. An increase in income will lead to an increase in the demand for money, depicted by a rightward shift in the money demand curve, a movement from A to C in Exhibit 1.

## The Supply of Money

The supply of money is largely governed by the monetary policies of the central bank. Whether interest rates are 4 percent or 14 percent, banks seeking to maximize profits will increase lending as long as they have reserves above their desired level. Even a 4 percent return on loans provides more profit than maintaining those excess reserves in noninterest-bearing cash. Given this fact, the money supply is effectively almost perfectly inelastic with respect to interest rates over their plausible range. Therefore, in Exhibit 2, we draw the money supply curve as vertical, other things equal, with changes in Bank of Canada policies acting to shift the money supply curve.

**section 13.1**
Exhibit 1

**Money Demand, Interest Rates, and Income**

An increase in the level of income will increase the amount of money that people want to hold for transaction purposes at any given interest rate; therefore it shifts the demand curve for money to the right, from $MD_0$ to $MD_1$. The demand for money curve is downward sloping because at the lower nominal interest rate, the opportunity cost of holding money is lower.

| **section 13.1**<br>Exhibit 2 | **Changes in the Money**<br>**Market Equilibrium** |
|---|---|

Combining the money demand and money supply curves, money market equilibrium occurs at that nominal interest rate where the quantity of money demanded equals the quantity of money supplied, initially at point A and interest rate $i_0$. An increase in income will shift the money demand curve to the right, from $MD_0$ to $MD_1$, raising the interest rate from $i_0$ to $i_1$ and resulting in a new equilibrium at point B. If the economy is presently at point B, an increase in the money supply resulting from expansionary monetary policies (e.g., the Bank of Canada buying bonds or lowering its target for the overnight interest rate) will shift the money supply curve to the right (from $MS_0$ to $MS_1$), lowering the nominal interest rate (from $i_1$ to $i_2$) and shifting the equilibrium to point C.

## Changes in Money Demand and Money Supply and the Nominal Interest Rate

Equilibrium in the money market is found by combining the money demand and money supply curves in Exhibit 2. Money market equilibrium occurs at that *nominal* interest rate, where the quantity of money demanded equals the quantity of money supplied. Initially, the money market is in equilibrium, at point A in Exhibit 2.

For example, rising national income increases the demand for money, shifting the money demand curve to the right from $MD_0$ to $MD_1$, and leading to a new higher equilibrium interest rate. If the economy is now at point B, an increase in the money supply (e.g., the Bank of Canada buys bonds) will shift the money supply curve to the right from $MS_0$ to $MS_1$, lowering the nominal rate of interest from $i_1$ to $i_2$, and shifting the equilibrium to point C.

## HOW DOES THE BANK OF CANADA AFFECT RGDP IN THE SHORT RUN?

### The Bank of Canada Increases the Money Supply

Suppose the economy is headed for a recession and the Bank of Canada wants to pursue an expansionary monetary policy to increase aggregate demand. It will buy bonds on the open market or it will lower its target for the overnight interest rate. When the Bank of Canada uses either of these tools, the money supply increases. The immediate impact of expansionary monetary policy is to decrease the interest rates, as seen in Exhibit 3(a). The lower interest rate, or the fall in the cost of borrowing money, then leads to an increase in aggregate demand for goods and services at the current price level. The lower interest rate will increase home sales, car sales, business investments, and so on. The increase in the money supply will lead to lower interest rates and an increase in aggregate demand, as seen in Exhibit 3(b).

### The Bank of Canada Lowers the Money Supply

Now suppose the Bank of Canada wants to contain an overheated economy—that is, pursue a contractionary monetary policy to reduce aggregate demand. It will sell bonds on the open market or it will raise its target for the overnight interest rate. The use of either of these tools leads to a reduction in the money supply or a leftward shift, as seen in the money market in Exhibit 4(a). The reduction of the money supply leads to an increase in the interest rate in the money market. The higher interest rate, or the rise in the cost of borrowing money, then leads to a reduction in aggregate demand for goods and services, as seen in Exhibit 4(b). That is, the higher interest rate will lead to a decrease in home sales, car sales, business investments, and so on. In sum, lowering of the money supply by the Bank of Canada leads to a higher interest rate and a reduction in aggregate demand, at least in the short run.

**The Bank of Canada Increases the Money Supply**

**a. Money Market**

**b. *AD/AS* Model**

If the Bank of Canada is pursuing an expansionary monetary policy (increasing the money supply), this will lower the interest rates, as seen in Exhibit 3(a). At lower interest rates, households and businesses will invest more and buy more goods and services, shifting the aggregate demand curve to the right, as seen in Exhibit 3(b).

**The Bank of Canada Decreases the Money Supply**

**a. Money Market**

**b. *AD/AS* Model**

If the Bank of Canada pursues a contractionary monetary policy (decreasing the money supply), this will lead to a reduction in the money supply or a leftward shift, as seen in the money market in Exhibit 4(a). The reduction of the money supply leads to an increase in the interest rate in the money market. The higher interest rate, or the rise in the cost of borrowing money, then leads to a reduction in aggregate demand for goods and services, as seen in Exhibit 4(b).

**section 13.1**
Exhibit 5

Bank of Canada Targeting:
Money Supply vs. the
Interest Rate

When the demand curve for money shifts out, the Bank
of Canada must either settle for a higher interest rate, a
greater money supply, or both. The Bank of Canada cannot
completely control the growth in the money supply and the
interest rate. If it attempts to keep the interest rate steady,
it must increase the growth in the money supply. And if it
tries to keep the growth of the money supply in check, the
interest rate will rise.

## DOES THE BANK OF CANADA TARGET THE MONEY SUPPLY OR THE INTEREST RATE?

Some economists believe the Bank of Canada should try
to control the money supply. Other economists believe
the Bank of Canada should try to control the interest
rate. Unfortunately, the Bank of Canada cannot do
both—it must pick one or the other.

The economy is initially at point A in Exhibit 5,
where the interest rate is $i_0$ and the quantity of money
is at $Q_0$. Now suppose the demand for money was to
increase because of an increase in national income, or
an increase in the price level, or overall, people want
to hold more money. As a result, the demand curve for
money would shift to the right from $MD_0$ to $MD_1$. If
the Bank of Canada decides it does not want the money
supply to increase, it can pursue a no-monetary-growth
policy; this will lead to an increase in the interest rate to
$i_1$ at point C in Exhibit 5. The Bank of Canada could
also try to keep the interest rate stable at $i_0$, but it can
do so only by increasing the growth in the money supply
through expansionary monetary policy. Since the Bank
of Canada cannot simultaneously pursue a no-monetary-
growth policy and an expansionary monetary policy,
it must choose a higher interest rate or a greater money
supply or some combination. The Bank of Canada cannot
completely control both the growth in the money supply
and the interest rate. If it attempts to keep the interest rate
steady in the face of increased money demand, it must increase the growth in the money
supply. And if it tries to keep the growth of the money supply in check in the face of
increased money demand, the interest rate will rise.

### The Problem

The problem with targeting the money supply is that the demand for money fluctuates considerably in the short run. Focusing on the growth in the money supply when
the demand for money is changing unpredictably will lead to large fluctuations in
the interest rate. These erratic changes in the interest rate could seriously disrupt the
investment climate.

Keeping interest rates in check would also create problems. For example, when the
economy grows, the demand for money also grows, so the Bank of Canada would have
to increase the money supply to keep interest rates from rising. And if the economy
was in a recession, the Bank of Canada would have to contract the money supply to
keep the interest rate from falling. This would lead to the wrong policy prescription—
expanding the money supply during a boom would eventually lead to inflation and
contracting the money supply during a recession would make the recession even worse.

### WHICH INTEREST RATE DOES THE BANK OF CANADA TARGET?

The Bank of Canada targets the overnight interest rate. Remember, the overnight
interest rate is the interest rate that chartered banks charge each other for one-day
loans. A bank that may be short of reserves might borrow from another bank that has
excess reserves. The Bank of Canada has been targeting the overnight interest rate since

about 1996. Announcements regarding the overnight interest rate—whether it will be increased, decreased, or stay the same—are made by the Bank of Canada on eight prespecified dates during the year.

Monetary policy actions can be conveyed through either the money supply or the interest rate. That is, if the Bank of Canada wants to pursue a contractionary monetary policy, this can be thought of as a reduction in the money supply or a higher interest rate. And, if the Bank of Canada wants to pursue an expansionary monetary policy, this can be thought of as an increase in the money supply or a lower interest rate. So why is the interest rate used? First, as we mentioned earlier, changes in the demand for money can significantly affect money supply targets. Second, many economists believe that the primary effects of monetary policy are felt through the interest rate. Finally, people are more familiar with changes in interest rates than changes in the money supply.

## DOES THE BANK OF CANADA INFLUENCE THE REAL INTEREST RATE IN THE SHORT RUN?

In Chapter 8, we saw how the equilibrium real interest rate was found at the intersection of the investment demand curve and the saving supply curve in the saving and investment market. In this chapter, we have seen how the equilibrium nominal interest rate is found at the intersection of the demand for money and the supply of money in the money market. Both are important, and the saving and investment market and the money market are interconnected.

Most economists believe that in the short run the Bank of Canada can control the nominal interest rate and the real interest rate. Recall that the *real interest rate is equal to the nominal interest rate minus the expected inflation rate*. So a change in the nominal interest rate tends to change the real interest rate by the same amount because the expected inflation rate is slow to change in the short run. That is, if the expected inflation rate does not change, there is a direct relationship between the nominal and real interest rates; a 1 percent reduction in the nominal interest rate will generally lead to a 1 percent reduction in the real interest rate in the short run. However, in the long run, over several years after the inflation rate has adjusted, the equilibrium real interest rate is found by the intersection of the saving supply curve and investment demand curve.

## SECTION CHECK

- The money market is the market where money demand and money supply determine the equilibrium interest rate. Money demand has three possible motives: transaction purposes, precautionary reasons, and asset purposes. The quantity of money demanded varies inversely with interest rates and directly with income. The supply of money is effectively almost perfectly inelastic with respect to interest rates over their plausible range, as controlled by Bank of Canada policies.
- When the Bank of Canada sells bonds to the private sector or raises its target for the overnight interest rate, this leads to a reduction in the money supply, which in turn leads to a higher interest rate and a reduction in aggregate demand, at least in the short run. When the Bank of Canada buys bonds or lowers its target for the overnight interest rate, the money supply increases. The increase in the money supply will lead to lower interest rates and an increase in aggregate demand.
- Since the Bank of Canada cannot completely control both the growth of the money supply and the interest rate, it must choose which target to manage.
- The Bank of Canada signals its intended monetary policy through the overnight interest rate target it sets.
- Since a change in the nominal interest rate tends to change the real interest rate by the same amount in the short run, most economists believe the Bank of Canada can control both the nominal and real interest rates in the short run.

# Expansionary and Contractionary Monetary Policy

● How does expansionary monetary policy work in a recessionary gap?
● How does contractionary monetary policy work in an inflationary gap?
● How does monetary policy work in the open economy?

## HOW DOES EXPANSIONARY MONETARY POLICY WORK IN A RECESSIONARY GAP?

Suppose the initial equilibrium is $E_0$, the point at which $AD_0$ intersects the short-run aggregate supply curve in Exhibit 1(c). At this point, output is equal to $RGDP_0$ and the price level is $PL_0$. If the Bank of Canada engages in expansionary monetary policy to combat a recessionary gap, the increase in the money supply will lower the interest rate, as seen in Exhibit 1(a). The lower interest rate leads to an increase in investment demanded, as seen in Exhibit 1(b). For example, business executives invest in new plant and equipment whereas individuals increase their investment in housing at the lower interest rate. In short, lower interest rates lead to greater investment spending. Since investment spending is one of the components of aggregate demand $[C + I + G + (X - M)]$, when interest rates fall, total expenditures rise. That is, as investment expenditures increase, the aggregate demand curve shifts from $AD_0$ to $AD_1$, as seen in Exhibit 1(c). The increase in aggregate expenditures then triggers the multiplier effect, which shifts aggregate demand even further, from $AD_1$ to $AD_2$. The result is greater RGDP and a higher price level, at $E_2$. In this case, the Bank of Canada has eliminated the recession and RGDP is equal to the potential level of output at $RGDP_{NR}$.

As seen in Exhibit 2, during 2001, the Bank of Canada aggressively lowered its target for the overnight interest rate to stimulate aggregate demand when faced with a slowing economy. Between January 2001 and January 2002, the Bank of Canada cut

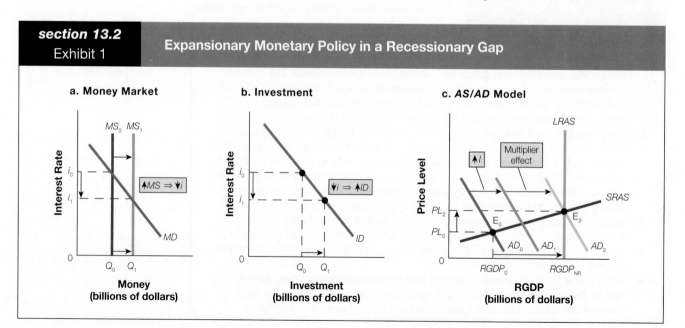

**section 13.2**
Exhibit 1

**Expansionary Monetary Policy in a Recessionary Gap**

**a. Money Market**

**b. Investment**

**c. *AS/AD* Model**

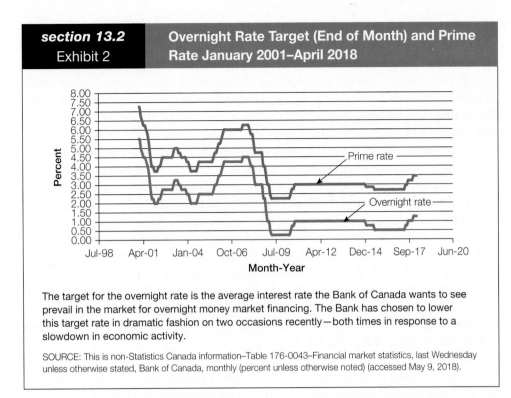

**section 13.2**
Exhibit 2

**Overnight Rate Target (End of Month) and Prime Rate January 2001–April 2018**

The target for the overnight rate is the average interest rate the Bank of Canada wants to see prevail in the market for overnight money market financing. The Bank has chosen to lower this target rate in dramatic fashion on two occasions recently—both times in response to a slowdown in economic activity.

SOURCE: This is non-Statistics Canada information–Table 176-0043–Financial market statistics, last Wednesday unless otherwise stated, Bank of Canada, monthly (percent unless otherwise noted) (accessed May 9, 2018).

its overnight target rate by 3.5 percentage points, from 5.50 percent to 2.00 percent, clearly demonstrating that it was concerned that the economy was dangerously close to falling into a recession.

By 2004, stronger economic performance led to increases of the target overnight rate to near historic levels and by July of 2007, the target overnight rate had reached 4.50 percent, with the prime interest rate reaching 6.25 percent. However, with the onset of the global financial crisis, massive rate reductions occurred, and by April of 2009, the overnight target rate had hit an unprecedented low of just 0.25 percent, with the prime interest rate dropping to 2.25 percent.

As the Canadian economy began to slowly recover, small increases in both the target overnight rate and the prime interest rate did occur. By September of 2010, the Bank of Canada had increased its target overnight rate to 1.0 percent, and the prime interest rate had increased to 3.0 percent. However, the fragility of the global economy and slowing economic growth in Canada resulted in a return to lower overnight rates, as well as a lower prime interest rate. By July of 2015, the overnight target rate had been lowered down to 0.50 percent and the prime interest rate had fallen to 2.70 percent. More recently, strong economic growth in the United States and an improvement in Canadian economic projections have seen both the overnight target rate and the prime interest rise. In April 2018, the overnight target rate sat at 1.25 percent and the prime interest rate was 3.45 percent.

## The 2008 to 2009 Recession

Historically low interest rates in the United States in the early 2000s, along with relaxed lending standards and the introduction of innovative adjustable-rate mortgages, led to a massive U.S. housing bubble between 2000 and 2006. By 2005, however, the Federal Reserve had become concerned with rising housing prices and began to raise short-term interest rates. Higher interest rates and falling housing prices, however, were a recipe for disaster and, consequently, many U.S. homes went into default and foreclosure.

The collapse of the U.S housing market was a huge hit for the U.S. economy and by December of 2007, the United States was officially in a recession. The Canadian economy would soon follow by the fourth quarter of 2008.

When housing prices fell and mortgage delinquencies soared in the United States, securities that had been backed by these subprime mortgages lost most of their value. When subprime borrowers defaulted, the result was a large decline in the capital of many banks and financial institutions in the United States, which in turn tightened credit around the world. Financial markets depend on lenders making funds available to borrowers, but when lenders become reluctant to make loans, it becomes difficult to assess credit risk. This is exactly what happened in 2008, which led central banks from around the world (including the Bank of Canada) to pour hundreds of billions of dollars (and euros, pounds, etc.) into credit markets to ease the pain of the financial crisis.

Several factors contributed to the financial crisis. First, there was a dramatic decline in the U.S. housing market. Second, many financial institutions became insolvent as a result of investments in the U.S. real estate market. Third, the financial crisis led to a decline in confidence and a credit crunch. Because a number of large global financial institutions were in trouble, many borrowers had a difficult time securing a loan, even for promising investment projects. This led to a reduction in overall demand for goods and services in the global economy.

As was first detailed in Chapter 10, the 2008 to 2009 recession resulted in an unprecedented fiscal policy response by the Canadian government. Did the government also introduce monetary policy to combat this severe economic downturn? The answer to this question is a resounding *yes*! Accompanying the Canadian government's fiscal policy response, the Bank of Canada, in unison with central banks around the world, undertook dramatic steps to lower interest rates by increasing liquidity in the financial system.

As seen in Exhibit 2, the Bank of Canada reduced its target overnight interest rate from a high of 4.5 percent in November of 2007 to just 0.25 percent by August 2009. One significant impact of this dramatic reduction in the target overnight interest rate was the decline in the prime interest rate—the benchmark rate that chartered banks use when setting both residential and commercial interest rates (see Exhibit 2). The Bank of Canada maintained this historically low level for the target overnight interest rate for over a year before beginning to slowly move it upward.

## HOW DOES CONTRACTIONARY MONETARY POLICY WORK IN AN INFLATIONARY GAP?

The Bank of Canada may engage in contractionary monetary policy if the economy faces an inflationary gap. Suppose the economy is at initial short-run equilibrium, $E_0$, in Exhibit 3(c). In order to combat inflation, suppose the Bank of Canada engages in either an open market sale of bonds or an increase in its target for the overnight interest rate. This would lead to a decrease in the money supply, shifting the $MS_0$ leftward to $MS_1$, causing the interest rate to rise from $i_0$ to $i_1$, as seen in Exhibit 3(a). The higher interest rate leads to a decrease in the quantity of investment demanded, from $Q_0$ to $Q_1$, as seen in Exhibit 3(b). Investment expenditures fall as firms find it more costly to invest in plant and equipment and households find it more costly to finance new homes. Since the decrease in investment spending causes a reduction in aggregate expenditures, the aggregate demand curve shifts leftward from $AD_0$ to $AD_1$ in Exhibit 3(c). The decrease in aggregate expenditures triggers the multiplier effect that reduces aggregate demand even further, shifting the aggregate demand curve from $AD_1$ to $AD_2$. The result is a lower RGDP and a lower price level, at $E_2$. The economy is now at $RGDP_{NR}$, where RGDP equals the potential level of output.

**section 13.2**
Exhibit 3

**Contractionary Monetary Policy in an Inflationary Gap**

## HOW DOES MONETARY POLICY WORK IN THE OPEN ECONOMY?

For simplicity we have assumed that the global economy does not impact Canadian monetary policy. This is incorrect. Suppose the Bank of Canada decides to pursue an expansionary policy by buying bonds on the open market. As we have seen, if the Bank of Canada buys bonds on the open market or lowers its target for the overnight interest rate, the immediate effect is that the money supply will increase and the interest rate in Canada will fall. As some Canadian investors now seek to invest funds in foreign markets, they will exchange Canadian dollars for foreign currency, leading to a depreciation of the dollar (a decrease in the value of the dollar). The depreciation of the dollar makes Canadian goods and services more attractive to foreign buyers, and foreign goods and services relatively less attractive to Canadian buyers. That is, there is an increase in net exports—fewer imports and more exports—and an increase in RGDP in the short run.

Similarly, if the Bank of Canada reduces the money supply and causes Canadian interest rates to rise, foreign investors will convert their currencies into Canadian dollars to take advantage of the relatively higher interest rates in Canada. This will lead to an appreciation of the dollar (an increase in the value of the dollar). The appreciation of the dollar will make Canadian goods and services relatively more expensive to foreign buyers, and foreign goods and services relatively cheaper to Canadian buyers. This leads to a decrease in net exports and a reduction in RGDP in the short run.

Thus, you can see that in an open economy, like Canada's, monetary policy operates on aggregate demand through two channels: the interest rate and the exchange rate. An expansionary monetary policy causes interest rates to fall and the exchange rate to depreciate, both of which, in turn, cause aggregate demand to increase. Similarly, a contractionary monetary policy causes interest rates to rise and the exchange rate to appreciate, both of which, in turn, cause aggregate demand to decrease.

## DEBATE

### SHOULD BANK OF CANADA APPOINTMENTS REMAIN OUT OF VOTERS' HANDS?

### For:

Both fiscal policy and monetary policy are best served by keeping the two apart. The Bank of Canada is Canada's central bank and its main responsibility is monetary policy. It carries out this responsibility by using a variety of tools, the most important of which is its ability to target the overnight interest rate. The combination of these tools helps the Bank, in conjunction with the government's fiscal policy, to meet the economic goals of the nation.

Fiscal policy uses the political process of the government to adjust spending and taxes. It has been a tradition to separate the political decisions of fiscal policy from those of the more staid decisions of the Bank, ensuring that the conservative nature of monetary policy is not marginalized by self-serving politicians setting unreasonable fiscal policy.

But since 2008, there have been political rumblings that the central bank should be more accountable to the citizens. Politicians, though, are self-serving because their goal is to get re-elected—they will prefer to lower taxes and use spending to entice the electorate to vote for them. While the central bank can use monetary policy to counter questionable policies by politicians, especially around election time, the need for independence is even more critical in times when the economy is under pressure.

Also, should membership in the Bank become an elected position? The best banker will not necessarily get elected, but certainly the most popular one will. The economy is already represented by elected individuals who do their best to ensure that economic goals are met. If the best banker is appointed through a vetting process made up of elected and appointed officials, presumably the qualifications of the banker would be of great importance.

There is also the argument that those who feel well qualified may not want to put their name forward in a political process. Further, in making economic decisions, banks employ knowledgeable professionals versed in economics and monetary policy. On the other hand, with politicians there are no guarantees that they understand the complexities of the issues. Surely it's clear that central bankers need to be free from the political process.

### Against:

Fiscal policy has to mesh with monetary policy, and without some integration, the two policies can work against one another. So individuals who have similar views should have the opportunity to work with each other, and that opportunity is best done through the political process, where in the end the electorate makes the decision about who serves.

At the moment, the Bank of Canada makes decisions that affect all of society, yet answers only to a few politically nonaccountable individuals. Canadians should expect that those who make such public decisions be answerable to the public.

There is no guarantee that the best individual is appointed to the Bank—appointments actually may have less accountability to the public than would be preferred. It can also be argued that these appointments may not include methods for removal if the appointed banker makes grievous errors and actually harms the economy.

On the one hand this independence may be preferred, but when there are errors in appointments, it may be virtually impossible to remove individuals from their positions. The best process for this may be the political process.

### Questions:

1. Without central bank freedom from the political process, what types of situations might develop that would be harmful to the economy?
2. On the other hand, what are some reasons that would justify some political influence in central bank policy?

## SECTION CHECK

- An expansionary monetary policy can combat a recessionary gap. By increasing the money supply, the Bank of Canada can lower interest rates, thereby causing an increase in real GDP and the price level.
- A contractionary monetary policy can close an inflationary gap. By reducing the money supply, the Bank of Canada can raise interest rates, thereby causing a decline in real GDP and the price level.
- In the open economy, interest rate changes can impact exchange rates. Higher interest rates produced by contractionary monetary policy lead to an appreciation of the Canadian dollar. This appreciation can cause net exports to decline and RGDP to be reduced in the short run. Expansionary monetary policy, having the opposite effect, can increase net exports and expand RGDP in the short run.

# Problems in Implementing Monetary and Fiscal Policy

- What problems exist in implementing monetary and fiscal policy?

## WHAT PROBLEMS EXIST IN IMPLEMENTING MONETARY AND FISCAL POLICY?

The lag problem inherent in adopting fiscal policy changes is much less acute for monetary policy, largely because the decisions are not slowed by the same budgetary process. The Bank of Canada, because of its independence, can act very quickly in undertaking open market operations. However, the length and variability of the impact lag before its effects on output and employment are felt are still significant, and the time before the full price level effects are felt is even longer and more variable. The major effects of a change in monetary policy on growth in the overall production of goods and services and on inflation are usually spread over six to eight quarters (18 to 24 months).

### Chartered Banks and Monetary Policy

One limitation of monetary policy is that it ultimately must be carried out through the banking system. The central bank can change the environment in which banks act, but the banks themselves must take the steps necessary to increase or decrease the money supply. Usually, when the Bank of Canada is trying to constrain monetary expansion, there is no difficulty in getting chartered banks to make appropriate responses. If the Bank of Canada sells bonds and/or raises the target for the overnight interest rate, banks will call in loans that are due for collection, and in the process of collecting loans, they lower the money supply.

When the Bank of Canada wants to induce monetary expansion, however, it can provide banks with excess reserves (by buying government bonds), but it cannot force the banks to make loans, thereby creating new money. Ordinarily, of course, banks want to convert their excess reserves to interest-earning income by making loans. But in a deep recession or depression, banks might be hesitant to make enough loans to put all those reserves to work, fearing that they will not be repaid. Their pessimism might lead them to perceive that the risks of making loans to many normally creditworthy borrowers outweigh any potential interest earnings (particularly at the low real interest rates that are characteristic of depressed times).

Some economists have argued that banks maintaining excess reserves rather than loaning them out was, in fact, one of the monetary problems that arose during the Great Recession and the financial crisis of 2008–09.

### Quantitative Easing

As illustrated in Section 13.2, Exhibit 2, the Bank of Canada responded to the global financial crisis by slashing its target for the overnight interest rate to levels never seen before. However, in doing so, the Bank of Canada encountered a previously unforeseen policy dilemma. By lowering the target for the overnight interest rate by as much as it did, the Bank of Canada had effectively run out of room to use this policy tool to bring about more monetary stimulus. The Bank could not lower the target for the overnight rate any further, because it would fall below zero.

With its conventional policy tool constrained by this effective lower boundary, the Bank was forced to consider unconventional monetary policy alternatives. One such alternative was **quantitative easing**, the purchase of private- and public-sector securities by the central bank. Instead of buying just short-term securities (Treasury bills), the Bank of Canada would buy longer-term securities, such as ten-year Government of Canada bonds from various financial intermediaries. These purchases by the Bank would drive down long-term interest rates, which in turn would help to stimulate the demand in housing and other private sector areas. In addition to lower long-term interest rates, these large-scale asset purchases would inject additional central bank reserves into the financial system, which deposit-taking institutions could use to generate additional loans.

While quantitative easing was not used by the Bank of Canada during the global financial crisis, the central banks in the United States, Europe, England, and Japan were forced to rely quite heavily of this program, in addition to other unconventional monetary policies. At least for now, according to the Bank of Canada, quantitative easing remains a monetary policy tool reserved for only the most extraordinary of circumstances.

**quantitative easing**
*the purchase of private- and public-sector securities by the central bank*

### Fiscal and Monetary Coordination Problems

Another possible problem that arises out of existing institutional policymaking arrangements is the coordination of fiscal and monetary policy. The Canadian government makes fiscal policy decisions, whereas monetary policy decision making is in the hands of the Bank of Canada. A macroeconomic problem arises if the federal government's fiscal decision makers differ with the Bank of Canada's monetary decision makers on policy objectives or targets. For example, the Bank of Canada may be more concerned about keeping inflation low, whereas fiscal policymakers may be more concerned about keeping unemployment low.

Some people believe that monetary policy should be more directly controlled by the federal government so that all macroeconomic policy will be determined more directly by the political process. Others, however, argue that it is dangerous to turn over control of the nation's money supply to politicians, rather than allowing decisions to be made by an independent central bank that is more focused on price stability and more insulated from political pressures.

### The Shape of the Aggregate Supply Curve and Policy Implications

Many economists argue that the short-run aggregate supply curve is relatively flat at very low levels of real GDP, when the economy has substantial excess capacity, and very steep when the economy is near maximum capacity, as shown in Exhibits 1 and 2.

Why is the *SRAS* curve in Exhibit 1 flat over the range where there is considerable excess capacity? Firms are operating well below their potential output at $RGDP_{NR}$, so the marginal cost of producing more rises little as output expands. Firms can also hire more labour without increasing the wage rate. With many idle

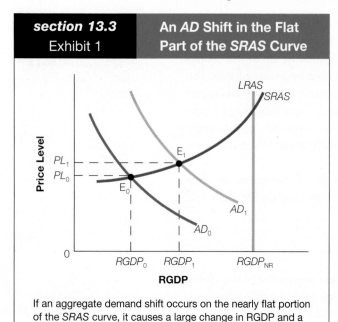

**section 13.3**
Exhibit 1

**An *AD* Shift in the Flat Part of the *SRAS* Curve**

If an aggregate demand shift occurs on the nearly flat portion of the *SRAS* curve, it causes a large change in RGDP and a small change in the price level.

resources, producers are willing to sell additional output at current prices because there are few shortages to push prices upward. In addition, many unemployed workers are willing to work at the going wage rate, which diminishes the power of workers to increase wages. In short, when the economy is operating at levels significantly lower than full-employment output, input prices are sticky (relatively inflexible). Empirical evidence for the period 1983–87, when the Canadian economy was experiencing significant unemployment, appears to confirm that the short-run aggregate supply curve was very flat when the economy was operating with significant excess capacity.

Near the top of the *SRAS* curve, however, the economy is operating close to maximum capacity (and beyond the output level that could be sustained over time). That is, at this level of output, it will be very difficult or impossible for firms to expand output any further—firms may already be running double shifts and paying overtime. At this point, an increase in aggregate demand will be met almost exclusively with a higher price level in the short run.

In short, if the government is using fiscal and/or monetary policy to stimulate aggregate demand, it must carefully assess where it is operating on the *SRAS* curve. As we have seen in Exhibit 1, if the economy is operating on the flat portion of the *SRAS* curve, far from full capacity, an increase in the money supply, a tax cut, or an increase in government spending will result in an increase in output but little change in the price level—a movement from $E_0$ to $E_1$ in Exhibit 1. In this case, the expansionary policy works well: higher RGDP and employment with little change in the price level. However, if the shift in aggregate demand occurs when the economy is operating near maximum capacity, the result will be a substantial increase in the price level with very little change in the output level—a movement from $E_2$ to $E_3$ in Exhibit 2. That is, if the economy is operating on the steep portion of the *SRAS* curve, expansionary policy does not work well.

Furthermore, what if the expansionary policy involves an increase in government spending, with no change in the money supply? If the economy is operating in the steep portion of the *SRAS* curve, the increase in *AD* largely causes the price level to rise. The increase in the price level leads to an increase in the demand for money and higher interest rates, which act to crowd out consumer and business investment. This also undermines the effectiveness of the government policy.

It is also easy to see in Exhibits 1 and 2 that contractionary monetary or fiscal policy (a tax increase, a decrease in government spending, and/or a decrease in the money supply) to combat inflation is more effective in the steep region of the *SRAS* curve than in the flat region. In the steep region, contractionary monetary and/or fiscal policy results in a large fall in the price level and a small change in real GDP; in the flat region of the *SRAS* curve, the contractionary policy would result in a large decrease in output and a small change in the price level.

| **section 13.3** Exhibit 2 | **An *AD* Shift in the Steep Part of the *SRAS* Curve** |
|---|---|

If an aggregate demand shift occurs when the economy is operating at the steep portion of the *SRAS* curve, it causes a very small change in output and a large change in the price level.

**Some economists believe that fine-tuning the economy is like driving a car with an unpredictable steering lag on a winding road.**

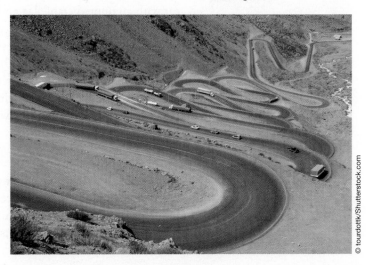

© tourdottk/Shutterstock.com

## Overall Problems with Monetary and Fiscal Policy

Much of macroeconomic policy in this country is driven by the idea that the federal government can counteract economic fluctuations: stimulating the economy (with increased government purchases, tax cuts, transfer payment increases, and easy money) when it is weak, and restraining it when it is overheating. But policymakers must adopt the right policies in the right amounts at the right time for such "stabilization" to do more good than harm. And for this, government policymakers need far more accurate and timely information than experts can give them.

First, economists must know not only which way the economy is heading, but also how rapidly. And the unvarnished truth is that in our incredibly complicated world, no one knows exactly what the economy will do, no matter how sophisticated the econometric models used. It has often been said, and not completely in jest, that the purpose of economic forecasting is to make astrology look respectable.

But let's assume that economists can outperform astrologers at forecasting. Indeed, let's be completely unrealistic and assume that economists can provide completely accurate economic forecasts of what will happen if macroeconomic policies are unchanged. Even then, they could not be certain of how best to promote stable economic growth.

If economists knew, for example, that the economy was going to dip into another recession in six months, they would then need to know exactly how much each possible policy would spur activity in order to keep the economy stable. But such precision is unattainable, given the complex forecasting problems faced. Furthermore, despite assurances to the contrary, economists aren't always sure what effect a policy will have on the economy. Will an increase in government purchases quicken economic growth? It is widely assumed so. But how much? And increasing government purchases increases the budget deficit, which could send a frightening signal to the bond markets. The result can be to drive up interest rates and choke off economic activity. So even when policymakers know which direction to nudge the economy, they can't be sure which policy levers to pull, or how hard to pull them, to fine-tune the economy to stable economic growth.

But let's further assume that policymakers know when the economy will need a boost, and also which policy will provide the right boost. A third crucial consideration is how long it will take for a policy to have an effect on the economy. The trouble is that, even when increased government purchases or expansionary monetary policy does give the economy a boost, no one knows precisely how long it will take to do so. The boost may come very quickly, or many months (or even years) in the future, when it may add inflationary pressures to an economy that is already overheating, rather than helping the economy recover from a recession.

In this way, macroeconomic policymaking is like driving down a twisting road in a car with an unpredictable lag and degree of response in the steering mechanism. If you turn the wheel to the right, the car will eventually veer to the right, but you don't know exactly when or how much. In short, there are severe practical difficulties in trying to fine-tune the economy. Even the best forecasting models and methods are far from perfect. Economists are not exactly sure where the economy is or where or how fast it is going, making it very difficult to prescribe an effective policy. Even if we do know where the economy is headed, we cannot be sure how large a policy's effect will be or when it will take effect.

**Unexpected Global and Technological Events**  The Bank of Canada must take into account the influences of many different factors that can either offset or reinforce monetary policy. This isn't easy because sometimes these developments occur unexpectedly, and because the size and timing of their effects are difficult to estimate.

For example, during the 1997 to 98 currency crisis in East Asia, economic activity in several countries in that region either slowed or declined. This led to a reduction in the aggregate demand for Canadian goods and services. In addition, the foreign exchange value of most of their currencies depreciated, and this made Asian-produced goods less expensive for us to buy and Canadian-produced goods more expensive in Asian countries. Both of these factors would reduce aggregate demand in Canada and lower output and employment. So the Bank of Canada must consider these global events in formulating its monetary policy.

During the late 1990s, the Canadian economy experienced a productivity increase through high-tech and other developments. This "new" economy increased productivity growth, allowing for greater economic growth without creating inflationary pressures. The Bank of Canada was then faced with estimating how fast productivity was increasing and whether those increases were temporary or permanent. Not an easy task.

By 2007, the Canadian economy was facing a new set of global challenges—the Canadian dollar was trading around par with its American counterpart (a reality that had last occurred during the mid-1970s), the U.S. economy was experiencing an economic slowdown, and oil prices had risen to near-record levels. An added complication for the Bank of Canada was the fact that, unlike the 1970s, the high oil prices had not produced strong inflationary expectations for consumers. To successfully navigate this set of challenges, the Bank of Canada would have to carefully consider a wide range of policy options.

By the end of 2007 and into 2008, the Canadian economy had begun to experience the effects of the global economic crisis. The U.S. economy, by this time, was already in the grip of a major recession and global financial markets were experiencing a severe financial crisis. The coordinated response of expansionary fiscal policy and expansionary monetary policy from the Government of Canada and the Bank of Canada is widely believed to have greatly minimized the recessionary effects of the global economic crisis for Canada.

## SECTION CHECK

- Monetary policy faces somewhat different implementation problems than fiscal policy. Both face difficult forecasting and lag problems, but the Bank of Canada can take action much more quickly. However, the effectiveness of monetary policy depends largely on the reaction of the private banking system to its policy changes. In Canada, monetary and fiscal policies are carried out by different decision makers, thus requiring cooperation and coordination for effective policy implementation.

# The Phillips Curve

**section**
**13.4**

- What is the Phillips curve?
- How does the Phillips curve relate to the aggregate supply and demand model?

We usually think of inflation as an evil—higher prices mean lower real incomes for people on fixed incomes, whereas those with the power to raise the prices charged for goods or services they provide may actually benefit. Nevertheless, some economists believe that in the short run, inflation could actually help eliminate unemployment. For example, if output prices rise but money wages do not go up as quickly or as much, real wages fall. At the lower real wage, unemployment is less because the lower wage makes it profitable to hire more, now cheaper, employees than before. The result is real wages that are closer to the full-employment equilibrium wage that clears the labour market. Hence, with increased inflation, one might expect lower unemployment in the short run. In the long run, there is no trade-off between unemployment and inflation. In the long run, output is determined by the *LRAS* curve, and unemployment is at its natural rate.

## WHAT IS THE PHILLIPS CURVE?

An inverse short-run relationship between the rate of unemployment and the changing level of prices has been observed in many periods and places in history. Credit for identifying this relationship generally goes to British economist A. H. Phillips, who in the late 1950s published a paper setting forth what has since been called the *Phillips curve.* Phillips and many others since have suggested that at higher rates of inflation, the rate of unemployment is lower, whereas during periods of relatively stable or falling prices, unemployment is substantial. In summary, the cost of lower unemployment appears to be greater inflation, and the cost of greater price stability appears to be higher unemployment, at least in the short run.

Exhibit 1 shows the actual inflation–unemployment relationship for Canada for the 1960s. The points in this graph represent the combination of the inflation rate and the rate of unemployment for the period 1960 to 1969. The curved line—the Phillips curve—is the smooth line that best fits the data points.

**section 13.4**
Exhibit 1

**The Phillips Curve (Canada), 1960–69**

The Phillips curve illustrates an inverse relationship between the rate of unemployment and the rate of inflation. The slope of the Phillips curve becomes more steep as the unemployment rate drops, indicating that at low unemployment rates, further decreases in unemployment can occur only if the economy can accept much larger increases in inflation rates.

## The Slope of the Phillips Curve

In examining Exhibit 1, it is evident that the slope of the Phillips curve is not the same throughout its length. The curve is steeper at higher rates of inflation and lower levels of unemployment. This relationship suggests that once the economy has relatively low unemployment rates, further reductions in the unemployment rate can occur only if the economy can accept larger increases in the inflation rate. Once the unemployment rate is low, it takes larger and larger doses of inflation to eliminate a given quantity of unemployment. Presumably, at lower unemployment rates, an increased part of the economy is already operating at or near full capacity. Further fiscal or monetary stimulus primarily triggers inflationary pressures in sectors already at capacity, while eliminating decreasing amounts of unemployment in those sectors where some excess capacity and unemployment still exist.

## HOW DOES THE PHILLIPS CURVE RELATE TO THE AGGREGATE SUPPLY AND DEMAND MODEL?

In Exhibit 2, we see the relationship between aggregate supply and demand analysis and the Phillips curve. Suppose the economy moved from a 2 percent annual inflation rate to a 4 percent inflation rate, and the unemployment rate simultaneously fell from 5 percent to 4 percent. In the Phillips curve, we see this change as a move up the curve from point A to point B in Exhibit 2(a). We can see a similar relationship in the *AD/AS* model in Exhibit 2(b). Imagine that an increase in aggregate demand occurs. Consequently, the price level increases from $PL_0$ to $PL_1$ (the inflation rate rises) and output increases from $RGDP_0$ to $RGDP_1$ (the unemployment rate falls). To increase output, firms employ more workers, so employment increases and unemployment falls—the movement from point A to point B in Exhibit 2(b).

| section 13.4 Exhibit 2 | The Phillips Curve and the *AD/AS* Curves |
| --- | --- |

**a. Phillips Curve**

**b. Aggregate Supply and Demand**

As shown in Exhibit 2(b), if the aggregate supply curve is positively sloped, an increase in aggregate demand will cause higher prices and higher output (lower unemployment); a decrease in aggregate demand will cause lower prices and lower output (higher unemployment). This same trade-off is illustrated in the Phillips curve in Exhibit 2(a), in the shift from point A to point B.

# Business *CONNECTION*

## GETTING A JUMP ON INFLATION IN MODERN TIMES

Monetary policies are policies that the government uses to control the nation's money supply. In Canada, this control is delegated to the Bank of Canada. The central bank's policies in regard to the money supply have a direct impact on short-run real interest rates and, accordingly, on at least two of the components of aggregate demand (the total demand for all of the final goods and services in the economy): consumer expenditure and business investment. A business with an eye on revenues will always be concerned about the demand for its goods or services. Many businesses producing big-ticket items—such as housing, cars, and appliances—find revenues extremely sensitive to interest rates, because purchasers often need to finance purchases with borrowed funds.

Sales are also extremely sensitive to the overall demand resulting from the government's fiscal policies. How can business read the road ahead regarding fiscal and monetary policies? The fact is that this area of macroeconomics is fraught with complexity for business. Unfortunately, independent businesses can't change macroeconomic policy—they can only consider the economic climate and hope to make wise decisions. Policymakers have great difficulty predicting the impact that various policy approaches will have on the economy and in forecasting when the expected outcomes will come about. Businesses find it almost impossible to gauge the collective impact that government and central bank policy decisions will have on costs of operations, revenue levels, and profitability. There are some pockets of reliable economic theory, such as the Phillips curve (the inverse relationship between the rate of unemployment and the rate of inflation), but such theories may have to be updated.

The work of economist A. H. Phillips suggested that there is a trade-off between inflation and unemployment in the short term. Basically, the cost of lower unemployment appears to be greater inflation, and the cost of greater price stability appears to be higher unemployment. Firms recognize that, when faced with a recessionary gap, governments use expansionary monetary policy to reduce unemployment—resulting in a gradual increase in the inflation rate. As attempts are made to further reduce unemployment, the rate of inflation is likely to increase more sharply.

But what happens when expansionary policies don't produce the stimulation in the economy as predicted? This might be the case currently, in the wake of unprecedented levels of monetary injections that were made to stimulate economies that had been under strain since the 2008 start of the Great Recession. The anemic growth rates, coupled with higher rates of unemployment (where some economists predict the natural rate of unemployment has increased) have kept inflation rates at, or near, record lows. Consumers might welcome such lows levels on the consumption side (because of lower or more stable prices), but they certainly won't appreciate the impact on real wages (because the low inflation rates will dampen wage growth). Couple that with increases in productivity through automation and mechanization, and there is notable downward pressure on employment rates. If this situation carries on, although firms may enjoy stable input prices, they will find it difficult to raise their own selling prices and will surely find fewer consumers willing or able to purchase. What's more, without modest increases in inflation, firms won't be able to afford the significant costs of R&D that could propel their product lines.

While many have doubted the likelihood of longer-term stagnation, we only have to look at Japan's past generation of anemic growth and see the damage inflicted on that economy. A further investigation is warranted with the current situation in the European Union. Inflation had plummeted to 0.5 percent in May 2014.* Reza Moghadam, director of the European Department at the International Monetary Fund, coined the term "lowflation" to describe the EU's dilemma—a period of stagnation caused by low inflation and high debt that burdens economic growth. Given the choice, firms would much prefer the perils of high inflation over lowflation or deflation, which are harder to control.

1. It is suggested that fiscal policy has a more immediate and dramatic effect on the economy than does monetary policy. Do you think business owners prefer one over the other? Why?

2. One of the most contentious issues facing manufacturing businesses in Canada is the preference of the Bank of Canada to raise the value of the Canadian dollar through its intervention in the market. What is your opinion of this strategy?

3. Do you think that innovation reaches a point where most consumers experience marginal benefit? If this is the case, what do you think the appropriate monetary policy response would be?

---

*Eurostat Press Office. *Eurostat News Release*, June 3, 2014, "Euro area annual inflation down to 0.5%—May 2014."

## SECTION CHECK

- The inverse relationship between the rate of unemployment and the rate of inflation is called the *Phillips curve.*
- The Phillips curve relationship can also be seen indirectly from the *AD/AS* model.

# For Your Review

## *Section 13.1*

1. Why would both the transaction motive and the precautionary motive for holding money tend to vary directly with the price level? Why would the quantity of money people want to hold for both motives tend to vary inversely with interest rates?

2. How does a higher price level affect the money market? How does it affect aggregate demand?

3. If the earnings available on other financial assets rose, would you want to hold more or less money? Why?

4. What is the motive for holding money in each of the following cases (precautionary, transaction, or asset)?

    a. Concerned about the fluctuations of the stock market, you sell stock and keep cash in your brokerage account.

    b. You keep ten $20 bills in your earthquake-preparedness kit.

    c. You go to Vancouver with a large sum of money in order to complete your holiday shopping.

    d. You keep $20 in your glove compartment just in case you run out of gas.

5. Using the following diagrams, respond to the following instructions.

    a. Show the effects in each of the indicated markets of an open market purchase of government bonds by the Bank of Canada.

    b. Show the effects in each of the indicated markets of an open market sale of government bonds by the Bank of Canada.

## Section 13.2

6. During the Great Depression in Canada in 1933, the price level fell, real GDP fell, and unemployment reached almost 20 percent. Investment fell and the money supply fell. Show the effect of these changes from a vibrant 1929 economy to a battered 1933 economy using the *AD/AS* model? What would have been the appropriate monetary policy response in 1933?

7. Using the following diagram, respond to the following instructions.

a. On the diagram, illustrate the short-run effects of an increase in aggregate demand caused by expanding the money supply.

b. On the diagram, illustrate the long-run effects of an increase in aggregate demand caused by expanding the money supply.

8. Predict the impact of a decrease in the money supply on the following variables in the short run and in the long run.

a. the inflation rate

b. the unemployment rate

c. real output

9. How will an expansionary monetary policy affect RGDP and the price level at less than full employment?

10. How will a contractionary monetary policy affect RGDP and the price level at a point beyond full employment?

## Section 13.3

11. Why does the effect of a given increase in aggregate demand have a larger effect on real output in the short run, the more excess capacity exists in the economy?

12. How does the slope of the short-run aggregate supply curve depend on the degree of excess capacity in the economy?

13. If fiscal policy was expansionary, but the Bank of Canada wanted to counteract the fiscal policy effect on aggregate demand, what could it do?

14. Why is the lag time for adopting policy changes shorter for monetary policy than for fiscal policy?

15. Why would a banking system that wanted to keep some excess reserves rather than lending out all of them hinder the Bank of Canada's ability to increase the money supply?

## Section 13.4

16. Suppose the following data represent points along a short-run Phillips curve. Are the data consistent with what you would expect? Why or why not?

|  | Inflation Rate (%) | Unemployment Rate (%) |
|---|---|---|
| A | 0 | 5.0 |
| B | 1 | 4.5 |
| C | 2 | 3.75 |
| D | 3 | 2.75 |
| E | 4 | 1.5 |

17. Why does a movement up and to the left along a Phillips curve correspond to a movement up and to the right along a short-run aggregate supply curve?

18. For a given upward-sloping, short-run aggregate supply curve, how does an increase in aggregate demand correspond to a movement up and to the left along a Phillips curve?

19. What is the argument for why the Phillips curve is relatively steeper at lower rates of unemployment and higher rates of inflation?

# International Trade

## section 14.1 Canada's Merchandise Trade

- Who are Canada's trading partners?
- What does Canada import and export?

### WHO ARE CANADA'S TRADING PARTNERS?

In its early history, Canadian international trade was largely directed toward Europe and to Great Britain, in particular. Now Canada trades with a vast number of countries. Exhibit 1 shows the country's most important trading partners. The United States is Canada's most important trading partner, accounting for an enormous 75 percent of our exports of goods and 65 percent of our imports of goods. Trade with countries of the European Union (EU) and China is also particularly important.

The extent to which the overall health of the Canadian economy is dependent on both exports and imports cannot be understated. However, as Exhibit 2 illustrates, Canada is not alone in its significant involvement in global trade. Several economies (most notably the United States, the European Union, China, Germany, and the United Kingdom) trade on a magnitude that is several times greater than that of the Canadian economy.

In terms of the extent to which the Canadian economy contributes to global trade, Canada is ranked tenth in terms of global imports and just outside the top ten economies in terms of global exports. In 2016, the Canadian economy accounted for 2.4 percent of global exports and 2.6 percent of global imports.

### WHAT DOES CANADA IMPORT AND EXPORT?

Throughout its history, Canada has been a large exporter of natural resource-based products to the rest of the world. As Exhibit 3 shows, Canada's exports of natural resource-based products (including farm, fishing, and intermediate food products; energy products; mineral products; basic and industrial chemical, plastic, and rubber

| section 14.1 Exhibit 1 | Major Canadian Trading Partners |
| --- | --- |

**Top Trading Partners—Exports of Goods in 2017**

| Rank | Country | % of Total |
| --- | --- | --- |
| 1 | United States | 74.7 |
| 2 | European Union | 7.9 |
| 3 | China | 4.5 |
| 4 | Other countries | 12.9 |

**Top Trading Partners—Imports of Goods in 2017**

| Rank | Country | % of Total |
| --- | --- | --- |
| 1 | United States | 64.6 |
| 2 | European Union | 9.9 |
| 3 | China | 7.4 |
| 4 | Other countries | 18.1 |

SOURCE: Based on Statistics Canada, Table 228-0069–Merchandise imports, exports, and trade balance, customs and balance of payments basis for all countries, by seasonal adjustment and principal trading. Reproduced and distributed on an "as is" basis with the permission of Statistics Canada.

| section 14.1 Exhibit 2 | Amounts of Merchandise Exports and Imports: Selected Developed Countries, 2016 |
| --- | --- |

**Exports**

| Rank | Country | Amount (current U.S. $billions) | % of World Exports |
| --- | --- | --- | --- |
| 1 | European Union* | $5379.3 | 33.5% |
| 2 | China | 2097.6 | 13.1 |
| 3 | United States | 1451.0 | 9.0 |
| 4 | Germany | 1337.9 | 8.3 |
| 5 | Japan | 644.9 | 4.0 |
| 6 | Netherlands | 571.4 | 3.6 |
| 7 | Hong Kong | 516.7 | 3.2 |
| 8 | France | 501.2 | 3.1 |
| 9 | South Korea | 495.4 | 3.1 |
| 10 | Italy | 461.7 | 2.9 |
| 11 | United Kingdom | 409.8 | 2.5 |
| 12 | Belgium | 398.0 | 2.5 |
| **13** | **Canada** | **$390.3** | **2.4%** |

**Imports**

| Rank | Country | Amount (current U.S. $billions) | % of World Imports |
| --- | --- | --- | --- |
| 1 | European Union | $5256.3 | 32.4% |
| 2 | United States | 2250.2 | 13.9 |
| 3 | China | 1587.9 | 9.8 |
| 4 | Germany | 1055.5 | 6.5 |
| 5 | United Kingdom | 636.4 | 3.9 |
| 6 | Japan | 607.6 | 3.7 |
| 7 | France | 573.0 | 3.5 |
| 8 | Hong Kong | 547.3 | 3.4 |
| 9 | Netherlands | 505.1 | 3.1 |
| **10** | **Canada** | **$416.6** | **2.6%** |

*The political and economic association comprising 28 central European countries.

SOURCE: World development indicators: World Bank, http://www.worldbank.org/Data Bank; export data: Author notes, World Bank, https://data.worldbank.org/indicator/TX.VAL.MRCH.CD.WT?view=chart; import data: World Bank, https://data.worldbank.org/indicator/TM.VAL.MRCH.CD.WT?view=chart.

products; and forestry products) total nearly $290 billion, or over 50 percent of our exports of goods. However, Canada's exports of industrial machinery, electrical equipment, motor vehicles, aircraft and other transportation equipment, and consumer goods total nearly $250 billion, or about 45 percent of our exports of goods.

On the import side, Canada's imports are much more concentrated on finished goods. Imports of electronic and electrical equipment, motor vehicles, and consumer goods total $66 billion, $112 billion, and $124 billion, respectively, and account for more than half of all imports of goods.

Canada's Exports and Imports by Category of Good, 2017

| | Exports ($billions) | % of Total | Imports ($billions) | % of Total | Trade Balance ($billions) |
|---|---|---|---|---|---|
| Farm, fishing, and intermediate food products | $33.2 | 6.0% | $17.1 | 3.0% | $16.1 |
| Energy products | 94.8 | 17.3 | 31.9 | 5.6 | 62.9 |
| Metal ores and nonmetallic minerals | 18.3 | 3.3 | 12.8 | 2.2 | 5.5 |
| Metal and nonmetallic mineral products | 63.7 | 11.6 | 44.0 | 7.7 | 19.7 |
| Basic and industrial chemical, plastic, and rubber products | 34.9 | 6.3 | 47.6 | 8.3 | −12.7 |
| Forestry products and building and packaging materials | 42.8 | 7.8 | 24.8 | 4.3 | 18.0 |
| Industrial machinery, equipment, and parts | 34.6 | 6.3 | 54.2 | 9.5 | −19.6 |
| Electronic and electrical equipment and parts | 27.5 | 5.0 | 66.0 | 11.5 | −38.5 |
| Motor vehicles and parts | 92.8 | 16.9 | 111.7 | 19.5 | −18.9 |
| Aircraft and other transportation equipment and parts | 22.4 | 4.1 | 20.9 | 3.6 | 1.5 |
| Consumer goods | 69.9 | 12.7 | 123.5 | 21.5 | −53.6 |
| Other transactions and adjustments | $14.9 | 2.7% | $18.9 | 3.3% | −$4.0 |

SOURCE: Statistics Canada, Table 380-0064–Gross domestic product, expenditure-based, annual (dollars unless otherwise noted). Reproduced and distributed on an "as is" basis with the permission of Statistics Canada.

When we compare the trade balance (exports of goods minus imports of goods) for the major categories of goods, we can see that the largest trade surpluses exist for energy products ($62.9 billion) and metal and nonmetallic mineral products ($19.7 billion). By far, the largest trade deficit is in the consumer goods category ($53.6 billion).

## Business *CONNECTION*

### WHAT A DIFFERENCE A FEW YEARS MAKE IN BUSINESS AND POLITICS

It was just a few years back in this very chapter's Business Connection feature that we were discussing what businesses could do to expand their reach into new and distant markets. While business owners and managers seek opportunities to expand their sales due to declining demand in home markets, the arrival of a new populism in political circles will make international trade more difficult, and likely much more expensive. A few years ago, nations were looking to expand their free trade agreements. However, more recently, the United States leads a number of nations in pulling out of these agreements and forcing inequitable agreements onto trading partners that want to access the U.S. domestic markets.

Will this recent trend toward protectionist policies be short-lived, or is this anti-trade sentiment an indicator of a longer term reality? Who knows for sure? The only thing that is for sure is that owners and managers need to deal with what they know now and add to that knowledge to solidify their viability internationally.

For example, if a company is thinking of entering international markets, it needs to consider the business climate of the host country. Many experienced business-people have encountered cultural, legal, and economic roadblocks as they tried to penetrate foreign markets. Couple that with the imposition of import tariffs or quotas on the home front, and international trade can become a virtual minefield of uncertainties. However, managers can help themselves by focusing on key questions before committing to international trade. For instance,

1. First and foremost, is there a demand for the firm's product or service in the host country's target market? Until a business is satisfied that there is foreign demand or that it can cultivate such demand, it should avoid venturing into a foreign market.

2. Do the current political policies allow for competition once various tariffs or quotas are taken into account? Managers need to keep in mind that just because a current climate indicates "no," it does not mean "not ever." Governments and their administrations ebb and flow, and a prudent manager recognizes opportunities where others don't.

3. Can the firm customize its products to suit the demands of the foreign customers while achieving attractive profit margins?

4. Is gross domestic product in the host country growing? What is the withholding tax rate?

5. Will the firm be able to hire people with the necessary skills and knowledge to conduct business in the host country?

6. Can the firm protect its intellectual property (IP) rights in the foreign country? These IP rights are quickly becoming the foundational assets for most firms, and despite the lure of access to larger markets, revenues (and, therefore, any profit) might be put in danger by the loss of the company's competitive advantage should control of IP be lost. The protection of IP is fast becoming one of the key hurdles governments have to overcome to protect their domestic firms.

If the answers to the above questions are favourable, an attempt to enter a foreign market might be operationally feasible.

The next step is to evaluate the likelihood of earning profits. In this area, the firm needs to assess the political and the financial risks. The traditional factors in evaluating broad political risks include the attitude of local consumers toward purchasing foreign-produced or foreign-branded goods, the host government's position toward multinational corporations, wars or threat of wars, and bureaucratic problems and corruption. In considering the broad financial risk involved in conducting business, the host country's growth in gross domestic product, prevailing interest rates, rates of unemployment, and rate of inflation (or deflation) need to be taken into account.

Prudent business leaders recognize that sound business decisions can be easily quashed by sometimes illogical or irrational political decisions. Larger companies are probably better positioned from a resource-based perspective to assess the levels of risk involved. This should not discourage small- and medium-sized enterprises (SMEs)—which may be much more innovative and nimble—from considering international trade. Remember, there is a positive correlation between the level of risk one is willing to take and the level of return available for those who can take advantage of or successfully navigate that risk.

1. Do you think the current economic climate, in which some countries are attempting to protect their domestic markets at all costs, is preferable to the expansion of free trade pacts? Or do you think that free trade among all nations will lead to higher levels of prosperity? Should individual nations put their domestic priorities ahead of international priorities?

2. Should countries that have excess resources expect to be able to keep those resources to themselves and not trade them? How do your thoughts on that square with the fact that Canada has some of the world's largest supplies of fresh water, while others (such as the United States and Mexico) are finding it increasingly difficult to maintain and manage their supplies? Should nations be forced to trade in necessities to keep other nations viable?

3. One of Canada's current impediments in getting a free trade agreement with the European Union is the government's quotas that protect some domestic industries (dairy, poultry, etc.). While the businesses that are directly benefiting from the quotas would be in full support, how do you think other firms feel about the quotas? What would their rationale be for either supporting or not supporting these types of quotas?

## SECTION CHECK

- Our most important trading partner, the United States, accounts for 75 percent of our exports and 65 percent of our imports. Trade with China and the countries of the European Union is also particularly important to Canada.
- Exports of natural resource-based products make up over one-half of our export of goods. Our imports are concentrated in finished goods, like electronic and electrical equipment, motor vehicles, and consumer goods.

# International Trade Agreements

- What has been the impact of international trade on Canada?
- What international trade agreements is Canada involved in?

## WHAT HAS BEEN THE IMPACT OF INTERNATIONAL TRADE ON CANADA?

In a typical year, about 15 percent of the world's output is traded in international markets. Of course, the importance of the international sector varies enormously from country to country. Some nations are almost closed economies (no interaction with other economies), with foreign trade equalling only a very small portion (perhaps 5 percent) of total output. The impact of international trade on the Canadian economy is illustrated in Exhibit 1, which shows the current dollar value of Canadian exports and imports of goods and services as a percentage of GDP.

As Exhibit 1 illustrates, the importance of international trade has grown over time for Canada. In the 1960s, imports plus exports accounted for around 40 percent of annual national income. This figure increased to more than 80 percent by 2000. Since then, however, the share of GDP represented by international trade has steadily declined. Currently, international trade represents less than 65 percent of annual national income. In the United States, by contrast, the 2017 figure for exports was only 12 percent of GDP while the figure for imports was just 15 percent of GDP. These figures together indicate that international trade represented just 27 percent of annual national income in the United States.

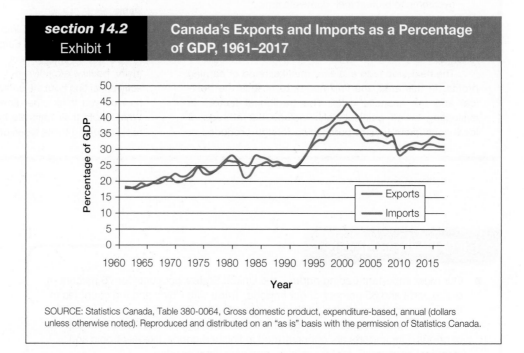

| section 14.2 Exhibit 1 | Canada's Exports and Imports as a Percentage of GDP, 1961–2017 |
|---|---|

SOURCE: Statistics Canada, Table 380-0064, Gross domestic product, expenditure-based, annual (dollars unless otherwise noted). Reproduced and distributed on an "as is" basis with the permission of Statistics Canada.

## WHAT INTERNATIONAL TRADE AGREEMENTS IS CANADA INVOLVED IN?

International trade agreements have been a positive force in expanding global trade, thereby contributing to economic growth and prosperity in countries covered by such agreements. Government trade policies have contributed to the remarkable rise in international trade for Canada. Listed below are the major trade agreements to which Canada is a participant.

## The General Agreement on Tariffs and Trade

Canada and 22 other nations in 1947 signed the General Agreement on Tariffs and Trade (GATT). The objective of the GATT was to reduce barriers to international trade, such as tariffs (taxes on imported goods) and quotas (government-imposed restrictions on the quantity of imports allowed). The GATT was based on a few key principles. First, each member nation was to apply any tariffs equally to all countries—that is, in a nondiscriminatory manner. Second, reductions in tariffs were to be the result of multilateral negotiations. And third, quotas were to be eliminated and replaced by tariffs. (We will examine the economic impact of tariffs and quotas later in this chapter.)

Eight rounds of multilateral negotiations took place under the GATT, with the last round of negotiations, called the Uruguay Round, taking effect in 1995. That agreement eliminated or reduced trade barriers on a wide range of goods and services. It also gave the world's poorer countries greater access to markets for textiles and garments in developed (richer) nations. On the agricultural side, export subsidies were to be reduced and import quotas on agricultural products were to be replaced by tariffs. Canadian egg and dairy farmers had their trade protection from quotas replaced by high tariffs. Although this has protected Canadian farmers in the short run, as these tariffs are reduced over time, we would expect a higher level of Canadian imports of these products.

## The World Trade Organization

In 1995, the GATT was replaced by the World Trade Organization (WTO), another multilateral trade organization. The WTO has over 140 nations as members, who negotiate in areas such as liberalizing trade in services, protecting intellectual property rights, and giving fair treatment to foreign investment. Member countries have their international trade disputes resolved by a WTO arbitration board. When the board makes its ruling, the losing country must comply with the ruling. If it does not comply, the winning country can impose trade sanctions on the losing country.

The Doha Development Round, which began in November 2001, is the current negotiation round for the WTO members. The aim of this latest round is "to achieve major reform to the international trade system through the introduction of lower trade barriers and revised trade rules." Unfortunately, at a WTO meeting in mid-December 2015, trade ministers failed to agree that negotiations should keep going, effectively paralyzing the negotiations and killing the round. The most significant differences are between developed nations led by the European Union and the United States and the major developing nations led primarily by China and India. Issues of access to domestic markets for manufactured goods and agricultural subsidies are proving the most difficult for WTO members to resolve.

Despite positive words from outgoing Director-General Pascal Lamy describing the Doha Round as having "strengthened the WTO as a global trade body, as a major pillar of global economic governance," many see the WTO as an organization in crisis. Since September 2013, the director-general has been Roberto Azevêdo of Brazil.

## North American Free Trade Agreement

Canada's first major bilateral trade agreement was the Canada–U.S. Free Trade Agreement (FTA), which came into effect in 1989. It called for the reduction or elimination of tariffs and other barriers to trade, free trade in energy products, freer trade in services, and a reduction in subsidies. As well, it set up a dispute-settlement mechanism to resolve trade disputes between the two countries. This free trade agreement, in particular, has had a significant impact on the volume of exports and imports for Canada. From 1989 to 2000, Canadian exports and imports increased sharply, as shown in Exhibit 1, with virtually all of this increase the result of increased trade with the United States.

In 1994, the Canada–U.S. FTA was replaced by the North American Free Trade Agreement (NAFTA), creating a trading bloc for Canada, the United States, and Mexico. NAFTA's objectives have been to eliminate trade barriers among the three countries, promote fair competition, increase investment opportunities, protect intellectual property rights, and resolve trade disputes.

Since 1994, as expected, Canada's exports and imports with the United States and Mexico have increased substantially. There have been concerns, however, about the impact of free trade with Mexico on Canadian industries and workers. Mexico's lower labour and environmental standards, as well as fears that Canadian businesses would relocate to Mexico to take advantage of the lower wages there, are often discussed. Economists, however, have tried to emphasize the benefits to Canada of freer trade that result from increased specialization and exchange (a topic we look at in the next section). There certainly have been labour market adjustments in Canada since NAFTA, as some Canadian industries have become smaller, resulting in reduced employment in those sectors. At the same time, however, the United States and Mexico represent a combined market of more than 400 million people, providing many Canadian businesses with the opportunity to expand their sales and create additional jobs in Canada.

## Other Trade Agreements

In addition to NAFTA, Canada has entered into the following bilateral agreements: Canada–Israel FTA, 1997; Canada–Chile FTA, 1997; Canada–Costa Rica FTA, 2002; Canada–European FTA, 2009; Canada–Peru FTA, 2009; Canada–Colombia FTA, 2011; Canada–Jordan FTA, 2012; Canada–Panama FTA, 2013; Canada–Honduras FTA, 2014; Canada–Korea FTA, 2015; Canada–Ukraine FTA, 2017; and the Canada–European Union Comprehensive Economic and Trade Agreement (CETA), 2017.

Negotiations involving Canada and the resurrected Trans-Pacific Partnership, now officially known as the Comprehensive and Progressive Agreement for Trans-Pacific Partnership (CPTPP), have been concluded. This trade agreement came into force for Canada on December 30, 2018.

The CPTPP specifically represents a free trade agreement of particular importance to Canada. The partnership would create an 11-nation free trade zone around the

Pacific; the economies involved account for nearly 500 million people and a combined GDP of $13.5 trillion. This "mega-deal," one of the world's largest trade agreements, will undoubtedly have a dramatic impact not only on international trade for Canada but likely also on the Canadian economy as a whole.

## DEBATE

### SHOULD CANADA CUT BACK ON TRADE WITH CHINA?

**For:**

China has become the manufacturing locale for the world, and a vast amount of consumer goods that Canadians buy come from there. The goods are of good quality and provide Canadians with relatively lower costs than if they were manufactured in North America, but because they aren't made in North America, the jobs that were once involved in making those products have left for China and elsewhere. The paradox is that the more jobs we lose, the more those jobless individuals rely on the lower-cost goods.

By 2012, annual Canada–China trade totalled $70 billion, of which $50 billion was Canadian imports—which left only $20 billion worth of goods going to China. Of that $20 billion, over 90 percent was from basic resources (ore, wood/wood pulp, grains/seeds, and petroleum energy products), which account for very little employment for the dollar amount traded. On the other hand, of the $50 billion imported, those goods were primarily manufactured goods with just electronics and machinery valued at over $23 billion. There were virtually no goods entering Canada that were not "value-added" products, so virtually all of the $50 billion meant jobs going to China, and very few jobs in return.

Canada can't sustain trade deficits at this level in the medium and long term—trade has to account for jobs, not just revenue for corporations. Corporations and owners of capital argue that trade is good for Canada—that a nation with 1.3 billion people offers great opportunities for Canadian goods. But some questions are: Do Canadian companies actually get access to those markets? Do they do so on a level playing field, or do they have to pay for access through tariffs and quotas? Who are the companies that get access—are they small to medium-sized companies, or is it multinationals who themselves are not owned by Canadians and take profits out of Canada?

There is some concern too that the tremendous trade imbalance between Canada and China allows the Chinese to take their Canadian dollars and purchase valuable land and resources within Canada.

The lure of short-term benefits of lower-cost products will be an immense cost to future Canadian generations. Surely it's clear that Canada should cut back on trade with China.

**Against:**

Canada is part of the global economy, and being internally focused would eventually cost Canada jobs. The Canadian population is just 2.5 percent of China's. If Canadians hope to increase their wealth, they will have to have access to a market much larger than their own.

It's not just the size of the market that's appealing to Canadian companies, but who the market is made up of. The per capita income in China is only $7000 a year, and as the economy in China grows, so will the wealth of the citizens who will then be able to buy more consumer goods. It's this emerging market that is so attractive to North American companies.

Others may argue that it's vital for Canada to continue to trade with China because our own markets are becoming saturated, and that firms that can't find new markets to make up for the loss of sales from domestic markets are doomed to fail. If Canada chooses not to trade with China, what other alternative do these producers have?

Another argument for continuing trade with China is rather perverse: It is that China has so much foreign credit that any decision by North American governments to regulate or reduce trade with China may have a major impact on political relations with China. Given the economic power of China, no country would feel confident in risking regulations to find out what those consequences would actually be. The impact on the North American economy could be big enough to cause a significant recession.

**Questions:**

1. What will the costs be if Canada continues on its present path?
2. Are there other key arguments to support the statement that Canada should cut back on trade with China?
3. What are other strong arguments for not cutting back on trade with China?
4. Arguing to cease trading may be unreasonable, so how could Canada use tariffs or quotas to even the trade balance between the countries?

## section 14.3

# Comparative Advantage and Gains from Trade

- Why do economies trade?
- What is the principle of comparative advantage?

### WHY DO ECONOMIES TRADE?

Using simple logic, we conclude that the very existence of trade suggests that trade is economically beneficial. This is true if one assumes that people are utility maximizers, are rational and intelligent, and engage in trade on a voluntary basis. Because almost all trade is voluntary, it would seem that trade occurs because the participants feel that they are better off because of the trade. Both participants of an exchange of goods and services anticipate an improvement in their economic welfare. Sometimes, of course, anticipations are not realized (because the world is uncertain), but the motive behind trade remains an expectation of some enhancement in utility or satisfaction by both parties.

Granted, "trade must be good because people do it" is a rather simplistic explanation. The classical economist David Ricardo is usually given most of the credit for developing the economic theory that more precisely explains how trade can be mutually beneficial to both parties, raising output and income levels in the entire trading area.

### WHAT IS THE PRINCIPLE OF COMPARATIVE ADVANTAGE?

David Ricardo's theory of international trade centres on the concept of comparative advantage.* A person, a region, or a country can gain by specializing in the production of the good in which they have a comparative advantage. A comparative advantage occurs when a person or a country can produce a good or service at a lower opportunity cost than others can. In other words, a country or a region should specialize in producing and selling those items that it can produce at a lower opportunity cost than other regions or countries.

---

*See *Famous Economists* at http://www.famouseconomists.net/david-ricardo.

## Absolute Advantage vs. Comparative Advantage

A common point of confusion regarding specialization and trade involves the concepts of absolute advantage and comparative advantage. **Absolute advantage** refers to the ability of a party (nation, region, or individual) to produce more of a good or service while using the same amount of inputs. That is, having an absolute advantage means a nation can produce a good or service more cheaply than other nations. The danger in using the concept of absolute advantage in determining what a nation should specialize in and trade is that a nation could actually lack an absolute advantage in anything. In this case, according to the theory of absolute advantage, the nation would not be involved in trade at all and the case for free trade collapses. By contrast, comparative advantage is never absent; even if a nation is bad at everything, it will still possess a comparative advantage at something.

To help distinguish between these two important concepts, consider the following example. Canada may be able to produce more clothing per worker than India, but that does not mean Canada should necessarily sell clothing to India. Indeed, Canada has an absolute advantage or productive advantage over India in nearly every good, given the higher levels of output per person in Canada. Yet India's disadvantage in producing some goods is much less than for others. In goods where India's productivity is only slightly less than that of Canada, such as perhaps in clothing, it probably has a comparative advantage over Canada. How? For a highly productive nation to produce goods in which it is only marginally more productive than other nations, the nation must take resources from the production of other goods in which its productive abilities are markedly greater. As a result, the opportunity costs in India of making clothing may be less than in Canada. With that, both can gain from trade, despite potential absolute advantages for every good in Canada.

## Comparative Advantage and the Production Possibilities Curve

To help illustrate the concepts involved, the principle of comparative advantage can be applied to trading areas. In fact, trade has evolved in large part because different geographic areas have different resources and therefore different production possibilities. In Exhibit 1, we show the production possibilities curves (PPCs) for two trading areas. A "trading area" may be a locality, a region, or (as in this example) a nation. We see that if Canada devotes all of its resources to producing food, it can produce 40 kilograms of food per day; if it devotes all of its resources to producing cloth, it can produce 100 metres of cloth per day. We also see that when India uses all of its resources to produce food, it can produce only 30 kilograms per day, and when it uses all of its resources to produce cloth, it can produce 30 metres per day.

Canada and India have various potential combinations of food and cloth that they can produce. For each region, the cost of producing more food is the output of cloth that must be forgone, and vice versa. We see in Exhibit 1 that Canada can produce more food (40 kilograms per day) and more cloth (100 metres per day) than India can (30 kilograms and 30 metres per day, respectively), perhaps reflecting better resources (more or better labour, more land, and so on). This means that Canada has an absolute advantage in both products.

Suppose that, before specialization, Canada chooses to produce 75 metres of cloth and 10 kilograms of food per day. Similarly, suppose India decides to produce 12 metres of cloth and 18 kilograms of food per day. Collectively, then, the two areas are producing 87 metres of cloth (75 + 12) and 28 kilograms of food (10 + 18) per day before specialization.

Looking at Exhibit 2, now suppose the two nations specialize. Canada decides to specialize in cloth and devotes all its resources to making that product. As a result,

**absolute advantage**
*the ability of a party (nation, region, or individual) to produce more of a good or service while using the same amount of inputs*

**section 14.3**
Exhibit 1

**Production Possibilities, Canada and India**

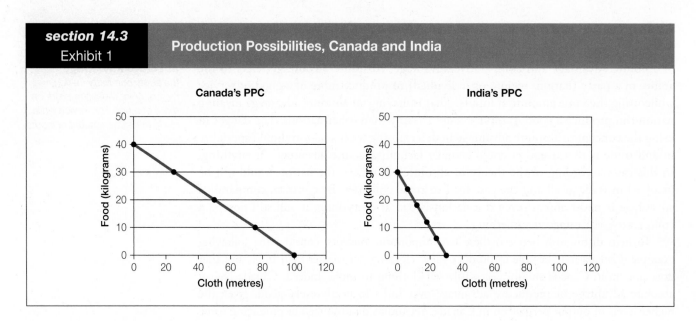

**section 14.3**
Exhibit 2

**Specialization and Trade**

| Region | Food | Cloth |
|--------|------|-------|
| Canada | (kilograms per day) | (metres per day) |
| | 0 | 100 |
| | 10 | 75 |
| | 20 | 50 |
| | 30 | 25 |
| | 40 | 0 |
| India | 0 | 30 |
| | 6 | 24 |
| | 12 | 18 |
| | 18 | 12 |
| | 24 | 6 |
| | 30 | 0 |
| **Before Specialization** | | |
| Canada | 10 | 75 |
| India | 18 | 12 |
| Total | 28 | 87 |
| **After Specialization** | | |
| Canada | 0 | 100 |
| India | 30 | 0 |
| Total | 30 | 100 |

cloth output in Canada rises to 100 metres per day, some of which is sold to India. India, in turn, devotes all its resources to food, producing 30 kilograms of food per day and selling some of it to Canada. Together, the two nations are producing more of both cloth and food than before—100 metres instead of 87 metres of cloth and 30 kilograms instead of 28 kilograms of food per day. Both areas could, as a result, have more of both products than before they began specializing and trading.

How can this happen? In Canada, the opportunity cost of producing food is very high—25 metres of cloth must be forgone to get 10 more kilograms of food. The cost of 1 kilogram of food is 2.5 metres of cloth (25 divided by 10). In India, by contrast, the opportunity cost of producing 6 more kilograms of food is 6 metres of cloth that must be forgone; so the cost of 1 kilogram of food is 1 metre of cloth. In Canada, a kilogram of food costs 2.5 metres of cloth, whereas in India the same amount of food costs only 1 metre of cloth. Food is more costly in Canada in terms of cloth forgone than in India, so India has a comparative advantage in food even though Canada has an absolute advantage in food.

With respect to cloth production, an increase in output by 25 metres, say, from 25 to 50 metres, costs 10 kilograms of food forgone in Canada. The cost of 1 more metre of cloth is 0.4 kilograms of food (10 divided by 25). In India, the cost of 1 metre of cloth is 1 kilogram of food. Cloth is more costly (in terms of opportunity cost) in India and cheaper in Canada, so Canada has a comparative advantage in the production of cloth.

Thus, by specializing in products in which it has a comparative advantage, an area has the potential of consuming more goods and services, assuming it trades the additional output for other desirable goods and services that others can produce at a lower opportunity cost. In the scenario presented here, the people in Canada would specialize in cloth, and the people in India would specialize in food. If Canada exports 20 metres of cloth and imports 11 kilograms of food, it can consume 80 metres of cloth and 11 kilograms of food after trade. Likewise, if India exports 11 kilograms of food and imports 20 metres of cloth, it can consume 20 metres of cloth and 19 kilograms of food after trade. We can see from this example that specialization increases both the division of labour and the interdependence among nations.

## SECTION CHECK

- ■ Voluntary trade occurs because the participants feel that they are better off because of the trade.
- ■ A nation, a geographic area, or even a person can gain from trade if the good or service is produced relatively cheaper than anyone else can produce it. That is, an area should specialize in producing and selling those items that it can produce at a lower opportunity cost than others. Through trade and specialization in products in which it has a comparative advantage, a country can enjoy a greater array of goods and services at a lower cost.

# Supply and Demand in International Trade

- ● What are consumer surplus and producer surplus?
- ● Who benefits and who loses when a country becomes an exporter?
- ● Who benefits and who loses when a country becomes an importer?

## WHAT ARE CONSUMER SURPLUS AND PRODUCER SURPLUS?

The difference between what the consumer is willing and able to pay and what the consumer actually pays for a quantity of a good or service is called **consumer surplus**. The difference between the lowest price at which a supplier is willing and able to supply a good or service and the actual price received for a given quantity of a good or service is called **producer surplus**. With the tools of consumer and producer surplus, we can better analyze the impact of trade. Who gains? Who loses? What happens to net welfare?

The demand curve represents maximum prices that consumers are willing and able to pay for different quantities of a good or service; the supply curve represents minimum prices that suppliers require to be willing to supply different quantities of that good or service. In Exhibit 1, for example, for the first unit of output, the consumer is willing to pay up to $7 and the producer would demand at least $1 for producing that unit. However, the equilibrium price is $4, as indicated by the intersection of the supply and demand curves. It is clear that the two would gain from getting together

**consumer surplus**
*the difference between what the consumer is willing and able to pay and what the consumer actually pays for a quantity of a good or service*

**producer surplus**
*the difference between the lowest price at which a supplier is willing and able to supply a good or service and the actual price received for a given quantity of a good or service*

**section 14.4**
Exhibit 1

**Consumer and Producer Surplus**

Consumer surplus is the difference between the price a consumer has to pay ($4) and the price the consumer is willing to pay. For unit 1, consumer surplus is $3 ($7 − $4). Producer surplus is the difference between the price a seller receives for selling a good or service ($4) and the price at which he is willing to supply that good or service. For unit 1, producer surplus is $3 ($4 − $1).

and trading that unit because the consumer would receive $3 of consumer surplus ($7 − $4) and the producer would receive $3 of producer surplus ($4 − $1). Both would also benefit from trading the second and third units of output—in fact, from every unit up to the equilibrium output. Once the equilibrium output is reached at the equilibrium price, all of the mutually beneficial opportunities from trade between suppliers and demanders will have taken place; the sum of consumer surplus and producer surplus is maximized.

It is important to recognize that the total gains to the economy from trade are the sum of consumer and producer surplus. That is, consumers benefit from additional amounts of consumer surplus and producers benefit from additional amounts of producer surplus.

## WHO BENEFITS AND WHO LOSES WHEN A COUNTRY BECOMES AN EXPORTER?

Using the concepts of consumer and producer surplus, we can graphically show the net benefits of free trade. Imagine an economy with no trade, where the equilibrium price, $P_{BT}$, and the equilibrium quantity, $Q_{BT}$, of wheat are determined exclusively in the domestic economy, as seen in Exhibit 2. Say that this imaginary economy decides to engage in free trade. You can see that the world price (established in the world market for wheat), $P_{WORLD}$, is higher than the domestic price before trade, $P_{BT}$. In other words, the domestic economy has a comparative advantage in wheat because it can produce wheat at a lower relative price than the rest of the world. So this wheat-producing country sells some wheat to the domestic market and some wheat to the world market, all at the going world price.

The price after trade $(P_{AT})$ is higher than the price before trade $(P_{BT})$. Because the world market is huge, the demand from the rest of the world at the world price $(P_{WORLD})$ is assumed to be perfectly elastic. That is, domestic wheat farmers can sell all the wheat they want at the world price. If you were a wheat farmer in Saskatchewan, would you rather sell all of your bushels of wheat at the higher world price or the lower domestic price? As a wheat farmer, you would surely prefer the higher world price. But this is not

**In 1994, the North American Free Trade Agreement (NAFTA) went into effect. This lowered the trade barriers among Mexico, Canada, and the United States. Proponents of freer trade, especially economists, viewed the agreement as a way to gain greater wealth through specialization and trade for all three countries. Opponents thought the agreement would take away Canadian and U.S. jobs and lower living standards.**

| section 14.4 Exhibit 2 | Free Trade and Exports |
|---|---|

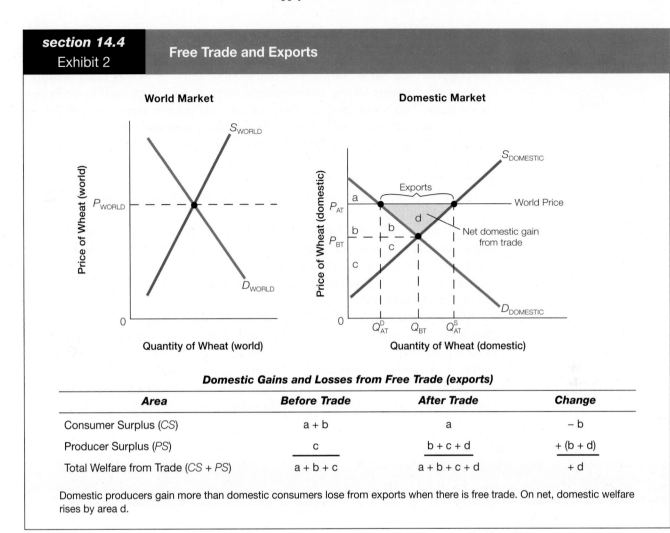

### Domestic Gains and Losses from Free Trade (exports)

| Area | Before Trade | After Trade | Change |
|---|---|---|---|
| Consumer Surplus (*CS*) | a + b | a | – b |
| Producer Surplus (*PS*) | c | b + c + d | + (b + d) |
| Total Welfare from Trade (*CS* + *PS*) | a + b + c | a + b + c + d | + d |

Domestic producers gain more than domestic consumers lose from exports when there is free trade. On net, domestic welfare rises by area d.

good news for domestic cereal and bread eaters, who now have to pay more for products made with wheat, because $P_{AT}$ is greater than $P_{BT}$.

Graphically, we can see how free trade and exports affect both domestic consumers and domestic producers. At the higher world price, $P_{AT}$, domestic producers supply $Q^S_{AT}$, whereas domestic consumers demand $Q^D_{AT}$. The difference between these two quantities is the amount of wheat exported to the world market. At the higher world price, $P_{AT}$, domestic wheat producers are receiving larger amounts of producer surplus. Before trade, they received a surplus equal to area c; after trade, they received surplus b + c + d, for a net gain of area b + d. However, part of the domestic producers' gain comes at domestic consumers' expense. Specifically, consumers had a consumer surplus equal to area a + b before the trade (at $P_{BT}$), but they now have only area a (at $P_{AT}$)—a loss of area b.

Area b reflects a redistribution of income because producers are gaining exactly what consumers are losing. Is that good or bad? We can't say objectively whether consumers or producers are more deserving. However, the net benefits from allowing free trade and exports are clearly visible in area d. Without free trade, no one gets area d. That is, on net, members of the domestic society gain when domestic wheat producers are able to sell their wheat at the higher world price. Although domestic wheat consumers lose from the free trade, those negative effects are more than offset by the positive gains captured by producers. Area d is the net increase in domestic welfare (the welfare gain) from free trade and exports.

## WHO BENEFITS AND WHO LOSES WHEN A COUNTRY BECOMES AN IMPORTER?

Now suppose that our economy does not produce shirts as well as other countries of the world. In other words, other countries have a comparative advantage in producing shirts. This means that the domestic price for shirts is above the world price. This scenario is illustrated in Exhibit 3. At the new, lower world price, the domestic producer will supply quantity $Q_{AT}^S$. However, at the lower world price, the domestic producers will not produce the entire amount demanded by domestic consumers, $Q_{AT}^D$. At the world price, reflecting the world supply and demand for shirts, the difference between what is domestically supplied and what is domestically demanded is supplied by imports.

At the world price (established in the world market for shirts), we assume the world supply curve to the domestic market is perfectly elastic—that the producers of the world can supply all that domestic consumers are willing to buy at the going price. At the world price, $Q_{AT}^S$ is supplied by domestic producers and the difference between $Q_{AT}^D$ and $Q_{AT}^S$ is imported from other countries.

Who wins and who loses from free trade and imports? Domestic consumers benefit from paying a lower price for shirts. In Exhibit 3, before trade, consumers received only area a in consumer surplus. After trade, the price fell and quantity purchased increased, causing the area of consumer surplus to increase from area a to area a + b + d, a gain of b + d. Domestic producers lose because they are now selling their shirts at the lower world price, $P_{AT}$. The producer surplus before trade was b + c. After trade, the producer

### section 14.4
Exhibit 3        **Free Trade and Imports**

#### *Domestic Gains and Losses from Free Trade (imports)*

| Area | Before Trade | After Trade | Change |
|---|---|---|---|
| Consumer Surplus (*CS*) | a | a + b + d | + (b + d) |
| Producer Surplus (*PS*) | b + c | c | – b |
| Total Welfare from Trade (*CS* + *PS*) | a + b + c | a + b + c + d | + d |

Domestic consumers gain more than domestic producers lose from imports when there is free trade. On net, domestic welfare rises by area d.

surplus falls to area c, reducing producer surplus by area b. Area b, then, represents a redistribution from producers to consumers, but area d is the net increase in domestic welfare (the welfare gain) from free trade and imports.

## SECTION CHECK

■ The difference between what a consumer is willing and able to pay and what a consumer actually has to pay is called *consumer surplus*. The difference between what a supplier is willing and able to receive and the price a supplier actually receives for selling a good or service is called *producer surplus*.
■ With free trade and exports, domestic producers gain more than domestic consumers lose.
■ With free trade and imports, domestic consumers gain more than domestic producers lose.

# Tariffs, Import Quotas, and Subsidies

● What is a tariff?
● What is the impact of tariffs on the domestic economy?
● What are some arguments in favour of tariffs?
● What are import quotas?
● What is the impact of import quotas on the domestic economy?
● What is the economic impact of subsidies?

## WHAT IS A TARIFF?

A **tariff** is a tax on imported goods. Tariffs are usually relatively small revenue producers that retard the expansion of trade. They bring about higher prices and revenues to domestic producers, and lower sales and revenues to foreign producers. Moreover, tariffs lead to higher prices for domestic consumers. In fact, the gains to producers are more than offset by the loss to consumers. Let us see how this works graphically.

**tariff**
*a tax on imported goods*

## WHAT IS THE IMPACT OF TARIFFS ON THE DOMESTIC ECONOMY?

The domestic economic impact of tariffs is presented in Exhibit 1, which illustrates the supply and demand curves for domestic consumers and producers of shoes. In a typical international supply and demand illustration, the intersection of the world supply and demand curves would determine the domestic market price. However, with import tariffs, the domestic price of shoes is greater than the world price, as in Exhibit 1. We consider the world supply curve ($S_{WORLD}$) to domestic consumers to be perfectly elastic; that is, we can buy all we want at the world price ($P_{WORLD}$). At the world price, domestic producers are willing to provide only quantity $Q_S$, but domestic consumers are willing to buy quantity $Q_D$—more than domestic producers are willing to supply. Imports make up the difference.

**section 14.5**
Exhibit 1

**Free Trade and Tariffs**

**Gains and Losses from Tariffs**

| Area | Before Tariff | After Tariff | Change |
|------|---------------|--------------|--------|
| Consumer Surplus (CS) | a + b + c + d + e | a | – (b + c + d + e) |
| Producer Surplus (PS) | f | b + f | + b |
| Government Revenues (Tariff) | — | d | + d |
| Total Welfare from Tariff (CS + PS + Tariff Revenues) | a + b + c + d + e + f | a + b + d + f | – (c + e) |

In the case of a tariff, we see that consumers lose more than producers and government gain. On net, the deadweight loss associated with the new tariff is represented by area c + e.

As you can see in Exhibit 1, the imposition of the tariff shifts up the perfectly elastic supply curve from foreigners to domestic consumers from $S_{WORLD}$ to $S_{WORLD + TARIFF}$, but it does not alter the domestic supply or demand curve. At the resulting higher domestic price ($P_{W+T}$), domestic suppliers are willing to supply more, $Q'_S$, but domestic consumers are willing to buy less, $Q'_D$, reducing the quantity of imported shoes. Overall, then, tariffs lead to (1) a smaller total quantity sold; (2) a higher price for shoes for domestic consumers; (3) greater sales of shoes at higher prices for domestic producers; and (4) lower sales of foreign shoes.

Although domestic producers do gain more sales and higher earnings, consumers lose much more. The increase in price from the tariff results in a loss in consumer surplus, as shown in Exhibit 1. After the tariff, shoe prices rise to $P_{W+T}$ and, consequently, consumer surplus falls by area b + c + d + e, representing the welfare loss to consumers from the tariff. Area b in Exhibit 1 shows the gain to domestic producers as a result of the tariff. That is, at the higher price, domestic producers are willing to supply more shoes, representing a welfare gain to producers resulting from the tariff. As a result of the tariff revenues, government gains area d. This is the import tariff—the revenue government collects on imports. However, we see from Exhibit 1 that consumers lose more than producers and government gain from the tariff. That is, on net, the deadweight loss associated with the tariff is represented by area c + e.

## WHAT ARE SOME ARGUMENTS IN FAVOUR OF TARIFFS?

Despite the preceding arguments against trade restrictions, they continue to be levied. Some rationale for their existence is necessary. Four common arguments for the use of trade restrictions deserve our critical examination.

### Temporary Trade Restrictions Help Infant Industries Grow

A country might argue that a protective tariff will allow a new industry to more quickly reach a scale of operation at which economies of scale and production efficiencies can be realized. That is, temporarily shielding the young industry from competition from foreign firms will allow the infant industry a chance to grow. With the early protection, these firms will eventually be able to compete effectively in the global market. It is presumed that without this protection, the industry could never get on its feet. At first hearing, the argument sounds valid, but there are many problems with it. How do you identify "infant industries" that genuinely have potential economies of scale and will quickly become efficient with protection? We do not know the long-run average total cost curves of industries, a necessary piece of information. Moreover, if firms and governments are truly convinced of the advantages of allowing an industry to reach a large scale, would it not be wise to make massive loans to the industry, allowing it to instantly begin large-scale production rather than slowly and at the expense of consumers? In other words, the goal of allowing the industry to reach its efficient size can be reached without protection. Finally, the history of infant industry tariffs suggests that the tariffs often linger long after the industry is mature and no longer in need of protection.

### Tariffs Can Reduce Domestic Unemployment

Exhibit 1 showed how tariffs increase output by domestic producers, thus leading to increased employment and reduced unemployment in industries where tariffs were imposed. Yet the overall employment effects of a tariff imposition are not likely to be positive; the argument is incorrect. Why? First, the imposition of a tariff by Canada on, say, foreign steel is going to be noticed in the countries adversely affected by the tariff. If a new tariff on steel lowers Japanese steel sales to Canada, the Japanese likely will retaliate by imposing tariffs on Canadian exports to Japan, for example, on beef exports. The retaliatory tariff will lower Canadian sales of beef and thus decrease employment in the Canadian beef industry. As a result, the gain in employment in the steel industry will be offset by a loss of employment elsewhere.

Even if the other countries did not retaliate, Canadian employment would likely suffer outside the industry being protected. The way that other countries pay for Canadian goods is by getting Canadian dollars from sales to Canada—imports to us. If new tariffs lead to restrictions on imports, fewer Canadian dollars will be flowing overseas in payment for imports, which means that foreigners will have fewer Canadian dollars available to buy our exports. Other things being equal, this will tend to reduce our exports, thus creating unemployment in the export industries.

### Tariffs Are Necessary for National Security Reasons

Sometimes it is argued that tariffs are a means of preventing a nation from becoming too dependent on foreign suppliers of goods vital to national security. That is, by making foreign goods more expensive, we can protect domestic suppliers. For example, if oil is vital to running planes and tanks, a cut-off of foreign supplies of oil during wartime could cripple a nation's defences.

The national security argument is usually not valid. If a nation's own resources are depletable, tariff-imposed reliance on domestic supplies will hasten depletion of domestic reserves, making the country even *more* dependent on imports in the future. If we impose a high tariff on foreign oil to protect domestic producers, we will increase domestic output of oil in the short run, but in the process, we will deplete the stockpile of available reserves. Thus, the defence argument is often of questionable validity. From a defence standpoint, it makes more sense to use foreign oil in peacetime and perhaps stockpile "insurance" supplies so that larger domestic supplies would be available during wars.

## Tariffs Are Necessary to Protect against Dumping

*Dumping* occurs when a foreign country sells its products at prices below the country's costs or below the prices for which the products are sold on the domestic market. For example, the Japanese government has been accused for years of subsidizing Japanese steel producers while they attempt to gain a greater share of the world steel market and greater market power. That is, using this strategy, the short-term losses from selling below cost may be offset by the long-term economic profits. Some have argued that tariffs are needed to protect domestic producers against low-cost dumpers because the tariffs will raise the cost to foreign producers and offset the producers' cost advantage.

Canada has anti-dumping laws; if a Canadian producer suspects that imported goods are being dumped or subsidized, they can file a written complaint with the Canadian Border Services Agency (CBSA). It is then up to the Canadian International Trade Tribunal to establish if the dumping or subsidizing is causing injury to Canadian industry. If the Tribunal finds such evidence, the CBSA is then given the authority to impose anti-dumping or countervailing duties on the dumped or subsidized imports. The duties are designed to raise the price of the foreign goods that are being dumped or subsidized and give Canadian industry an opportunity to compete fairly with the imported goods.

## WHAT ARE IMPORT QUOTAS?

**import quota**
*a legal limit on the imported quantity of a good that is produced abroad and can be sold in domestic markets*

An **import quota** is a legal limit on the imported quantity of a good that is produced abroad and can be sold in domestic markets. Like tariffs, import quotas directly restrict imports, leading to reductions in trade and thus preventing nations from fully realizing their comparative advantage. The case for quotas is probably even weaker than the case for tariffs. Suppose that the Japanese have been sending 50 000 cars annually to Canada but now are told that, because of quota restrictions, they can send only 30 000 cars. If the Japanese manufacturers are allowed to determine how the quantity reduction is to occur, they will likely collude, leading to higher prices. Suppose that each producer is simply told to reduce sales by 40 percent. They will substantially raise the price of the cars to Canadians above what the 50 000 original buyers would have paid for them.

## The Government Does Not Collect Revenues from Import Quotas

Unlike what occurs with a tariff, the Canadian government does not collect any revenue as a result of the import quota. Despite the higher prices, the loss in consumer surplus, and the loss in government revenue, quotas come about because people often view them as being less "protectionist" than tariffs—the traditional, most maligned form of protection.

Besides the rather blunt means of curtailing imports by using tariffs and quotas, nations have devised still other, more subtle means to restrict international trade. For example, nations sometimes impose product standards, ostensibly to protect consumers against inferior merchandise. Effectively, however, sometimes those standards are simply a means to restrict foreign competition. For example, France might keep certain kinds of wine out of the country on the grounds that the wines were made with allegedly inferior grapes or had an inappropriate alcoholic content. Likewise, Canada might prohibit automobile imports that do not meet certain standards in terms of pollutants, safety, and fuel efficiency. Even if these standards are not intended to restrict foreign competition, the regulations may nonetheless have that impact, restricting consumer choice.

## WHAT IS THE IMPACT OF IMPORT QUOTAS ON THE DOMESTIC ECONOMY?

The domestic economic impact of an import quota on autos is presented in Exhibit 2. The introduction of an import quota increases the price from the world price, $P_W$ (established in the world market for autos) to $P_{W+Q}$. The quota causes the price to rise

**section 14.5**
Exhibit 2

**Free Trade and Import Quotas**

*Gains and Losses from Import Quotas*

| Area | Before Quota | After Quota | Change |
|------|:---:|:---:|:---:|
| Consumer Surplus (*CS*) | a + b + c + d + e | a | − (b + c + d + e) |
| Producer Surplus (*PS*) | f | b + f | + b |
| Total Welfare (*CS* + *PS*) from Quota | a + b + c + d + e + f | a + b + f | − (c + d + e) |

With an import quota, the price rises from $P_W$ to $P_{W+Q}$. Compared to free trade, consumers lose area b + c + d + e and producers gain area b. The deadweight loss from the quota is area c + d + e. Under quotas, consumers lose and producers gain. The difference in deadweight loss between quotas and tariffs is area d that the government is not able to pick up with import quotas.

above the world price. The domestic quantity demanded falls and the domestic quantity supplied rises. Consequently, the number of imports is much smaller than it would be without the import quota. Compared to free trade, domestic producers are better off but domestic consumers are worse off. Specifically, the import quota results in a gain in producer surplus of area b and a loss in consumer surplus of area b + c + d + e. However, unlike the tariff case, where the government gains area d in revenues, the government does not gain any revenues with a quota. Consequently, the deadweight loss is even greater with quotas than with tariffs. That is, on net, the deadweight loss associated with the quota is represented by area c + d + e. Recall that the deadweight loss was only c + e for tariffs.

If tariffs and import quotas hurt importing countries, why do they exist? The reason they exist is that producers can make large profits or "rents" from tariffs and import quotas. Economists call producer efforts to gain profits from government protection **rent seeking**. Because this is money, time, and effort that could have been spent producing something else rather than spent on lobbying efforts, the deadweight loss from tariffs and quotas that we just illustrated will likely understate the true deadweight loss to society.

**rent seeking**

*producer efforts to gain profits from government protections such as tariffs and import quotas*

## WHAT IS THE ECONOMIC IMPACT OF SUBSIDIES?

**subsidy**

*a program of financial assistance paid out to producers*

Working in the opposite direction to a tariff or import quota, a **subsidy** is a program of financial assistance paid out to producers in a particular industry. As a form of protectionism or trade barrier, subsidies artificially make domestic goods and services competitive against imports. Specifically, an export subsidy involves giving revenue to producers for each exported unit of output, therefore encouraging producers to export. Although not a barrier to trade like tariffs and quotas, objections can be raised that subsidies distort trade patterns and lead to inefficiencies. How does this happen? With subsidies, producers will export goods not because their costs are lower than that of a foreign competitor, but because their costs have been artificially reduced by government action, transferring income from taxpayers to the exporter. The subsidy does not reduce the actual labour, raw material, technology, entrepreneurship, and capital costs of production—society has the same opportunity costs as before. A nation's taxpayers end up subsidizing the output of producers who, relative to producers in other countries, are inefficient. The nation, then, exports products in which it does not have a comparative advantage. Gains from trade in terms of world output are reduced by such subsidies. Thus, subsidies, usually defended as a means of increasing exports and improving a nation's international financial position, are usually of dubious worth to the world economy and even to the economy doing the subsidizing.

Several Canadian subsidy programs have drawn the criticism of other economies. The most controversial of these are the ones provided to our agricultural, forest products, and mining and steel industries.

According to the World Bank and the International Monetary Fund, world trade has benefited enormously from greater trade openness since 1950. Tariffs on goods have fallen from a worldwide average of 26 percent to less than 9 percent. On average, trade has grown more than twice as fast as output. While tariff use has declined, the incidence of nontariff barriers such as import quotas and export subsidies has risen sharply, indicating that there is still work to be done.

## SECTION CHECK

- A tariff is a tax on imported goods.
- Tariffs bring about higher prices and revenues to domestic producers, and lower sales and revenues to foreign producers. Tariffs lead to higher prices and reduce consumer surplus for domestic consumers. Tariffs result in a net loss in welfare because the loss in consumer surplus is greater than the gain to producers and the government.
- Arguments in favour of the use of tariffs include: tariffs help infant industries grow; tariffs can reduce domestic unemployment; tariffs are necessary for national security reasons; and tariffs protect against dumping.
- Import quotas are legal limits on the quantity of an imported good that can be produced abroad and sold in domestic markets.
- Like tariffs, import quotas restrict imports, lowering consumer surplus and preventing countries from fully realizing their comparative advantage. There is a net loss in welfare from quotas, but it is proportionately larger than for a tariff because there are no government revenues.
- Sometimes government tries to encourage production of a certain good by subsidizing its production with taxpayer dollars. Because subsidies stimulate exports, they are not a barrier to trade like tariffs and import quotas. However, they do distort trade patterns and cause overall inefficiencies.

# For Your Review

## Section 14.1

1. What is the major difference between the nature of Canadian exports and imports?

2. Why would Canadian producers and consumers be more concerned about American trade restrictions than Swedish trade restrictions?

## Section 14.2

3. Why is it important to understand the effects of international trade?

4. The North American Free Trade Agreement (NAFTA) is an agreement among Canada, the United States, and Mexico to reduce trade barriers and promote the free flow of goods and services across borders. Some Canadian labour groups were opposed to NAFTA. Can you explain why? Can you predict how NAFTA might affect the nature and production methods of goods and services produced in the participating countries?

## Section 14.3

5. Bud and Larry have been shipwrecked on a deserted island. Their economic activity consists of either gathering berries or fishing. We know that Bud can catch four fish in one hour or harvest two buckets of berries. In the same time, Larry can catch two fish or harvest two buckets of berries.

a. Fill in the following table assuming that they *each* spend four hours a day fishing and four hours a day harvesting berries.

|  | Fish per Day | Buckets of Berries per Day |
|---|---|---|
| Bud | _____ | _____ |
| Larry | _____ | _____ |
| Total | _____ | _____ |

b. If Bud and Larry don't trade with each other, who is better off? Why?

c. Assume that Larry and Bud operate on straight-line production possibilities curves. Fill in the following table:

|  | Opportunity Cost of a Bucket of Berries | Opportunity Cost of a Fish |
|---|---|---|
| Bud | _____ | _____ |
| Larry | _____ | _____ |

d. If they trade, who has the comparative advantage in fish? In berries?

e. If Larry and Bud specialize in and trade the good in which they have a comparative advantage, how much of each good will be produced in an eight-hour day? What are the gains from trade?

6. Suppose Canada can produce cars at an opportunity cost of 2 computers for each car it produces. Suppose Mexico can produce cars at an opportunity cost of 8 computers for each car it produces. Indicate how both countries can gain from free trade.

7. The following represents the production possibilities in two countries.

| Country A | | Country B | |
|---|---|---|---|
| Good X | Good Y | Good X | Good Y |
| 0 | 32 | 0 | 24 |
| 4 | 24 | 4 | 18 |
| 8 | 16 | 8 | 12 |
| 12 | 8 | 12 | 6 |
| 16 | 0 | 16 | 0 |

Which country has a comparative advantage at producing Good X? How can you tell? Which country has a comparative advantage at producing Good Y?

8. Evaluate the following statement: "Canada has an absolute advantage in growing wheat. Therefore, it must have a comparative advantage in growing wheat."

9. Assume that Freeland could produce 8 units of X and no Y, 16 units of Y and no X, or any linear combination in between, and Braveburg could produce 32 units of X and no Y, 48 units of Y and no X, or any linear combination in between.

   a. What is the opportunity cost of producing X in Freeland? In Braveburg?

   b. If Freeland and Braveburg specialize according to comparative advantage, in which directions will traded goods flow?

   c. If trade occurs, what will be the terms of trade between X and Y?

   d. How large would transaction costs, transportation costs, or tariffs have to be to eliminate trade between Freeland and Braveburg?

10. If country A is the lower opportunity cost producer of X and country B is the lowest opportunity cost producer of Y, what happens to their absolute and comparative advantages if country A suddenly becomes three times more productive at producing both X and Y than it was before?

## Section 14.4

11. How does voluntary trade generate both consumer and producer surplus?

12. To protect its domestic apple industry, Botswana has for many years prevented international trade in apples. The following graph represents the Botswana domestic market for apples. $P_{BT}$ is the current price, and $P_{AT}$ is the world price.

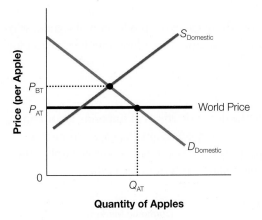

   a. If the government allows world trade in apples, what will happen to the price of apples in Botswana? Why?

   b. Indicate the amount of apples domestic producers produce after there is trade in apples as $Q_{DT}$. How many apples are imported?

   c. Trade in imports causes producer surplus to be reduced. Describe this area on the graph.

   d. The gains from trade equal the amount that increased consumer surplus exceeds the loss in producer surplus. Describe this area on the graph.

   e. Explain why consumers in Botswana would still be better off if they were required to compensate producers for their lost producer surplus.

13. Using the following graph, illustrate the domestic effects of opening up the domestic market to international trade on the domestic price, the domestic quantity

purchased, the domestic quantity produced, imports or exports, consumer surplus, producer surplus, and the total welfare gain from trade.

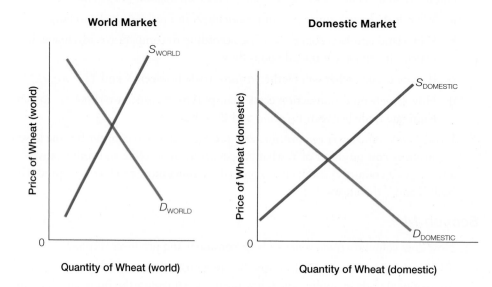

14. When a country has a comparative advantage in the production of a good, why do domestic producers gain more than domestic consumers lose from free international trade?

15. When a country has a comparative disadvantage in the production of a good, why do domestic consumers gain more than domestic producers lose from free international trade?

## Section 14.5

16. Use the following graph to illustrate the domestic effects of imposing a tariff on imports on the domestic price, the domestic quantity purchased, the domestic quantity produced, the level of imports, consumer surplus, producer surplus, the tariff revenue generated, and the total welfare effect from the tariff.

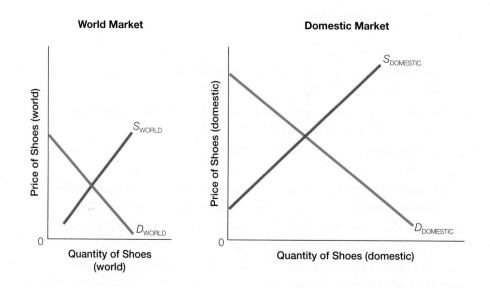

17. Why do tariffs increase domestic producer surplus but decrease domestic consumer surplus?

18. How do import tariffs increase employment in "protected" industries but at the expense of a likely decrease in employment overall?

19. Why does rent seeking imply that the traditional measure of deadweight loss from tariffs and quotas will likely understate the true deadweight loss to society?

20. Would you be in favour of freer trade or against it in the following circumstances?

    a. The move to freer trade is in another country and you are an exporter to that country.

    b. The move to freer trade is in your country and you compete with imports from other countries.

    c. The move to freer trade is in your country and you import parts for products you sell domestically.

21. Why is the domestic argument for import quotas weaker than the case for tariffs?

## section

## 15.1

# The Balance of Payments

- What is the balance of payments?
- What is the current account?
- What is the capital account?
- What is the statistical discrepancy?

## WHAT IS THE BALANCE OF PAYMENTS?

**balance of payments**
*the record of international transactions of a nation over a year*

The record of the international transactions of a nation over a year is called the **balance of payments**. The balance of payments is a statement that records all the exchanges requiring an outflow of funds to foreign nations or an inflow of funds from other nations. Just as an examination of gross domestic product accounts gives us some idea of the economic health and vitality of a nation, the balance of payments provides information about a nation's world trade position. The balance of payments is divided into three main sections: the current account, the capital account, and an "error term" called the *statistical discrepancy*. These are shown in Exhibit 1. Let us look at each of these components beginning with the current account, which is largely made up of imports and exports of goods and services.

## WHAT IS THE CURRENT ACCOUNT?

### Export Goods and the Current Account

**current account**
*a record of a country's imports and exports of goods and services, net primary income, and net secondary income*

The **current account** is a record of a country's imports and exports of goods and services, net primary income, and net secondary income. Any time that a foreign buyer purchases a good from a Canadian producer, the foreign buyer must pay the Canadian producer for the good. Usually, the foreigner must pay for the good in Canadian dollars because the seller wants to pay his workers and for other inputs with dollars. This requires the foreign buyer to exchange units of his currency with a foreign exchange dealer for Canadian dollars. Because Canada obtains foreign currency, exports of Canadian goods abroad are considered a receipt or plus (+) item in the Canadian balance of payments.

| | | | |
|---|---|---|---|
| **section 15.1**<br>Exhibit 1 | **Canadian Balance of Payments, 2017 (billions of dollars)** | | |

**Type of Transaction**

| Current Account | | Capital Account | |
|---|---|---|---|
| 1. Exports of goods | $550 | 10. Net acquisition of financial assets | $−224 |
| 2. Imports of goods | −573 | 11. Net incurrence of liabilities | 280 |
| 3. Merchandise trade balance<br>(lines 1 + 2) | −23 | 12. Financial account balance<br>(lines 10 + 11) | 56 |
| 4. Exports of services | 113 | 13. Statistical discrepancy | 7 |
| 5. Imports of services | −138 | 14. Net balance<br>(lines 9 + 12 + 13) | $0 |
| 6. Services trade balance<br>(lines 4 + 5) | −25 | | |
| 7. Net primary income | −12 | | |
| 8. Net secondary income | −3 | | |
| 9. Current account balance (lines<br>3 + 6 + 7 + 8) | −63 | | |

SOURCES: Based on current account data: Statistics Canada, Table 376-0101–Balance of international payments, current account and capital account, annual (dollars); capital account data: Statistics Canada, Table 376-0104–Balance of international payments, financial account, annual (dollars).

## Import Goods and the Current Account

When a Canadian consumer buys an imported good, however, the reverse is true: The Canadian importer usually must pay the foreign producer in the foreign nation's currency. Typically, the Canadian buyer will go to a foreign exchange dealer and exchange Canadian dollars for units of that foreign currency. Imports are thus a payment (−) item in the balance of payments, because Canada loses foreign currency in order to buy imports.

## Services and the Current Account

Although imports and exports of goods are the largest components of the balance of payments, they are not the only ones. Nations import and export services as well. A particularly important service is tourism. When Canadian tourists go abroad, they are buying foreign-produced services. Those services include the use of hotels, sightseeing tours, restaurants, and so forth. In the current account, these services are included in imports. On the other hand, foreign tourism in Canada provides us with foreign currencies, so they are included in exports.

## Net Primary and Net Secondary Income

Another item that affects the current account is net primary income—Canadian investors hold foreign assets

**When a foreign tourist visits the CN Tower in Toronto, how does that affect the current account? Tourism provides Canada with foreign currency, which is included in exports.**

ROYALTY-FREE/CORBIS

and foreign investors hold Canadian assets. When Canadian investors hold foreign assets, they earn investment income in the form of interest and dividends, which is a receipt item. When foreign investors hold Canadian assets, they earn investment income in the form of interest and dividends, which is a payment item. In Exhibit 1, investment income paid to foreigners on their Canadian assets exceeded the investment income received by Canadians on their foreign assets by $12 billion.

There is also net secondary income in the current account, which is largely private and government grants and gifts to and from other countries. When the Canadian government gives foreign aid to another country, this creates a payment in the Canadian balance of payments. Private gifts, such as Canadian individuals receiving money from relatives or friends in foreign countries, show up in the current account as a receipt item.

## Current Account Balance

The balance on the current account is the net amount of receipts or payments after adding up all transactions of goods (merchandise imports and exports), services, net primary income, and net secondary income. If the sum of receipts exceeds the sum of payments, the nation is said to be running a surplus on the current account. If payments exceed receipts, however, the nation is running a deficit on the current account.

The current account balance for 2017 is presented in Exhibit 1. Note that exports and imports of goods were by far the largest receipts and payments. Note also that Canadian imports of goods were $23 billion more than Canadian exports of goods. Canada, therefore, experienced a $23 billion deficit in the merchandise trade balance. In addition to this $23 billion merchandise trade deficit was a $25 billion deficit in the services trade balance. When the $12 billion net primary income and the $3 billion net secondary income are also included, the overall current account deficit was $63 billion.

## WHAT IS THE CAPITAL ACCOUNT?

How was this deficit on the current account financed? We borrowed from the rest of the world. The current account deficit is reflected by movements of financial, or capital, assets. These transactions are recorded in the *capital account*, so a current account deficit is financed by a capital account surplus. In short, the **capital account** is a record of the foreign purchases or assets in the domestic economy (a monetary inflow) and domestic purchases of assets abroad (a monetary outflow).

**capital account**
*a record of the foreign purchases or assets in the domestic economy (a monetary inflow) and domestic purchases of assets abroad (a monetary outflow)*

## Capital Account Transactions

Capital account transactions include items such as international bank loans, purchases of corporate stocks and bonds, government bond purchases, and direct investments in foreign subsidiary companies. In Exhibit 1, we see that Canadians purchased an additional $224 billion of foreign assets in 2017, which was a payment because Canada lost foreign currency. On the other hand, foreigners purchased an additional $280 billion of Canadian assets in 2017 which was a receipt because it provided Canadians with foreign currency. On balance, then, there was a surplus in the capital account from capital movements of $56 billion, offsetting the $63 billion deficit in the current account.

It is important to highlight one particular capital account transaction: purchases and sales of foreign currencies by the Bank of Canada in the foreign exchange market. The Bank of Canada can intervene in the foreign exchange market to counter disruptive short-term movements in the external value of the Canadian dollar. For example, to moderate a decline in the value of the Canadian dollar, the Bank of Canada can sell foreign currency (usually U.S. dollars) and buy Canadian dollars on the foreign exchange market, thereby putting upward pressure on the Canadian dollar. Similarly, if the Canadian dollar is appreciating too rapidly, the Bank of Canada can buy foreign currency (usually U.S. dollars) and sell Canadian dollars on the foreign exchange market, thereby putting downward pressure on the Canadian dollar. These purchases and sales of foreign currencies by the Bank of Canada affect the level of Canada's official international reserves (the Government of Canada's holdings of foreign currencies), and these transactions are recorded in the capital account of the balance of payments.

## WHAT IS THE STATISTICAL DISCREPANCY?

In the final analysis, it is true that the overall balance of payments account must balance so that receipts and payments are equal. Why is this so? Because every unit of foreign currency used (payment) must have a source (receipt). We can see that the current account deficit ($63 billion payment) does not exactly equal the capital account surplus ($56 billion receipt). That is because there are considerable international flows of goods and capital that government authorities are unable to measure and record (e.g., smuggling of goods, or undeclared financial investments). These "errors" are entered into the balance of payments as the statistical discrepancy. In Exhibit 1, the statistical discrepancy was $7 billion (receipt). By including the statistical discrepancy with the current account balance and the capital account balance, the overall balance of payments does balance.

## Balance of Payments: A Useful Analogy

In concept, the international balance of payments is similar to the personal financial transactions of individuals. Each individual has his or her own "balance of payments," reflecting that person's trading with other economic units: other individuals, corporations, or governments. People earn income or credits by "exporting" their labour service to other economic units, or by receiving investment income (a return on capital services). Against that, they "import" goods from other economic units; we call these imports *consumption*. This negative item is sometimes augmented by payments made to outsiders (e.g., banks) on loans, and so forth. Fund transfers, such as gifts to children or charities, are other payment items (or receipt items for recipients of the assistance).

As individuals, if our spending on our consumption ("imports") exceeds our income from our "exports" of our labour and capital services, we have a "deficit" that must be financed by borrowing or selling assets. On the other hand, if we "export" more than we "import," we can make new investments and/or increase our "reserves" (savings and investment holdings). Like nations, individuals who run a deficit in daily transactions must make up for it through accommodating transactions (e.g., borrowing or reducing their savings or investment holdings) to bring about an ultimate balance of receipts and payments to their personal account. Likewise, individuals who run a surplus in daily transactions must make new investments and/or increase their savings and investment holdings to bring about a balance of receipts and payments.

In summary, the international balance of payments works like this: A country that runs a current account surplus lends that surplus to the rest of the world, creating a capital account deficit; a country that runs a current account deficit finances that deficit by borrowing from the rest of the world, thus creating a capital account surplus.

## section 15.2

# Exchange Rates

- What are exchange rates?
- How are exchange rates determined?

When Canadian consumers buy goods from people in other countries, the sellers of those goods want to be paid in their own domestic currencies. Canadian consumers, then, must first exchange Canadian dollars for the seller's currency in order to pay for those goods. Canadian importers must, therefore, constantly buy U.S. dollars, yen, euros, pesos, and other currencies in order to finance their purchases. Similarly, people in other countries buying Canadian goods must sell their currencies to obtain Canadian dollars in order to pay for those goods.

## WHAT ARE EXCHANGE RATES?

**exchange rate**
*the price of one unit of a country's currency in terms of another country's currency*

The price of one unit of a country's currency in terms of another country's currency is called the **exchange rate**. If a Canadian importer has agreed to pay euros (the currency of the European Union) to buy a BMW M6 made in southern Bavaria, Germany, she would then have to exchange Canadian dollars for euros. If it takes $2 to buy 1 euro, then the exchange rate is $2 per euro. From the German perspective, the exchange rate is 0.50 euros per Canadian dollar.

Exhibit 1 shows the exchange rate for the Canadian dollar against the currencies of some of our major trading partners. The exchange rates listed were the average exchange rates for the year 2017. It took 0.7701 U.S. dollars to buy one Canadian dollar (i.e., the exchange rate of the Canadian dollar in terms of the U.S. dollar). Conversely, it took 1.2985 Canadian dollars to buy one U.S. dollar (i.e., the exchange rate of the U.S. dollar in terms of the Canadian dollar). Note carefully that 1.2985 equals 1 divided by 0.7701. Similarly, it took 86.3558 Japanese yen to buy one Canadian dollar, and it took 0.01158 Canadian dollars (1 divided by 86.3558) to buy one Japanese yen.

**currency appreciation**
*an increase in the value of a currency*

A review of exchange rates over time will reveal that they are not constant: They can increase and decrease. An increase in the value of a currency is referred to as **currency appreciation**. For example, suppose the exchange rate rises from 40 to 50 Russian rubles

| | | Units of Foreign Currency per Canadian Dollar | Canadian Dollars per Unit of Foreign Currency |
|---|---|---|---|
| **Country** | **Currency** | | |
| Australia | Dollar | 1.0049 | 0.9951 |
| China | Renminbi | 5.2056 | 0.1921 |
| European Monetary Union | Euro | 0.6826 | 1.465 |
| Hong Kong | Dollar | 6.0003 | 0.166659 |
| India | Rupee | 50.1253 | 0.01995 |
| Japan | Yen | 86.3558 | 0.01158 |
| Mexico | Peso | 14.5264 | 0.06884 |
| New Zealand | Dollar | 1.0835 | 0.9229 |
| Norway | Krone | 6.3694 | 0.157 |
| Russia | Ruble | 44.8833 | 0.02228 |
| South Korea | Won | 870.3220 | 0.001149 |
| Sweden | Krona | 6.5789 | 0.152 |
| Switzerland | Franc | 0.7582 | 1.3189 |
| United Kingdom | Pound | 0.5981 | 1.672 |
| United States | Dollar | 0.7701 | 1.2985 |

**section 15.2**
Exhibit 1       **Exchange Rates for the Canadian Dollar in 2017**

SOURCE: Bank of Canada Financial Markets Department, *Year Average of Exchange Rates, 2017.*

per Canadian dollar. Since you can now get more Russian rubles for each Canadian dollar, the dollar is said to have appreciated. A decrease in the value of a currency is referred to as **currency depreciation**. If the exchange rate falls from 15 to 10 Mexican pesos per Canadian dollar, the dollar is said to have depreciated.

**currency depreciation**
*a decrease in the value of a currency*

**The euro makes it easy to compare prices for the same goods in different European countries using this currency. For example, if you use mail order or shop on the Internet, it is easier to spot the bargains between countries.**

### Changes in Exchange Rates Affect the Domestic Demand for Foreign Goods

Prices of goods in their currencies combine with exchange rates to determine the domestic price of foreign goods. Suppose the BMW M6 sells for 128 000 euros in Germany. What is the price to Canadian consumers? Let us assume that tariffs and other transaction costs are zero. If the exchange rate is $2 = 1 euro, then the equivalent Canadian dollar price of the BMW M6 is 128 000 euros times $2 per euro, or $256 000. If the exchange rate was to change to $3 = 1 euro, fewer cars would be demanded in Canada, because the effective Canadian dollar price of the cars would rise to $384 000 (128 000 euros times $3 per euro). The new higher relative value of a euro compared to the dollar (or equivalently, the lower relative value of a dollar compared to the euro) would lead to a reduction in Canadian demand for German-made cars.

© Fingerhut/Shutterstock.com

## DEBATE

## IS A LOW LOONIE GOOD FOR CANADA'S ECONOMY?

### For:

Canada has long enjoyed a "discounted dollar," which gives Canadian exporters an artificial competitive advantage by making their goods seem to have more value simply because of the lower cost. It's as if Canadian products are "on sale" to the rest of the world.

Over the course of the last decade, Canadians have seen their dollar fluctuate between US$0.69 and US$1.03. This is a wild swing that has major effects on our economy. According to *The Globe and Mail*, experts tend to agree that a US$0.90 dollar is close to fair value.*

Those who trade with Canada desire a low Canadian dollar—it keeps the prices of Canadian products down and is more of a value to those who buy our goods. Trade unions and Canadian manufacturing firms enjoy the benefits of a low dollar because it provides the illusion of value. Surely it's clear that a low loonie is good for Canada's economy.

### Against:

A rising Canadian dollar sends a message to the world—that the Canadian economy and Canadian products are strong and desirable. A high dollar value is also much better for a resource-based economy. Canada has many resource-based firms that rely on the "value-added" (the difference between the sale price and the production cost of a product), and they would like to sell their products at the highest Canadian dollar price they can. It simply

_____
*B. McKenna. "Why a lower loonie is (mostly) good for Canada." *The Globe and Mail* (January 11, 2014).

brings them the most revenues possible when they sell to foreign entities.

When the dollar is low, it's as if the product is discounted to the world. A low dollar may be seen as a negative to Canadian manufacturing firms (although many firms would disagree). This is because when the dollar is low, those firms sell more products internationally, but it's the value of the dollar that sells the product, not necessarily the value of the product itself.

When the dollar appreciates, those firms find it difficult to compete. They should take the opportunity to improve their firms' productivity when they are selling more in preparation for when the value of the Canadian dollar eventually appreciates.

A low Canadian dollar is bad for the migrating seniors who head south each year and it's bad for cross-border shoppers—they have to spend more Canadian dollars to pay for the goods they buy in the United States. All in all, surely a high loonie is preferable.

### Questions

1. Is a low loonie good for the long-term viability of a firm? Why or why not?
2. Who are the other stakeholders that would benefit from a low dollar? What are some other reasons to justify their views?
3. What is the impact on the goals of growth, employment, and inflation when the dollar value is higher?
4. What are other reasons why Canada should embrace the rising dollar?
5. Is the statement made in *The Globe and Mail* article sound? Why or why not?

## The Demand for a Foreign Currency

**derived demand**
*the demand for an input derived from consumers' demand for the good or service produced with that input*

The demand for foreign currencies is an example of what economists call a **derived demand**—a demand for an input derived from consumers' demand for the good or service produced with that input. Specifically, the demand for foreign currency is derived from the demand for foreign goods and services or for foreign assets. The more foreign goods are demanded, the more of that foreign currency will be needed to pay for those goods. Such an increased demand for the currency will push up the exchange rate of that currency relative to other currencies.

## The Supply of a Foreign Currency

Similarly, the supply of foreign currency is provided by foreigners who want to buy the exports of another nation. For example, the more that foreigners demand Canadian products, the more of their currencies they will supply in exchange for Canadian dollars, which they use to buy our products.

# HOW ARE EXCHANGE RATES DETERMINED?

We know that the demand for foreign currencies is derived in part from the demand for foreign goods, but how does that affect the exchange rate? Just as in the product market, the answer lies with the forces of supply and demand. In this case, it is the supply of and demand for a foreign currency that determine the equilibrium price (exchange rate) of that currency.

## The Demand Curve for a Foreign Currency

As Exhibit 2 shows, the demand curve for a foreign currency—the euro, for example— is downward sloping, just as a demand curve is in product markets. In this case, how- ever, the demand curve has a negative slope because as the price of the euro falls relative to the Canadian dollar (i.e., the euro depreciates in value), European products become relatively cheaper for Canadian consumers, who therefore buy more European goods. To do so, the quantity of euros demanded by Canadian consumers will increase to buy more European goods as the price of the euro falls. This is why the demand for foreign currencies is considered to be a derived demand.

## The Supply Curve for a Foreign Currency

The supply curve for a foreign currency is upward sloping, just as a supply curve is in product markets. In this case, as the price of the euro increases relative to the Canadian dollar (i.e., the euro appreciates in value), Canadian products will become relatively cheaper for European buyers and they will increase the quantity of dollars they demand. Europeans will, therefore, increase the quantity of euros supplied to the foreign exchange market by buying more Canadian products. Hence, the supply curve is upward sloping.

## Equilibrium in the Foreign Exchange Market

Equilibrium is reached where the demand and supply curves for a given currency inter- sect. In Exhibit 2, the equilibrium price of a euro is $1.20. As in the product market, if the Canadian dollar price of euros is higher than the equilibrium price, an excess

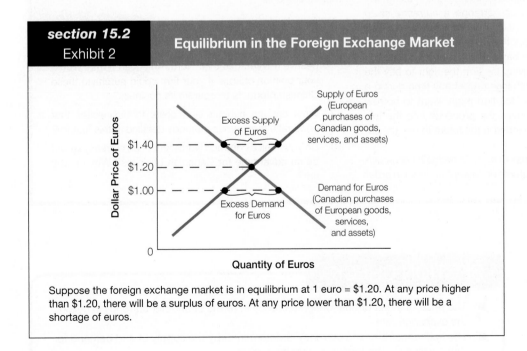

**section 15.2**
Exhibit 2

**Equilibrium in the Foreign Exchange Market**

Suppose the foreign exchange market is in equilibrium at 1 euro = $1.20. At any price higher than $1.20, there will be a surplus of euros. At any price lower than $1.20, there will be a shortage of euros.

quantity of euros will be supplied at that price, or a surplus of euros. Competition among euro sellers will push the price of euros down toward equilibrium. Likewise, if the dollar price of euros is lower than the equilibrium price, an excess quantity of euros will be demanded at that price, or a shortage of euros. Competition among euro buyers will push the price of euros up toward equilibrium.

## Business *CONNECTION*

### MANAGING TRANSACTION RISKS

Companies that trade internationally incur transaction fees, amounts payable and amounts receivable that expose the firm's cash flow to fluctuations in exchange rates. The risk is that the amount payable might increase if the foreign currency actually appreciates in value relative to the domestic currency between the time the payable was incurred and the date of payment. Similarly, if the international transaction results in an amount receivable, the foreign exchange risk is the risk that the amount to be received might drop in value if the foreign currency actually depreciates in value relative to the domestic currency between the time the receivable was incurred and the actual date of receipt.

What can businesses do to manage transaction exposure to fluctuations in foreign currencies? First, on an ongoing basis, the business should try to measure the net exposure it has to each foreign currency. The net exposure for each currency in a period is the amounts receivable less the amounts payable. Once this net amount is determined for each currency, the firm can manage the exposure using a variety of methods. For example, if the net amount is payable, the firm can buy a *futures* or *forward contract* to obtain the currency at a predetermined exchange rate in the future.

Alternatively, the firm can arrange a *currency swap* (involving the exchange of principal and/or interest on a loan in one currency for that in another currency) through a financial intermediary such as a bank, or it can buy a *call option* on the foreign currency (giving the firm the right to buy the currency at a specified exchange rate at any time during a specified period). At times, the firm might want to borrow its home currency and convert the proceeds into the foreign currency that will be needed in the future to pay the net amount payable.

*Hedging* reduces the risk of loss. To hedge a net receivable, the firm could sell a futures or forward contract in order to sell the currency at a predetermined exchange rate in the future. (Futures contracts and forward contracts normally yield similar results, but forward contracts are private agreements and so are more flexible than standardized futures contracts.) As in the case of payables, the firm could arrange a currency swap through a financial intermediary such as a bank, or sell a *put option* (which gives the holder the right to sell at a specified price within a fixed period) on the foreign currency. The firm could also consider borrowing the foreign currency and converting the proceeds into its domestic currency, repaying the loan with the net receivable in due course.

With some forward planning, the transaction risk associated with fluctuations in exchange rates can be lessened. This is especially important for companies that operate in nations that have significant amounts of foreign trade, and even for small- and medium-sized businesses that don't have any appreciable direct foreign trade. With the state of the world's global economy, no country and certainly no firm is immune to currency fluctuations. These days, all firms must understand the way that world currencies can affect their operations.

1. As a business owner interested in doing business in China, how do you feel about the Chinese government holding its currency at low rates to have competitive advantages over North American firms? Would your opinion change if your firm could purchase these Chinese products to operate its business?

2. What are the benefits and costs to businesses that undertake the various methods detailed in this feature?

3. Do you think a common North American currency would be an advantage for Canadian business? Why or why not?

## SECTION CHECK

- The price of a unit of one foreign currency in terms of another currency is called the *exchange rate.*
- The exchange rate for a currency is determined by the supply of and demand for that currency in the foreign exchange market.

# Equilibrium Changes in the Foreign Exchange Market

**section**
**15.3**

● What are the major determinants in the foreign exchange market?

## WHAT ARE THE MAJOR DETERMINANTS IN THE FOREIGN EXCHANGE MARKET?

The equilibrium exchange rate of a currency changes many times daily. Sometimes, these changes can be quite significant. Any force that shifts either the demand for or supply of a currency will shift the equilibrium in the foreign exchange market, leading to a new exchange rate. These factors include changes in consumer tastes for goods, changes in income, changes in tariffs, changes in relative interest rates, changes in relative inflation rates, and speculation.

### Increased Tastes for Foreign Goods

Because the demand for foreign currencies is derived from the demand for foreign goods, any change in the demand for foreign goods will shift the demand schedule for foreign currency in the same direction. For example, if a cuckoo clock revolution sweeps through Canada, German producers would have reason to celebrate, knowing that many Canadian buyers will turn to Germany for their cuckoo clocks. The Germans, however, will accept payment only in the form of euros, so Canadian consumers and retailers must convert their dollars into euros before they can purchase their clocks. The increased taste for European goods in Canada would, therefore, lead to an increased demand for euros. As shown in Exhibit 1, this increased demand for

| **section 15.3** Exhibit 1 | Impact on the Foreign Exchange Market of a Canadian Change in Taste, Income Increase, or Tariff Decrease |
| --- | --- |

An increase in taste for European goods, an increase in Canadian income, and a decrease in Canadian tariffs all have the potential to cause an increase in demand for euros, shifting the demand for euros to the right and leading to a higher equilibrium exchange rate.

**What impact will an increase in travel to Paris by Canadian consumers have on the Canadian dollar price of euros? In order for a consumer to buy souvenirs at the Eiffel Tower, she will need to exchange dollars for euros. This would increase the demand for euros and result in a new higher dollar price of euros.**

euros shifts the demand curve to the right, resulting in a new, higher equilibrium dollar price of euros.

## Canadian Income Increases or Reductions in Canadian Tariffs

Any change in the average income of Canadian consumers will also change the equilibrium exchange rate, *ceteris paribus*. If, on the whole, incomes increased in Canada, Canadians would buy more goods, including imported goods, so more European goods would be bought. This increased demand for European goods would lead to an increased demand for euros, resulting in a higher exchange rate for the euro. A decrease in Canadian tariffs on European goods would tend to have the same effect as an increase in incomes by making European goods more affordable. As Exhibit 1 shows, this would again lead to an increased demand for European goods and a higher equilibrium exchange rate for the euro.

## Changes in European Income, Tariffs, or Tastes

If European incomes rose, European tariffs on Canadian goods fell, or European tastes for Canadian goods increased, the supply of euros in the foreign exchange market would increase. Any of these changes would cause Europeans to demand more Canadian goods, and therefore more Canadian dollars in order to purchase those goods. To obtain those added dollars, Europeans must exchange more of their euros, increasing the supply of euros on the foreign exchange market. As Exhibit 2 demonstrates, the effect of this would be a rightward shift in the euro supply curve, leading to a new equilibrium at a lower exchange rate for the euro.

**section 15.3**
Exhibit 2

**Impact on the Foreign Exchange Market of European Change in Taste, Income Increase, or Tariff Decrease**

If European incomes increased, European tariffs on Canadian goods fell, or European tastes for Canadian goods increased, the supply of euros would increase. The increase in demand for dollars would cause an increase in the supply of euros, shifting it to the right, from $S_0$ to $S_1$, and leading to a lower exchange rate for the euro.

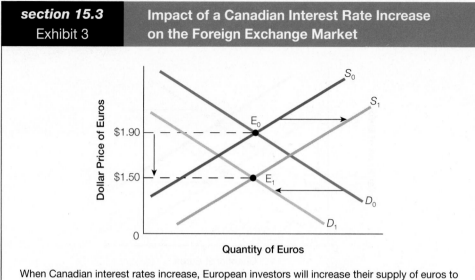

| **section 15.3** Exhibit 3 | **Impact of a Canadian Interest Rate Increase on the Foreign Exchange Market** |

When Canadian interest rates increase, European investors will increase their supply of euros to buy dollars—the supply curve of euros increases from $S_0$ to $S_1$. In addition, Canadian investors will also shift their investments away from Europe, decreasing their demand for euros and shifting the demand curve from $D_0$ to $D_1$. This will lead to a depreciation of the euro and an appreciation of the dollar.

## Changes in Relative Interest Rates

If interest rates in Canada were to increase relative to, say, European interest rates, other things equal, the rate of return on Canadian bonds would increase relative to that on European bonds. European investors would thus increase their demand for Canadian bonds, and therefore offer euros for sale to buy dollars to buy Canadian bonds, shifting the supply curve for euros to the right, from $S_0$ to $S_1$ in Exhibit 3.

In this scenario, Canadian investors would also shift their investments away from Europe by decreasing their demand for euros, from $D_0$ to $D_1$ in Exhibit 3. A subsequent lower equilibrium exchange rate ($1.50) would result for the euro due to an increase in the Canadian interest rate. That is, the euro would depreciate. In short, the higher Canadian interest rate would attract more investment to Canada and lead to a relative appreciation of the dollar and a relative depreciation of the euro.

You may remember this analysis from our discussion of monetary policy in the open economy in Chapter 13. When the Bank of Canada runs a contractionary monetary policy and causes Canadian interest rates to rise, the Canadian dollar appreciates, which leads to a decrease in net exports and a reduction in real GDP in the short run.

## Changes in Relative Inflation Rates

If Europe experienced an inflation rate greater than that experienced in Canada, other things being equal, what would happen to the exchange rate? In this case, European products would become relatively more expensive for Canadian consumers. Canadians would decrease the quantity of European goods demanded and, therefore, decrease their demand for euros. The result would be a leftward shift of the demand curve for euros.

**Impact of European Inflation Rate Increase on the Foreign Exchange Market**

If Europe experienced a higher inflation rate than Canada, European products would become relatively more expensive to Canadian consumers. As a result, those consumers would demand fewer euros, shifting the demand for euros to the left, from $D_0$ to $D_1$. At the same time, Canadian goods would become relatively cheaper to Europeans, who would then buy more dollars by supplying euros, shifting the euro supply curve to the right, from $S_0$ to $S_1$. The result: a new lower equilibrium exchange rate for the euro.

On the other side of the Atlantic, Canadian goods would become relatively cheaper for Europeans, leading Europeans to increase the quantity of Canadian goods demanded and, therefore, to demand more Canadian dollars. This increased demand for dollars translates into an increased supply of euros, shifting the supply curve for euros rightward. Exhibit 4 shows the shifts of the supply and demand curves and the new lower equilibrium exchange rate for the euro resulting from the higher European inflation rate.

## Expectations and Speculation

Every trading day, billions of Canadian dollars trade hands in the foreign exchange markets. Suppose currency traders believed Canada was going to experience more rapid inflation in the future than Japan. If currency speculators believe that the value of the dollar will soon be falling because of the anticipated rise in the Canadian inflation rate, those traders that are holding dollars will convert them to yen. This leads to an increase in the demand for yen—the yen appreciates and the dollar depreciates relative to the yen, *ceteris paribus*. In short, if speculators believe that the price of a country's currency is going to rise, they will buy more of that currency, pushing up the price and causing the country's currency to appreciate.

## SECTION CHECK

- Any force that shifts either the demand or supply curves for a foreign currency will shift the equilibrium in the foreign exchange market and lead to a new exchange rate. Changes in tastes, tariffs, income levels, relative interest rates, relative inflation rates, or speculation will cause the demand for and supply of a currency to shift.

# Flexible Exchange Rates

- How are exchange rates determined today?
- What are the advantages of a flexible exchange rate system?
- What are the disadvantages of a flexible exchange rate system?

## HOW ARE EXCHANGE RATES DETERMINED TODAY?

Since 1973, the world has essentially operated on a system of flexible exchange rates. With flexible exchange rates, currency prices are allowed to fluctuate with changes in supply and demand, without governments stepping in to prevent those changes. Prior to 1973, governments operated under what was called the *Bretton Woods fixed exchange rate system*, in which they would maintain a stable exchange rate by buying or selling currencies or reserves to bring demand and supply for their currencies together at the fixed exchange rate. The present system of flexible exchange rates evolved out of the Bretton Woods fixed-rate system and occurred by accident, not design. Governments were unable to agree on an alternative fixed-rate approach when the Bretton Woods system collapsed, so nations simply let market forces determine currency values.

## Government Intervention in the Exchange Rate System

To be sure, governments sensitive to sharp changes in the exchange value of their currencies do still intervene from time to time to prop up their currency's exchange rate if it is considered to be too low or falling too rapidly, or to depress its exchange rate if it is considered to be too high or rising too rapidly. However, present-day fluctuations in exchange rates are not determined solely by market forces. Economists sometimes say that the current exchange rate system is a **dirty float system**, meaning that fluctuations in currency values are partly determined by market forces and partly influenced by government intervention. Over the years, however, such governmental support attempts have been insufficient to dramatically alter exchange rates for long, and currency exchange rates have changed dramatically.

When exchange rates change, they affect not only the currency market but the product markets as well. For example, if Canadian consumers were to receive fewer and fewer British pounds and Japanese yen per Canadian dollar, the effect would be an increasing price for foreign imports, *ceteris paribus*. It would now take a greater number of dollars to buy a given number of yen or pounds, which Canadian consumers use to purchase those foreign products. It would, however, lower the cost of Canadian exports to foreigners. If, however, the dollar increased in value relative to other currencies, then the relative price of foreign goods would decrease, *ceteris paribus*. But foreigners would find that Canadian goods were more expensive in terms of their own currency prices, and, as a result, would import fewer Canadian products.

**dirty float system**
*a description of the exchange rate system that means that fluctuations in currency values are partly determined by market forces and partly influenced by government intervention*

**The exchange rate is the rate at which one country's currency can be traded for another country's currency. Under a flexible-rate system, the government allows the forces of supply and demand to determine the exchange rate. Changes in exchange rates occur daily or even hourly.**

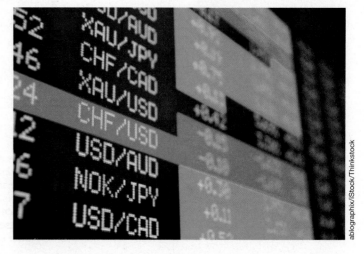

ablographix/iStock/Thinkstock

## WHAT ARE THE ADVANTAGES OF A FLEXIBLE EXCHANGE RATE SYSTEM?

As mentioned earlier, the present system of flexible exchange rates was not planned. Indeed, most central bankers thought that a system where rates were not fixed would lead to chaos. What in fact has happened? Since the advent of flexible exchange rates, world trade has not only continued but expanded. Over a one-year period, the world economy adjusted to the shock of a fourfold increase in the price of its most important internationally traded commodity, oil. Although the OPEC oil cartel's price increase certainly had adverse economic effects, it did so without paralyzing the economy of any one nation.

The most important advantage of the flexible-rate system is that the recurrent crises that led to speculative rampages and major currency revaluations under the Bretton Woods fixed-rate system have significantly diminished. Under the fixed-rate system, price changes in currencies came infrequently, but when they came, they were large: 20 percent or 30 percent changes overnight were fairly common. Now, price changes occur daily or even hourly, but each change is much smaller, with major changes in exchange rates typically occurring only over periods of months or years.

### Fixed Exchange Rates Can Result in Currency Shortages

Perhaps the most significant problem with a fixed-rate system is that it can result in currency shortages, just as domestic price and wage controls lead to shortages. Suppose we had a fixed-rate system with the price of one euro set at $1, as shown in Exhibit 1. In this example, the original quantity of euros demanded and supplied is indicated by curves $D_0$ and $S$, so $1 is the equilibrium price. That is, at a price of $1, the quantity of euros demanded (by Canadian importers of European products and others wanting euros) equals the quantity supplied (by European importers of Canadian products and others).

**section 15.4**
Exhibit 1                **How Fixed Exchange Rates Work**

An increase in demand for euros shifts the demand curve to the right, from $D_0$ to $D_1$. Under a fixed-rate system, this increase in demand results in a shortage of euros at the equilibrium price of $1, because the quantity demanded at this price, $Q_1$, is greater than the quantity supplied, $Q_0$. If the exchange rate is flexible, however, no shortage develops. Instead, the increase in demand forces the exchange rate higher, to $1.50. At this higher exchange rate, the quantity of euros demanded doesn't increase as much, and the quantity of euros supplied increases as a result of the now relatively lower cost of imports from Canada.

Suppose that some event happens to increase Canadian demand for Dutch goods. For this example, let us assume that Royal Dutch Shell discovers new oil reserves in the North Sea and thus has a new product to export. As Canadian consumers begin to demand Royal Dutch Shell oil, the demand for euros increases. That is, at any given dollar price of euros, Canadian consumers want more euros, shifting the demand curve to the right, to $D_1$. Under a fixed exchange rate system, the dollar price of euros must remain at $1, where the quantity of euros demanded, $Q_1$, now exceeds the quantity supplied, $Q_0$. The result is a shortage of euros—a shortage that must be corrected in some way. As a solution to the shortage, Canada may borrow euros from the Netherlands, or perhaps ship the Netherlands some of its reserves of gold. The ability to continually make up the shortage (deficit) in this manner, however, is limited, particularly if the deficit persists for a substantial period of time.

## Flexible Rates Solve the Currency Shortage Problem

Under flexible exchange rates, a change in the supply or demand for euros does not pose a problem. Because rates are allowed to change, the rising Canadian demand for European goods (and thus for euros) would lead to a new equilibrium price for euros, say, at $1.50. At this higher price, European goods are more costly to Canadian buyers. Some of the increase in demand for European imports, then, is offset by a decrease in quantity demanded resulting from higher import prices. Similarly, the change in the exchange rate will make Canadian goods cheaper to Europeans, thus increasing Canadian exports and, with that, the quantity of euros supplied. For example, a $40 software program that cost Europeans 40 euros when the exchange rate was $1 per euro costs less than 27 euros when the exchange rate increases to $1.50 per euro ($40 divided by $1.50).

## Flexible Rates Affect Macroeconomic Policies

With flexible exchange rates, the imbalance between debits and credits arising from shifts in currency demand and/or supply is accommodated by changes in currency prices, rather than through the special financial borrowings or reserve movements necessary with fixed rates. In a pure flexible exchange rate system, deficits and surpluses in the balance of payments tend to disappear automatically. The market mechanism itself is able to address world trade imbalances, dispensing with the need for bureaucrats attempting to achieve some administratively determined price. Moreover, the need to use restrictive monetary and/or fiscal policy to end such an imbalance while maintaining a fixed exchange rate is alleviated. Nations are thus able to feel less constraint in carrying out internal macroeconomic policies under flexible exchange rates. For these reasons, many economists welcomed the collapse of the Bretton Woods system and the failure to arrive at a new system of fixed or quasi-fixed exchange rates.

## WHAT ARE THE DISADVANTAGES OF A FLEXIBLE EXCHANGE RATE SYSTEM?

Despite the fact that world trade has grown and dealing with balance-of-payments problems has become less difficult, flexible exchange rates have not been universally endorsed by everyone. Several disadvantages of this system have been cited.

## Flexible Rates and World Trade

Traditionally, the major objection to flexible rates was that they introduce considerable uncertainty into international trade. For example, if you order some perfume from France with a commitment to pay 1000 euros in three months, you are not certain what the dollar price of euros, and therefore of the perfume, will be three months from now because the exchange rate is constantly fluctuating. Because people prefer certainty to uncertainty and are generally risk-averse, this uncertainty raises the costs of international transactions. As a result, flexible exchange rates can reduce the volume of trade, thus reducing the potential gains from international specialization.

Proponents of flexible rates have three answers to this argument. First, the empirical evidence shows that international trade has, in fact, grown in volume faster since the introduction of flexible rates. The exchange rate risk of trade has not had any major adverse effect. Second, it is possible to, in effect, buy insurance against the proposed adverse effect of currency fluctuations. Rather than buying currencies for immediate use in what is called the *spot market* for foreign currencies, one can contract today to buy foreign currencies in the future at a set exchange rate in the forward or futures market. By using this market, a perfume importer can buy euros now for delivery to her in three months; in doing so, she can be certain of the dollar price she is paying for the perfume. Since floating exchange rates began, booming futures markets in foreign currencies have opened in Toronto, Chicago, New York, and other foreign financial centres. The third argument is that the alleged certainty of currency prices under the old Bretton Woods system was fictitious because the possibility existed that nations might, at their whim, drastically revalue their currencies to deal with their own fundamental balance-of-payments problems. Proponents of flexible rates, then, argue that they are therefore no less disruptive to trade than fixed rates.

## Flexible Rates and Inflation

A second, more valid criticism of flexible exchange rates is that they can contribute to inflationary pressures. Under fixed rates, domestic monetary and fiscal authorities have an incentive to constrain their domestic prices because lower domestic prices increase the attractiveness of exported goods. This discipline is not present to the same extent with flexible rates. The consequence of a sharp monetary or fiscal expansion under flexible rates would be a decline in the value of one's currency relative to those of other countries.

Advocates of flexible rates would argue that inflation need not occur under flexible rates. Flexible rates do not cause inflation; rather, it is caused by the expansionary macroeconomic policies of governments and central banks. Actually, flexible rates give government decision makers greater freedom of action than do fixed rates; whether decision makers act responsibly is determined not by exchange rates but by domestic policies.

---

## SECTION CHECK

- Flexible rates are free to fluctuate based on market transactions, but governments occasionally intervene to increase or depress the price of their currencies.
- Changes in exchange rates occur more often under a flexible-rate system, but the changes are much smaller than the large overnight revaluations of currencies that occurred under the fixed-rate system. Under a fixed-rate system, the supply and demand for currencies shift, but currency prices are not allowed to shift to the new equilibrium, leading to surpluses and shortages of currencies.
- The main arguments presented against flexible exchange rates are that international trade levels will be diminished due to uncertainty of future currency prices and that the flexible rates would lead to inflation. Proponents of flexible exchange rates have strong counterarguments to those views.

# For Your Review

## Section 15.1

1. Indicate whether each of the following represents a receipt or payment in the Canadian current account.

   a. A Canadian imports a BMW from Germany.

   b. A Japanese company purchases software from a Canadian company.

   c. Canada gives $100 million in financial aid to Afghanistan.

   d. A Canadian company sells lumber to the United Kingdom.

2. Indicate whether each of the following represents a receipt or a payment in the Canadian capital account.

   a. A French bank purchases $100 000 worth of Canadian government bonds.

   b. Toronto Dominion Bank purchases a U.S. financial services company.

   c. A Canadian resident buys company shares in the Japanese stock market.

   d. A Japanese company purchases a shopping mall in Vancouver.

3. How is each of the following events likely to affect the Canadian merchandise trade balance?

   a. The European price level increases relative to the Canadian price level.

   b. The Canadian dollar appreciates in value relative to the currencies of its trading partners.

   c. The Canadian government offers subsidies to firms that export goods.

   d. The Canadian government imposes tariffs on imported goods.

   e. The United States experiences a severe recession.

4. How is each of the following classified, as a payment or as a receipt, in the Canadian balance-of-payments accounts?

| | **Receipt** | **Payment** |
|---|---|---|
| a. Canadians buy autos from Japan. | _____ | _____ |
| b. Canadian tourists travel to Japan. | _____ | _____ |
| c. Japanese consumers buy rice grown in Canada. | _____ | _____ |
| d. Canada gives foreign aid to Rwanda. | _____ | _____ |
| e. Lululemon, a Canadian company, earns profits in France. | _____ | _____ |
| f. Royal Dutch Shell earns profits from its Canadian operations. | _____ | _____ |
| g. Bombardier builds a new plant in Vietnam. | _____ | _____ |
| h. Japanese investors purchase Canadian government bonds. | _____ | _____ |

5. Following is a list of balance-of-payments figures for the economy of Bravo. All figures are in millions. Using this data, construct Bravo's balance of payments.

| | |
|---|---|
| Exports of goods | $50 |
| Merchandise trade balance | 10 |
| Net acquisition of financial assets | –45 |
| Imports of services | 20 |
| Net primary income | 5 |
| Exports of services | 10 |
| Financial account balance | 15 |
| Net secondary income | –15 |

6. Following is a list of balance of payments figures for the economy of Delta. All figures are in millions. Using this data, construct Delta's balance of payments.

| | |
|---|---|
| Exports of services | $320 |
| Imports of goods | 470 |
| Net secondary income | 30 |
| Net incurrence of liabilities | 160 |
| Imports of services | 410 |
| Exports of goods | 530 |
| Statistical discrepancy | 10 |
| Current account balance | 60 |

## Section 15.2

7. Assume that a product sells for $100 in Canada.

    a. If the exchange rate between British pounds and Canadian dollars is $2 per pound, what would be the price of the product in the United Kingdom?

    b. If the exchange rate between Mexican pesos and Canadian dollars is 8 pesos per dollar, what would be the price of the product in Mexico?

    c. In which direction would the price of the $100 Canadian product change in a foreign country if Canadians' tastes for foreign products increased?

    d. In which direction would the price of the $100 Canadian product change in a foreign country if incomes in the foreign country fell?

    e. In which direction would the price of the $100 Canadian product change in a foreign country if interest rates in Canada fell relative to interest rates in other countries?

8. Why is a strong Canadian dollar a mixed blessing?

9. When a Canadian dollar buys relatively more British pounds, why does the cost of imports from England fall in Canada?

10. How does an increase in domestic demand for foreign goods and services increase the demand for those foreign currencies?

11. As euros become cheaper relative to the Canadian dollar, why does the quantity of euros demanded by Canadians increase? Why doesn't the demand for euros increase as a result?

## Section 15.3

12. How is each of the following events likely to affect the value of the Canadian dollar relative to the euro?

    a. Interest rates in the European Union increase relative to those in Canada.

    b. The European Union price level rises relative to the Canadian price level.

    c. The Bank of Canada intervenes by buying Canadian dollars on the foreign exchange market.

    d. The price level in Canada rises relative to the price level in Europe.

13. What happens to the supply curve for Canadian dollars in the foreign exchange market under the following conditions?

    a. Canadians choose to buy more Chinese consumer products, instead of buying Canadian-made products.

    b. A Canadian mutual fund decides to sell its shares in Microsoft, deciding instead to invest in Government of Canada bonds.

14. How would each of the following affect the supply of euros, the demand for euros, and the dollar price of euros?

| Change | Supply of Euros | Demand for Euros | Dollar Price of Euros |
|---|---|---|---|
| Reduced Canadian tastes for European goods | | | |
| Increased incomes in Canada | | | |
| Increased Canadian interest rates | | | |
| Decreased inflation in Europe | | | |
| Reduced Canadian tariffs on imports | | | |
| Increased European tastes for Canadian goods | | | |

15. How would each of the following events impact the foreign exchange market?

    a. Canadian travel to Europe increases.

    b. Japanese investors purchase Canadian company shares.

    c. Canadian interest rates abruptly increase relative to world interest rates.

    d. Other countries become less politically and economically stable relative to Canada.

## Section 15.4

16. What will happen to the supply of dollars, the demand for dollars, and the equilibrium exchange rate of the dollar in each of the following cases?

| | Event | Supply of Dollars | Demand for Dollars | Equilibrium Exchange Rate |
|---|---|---|---|---|
| a. | Canadians buy more European goods | | | |
| b. | Europeans invest in Canadian stock markets | | | |
| c. | European tourists flock to Canada | | | |
| d. | Europeans buy Government of Canada bonds | | | |
| e. | Canadian tourists flock to Europe | | | |

17. If the demand for a domestic currency decreases in a country using a fixed exchange rate system, what must the central bank do to keep the currency value steady?

18. What is the uncertainty argument against flexible exchange rates? What evidence do proponents of flexible exchange rates cite in response?

# Answers to Odd-Numbered Problems

## CHAPTER 1: THE ROLE AND METHOD OF ECONOMICS

1. The definition of *economics* must recognize the central parts of the economist's point of view: Resources are scarce, scarcity forces us to make choices, and the cost of any choice is the cost of the lost opportunity with the highest value.

3. **a.** The first is positive and the other is normative. The first statement (a positive statement) expresses a fact or a testable theory that a higher income tax rate would generate increased tax revenues. The second statement (a normative statement) expresses an opinion regarding how any additional tax revenues should be used.
   **b.** Both are normative statements that express opinions. The first regards the relative value of studying physics as opposed to studying sociology, and the second regards the value of studying either physics or sociology.
   **c.** Both statements are positive. They are expressions of facts or testable theories regarding the relationship between the price of wheat and how much wheat will be purchased and produced.
   **d.** The first is positive and the other is normative. The first statement (positive) expresses a fact or testable theory regarding the relationship between the price of butter and how much will be purchased. The second statement (normative) is an expression of opinion about the social value of buying butter.
   **e.** Both statements are positive. They are expressions of fact or testable theory regarding demographic change.

5. **a.** This involves confusing correlation with causation.
   **b.** This involves confusing correlation with causation.
   **c.** This involves the fallacy of composition.
   **d.** This is a violation of the *ceteris paribus* conditions.
   **e.** There is no fallacy in this statement.

7. Economics is concerned with reaching generalizations about human behaviour. If you generalize on the basis of observed individual behavior, you risk committing the fallacy of composition. Generalizations based on observed group behaviour are likely to be both more realistic and useful (reliable).

9. The automobile freed Canadians to travel and helped to create the tourism business. New wants included motels, resorts, and theme parks. The increased importance of automobile and truck transportation also created the desire for more and better roads and highways. The automobile also allowed people to live farther from where they worked, so that people wanted more land and newer houses.

11. Since Sarah's time is probably worth more during the school year (it would cost part of her salary), the opportunity cost of the trip is higher in February than in July.

13. **a.** The opportunity cost of going to college or university includes the income you could have earned by working instead; it also includes the money spent on school-specific expenses like tuition and textbooks. Room and board and transportation would not necessarily be included, since you would need those services even if you were not going to school.
   **b.** The opportunity cost of missing a lecture includes the potential damage to one's grade in a course from not being present while important subject material is covered, as well as the knowledge's forgone value in the "real world." The magnitude of the opportunity cost depends partly on how much essential information the instructor provides during the missed class session or if any activities were conducted.
   **c.** The opportunity cost of spending $100 today is the $105 you could have spent next year. If you are withdrawing the money just to have cash in your pocket, the opportunity cost of holding money is the 5 percent interest you could have been earning.

   **d.** The opportunity cost of snowboarding the weekend before final examinations is the expected reduction in grades that will result, in addition to the cost of a lift ticket.

15. One of the most important resources used raising children has historically been the mother's time. As opportunities for women to hold jobs, start businesses, and participate in political life increase, the cost of using women's time for raising children increases. As the cost of the mother's time rises, fewer children are born.

17. **a.** $57; $88
   **b.** 43; 44; he would produce widgets as long as the price (marginal benefit) exceeded the marginal cost.

19. Marginal thinking involves incremental changes to a plan of action. All of the activities listed involve marginal thinking. When studying, one chooses whether or not to study for one more hour; when eating, one chooses whether or not to consume one more portion; when driving, one chooses whether or not to travel one more kilometre (or one more kilometre per hour); when shopping, one chooses whether or not to buy one more item or visit one more store; when getting ready for a night out, one chooses whether or not to spend another minute styling one's hair.

21. Positive incentives are those that either increase benefits or reduce costs and thus tend to increase the level of an activity. Both of the following are examples of positive incentives: (b) a trip to Hawaii paid for by your parents or significant other for earning an A in your economics course; (d) a subsidy for installing solar panels on your house. Negative incentives either reduce benefits or increase costs, and thus tend to decrease the level of the related activity or behaviour. Both of the following are examples of negative incentives: (a) a fine for not cleaning up after your dog defecates in the park; (c) a higher tax on cigarettes and alcohol.

23. The Chinese government was attempting to promote population control. As the world's most populated country, China has historically struggled with controlling population growth in its attempts to manage economic growth and national standards of living. The sanctions and penalties associated with not following the one-child policy would be considered negative incentives designed to discourage couples from having more than one child. The rewards and honours associated with following the policy would be considered positive incentives designed to promote adherence to the policy.

25. The opportunity cost to Fran of growing soybeans is the lost value because she can't grow corn. This opportunity cost is equal to $1800 (3000 kg × $0.60/kg). The opportunity cost of growing corn is the lost opportunity to grow and sell soybeans, which is equal to $2250 (1500 kg × $1.50/kg). Fran should specialize in soybeans, which is the crop with the lower opportunity cost. For each hectare of corn that Fran converts to soybeans, she will gain $450.

27. **a.** If the country or region with the lower opportunity cost produces the good, the opportunity cost of consuming that good is minimized.
   **b.** Trade allows people, regions, and countries to specialize in producing those goods in which they have the lowest opportunity cost, so reducing trade restrictions will encourage specialization, thereby increasing efficiency.

29. No, Karl is wrong. Markets provide important signals, and the signal being sent in this situation is that Adam should look for some other way to support his ambitions, something that society values. Remember the function of consumer sovereignty in the marketplace. Clearly, consumers were not voting for Adam's art.

## CHAPTER 1 APPENDIX: WORKING WITH GRAPHS

1. **A.** (−2, 2)
   **B.** (2, 1)
   **C.** (3, 2)

   **D.** (−1, −2)
   **E.** (2, −1)
   **F.** (−2, −1)
**3.** **a.** Semester 1
  **b.** Semesters 3 and 4
  **c.** Semester 2
  **d.** Total number of boys: 372; total number of girls: 366
**5.** **a.** 2
  **b.** −3
  **c.** −0.5
  **d.** Undefined
  **e.** 0

# CHAPTER 2: SCARCITY, TRADE-OFFS, AND PRODUCTION POSSIBILITIES

**1.** **a.**

  **b.** 1 side of beef; 6 kegs of beer; 9 kegs of beer
  **c.** 35 kegs of beer
  **d.** No; that combination is inside the production possibilities curve, which means more of one good could be produced without giving up any production of the other good.
  **e.** No; that combination is beyond the production possibilities curve and therefore unattainable.
**3.** This is the law of increasing opportunity cost in action. As you planted more and more of your land in wheat, you would move into some of the less fertile land and, consequently, wheat yields on this additional land would fall. If you were to go so far as to plant the entire island with wheat, you would find that some of the less fertile land would yield virtually no extra wheat. It would, however, have been great for cattle grazing—a large loss. So the opportunity cost of using that marginal land for wheat rather than cattle grazing would be very high.

**5.** **a.**

**b.**

| | A | B | C | D | E | F |
|---|---|---|---|---|---|---|
| | | −3 | | −6 | | −9 | | −12 | | −15 | | |
| | | | | | | | | | | | |
| Cheese | 45 | | 42 | | 36 | | 27 | | 15 | | 0 |
| Tractors | 0 | | 10 | | 20 | | 30 | | 40 | | 50 |
| | | +10 | | +10 | | +10 | | +10 | | +10 | |

As indicated in the table above, if the province of Quebec is to continually increase tractor production by 10 tractors it must give up increasing amounts of cheese—thus illustrating the law of increasing opportunity cost.

  **c.**

  **d.** The alteration in production from production alternative B to alternative E represents an increase in capital goods and a decrease in consumption goods. As a result, the prediction would be that the province of Quebec would experience greater economic growth in the future.
**7.** Investment in capital goods increases the future productive potential of an economy. Economy A will grow more rapidly, shifting the production possibilities curve outward to a greater extent over time, if it invests in a higher proportion of capital goods than does Economy B.

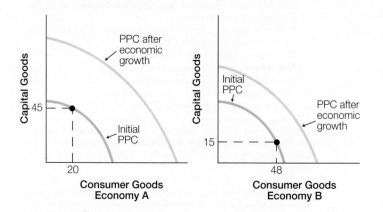

**9.** **a.** A country will fail to grow if its sacrificed consumption is spent in other countries.
  **b.** A country will fail to grow if it chooses not to sacrifice because it cares so much about current consumption.
  **c.** Growth will be limited if a country does not invest in human capital.
  **d.** A country will fail to grow if its sacrificed consumption is spent on goods other than capital goods.

11. The definition of a market focuses on the process of exchange not on the physical location where the exchange takes place. Therefore, even though online buyers and sellers are never actually in the same place, their behaviour still constitutes a market transaction due to the fact that goods and services are being exchanged.

13. Options (a), (b), and (c) would cause increases in the relative value and price of potatoes. In option (d), the reduction in the prices of potato substitutes would make alternatives more attractive and reduce the relative value and price of potatoes.

15. The market is global. Manufacturers sell to dealers throughout the world. Transportation costs are low relative to the costs of a laptop computer. Middlepersons make information about prices and quality easily available.

17. **a.** Product market
    **b.** Factor market
    **c.** Product market
    **d.** Factor market

    Furniture is a good purchased in the product market from firms. Labour is a resource that households sell to firms in the factor market. Restaurant food is a good purchased by consumers in the product market. Finally, Billy's entrepreneurial resource is paid a profit, which is the amount left over after all his other costs have been paid. This takes place in the factor market.

# CHAPTER 3: SUPPLY AND DEMAND

1. **a.**

| P | $Q_D$ |
|---|---|
| $5 | 4 |
| 4 | 8 |
| 3 | 12 |
| 2 | 16 |
| 1 | 20 |

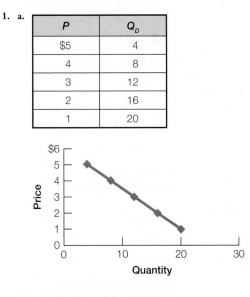

**b.**

| P | $Q_D$ |
|---|---|
| $5 | 6 |
| 4 | 12 |
| 3 | 18 |
| 2 | 24 |
| 1 | 30 |

**c.**

| P | $Q_D$ |
|---|---|
| $5 | 5 |
| 4 | 10 |
| 3 | 15 |
| 2 | 20 |
| 1 | 25 |

3.

5. **a.** Demand decreases (Determinant: Price of substitute falls)
   **b.** Demand decreases (Determinant: Price of complement rises)
   **c.** Demand increases (Determinant variable: Taste and preference increase)
   **d.** Demand increases (Determinant: Number of consumers increases)

7. **a.** Point B represents an increase in quantity demanded.
   **b.** Point E represents an increase in demand.
   **c.** Point F represents a decrease in demand.
   **d.** Point C represents a decrease in quantity demanded.

9. **a.** Hamburgers and ketchup are complements. An increase in the price of hamburger will decrease the demand for ketchup.

**b.** Coca-Cola and Pepsi are substitutes. An increase in the price of Coca-Cola will increase the demand for Pepsi.

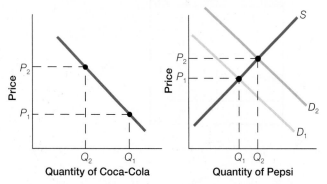

**c.** iPhones and iPhone cases are complements. An increase in the price of iPhones will decrease the demand for iPhone cases.

**d.** Golf clubs and golf balls are complements. An increase in the price of golf clubs will decrease the demand for golf balls, *ceteris paribus*.

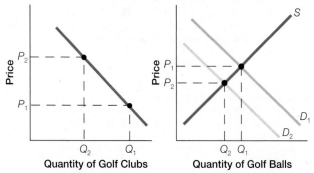

**e.** Assuming that skateboards and razor scooters are substitutes, an increase in the price of skateboards will increase the demand for razor scooters.

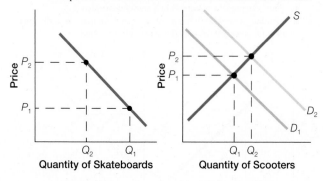

**11. a.** The shift from $D_0$ to $D_1$ is called an *increase in demand*.
  **b.** The movement from B to A is called a *decrease in the quantity demanded*.
  **c.** The movement from A to B is called an *increase in the quantity demanded*.
  **d.** The shift from $D_1$ to $D_0$ is called a *decrease in demand*.

**13.** The market price of wheat would have to rise for Felix to have the incentive to produce from the second field. Because costs are higher in the second field, Felix must receive a higher price to compensate him for his higher costs.

**15.**

| Quantity Supplied (barrels per month) | | | | |
|---|---|---|---|---|
| Price ($ per barrel) | Rolling Rock | Armadillo Oil | Pecos Petroleum | Market |
| $5 | 10 000 | 8 000 | 2 000 | 20 000 |
| 10 | 15 000 | 10 000 | 5 000 | 30 000 |
| 15 | 20 000 | 12 000 | 8 000 | 40 000 |
| 20 | 25 000 | 14 000 | 11 000 | 50 000 |
| 25 | 30 000 | 16 000 | 14 000 | 60 000 |

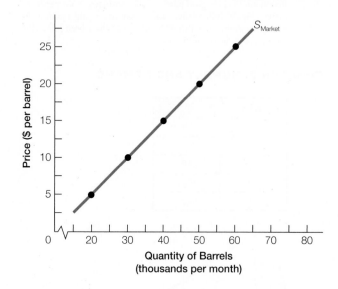

**17. a.** The shift from $S_0$ to $S_1$ is called an *increase in supply*.
  **b.** The movement from A to B is called an *increase in the quantity supplied*.
  **c.** The movement from B to A is called a *decrease in the quantity supplied*.
  **d.** The shift from $S_1$ to $S_0$ is called a *decrease in supply*.

**19. a.** An increase in the price of corn would increase the quantity of corn supplied, but not the supply of corn. This is because a change in the price of corn causes the market for corn to experience a movement in supply (as opposed to a shift in supply).
  **b.** An increase in the price of corn would decrease the supply of wheat, which is a substitute in production to corn. This is because a change in the price of corn—a substitute in production with wheat—causes the market for wheat to experience a shift in supply (as opposed to a movement).

**21. a.** Supply decreases (Determinant: Bad weather)
  **b.** Supply decreases (Determinant: Input prices rise)
  **c.** Supply increases (Determinant: Subsidies)
  **d.** Supply increases (Determinant: Technology advance)
  **e.** Supply decreases today (Determinant: Expected future price increases)

**23. a.** Point B represents an increase in quantity supplied
  **b.** Point C represents an increase in supply
  **c.** Point D represents a decrease in quantity supplied
  **d.** Point E represents a decrease in supply

**25.** An increase in wages, or any other input price, would decrease the supply of guitars (the supply curve would shift to the left), making fewer guitars available for sale at any given price, by raising the opportunity cost of producing guitars.

## CHAPTER 4: BRINGING SUPPLY AND DEMAND TOGETHER

1. When a price is above the equilibrium price, the quantity of a good or service willingly supplied by sellers exceeds the quantity willingly demanded by buyers. If sellers want to sell a greater quantity of goods or services, it is necessary to reduce the price (or otherwise improve the terms of sale, such as with free delivery or lower interest rate financing) in order to induce buyers to make additional purchases. Market forces thus exert a downward pressure on price in the direction of equilibrium price. A surplus is eliminated once price falls to the equilibrium price.

   If a price is below the equilibrium price, then the quantity of a good or service willingly demanded by buyers exceeds the quantity willingly supplied by sellers. In order to induce sellers to provide a greater quantity to the market-place, it is necessary for buyers to offer a higher price for the good or service. Market forces exert upward pressure on price in the direction of the equilibrium. A shortage is eliminated once price increases to the equilibrium price.

3. **a.** Equilibrium price = $400; Equilibrium quantity = 6.3 million units
   **b.** A shortage exists at any price below $400; market forces would raise the price of a tablet computer up to $400 to self-regulate a solution to this shortage situation.
   **c.** A surplus exists at any price above $400; market forces would lower the price of a tablet computer down to $400 to self-regulate a solution to this surplus situation.

5. **a.**

   **b.** $7; 40 units traded.
   **c.** Surplus. At $9, above the equilibrium price, there will be a surplus of 30 units of Z [the quantity supplied at $9 (50) minus the quantity demanded at $9 (20)].
   **d.** Shortage. At $3, below the equilibrium price, there will be a shortage of 60 units of Z [the quantity demanded at $3 (80) minus the quantity supplied at $3 (20)].
   **e.** $8, with 45 units traded (at the new supply and demand intersection).
   **f.** $6, with 50 units traded (at the new supply and demand intersection).

7. An increase in supply increases the quantity supplied at the original equilibrium price, but it does not change the quantity demanded at that price, meaning that it would create a surplus at the original equilibrium price.

9. **a.** Effect on the hamburger market of an increase in the price of hot dogs:

   **Hamburger Market**

**b.** Effect on cab trips of a decrease in the number of taxi companies:

**Halifax Cab Trips**

**c.** Effect of El Niño rainstorm destruction of strawberry crops:

**Supply of Strawberry Crops**

11. Even though the tuition "price" is the same in both cases, student demand for 10 a.m. classes is typically greater than for 8 a.m. classes. Students often prefer to sleep in later than punctual attendance at an 8 a.m. class would allow. A shortage of 10 a.m. class spaces relative to demand is the likely result. There may be a surplus of class spaces in 8 a.m. courses if the demand for early-morning classes is sufficiently low.

13. Fresh fruit is less expensive in the summer because the supply curve for fresh fruit shifts rightward in the summer, thus lowering equilibrium price and increasing equilibrium quantity.
   - This event is supply-side, since it deals with how growers are making product available for sale.
   - The event is a shift since the price of fresh fruit is not independently changing in the question.
   - The event is expansionary, since Canadian producers are seen as being able to make more fresh fruit available in the summer, when it is in season, as opposed to in the winter.

**Quantity of Fresh Fruit**

**15. a.** To get to point A would require a decrease in supply; to get to point B would require a decrease in supply and an increase in demand; to get to point C would require an increase in demand; to get to point D would require a decrease in supply and a decrease in demand; point E is the current equilibrium; to get to point F would require an increase in supply and an increase in demand; to get to point G would require a decrease in demand; to get to point H would require an increase in supply and a decrease in demand; and to get to point I would require an increase in supply.

**b.** The new equilibrium would be point F, because it is an increase in supply and an increase in demand. Equilibrium quantity would increase and if the magnitude of the demand and supply changes were equal, equilibrium price would remain constant.

**c.** Indeterminate; because one of the changes decreases supply and the other increases supply, we don't know what the net effect is on supply. If the effects were of the exact same magnitude, the result would be E; if the increase in supply was greater than the decrease in supply, the answer would be I; if the decrease in supply was greater than the increase in supply, the answer would be A.

**d.** C; A; A.

**e.** G; I; G.

**17.**

**a.** If the price ceiling is raised, the quantity supplied increases, the quantity demanded decreases, and the shortage is reduced; if the price ceiling is lowered, the quantity supplied decreases, the quantity demanded increases, and the shortage is increased.

**b.** The quantity supplied does not change, the quantity demanded increases, and the shortage is increased.

**c.** The quantity supplied increases, the quantity demanded does not change, and the shortage is decreased.

**19.** A price floor set above the equilibrium price for dairy products would result in a surplus. A price floor set below the equilibrium price would have no impact on the price or quantity of dairy products traded. (A price floor is a minimum allowed price, not a mandated market price.)

## CHAPTER 5: INTRODUCTION TO THE MACROECONOMY

**1.** Answers will vary based on information obtained at the time.

**3. a.** 80 percent (160 million/200 million)

**b.** 70 percent (140 million/200 million)

**c.** The labour force participation rate would become 65 percent (130 million/200 million).

**d.** Nothing; neither the adult population nor the size of the labour force would change.

**5. a.** Sam is a discouraged worker who is not actively seeking work and is therefore not considered to be unemployed.

**b.** The 12-year-old is under 15 years of age and therefore is not considered to be part of the labour force.

**c.** The factory worker is unemployed as long as she is looking for work.

**d.** The receptionist is considered to be employed, even though she would like to work more hours each week.

**e.** The high-school graduate is not actively seeking work and therefore is not considered to be unemployed.

**7.** Full-time students are not considered part of the labour force, so the labour force, the number officially unemployed, and the unemployment rate would all fall if a substantial group of unemployed people became full-time students.

**9. a.** Frictional; increase

**b.** Seasonal; increase

**c.** Frictional; decrease

**d.** Structural; increase

**e.** Structural; decrease

**f.** Cyclical; increase

**11. a.** A natural rate of 6 percent would account for the sum of structural and frictional unemployment. The additional 2 percent of unemployment above the natural rate would be attributed to cyclical unemployment.

**b.** Since cyclical unemployment cannot be negative, the only way actual unemployment can fall below the natural rate is if either structural or frictional levels of unemployment fall below their maximums (that is, below-average levels of either structural or frictional unemployment).

**13.** In a period of plentiful jobs, frictional unemployment can be higher because job opportunities are more plentiful. The fact that there is the potential of getting a better job stimulates mobility between jobs, which, in turn, increases frictional unemployment.

**15. a.** Retirees on fixed incomes: Hurt
Workers: Hurt (unless wages kept up with inflation)
Debtors: Help
Creditors: Hurt
Shoe-leather costs: Increase
Menu costs: Increase

**b.** Workers, debtors, and creditors would be unaffected. If retirees stayed on their fixed incomes, they would be hurt. Shoe-leather costs would be unaffected but menu costs would rise.

**17.** Price index 2016 = \$16/\$16 × 100 = 100
Price index 2017 = \$17.28/\$16 × 100 = 108
Price index 2018 = \$20/\$16 × 100 = 125
Inflation rate 2016–17 = (108 − 100)/100 = 8 percent
Inflation rate 2016–18 = (125 − 100)/100 = 25 percent
Inflation rate 2017–18 = (125 − 108)/108 = 15.7 percent

**19.** Unanticipated inflation would have a larger impact because it creates additional uncertainty and complicates business planning, and the risk discourages investment, which reduces economic growth.

**21.** Expansion phase

**23. a.** Year 3

**b.** Years 4, 5, and 6

**c.** Year 7

**d.** Years 1, 2, 8, 9, and 10

## CHAPTER 6: MEASURING ECONOMIC PERFORMANCE

**1.** The following are included in Canadian GDP calculations:

**a.** Cleaning services performed by a cleaning company

**d.** Prescription drugs manufactured in Canada and sold at a local pharmacy

**g.** Toxic waste cleanup performed by a local company

**h.** Car parts manufactured in Canada for assembly of a car in Mexico

**3.** Existing homes and used cars were both produced in the past and therefore aren't counted as part of current GDP. However, the services provided this year by real estate agents and used-car dealers are currently produced, so the market value of those services, measured by real estate agent commissions and the profits earned by used-car dealers, are included in GDP.

**5. a.** Ministry of Transportation snow-clearing services: Government spending

**b.** Automobiles exported to Europe: Exports

**c.** Refrigerator: Consumption (consumer durables)

**d.** Newly constructed four-bedroom house: Investment

**e.** Restaurant meal: Consumption

**f.** Additions to inventory at a furniture store: Investment

**g.** Purchases of new computers by Statistics Canada: Government spending

**h.** New steel mill: Investment

**7.**

| | |
|---|---|
| Consumption | $6500 |
| Consumption of durable goods | $1200 |
| Consumption of semi-durable goods | $1100 |
| Consumption of nonduable goods | $1800 |
| Consumption of services | $2400 |
| Investment | $1400 |
| Fixed investment | $ 800 |
| Inventory investment | $ 600 |
| Government expenditures on goods and services | $1600 |
| Government transfer payments | $ 500 |
| Exports | $ 500 |
| Imports | $ 650 |
| Net exports | −$150 |
| GDP | **$9350** |

**9.** Economic forecasters focus so much on consumption purchases and their determinants because consumption purchases are by far the largest component of GDP (in Canada, nearly 60 percent); what happens to consumption purchases is therefore crucial to what happens to GDP.

**11.**

| | |
|---|---|
| Personal consumption expenditures | $210 |
| Gross investment | 100 |
| Government current purchases of goods and services | 60 |
| Exports | 10 |
| Imports | (20) |
| **GDP–Expenditure Approach** | **$360** |
| Compensation of employees | $210 |
| Corporation profits before taxes | 62 |
| Net mixed income | 21 |
| Indirect taxes (less subsidies) | 35 |
| Capital consumption allowances (depreciation) | 32 |
| **GDP–Income Approach** | **$360** |

**13.**

| Year | Nominal GDP | Real GDP |
|---|---|---|
| 2014 | ($720 billion/100) × 100 = $720 billion | |
| 2015 | ($750 billion/102) × 100 = approximately $735 billion | |
| 2016 | ($800 billion/110) × 100 = approximately $727 billion | |
| 2017 | ($900 billion/114) × 100 = approximately $789 billion | |
| 2018 | ($960 billion/120) × 100 = $800 billion | |

The real economic growth rate for 2018 was 1.4 percent:

$$\left(\frac{\$800 - \$789}{\$789}\right) \times 100 = 1.4\%$$

**15. a.**

| Year | Nominal GDP (in millions of $) | GDP Deflator | Real GDP (in millions of $) |
|---|---|---|---|
| 2013 | 3237.0 | 93.3 | 3469.5 |
| 2014 | 3156.4 | 97.2 | 3247.3 |
| 2015 | 2995.3 | 100 | 2995.3 |
| 2016 | 3376.2 | 103.2 | 3271.5 |
| 2017 | 3517.6 | 101.4 | 3469.0 |
| 2018 | 3797.3 | 102.6 | 3701.1 |

**b.** The base year is 2015 (identified by the GDP deflator value of 100). The significance of the year 2015 is that the conversion of nominal GDP values into real GDP involves the conversion of current dollar output (nominal GDP) to constant dollar output (real GDP). The constant dollars that real GDP is measured in is 2015 dollars.

**c.** Looking at the behaviour of real GDP between 2013–14, the following trends are apparent: 2013–15, real GDP (production) is falling; 2015–18, real GDP (production) is rising.

**17. a.** Next year's real GDP can exceed next year's nominal GDP, but only if the price level falls. If the price level rises, next year's nominal GDP will exceed next year's real GDP.

**b.** Yes. It will happen when the population growth rate exceeds the growth rate of real GDP.

**c.** Since only what is produced can be consumed, if we measured all sources of output accurately, real per capita consumption possibilities can expand only when real per capita GDP grows. However, if, say, the underground (therefore, unmeasured) economy grew fast enough, real per capita consumption possibilities could increase despite measured decreases in real per capita GDP.

**d.** Leisure is valuable but its value is not counted in GDP. So changing amounts of leisure over time will not be accurately incorporated into GDP measures. Further, while a decrease in leisure (an increase in labour market work) would increase measured GDP, people would be better off only if their real after-tax wages were higher than the value of the leisure they gave up, which is not always the case (especially when workers don't take into account the fact that, as their wages increase, so do the prices of goods and services).

**19.** Since nonmarket activities are not included in GDP, GDP statistics understate the true value of total output more for developing economies than for developed economies. This statistical bias tends to make developed economies (with their smaller shares of nonmarket activities) look more productive relative to developing economies (with larger shares of nonmarket activities).

## CHAPTER 7: ECONOMIC GROWTH IN THE GLOBAL ECONOMY

**1. a.**

| | | |
|---|---|---|
| 0.5 percent | 140 | years |
| 1.0 percent | 70 | years |
| 1.4 percent | 50 | years |
| 2.0 percent | 35 | years |
| 2.8 percent | 25 | years |
| 3.5 percent | 20 | years |
| 7.0 percent | 10 | years |

**b.**

| | |
|---|---|
| 1.4 percent | $200 billion |
| 2.8 percent | $400 billion |
| 7.0 percent | $3200 billion |

**3. a.** Using the Rule of 70, Country A's real per capita GDP would double every 50 years (70/1.4) and Country B's real per capita GDP would double every 25 years (70/2.8). In the course of 100 years, Country B's real per capita GDP would double 4 times, while Country A's would double only 2 times. If they started at the same size, Country B's real per capita GDP would be 4 times that of Country A after that period of time, but since Country B started out one-fourth as large as Country A, their real per capita GDP would end up the same size in 100 years.

**b.** At 2.8 percent annual growth, Country A's real per capita GDP would double every 25 years, or 4 times in a century. At 3.5 percent annual growth, Country B's real per capita GDP would double every 20 years, or 5 times in a century. As a result, Country B's real per capita GDP would be twice that of Country A after a century.

**5.** Building dikes in Holland increased the quantity of usable land the Dutch had to work with; an increase in the amount of usable natural resources shifts a country's production possibilities curve outward.

**7.** It depends. Both capital investment and human capital investment increase productivity, so the answer depends on which is more productive in a given case. If education (human capital investment) is more productive, shifting from capital investment to human capital investment would increase the growth rate of real per capita GDP. If education (human capital investment) is less productive, shifting from capital investment to human capital investment would decrease the growth rate of real per capita GDP.

**9.** Each of the following will likely improve the productivity of labour:

**a.** On-the-job experience

**b.** College education

**d.** Improvements in management of resources

**11.**

|  | Real GDP Growth | Real GDP Growth per Capita |
|---|---|---|
| An increase in population | Increase | Indeterminate |
| An increase in labour force participation | Increase | Increase |
| An increase in population and labour force participation | Increase | Increase |
| An increase in current consumption | Decrease | Decrease |
| An increase in technology | Increase | Decrease |
| An increase in illiteracy | Decrease | Decrease |
| An increase in tax rates | Decrease | Decrease |
| An increase in productivity | Increase | Increase |
| An increase in tariffs on imported goods | Decrease | Decrease |
| An earlier retirement age in the country | Decrease | Decrease |
| An increase in technology and a decrease in labour force participation | Indeterminant | Indeterminant |
| An earlier retirement age and an increase in the capital stock | Indeterminant | Indeterminant |

**13.** Permanently lower marginal tax rates would increase the after-tax rate of return to each of these productive activities, which, over time, would increase the levels of the capital stock, education, and technology, and the amount of developed natural resources.

**15.**
  **a.** Real GDP will grow while real GDP per capita falls whenever the population growth rate exceeds the growth rate of real GDP.
  **b.** Country A has a higher real per capita GDP growth rate of 2 percent (4 percent real GDP growth minus 2 percent population growth). Country B's real per capita GDP growth rate is 1 percent (6 percent real GDP growth minus 5 percent population growth).

**17.** In countries with a fixed supply of land and little, if any, technological advance, Malthus's assumptions are not far from reality. Population control is one way to hold down the rate of population increase, to prevent the Malthusian subsistence wage result.

## CHAPTER 8: AGGREGATE DEMAND

**1.**
  **a.** 0.90
  **b.** 0.80
  **c.** 0.60
  **d.** $300\,000$; 0.75
  **e.** $120\,000$; 1.2

**3.**
  **a.** The quantity of investment demanded increases but the investment demand curve does not shift.
  **b.** The investment demand curve shifts to the left.
  **c.** The investment demand curve shifts to the right.
  **d.** The quantity of saving supplied increases but the saving supply curve does not shift.
  **e.** The saving supply curve shifts to the right.

**5.** An increase in current disposable income would cause an increase in private saving, shifting the saving supply curve to the right. A decrease in new technologies creating investment opportunities would shift the investment demand curve to the left, moving the equilibrium down along the saving supply curve but not shifting it.

**7.** In a simple closed economy, exports ($X$) and imports ($M$) are both zero. Therefore, $GDP - C - G$ is what is left over from income ($GDP$) after spending on consumption ($C$) and government purchases ($G$), which is what is available for investment ($I$). But in equilibrium, investment ($I$) must equal saving ($S$).

**9.** The aggregate demand curve shows what happens to the total quantity of all real goods and services demanded in the economy as a whole (i.e., the quantity of real GDP demanded) at different price levels. The downward slope of the aggregate demand curve is explained by the real wealth effect, the interest rate effect, and the open economy effect. All three effects tell us that as the price level in the economy increases, the various components of aggregate demand [$C$, $I$, and ($X - M$)] will decline.

**11.** A reduced price level increases the real value of people's currency holdings; as their wealth increases, so does the quantity of real goods and services demanded, particularly consumption goods. As a result, the aggregate demand curve, which represents the relationship between the price level and the quantity of real goods and services demanded, slopes downward.

**13.** The open economy effect occurs when a higher domestic price level raises the prices of domestically produced goods relative to the prices of imported goods. This reduces the quantity of domestically produced goods demanded (by both citizens and foreigners) as relatively cheaper foreign-made goods are substituted for them. As a result, the aggregate demand curve, which represents the relationship between the price level and the quantity of real goods and services demanded, slopes downward.

**15.** A rapid depletion of inventories is consistent with a rightward shift of the aggregate demand curve. As a result of an increase in aggregate demand, both output and investment are likely to increase.

**17.**
  **a.** Investment expenditures will increase.
  **b.** Investment expenditures will decrease.
  **c.** Investment expenditures will decrease.
  **d.** Investment expenditures will decrease.

**19.** Any recession in the United States reduces the incomes of Americans. As a result, Americans probably buy fewer Canadian goods and services, decreasing Canadian exports and aggregate demand.

## CHAPTER 9: AGGREGATE SUPPLY AND MACROECONOMIC EQUILIBRIUM

**1.** This is an example of the misperception effect. The misperception effect implies an upward sloping short-run aggregate supply curve.

**3.** Profit incentives are the key to understanding what happens to real output as the price level changes in the short run (before input prices completely adjust to the price level). When the prices of outputs rise relative to the prices of inputs (costs), as when aggregate demand increases in the short run, profit margins increase, which increases the incentives to produce, which leads to increased real output. When the prices of outputs fall relative to the prices of inputs (costs), as when aggregate demand decreases in the short run, profit margins decrease, which decreases the incentives to produce, which leads to decreased real output.

**5.**
  **a.** Shift *SRAS* to the right.
  **b.** Shift *SRAS* to the left.
  **c.** Shift *SRAS* to the right.
  **d.** No shift of the *SRAS* occurs (aggregate demand increases and there is a movement up along the *SRAS*).
  **e.** Shift *SRAS* to the left.

**7.**
  **a.** A decrease in *SRAS*
  **b.** A decrease in both *SRAS* and *LRAS*
  **c.** A decrease in *SRAS*
  **d.** An increase in both *SRAS* and *LRAS*

**9. a.**

With greater confidence in the economy, consumers would undertake more consumption. This increase in consumption would cause aggregate demand to increase. The price level increases, real output increases, employment increases, and unemployment decreases.

**b.**

The price level ends up higher, real output ends up back where it began at potential output, employment ends up back where it began at full employment, and unemployment ends up back where it began at the natural rate of unemployment.

**11. a.**

**b.**

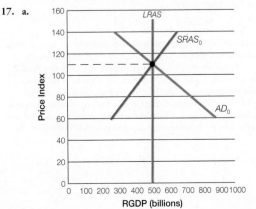

In the long run, the price level will end up lower than before, but real output and unemployment will return to their long-run equilibrium levels.

**13.** Cost-push inflation occurs when the short-run aggregate supply curve shifts to the left, pushing up prices. Demand-pull inflation occurs when the aggregate demand curve shifts to the right, pulling up prices. Examples will vary. Cost-push inflation may be caused by an increase in input prices, such as the price of crude oil or wages. Demand-pull inflation may be caused by an increase in consumer confidence or a decrease in taxes.

**15.** Sticky prices and wages is a term for input prices and wages that may be very slow to adjust in the downward direction. This delay in adjustment may cause the economy's self-adjustment mechanism to a recessionary gap to take a substantial amount of time.

**17. a.**

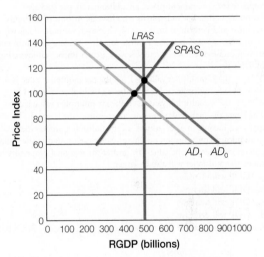

**b.** The equilibrium price level is 110 and the equilibrium level of real GDP is \$500 billion.

**c.** As the initial equilibrium (a short-run equilibrium) occurs at potential output, the economy is initially experiencing neither a recessionary nor an inflationary gap.

**d.**

| Price Index | $AD_0$ (billions) | $AS_0$ (billions) | $AD_1$ (billions) |
|:---:|:---:|:---:|:---:|
| 60 | \$875 | \$250 | \$750 |
| 70 | 800 | 300 | 675 |
| 80 | 725 | 350 | 600 |
| 90 | 650 | 400 | 525 |
| 100 | 575 | 450 | 450 |
| 110 | 500 | 500 | 375 |
| 120 | 425 | 550 | 300 |
| 130 | 350 | 600 | 225 |
| 140 | 275 | 650 | 150 |

New equilibrium price level is 100; equilibrium level of real GDP is \$450 billion.

**e.** At this short-run equilibrium, the economy of Adanac is experiencing a \$50 billion recessionary gap.

## CHAPTER 9 APPENDIX: THE KEYNESIAN AGGREGATE EXPENDITURE MODEL

**1. a.** An increase in interest rates
   **c.** A decrease in disposable income
   **d.** An increase in income taxes

**3. a.** An increase in consumer optimism
   **c.** An increase in the sale of exports
   **e.** An increase in government spending due to the outbreak of war

**5.** Both an increase in real wealth and more optimistic expectations would increase autonomous consumption, so together they must also increase autonomous consumption.

**7.** If the value of a consumer's stock market investments rose, it would increase autonomous consumption, but if household debt rose, it would reduce autonomous consumption. Since these effects are in opposite directions, the net effect would be indeterminate without more information.

**9.** If *MPC* was greater than one, the aggregate expenditure line would never intersect the 45-degree expenditure equals output line, so there would not be any stable equilibrium.

11. An increase in planned investment shifts up the aggregate expenditure line, increasing the equilibrium level of real GDP. An unplanned increase in investment, however, indicates that real GDP is greater than its equilibrium level, which will lead to a decrease in real GDP toward that equilibrium level.

13. An increase in unplanned investment would indicate real GDP was greater than its equilibrium level, leading to a decrease in real GDP produced. In contrast, an increase in planned investment would increase planned expenditures, tending to increase real GDP produced.

15. Net exports would decrease by $100 million, which would decrease autonomous expenditures by $100 million. Income would fall by

$$\$100 \text{ million} \times \left( \frac{1}{1 - 0.9} \right) = \$1 \text{ billion.}$$

## CHAPTER 10: FISCAL POLICY

1. **a.** An increase in government spending would decrease a budget surplus.
   **b.** An increase in government spending would increase aggregate demand.
   **c.** When the threat of a recession is developing

3. **a.** An increase in taxes would decrease a budget deficit.
   **b.** An increase in taxes would decrease aggregate demand.
   **c.** When the threat of an unsustainable, inflationary boom is likely

5. Suppose the government places an additional $1 per package tax on cigarettes. For individuals who have an income of $50, this amounts to 2 percent of their income; however, for individuals who have an income of $100, the tax amounts to only 1 percent. Uniform taxes, such as excise taxes on cigarettes, have a greater impact on lower-income individuals.

7. $MPC = 0.25$, multiplier value is 1.33, the tax multiplier value is 0.33
   $MPC = 0.5$, multiplier value is 2, the tax multiplier value is 1
   $MPC = 0.75$, multiplier value is 4, the tax multiplier value is 3

9. The larger the marginal propensity to consume, the larger the fraction of increased income in each "round" of the multiplier process that will go to additional consumption purchases. Since each round of the multiplier process will therefore be larger the greater the marginal propensity to consume, the multiplier will also be larger.

11. **a.** GDP will increase.
    **b.** GDP will decrease.
    **c.** GDP will increase.
    **d.** GDP will decrease.

13. A reduction in taxes of $10 billion; a reduction in taxes of $15.5 billion.

15.

**RGDP**

An economy can operate above the full employment level of output temporarily by using resources intensively. For example, factories can run three shifts per day, instead of two. Employees can be asked to work more hours each week. Firms can attempt to lure workers away from other firms by offering higher wages. As firms compete for scarce resources to maintain high levels of production, there will be upward pressure on input prices. When that occurs, the short-run aggregate supply curve will

shift to the left, moving the economy back toward full employment and the economy will experience inflation. The government may be able to prevent inflation from occurring by decreasing government spending. To determine the correct magnitude, the government would need to know the size of the multiplier and then use this value to determine the appropriate reduction in government spending to eliminate the $25 billion inflationary gap.

17. **a.** At point $E_3$
    **b.** The economy would end up at a long-run equilibrium at point $E_2$.
    **c.** The economy would end up at a long-run equilibrium at point $E_0$.
    **d.** At point $E_1$
    **e.** The economy would end up in long-run equilibrium at point $E_0$.
    **f.** The economy would end up in long-run equilibrium at point $E_2$.

19. Discretionary fiscal policy requires new policies to be made, so it is subject to time lags in deciding what the problem is and what to do about it, and in implementing a solution. Since automatic stabilizers do not require new policy to be adopted, those lags do not handicap it in the same way.

21. Some taxes, such as progressive income taxes and corporate profits taxes, automatically increase as the economy grows, and this increase in taxes restrains disposable income and the growth of aggregate demand below what it would have been otherwise. Similarly, these taxes automatically decrease in recessions, and this decrease in taxes increases disposable income and acts as a partial offset to the fall in aggregate demand. The result is reduced business cycle instability. Some transfer payment programs, such as Employment Insurance (EI), act as automatic stabilizers because when business cycle conditions worsen, people can start receiving increased transfer payments as soon as they become eligible (e.g., lose their jobs, in the case of EI). The same is true of some other welfare-type programs, such as the Canada Child Benefit (CCB).

23. **a.** An increase in government purchases increases the government budget deficit. The increased government borrowing increases the demand for loanable funds, which increases real interest rates, other things equal, which reduces, or crowds out, some of the investment that would otherwise have taken place.
    **b.** The crowding-out of investment increases the more that interest rates are bid up by the government borrowing and the more that investment falls as a result of increased interest rates.
    **c.** The greater the crowding-out effect, the smaller the net effect of a given increase in government purchases on aggregate demand.

25. In the short run, deficit reduction is contradictory fiscal policy; either tax increases and/or a reduction in government purchases will shift the aggregate demand curve to the left, and a lower price level and lower RGDP will result.

**RGDP**

27. Arguments can be made that the generation of taxpayers living at the time that the debt is issued shoulders the true cost of the debt, because the debt permits the government to take command of resources that would be available for other, private uses. However, the issuance of debt does involve some intergenerational transfer of incomes. Long after federal debt is issued, new generations of taxpayers are making interest payments to people of the generation that bought the bonds issued to finance that debt. If public debt is created intelligently, however, the "burden" of the

debt should be less than the benefits derived from the resources acquired as a result; this is particularly true when the debt allows for an expansion in real economic activity or for the development of vital infrastructure for the future.

# CHAPTER 11 MONEY AND THE BANKING SYSTEM

1. An economics professor might find it difficult to locate a trading partner willing to listen to economics lectures or receive economic advice in exchange for a new car. There may be significant search costs involved in locating such a trading partner. The professor might have to provide lectures in exchange for goods that are not desired, hoping that ultimately, after perhaps a series of trades, to be able to obtain a new car.

3. Having some good function as money lowers transaction costs, allowing increasing specialization and exchange to create increasing wealth for a society. That increase in wealth made possible by using money is why virtually all societies create something to function as money.

5. ATMs and online banking have made it far easier to convert savings accounts into chequing accounts, so savings accounts have become more liquid as a result.

7. Credit cards are not money. They are actually guaranteed loans available on demand to users, which can be activated by consumers. Credit cards are convenient substitutes for making transactions directly with money; that is, they are substitutes for the use of money in exchange.

9. Banks make money (profits) by loaning out their deposits at a higher interest rate than they pay their depositors. However, it is the extension of new loans in search of profits that creates new demand deposits, thereby increasing the stock of money.

11. A new $10 000 deposit adds that amount to both your demand deposit account and to the reserves of your bank. But only a fraction of the added reserves are required by the addition to your demand deposit account. The rest are excess reserves, which the bank will look to convert to interest-earning loans or other assets.

13. **a.**

| 10 percent | $10 000 |
|---|---|
| 15 percent | Zero (it has zero excess reserves) |
| 20 percent | Zero (it has insufficient reserves) |

**b.**

| 10 percent | $46 000 |
|---|---|
| 15 percent | $34 000 |
| 20 percent | $22 000 |

15. **a.** $45 000 ($4500 × 1/0.10)

**b.** If the bank had no excess reserves, the withdrawal would result in the bank having insufficient reserves to support its demand deposits. In this situation, the bank would have to either sell other assets or reduce the amount of existing loans to make up the reserve shortfall. If the bank had excess reserves, the withdrawal would result in these funds being used to meet that requirement in place of potential deposit creation. In this case, the resulting loss in potential deposit creation would be $500 ($50 × 1/0.10).

**c.** While the balance sheets of the individual banks are affected, there is no change in the level of demand deposits in the overall banking system.

17. Excess reserves equal $300 000. The potential expansion in demand deposits from loaning out these excess reserves equals $3 000 000 ($300 000 × 1/0.10).

## 10 Percent Desired Reserve Ratio

| Bank Balance Sheet (revised) | | | |
|---|---|---|---|
| **Assets** | | **Liabilities** | |
| Reserves | $ 500 000 | Demand deposits | $2 000 000 |
| Loans | 1 600 000 | Demand deposits (new) | 3 000 000 |
| Loans (new) | 3 000 000 | Total Liabilities | $5 000 000 |
| Buildings | 1 200 000 | Capital | 1 300 000 |
| **Total Assets** | **$6 300 000** | **Total Liabilities and Capital** | **$6 300 000** |

19. Excess reserves equal $50 000. The potential expansion in demand deposits from loaning out these excess reserves equals $250 000 ($50 000 × 1/0.20).

## 20 Percent Desired Reserve Ratio

| Bank Balance Sheet (revised) | | | |
|---|---|---|---|
| **Assets** | | **Liabilities** | |
| Reserves | $ 750 000 | Demand deposits | $3 500 000 |
| Loans | 2 500 000 | Demand deposits (new) | 250 000 |
| Loans (new) | 250 000 | Total Liabilities | $3 750 000 |
| Buildings | 1 250 000 | Capital | 1 000 000 |
| **Total Assets** | **$4 750 000** | **Total Liabilities and Capital** | **$4 750 000** |

# CHAPTER 12 THE BANK OF CANADA

1. The following are functions of the Bank of Canada:
   **b.** Lender of last resort
   **d.** Issue currency
   **e.** Regulate the money supply
   **f.** Loan reserves to banks
   **g.** Act as the bank for the Canadian government

3.

| Nonbank Public | | | |
|---|---|---|---|
| **Assets** | | **Liabilities** | |
| Securities | −$10 million | | |
| Demand deposits | +$10 million | | |

| Banking System | | | | Bank of Canada | | | |
|---|---|---|---|---|---|---|---|
| **Assets** | | **Liabilities** | | **Assets** | | **Liabilities** | |
| Reserves | +$10 million | Demand deposits | +$10 million | Securities | +$10 million | Reserves of banking system | +$10 million |

### 5 Percent Desired Reserve Ratio

| Banking System | | | |
|---|---|---|---|
| **Assets** | | **Liabilities** | |
| Reserves | $500 000 | Demand deposits | $10 million |
| Excess reserves | $9 500 000 | | |

Potential deposit creation      = $190 million ($9.5 million × 1/0.05)
(Bank system lending)
Initial demand deposit      = $10 million

Potential increase in money supply = $200 million

### 25 Percent Desired Reserve Ratio

| Banking System | | | |
|---|---|---|---|
| **Assets** | | **Liabilities** | |
| Reserves | $2 500 000 | Demand deposits | $10 million |
| Excess reserves | $7 500 000 | | |

Potential deposit creation      = $30 million ($7.5 million × 1/0.25)
(Bank system lending)
Initial demand deposit      = $10 million

Potential increase in money supply = $40 million

5. The potential change in the money supply is $250 000 ($50 000 × 1/0.20).
7. If the bank increases the desired reserve ratio to 12.5 percent, there would be insufficient reserves for the $1 000 000 in deposits by an amount of $25 000. The $100 000 in reserves would support only $800 000 in deposits, so this would decrease the money supply by $200 000. To acquire the additional desired reserves, the bank could sell securities or lower the amount of loans it has previously issued.
9. When the Bank of Canada pays for an open market purchase and its cheque (electronic payment) clears, it will add that amount of new reserves to the bank where the payment is deposited by the seller. The excess reserves created by that process lead to an expansion of bank loans of those reserves, creating additional demand deposits and therefore additional money.
11. **a.** $M \times V = P \times Q$
    **b.** Nominal GDP would double.
    **c.** The price level would double.
    **d.** Nominal GDP would double.
    **e.** Nominal GDP would remain unchanged.
13. If the money supply is $50 billion and velocity is 2 (so that $M \times V =$ $100 billion), the product of the price level and real output ($P \times Q$, or nominal output), must also be $100 billion. If the price level is 10, real GDP would equal the $10 billion (nominal output divided by the price level of 10, or $10 billion).

## CHAPTER 13: MONETARY POLICY

1. The higher the price level, the more money will be needed to conduct a given real value of transactions or for "just in case" precautionary purposes, so the demand for money for such purposes will be roughly proportionate to the price level. People will want to hold less money for either purpose when the opportunity cost of holding money—the interest rate—is higher.
3. Since holding wealth in the form of other financial assets is the alternative to holding it in the form of money, nonmoney financial assets are substitutes for holding money. When the earnings (interest) available on alternative financial assets rise, the opportunity cost of holding money instead also rises; so you would want to hold less money, other things being equal.

5. **a.**

**b.**

7. **a.**

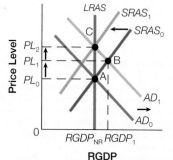

The short-run result is indicated by the movement from point A to point B in the diagram above.

**b.**

The long-run result is indicated by the movement from point B to point C in the diagram above.

9. An expansionary monetary policy shifts aggregate demand to the right. Starting from less than full employment, the result will be an increase in the price level, an increase in real output, and a decrease in unemployment as the economy moves up along the short-run aggregate supply curve. This increased output will be sustainable if it does not exceed the natural level of real output.
11. The more excess capacity there is in the economy, the flatter the short-run aggregate supply curve over that range of output. Therefore, the more excess capacity there is in the economy, a given shift in aggregate demand will result in a larger effect on real output and a smaller effect on price level.
13. Expansionary fiscal policy would increase aggregate demand. To counteract that fiscal policy effect on aggregate demand, the Bank of Canada would want to adopt contractionary monetary policy (through an open market sale of government securities and/or an increase in the target for the overnight interest rate), which would tend to reduce aggregate demand, other things being equal.

**15.** A desire on the part of the banking system to keep some excess reserves would reduce the money supply, other things being equal. The retention of some excess reserves essentially equates to a higher desired reserve ratio (R), which would have a negative effect on the size of the money multiplier. Such a change would thus at least partly offset the effects of the Bank of Canada's expansionary policy changes, which would hinder the Bank of Canada's ability to successfully use expansionary monetary policy to increase the money supply.

**17.** A movement up and to the left along a Phillips curve indicates an increase in inflation and a reduction in unemployment. A movement up and to the right along a short-run aggregate supply curve (achieved by a rightward shift in aggregate demand) indicates a price level increase (higher inflation) and an increase in RGDP (lower unemployment).

**19.** The argument is that once capacity utilization is high and unemployment is low, an increased part of the economy is already operating at or near full capacity; further fiscal or monetary policy stimulus primarily triggers inflationary pressures in sectors already at capacity, while eliminating decreasing amounts of unemployment in those fewer sectors where excess capacity and high unemployment still exist.

## CHAPTER 14: INTERNATIONAL TRADE

**1.** The nature of Canadian exports has been, and continues to be, predominantly natural resource–based products (energy products, and forestry and mineral products). As for imports, the Canadian economy imports predominantly finished goods (automotive products, consumer electronic and electrical equipment, motor vehicles, and consumer goods).

**3.** All countries are significantly affected by international trade, although the magnitude of the international trade sector varies substantially by country. International connections mean that any of a large number of disturbances that originate elsewhere may have important consequences for the domestic economy.

**5. a.**

|       | Fish per Day | Buckets of Berries per Day |
|-------|--------------|----------------------------|
| Bud   | 16           | 8                          |
| Larry | 8            | 8                          |
| Total | 24           | 16                         |

**b.** Bud is better off because he can produce and consume more fish while producing the same quantity of berries.

**c.**

|       | Opportunity Cost of a Bucket of Berries | Opportunity Cost of a Fish |
|-------|------------------------------------------|----------------------------|
| Bud   | 2 fish                                   | 1/2 bucket of berries      |
| Larry | 1 fish                                   | 1 bucket of berries        |

**d.** Bud has a comparative advantage in fishing and Larry has a comparative advantage in picking berries.

**e.** A total of 32 fish and 16 buckets of berries will be produced. There will be 8 more fish and no fewer berries produced if they both completely specialize according to their comparative advantage.

**7.** Country B has a comparative advantage over the production of Good X because its opportunity cost of producing 1 unit of Good X is only 1.5 units of Good Y versus 2 units of Good Y in country A. Country A has a comparative advantage in the production of Good Y.

**9. a.** The opportunity cost of producing X in Freeland is 2Y. The opportunity cost of producing X in Braveburg is 1.5Y.

   **b.** Since Braveburg has a comparative advantage in producing X, it will ship X to Freeland in exchange for Y produced in Freeland.

   **c.** The terms of trade will have to be between 1.5Y per X and 2Y per X (the opportunity costs of producing X in the two countries).

   **d.** Transaction costs, transportation costs, or tariffs greater than the net gains from trade (0.5 units of Y per X traded) would eliminate trade between Freeland and Braveburg.

**11.** Voluntary trade generates consumer surplus because a rational consumer would not purchase if he did not value the benefits of the purchase at greater than its cost, and consumer surplus is the difference between that

value and the cost he is forced to pay. Voluntary trade generates producer surplus because a rational producer would not sell additional units unless the price he received was greater than his marginal cost, and producer surplus is the difference between the revenues received and the costs producers must bear to produce the goods that generate those revenues.

**13.**

| Domestic Gains and Losses from Free Trade (exports) ||||
|------|-------------|------------|--------|
| Area | Before Trade | After Trade | Change |
| Consumer surplus (CS) | a + b | a | −b |
| Producer surplus (PS) | c | b + c + d | +(b + d) |
| Total welfare from trade (CS + PS) | a + b + c | a + b + c + d | +d |

**15.** When a country has a comparative disadvantage in producing a good, the marginal cost of importing is the world price, which is less than the additional value (along the domestic demand curve) for those units of expanded domestic consumption and less than the marginal cost of the domestic production crowded out. Therefore, there are net domestic gains to international trade (the gains to domestic consumers exceed the losses to domestic producers).

**17.** Tariffs raise the price of imported goods to domestic consumers, resulting in higher prices received by domestic producers as well. As a result, the higher price reduces domestic consumer surplus but increases domestic producer surplus.

**19.** The resources used in lobbying government in favour of zero-sum or negative-sum protectionism produce nothing of value, and so are losses from society's point of view. Those resources used up must be added to the traditional welfare cost measures. That is, the deadweight loss normally associated with tariffs and import quotas will likely underestimate the actual deadweight loss to society of these policies due to these additional resource costs.

**21.** Tariffs at least use the price system as the basis of trade. Tariff revenues end up in a country's treasury, where they can be used to produce benefits for the country's citizens or to reduce the domestic tax burden. Import quotas, however, transfer most of those benefits to foreign producers as the higher prices they receive.

## CHAPTER 15: INTERNATIONAL FINANCE

**1. a.** Payment
   **b.** Receipt
   **c.** Payment
   **d.** Receipt

**3. a.** Canadian exports will increase, imports decrease, and the trade deficit (surplus) will decrease (increase).
   **b.** Canadian exports will decrease, imports increase, and the trade deficit (surplus) will increase (decrease).
   **c.** Canadian exports will increase and the trade deficit (surplus) will decrease (increase).
   **d.** Canadian imports will decrease and the trade deficit (surplus) will decrease (increase).
   **e.** Canadian exports will decrease, imports increase, and the trade deficit (surplus) will increase (decrease).

**5.**

| Current Account | | | Capital Account | | |
|---|---|---|---|---|---|
| Exports of goods | $50 | | Net acquisition of financial assets | −$45 | |
| Imports of goods | 40 | | Net incurrence of liabilities | 60 | |
| Merchandise trade balance | | 10 | | | |
| Exports of services | 10 | | Financial account balance | | 15 |
| Import of services | 20 | | Statistical discrepancy | | −5 |
| Services trade balance | | −10 | | | |
| Net primary income | | 5 | Net balance | | $0 |
| Net secondary income | | −15 | | | |
| Current account balance | | −10 | | | |

**7. a.** 50 pounds
　**b.** 800 pesos
　**c.** The Canadian dollar would depreciate, making the Canadian product cheaper in the other country.
　**d.** The Canadian dollar would depreciate, making the Canadian product cheaper in the other country.
　**e.** The Canadian dollar would depreciate, making the Canadian product cheaper in the other country.

**9.** When a Canadian dollar buys relatively more British pounds, the cost of imports from England falls in Canada because it takes fewer Canadian dollars to buy a given number of British pounds to pay English producers. In other words, the price in Canadian dollars of English goods and services has fallen.

**11.** As euros become cheaper relative to the Canadian dollar, European products become relatively more inexpensive to Canadians, who therefore buy more European goods and services. To do so, the quantity of euros demanded by Canadian consumers will rise to buy them, as the price (exchange rate) for euros falls. The demand (as opposed to quantity demanded) of euros doesn't increase because this represents a movement along the demand curve for euros caused by a change in exchange rates, rather than a change in demand for euros caused by some other factor.

**13. a.** The supply curve for Canadian dollars shifts to the right.
　**b.** The supply curve for Canadian dollars shifts to the left.

**15. a.** Demand for euros increases (demand shifts right in the euro market), the Canadian dollar will depreciate, and the euro will appreciate, *ceteris paribus.*
　**b.** Demand for dollars increases (demand shifts right in the dollar market), the dollar will appreciate, and the yen will depreciate, *ceteris paribus.* Alternatively, you could think of this as an increase in supply in the yen market.
　**c.** International investors will increase their demand for dollars in the dollar market to take advantage of the higher interest rate. The dollar will appreciate relative to other foreign currencies, *ceteris paribus.*
　**d.** More foreign investors will want to buy Canadian assets, causing an increase in demand for dollars. The dollar will appreciate relative to other foreign currencies.

**17.** The central bank must purchase the currency using foreign reserve assets to prevent its currency from falling in value relative to foreign currencies.

# Glossary

**absolute advantage** the ability of a party (nation, region, or individual) to produce more of a good or service while using the same amount of inputs (p. 341)

**aggregate** the total amount—such as the aggregate level of output (p. 3)

**aggregate demand (*AD*)** the total demand for all final goods and services in the economy (p. 192)

**aggregate demand curve** a graphical representation that shows the inverse relationship between the price level and RGDP demanded (p. 201)

**aggregate supply (*AS*) curve** a graphical representation that shows the positive relationship between the price level and real gross domestic product supplied (p. 211)

**automatic stabilizers** changes in government spending or tax collections that automatically help counter business cycle fluctuations (p. 256)

**autonomous determinants of consumption expenditures** expenditures not dependent on the level of current disposable income (p. 233)

**average propensity to consume (*APC*)** the fraction of total disposable income that households spend on consumption (p. 193)

**bads** items that we do not desire or want (p. 11)

**balance of payments** the record of international transactions of a nation over a year (p. 358)

**balance sheet** a financial record that indicates the balance between a bank's assets and its liabilities plus capital (p. 281)

**bank rate** the interest rate that the Bank of Canada charges major financial institutions on the loans it extends to them (p. 301)

**bankers' deposit rate** the interest rate that the Bank of Canada pays major financial institutions on surplus funds deposited at the Bank of Canada (p. 301)

**bar graph** represents data using vertical bars rising from the horizontal axis (p. 32)

**barter** direct exchange of goods and services without the use of money (p. 271)

**boom** prolonged expansion in economic activity (p. 139)

**budget deficit** Government spending exceeds tax revenues for a given fiscal year. (p. 244)

**budget surplus** Tax revenues are greater than government expenditures for a given fiscal year. (p. 244)

**business cycles** short-term fluctuations in the economy relative to the long-term trend in output (p. 136)

**capital** the equipment and structures used to produce goods and services (p. 10)

**capital account** a record of the foreign purchases or assets in the domestic economy (a monetary inflow) and domestic purchases of assets abroad (a monetary outflow) (p. 360)

**capital-intensive** production that uses a large amount of capital (p. 24)

**causation** when one event causes another event to occur (p. 7)

*ceteris paribus* holding everything else constant (p. 5)

**change in demand** a change in a determinant of demand leads to a change in demand, a shift of the entire demand curve (p. 70)

**change in quantity demanded** a change in a good's price leads to a change in quantity demanded, a move along a given demand curve (p. 70)

**chartered banks** financial institutions that accept deposits and make loans (p. 279)

**circular flow model of income and output** an illustration of the continuous flow of goods, services, inputs, and payments between firms and households (p. 58)

**command economy** The government uses central planning to coordinate most economic activities. (p. 23)

**comparative advantage** occurs when a person or a country can produce a good or service at a lower opportunity cost than others can (p. 21)

**complement** An increase (a decrease) in the price of one good causes a decrease (an increase) in the demand of another good. (p. 71)

**Consumer Price Index (CPI)** a measure of the prices of a basket of consumable goods and services that serves to gauge inflation (p. 129)

**consumer sovereignty** Consumers vote on economic affairs with their dollars in a market economy. (p. 23)

**consumer surplus** the difference between what the consumer is willing and able to pay and what the consumer actually pays for a quantity of a good or service (p. 343)

**consumption (*C*)** purchases of consumer goods and services by households (p. 150)

**contraction** when the economy's output is falling—measured from the peak to the trough (p. 137)

**contractionary fiscal policy** use of fiscal policy tools to reduce output by decreasing government spending and/or increasing taxes (p. 244)

**correlation** two events that usually occur together (p. 7)

**cost-push inflation** a price level increase due to a negative supply shock or increase in input prices (p. 220)

**crowding-out effect** theory that government borrowing drives up the interest rate, lowering consumption by households and investment spending by firms (p. 258)

**currency** coins and banknotes that an institution or government has created to be used in the trading of goods and services and the payment of debts (p. 273)

**currency appreciation** an increase in the value of a currency (p. 362)

**currency depreciation** a decrease in the value of a currency (p. 363)

**current account** a record of a country's imports and exports of goods and services, net primary income, and net secondary income (p. 358)

**cyclical unemployment** unemployment due to short-term cyclical fluctuations in the economy (p. 125)

**deflation** a decrease in the overall price level (p. 128)

**demand** the quantity of a good or service that consumers are both willing and able to purchase over a period of time at various prices (p. 66)

**demand deposits** balances in bank accounts that depositors can access on demand (p. 274)

**demand-pull inflation** a price level increase due to an increase in aggregate demand (p. 219)

**depression** a severe recession (p. 139)

**derived demand** the demand for an input derived from consumers' demand for the good or service produced with that input (p. 364)

**desired reserve ratio** the percentage of deposits that a bank chooses to hold as cash reserves (p. 283)

**dirty float system** a description of the exchange rate system that means that fluctuations in currency values are partly determined by market forces and partly influenced by government intervention (p. 371)

**discouraged workers** people who have left the labour force because they could not find work (p. 120)

**disposable income** the personal income available after taxes (p. 157)

**dissaving** consuming more than total available income (p. 200)

**double counting** adding the value of a good or service twice by mistakenly counting intermediate goods and services in GDP (p. 148)

**durable goods** consumer goods that can be used repeatedly for more than one year, such as automobiles (p. 151)

**economic growth** an upward trend in the real per capita output of goods and services (p. 173)

**economics** the study of the allocation of our limited resources to satisfy our unlimited wants (p. 1)

**efficiency** getting the most from society's scarce resources (p. 54)

**empirical analysis** the examination of data to see if the hypothesis fits well with the facts (p. 5)

**employee compensation** all compensation paid to employees, including wages and salaries and the employers' social contributions (p. 156)

**entrepreneurship** the process of combining labour, land, and capital together to produce goods and services (p. 10)

**equilibrium price** the price at the intersection of the market supply and demand curves; at this price, the quantity demanded equals the quantity supplied (p. 94)

**equilibrium quantity** the quantity at the intersection of the market supply and demand curves; at this quantity, the quantity demanded equals the quantity supplied (p. 94)

**excess reserves** cash reserves that are in excess of desired reserves (p. 283)

**exchange rate** the price of one unit of a country's currency in terms of another country's currency (p. 362)

**excise tax** a sales tax on individual products such as alcohol, tobacco, and gasoline (p. 248)

**expansion** when output (real GDP) is rising significantly—the period between the trough of a recession and the next peak (p. 137)

**expansionary fiscal policy** use of fiscal policy tools to foster increased output by increasing government spending and/or lowering taxes (p. 244)

**expenditure approach** calculation of GDP by adding up how much market participants spend on final goods and services over a period of time (p. 150)

**expenditure multiplier** the multiplier that considers only the impact of consumption changes on aggregate expenditures (p. 239)

**exports (X)** the value of foreign expenditure on domestically produced goods and services (p. 153)

**factor (input) markets** the market in which households sell the use of their inputs (capital, land, labour, and entrepreneurship) to firms (p. 58)

**factor payments** wages (salaries), rent, interest payments, and profits paid to the owners of productive resources (p. 156)

**fallacy of composition** Even if something is true for an individual, it is not necessarily true for a group. (p. 7)

**fiat money** a means of exchange established by government declaration (p. 274)

**fiscal policy** use of government spending and/or taxes to alter RGDP and the price level (p. 243)

**fixed investments** all new spending on capital goods by producers (p. 152)

**fractional reserve system** a system in which banks hold reserves equal to some fraction of their demand deposits (p. 281)

**frictional unemployment** the temporary unemployment that results from workers searching for suitable jobs and firms looking for suitable workers (p. 123)

**GDP deflator** a price index that helps to measure the average price level of all final goods and services produced in the economy (p. 158)

**gold standard** a monetary system that defines the value of the dollar as equivalent in value to a certain amount of gold, thereby allowing direct convertibility from currency to gold (p. 278)

**goods** items we value or desire (p. 11)

**goods and services flow** the continuous flow of inputs and outputs in an economy (p. 58)

**gross domestic product (GDP)** the measure of economic performance based on the value of all final goods and services produced in a country during a given period of time (p. 148)

**human capital** the productive knowledge and skill people receive from education and on-the-job training (p. 10)

**hyperinflation** extremely high rates of inflation for a sustained period of time (p. 133)

**hypothesis** a testable proposition (p. 5)

**import quota** a legal limit on the imported quantity of a good that is produced abroad and can be sold in domestic markets (p. 350)

**imports (M)** the value of domestic expenditure on foreign-produced goods and services (p. 153)

**income approach** calculation of GDP based on the summation of incomes received by the owners of resources used in the production of goods and services (p. 155)

**income effect** At higher prices, buyers feel poorer, causing a lowering of quantity demanded. (p. 67)

**income flow** the continuous flow of income and expenditure in an economy (p. 58)

**individual demand curve** a graphical representation that shows the inverse relationship between price and quantity demanded (p. 67)

**individual demand schedule** a table that shows the relationship between price and quantity demanded (p. 67)

**individual supply curve** a graphical representation that shows the positive relationship between price and quantity supplied (p. 78)

**inferior good** If income increases, the demand for a good decreases; if income decreases, the demand for a good increases. (p. 72)

**inflation** a continuous rise in the overall price level (p. 128)

**inflationary gap** an output gap that occurs when the actual output is greater than the potential output (p. 219)

**innovation** applications of new knowledge that create new products or improve existing products (p. 179)

**inventory investment** all purchases by businesses that add to the stocks of goods kept by the firm to meet consumer demand (p. 152)

**investment (I)** the creation of capital goods to augment future production (p. 152)

**labour** the physical and mental effort used by people in the production of goods and services (p. 10)

**labour force** persons 15 years of age and over who are employed or are unemployed and seeking work (p. 117)

**labour force participation rate** the percentage of the population (aged 15 years and over) in the labour force (p. 121)

**labour-intensive** production that uses a large amount of labour (p. 24)

**land** the natural resources used in the production of goods and services (p. 10)

**law of demand** the quantity of a good or service demanded varies inversely (negatively) with its price, *ceteris paribus* (p. 66)

**law of increasing opportunity cost** As more of one item is produced by an economy, the opportunity cost of additional units of that product rises. (p. 46)

**law of supply** The higher (lower) the price of the good, the greater (smaller) the quantity supplied, *ceteris paribus.* (p. 77)

**leading economic indicators** factors that typically change before changes in economic activity (p. 140)

**legal tender** coins and banknotes officially declared to be acceptable for the settlement of debts incurred in financial transactions (p. 273)

**leverage** the use of borrowed money for the purpose of investing (p. 283)

**leverage ratio** the ratio of total assets to bank capital (p. 284)

**liquidity** the ease with which one asset can be converted into another asset or into goods and services (p. 276)

**long-run aggregate supply (LRAS) curve** the graphical relationship between RGDP and the price level when output prices and input prices can fully adjust to economic changes (p. 211)

**M2** currency outside chartered banks plus demand and savings deposits at chartered banks (p. 276)

**M2+** M2 plus demand and savings deposits at trust companies, mortgage loan companies, credit unions, caisses populaires, and other financial institutions (p. 276)

**macroeconomics** the study of the aggregate economy, including the topics of inflation, unemployment, and economic growth (p. 3)

**marginal propensity to consume (MPC)** the additional consumption resulting from an additional dollar of disposable income (pp. 194, 233)

**marginal propensity to save (MPS)** the additional saving that results from an additional dollar of income (p. 233)

**marginal thinking** focusing on the additional, or incremental, choices (p. 15)

**market** the process of buyers and sellers exchanging goods and services (p. 53)

**market demand curve** the horizontal summation of individual demand curves (p. 68)

**market economy** Goods and services are allocated based on the private decisions of consumers, input suppliers, and firms. (p. 24)

**market equilibrium** the point at which the market supply and the market demand curves intersect (p. 94)

**market failure** when the economy fails to allocate resources efficiently on its own (p. 56)

**market supply curve** the horizontal summation of individual supply curves (p. 78)

**means of deferred payment** the attribute of money that makes it easier to borrow and to repay loans (p. 273)

**measure of value** money as a common "ruler" of worth allowing for the comparison of diverse goods and services (p. 272)

**medium of exchange** the primary function of money, which is to facilitate transactions and lower transactions costs (p. 271)

**menu costs** the costs incurred by a firm as a result of changing its listed prices (p. 134)

**microeconomics** the study of the smaller units within the economy, including the topics of household and firm behaviour and how they interact in the marketplace (p. 3)

**mixed economy** Government and the private sector together determine the allocation of resources. (p. 24)

**monetary policy** the policy decisions that the Bank of Canada makes in managing the money supply and interest rates, consistent with its inflation-control objective (p. 300)

**money** anything generally accepted in exchange for goods or services (p. 271)

**money market** market in which money demand and money supply determine the equilibrium nominal interest rate (p. 310)

**money multiplier** measures the potential amount of demand deposit money that the banking system generates with each dollar of reserves (p. 287)

**multiplier effect** a chain reaction of additional income and purchases that results in total purchases that are greater than the initial increase in purchases (p. 250)

**national income accounting** a uniform means of measuring economic performance (p. 147)

**national saving** the sum of both private and public saving (p. 198)

**natural rate of unemployment** the amount of unemployment that is unavoidable, equal to the sum of frictional and structural unemployment when they are at a maximum (p. 125)

**negative incentives** incentives that either increase costs or reduce benefits, resulting in a decrease in the activity or behaviour (p. 19)

**negative relationship** when two variables change in opposite directions (p. 34)

**net benefits** the difference between the expected marginal benefits and expected marginal costs (p. 16)

**net domestic income at factor cost** a measure of income earned by the owners of factors of production (p. 156)

**net exports (X − M)** the value of total exports minus total imports (pp. 153, 195)

**net mixed income** the income of unincorporated businesses generated from the production of goods and services (p. 156)

**net operating surplus: corporations** the income of corporations and government business enterprises resulting from the production of goods and services (p. 156)

**nominal interest rate** the reported interest rate that is not adjusted for inflation (p. 134)

**nondurable goods** tangible consumer items that are typically consumed or used only once, such as food (p. 151)

**normal good** If income increases, the demand for a good increases; if income decreases, the demand for a good decreases. (p. 72)

**normative analysis** a subjective, biased approach (p. 8)

**open economy** a type of model that includes international trade effects (p. 194)

**open market operations** purchase and sale of government securities by the Bank of Canada (p. 301)

**opportunity cost** the highest or best forgone opportunity resulting from a decision (p. 13)

**overnight interest rate** the interest rate that major financial institutions charge each other for one-day loans (p. 300)

**peak** the point in time when the expansion comes to an end, when output is at the highest point in the cycle (p. 137)

**personal income** the amount of income received by households before taxes (p. 157)

**pie chart** a circle divided into proportionate slices that represent various quantities that add up to 100 percent (p. 32)

**positive analysis** an objective, value-free approach, utilizing the scientific method (p. 8)

**positive incentives** incentives that either reduce costs or increase benefits, resulting in an increase in the activity or behaviour (p. 19)

**positive relationship** when two variables change in the same direction (p. 34)

**potential output** the amount of real output the economy would produce if its labour and other resources were fully employed—that is, at the natural rate of unemployment (p. 126)

**price ceiling** a legally established maximum price (p. 104)

**price controls** government-mandated minimum and maximum prices (p. 104)

**price floor** a legally established minimum price (p. 104)

**price index** a measure of the trend in prices for a certain bundle of goods and services over a given time period (p. 128)

**price level** the average level of prices in the economy (p. 128)

**private saving** the amount of income that households have left over after consumption and taxes (p. 198)

**producer goods** capital goods that increase future production capabilities (p. 152)

**producer surplus** the difference between the lowest price at which a supplier is willing and able to supply a good or service and the actual price received for a given quantity of a good or service (p. 343)

**product markets** the markets for consumer goods and services (p. 58)

**production possibilities curve** the potential total output combinations of any two goods for an economy, given the inputs and technology available (p. 43)

**productivity** the amount of goods and services a worker can produce per hour (p. 176)

**progressive tax** The amount of an individual's tax rises as a proportion of income, as the person's income rises. (p. 247)

**proportional tax** designed so that all taxpayers are subject to the tax rate, regardless of earnings (p. 248)

**public saving** the amount of income that the government has left over after paying for its spending (p. 198)

**quantitative easing** the purchase of private- and public-sector securities by the central bank (p. 322)

**quantity theory of money and prices** a theory of the connection between the money supply and the price level when the velocity of money is constant (p. 306)

**real gross domestic product (RGDP)** the total value of all final goods and services produced in a given time period, such as a year or a quarter, adjusted for inflation (p. 116)

**real gross domestic product per capita** real output of goods and services per person (p. 160)

**real interest rate** the nominal interest rate minus the inflation rate (p. 134)

**recession** a period of significant decline in output and employment (p. 137)

**recessionary gap** an output gap that occurs when the actual output is less than the potential output (p. 219)

**regressive tax** The amount of an individual's tax falls as a proportion of income, as the person's income rises. (p. 248)

**relative price** the price of a specific good compared to the prices of other goods (p. 128)

**rent seeking** producer efforts to gain profits from government protections such as tariffs and import quotas (p. 352)

**research and development (R&D)** activities undertaken to create new products and processes that will lead to technological progress (p. 181)

**resources** inputs used to produce goods and services (p. 1)

**rule of rational choice** Individuals will pursue an activity if the expected marginal benefits are greater than the expected marginal costs. (p. 15)

**savings deposits** financial institution accounts containing funds that cannot be used directly for payment (p. 275)

**scarcity** the situation that exists when human wants exceed available resources (p. 10)

**semi-durable goods** consumer items that can be used more than once and have an expected lifetime of around one year, such as clothing (p. 151)

**services** intangible acts that people want (p. 11)

**shocks** unexpected aggregate supply or aggregate demand changes (p. 218)

**shoe-leather cost** the time and inconvenience cost incurred when individuals reduce their money holdings because of inflation (p. 134)

**shortage** where quantity demanded exceeds quantity supplied (p. 95)

**short-run aggregate supply (*SRAS*) curve** the graphical relationship between RGDP and the price level when output prices can change but input prices are unable to adjust (p. 211)

**slope** the ratio of rise (change in the *Y* variable) over the run (change in the *X* variable) (p. 38)

**specializing** concentrating on the production of one, or a few, goods or services (p. 21)

**stagflation** a situation in which lower growth and higher prices occur together (p. 220)

**store of value** Money provides a means of saving or accumulating purchasing power from the present and transferring it to the future. (p. 272)

**structural unemployment** unemployment that occurs due to a lack of skills necessary for available jobs (p. 124)

**subsidy** a program of financial assistance paid out to producers (p. 352)

**substitute** An increase (a decrease) in the price of one good causes an increase (a decrease) in the demand for another good. (p. 71)

**substitution effect** At higher prices, buyers increasingly substitute other goods for the good that now has a higher relative price. (p. 67)

**supply** the quantity of a good or service that producers are both willing and able to make available for sale (p. 77)

**surplus** where quantity supplied exceeds quantity demanded (p. 95)

**tariff** a tax on imported goods (p. 347)

**the economic problem** Scarcity forces us to choose, and choices are costly because we must give up other opportunities that we value. (p. 1)

**theory** an established explanation that accounts for known facts or phenomena (p. 4)

**time-series graph** shows changes in the value of a variable over time (p. 32)

**trough** the point in time when output stops declining; it is the moment when business activity is at its lowest point in the cycle (p. 137)

**underemployment** a situation in which workers have skills higher than necessary for a job (p. 120)

**unemployment rate** the percentage of the people in the labour force who are unemployed (p. 118)

**unintended consequences** the secondary effects of an action that may occur after the initial effects (p. 108)

**unplanned inventory investment** collection of inventory that results when people do not buy the products firms are producing (p. 238)

**variable** something that is measured by a number, such as your height (p. 33)

**velocity of money (*V*)** the average number of times that a dollar is used in purchasing final goods or services in a one-year period (p. 306)

**wage and price inflexibility** the tendency for prices and wages to only adjust slowly downward to changes in the economy (p. 222)

***X*-axis** the horizontal axis on a graph (p. 32)

***Y*-axis** the vertical axis on a graph (p. 32)

# Index

# The Role and Method of Economics

## Section 1.1 Economics: A Brief Introduction

- *What is economics?*

  Economics is the study of the allocation of our limited resources to satisfy our unlimited wants.

- *Why study economics?*

  Economics is a problem-solving science that teaches you to ask intelligent questions.

- *What distinguishes macroeconomics from microeconomics?*

  Macroeconomics deals with the aggregate, or total, economy, while microeconomics focuses on smaller units within the economy.

## Section 1.2 Economic Theory

- *What are economic theories?*

  Economic theories are statements used to explain and predict patterns of human behaviour.

- *Why do we need to abstract?*

  Economic theories, through abstractions, provide a broad view of human economic behaviour.

- *What is a hypothesis?*

  A hypothesis makes a prediction about human behaviour and is then tested.

- *What is the ceteris paribus assumption?*

  In order to isolate the effects of one variable on another, we use the *ceteris paribus* assumption.

- *Why are observations and predictions harder in the social sciences?*

  With its focus on human behaviour, which is more variable and less predictable, observation and prediction are more difficult in the social sciences.

- *What distinguishes between correlation and causation?*

  The fact that two events are related does not mean that one caused the other to occur.

- *What are positive analysis and normative analysis?*

  Positive analysis is objective and value-free, while normative analysis involves value judgments and opinions about the desirability of various actions.

## Section 1.3 Scarcity

- *What is scarcity?*

  Scarcity exists when our wants exceed the available resources of land, labour, capital, and entrepreneurship.

- *What are goods and services?*

  Goods and services are things that we value.

## Section 1.4 Opportunity Cost

- *Why do we have to make choices?*

  Scarcity means we all have to make choices.

- *What do we give up when we have to choose?*

  When we are forced to choose, we give up the next highest-valued alternative.

## Key Terms

**economics** *the study of the allocation of our limited resources to satisfy our unlimited wants. p. 1*

**resources** *inputs used to produce goods and services p. 1*

**the economic problem** *Scarcity forces us to choose, and choices are costly because we must give up other opportunities that we value. p. 1*

**macroeconomics** *the study of the aggregate economy, including the topics of inflation, unemployment, and economic growth p. 3*

**aggregate** *the total amount—such as the aggregate level of output p. 3*

**microeconomics** *the study of the smaller units within the economy, including the topics of household and firm behaviour and how they interact in the marketplace p. 3*

**theory** *an established explanation that accounts for known facts or phenomena p. 4*

**hypothesis** *a testable proposition p. 5*

**empirical analysis** *the examination of data to see if the hypothesis fits well with the facts p. 5*

**ceteris paribus** *holding everything else constant p. 5*

**correlation** *two events that usually occur together p. 7*

**causation** *when one event causes another event to occur p. 7*

**fallacy of composition** *Even if something is true for an individual, it is not necessarily true for a group. p. 7*

**positive analysis** *an objective, value-free approach, utilizing the scientific method p. 8*

**normative analysis** *a subjective, biased approach p. 8*

**scarcity** *the situation that exists when human wants exceed available resources p. 10*

- *Why are "free" lunches not free?*

Because the production of any good uses up some of society's resources, there is no such thing as a free lunch.

## Section 1.5 Marginal Thinking

- *What do we mean by marginal thinking?*

Economists are usually interested in the effects of additional, or incremental, changes in a given situation.

- *What is the rule of rational choice?*

The rule of rational choice states that individuals will pursue an activity if they expect the marginal benefits to be greater than the marginal costs, or $E(MB) > E(MC)$.

## Section 1.6 Incentives Matter

- *Can we predict how people will respond to changes in incentives?*

Incentives change the expected marginal benefits and expected marginal costs of certain behaviour. Therefore, when people are acting rationally, they respond to incentives in predictable ways.

- *What are positive and negative incentives?*

A negative incentive increases costs or reduces benefits, thus discouraging consumption or production, while a positive incentive decreases costs or increases benefits, thus encouraging consumption or production.

## Section 1.7 Specialization and Trade

- *Why do people specialize?*

Specialization is important for individuals, businesses, regions, and nations. It allows them to make the best use of their limited resources.

- *How do specialization and trade lead to greater wealth and prosperity?*

Specialization and trade increase wealth by allowing a person, a region, or a nation to specialize in those products that it produces at a lower opportunity cost and to trade for those products that others produce at a lower opportunity cost.

## Section 1.8 The Three Economic Questions Every Society Faces

- *What is to be produced?*

Every economy has to decide what to produce. In a decentralized market economy, millions of buyers and sellers determine what and how much to produce. In a mixed economy, the government and the private sector determine the allocation of resources.

- *How are the goods and services to be produced?*

The best form of production is the one that conserves the relatively scarce (more costly) resources and uses more of the abundant (less costly) resources. When capital is relatively scarce and labour is plentiful, production tends to be labour-intensive. When capital is relatively abundant and labour is relatively scarce, production tends to be capital-intensive.

- *Who will get the goods and services?*

In a market economy, the amount of goods and services one is able to obtain depends on one's income. The amount of one's income depends on the quantity and the quality of the scarce resources that the individual controls.

# Scarcity, Trade-Offs, and Production Possibilities

## Section 2.1 The Production Possibilities Curve

- *What is a production possibilities curve?*

  A production possibilities curve represents the potential total output combinations of any two goods available to a society, given its resources and existing technology.

- *What is efficiency?*

  Efficiency requires society to use its resources to the fullest extent—no wasted resources. If the economy is operating within the production possibilities curve, the economy is operating inefficiently.

- *How is opportunity cost measured?*

  The cost of altering production within the production possibilities curve framework, at efficiency, is measured in forgone units of the sole alternative.

- *What is the law of increasing opportunity costs?*

  A bowed production possibilities curve means that the opportunity costs of producing additional units of a good rise as society produces more of that good (the law of increasing opportunity costs).

## Section 2.2 Economic Growth and the Production Possibilities Curve

- *How do we show economic growth on the production possibilities curve?*

  Economic growth is represented by an outward shift of the production possibilities curve, indicating the possibility of producing more of all goods. Despite this, scarcity inevitably remains a fact of life.

- *How can we summarize the production possibilities curve?*

  The production possibilities model is an effective way of illustrating the economic concepts of scarcity, choice, opportunity costs, efficiency, and economic growth.

## Section 2.3 Market Prices Coordinate Economic Activity

- *What is a market?*

  Markets consist of buyers and sellers exchanging goods and services with one another.

- *What are the roles of buyers and sellers in a market?*

  Buyers determine the demand side of the market and sellers determine the supply side of the market.

- *How does a market system allocate scarce resources?*

  Through voluntary exchange and the price system, the market system provides a way for producers and consumers to allocate scarce resources.

- *What is a market failure?*

  A market failure occurs when an economy fails to allocate resources efficiently on its own.

## Key Terms

**production possibilities curve** *the potential total output combinations of any two goods for an economy, given the inputs and technology available* p. 43

**law of increasing opportunity cost** *As more of one item is produced by an economy, the opportunity cost of additional units of that product rises.* p. 46

**market** *the process of buyers and sellers exchanging goods and services* p. 53

**efficiency** *getting the most from society's scarce resources* p. 54

**market failure** *when the economy fails to allocate resources efficiently on its own* p. 56

**product markets** *the markets for consumer goods and services* p. 58

**factor (input) markets** *the market where households sell the use of their inputs (capital, land, labour, and entrepreneurship) to firms* p. 58

**goods and services flow** *the continuous flow of inputs and outputs in an economy* p. 58

**income flow** *the continuous flow of income and expenditure in an economy* p. 58

**circular flow model of income and output** *an illustration of the continuous flow of goods, services, inputs, and payments between firms and households* p. 58

## Key Exhibits/ Graphs

## Section 2.4 The Circular Flow Model

- *What are product markets?*

  In the product market, households are buyers and firms are sellers.

- *What are factor markets?*

  In the factor markets, households are the sellers and firms are the buyers.

- *What is the goods and services flow?*

  The goods and services flow represents the continuous flow of inputs and outputs in an economy.

- *What is the income flow?*

  The income flow represents the continuous flow of income and expenditure in an economy.

- *What is the circular flow model?*

  The circular flow model illustrates the flow of goods, services, and payments among firms and households.

# Supply and Demand

## Section 3.1 Demand

- *What is the law of demand?*

  The law of demand states that when the price of a good falls (rises), the quantity demanded rises (falls), *ceteris paribus*.

- *What is an individual demand schedule and curve?*

  An individual demand schedule is a table that shows the relationship between the price of a good and the quantity demanded.

- *What is a market demand curve?*

  A market demand curve shows the amount of a good that all the buyers in the market would be willing and able to buy at various prices.

## Section 3.2 Shifts in the Demand Curve

- *What is the difference between a change in demand and a change in quantity demanded?*

  A change in the quantity demanded describes a movement along a given demand curve in response to a change in the price of the good. A change in demand shifts the entire demand curve in response to a change in some determinant of demand.

- *What are the determinants of demand?*

  Some possible determinants of demand (demand shifters) are the prices of related goods, income, number of buyers, tastes, and expectations.

- *Can we review the distinction between changes in demand and changes in quantity demanded?*

### Change in Variable and Change in Demand

| Variable | Change in Variable | Change in Demand |
|---|:---:|:---:|
| 1. Price of a complement good | ↑ | ↓ |
| 2. Price of a substitute good | ↑ | ↑ |
| 3. Income (normal good) | ↑ | ↑ |
| 4. Income (inferior good) | ↑ | ↓ |
| 5. Number of buyers | ↑ | ↑ |
| 6. Tastes and preferences | ↑ | ↑ |
| 7. Expected future price | ↑ | ↑ |

## Key Terms

**demand** *the quantity of a good or service that consumers are both willing and able to purchase over a period of time at various prices* p. 66

**law of demand** *the quantity of a good or service demanded varies inversely (negatively) with its price, ceteris paribus* p. 66

**substitution effect** *At higher prices, buyers increasingly substitute other goods for the good that now has a higher relative price.* p. 67

**income effect** *At higher prices, buyers feel poorer, causing a lowering of quantity demanded.* p. 67

**individual demand schedule** *a table that shows the relationship between price and quantity demanded* p. 67

**individual demand curve** *a graphical representation that shows the inverse relationship between price and quantity demanded* p. 67

**market demand curve** *the horizontal summation of individual demand curves* p. 68

**change in quantity demanded** *a change in a good's price leads to a change in quantity demanded, a move along a given demand curve* p. 70

**change in demand** *a change in a determinant of demand leads to a change in demand, a shift of the entire demand curve* p. 70

**substitute** *An increase (a decrease) in the price of one good causes an increase (a decrease) in the demand for another good.* p. 71

**complement** *An increase (a decrease) in the price of one good causes a decrease (an increase) in the demand of another good.* p. 71

**normal good** *If income increases, the demand for a good increases; if income decreases, the demand for a good decreases.* p. 72

**inferior good** *If income increases, the demand for a good decreases; if income decreases, the demand for a good increases.* p. 72

**supply** *the quantity of a good or service that producers are both willing and able to make available for sale* p. 77

**law of supply** *The higher (lower) the price of the good, the greater (smaller) the quantity supplied, ceteris paribus.* p. 77

**individual supply curve** *a graphical representation that shows the positive relationship between the price and the quantity supplied* p. 78

**market supply curve** *the horizontal summation of individual supply curves* p. 78

## Key Exhibits/ Graphs

## Section 3.3 Supply

• *What is the law of supply?*

The law of supply states that the higher (lower) the price of the good, the greater (smaller) the quantity supplied.

• *What is an individual supply curve?*

The individual supply curve shows the positive relationship between the price and quantity supplied of a given good or service.

• *What is a market supply curve?*

The market supply curve is a graphical representation of the amount of goods and services that suppliers are willing and able to supply at various prices.

## Section 3.4 Shifts in the Supply Curve

• *What is the difference between a change in supply and a change in quantity supplied?*

A movement along a given supply curve is caused by a change in the price of the good in question. A shift of the entire supply curve is called a *change in supply*.

• *What are the determinants of supply?*

Input prices, the prices of related products, expectations, the number of suppliers, technology, regulation, taxes and subsidies, and weather can all lead to changes in supply (shifts in supply).

• *Can we review the distinction between a change in supply and a change in quantity supplied?*

### Change in Variable and Change in Supply

| Variable | Change in Variable | Change in Supply |
|---|---|---|
| 1. Input prices | ↑ | ↓ |
| 2. Price of substitute in production | ↑ | ↓ |
| 3. Price of complement in production | ↑ | ↑ |
| 4. Expected future price | ↑ | ↓ |
| 5. Number of suppliers | ↑ | ↑ |
| 6. Government regulation | ↑ | ↓ |
| 7. Taxes | ↑ | ↓ |
| 8. Subsidies | ↑ | ↑ |
| 9. Technology | ↑ | ↑ |

# Chapter in Review

## Bringing Supply and Demand Together

### Section 4.1 Market Equilibrium Price and Quantity

- *What are the equilibrium price and the equilibrium quantity?*

  The intersection of the supply and demand curve shows the equilibrium price and equilibrium quantity in a market.

- *What is a shortage and what is a surplus?*

  A surplus is where quantity supplied exceeds quantity demanded. A shortage is where quantity demanded exceeds quantity supplied.

### Section 4.2 Changes in Equilibrium Price and Quantity

- *What happens to equilibrium price and equilibrium quantity when the demand curve shifts?*

  Changes in demand will cause a change in the equilibrium price and quantity, *ceteris paribus.* An increase (decrease) in demand will cause an increase (decrease) in both equilibrium price and equilibrium quantity.

- *What happens to equilibrium price and equilibrium quantity when the supply curve shifts?*

  Changes in supply will cause a change in the equilibrium price and quantity, *ceteris paribus.* An increase (decrease) in supply will cause a decrease (increase) in equilibrium price and an increase (decrease) in equilibrium quantity.

- *What happens when both supply and demand shift in the same time period?*

  When there are simultaneous shifts in both supply and demand curves, either the equilibrium price or the equilibrium quantity will be indeterminate without more information.

### Section 4.3 Price Controls

- *What are price controls?*

  Price controls involve government mandates to keep prices above or below the market-determined equilibrium price.

- *What are price ceilings?*

  Price ceilings are government-imposed maximum prices. When price ceilings are set below the equilibrium price, shortages will result.

- *What are price floors?*

  Price floors are government-imposed minimum prices. When price floors are set above the equilibrium price, surpluses will result.

## Key Terms

**market equilibrium**  *the point at which the market supply and the market demand curves intersect  p. 94*

**equilibrium price**  *the price at the intersection of the market supply and demand curves; at this price the quantity demanded equals the quantity supplied  p. 94*

**equilibrium quantity**  *the quantity at the intersection of the market supply and demand curves; at this quantity, the quantity demanded equals the quantity supplied  p. 94*

**surplus**  *where quantity supplied exceeds quantity demanded  p. 95*

**shortage**  *where quantity demanded exceeds quantity supplied  p. 95*

**price controls**  *government-mandated minimum and maximum prices  p. 104*

**price ceiling**  *a legally established maximum price  p. 104*

**price floor**  *a legally established minimum price  p. 104*

**unintended consequences**  *the secondary effects of an action that may occur after the initial effects  p. 108*

## Key Exhibits/ Graphs

Section 4.1, Exhibit 1
Section 4.2, Exhibit 6
Section 4.2, Exhibit 7
Section 4.3, Exhibit 1
Section 4.3, Exhibit 2

# Notes

# Chapter in Review

## Introduction to the Macroeconomy

### Section 5.1 Macroeconomic Goals

- *What are the three major macroeconomic goals in Canada?*

  The three major macroeconomic goals in Canada are employment, price-level stability, and economic growth.

- *Are these macroeconomic goals universal?*

  Individuals have their own reasons for valuing certain goals more than others. As a result, there is debate as to what is most important for an economy.

### Section 5.2 Employment and Unemployment

- *What is the unemployment rate?*

  The unemployment rate is found by taking the number of people officially unemployed and dividing by the number in the labour force. Unemployment rates are higher for teenagers, men, and those living in eastern Canada.

- *Are unemployment statistics accurate reflections of the labour market?*

  No. The overall accuracy of the unemployment rate is impacted by factors such as discouraged workers, the treatment of part-time work, and the underground economy.

- *How long is someone typically unemployed?*

  Most people who become unemployed will find jobs soon. Yet, at the same time, most of the unemployment problem is a result of a relatively few people who are jobless for long periods of time.

- *What is the labour force participation rate?*

  Labour force participation measures the percentage of the adult population that is participating in the labour force. In Canada, women's labour force participation has increased dramatically over the past 40 years.

### Section 5.3 Different Types of Unemployment

- *What is frictional unemployment?*

  Frictional employment is temporary unemployment that results from workers searching for suitable jobs and firms looking for suitable workers.

- *What is structural unemployment?*

  Structural unemployment results when people who are looking for jobs lack the required skills for the jobs that are available, or a long-term change in demand occurs.

- *What is cyclical unemployment?*

  Cyclical unemployment is caused by short-term cyclical fluctuations in the economy, such as recessions.

- *What is the natural rate of unemployment?*

  When cyclical unemployment is eliminated, our economy is said to be operating at full employment, or at a natural rate of unemployment.

## Key Terms

**real gross domestic product (RGDP)** *the total value of all final goods and services produced in a given time period, such as a year or a quarter, adjusted for inflation* p. 116

**labour force** *persons 15 years of age and over who are employed or are unemployed and seeking work* p. 117

**unemployment rate** *the percentage of the people in the labour force who are unemployed* p. 118

**discouraged workers** *people who have left the labour force because they could not find work* p. 120

**underemployment** *a situation in which workers have skills higher than necessary for a job* p. 120

**labour force participation rate** *the percentage of the population (aged 15 years and over) in the labour force* p. 121

**frictional unemployment** *temporary unemployment that results from workers searching for suitable jobs and firms looking for suitable workers* p. 123

**structural unemployment** *unemployment that occurs due to a lack of skills necessary for available jobs* p. 124

**cyclical unemployment** *unemployment due to short-term cyclical fluctuations in the economy* p. 125

**natural rate of unemployment** *the amount of unemployment that is unavoidable, equal to the sum of frictional and structural unemployment when they are at a maximum* p. 125

**potential output** *the amount of real output the economy would produce if its labour and other resources were fully employed— that is, at the natural rate of unemployment* p. 126

## Section 5.4 Inflation

• *Why is the overall price level important?*

Price-level stability is a desirable goal because it limits inflationary costs. A continuous rise in the price level defines the case of inflation, whereas a fall in the overall price level defines the case for deflation.

• *How is inflation measured using the Consumer Price Index (CPI)?*

A price index allows us to compare prices paid for goods and services over time. The Consumer Price Index (CPI) is the best-known price index.

• *Is the CPI accurate?*

The substitution bias, quality bias, new outlet bias, and new product bias are all reasons why the CPI overstates the true inflation rate.

• *Who are the winners and losers during inflation?*

Inflation generally hurts creditors and those on fixed incomes and pensions; debtors generally benefit from inflation.

• *What are the costs of inflation?*

Unanticipated inflation causes unpredictable transfers of wealth and reduces the efficiency of the market system by distorting price signals.

• *What is the relationship between inflation and interest rates?*

The nominal interest rate is the actual amount of interest you pay. The real interest rate is the nominal rate minus the inflation rate. Inflationary expectations tend to increase nominal interest rates.

## Section 5.5 Economic Fluctuations

• *What are short-term economic fluctuations?*

Business cycles (or economic fluctuations) are short-term fluctuations in the amount of economic activity, relative to the long-term growth trend in output.

• *What are the four phases of a business cycle?*

The four phases of a business cycle are expansion, peak, contraction, and trough.

• *How long does a business cycle last?*

Recessions occur during the contraction phase of a business cycle. Severe, long-term recessions are called *depressions*, while prolonged expansions are referred to as *booms*. The economy often goes through short-term contractions even during a long-term growth trend. Overall, the duration of any one business is uncertain.

## Key Equations

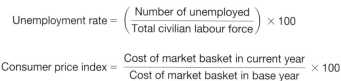

$$\text{Unemployment rate} = \left( \frac{\text{Number of unemployed}}{\text{Total civilian labour force}} \right) \times 100$$

$$\text{Consumer price index} = \frac{\text{Cost of market basket in current year}}{\text{Cost of market basket in base year}} \times 100$$

$$\text{Real interest rate} = \text{Nominal interest rate} - \text{Inflation rate}$$

## Key Exhibits/Graphs

Section 5.5, Exhibit 2

# Measuring Economic Performance

## Section 6.1 National Income Accounting: Measuring Economic Performance

- *Why do we measure our economy's performance?*

  We measure our economy's status in order to see how its performance has changed over time. These economic measurements are important to government officials, private businesses, and investors.

- *What is gross domestic product (GDP)?*

  Gross domestic product (GDP) is the value of all final goods and services produced within a country during a given time period. The two different ways to measure GDP are the expenditure approach and the income approach.

## Section 6.2 The Expenditure Approach to Measuring GDP

- *What is the expenditure approach to measuring GDP?*

  The expenditure approach to measuring GDP involves adding up the purchases of final goods and services by market participants. Four categories of spending are used in the GDP calculation: consumption (C), investment (I), government purchases (G), and net exports (X – M).

- *What is consumption (C)?*

  Consumption includes spending on nondurable consumer goods—tangible items that are usually consumed or used only once; semi-durable goods—items that can be used more than once and have an expected lifetime of around one year; durable consumer goods—items that can be used repeatedly for more than one year; and services—intangible items of value.

- *What is investment (I)?*

  Fixed investment includes all spending on capital goods, such as machinery, tools, and buildings. Inventory investment includes the net expenditures by businesses to increase their inventories.

- *What are government purchases (G)?*

  Purchases of goods and services are the only part of government spending included in GDP. Transfer payments are not included in these calculations because that spending is not payment for a newly produced good or service.

- *What are net exports (X – M)?*

  Net exports are calculated by subtracting total imports from total exports.

## Section 6.3 The Income Approach to Measuring GDP

- *What is the income approach to measuring GDP?*

  The income approach to measuring GDP involves summing the incomes received by the producers of goods and services. These payments to the owners of productive resources are also known as *factor payments*. The income approach to GDP adds together wages and salaries, corporate profits, interest income, and net income of farm and unincorporated businesses to obtain net domestic income at factor cost. Adding indirect taxes less subsidies and depreciation to net domestic income gives GDP.

- *What do personal income and disposable income measure?*

  Personal income measures the amount of income received by households (including transfer payments) before taxes. Disposable income is the personal income available after taxes.

## Key Terms

**national income accounting** *a uniform means of measuring economic performance* p. 147

**gross domestic product (GDP)** *the measure of economic performance based on the value of all final goods and services produced in a country in a given period of time* p. 148

**double counting** *adding the value of a good or service twice by mistakenly counting intermediate goods and services in GDP* p. 148

**expenditure approach** *calculation of GDP by adding up how much market participants spend on final goods and services over a period of time* p. 150

**consumption (C)** *purchases of consumer goods and services by households* p. 150

**nondurable goods** *tangible consumer items that are typically consumed or used only once, such as food* p. 151

**semi-durable goods** *consumer items that can be used more than once and have an expected lifetime of around one year, such as clothing* p. 151

**durable goods** *consumer goods that can be used repeatedly for more than one year, such as automobiles* p. 151

**investment (I)** *the creation of capital goods to augment future production* p. 152

**fixed investments** *all new spending on capital goods by producers* p. 152

**producer goods** *capital goods that increase future production capabilities* p. 152

**inventory investment** *all purchases by businesses that add to the stocks of goods kept by the firm to meet consumer demand* p. 152

## Key Exhibits/ Graphs

## Section 6.4 Issues with Calculating an Accurate GDP

- *What are the problems with GDP in measuring output?*

  It is difficult to compare nominal GDP over time because of the changing value of money over time.

- *How is real GDP calculated?*

  The GDP deflator is a price index that measures the average level of prices of all final goods and services produced in the economy. It is used to convert nominal measures of GDP into equivalent real measures of GDP.

- *What is real GDP per capita?*

  Real GDP per capita is real output of goods and services per person. In some cases, real GDP may increase, but real GDP per capita may actually drop as a result of population growth.

## Section 6.5 Problems with GDP as a Measure of Economic Welfare

- *What are some of the deficiencies of GDP as a measure of economic welfare?*

  Several factors make it difficult to use GDP as a welfare indicator, including nonmarket transactions, the underground economy, leisure, and externalities. Nonmarket transactions are the exchanges of goods and services that do not occur in traditional markets, so no money is exchanged. The underground economy is the unreported production and income that come from certain legal and illegal activities. The presence of positive and negative externalities also make it difficult to measure GDP accurately.

## Key Equations

$$GDP = C + I + G + (X - M)$$

$$Net\ investment = Gross\ investment - Depreciation$$

$$Real\ GDP = \frac{Nominal\ GDP}{GDP\ deflator} \times 100$$

## Economic Growth in the Global Economy

### Section 7.1 Economic Growth

- *How does economic growth differ from the business cycle?*

  Economic growth refers to the long-run trend rate of growth for an economy. Business cycles refer to the short-run fluctuations in economic activity around this trend rate of growth.

- *What is economic growth?*

  Economic growth is usually measured by the annual percentage change in real output of goods and services per capita. Improvements in and greater stocks of land, labour, capital, and entrepreneurial activity will lead to greater economic growth and shift the production possibilities curve outward.

- *What is the Rule of 70?*

  According to the Rule of 70, if you take a nation's growth rate and divide it into 70, you have the approximate time it will take to double the income level.

### Section 7.2 Determinants of Economic Growth

- *What factors contribute to economic growth?*

  The factors that contribute to economic growth are the same factors that determine growth in productivity. They include physical capital, quantity and quality of labour resources, natural resources, and technology.

### Section 7.3 Public Policy and Economic Growth

- *What policies can a nation pursue to increase economic growth?*

  Generally speaking, those policies and institutional structures that promote higher levels of saving, more research and development, better protection of private property rights, freer trade, and more education will lead to greater economic growth.

- *Can rates of economic growth between different economies converge?*

  While certain factors such as the ability to adopt existing technology would seem to allow developing nations to grow faster than developed nations, population growth and low literacy rates tend to have the opposite effect. Therefore, there seems to be no clear indication that rates of economic growth between economies will converge

### Section 7.4 Population and Economic Growth

- *What is the effect of population growth on per capita economic growth?*

  Population growth may increase per capita output in resource-rich countries such as Canada, the United States, Australia, and Saudi Arabia, because they have more resources for each labourer to produce with. They are more likely to be able to exploit economies of large-scale production, and they are more likely to have rapidly expanding technology.

- *What is the Malthusian prediction?*

  The Malthusian prediction was that, due to limited productive resources and rapid population growth, eventually per capita economic growth would become negative.

## Key Terms

**economic growth** *an upward trend in the real per capita output of goods and services* p. 173

**productivity** *the amount of goods and services a worker can produce per hour* p. 176

**innovation** *applications of new knowledge that create new products or improve existing products* p. 179

**research and development (R&D)** *activities undertaken to create new products and processes that will lead to technological progress* p. 181

## Key Exhibits/ Graphs

Section 7.1, Exhibit 1
Section 7.1, Exhibit 2
Section 7.2, Exhibit 1

# Notes

# Chapter in Review

## Aggregate Demand

### Section 8.1 The Determinants of Aggregate Demand

* *What is aggregate demand?*

    Aggregate demand is the sum of the demand for all final goods and services in the economy. It can also be seen as the quantity of real GDP demanded at different price levels.

* *What is consumption?*

    Consumption—the purchases of consumer goods and services by households—is the largest component of aggregate demand. Empirical evidence suggests that consumption increases directly with any increase in income.

* *What is investment?*

    Investment spending refers to the purchases of investment goods such as machinery and equipment. Changes in investment spending are often responsible for changes in the level of economic activity.

* *What are government purchases?*

    Government purchases are made up of federal, provincial and territorial, and local purchases of goods and services.

* *What are net exports?*

    Net exports are the difference between the value of total exports and the value of total imports.

### Section 8.2 The Investment and Saving Market

* *What is the investment demand curve?*

    The investment demand curve is downward sloping, reflecting the fact that the quantity of investment demanded varies inversely with the real interest rate. Technology, inventories, expectations, and business taxes can shift the investment demand curve at a given real interest rate.

* *What is the saving supply curve?*

    The supply of national saving is composed of both private saving and public saving. The saving supply curve is upward sloping, reflecting the fact that the quantity of savings is positively related to the real interest rate. Two noninterest determinants of the saving supply curve are disposable (after-tax) income and expected future earnings.

* *How is equilibrium determined in the investment and saving market?*

    In equilibrium, desired investment equals desired national saving at the intersection of the investment demand curve and the saving supply curve. A surplus of saving will occur at real interest rates above equilibrium and shortages of saving will occur at real interest rates below equilibrium.

* *What effect do budget surpluses and budget deficits have on the investment and saving market?*

    Budget surpluses lead to an increase in national saving, a lowering of the real interest rate and an increase in the quantity of saving and investment. Budget deficits reduce national saving, increase the real interest rate, and lower the quantity of saving and investment.

## Key Terms

**aggregate demand** $(AD)$ *the total demand for all final goods and services in the economy* p. 192

**average propensity to consume** $(APC)$ *the fraction of total disposable income that households spend on consumption* p. 193

**marginal propensity to consume** $(MPC)$ *the additional consumption resulting from an additional dollar of disposable income* p. 194

**open economy** *a type of model that includes international trade effects* p. 194

**net exports** $(X - M)$ *the value of total exports minus total imports* p. 195

**private saving** *the amount of income that households have left over after consumption and taxes* p. 198

**public saving** *the amount of income that the government has left over after paying for its spending* p. 198

**national saving** *the sum of both private and public saving* p. 198

**dissaving** *consuming more than total available income* p. 200

**aggregate demand curve** *a graphical representation that shows the inverse relationship between the price level and RGDP demanded* p. 201

## Key Exhibits/ Graphs

## Section 8.3 The Aggregate Demand Curve

- *How is the quantity of real GDP demanded affected by the price level?*

  An increase in the price level causes RGDP demanded to fall. Conversely, if there is a reduction in the price level, quantity demanded of RGDP increases.

- *Why is the aggregate demand curve negatively sloped?*

  The aggregate demand curve is downward sloping because of the real wealth effect, the interest rate effect, and the open economy effect.

## Section 8.4 Shifts in the Aggregate Demand Curve

- *What variables cause the aggregate demand curve to shift?*

  A change in the price level causes a movement along the aggregate demand curve, not a shift in the aggregate demand curve. Aggregate demand is made up of total spending, or $C + I + G + (X - M)$. Any change in these factors will cause the aggregate demand curve to shift. A change in the price level causes a movement along the aggregate demand curve, but not a shift in the aggregate demand curve.

- *Can we review the determinants that change aggregate demand?*

| Variable | Change in Variable | Change in Aggregate Demand |
|---|---|---|
| 1. Consumption (C) | ↑ | ↑ |
| 2. Investment (I) | ↑ | ↑ |
| 3. Government purchases (G) | ↑ | ↑ |
| 4. Exports (X) | ↑ | ↑ |
| 5. Imports (M) | ↑ | ↓ |
| 6. Net exports (X – M) | ↑ | ↑ |

## Key Equations

$$MPC = \frac{\text{Change in consumption}}{\text{Change in disposable income}}$$

$$APC = \frac{\text{Consumption}}{\text{Disposable income}}$$

$$S = (GDP - C - T) + (T - G)$$

# Chapter in Review

## Aggregate Supply and Macroeconomic Equilibrium

### Section 9.1 The Aggregate Supply Curve

- *What is the aggregate supply curve?*

  The aggregate supply curve is the relationship between the overall price level and the total quantity of final goods and services that suppliers are *willing and able* to produce.

- *Why is the short-run aggregate supply curve positively sloped?*

  The short-run aggregate supply curve measures how much RGDP suppliers are willing to produce at different price levels when input prices are unable to adjust. For this reason, producers can make a profit by expanding production when the price level rises. Producers also may be fooled into thinking that the relative price of the item they are producing is rising, so they increase production.

- *Why is the long-run aggregate supply curve vertical at the natural rate of output?*

  In the long run, the aggregate supply curve is vertical. In the long run, input prices change proportionally with output prices. The position of the *LRAS* curve is determined by the level of capital, land, labour, entrepreneurship, and technology at the natural rate of output, $RGDP_{NR}$.

### Section 9.2 Shifts in the Aggregate Supply Curve

- *What factors of production affect the short-run and the long-run aggregate supply curves?*

  Any increase in the quantity of any of the factors of production—capital, land, labour, entrepreneurship, or technology—available will cause both the long-run and short-run aggregate supply curves to shift to the right. A decrease in any of these factors will shift both of the aggregate supply curves to the left.

- *What factors exclusively shift the short-run aggregate supply curve?*

  Changes in wages and other input price, productivity, and temporary supply shocks shift the short-run aggregate supply curve but do not affect the long-run aggregate supply curve.

- *Can we review the determinants that change aggregate supply?*

| Variable | Change in Variable | Change in SRAS | Change in LRAS |
|---|:---:|:---:|:---:|
| 1. Costs | | | |
| • Wages | ↑ | ↓ | n/c* |
| • Other input prices | ↑ | ↓ | n/c* |
| 2. Government policy | | | |
| • Taxes | ↑ | ↓ | ↓ |
| • Regulatory framework | ↑ | ↓ | ↓ |
| • Trade barriers | ↑ | ↓ | ↓ |
| • Waste and inefficiency | ↑ | ↓ | ↓ |
| 3. Economic growth | | | |
| • Quantity of human capital | ↑ | ↑ | ↑ |
| • Quantity of physical capital | ↑ | ↑ | ↑ |
| • Technology and entrepreneurship | ↑ | ↑ | ↑ |
| • Labour productivity | ↑ | ↑ | ↑ |
| 4. Other | | | |
| • Unfavourable weather | ↑ | ↓ | n/c* |
| • Natural disasters, war | ↑ | ↓ | n/c* |
| n/c* — The curve does not shift unless the variable change is permanent. | | | |

## Key Terms

**aggregate supply (*AS*) curve** *a graphical representation that shows the positive relationship between the price level and real gross domestic product supplied  p. 211*

**short-run aggregate supply (*SRAS*) curve** *the graphical relationship between RGDP and the price level when output prices can change but input prices are unable to adjust  p. 211*

**long-run aggregate supply (*LRAS*) curve** *the graphical relationship between RGDP and the price level when output prices and input prices can fully adjust to economic changes  p. 211*

**shocks** *unexpected aggregate supply or aggregate demand changes  p. 218*

**recessionary gap** *an output gap that occurs when the actual output is less than the potential output  p. 219*

**inflationary gap** *an output gap that occurs when the actual output is greater than the potential output  p. 219*

**demand-pull inflation** *a price level increase due to an increase in aggregate demand  p. 219*

**stagflation** *a situation in which lower growth and higher prices occur together  p. 220*

**cost-push inflation** *a price level increase due to a negative supply shock or increases in input prices  p. 220*

**wage and price inflexibility** *the tendency for prices and wages to only adjust slowly downward to changes in the economy  p. 222*

**autonomous determinants of consumption expenditures** *expenditures not dependent on the level of current disposable income  p. 233*

## Key Exhibits/ Graphs

## Section 9.3 Macroeconomic Equilibrium

- *How is macroeconomic equilibrium determined?*

  Short-run macroeconomic equilibrium is shown by the intersection of the aggregate demand curve and the short-run aggregate supply curve. A short-run equilibrium is also a long-run equilibrium only if it is at potential output on the long-run aggregate supply curve.

- *What are recessionary and inflationary gaps?*

  If short-run equilibrium occurs at less than the potential output of the economy, $RGDP_{NR}$, there is a recessionary gap. If short-run equilibrium temporarily occurs beyond $RGDP_{NR}$, there is an inflationary gap.

- *How can the economy self-correct to a recessionary gap?*

  It is possible for the economy to self-correct from a recessionary gap through declining wages and prices. The short-run aggregate supply curve eventually increases, returning the economy to the long-run equilibrium, at $RGDP_{NR}$, at a lower price level.

- *How can the economy self-correct to an inflationary gap?*

  It is possible for the economy to self-correct from an inflationary gap through increasing wages and prices. The short-run aggregate supply curve ultimately decreases, returning the economy to the long-run equilibrium, at $RGDP_{NR}$, at a higher price level.

# chapter 10

# Chapter in Review

# Fiscal Policy

## Section 10.1 Fiscal Policy

- *What is fiscal policy?*

  Fiscal policy is the use of government spending on goods and services and/or taxes to affect aggregate demand and to alter RGDP and the price level.

- *How does fiscal policy affect the government's budget?*

  Expansionary fiscal policies will increase the budget deficit (or reduce a budget surplus) through greater government spending, lower taxes, or both. Contractionary fiscal policies will increase a budget surplus (or reduce a budget deficit) through reduced government spending, higher taxes, or both.

## Section 10.2 Government: Spending and Taxation

- *What are the major categories of government spending?*

  Twenty-nine percent of federal government spending is in the form of major transfers to persons, such as Employment Insurance and Old Age Security programs. Other major expenditures are transfers to other levels of government (22 percent) and expenditures associated with the operation of other departments and agencies (17 percent).

- *What are the major sources of government revenue?*

  The largest source of federal revenue is income taxes on individuals and corporations (49 percent and 14 percent, respectively). Other taxes and duties collected by the federal government account for 18 percent of revenue.

## Section 10.3 The Multiplier Effect

- *What is the multiplier effect?*

  The multiplier effect is a chain reaction of additional income and purchases that results in total purchases that are greater than the initial increase in purchases.

- *What impact does the multiplier effect have on the aggregate demand curve?*

  Initially, the *AD* curve shifts rightward by the amount of the original increase in expenditure. The multiplier effect has the effect of shifting the *AD* curve farther rightward.

- *What impact does the multiplier effect have on tax cuts?*

  Because taxes have only an indirect impact on aggregate demand, the tax multiplier is smaller than the government spending multiplier.

- *What factors can potentially reduce the size of the multiplier?*

  Because of a time lag, the full impact of the multiplier effect on GDP may not be felt until a year or more after the initial purchase. Also, the ultimate size of the multiplier may be reduced by increases in savings rates, taxes, and money spent on imported goods.

## Section 10.4 Fiscal Policy and the AD/AS Model

- *How can fiscal policy alleviate a recessionary gap?*

  A government decision to spend more and/or cut taxes would increase total purchases and shift out the aggregate demand curve. If the correct magnitude of expansionary fiscal policy is used in a recession, it could potentially bring the economy to full employment at a higher price level.

## Key Terms

**fiscal policy** *use of government spending and/or taxes to alter RGDP and the price level*  p. 243

**budget deficit** *Government spending exceeds tax revenues for a given fiscal year.*  p. 244

**budget surplus** *Tax revenues are greater than government expenditures for a given fiscal year.*  p. 244

**expansionary fiscal policy** *use of fiscal policy tools to foster increased output by increasing government spending and/or lowering taxes*  p. 244

**contractionary fiscal policy** *use of fiscal policy tools to reduce output by decreasing government spending and/or increasing taxes*  p. 244

**progressive tax** *The amount of an individual's tax rises as a proportion of income, as the person's income rises.*  p. 247

**excise tax** *a sales tax on individual products such as alcohol, tobacco, and gasoline*  p. 248

**regressive tax** *The amount of an individual's tax falls as a proportion of income, as the person's income rises.*  p. 248

**proportional tax** *designed so that all taxpayers are subject to the tax rate, regardless of earnings*  p. 248

**multiplier effect** *a chain reaction of additional income and purchases that results in total purchases that are greater than the initial increase in purchases*  p. 250

**automatic stabilizers** *changes in government spending or tax collection that automatically help counter business cycle fluctuations*  p. 256

**crowding-out effect** *theory that government borrowing drives up the interest rate, lowering consumption by households and investment spending by firms*  p. 258

- *How can fiscal policy alleviate an inflationary gap?*

  Use of the correct magnitude of contractionary fiscal policy in an inflationary boom could potentially bring the economy back to full employment at a lower price level.

## Section 10.5 Automatic Stabilizers

- *What are automatic stabilizers?*

  Automatic stabilizers are changes in government transfer payments or tax collections that happen automatically and have effects that vary inversely with business cycles.

- *How does the tax system stabilize the economy?*

  The tax system is the most important automatic stabilizer; it has the greatest ability to smooth out swings in GDP during business cycles. Other automatic stabilizers are Employment Insurance and social assistance payments.

## Section 10.6 Possible Obstacles to Effective Fiscal Policy

- *How does the crowding-out effect limit the economic impact of expansionary fiscal policy?*

  The crowding-out effect states that as the government borrows to finance the budget deficit, it drives up the interest rates and crowds out private investment spending. If crowding-out causes a higher Canadian interest rate, it will attract foreign funds. In order to invest in the Canadian economy, foreigners will have to first convert their currencies into Canadian dollars. The increase in the demand for dollars relative to other currencies will cause the dollar to appreciate in value, making imports relatively cheaper in Canada and Canadian exports relatively more expensive in other countries. This will cause net exports $(X - M)$ to fall. This is the crowding-out effect in the open economy.

- *How do time lags in policy implementation affect policy effectiveness?*

  The time lag between when a fiscal policy may be needed and when it eventually affects the economy is considerable. Time lags are generally grouped in three classifications: recognition lags, implementation lags, and impact lags.

## Section 10.7 The Federal Government Debt

- *How is the budget deficit financed?*

  The budget deficit is financed by issuing debt.

- *What has happened to the federal budget balance?*

  Improvement in the federal budget balance since the mid-1990s resulted from economic growth, increased tax revenues, and the efforts of the federal government to control the growth of government spending.

- *What is the impact of reducing a budget deficit?*

  In the short run, reducing a budget deficit can lead to a recession (if not offset by expansionary monetary policy). In the long run, however, deficit reduction increases economic growth and lowers the price level.

- *How much is the burden of government debt in Canada?*

  With greater fiscal responsibility and increased economic growth, Canada has managed to lower its debt–GDP ratio (the international measure of debt burden).

## Key Equations

$$\text{Multiplier} = \frac{1}{1 - MPC}$$

$$\text{Tax multiplier} = -\frac{MPC}{1 - MPC}$$

## Money and the Banking System

### Section 11.1 What Is Money?

- *What is money?*

  Money is anything that is generally accepted in exchange for goods or services.

- *What are the four functions of money?*

  The four important functions of money are money as a medium of exchange, money as a store of value, money as a unit of account, and money as a means of deferred payment.

### Section 11.2 Measuring Money

- *What is currency?*

  *Currency* refers to the coins and banknotes that are issued by institutions and governments to facilitate the trading of goods and services and the payment of debts. Canadian currency consists of Government of Canada-issued banknotes and coins, and demand and savings deposits held in various financial institutions.

- *What are demand and savings deposits?*

  Demand and savings deposits are two types of bank accounts. Demand deposits are balances in financial institution accounts that depositors can access on demand, while savings deposits are deposited funds that cannot be used directly for payment.

- *What is liquidity?*

  The ease with which one asset can be converted into another asset or into goods and services is called *liquidity*.

- *How is the money supply measured?*

  M2 is made up of currency outside chartered banks plus demand and savings deposits at chartered banks. M2+ includes M2 plus demand and savings deposits at trust companies, mortgage loan companies, credit unions, caisses populaires, and other financial institutions.

- *What backs the money supply?*

  Money is backed by our faith that others will accept it from us in exchange for goods and services.

### Section 11.3 How Banks Create Money

- *What types of financial institutions exist in Canada?*

  While a variety of financial intermediaries exist in the Canadian financial system, the financial sector is dominated by deposit-accepting institutions—banks. The Canadian banking industry itself is dominated by six large chartered banks. The "Big Six" hold the majority of the financial assets in the banking industry.

- *How do banks create money?*

  Money is created when banks make loans. Borrowers receive newly created demand deposits.

- *What does a bank balance sheet look like?*

  A bank balance sheet is a financial record that indicates the balance between a bank's assets and its liabilities plus capital. A bank's largest asset is loans and its largest liability is deposits.

- *What is a desired reserve ratio?*

  A desired reserve ratio is the percentage of deposits a bank chooses to keep on hand in the form of cash reserves.

### Key Terms

**money** *anything generally accepted in exchange for goods or services  p. 271*

**medium of exchange** *the primary function of money, which is to facilitate transactions and lower transaction costs  p. 271*

**barter** *direct exchange of goods and services without the use of money  p. 271*

**measure of value** *money as a common "ruler" of worth allowing for the comparison of diverse goods and services  p. 272*

**store of value** *Money provides a means of saving or accumulating purchasing power from the present and transferring it to the future.  p. 272*

**means of deferred payment** *the attribute of money that makes it easier to borrow and to repay loans  p. 273*

**currency** *coins and banknotes that an institution or government has created to be used in the trading of goods and services and the payment of debts  p. 273*

**legal tender** *coins and banknotes officially declared to be acceptable for the settlement of debts incurred in financial transactions  p. 273*

**fiat money** *a means of exchange established by government declaration  p. 274*

**demand deposits** *balances in bank accounts that depositors can access on demand  p. 274*

**savings deposits** *financial institution accounts containing funds that cannot be used directly for payment  p. 275*

**liquidity** *the ease with which one asset can be converted into another asset or into goods and services  p. 276*

**M2** *currency outside chartered banks plus demand and savings deposits at chartered banks  p. 276*

## Key Exhibits/ Graphs

## Section 11.4 The Money Multiplier

- *How does the multiple expansion of the money supply process work?*

  New loans mean new money (demand deposits), which can increase spending as well as the money supply. New loans also create excess reserves in other banks, which leads to still further increases in both loans and the money supply.

- *What is the money multiplier?*

  The money multiplier is equal to 1 divided by the desired reserve ratio.

- *Why is it only "potential" money creation?*

  The banking system as a whole can potentially create new money equal to several times the amount of new reserves—as determined by the money multiplier. However, due to various leakages and time lags, the actual monetary impact of an initial deposit created out of excess reserves within a short period of time will be less than that calculated by the money multiplier.

### Key Equations

$$\text{Money multiplier} = \frac{1}{\text{Desired reserve ratio}}$$

$$\text{Potential deposit creation} = \text{Excess reserves} \times \text{Money multiplier}$$

# The Bank of Canada

## Section 12.1 The Bank of Canada

- *What is the Bank of Canada?*

    The Bank of Canada is Canada's central bank. It is owned by the federal government, which has final responsibility for the Bank of Canada's policies. Despite this goal dependence, the governor of the Bank of Canada has considerable independence in formulating the Bank of Canada's monetary policy.

- *What are the main responsibilities of the Bank of Canada?*

    The Bank of Canada has four main areas of responsibility: currency, funds management, the financial system, and monetary policy.

## Section 12.2 Tools of the Bank of Canada

- *What are the tools of the Bank of Canada?*

    The two major tools of the Bank of Canada are open market operations and changing the target for the overnight interest rate.

- *What is the Bank of Canada's approach to monetary policy?*

    The Bank of Canada will raise the target for the overnight interest rate in response to an expectation of inflation above the 2 percent control target. A higher target for the overnight interest rate will raise other commercial interest rates and the exchange rate for the Canadian dollar, thus lowering overall economic demand. This reduction in overall demand will have the effect of returning the rate of inflation back to its 2 percent target. If the Bank of Canada expects the rate of inflation to fall below its 2 percent control target, it will lower the target for the overnight interest rate. The resulting lower commercial interest rates and exchange rate for the Canadian dollar will lead to greater overall demand in the economy, thus increasing the inflation rate back toward the 2 percent target.

## Section 12.3 Money and Inflation

- *What is the equation of exchange?*

    The equation of exchange is expressed as $M \times V = P \times Q$, where $M$ is the money supply, $V$ is the velocity of money, $P$ is the average level of prices of final goods and services, and $Q$ is real GDP in a given year.

- *What is the quantity theory of money and prices?*

    The theory that draws a connection between the money supply and the price level when the velocity of money is constant is referred to as the *quantity theory of money and prices*.

## Key Equations

$$M \times V = P \times Q$$

$$V = \frac{P \times Q}{M}$$

## Key Terms

**monetary policy** *the policy decisions that the Bank of Canada makes in managing the money supply and interest rates, consistent with its inflation-control objective* p. 300

**overnight interest rate** *the interest rate that major financial institutions charge each other for one-day loans* p. 300

**bank rate** *the interest rate that the Bank of Canada charges major financial institutions on the loans it extends to them* p. 301

**bankers' deposit rate** *the interest rate Bank of Canada pays major financial institutions on surplus funds deposited at the Bank of Canada* p. 301

**open market operations** *purchase and sale of government securities by the Bank of Canada* p. 301

**velocity of money ($V$)** *the average number of times that a dollar is used in purchasing final goods or services in a one-year period* p. 306

**quantity theory of money and prices** *a theory of the connection between the money supply and the price level when the velocity of money is constant* p. 306

## Key Exhibits/ Graphs

Section 12.2, Exhibit 1

# Notes

## Monetary Policy

### Section 13.1 Money, Interest Rates, and Aggregate Demand

- *What determines the money market?*

  The money market is the market in which money demand and money supply determine the equilibrium interest rate. Money demand has three possible motives: transaction purposes, precautionary reasons, and asset purposes. The quantity of money demanded varies inversely with interest rates and directly with income. The supply of money is effectively almost perfectly inelastic with respect to interest rates over their plausible range, as controlled by Bank of Canada policies.

- *How does the Bank of Canada affect RGDP in the short run?*

  When the Bank of Canada sells bonds to the private sector or raises its target for the overnight interest rate, there is a reduction in the money supply, which in turn leads to a higher interest rate and a reduction in aggregate demand, at least in the short run. When the Bank of Canada buys bonds or lowers its target for the overnight interest rate, the money supply increases. The increase in the money supply will lead to lower interest rates and an increase in aggregate demand.

- *Does the Bank of Canada target the money supply or the interest rate?*

  Since the Bank of Canada cannot completely control both the growth of the money supply and the interest rate, it must choose which target to manage.

- *Which interest rate does the Bank of Canada target?*

  The Bank of Canada signals its intended monetary policy through the overnight interest rate target that it sets.

- *Does the Bank of Canada influence the real interest rate in the short run?*

  Since a change in the nominal interest rate tends to change the real interest rate by the same amount in the short run, most economists believe the Bank of Canada can control both the nominal and real interest rates (in the short run).

### Section 13.2 Expansionary and Contractionary Monetary Policy

- *How does expansionary monetary policy work in a recessionary gap?*

  An expansionary monetary policy can combat a recessionary gap. By increasing the money supply, the Bank of Canada can lower interest rates, thereby causing an increase in real GDP and the price level.

- *How does contractionary monetary policy work in an inflationary gap?*

  A contractionary monetary policy can close an inflationary gap. By reducing the money supply, the Bank of Canada can raise interest rates, thereby causing a decline in real GDP and the price level.

- *How does monetary policy work in the open economy?*

  In the open economy, interest rate changes can impact exchange rates. Higher interest rates produced by contractionary monetary policy lead to an appreciation of the Canadian dollar. This appreciation can cause net exports to decline and RGDP to be reduced in the short run. Expansionary monetary policy, having the opposite effect, can increase net exports and expand RGDP in the short run.

## Key Terms

**money market** *market in which money demand and money supply determine the equilibrium nominal interest rate* p. 310

**quantitative easing** *the purchase of private- and public-sector securities by the central bank* p. 322

## Key Exhibits/ Graphs

Section 13.1, Exhibit 2
Section 13.1, Exhibit 3
Section 13.1, Exhibit 4
Section 13.2, Exhibit 1
Section 13.2, Exhibit 2
Section 13.2, Exhibit 3

### Section 13.3 Problems in Implementing Monetary and Fiscal Policy

- *What problems exist in implementing monetary and fiscal policy?*

  Monetary policy faces somewhat different implementation problems than fiscal policy. Both face difficult forecasting and lag problems, but the Bank of Canada can take action much more quickly. However, its effectiveness depends largely on the reaction of the private banking system to its policy changes. In Canada, monetary and fiscal policy are carried out by different decision makers, thus requiring cooperation and coordination for effective policy implementation.

### Section 13.4 The Phillips Curve

- *What is the Phillips curve?*

  The inverse relationship between the rate of unemployment and the rate of inflation is called the *Phillips curve*.

- *How does the Phillips curve relate to the aggregate supply and demand model?*

  When the aggregate supply curve is positively sloped, an increase in aggregate demand will cause higher prices and higher output (lower unemployment). A decrease in aggregate demand will cause lower prices and lower output (higher unemployment).

# International Trade

## Section 14.1 Canada's Merchandise Trade

- *Who are Canada's trading partners?*

  Our most important trading partner, the United States, accounts for 75 percent of our exports and 65 percent of our imports. Trade with the countries of the European Union (EU) and China is also particularly important to Canada.

- *What does Canada import and export?*

  Exports of natural resource-based products make up over 50 percent of our exports of goods. Our imports are concentrated in finished goods, like electronic and electrical equipment, motor vehicles, and consumer goods.

## Section 14.2 International Trade Agreements

- *What has been the impact of international trade on Canada?*

  The volume of international trade has increased substantially in Canada over the past 60 years. During that time, exports plus imports have grown from about 40 percent of GDP to over 80 percent. Recently, however, international trade represents less than 65 percent of annual national income.

- *What international trade agreements is Canada involved in?*

  The numerous trade agreements in which Canada is an active participant range from multilateral global trade agreements (such as GATT/WTO) to regional agreements (such as the Canada–European Union Comprehensive Economic and Trade Agreement (CETA)). This substantial involvement is a major reason why Canada has experienced sustained international trade.

## Section 14.3 Comparative Advantage and Gains from Trade

- *Why do economies trade?*

  Voluntary trade occurs because the participants feel that they are better off because of the trade.

- *What is the principle of comparative advantage?*

  A nation, a geographic area, or even a person can gain from trade if the good or service is produced relatively cheaper than anyone else can produce it. So an area should specialize in producing and selling those items that it can produce at a lower opportunity cost than others can. Through trade and specialization in products in which it has a comparative advantage, a country can enjoy a greater array of goods and services at a lower cost.

## Section 14.4 Supply and Demand in International Trade

- *What are consumer surplus and producer surplus?*

  The difference between what a consumer is willing and able to pay and what a consumer actually has to pay is called *consumer surplus*. The difference between what a supplier is willing and able to receive and the price a supplier actually receives for selling a good or service is called *producer surplus*.

## Key Terms

**absolute advantage** *the ability of a party (nation, region, or individual) to produce more of a good or service while using the same amount of inputs* p. 341

**consumer surplus** *the difference between what the consumer is willing and able to pay and what the consumer actually pays for a quantity of a good or service* p. 343

**producer surplus** *the difference between the lowest price at which a supplier is willing and able to supply a good or service and the actual price received for a given quantity of a good or service* p. 343

**tariff** *a tax on imported goods* p. 347

**import quota** *a legal limit on the imported quantity of a good that is produced abroad and can be sold in domestic markets* p. 350

**rent seeking** *producer efforts to gain profits from government protections such as tariffs and import quotas* p. 352

**subsidy** *a program of financial assistance paid out to producers* p. 352

## Key Exhibits/ Graphs

Section 14.4, Exhibit 2
Section 14.4, Exhibit 3
Section 14.5, Exhibit 1
Section 14.5, Exhibit 2

- *Who benefits and who loses when a country becomes an exporter?*

  With free trade and exports, domestic producers gain more than domestic consumers lose.

- *Who benefits and who loses when a country becomes an importer?*

  With free trade and imports, domestic consumers gain more than domestic producers lose.

## Section 14.5 Tariffs, Import Quotas, and Subsidies

- *What is a tariff?*

  A tariff is a tax on imported goods.

- *What is the impact of tariffs on the domestic economy?*

  Tariffs bring about higher prices and revenues to domestic producers, and lower sales and revenues to foreign producers. Tariffs lead to higher prices and reduce consumer surplus for domestic consumers. Tariffs result in a net loss in welfare because the loss in consumer surplus is greater than the gain to producers and the government.

- *What are some arguments in favour of tariffs?*

  Arguments for the use of tariffs include: Tariffs help infant industries grow, they can reduce domestic unemployment, they are necessary for national security reasons, and they protect against dumping.

- *What are import quotas?*

  Import quotas are legal limits on the quantity of an imported good that can be produced abroad and sold in domestic markets.

- *What is the impact of import quotas on the domestic economy?*

  Like tariffs, import quotas restrict imports, lowering consumer surplus and preventing countries from fully realizing their comparative advantage. There is a net loss in welfare from quotas, but it is proportionately larger than for tariffs because there are no government revenues.

- *What is the economic impact of subsidies?*

  Sometimes a government tries to encourage production of a certain good by subsidizing its production with taxpayer dollars. Because subsidies stimulate exports, they are not a barrier to trade like tariffs and import quotas are. However, they do distort trade patterns and cause overall inefficiencies.

# International Finance

## Section 15.1 The Balance of Payments

- *What is the balance of payments?*

  The balance of payments is the record of all of the international financial transactions of a nation for any given year.

- *What is the current account?*

  The current account is a record of a country's imports and exports of goods and services, net primary income, and net secondary income. If the sum of receipts exceeds the sum of payments for all transactions of goods, services, primary income, and secondary income, the current account is in surplus. If the opposite is true, the account is in deficit.

- *What is the capital account?*

  The capital account records the foreign purchases or assets in Canada and Canadian purchases of assets abroad. Capital account surpluses finance current deficits.

- *What is the statistical discrepancy?*

  To ensure that the balance of payments account does in fact balance, an "error" category—the statistical discrepancy—is included.

## Section 15.2 Exchange Rates

- *What are exchange rates?*

  The price of a unit of one foreign currency in terms of another currency is called the *exchange rate*.

- *How are exchange rates determined?*

  The exchange rate for a currency is determined by the supply of and demand for that currency in the foreign exchange market.

## Section 15.3 Equilibrium Changes in the Foreign Exchange Market

- *What are the major determinants in the foreign exchange market?*

  Any force that shifts either the demand or the supply curves for a foreign currency will shift the equilibrium in the foreign exchange market and lead to a new exchange rate. Changes in tastes, tariffs, income levels, relative interest rates, relative inflation rates, or speculation will cause the demand for and supply of a currency to shift.

## Section 15.4 Flexible Exchange Rates

- *How are exchange rates determined today?*

  Today, rates are free to fluctuate based on market transactions, but governments occasionally intervene to increase or depress the price of their currencies.

- *What are the advantages of a flexible exchange rate system?*

  Changes in exchange rates occur more often under a flexible-rate system but the changes are much smaller than the large overnight revaluations of currencies that occurred under the fixed-rate system. Under a fixed-rate system, the supply and demand for currencies shift, but currency prices are not allowed to shift to the new equilibrium, leading to surpluses and shortages of currencies.

- *What are the disadvantages of a flexible exchange rate system?*

  The main arguments presented against flexible exchange rates are that international trade levels could be diminished due to uncertainty of future currency prices and that the flexible rates would lead to inflation. Proponents of flexible exchange rates have strong counterarguments to those views.

## Key Terms

**balance of payments** *the record of international transactions of a nation over a year* p. 358

**current account** *a record of a country's imports and exports of goods and services, net investment income, and net income* p. 358

**capital account** *a record of the foreign purchases or assets in the domestic economy (a monetary inflow) and domestic purchases of assets abroad (a monetary outflow)* p. 360

**exchange rate** *the price of one unit of a country's currency in terms of another country's currency* p. 362

**currency appreciation** *an increase in the value of a currency* p. 362

**currency depreciation** *a decrease in the value of a currency* p. 363

**derived demand** *the demand for an input derived from consumers' demand for the good or service produced with that input* p. 364

**dirty float system** *a description of the exchange rate system that means that fluctuations in currency values are partly determined by market forces and partly influenced by government intervention* p. 371

## Key Exhibits/ Graphs

Section 15.2, Exhibit 2
Section 15.4, Exhibit 1

# Notes

# Notes

# Notes